Medieval Parks
of Hertfordshire

Medieval Parks
of Hertfordshire

Anne Rowe

HERTFORDSHIRE PUBLICATIONS
an imprint of
University of Hertfordshire Press

First published in Great Britain in 2009 by
Hertfordshire Publications
an imprint of
University of Hertfordshire Press
College Lane
Hatfield
Hertfordshire, AL10 9AB

British Library Cataloguing in Publication Data
A catalogue record for this book is available from the British Library

ISBN 978-1-912260-10-2

Design by Mathew Lyons
Printed in Great Britain by Hobbs The Printers Ltd

Dedicated to my parents,
Beryl and Brian Lister

Contents

List of Figures *viii*
Abbreviations *x*
Dates, units of measurement and money *xi*
Acknowledgements *xii*
Preface *xiii*

Part I Introduction: Medieval parks of Hertfordshire
Hertfordshire – a parky county? 4
The sources 5
The chronology of medieval park creation in Hertfordshire 7
The longevity of Hertfordshire's medieval parks 8
The park creators 9
The spatial relationship between the lord's residence and his park 12
The geographical distribution of medieval parks in Hertfordshire 14
The distribution of woodland 14
Settlement patterns and lordship 16
Parks in the Hertfordshire landscape 17
The park residents 21
The economic viability of parks 24
Park management 28
Park lodges 34
Park personnel 36

Part II Gazetteer of medieval parks in Hertfordshire
Introduction 42
Gazetteer 44

Glossary 232
Bibliography 234
Index 243

List of Figures

1. First documentary references to parks in Hertfordshire 5
2. Minimum and likely numbers of deer parks in Hertfordshire 1200–1500 9
3. Medieval parks and the social status of their owners 10
4. The geographical distribution of Hertfordshire's medieval parks 15
5. Domesday woodland in Hertfordshire 16
6. The distribution of Hertfordshire's population in 1086 18
7. The land-holdings of the major religious houses in medieval Hertfordshire 19
8. The distribution of parks in relation to the county's relief 20
9. The main revenues and costs of the park of the bishops of Ely
   at Little Hadham during the fourteenth and fifteenth centuries 23
10. Some costs and revenues of Hertfordshire parks in the last quarters of
   the fourteenth and fifteenth centuries 25
11. The relationship between the size and longevity of Hertfordshire's parks 26
12. Key map showing Hertfordshire's medieval parks with their parishes 43
13. Aerial photograph of the former Punsho park, 1946 47
14. Detail of map of Scales Park, 1741 54
15. View along the southern boundary of Scales Park, Barkway 55
16. View across the former Benington park 56
17. View along boundary bank of Benington park 58
18. Detail of Norden's county map, 1598, showing Bishop's Stortford park 68
19. Aerial photograph of Bishop's Stortford park, 1946 71
20. Detail of Saxton's county map, 1577, showing Cheshunt park 78
21. Detail of Morden's county map, 1722, showing 'Barham Wood' 89
22. View across the former Bedwell park 92
23. Detail of Saxton's county map, 1577, showing east Hertfordshire 99
24. View across Whitehills golf course, the former Floodgacy park, Great Munden 104
25. Aerial photograph of the former Floodgacy park, 1946 105
26. Detail of Saxton's county map, 1577, showing the Hatfield area 113
27. View of the Halfwayoak Pond in Millwards Park 116
28. Detail of a map of Hertingfordbury Farm, 1732 125
29. Detail of the bird's-eye view of Hitchin by J. Drapentier, 1700 128
30. Boundary bank at Hoddesdonpark Wood 132
31. Hornbeams on the southern boundary of Hoddesdonpark Wood 132
32. Detail of Norden's county map, 1598, showing the parks at Hunsdon 138

33. Detail of Saxton's county map, 1577, showing the parks at Hunsdon 138

34. View of northern boundary of Hunsdon park 139

35. View of the landscape setting of Almshoe Bury 142

36. View of the possible former boundary of Almshoe park 144

37. View of Kimpton from the Park by Buckler, 1840 146

38. Aerial photograph of the former King's Langley park, 1947 153

39. View across the former Knebworth great park 157

40. Pollarded hornbeams in the present-day Knebworth Park 158

41. View of boundary earthworks at Ashridge park 164

42. Aerial photograph of the park of the bishops of Ely at Little Hadham, 1946 168

43. Aerial photograph of the former Munden park, 1946 174

44. View across Sandy Lodge golf course, the former park of The More 182

45. Detail of Saxton's county map, 1577, showing Tyttenhanger park 184

46. Detail of Dury and Andrews' county map, 1766, showing Tyttenhanger park 186

47. View along the eighteenth-century boundary of Tyttenhanger park 187

48. View of the bank bounding Green Wood, Childwick Green 188

49. Detail of Saxton's county map, 1577, showing Pisho and Shingle Hall parks 196

50. Detail of Norden's county map, 1598, showing the parks between
Bishop's Stortford and Hunsdon 198

51. An ancient pollard in the former Pisho park 201

52. Detail of Saxton's county map, 1577, showing Pendley park 214

53. Detail of Norden's county map, 1598, showing Pendley park 216

54. Aerial photograph of Pendley park, 1947 217

55. Engraving of Walkern Park, 1878 220

Cover illustration

A hunting scene forming part of the decorative border around the Hertford Borough Charter of 1605 [HALS Off Acc 216]. The artist may well have been depicting activities in the medieval park of Hertingfordbury, otherwise known as Hertford park, at the beginning of the seventeenth century. Note the palmate antlers of the fallow buck and the pollarded trees.

Abbreviations

A2A	Access to Archives
BL	British Library
c.	*circa*
Cal. Chart.	Calendar of Charter Rolls
Cal. Close	Calendar of Close Rolls
Cal. Inq.	Calendar of Inquisitions
Cal. Pat.	Calendar of Patent Rolls
CUL	Cambridge University Library
DoE	Department of the Environment
EPNS	English Place-Name Society
GIS	Geographical Information Systems
HALS	Hertfordshire Archives and Local Studies
HER	Historic Environment Record
HHA	Hatfield House Archive
OD	Ordnance Datum
OE	Old English
OS	Ordnance Survey
p.a.	per annum
TNA: PRO	The National Archives: Public Record Office
VCH	Victoria County History

Dates, units of measurement and money

In the medieval period, and until 1752, the new year was assumed to begin on 25 March (Lady Day), not 1 January. For dates lying between 1 January and 24 March before 1752 the convention is to record both years for clarity: for example, 1 February 1435/6. The accounting year usually ran from Michaelmas (29 September) to Michaelmas.

A perch (*pertica*) was a highly variable measure of between nine and twenty-six feet which became standardised at sixteen and a half feet. Different Hertfordshire manors appear to have used different measures, for example at King's Langley in 1360 a perch contained twenty feet whereas at Benington a perch contained eighteen feet as late as the sixteenth century. Some measurements quoted in this book in perches have been converted into metres using the standardised measure, but the reader should bear in mind that the conversions given are *very* approximate. A perch could also be called a rod or pole.

Area was measured in acres, roods and perches. An acre consisted of four roods and each rood contained forty perches.

Conversions
1 foot = 0.3 metres
1 furlong = 200 metres
1 mile = 1.6 kilometres
1 acre = 0.4 hectares
A pound (£) contained twenty shillings and one shilling (s) contained twelve pennies (d). 1 shilling = 5p

Acknowledgements

This book has been long in the making and many people have helped in different ways over the years. I would like to thank in particular Roger Beament for sources relating to Berkhamsted park, Nicholas Buxton for showing me around Easneye Park, Robert Dimsdale for permitting me to explore Scales Park and for providing me with additional information about its history, Heather Falvey for sharing her research on Moor Park and Berkhamsted, Sue Garside for sharing her knowledge of Hoddesdon, Janet Holt for sharing her research on Great Offley, David Perman for additional information relating to Ware park, Isobel Thompson and Alison Tinniswood in the Archaeology Unit at County Hall for their prompt and knowledgeable responses to my requests for information, and Angus Wainwright for permission to use his report on the history of the Ashridge estate. I am also very grateful to Twigs Way for publishing the results of her laborious search for park records in the calendars of medieval state records and for lending me her PhD thesis on parks in Cambridgeshire and Huntingdonshire.

Many people have helped me in my struggle to get to grips with medieval Latin documents. Particular thanks are due to Robin Harcourt Williams for patiently getting me started with the transcription and translation of manorial records in the Hatfield House Archives. Others who have helped with translation at various times include Sue Flood, Katrina Legg, Jonathan Mackman and Lee Prosser. I am especially grateful to Kate and Martin Banister who generously put their Latin expertise at my disposal and helped enormously with the compilation of the Glossary.

I am very grateful to Sue Flood, County Archivist, for permitting me to use digital copies of the original Ordnance Survey maps held in the Hertfordshire Archives which made the task of producing the maps for the gazetteer a great deal easier than it might have been. The staff of the Hertfordshire Archives and Local Studies library at County Hall are also to be warmly thanked for many years of helpful and efficient service.

Stephen Mileson, Hugh Prince and Tom Williamson kindly provided encouragement and valuable comments on draft sections of the Introduction. I am also grateful to Jane Housham and Sarah Elvins at the University of Hertfordshire Press for their friendly but professional expertise and for much practical support with the production of the gazetteer maps.

Finally, special thanks are due to my husband, Charlie, without whose whole-hearted support this book would never have been finished.

Preface

The seeds of this book were sown about twenty years ago when I worked for a short time in the Landscape Group at County Hall in Hertford. The Landscape Officer at the time was Andrew Clarke and he gave me the task of identifying areas of parkland which may have had their origins in the medieval period, the purpose of the project being to locate parts of the county of particular value for landscape history and ecology. Thus began my initiation into the world of archives with a nervous visit to the County Record Office, as it was then known. I had no idea what I was looking for, or how to set about finding it, but the thrill of examining old maps and struggling to read ancient documents has stayed with me ever since — I was hooked! One of the young archivists who helped me in those early days was Sue Flood, now County Archivist. Another young County Council employee who encouraged the project along was archaeologist Stewart Bryant, now County Archaeologist.

The seeds germinated a decade later when I undertook a course leading to a Master of Studies degree in English Local History at Cambridge University. I had the great good fortune to have as the supervisor of my research project Christopher Taylor, who helped me to unravel the landscape history of Hamels Park, a park created in east Hertfordshire in the late sixteenth/early seventeenth century. He taught me how to 'read' the humps and bumps in the landscape and interpret them with the aid of maps, aerial photographs and documentary sources.

The seedlings grew slowly and fitfully for several years as I gathered information and developed ideas on an *ad hoc* basis and it was Hugh Prince who galvanised me into some more concerted action when he proposed writing a series of articles on Hertfordshire's parks, to which I suggested adding some of my research on medieval parks. His initial idea then developed into a proposal for a joint book on the subject, which then further developed into two separate books as it became obvious that our ideas and research could not be confined to a single volume. Hugh's book *Parks in Hertfordshire since 1500* was published in March 2008.

Identifying medieval parks starts out a bit like stamp-collecting as one gleans references from a wide variety of documentary sources and compiles a list. The challenge is to put flesh on the bones by finding corroborative documentary evidence which might reveal when the park was created and by whom, how it was managed and how long it survived. Cartographic evidence, often in the form of field-names, combined with surviving field evidence can be sought and used to attempt to locate the former park geographically. Once this has been done for a substantial number of parks, it is possible to start looking for trends in the ways medieval park creators chose to locate their parks in the landscape according to both the physical and social geographical structures which existed at the time. Some of these trends were examined in a chapter on Hertfordshire's parks contributed to Robert Liddiard's book *The medieval park: new perspectives*, published in 2007. Since then, further research has led to the discovery of more parks and the exploration of additional themes relating to the history and development of medieval parks in the county which are contained in this book. Historical research is never 'finished'; there is always more information waiting to be found and I have no doubt that the list of medieval parks in Hertfordshire will continue to grow.

I have sought to combine my undergraduate training in the natural environment with my later studies in local and landscape history to compile a multi-disciplinary study which will be of value to both social and natural historians. The evidence presented here adds to a growing body of information about medieval parks in England and will, I hope, help to inform the studies of historians whose horizons rise above the level of a single county.

Exploring the county's medieval parks

One of the aims of this book is to encourage readers to get out into the Hertfordshire countryside and look for evidence of its management in the past. Unlike many of the parks with which we are familiar today, medieval parks were never open to the general public. The sites of many former parks can, however, be seen from public rights of way — roads and footpaths — which frequently developed around the peripheries of the parks and help to identify where their boundaries lay.

Anne Rowe
April 2008

Part One

Introduction: Medieval parks of Hertfordshire

MEDIEVAL PARKS HAVE LONG BEEN a subject of interest to landscape historians: once common features in the countryside, most parks ceased to exist centuries ago and yet many have left a variety of clues which enable landscape enthusiasts to determine where they used to be and thus to establish a link with the past. Parks created between the eleventh and fifteenth centuries bore little resemblance to the modern concept of a park, which could encompass everything from the beautifully designed landscape park of the eighteenth century through Victorian municipal parks to a twenty-first-century theme park. Our perception of what made a park in the Middle Ages has developed as new research has been published and it now seems that the notion of what constituted a park did not remain constant, even during the medieval period itself.

Central to the study of medieval parks is the question: what were they for? The traditional view – that they were the playgrounds of the wealthy, who spent their days on horseback hunting deer – has been seriously undermined by a lack of documentary evidence and the discovery that most parks were far too small to accommodate such activity. Nevertheless, the primary motivation for creating a park in the medieval period seems to have been the rearing and management of deer. Hunting for recreation was certainly enjoyed by the social elite in the largest parks but most deer were killed by professional huntsmen and parkers to provide a regular supply of venison for the park-owner.[1] 'Venison was the food of the rich, eaten on special occasions and given as a mark of particular favour', and owning a park was an indicator of high social status.[2]

In addition to being a status symbol, however, parks were functional economic units in the countryside. Many smaller parks were more venison farm than hunting park but they could also be managed to produce a regular supply of timber and wood, and to produce revenue from the leasing of grazing (agistment) and pannage rights. Parks were typically created by enclosing part of the manorial waste – the uncultivated land on the margins of the manor – a process which enabled a medieval lord to take control of important (and dwindling) resources of woodland and pasture, usually to the detriment of his tenants, who relied on the same resources for fuel and for grazing their livestock.[3]

Records of recreational hunting in Hertfordshire's parks are extremely rare – in fact the only two known examples occurred in July 1362, when the Black Prince permitted 'the bishop of Wircestre and Master John de Stretelee to take two bucks of grease' in Berkhamsted park, and in the mid-fifteenth century, when Queen Margaret of Anjou signalled her intention to hunt in Ware park by instructing the parker there to preserve the stocks of deer for her exclusive use.[4] Two earlier queens, Isabella and her daughter, Joan of Scotland, are known to have visited the parks at Almshoe and Maydencroft near Hitchin on consecutive days in July 1358 but there is no record of what they did there.[5] Given the advanced years and delicate health of Queen Isabella (she died just a few weeks later), a hunt on horseback seems unlikely. Such a hunt could, perhaps, be inferred from the record that in October 1295 Joan, Countess of Pembroke, was joined at Hertford castle by her pack of hunting dogs.[6]

Records of hunting by professional huntsmen are equally rare. In the summer of 1298, during a vacancy in the see, Edward I ordered that a hundred fallow bucks should be taken in the parks of the bishopric of Ely, salted, dried, packed in barrels and delivered to his larder in York.[7] Whether any of these deer were

---

1. J. Birrell, 'Deer and deer farming in medieval England', *Agricultural History Review*, 40 (1993), p. 122.

2. T. Williamson, 'Fish, fur and feather: Man and nature in the post-medieval landscape', in K. Barker and T. Darvill (eds.), *Making English landscapes* (Bournemouth, 1999), p. 93.

3. Birrell, 'Deer and deer farming', p. 112.

4. M.C.B. Dawes, *Register of Edward the Black Prince, part 4* (England) 1351–1365 (London, 1933), p. 458; C. Monro, *Letters of Queen Margaret of Anjou* (London, 1863), p. 91.

5. E.A. Bond, 'Notices of the last days of Isabella, Queen of Edward the second, drawn from an account of the expenses of her household', *Archaeologia*, 35 (1853), p. 462.

6. C.M. Woolgar, *The great household in late medieval England* (New Haven & London, 1999), p. 193.

taken in the Hertfordshire parks of the bishopric, at Hatfield or Little Hadham, is not recorded. In 1315 Edward II sent his professional huntsmen with their dogs to take deer in the park at Standon to provide venison for the next sitting of parliament at Westminster.[8] The abbot of St Albans, Thomas de la Mare, kept huntsmen and falconers on his staff in the second half of the fourteenth century, but no records of their activities in the abbey's parks appear to survive.[9]

It seems likely that hunting in parks took on a greater significance during the later Middle Ages, perhaps because there were so few wild deer remaining in the countryside, and a new style of hunting developed, more suited to the confines of a park, whereby deer were driven towards stationary bowmen waiting in a 'standing'.[10] This method of hunting may well have been popular in Hertfordshire's parks, but no evidence for it has been found before the sixteenth century. The gentler art of falconry was practised in the county's parks and has left slightly more evidence in the documentary record, if not in the landscape itself.

The visual relationship between the park and residence of the owner also changed during the Middle Ages. Early parks in Hertfordshire were generally distant from the residence, but in the fifteenth century houses commonly came to be sited within parks.[11] It is possible that the value of a park as a status symbol increased in the later Middle Ages – especially for those who had bought their way into the landowning classes.[12] On the other hand, some park owners seem to have focused on increasing income from their parks in the form of agistment or from sales of wood.

Parks, then, were multifunctional spaces and the emphasis placed on the different functions varied from park to park and shifted over time. One feature of parkland which remained relatively constant during the period, however, was its ecology. Most parkland comprised a complex mosaic of trees and pasture, maintained by grazing animals and by the pollarding of trees and coppicing of woodland. Many parks existed for several centuries and incorporated a remarkably rich and diverse range of habitats.[13] Only tiny fragments of Hertfordshire's once extensive parklands have survived to the present day – including, for example, some exceptional ancient pollarded hornbeams in a surviving area of pasture in Ware Park – and one of the objectives of this study has been to identify and record those fragments in the hope that they might be afforded extra protection in the future, perhaps forming the nuclei of local habitat restoration projects. The extensive wood-pastures of the past have all but disappeared from the county's countryside and any attempt to restore or recreate them, for the benefit of people and wildlife alike, should be encouraged.

Hertfordshire – a parky county?

At the end of the sixteenth century John Norden wrote of Hertfordshire, 'This Shire at this day is, and more hath beene heretofore, much repleat with parkes, woodes, and rivers'.[14] His map of the county (1598), together with the earlier map by Christopher Saxton (1577)[15] and the county history by Sir Henry Chauncy (1700), formed the basis for Evelyn Shirley's 1867 historical survey of the county's parks, in which he described 31 'principal' parks.[16] Several of these, however, were post-medieval in origin and, of the six deer parks he listed as existing in Hertfordshire in 1867, none was wholly medieval in origin, although those at Hatfield, Knebworth and Moor Park (Rickmansworth) probably incorporated parts of their medieval antecedents. James E. Harting, writing in 1881, drew upon the historical research of a wider range of antiquarians and was able to compile information on 44 deer parks in the county, of which ten were extant and about half had medieval origins.[17]

Nearly a century later Lionel Munby described Hertfordshire as 'a county of parks' and found evidence for about 40 medieval 'hunting parks or game preserves'.[18] Leonard Cantor's 1983 total of 44 medieval parks for Hertfordshire was derived, for the most part, from state records such as the Close, Charter and Patent Rolls and inquisitions *post mortem* (most of which were gleaned from the Victoria County History).[19] Oliver Rackham considered Hertfordshire 'the most parky county of all … with ninety known parks', but the source of this figure is a puzzle.[20]

7. *Cal. Close 1296-1302*, pp. 170 and 175.

8. *Cal. Close 1313–18*, pp. 140–1.

9. W. Page (ed.), *A history of the county of Hertford*, 4 (VCH, 1971), 4, p. 396 citing *Gesta abbat.* iii, pp. 390 and 400; Cott. MS. Nero, D vii, fol. 22d.

10. R. Almond, *Medieval hunting* (Stroud, 2003), pp. 82–3.

11. L.M. Cantor and J. Hatherly, 'The medieval parks of England', *Geography*, 64 (1979), p. 79; S.A. Mileson, 'The importance of parks in fifteenth-century society', in L. Clark (ed.), *The fifteenth century V* (Woodbridge, 2005), pp. 23–5.

12. S.A. Mileson, 'The sociology of park creation in medieval England', in R. Liddiard (ed.), *The medieval park: new perspectives* (Macclesfield, 2007), pp. 21, 23.

13. I.D. Rotherham, 'The historical ecology of medieval parks and the implications for conservation', in R. Liddiard (ed.), *The medieval park: new perspectives* (Macclesfield, 2007), pp. 79–91.

14. J. Norden, *A description of Hertfordshire* (Ware, 1598, reprinted 1903), p. 2.

15. J. Norden, *Hartford Shire* (1598); C. Saxton, *Hartfordiae Comitatus* (1577).

16. E. Shirley, *English deer parks* (London, 1867), pp. 79–81, citing H. Chauncy, *The historical antiquities of Hertfordshire* (London, 1700).

17. J.E. Harting, 'Hertfordshire deer-parks', *Transactions of the Hertfordshire Natural History Society*, 2 (1881), pp. 97–111. In addition to Chauncy, he cites N. Salmon, *The history of Hertfordshire* (London, 1728); R. Clutterbuck, *The history and antiquities of the county of Hertford*, 1–3 (London, 1815–27); J.E. Cussans, *History of Hertfordshire*, 1–3 (London, 1870–81).

18. L.M. Munby, *The Hertfordshire landscape* (London, 1977), p. 131.

19. L. Cantor, *The medieval parks of England: a gazetteer* (Loughborough, 1983), pp. 38–9 citing *VCH*, 2–4.

20. O. Rackham, *The history of the countryside* (1986; republished London, 1997), p. 123, citing Munby, *Hertfordshire landscape* (but Munby makes no such claim).

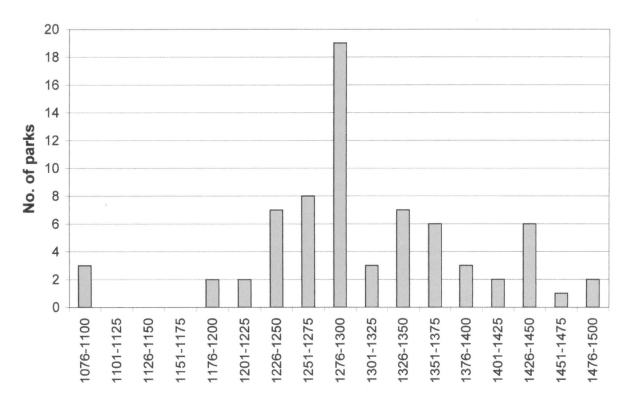

Figure 1. First documentary references to parks in Hertfordshire

Almost invariably, however, further research leads to the discovery of more parks and the lists of medieval parks have grown markedly in those counties whose parks have been investigated in recent decades. Hertfordshire is no exception and current research puts the total number of medieval parks in the county at about 70, but there may well be a few more awaiting discovery.

The sources

As Cantor wrote in 1983, 'the mapping of the English medieval park depends upon three major sources of evidence: documentary material; physical remains such as park banks and ancient woods; and field-, wood- and farm-names'.[21] Other clues to look for on maps are anomalous field patterns and disruptions to the local network of roads and footpaths.

Documentary evidence

The earliest documentary evidence for about 60 per cent of parks in Hertfordshire is found in the records of medieval government – primarily in the Calendars of Patent Rolls (11 parks), Charter Rolls (7) and Close Rolls (7) and in the manorial extents recorded in the inquisitions held after the death of a tenant-in-chief (6 parks). Seven parks were first recorded as a result of having been broken into and, in most cases, deer were stolen. Four of these park-breaks occurred between 1296 and 1300 at Hunsdon, Broadfield, Barkway and Gacelyn park (Hatfield). Licences to impark land were granted

for only nine of Hertfordshire's parks, the earliest of which was granted to the abbot of Waltham Holy Cross in 1332. Three licences were granted in the 1360s, at Oxhey (Watford), Albury and Kimpton, but the remaining five licences were granted in the first half of the fifteenth century at Bedwell (Essendon), The More (Rickmansworth), Pendley (Tring), Rye (Stanstead Abbots) and Shingle Hall (Sawbridgeworth).

The dates at which parks first made their appearance in the documentary record have been plotted in Figure 1. A gap of about a century follows the recording of the three Hertfordshire parks in the Domesday survey of 1086. This gap is most likely to reflect a lack of records rather than a lack of new parks. The chart shows a notable spike in the last quarter of the thirteenth century, when the number of parks appearing in the records for the first time rose dramatically. A similar peak has been observed in the neighbouring county of Cambridgeshire but also further away in Hampshire and East Yorkshire; the phenomenon probably had as much to do with advances in national administration and record-keeping as with an actual increase in park creation.[22] Many of the parks represented in the late thirteenth-century spike will have been created much earlier in the century, or even in the twelfth century. As Rosemary Hoppitt has recently emphasised, the recording of parks in government documents does not provide dating evidence for the *creation* of those parks and a closer examination of the documentary evidence 'is essential in order to establish a more reliable chronology of imparking'.[23]

21. Cantor, *The medieval parks of England*, p. 5.

22. T. Way, *A study of the impact of imparkment on the social landscape of Cambridgeshire and Huntingdonshire from c.1080 to 1760*, BAR British Series, 258 (1997), p. 21, quoting K. Bilikowski, *Hampshire's countryside heritage: historic parks and gardens* (Winchester, 1983) and S. Neave, *Medieval parks of East Yorkshire* (Beverley, 1991).

23. R. Hoppitt, 'Hunting Suffolk's parks: towards a reliable chronology of imparkment', in R. Liddiard (ed.), *The medieval park: new perspectives* (Macclesfield, 2007), p. 149.

The most informative source of evidence for the existence and management of medieval parks are manorial records, and especially the annual accounts drawn up by the manorial bailiff, reeve or other official. The preservation of these records is a matter of chance but many have survived and are accessible to the public in county record offices and in The National Archives at Kew. The manorial records for 34 parks on 24 Hertfordshire manors have been examined, most of which were located via the website of The National Archives, which provides access to catalogues of manorial records held in local archives via the Access to Archives (A2A) database and the Manorial Documents Register. The records for some manors continue into the sixteenth century and for two medieval parks (Ware and Hunsdon) the only useful manorial records date from the early sixteenth century but, nevertheless, shed light on the parks in the late medieval period. These records are of enormous value, not least because they can fill in the gaps between a park's appearances in the 'state' records and can sometimes confirm the presence of deer in the park.

Manorial accounts were compiled in Latin and gleaning information from them can seem a daunting prospect for the researcher with little or no knowledge of the language and, perhaps, a limited understanding of the way the medieval manor functioned. However, the accounts are set out in a reasonably standardised way and, with some background reading, guidance with palaeography, access to appropriate Latin word lists and *practice*, they can yield some fascinating details to reward one's efforts.

The presence of a parker in the fees and wages section of the account provides firm evidence of a functioning deer park (although the converse is not necessarily the case). As the park almost always formed part of the manorial demesne, any income derived from it appears under 'Issues of the manor' (*Exitus manerii*). The most common sources of income were payments for the right to graze livestock in the park (agistment) and the sale of wood and underwood from parkland trees, which were pollarded, or from woods within the park, which were coppiced. Pannage of pigs also features regularly in the accounts but produced income very irregularly. The costs of running the park were often recorded in a section of the account headed, unsurprisingly, 'Costs of the park' (*Custus parci*). Predominant amongst these costs were payments for repairs to the park boundary and, sometimes, the wage of the parker – although this was more often entered in the 'Wages' (*vadium*) section of the account. The principal inhabitants of the parks, the deer, were rarely recorded because they were not a source of income. There was no legal market in venison and park-owners seem to have thought solely in terms of producing deer for their own households or to give away as prestigious gifts as, for example, in December 1363 when the Black Prince ordered his parker at Berkhamsted to deliver three does to his near neighbour, Sir Walter de Aldebury.[24] Evidence of this gift-giving can be found in the accounts if costs were incurred in transporting the deer or venison, as was the case at Walkern in 1390/1, when William Holm was paid 5d for 'drawing 1

slaughtered deer up to Cambridge of the lord's gift to the Augustinian Friars there'; in 1449/50, the costs of obtaining deer from four local parks to restock the park at Great Munden were recorded.[25] Sometimes costs were incurred in providing fodder to maintain the deer herd during the winter and, occasionally, when grazing in the park was reserved exclusively for the deer, this was recorded in the accounts to explain the lack of income from agistment.

Physical evidence

During this study, the remains of sections of a boundary bank have been found at about one-third of medieval park sites in Hertfordshire. It should be stressed, however, that no systematic survey of the park boundaries has been undertaken and the surviving banks have been observed only from public rights of way. The proportion of parks for which at least part of the medieval boundary survives may, therefore, be significantly more than a third. Notable banks, which may have nothing to do with a former park, also survive around ancient woods (woodbanks) and on parish boundaries. In some cases the boundaries of park and parish and/or wood coincide and it is often impossible to tell which came first and which occasioned the creation of the earthwork. Some parish boundary banks – or woodbanks – may have been adopted and adapted to form later park boundaries, thus reducing the cost of the new park.

Most of the banks which remain are about 6m across and many have a ditch on one side. Very few, however, seem to conform to the textbook park boundary, with the ditch on the inside of the bank. Given the predominance of arable farming in much of modern Hertfordshire it is perhaps surprising that most park boundaries can still be traced on the ground at all, but the practice of ploughing up to the margins of fields may well account for the loss of many internal ditches, if indeed they did once exist. The most impressive park boundary earthworks which can be seen from a public footpath are at Benington Park, Bramfield Park Wood and Hoddesdonpark Wood.

Place-name evidence

Over 70 per cent of Hertfordshire's medieval parks are (or were) remembered in the names of fields and woods as well as in farm names, place-names and street names recorded on maps from the seventeenth century onwards. Park Street, south of St Albans, is perhaps the only settlement to be named after a park: it grew up along Roman Watling Street beside a medieval park belonging to the abbots of St Albans (Eywood park). There are, however, many park-related farm names in the county: there are (or were) 9 Park Farms and no fewer than 13 Lodge Farms, all established on former medieval parkland. Some of these parks may have survived into the post-medieval period, so the lodges commemorated in some of the names may not necessarily have medieval origins. Wood names include Old Park Wood (Cheshunt and Much Hadham), Bramfield Park Wood, Park Spring (Flamstead), Park Wood (Knebworth), Hailey Park Wood (Benington),

---

24. Dawes, *Register of the Black Prince, 4*, p. 517.

25. HALS DE/Hx/Z24 typed translation of account rolls of manor of Walkern, 1324–1432, pp. 84–5, quoting HALS 9357 bailiff's account for the manor of Walkern, 1390/1; TNA: PRO SC6/867/13 bailiff's account for Great Munden, 1449/50.

Lodge Hill Wood and New Lodge Wood (Berkhamsted) but, sadly, the woods at Much Hadham and Berkhamsted no longer exist. Park Lanes lead to, or around, the parks at Bramfield, Cheshunt (Brantingshay), Knebworth (great), Ware and Weston (great).

Field names are the most frequent reminder of a former park, the most interesting perhaps revealing the presence of a lodge. Examples include Lodge Croft and Lodge Yard Pasture (Bishop's Stortford), 'le logge' (Bushey), Lodge Pasture (Furneux Pelham), Lodge Field (Tyttenhanger) and Lodge Mead (Benington). The word 'laund' was a Norman-French word for an open, unwooded field or pasture and is often found in association with deer parks. The word evolved into our modern word 'lawn'. Laund (or lawn) field names have been found relating to eight former medieval parks including, for example, Launde Meadow (Benington), New Lodge Launde (Berkhamsted), Lower, Middle and Further Lawn (Knebworth), Postern Lawn (Bedwell) and The Lawn (Bishop's Stortford). The sites of former park gates can also be revealed in field names such as Park Gate Field (Bishop's Stortford) and Park Gate Close (Weston great park).

Occasionally, wood and field names provide the strongest evidence for a former park, as at Flamstead, where a wood called Park Spring, a collection of park field names and a boundary earthwork all seem to recall a park for which no documentary evidence has been found.

Cartographic evidence
In addition to recording features with park-related names, maps can also provide other clues to the existence of a former park. The creation of a park often caused paths and tracks to be diverted; ordinary folk were generally not permitted to pass through the park and, consequently, new routes developed around the outside of the park. Many of these routes have survived as lanes or public rights of way to this day and can be used to help identify former park boundaries.

Maps can also reveal variations in the character of field boundaries. Parks which fell out of use and were divided up into fields at any time from the seventeenth century onwards can sometimes be identified as areas with relatively large, straight-sided fields which are in marked contrast to the smaller, irregularly shaped fields immediately around them.

The chronology of medieval park creation in Hertfordshire
The earliest parks to be recorded in the county appear in entries in the Domesday Book of 1086 at St Albans, Ware and Benington, each of which was described as 'a park for woodland beasts'.[26] The holders of the three Domesday parks were all prestigious Norman lords, who had been granted the lands of high-ranking Saxons after the Conquest. Parks have long been considered a Norman introduction but recent work has determined that several were already in existence in England in the decades before 1066.[27] Although clear evidence

is lacking in Hertfordshire, it is possible that any, or all, of these Domesday parks had pre-Conquest origins and the question is examined for each park in its respective entry in the gazetteer.

Whether these three parks originated before or after the Norman Conquest will probably never be known, however, and a similar lack of evidence makes it impossible to ascertain how many parks were created in the county during the late eleventh and twelfth centuries. The first record we have of a park after Domesday dates from 1199, when the bishop of London granted some land out of his 'old park' in Much Hadham. The implication is that the park had been in existence for some time and had already been disparked or replaced. Another park likely to date from the twelfth century was at Cheshunt. The earliest reference to this park dates from 1226, when Alan de Bassingbourn held it by serjeanty, a position he had inherited from his father and his 'antecedants' before him. This suggests that at least three generations of men had held the park in this way by 1226.[28]

In the 80 years from 1220 to the end of the thirteenth century 37 parks appear in the documentary record for the first (and, in some cases, only) time. For none of these parks is the date of their creation recorded; we can only deduce that they were created before the date of their appearance in the historical record. Listed in the order in which they appear in the records, these parks were at Ardeley, Hatfield (great park), Cheshunt (old park), Weston (either great or Ipgrave park), Standon, Sawbridgeworth (Sayes), Bramfield, Clothall, Great Gaddesden, Hatfield (little park), St Albans (Derefold), Bishop's Stortford, Ayot St Lawrence, Little Gaddesden (Ashridge), Furneux Pelham, Boreham Wood, Little Hadham (Hadham Hall), Weston (either great or Ipgrave park), King's Langley (great park), Hoddesdon (Bassingbourne's park), Berkhamsted, Cheshunt (Brantingshay), Great Munden, Hertingfordbury (old park), Little Hadham, Hoddesdon (William of Louth's park), Sawbridgeworth (Pisho), Hunsdon, Eastwick, King's Langley (little park), Broadfield, Barkway (Scales), Knebworth (old park), Little Munden (two parks), Little Wymondley and Hatfield (Gacelyn).

In the first half of the fourteenth century another 10 parks were recorded for the first time at Standon (Milkley), Walkern, Hormead, Stanstead Abbots (Easneye), Cheshunt (Periers x2), Albury, Little Berkhamsted, Benington (Hayley) and Bishop's Stortford. Three of these parks were almost certainly created during this period: the abbot of Waltham Holy Cross obtained a licence 'to impark his wood of Isneye' in 1332; the creation of a new park was recorded in the accounts for Stortford manor in 1346/7; and the Walkern manorial accounts appear to record the creation of the park there in 1324/5.[29] Many of the remaining parks, however, could have been established during the previous century.

In the decades immediately after the Black Death (1349) three lay manorial lords obtained licences to enclose parks:

26. J. Morris (ed.), *Domesday Book: Hertfordshire*, (Chichester, 1976) 10,5; 26,1 and 36,7.
27. R. Liddiard, 'The deer parks of Domesday Book', *Landscapes*, 4, 1 (2003), pp. 4–23.
28. *Curia Regis Rolls of the reign of Henry III vol. XII 1225–1226* (London, 1957), p. 486.
29. *Cal. Pat. 1330–1334*, p. 259; TNA: PRO SC6/1140/2 minister's account for Bishop's Stortford, 1346/7; HALS 9325 bailiff's account for the manor of Walkern, 1324/5.

Roger de Louthe was granted permission to 'impark his woods of Gippes and Edeswyk' at Oxhey, Watford, in 1360; John de la Lee was licensed to enclose '300 acres of pasture and wood in his demesne lands, pastures and woods in the towns of Braughing and Albury' in 1366 (but may not actually have done so); and, in the same year, Sir Nigel Loring, chamberlain to the Black Prince, was licensed to enclose woods at Kimpton.[30] In each case the land being imparked was apparently not abandoned arable land but manorial 'waste'. Another seven parks were recorded for the first time in the second half of the fourteenth century at Hertingfordbury (new park), Ippollitts (Almshoe and Maydencroft), Knebworth (new park), Hitchin, St Albans (Childwick) and Flamstead, but some of these (notably Almshoe) may have been created significantly earlier.

In addition to the creation of three new parks, at least two parks were enlarged following the Black Death. These were both royal parks in the west of Hertfordshire and both were enlarged by enclosing land which had previously been cultivated: 54 acres of land and 10 acres of wood were added to Berkhamsted park by Edward the Black Prince in 1354 and at King's Langley Edward III added more lands to the park in the 1360s, including 160 acres of former arable land.[31]

The early fifteenth century saw another flurry of imparkment, starting with a licence granted to John Norbury to enclose 800 acres of his land at Bedwell in 1406.[32] The second quarter of the century saw the granting of a further four licences: for the enclosure of '600 acres of land in wood' in Rickmansworth and Watford to make a park at The More in 1426; for the enclosure of 200 acres of land at Pendley in Tring and Aldbury, in 1440; for the enclosure of a 157-acre park comprising land, meadow, pasture and wood on the Island of Rye beside the river Lea in Stanstead Abbots in 1443 and for the enclosure of a 520-acre park comprising land, meadow and wood in Sawbridgeworth and Thorley at Shingle Hall in 1447.[33] The parks at Bedwell, The More and Shingle Hall were amongst the eight largest medieval parks in the county and all five fifteenth-century parks for which licences were granted were created in association with a substantial house. Another two fifteenth-century parks were established, also in association with major houses, at Tyttenhanger (by the abbot of St Albans) and at Bushey (by the Earl of Salisbury).[34]

A further three parks were recorded for the first time in the late fifteenth century: the little park at Knebworth and the parks on the Hatfield manors of Symondshyde and Woodhall, bringing the total of parks known to have existed in Hertfordshire in the medieval period to just over 70.

The chance find of records of the parks at Symondshyde and Woodhall demonstrates that parks on smaller manors and sub-manors may well be under-recorded. Symondshyde and Woodhall were sub-manors of the manor of Hatfield, held of the bishops of Ely by tenants. There is very little documented history for either manor, perhaps because the tenant families

had little need for record-keeping or, if records were produced, they have not survived. Those few records which have been found were fortunately preserved and catalogued in the archive at Hatfield House – but only because both manors subsequently became part of the Hatfield House estate. Although there are no earlier records of these two parks, the evidence suggests that they are most likely to date from the fourteenth century or earlier.

One further line of enquiry is the list of persons named in the 1307 lay subsidy return for Hertfordshire, which includes 4 records of the locative surname 'ate parc' and 12 records of the occupational name 'le parker' or 'parker', providing corroborative evidence for 16 parks. For the six settlements of Baldock, King's Walden, Marston, Stocking Pelham, Totteridge and Widford these names are, so far, the only indication that there *may* once have been a medieval park in the vicinity: further research might reveal more evidence.

The longevity of Hertfordshire's medieval parks

Figure 2 provides a synopsis of the numbers of deer parks which were functioning in Hertfordshire during the thirteenth, fourteenth and fifteenth centuries. It shows the minimum number of parks (dark bars) in each decade based upon good documentary evidence but also includes an assumption of continuity for the more substantial parks when there is a gap in the records. The lighter sections of the bars represent the additional parks which were very likely to have been functioning but for which no evidence has been found in any particular decade. Thus, for example, the park at Maydencroft (Ippollitts), for which there is just one known record in 1358, is likely to have existed in the 1340s and the 1360s and not just in the 1350s. The park at Baud's manor, Little Hadham, was only recorded in 1275 and 1323 but, given the social status of the owners from the later fourteenth century onwards and the existence of a park in the sixteenth century, it seems very likely that the park would have continued in use to the end of the medieval period. Where the gap in the historical record spans about a century or more, the park has been classified as 'likely' to have continued in use, rather than 'definitely', as for example at Ayot St Lawrence (recorded in 1268 and 1367) and Furneux Pelham (recorded in 1274 and 1367/8).

Uncertainty also arises when it is not clear whether the park name continued in use after disparkment occurred. For example, references to the old park at Cheshunt occur regularly over the centuries but it is not clear whether or not it continued to hold deer, particularly after the establishment of a second park at Cheshunt in the late thirteenth century. It has, therefore, been classified as a 'likely', rather than a 'definite', park from 1230 to 1410. Of course, some parks are likely to have fallen out of use and then been restocked with deer during the course of their history but this can rarely be detected in the historical record. Only at Great Munden is it clear that the park was refurbished and restocked with deer in

30. *Cal. Chart. 1341–1417*, pp. 167, 192, 193–4.

31. *Cal. Pat. 1354–1358*, p. 137; *Cal. Pat. 1361–1364*, p. 93; *Cal. Close 1396–1399*, p. 107.

32. *Cal. Chart. 1341–1417*, p. 430.

33. *Cal. Pat. 1422–1429*, p. 351; *Cal. Chart. 1427–1516*, pp. 8, 38, 98.

34. H.T. Riley (ed.), *Annales Monasterii S. Albani a Johanne Amundesham, vol. 1, AD 793–1290* (London, 1870), p. 261.

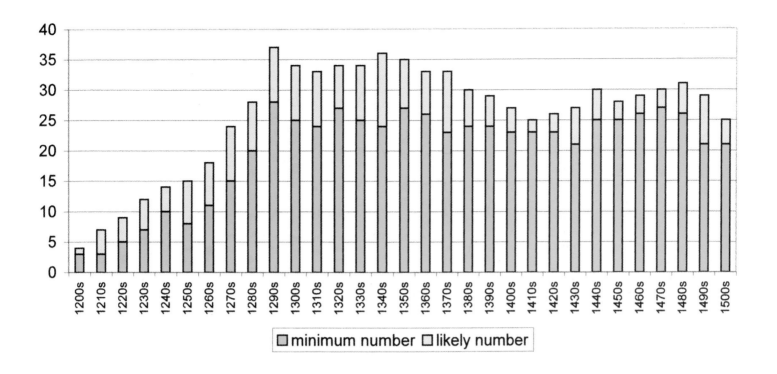

Figure 2. Minimum and likely numbers of deer parks in Hertfordshire 1200–1500

the 1440s, but the same process may also have occurred at Albury in the 1360s and at Furneux Pelham at some time during the fifteenth or early sixteenth centuries. There is, therefore, an element of uncertainty in the chart which has been minimised as much as possible but cannot be eliminated altogether. Rather than the absolute numbers, it is perhaps the trends over time which are the most important feature revealed by the chart and, if anything, the numbers of parks represented are likely to be underestimates.

The chart shows a steady increase in the numbers of parks in the county during the thirteenth century. This trend is no doubt real, but the apparently low park numbers early in the century are also likely to reflect a lack of records compiled during (and surviving from) that period: there may well have been more parks but the evidence simply does not exist. It seems that the number of parks rose to a peak of over 35 by the end of the thirteenth century and then fell very slightly to about 30–35 parks for most of the fourteenth century. During the last decades of the fourteenth century park numbers seem to have fallen to between 25 and 30, perhaps reaching a low point of 25 around 1410. Thereafter, the number of parks rose again to about 30 until the final decade of the fifteenth century, when numbers started to decline once more. Nevertheless, at least 23 of the county's medieval parks continued in use into the sixteenth century.

Perhaps the most remarkable feature of this chart is the apparent stability of park numbers over a period of two hundred years from 1300. Neither the deterioration in the climate in the decades around 1320 nor the social disaster caused by the Black Death in 1349 had a discernable effect on

the number of parks in the county. There was a core of about 16 manors which maintained at least one deer park throughout the fourteenth and fifteenth centuries. Between 60 and 70 per cent of the parks present in 1300 were still extant in 1450 and the losses were largely balanced by the creation of new parks. This accords with Stephen Mileson's estimation, based on research in Oxfordshire, Bedfordshire, Suffolk and Leicestershire, of 70 per cent park survival over the same period and confirms his view that the decline in park numbers from the mid-fourteenth century was much less significant than previously thought.[35]

The park creators

According to Leonard Cantor, a pioneer of medieval park studies, 'The Crown and the great magnates, lay and ecclesiastical, continued to be the owners of the largest numbers of parks throughout the middle ages'.[36] However, in counties like Leicestershire and Buckinghamshire he noted that 'long-established knightly families' were the predominant class of park-maker and this also seems to have been the case in Hertfordshire.[37]

Of the county's 70+ parks, only one was established by the crown, namely the park at King's Langley, which was made for Queen Eleanor by 1276. Two other parks, however, came to be held by the crown for much of the medieval period. Berkhamsted park was probably created by Edmund, Earl of Cornwall, before 1280 and passed to his cousin, Edward I, with Berkhamsted castle on his death in 1300. A park appears to have been established on the manor of Hertingfordbury before 1285 and, as a result of close family ties between the

35. Mileson, 'The importance of parks', p. 22; Cantor and Hatherly, 'Medieval parks of England', p. 73.

36. L.M. Cantor, 'Forests, chases, parks and warrens', in L.M. Cantor (ed.), *The English medieval landscape* (London, 1982), p. 76.

37. Cantor and Hatherly, 'Medieval parks of England', p. 78.

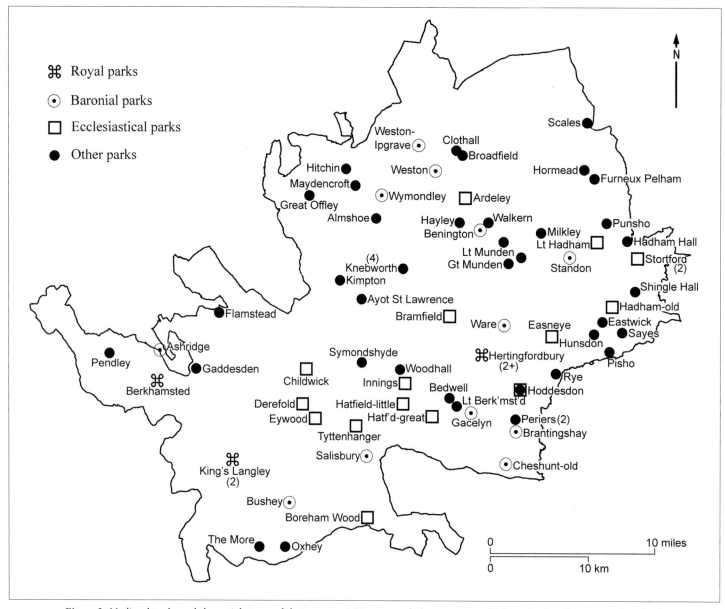

Figure 3. Medieval parks and the social status of their owners. NB some symbols represent multiple parks (number given in brackets). Further information can be found in the Gazetteer.

custodians of Hertford castle and subsequent holders of the manor of Hertingfordbury, the park (and its successors) came to be linked with the castle. Besides these three, a further 11 parks were created by members of the baronage and 16 by ecclesiastical institutions. The remaining 40 parks (57 per cent) were held by lesser lay lords (Figure 3).

The early parks were almost all established by leading barons and ecclesiastical figures. Besides Peter de Valognes, nephew of William the Conqueror, and Hugh de Grandmesnil, one of William's most trusted followers, who held the Domesday parks at Benington and Ware respectively, several other early parks occur on manors which were granted to high-ranking members of the Norman aristocracy after the Conquest. The manor of Cheshunt, where a park was first recorded in 1226, was held in 1086 by Count Alan, the son of the Duke of Brittany and son-in-law of William I. The manor

of Standon was held in 1086 by Rothais, the wife of Richard de Tonbridge, the head of a barony based at Clare in Suffolk. Gilbert de Clare became Earl of Gloucester *c*.1218 and may well have established the park which was recorded in the Standon manorial accounts in 1234/5.[38] Another branch of the de Clare family held Weston, whose illustrious twelfth-century lords included Gilbert, Earl of Clare and Pembroke, and William Marshal, Earl of Pembroke from 1199 and regent from 1216 until he died in 1219. A park was first recorded at Weston in 1231.[39]

Many of the manors on which these Norman aristocrats made their parks had several important features in common. Benington, Ware, Cheshunt, Standon and Weston were held before the Conquest by members of the English elite in the county: Aelmer of Benington, Askell of Ware, Edeva the Fair (Cheshunt), Archbishop Stigand (Standon), and Alstan, a

38. TNA: PRO SC6/1109/6 ministers' and receivers' accounts, Standon, 1233–37.
39. *Cal. Close 1227–1231*, p. 489.

thegn of King Edward (Weston). Benington, Ware, Cheshunt and Standon were all classified as 'Category 1' vills by Tom Williamson based on their Domesday entries: that is, they were all 'very large vills, assessed for taxation at more than ten hides, with simple tenurial structures' and 'contained only one manor or estate'.[40] Weston, the fifth manor in this group, was assessed at ten hides and also contained only one manor, but had lost several pieces of land to neighbouring vills by 1086. With the exception of Ashridge (created *c.*1270 by the Earl of Cornwall), all of the parks held by members of the Norman elite were located in the eastern two-thirds of the county and most were relatively large, containing between about 300 and 600 acres. Only two were small, both of which date from the late thirteenth century: Gacelyn, created by the Earl of Pembroke, covered 60 acres and Little Wymondley, created by Reginald de Argentein, covered about 50 acres.[41]

Of the religious houses, the abbots of Ely held the largest area of parkland in the county, probably totalling over 1,700 acres. The areas of two of the three parks on their manor of Hatfield were recorded in 1251: the great park was 1,000 acres (but possibly up to 1,860 acres) and the little park (later known as the middle or Millwards park) was 350 acres.[42] Innings park, containing 100 acres, was established next to their Hatfield residence probably in the late fifteenth century. In addition, they had a fourth park on their manor at Little Hadham by 1285, which may have covered 260 acres. The abbots of St Albans were also keen park-makers, establishing two parks less than half a mile from the abbey at Eywood and Derefold by the late eleventh and thirteenth centuries. A third park was recorded two miles (3km) away on their manor of Childwick in the late fourteenth century and a fourth was established three miles (5km) away at Tyttenhanger in the fifteenth century.[43] They also established two parks on their more distant manors of Boreham Wood and Bramfield, both probably in the thirteenth century. The parks ranged in size from about 80 acres at Bramfield to perhaps over 400 acres at Eywood, and possibly also at Boreham Wood: probably well over 1,000 acres in total. The bishops of London held Stortford, where they had a park of unknown size by 1263; this was replaced by a new park in 1346/7 which grew to cover nearly 300 acres.[44] The bishops also held Much Hadham, where they had a park of 190 acres which was described as 'old' in 1199 and was apparently disparked at an early date.[45] The canons of St Paul's, London, held the manor of Ardeley, where they had a park of 60 acres.[46] The abbots of Waltham created a park of about 130 acres at Easneye in Stanstead Abbots, and the dean of St Martin's-le-Grand, London, may have had a park in Hoddesdon.[47]

Most parks in the county, however, were created by ordinary lords of the manor, men like William de Say of Sawbridgeworth (whose park was first recorded in 1237), William de Ayot of Ayot St Lawrence (1268), Simon de Furneus of Furneux Pelham (1274) or Gerard de Furnival of Great Munden (1283). Some of these early manorial parks were relatively modest in size: for example, William de Say's park covered just 40 acres in 1295, and two parks belonging to Richard de Frevill of Little Munden contained 60 and 20 acres respectively in 1299.[48] Other manorial parks appear to have been significantly larger, but it is usually impossible to say whether they were that size when established or expanded from more modest beginnings during the medieval period. William de Say's park, for example, had grown to 60 acres by 1359 and probably covered over 100 acres by the late fifteenth century.[49] Larger manorial parks include Symondshyde (Hatfield) at 167 acres, Great Munden at 212 acres and Scales (Barkway) with 287 acres. The proportion of parks established by manorial lords gradually increased during the thirteenth century and from the late thirteenth century onwards they constituted the largest group of park-makers in the county.

Not all the park-makers were of 'long-established knightly families', however, and a few parks were created by royal courtiers on estates which they had acquired in the county. One such was the aforementioned Sir Nigel Loring, chamberlain to the Black Prince, whose family seat was in Bedfordshire but who was licensed to create a park at Kimpton in 1366.[50] Another servant of the crown was John Norbury, who had accumulated wealth as a successful soldier before settling into a career in royal administration. He acquired substantial estates in the south of the county and obtained a licence to enclose an 800-acre park at Bedwell (Essendon) in 1406.[51] Sir Andrew Ogard was a royal courtier who made his fortune working for the Duke of Bedford in

40. T. Williamson, *The origins of Hertfordshire* (Manchester, 2000), p. 157.

41. *Cal. Inq. post mortem, vol. 6, Edward II, 1316–1327*, p. 317; HALS 59336 inquisition *post mortem* of John de Argentein, 1423.

42. BL Cotton MS, Claudius C.xi survey of manors of bishopric of Ely, 1251, f.155.

43. J.R. Hunn, *Reconstruction and measurement of landscape change: a study of six parishes in the St Albans area*, BAR British Series, 236 (1994), pp. 176, 178–9.

44. P.J. Taylor, 'The estates of the bishopric of London from the seventh century to the early sixteenth century', (PhD thesis, London, 1976), p. 179; TNA: PRO SC6/1140/2 minister's account, 1346/7.

45. Page, *Hertford*, 4, p. 60.

46. W.H. Hale, *The Domesday of St Paul's of 1222* (Camden Society, 1858), p. 21.

47. *Cal. Pat. 1330–1334*, p. 259; *Cal. Close 1288–1296*, p. 64; because of the uncertainty, the park at Hoddesdon has not been included in the total created by ecclesiastical institutions.

48. *Cal. Inq. post mortem, vol. 3, Edward I, 1290–1300*, p. 170; Cussans, *History of Hertfordshire*, 2, p. 148 citing Chancery Inquisition *post mortem* 27 Edw. I no. 16 (TNA: PRO C133/87/15).

49. *Cal. Inq. post mortem, vol. 10, 33 Edward III, 1352–1361*, p. 403; HHA CP349, Survey of the estates of Robert Cecil carried out by Israel Amyce, 1600/01.

50. *Cal. Chart. 1341–1417*, pp. 193–4; C.L. Kingsford, 'Loring, Sir Neil [Nigel] (*c.*1315–1386)', rev. Richard Barber, *Oxford dictionary of national biography* (Oxford, 2004; online edn, October 2005), accessed online 18 July 2007.

51. *Cal. Chart. 1341–1417*, p. 430; P. Morgan, 'Norbury, John (*d.* 1414)', *Oxford dictionary of national biography* (Oxford, 2004; online edn, May 2006), accessed online 9 July 2007.

France and used it to purchase the manor of Rye (Stanstead Abbots) where he was licensed to create a park in 1443.[52]

Another social group which emerged as park-makers in the fifteenth century was composed of men who had made their wealth in trade and used it to buy their way into the landed classes.[53] The earliest example in Hertfordshire was William Flete, a London mercer, who was licensed to create a 600-acre park at his manor of The More, Rickmansworth, in 1426.[54] The next was Sir Robert Whittingham, a London merchant and financier who, like Sir Andrew Ogard, worked for the Duke of Bedford. He created a park at Pendley, near Tring, in the 1440s.[55]

Several magnates created more than one park on their manors. The earliest Hertfordshire example of this was probably at Hatfield, where the bishop of Ely had two parks by 1248.[56] The Duke of Brittany had two parks at Cheshunt by 1280, the countess of Pembroke had two parks at Weston by 1275 and Edward I had two parks on his manor at Langley by 1296.[57] These great landowners all had substantial areas of parkland by the end of the thirteenth century, but lesser men could also aspire to owning two parks, albeit on a smaller scale. Richard de Frevill had two parks of 60 and 20 acres at Little Munden in 1299, and on the manor of Periers in Cheshunt Richard de Periers had two parks containing 40 acres in 1335.[58] Two parks were recorded at Hertingfordbury in the middle of the fourteenth century, the second park perhaps being created by Queen Isabella as an appurtenance to Hertford castle, and several parks existed at Knebworth by the early fifteenth century.[59] Little parks, a fashionable adjunct to the lordly residence from the thirteenth century, appeared at Knebworth by 1481 and beside the bishop's palace at Hatfield by the beginning of the sixteenth century,[60] while an earlier example may have existed at Almshoe Bury (Ippollitts).

The spatial relationship between the lord's residence and his park

Most early medieval parks were located some distance away from the manorial halls of their owners.[61] From the fourteenth century, however, many royal residences were sited within parks and there are numerous examples nationally where the residence and park were located close together and where

there was a clear visual relationship between the two. This has led landscape historians to debate both the extent to which these particular park landscapes were deliberately designed to provide an attractive vista from the house, or to enhance the setting of the residence, and how this relationship may have changed during the medieval period.[62] Within Hertfordshire, the evidence suggests that only a small proportion of parks was established in close proximity to the owner's residence before the fifteenth century. On those few sites where park and residence were intervisible, however, the possibility that aesthetics, as well as convenience, played a part in determining their relative positions can be considered.

Of the 14 parks known to have been created in Hertfordshire by 1250, only the one at Ardeley was definitely located adjacent to the residence of the owner. The manor house, held by the canons of St Paul's from pre-Norman times, was said in 1222 to be surrounded by a park of 60 acres.[63] The great park at Weston may also have been established next to the manor house before 1250, or, if not, certainly before 1275. One of Weston's two parks had been established before 1231 by William Marshal, Earl of Pembroke, and the second had been created by 1275, when the pales around the garden in the 'great' park were repaired. The garden was presumably adjacent to the manor house and confirmation of the close proximity of the park occurs in a reference to the sale of dead wood and underwood 'in the park beside the house' in 1305/6. The manor house probably lay on the south side of the church in Court Close.[64] From here, the occupants of the house would have enjoyed lovely views over the rolling landscape of the great park, an important example, perhaps, of thirteenth-century landscape appreciation.

In the second half of the thirteenth century 27 parks appeared in the documentary record for the first time, of which four were close to the residence of the owner. Two of these, at Ashridge and at King's Langley, belonged to the social elite but the other two were established by lords of lower status at Ayot St Lawrence and Little Wymondley. The park at Ashridge was probably created by Edmund, Earl of Cornwall, during the 1270s. Although his main seat was at nearby Berkhamsted castle, Edmund appears to have been very fond

52. Page, W. (ed.), *A history of the county of Hertford*, 3 (VCH, 1912), p. 367.

53. Mileson, 'The importance of parks', p. 32.

54. *Cal. Pat. 1422–1429*, p. 351.

55. *Cal. Chart. 1427–1516*, p. 8; J. Stratford, 'Whittingham, Sir Robert (d. 1452)', *Oxford dictionary of national biography* (Oxford, 2004), accessed online 29 August 2007.

56. HHA Hatfield Manor Papers I, 1248–9, p. 47.

57. Cussans, *History of Hertfordshire*, 2, p. 208; TNA: PRO SC6/873/6 ministers' account for Weston, 1275/6; TNA: PRO SC6/1090/4 minister's account for King's Langley, 1296/7.

58. Cussans, *History of Hertfordshire*, 2, p. 148 citing Chan. Inq. p.m. 27 Edw. I no. 16; *Cal. Inq. post mortem, vol. 7, Edward III, 1327–1336*, p. 453.

59. *Cal. Pat. 1358–1361*, p. 97; HALS K102 bailiff's account for manor of Knebworth, 1401/2; K106 bailiff's account for manor of Knebworth, 1402/3.

60. HALS K124 bailiff's account for manor of Knebworth, 1481/2; HHA Hatfield Manor Papers II, November 1508, p. 587.

61. S. Lasdun, *The English park: royal, private and public* (London, 1991), p. 8; Hoppitt, 'Hunting Suffolk's parks', p. 162.

62. C. Taylor, 'Medieval ornamental landscapes', *Landscapes*, 1 (2000), pp. 38–55; A. Richardson, '"The king's chief delights": a landscape approach to the royal parks of post-Conquest England', in R. Liddiard (ed.), *The medieval park: new perspectives* (Macclesfield, 2007), pp. 27–48; A. Pluskowski, 'The social construction of medieval park ecosystems: an interdisciplinary perspective', in R. Liddiard (ed.), *The medieval park: new perspectives* (Macclesfield, 2007), p. 76.

63. Hale, *Domesday of St Paul's*, p. 21.

64. TNA: PRO SC6/873/6 and 22 minister's accounts, 1275/6 and 1305/6; HALS Acc 4283 plan by Henry Lily of the Township and Parish of Weston together with the Manor of Weston Argentines and Newberry, 1633.

of Ashridge and built himself a residence there, complete with gardens and a chapel, set within a park. By 1285 he had established a religious foundation in the park at Ashridge.[65] The manor of Langley was acquired by Queen Eleanor, who initiated the building which developed into a favourite residence of Edward II and subsequent medieval kings and queens. The park was first recorded in 1276 and was probably visible from the proto-palace because it incorporated 120 acres of former arable land which presumably lay close to the settlement, and palace, of Langley.[66] By 1296 there were at least two parks at Langley and they increased in size over the fourteenth century so that the palace was on the boundary of the park – as it may have been from the outset.[67]

Of the two less prestigious sites, the park at Ayot St Lawrence was probably created by William de Ayot, a steward of Henry III, between 1257 and 1268, and the manor house was probably located in, or on the boundary of, the park, which may have been about 135 acres in size.[68] The park at Little Wymondley was recorded in 1299 and was probably created after 1285 by Reginald de Argentein, the son of Sir Giles d'Argentein of Great Wymondley, a baronial leader whose own father had been a knight of the royal household and was descended from a line of sheriffs of Hertfordshire, Essex and Cambridgeshire. The manorial account rolls record that in 1369 a fence was made anew 'between the park and the lord's hall' and the location of the residence in the park (which probably covered only c.50 acres) is supported by field-name and map evidence.[69]

Another 'royal' establishment where it could be argued that the park formed an attractive setting for the residence was at Berkhamsted castle. However, the park created by Edmund, Earl of Cornwall, by about 1280 probably lay a short distance away on the hill to the north-west of the castle. It might have been visible from the castle but was probably not originally designed to enhance its setting. That probably occurred around 1340 when Edward III initiated a major programme of repairs to make the castle one of the chief residences of the royal family. An account of 1377/8 records the enclosing of 180 acres of land in 'Castelfeld' into the park at some (unspecified) time in the past and it seems likely that this was part of Edward III's works, intended to improve both the castle and its landscape.[70]

Of the 19 parks which appeared in the documentary record for the first time during the fourteenth century, only one was (probably) closely associated with the lord's residence: that at Almshoe Bury. The only record of this park was in 1358 when it was visited by Queen Isabella.[71] The present house incorporates the timber frame of an aisled hall house which has been dated to the mid-thirteenth century. The dog-tooth ornament on an arch-brace, together with records of a chapel on the manor, indicates a high-status residence which was probably built by Simon Fitz Adam, a sub-tenant of the manor, who settled the house on his wife at their marriage in 1241.[72] It seems very likely that Simon Fitz Adam could also have established Almshoe park in the middle of the thirteenth century and fragmentary documentary and field evidence suggests that the grand manor house sat in an inner or 'little' park in the midst of a larger area of parkland.

The spatial relationship between park and residence changed dramatically in the fifteenth century, when at least eight of the nine new parks recorded in Hertfordshire were established in association with a grand, usually new, house. John Norbury, who was licensed to create Bedwell park (Essendon and Little Berkhamsted) in 1406, had a house at Little Berkhamsted but where it lay in relation to the park is not known; there was, however, a high-status residence in the park by the early sixteenth century.[73] At The More (Rickmansworth) William Flete (along with others) was granted a charter in 1426 to crenellate the manor house and create the park. The park appears to have been established adjacent to the house, probably by Flete, but the crenellation did not take place until the 1450s, when it was undertaken by a subsequent owner, Sir Ralph Boteler, lord of Sudeley.[74] John of Wheathampstead, abbot of St Albans, established a park at Tyttenhanger (Ridge) in 1427 and the records of the abbey explicitly state that his intention was to enhance the setting and privacy of his country residence.[75] Another park which may have been established in the 1420s is reputed to have been laid out around Bushey Hall, a magnificent house started in 1428 by Thomas Earl of Salisbury, but little evidence remains to substantiate this.[76]

More parks were established around prestigious residences in the 1440s. In the process of laying out the parkland landscape around his new house at Pendley (Tring), Sir Robert Whittingham removed a thriving settlement and deprived the tenants of their grazing rights, the only known example of medieval settlement clearance to make a park in the county.[77] Sir Andrew Ogard's new park at The Rye in Stanstead Abbots formed the setting for his new (crenellated) house there and John Leventhorpe's new park seems to have surrounded his home at Shingle Hall (Sawbridgeworth).

65. TNA: PRO SC6/863/8 minister's account for Berkhamsted, 1272–1307; *Cal. Chart. 1257–1300*, p. 324.

66. L.M. Munby, *The history of King's Langley* (Workers' Educational Association, 1963), p. 11.

67. TNA: PRO SC6/1090/4 minister's account for Langley, 1296/7.

68. Page, *Hertford*, 3, p. 61.

69. N. Farris, *The Wymondleys* (Hertfordshire Publications, 1989), p. 189; H.W. Ridgeway, 'Argentine, Sir Giles d' (c.1210–1282)', *Oxford dictionary of national biography* (Oxford, September 2004; online edn, May 2007), accessed online 29 November 2007.

70. J.W. Cobb, *Two lectures on the history and antiquities of Berkhamsted* (London, 1883), p. 19; TNA: PRO SC6/863/12 receiver's account for Berkhamsted, 1377/8.

71. Bond, 'Notices of the last days of Isabella, Queen of Edward the second', p. 462.

72. J.T. Smith, *Hertfordshire houses: selective inventory* (London, 1993), p. 108.

73. *Cal. Chart. 1341–1417*, p. 430; J.S. Roskell, L. Clark and C. Rawcliffe, *The history of parliament: the House of Commons 1386–1421* (Stroud, 1992), p. 843; Page, *Hertford*, 3, p. 460.

74. *Cal. Pat. 1422–1429*, p. 351; *Cal. Pat. 1452–1461*, p. 422.

75. Riley, *Annales Monasterii*, p. 261.

76. G. Robinson, *Hertfordshire*, Barracuda Guide to County History, 3 (Chesham, 1978), p. 43.

A little park was recorded for the first time at Knebworth in 1481, a manor held by Sir John Barre of Ayot St Lawrence from 1443. The park lay beside the sixteenth-century house and, presumably, its fifteenth-century predecessor. One or more of the earlier parks at Knebworth may also have been visible from the house, but their precise locations are not known. A new park, known as Innings park, also appeared adjacent to the bishop of Ely's residence at Hatfield. It was first recorded in 1508 but was probably late medieval in origin. The earlier parks at Hatfield were a short distance away and can have made little impact on the view from the residence.

Several pre-existing parks also acquired new residences in the late medieval period. A new house was built by Thomas Baud MP at Little Hadham about 1440 on a site which later became the site of the sixteenth-century Hadham Hall.[78] Where the pre-1440 manor house stood is not known but the new house appears to have been located on the western boundary of the medieval park, which was first recorded in 1275. At Hunsdon the thirteenth-century park was expanded in 1445 and probably formed the setting for a new house built for Sir William Oldhall, chamberlain of Richard Duke of York, from 1447.[79] At Salisbury Hall (Shenley) a new house was built by Sir John Cuttes (who died in 1521) 'at Salisbury Park'.[80] This was presumably a pre-existing park established by an earl of Salisbury – perhaps the third earl, who lived there at the end of the fourteenth century, or subsequent earls who owned the estate in the fifteenth century.

The geographical distribution of medieval parks in Hertfordshire

Figure 4 shows that Hertfordshire's medieval parks were not evenly distributed throughout the county but appear to fall into two distinct zones: those in the south-western part of the county and those in the eastern and northern part of the county. Fifty-two of the parks lay in the east and north of the county; only 22 lay in the south-west. There appears to have been no significant difference in the sizes of the parks in the two zones but what is significant is the difference in the densities of park distribution.[81] In the eastern zone there were 5.4 parks per 10 kilometre square (25,000 acres), but in the western zone there were 3.2 parks per 10 kilometre square. That is, the density of parks in the eastern zone was nearly 1.7 times that in the western zone. The factors underlying this pattern of park distribution need to be carefully examined: much previous work on medieval parks in other parts of the country has found a strong link between parks and woodland, with well-wooded areas generally supporting higher densities of parks than thinly wooded areas.[82] In Hertfordshire, however, the explanation appears to be more complex than this because the most densely wooded part of the county in medieval times was the south-west.

The distribution of woodland

Several sources suggest that much of south-western Hertfordshire was still thickly wooded in the eleventh century. This area forms part of the Chiltern region and lay within what Rackham described as 'one of the largest wooded areas in England [which] extended from the Chiltern escarpment down the dip-slope almost to the gates of London'.[83] A medieval monk at the abbey of St Albans claimed that 'the whole of the Chilterns was a dense and impenetrable forest, full of wild and fierce beasts' until the eleventh century, while Abbot Leofstan (c.1048–1066) is said to have 'cleared the thick woods south of Watling Street from the Chilterns to London' in order to make the roads safer for travellers.[84] Further south, Offa's charter granting land in Aldenham to Westminster Abbey in AD 785 mentioned the density of the woods,[85] although several landscape features recorded in the boundary clause of this charter suggest a managed landscape of woods and clearings rather than an untamed wilderness. A similar landscape is suggested for the large estate further north at Wheathampstead in a charter confirming its ownership by Westminster Abbey in 1060.[86]

The Domesday survey of 1086 confirms the abundance of woodland in south-west Hertfordshire and also extending into north Middlesex, south Buckinghamshire and the southern tip of Bedfordshire. Within this area (measuring approximately 40 by 25 miles and centred on the Chilterns), Rackham has noted that settlements were relatively sparse but that 'nearly every one had wood, usually for at least 500 swine' (Figure 5).[87] The high swine numbers, and an absence of entries describing 'wood for fences', suggests that these woodlands were not intensively managed. The soils over much of this area are of poor quality for agriculture: those on the Chiltern dipslope are derived from clay-with-flints and those on the 'Southern Uplands' from London Clay (see Figures 5 and 8).

Despite the concentration of woodland in south-west Hertfordshire however, much of the remainder of the county was also relatively well-wooded in the late eleventh century.

77. Munby, *Hertfordshire landscape*, p. 133.

78. W. Minet, *Hadham Hall and the manor of Bawdes alias Hadham Parva* (1914), pp. 60–2.

79. Page, *Hertford*, 3, pp. 232, 329.

80. J. Chandler, *John Leland's itinerary: travels in Tudor England* (Stroud, 1998), pp. 245–6.

81. A. Rowe, 'The distribution of parks in Hertfordshire: landscape, lordship and woodland', in R. Liddiard (ed.), *The medieval park: new perspectives* (Macclesfield, 2007), p. 134.

82. Cantor and Hatherly, 'Medieval parks of England', pp. 74–5; Cantor, 'Forests, chases, parks and warrens', p. 77; O. Rackham, *Ancient woodland* (London, 1980; republished Dalbeattie, 2003), p. 191.

83. Rackham, *Ancient woodland*, p. 123.

84. A.E. Levett, *Studies in Manorial History* (Oxford, 1938), p. 180 quoting H.T. Riley (ed.), *Gesta abbatum monasterii Sancti Albani a Thoma Walsingham*, vol. 1, *AD 793–1290* (London, 1867; republished Germany, 1965), pp. 39–40.

85. W. De Gray Birch, *Cartularium Saxonicum: a collection of charters relating to Anglo-Saxon history*, 1 (London, 1885, reprinted 1964), p. 339.

86. Williamson, *Origins of Hertfordshire*, pp. 136–8.

87. Rackham, *Ancient woodland*, p. 123.

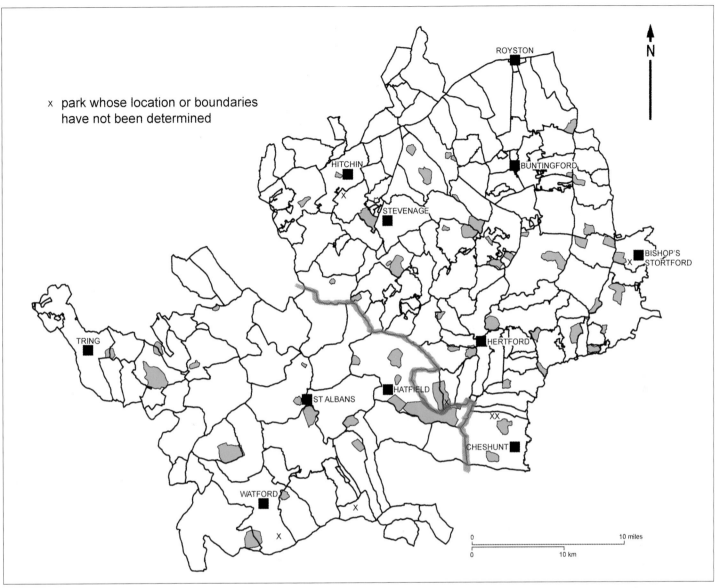

x park whose location or boundaries have not been determined

Figure 4. The geographical distribution of Hertfordshire's medieval parks. The grey line marks the hypothetical division between the south-western zone and the north-eastern zone. Please note that the areas of parkland plotted here correspond with all the parkland shown in the Gazetteer, including areas plotted with lower levels of confidence. Unlocated parks and those for which boundaries have not been determined are indicated with a cross. Further information on individual parks can be obtained from the relevant Gazetteer entry and readers should refer to the county key map on p.43, where the parishes containing parks are named.

Over three-quarters of the Hertfordshire manors recorded in Domesday Book – a higher proportion than any other county – had woodland.[88] The north-eastern two-thirds of the county was characterised by numerous small swine entries, plus a few large ones, and also a number of places with only 'wood for fences'. These records suggest that the woodland in this part of Hertfordshire was concentrated into relatively small pockets, many of which were intensively managed coppiced woods.

The woodland in this part of the county was not evenly distributed, however, and the northernmost strip of the county, in the parishes bordering east Bedfordshire and south Cambridgeshire, seems to have been virtually devoid of woodland, probably since prehistory. Here, only Pirton in the west and Ashwell in the north had significant numbers of pigs,

indicating woodland, in Domesday Book. To the south of this strip the land rises to the chalk ridge of the East Anglian Heights which extends as a boulder clay-covered plateau dipping gently southwards beneath north-east Hertfordshire. This area appears to have been well-wooded in Saxon times but the relatively fertile soils attracted settlement and by 1086 the ridge and the interfluves lying west and east of the upper Rib and Quin valleys were dotted with manors which had very little or no woodland, while thirteen holdings had only 'wood for fences'. In this area, centred on the medieval market town of Buntingford, most of the woodland seems to have been cleared before the Conquest and those small woods which survived were probably intensively managed by coppicing. No medieval parks were established in the Buntingford area, nor in the far north of the county.

88. Rackham, *Ancient woodland*, p. 123.

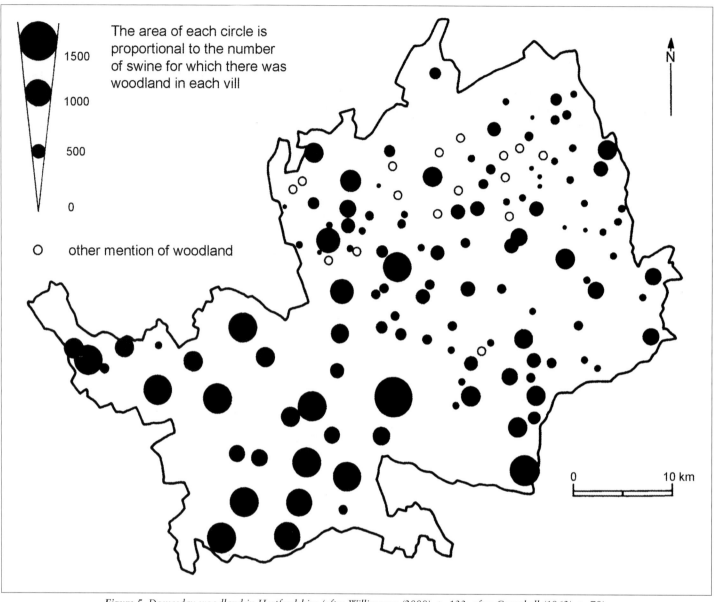

The area of each circle is proportional to the number of swine for which there was woodland in each vill

1500
1000
500
0

O   other mention of woodland

Figure 5. Domesday woodland in Hertfordshire (after Williamson (2000), p. 133; after Campbell (1962), p. 78).

In the far east of the county, particularly in the upper reaches of the Ash valley and on its interfluves to the south, and further west, on the broad plateau between the Beane and Rib valleys, woodland was much more abundant and several manors had Domesday swine counts which were comparable with the swine densities in the west of the county. Numerous parks were created in both of these areas. The watersheds between the Beane and the Mimram and between the Mimram and the Lea were also moderately well-wooded and a particularly high number of pigs – 1,000 – was recorded at Knebworth. This central and western part of the 'eastern zone' of the county also had a scatter of medieval parks but, in the far north-west, where there were also several well-wooded manors, parks were largely absent. Some of the most abundant woodland in the eastern zone was in the far south on the high ground covered with poorly draining and infertile soils derived from London Clay. There were several parks in this area, some of them particularly extensive.

Clearly there was a relationship between parks and woodland at a local level because, within the less well-wooded eastern zone of the county, parks were generally only established on those manors which had significant Domesday swine counts.

Indeed, those manors with the most abundant woodland in 1086, such as Knebworth or Standon, went on to become the sites of the most extensive medieval parks. No parks appear to have been established in areas with no woodland, or with only intensively managed woodland. However, there were many manors in the eastern zone which did have abundant woodland in 1086, such as King's Walden in the north-west (800 pigs) and Wormley in the south-east (600 pigs), as well as most of the manors in the western zone of the county, which did not, so far as we know, have medieval parks. So abundant woodland, although a desirable prerequisite, was not the primary factor influencing park creation in Hertfordshire, or there would have been far more parks in the west of the county where the woodland cover was densest. There must, therefore, have been other factors influencing the distribution of the county's medieval parks and perhaps the most important of these were settlement patterns and lordship.

Settlement patterns and lordship

The map in Figure 4 shows that parishes were not uniformly distributed across Hertfordshire: in the centre and east of the

16

county, where there were more parks, the parishes are small and densely packed: in the west, where there were fewer parks, the parishes are generally larger. Perhaps in order to understand the distribution of parks in Hertfordshire we first have to understand the reasons behind the variation in parish densities and the underlying pattern of settlement.

By late Saxon times the east and north of the county was already densely settled. Rising population levels had resulted in the gradual clearance of woodland cover, resulting in the scatter of relatively small woods indicated in Domesday Book (Figure 5). The density of the population in this part of the county in 1086 (9–13 recorded people per square mile) was comparable with the high levels recorded in much of East Anglia and is reflected in the multitude of small parishes and in the numerous manors recorded in Domesday Book. In the south-west of the county population density decreased sharply to two or three recorded people per square mile. In the far west, where the county extends over the chalk escarpment near Tring and into the clay vale of Aylesbury beyond, the recorded population rose again to nine per square mile (Figure 6).

The highest population densities, of 13 recorded people per square mile, were in the far north of the county and in the far east. In the north, where the fertile, well-drained soils of the chalk escarpment descend to the Bedfordshire lowlands, a classic 'Midland' pattern of settlement was established, with nucleated villages and 'regular' open-field systems. As we have seen, this area was almost devoid of woodland by the eleventh century and no parks were established there. By contrast, in the equally densely populated far east of the county, on the west flank of the Stort valley, nearly every parish contained a park by the end of the fifteenth century. The survival of significant woodland resources on the higher ground in these parishes, despite the high population levels, was no doubt a significant factor and the number of parks reflects the number of manors and lords wanting to enclose some of the woodland for themselves.

Between these two areas of maximum population density lies the bulk of northern and eastern Hertfordshire, where the majority of the county's medieval parks were established. Here there was an ancient, dispersed settlement pattern (with irregular field systems) which formed part of a much wider zone of 'ancient countryside' covering most of south-east England and southern parts of East Anglia.[89] The recorded population in 1086 was generally 9 per square mile rising to 11 per square mile east of the river Rib. Population levels grew rapidly between 1086 and 1307, probably more than doubling,[90] leading to a steady expansion of settlement and cultivation from the primary foci in the valleys up onto the clay-covered interfluves. Arable and pasture expanded at the expense of woods and wood-pasture, which survived longest on the higher ground furthest from the settlements.

By contrast, in the south-west of the county, as we have seen, there was abundant woodland and sparse settlement at the end of the Saxon period. Precisely because this area was relatively 'undeveloped', large tracts of it were donated to religious houses in the middle and late Saxon period. In AD 785 King Offa of Mercia granted land in Aldenham to Westminster Abbey and in AD 793 he founded the abbey at St Albans and provided it with a substantial endowment of land. The extensive Wheathampstead estate (including most of what later became the parish of Harpenden) was granted to Westminster Abbey *c*.AD 960 and Hatfield was given to King Edgar *c*.AD 970 and then granted to the abbey of Ely, which also acquired Totteridge in Saxon times.[91] Under the control of the monastic houses, primarily St Albans but also Westminster and Ely, these mid-Saxon landholdings in south and west Hertfordshire remained large and substantially intact after 1066 and evolved into the extensive parishes which exist today (Figure 7).

The main settlements on the Chiltern dipslope in the south-west were all located in the river valleys, leaving large areas of higher ground sparsely populated and covered in woods and pasture until after Domesday. As population levels rose during the early Middle Ages settlement began to spread over the higher ground and the woodland was gradually cleared, initially providing fuel and then food for the ever-growing London market. Only on the higher ground to the north did wood-pasture survive well into the Middle Ages, and much of that became incorporated into the medieval parks at Ashridge and Berkhamsted.

The extensive holdings of the abbeys of St Albans, Westminster and Ely allowed them to dominate much of south-west Hertfordshire. Although various abbots of St Albans and of Ely were keen park-enclosers, monastic owners had an inhibiting effect on park creation over most of their estates and, where those estates were particularly extensive, few parks were established. In contrast, north and east Hertfordshire was characterised by numerous smaller properties in the hands of lay owners, many of whom aspired to owning a park.[92] In summary then, the distribution of Hertfordshire's parks on the county scale had more to do with settlement and lordship than with woodland *per se*.

At the local level, however, woodland was a necessary ingredient of a medieval park and, where it was scarce or intensively managed, no parks were established. But, in areas with numerous manors where there *was* sufficient woodland to provide suitable habitat for deer, parks proliferated. Most parks seem to have been established in the thirteenth century, perhaps as a direct response by 'knightly families' to increasing pressure on woodland resources caused by rising population levels. Imparking allowed these manorial lords to take control of a rapidly dwindling resource. In the Stort valley four parks were first recorded in the thirteenth century: Sayes (1237), Stortford (1263), Pisho (1294) and Hunsdon (1296) and there may well have been a fifth at Eastwick.

Parks in the Hertfordshire landscape

The ways in which parks related to the natural landscape and to the social structures – the manors and parishes – which had been superimposed onto it are complex and interrelated. It is particularly striking that many medieval parks were located on

89. Rackham, *History of the countryside*, p. 3.
90. M. Bailey, 'Introduction', in J. Brooker and S. Flood (eds), *Hertfordshire lay subsidy rolls 1307 and 1334* (Hertfordshire Record Society, 1998), p. xxii.
91. Williamson, *Origins of Hertfordshire*, pp. 115, 118, 124, 129, 137.
92. Williamson, *Origins of Hertfordshire*, p. 181.

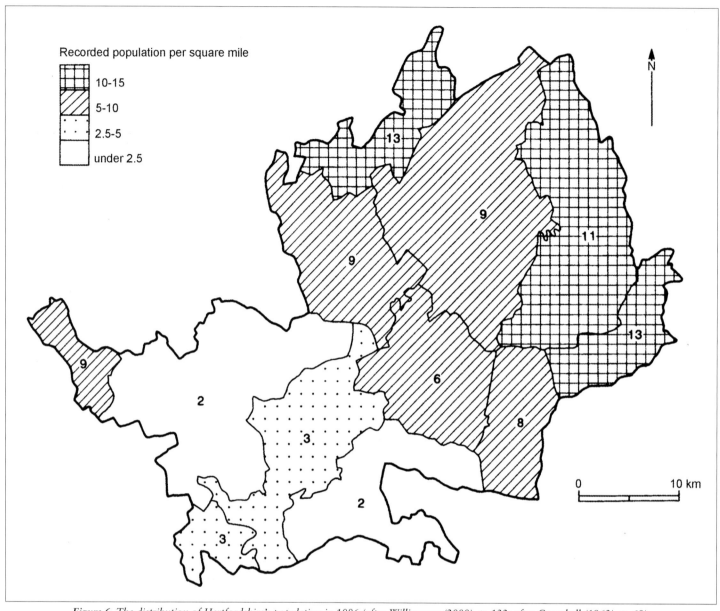

Figure 6. The distribution of Hertfordshire's population in 1086 (after Williamson (2000), p. 132; after Campbell (1962), p. 68).

high ground: about 70 per cent of Hertfordshire's medieval parks are located on high plateaux and watersheds and about a third are located on the highest land in their parishes. This relationship between parks and topography is most clearly demonstrated in the far east of the county, where six parks lay along the watershed between the river Rib (and its tributary the Quin) and the Ash and another eight parks lay on the watershed between the rivers Ash and Stort (Figure 8).

Further west, eight parks lay on the broad interfluve between the Rib and the Beane, but here a preference for locations close to the margin of the plateau is apparent. A similar distribution can be seen around the margins of high ground in the south-east of the county. The highest parks (over 150m) lay on the chalk ridge of the Chilterns at Ashridge, Berkhamsted and Flamstead. Rye park, located on the floodplain between the rivers Lea and Stort, was the only Hertfordshire park established on entirely low-lying ground; several others, such as Ware and Hertingfordbury, lay beside rivers but also incorporated land

which rose quite steeply above the floodplain.

Why was high ground the favoured location for so many parks? Perhaps the overriding reason was that it was often the only land left with the woodland cover needed to make a deer park. This was the result of a combination of natural and social factors: primary settlements often became established in river valleys close to the most fertile and easily worked land; the land further away, often on higher ground, became the manorial 'waste' – land not used for agriculture but nevertheless of value as common land for collecting firewood and grazing animals.[93] Being relatively high and exposed, and often with poorer soils, these sites were more likely to retain a covering of wood or heath than the rest of the parish. This largely unregulated land was particularly susceptible to enclosure, or 'privatisation', by a manorial lord seeking to establish a park and ensure his supply of timber and wood.

Apart from at a few high-status sites, like the royal parks at King's Langley and Berkhamsted, there is little evidence of

93. Cantor and Hatherly, 'Medieval parks of England', pp. 72, 74; Hoppitt, 'Hunting Suffolk's parks', p. 157.

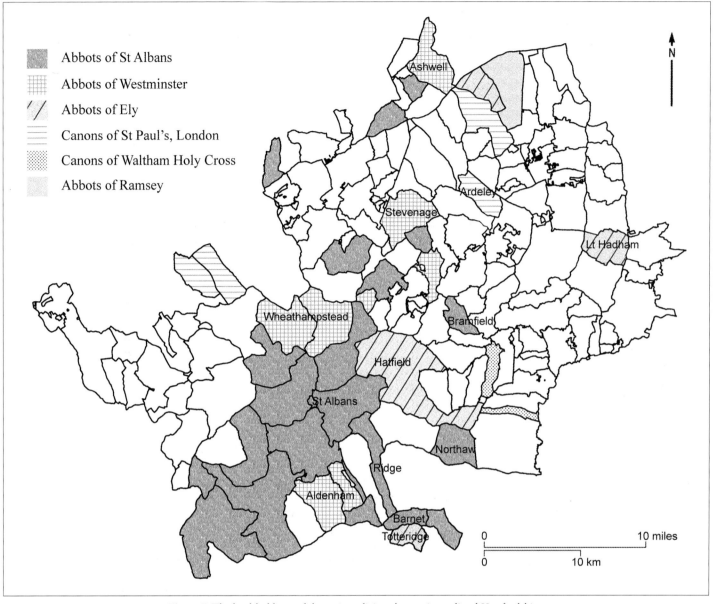

Figure 7. The land-holdings of the major religious houses in medieval Hertfordshire.

farmland being imparked in Hertfordshire. Assuming that the most fertile and easily cultivated land became farmland, this might also suggest that parks were located on poor-quality or topographically challenging land and that perhaps soil fertility was another environmental factor influencing the siting of parks. Natural soil fertility is governed by underlying geology and, although no detailed analysis has been undertaken for this study, it appears that many Hertfordshire parks did lie on relatively infertile soils.

Many parks in the north and east of the county were established on soils derived from boulder clay which, in the larger valleys, are fairly well-drained and were capable of supporting relatively high levels of population in the eleventh century (Figure 6). As we have seen, the parks in this part of the county were usually located on the interfluves – those relatively high fingers of level ground between the valleys where the heavy clay soils were prone to waterlogging and, consequently, were of limited agricultural value in the medieval period. Parks in other parts of the county also tended to be located on poor soils. For example, those on the Chiltern dipslope in the west of the county, such as Ashridge and

Berkhamsted, lay on moderately leached and acidic soils derived from clay-with-flints, and parks in the south of the county are frequently found to have lain on acid soils derived from pebbly gravels and waterlogged London Clays. Whether the soils within the parks were actually any worse than those in the remainder of the manor or parish, however, has yet to be examined in detail but there are some parks, such as Knebworth great park and Ipgrave park in Weston, where the underlying geology suggests that this may have been the case.

Within the natural and social frameworks which restricted the availability of land suitable for imparking, some manorial lords must have been able to exercise an element of choice in deciding the locations of their parks. Higher ground, remote from settlement and cultivation, offered opportunities for enjoyment of a challenging ride, extensive vistas and the 'natural' world, in addition to the opportunity to hunt game. The most impressive of the early parks in terms of landscape quality were Berkhamsted, Easneye (Stanstead Abbots), Standon, Walkern, Ware and Weston, but some of the fifteenth-century parks were equally striking, the best perhaps being Bedwell (Essendon).

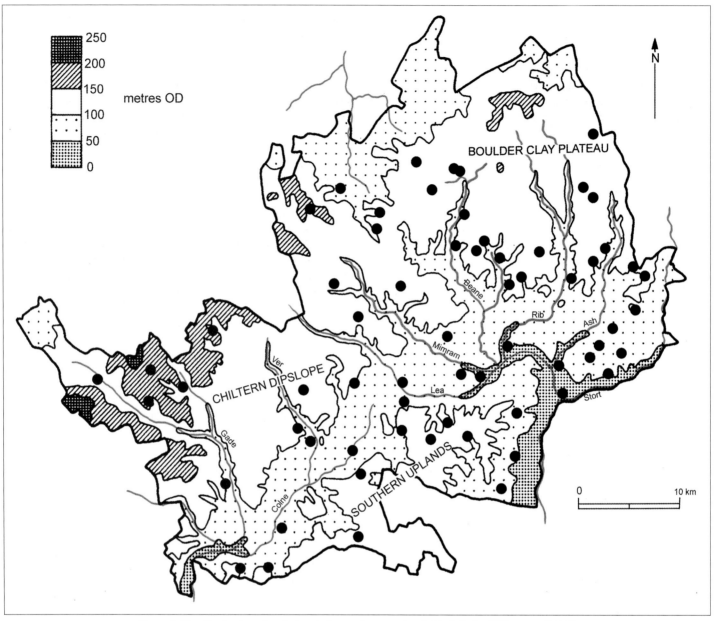

Figure 8. The distribution of parks in relation to the county's relief (relief after Williamson (2000)).

The affinity between medieval parks and high ground partly explains a close relationship between park and parish boundaries: two-thirds of Hertfordshire's parks lay on or at the parish boundary (Figure 4). This is because the boundaries between Saxon estates and, later, parishes often tended to follow the higher ground of the interfluves – usually the furthest point between neighbouring valley settlements. Some parish boundaries were marked by earth banks and these ready-made boundaries may have been an extra incentive for some manorial lords to locate their parks at the parish boundary, as they reduced the labour costs of constructing the park boundary. This may be another reason why high, remote corners of parishes seem to have been particularly susceptible to imparking, as, for example, at Stortford, Scales (Barkway) and Walkern.

The relationship between park and parish boundary can be particularly intriguing and sometimes it is impossible to determine which came first. The boundaries of a few parishes take tortuous detours to enclose pieces of land which presumably held a resource which was important to the landholder at the time the boundary was established. The best

example is at Great Munden where a southerly extension is joined to the rest of the parish by a narrow strip of land. The medieval park occupied most of that southerly extension and it is tempting to conclude that the important resource was an early park, or at least woodland which later became imparked. Similarly, the park of Pisho was located in a detached part of the parish of Sawbridgeworth, probably also an important area of woodland and wood-pasture which was subsequently enclosed to make a park.

About one third of Hertfordshire's parishes had a medieval park and several had more than one. There were no fewer than six parks in the large parish of Hatfield, and Cheshunt and Sawbridgeworth had, respectively, four and three medieval parks each. The number of parks in a parish was partly influenced by the number of manors it contained – the larger parishes tended to contain several manors, each of which could have had one or more parks.

The impact that the creation of a park had on the lives of ordinary people would have depended to a large extent on the acreage of the land enclosed. About half of Hertfordshire's

70+ parks were less than 200 acres in size and took up a relatively small proportion of the parishes in which they lay. The extents of a further 16 parks are not known but were probably relatively small, although the earliest park at Hertingfordbury and Oxhey park (Watford) might have been larger and it is possible that the abbot of St Alban's park at Boreham Wood took up a significant proportion of the parish of Elstree. Only seven parks are known to have extended over more than 500 acres and even here their effect on the local populace was probably variable. The royal parks at King's Langley (913 acres) and Berkhamsted (991 acres) must have had a considerable impact in their localities, as they took up 26 and 23 per cent of their respective parishes at their maximum extents. The effects of the much larger area of parkland owned by the bishops of Ely at Hatfield (perhaps over 2,300 acres) were mitigated by the fact that the parish was large and the manorial tenants retained common rights in the great park. Nevertheless, when the potential areas of the parks on the two sub-manors of Woodhall and Symondshyde, plus Gacelyn park, are taken into account, as much as 23 per cent of the parish of Hatfield could also have been parkland. Smaller parishes, such as Knebworth and Essendon, were perhaps even more severely affected when about 20 per cent of the land in each was enclosed into parks.

The Statute of Merton of 1236 clearly shows that imparking of land was causing major problems for manorial tenants dispossessed of woodland and heathland resources by the early thirteenth century. Under the terms of the Statute, lords of the manor were permitted to assart or impark waste only when other land was available to compensate holders of grazing and other rights, but how carefully this was observed in practice cannot be determined.[94] An examination of the frequency of park-breaking events in relation to the extent of parkland in a parish could be a potential area for future research, but determining the social effects of imparking is fraught with difficulty, not least because the lives of ordinary people rarely feature in the documentary records of the period.

The park residents
The deer
The Normans introduced the fallow deer (*Dama dama dama*), a native of the Mediterranean area, to Britain to stock their new deer parks. The fallow deer was considered better suited to living in an enclosed area than either of our native species, the red and roe deer. Most references to deer in documentary records are to fallow deer, usually in the form of *damus* (buck) or *dama* (doe) or some variant. Other deer species were rarely recorded: in fact just two references (one apiece) have been found to roe and red deer in the county's medieval parks. Roe deer were recorded in 1282, when a white doe and five white roe-bucks were obtained for Queen Eleanor's new park at Langley; and red deer were mentioned in 1427/8, when the abbot of St Albans stocked his new park at Tyttenhanger with both red and fallow deer.[95] The presence of red deer in the park at Standon in the early fourteenth century might also be inferred from an order issued by Edward II concerning the taking of forty hinds by his yeomen in three parks belonging to the late Gilbert de Clare.[96]

Medieval kings frequently granted deer to favoured subjects, which often necessitated transporting the animals long distances. The earliest known example in Hertfordshire was in 1241, when Henry III granted six fallow does and two bucks in 'Bernewud' to his cousin Stephen Longespee who had a (probably new) park at Great Gaddesden.[97] Bernwood was a royal forest about 23 miles (38km) away in Buckinghamshire and, apart from Whaddon Chase (also in Buckinghamshire), this was the closest royal forest to Gaddesden. The deer obtained to stock Queen Eleanor's park at Langley in 1276 had to travel much further: 30 fallow does were brought from her park at Odiham castle, Hampshire, in addition to the white roe-bucks, which came from Rugeley in the king's forest of Cannock, Staffordshire, in 1282.[98] In 1290 William of Louth was granted two fallow bucks and two does from the king's forest of Essex, which was only a few miles from William's park in Hoddesdon.[99]

Gifts of deer were also recorded between members of the nobility, but were perhaps most common at a local level between neighbouring manorial lords. These gifts appear in the records only because of the expenses incurred in catching and transporting the animals to their new park, which were entered in the bailiff's account for the relevant manor. The deer themselves had no monetary value because there was no (legal) market for them.[100] These recorded movements help to shed light on the varying fortunes of some parks over time. The earliest example found in Hertfordshire was the gift of 15 fallow does (*damas*) and 5 bucks (*damos*) made by Earl William Marshal from his park at Weston to Ranulf Briton before the earl died in 1231.[101] When Lord Morley needed to stock his park at Walkern in 1323/4 he was given two fallow deer from the nearby park at Great Munden and two from the East park at Little Munden by their respective owners.[102] Lord Morley's deer herd must have thrived because in 1367/8 13 deer were taken from Walkern to help restock the bishop of Ely's park at Little Hadham.[103] And in 1449/50 Sir John Fray

94. Cantor and Hatherly, 'Medieval parks of England', p. 76.

95. W. Page (ed.), *A history of the county of Hertford*, 2 (VCH, 1908), p. 237 citing *Cal. Close 1279–1288*, p. 148; Riley, *Annales Monasterii*, p. 261.

96. *Cal. Close 1313–1318*, p. 140.

97. *Cal. Close 1237–1242*, p. 332.

98. Odiham castle (and presumably its park) was assigned to Queen Eleanor in 1275 (W. Page (ed.), *A history of the county of Hampshire*, 4 (VCH, 1911), pp. 87–98); Rugeley was part of the king's forest of Cannock (L.M. Midgley (ed.), *A history of the county of Stafford*, 5 (VCH, 1959), pp. 49–63).

99. *Cal. Close 1288–1296*, p. 64.

100. Birrell, 'Deer and deer farming', p. 114.

101. Page, *Hertford*, 3, p. 173 quoting *Cal. Close 1227–1231*, p. 489. The location of Briton's park is not known.

102. HALS 9325 bailiff's account for Walkern, 1324/5.

103. HHA Court Rolls 11/4 fos. 103–5 bailiff's accounts for the bishops of Ely for Little Hadham, 1367/8.

obtained four deer from the parks of Weston, Knebworth, Hallingbury (Essex) and Benington to help restock his newly refurbished park at Great Munden.[104]

For much of the year the deer grazed on the pastures in the park. These pastures were often shared with livestock – usually cattle and horses – either belonging to the lord of the manor or to people who had paid for grazing rights (agistment), or both. The manorial accounts occasionally recorded no income from agistment because the grazing 'was reserved for the deer' (feris) as, for example, at King's Langley in 1324 when a summer drought caused a shortage of grass, or in Standon park in 1345 and in Bedwell and Sayes parks (both of which belonged to Sir William Say) in the later fifteenth century.[105]

The diet of the deer included browsewood, the foliage on branches cut from coppiced or pollarded trees: the 1484/5 accounts for both Great Munden and Sayes parks recorded 'underwood felled for sustenance of the deer in the park' and in 1435/6 'hornbeam cropp' was used to feed the deer in Little Hadham park in wintertime.[106] When grass was scarce in the growing season, cut branches were left on the ground so the deer would browse the leaves (the wood was later gathered for fuel). Alternatively, the branches could be cut in the summer and then stored as 'leafy hay' to be fed to the deer during the winter, as was mentioned in the account for Berkhamsted in 1408/9.[107] Cutting browsewood from either deciduous or evergreen trees in the park was the cheapest way of providing winter fodder for the deer.[108] But although the lopping of trees was regularly recorded, the Hertfordshire manorial accounts rarely specify that it was done in order to provide fodder for the deer, which makes it impossible to gauge the importance of this practice.

Hay was recorded much more frequently as winter fodder for the deer and was a regular and significant cost of the park in the Berkhamsted accounts. In September 1354 the receiver of Berkhamsted was ordered to buy hay to the value of 26s 8d for the sustenance of the deer in the park during the coming winter, and similar sums were spent on four cartloads in both 1388 and 1389.[109] From the turn of the fourteenth and fifteenth centuries the hay appears to have been home-grown on demesne meadows and only two cartloads were required each winter. Pea straw was also used as winter fodder for the Berkhamsted deer herd between 1388 and 1401 and a cart of white straw was purchased for 2 shillings to 'sustain the deer in the wintertime' in Little Hadham park in 1434/5.[110] At King's Langley 13s 3d was spent in the winter of 1315/6 and 12 shillings the following year on purchasing hay for the deer, and at Great Munden a cart of hay for the deer cost 4 shillings in the mid-fifteenth century.[111]

Some parks contained meadows which were used to provide hay for the deer in winter as, for example, at King's Langley in 1296/7, where eight acres of meadow in the park were valued at 20s 2d.[112] The hay meadow (falcabile) was given extra protection in 1305/6 when thorns were cut to reinforce the hedge between it and the great park to preserve the hay for the deer. In 1397 John of Gaunt issued a warrant to enclose an additional 25 acres of meadow into his park at Hertingfordbury, bringing the total to 51 acres. Nevertheless, a 6-acre meadow outside the park was still mown to make hay for the king's deer in the park in the fifteenth century.[113]

Occasionally the 'costs of the park' recorded in the manorial accounts reveal deer-related structures being made or repaired. A deerhouse (Le Derhows) was recorded at King's Langley in 1324 when the roof was repaired using 'fern' gathered by the roofer's assistant.[114] At Standon in 1363 a new 40-foot long 'rakk' was made for the deer (feris best') in the park and at Hertingfordbury a man spent ten days making 'rakes' for the deer in the park.[115] These were perhaps wooden feeding racks to prevent hay getting spoilt on the ground.

Care was taken to minimise disturbance to the deer at two crucial periods of the year: during fawning, which generally occurred in the fortnight either side of Midsummer Day (the 'fence month'); and during the rut, which lasted a month or more during the autumn.[116] Thus, at Berkhamsted in 1353, a man was permitted to collect leaves and dung from the park provided he avoided the fawning and rutting seasons.[117] The hunting of bucks most commonly took place in the summer, before the rut, when they were carrying the most venison and fat and were said to be 'in grease'. For example, on 1 August 1347 the Black Prince instructed Robert the parker to take a 'buck of grease' in Berkhamsted park and deliver it to the abbot of St Albans and, at the end of the same month, the parker and constable of the castle were ordered to take 'this season's grease' in the park, 'as shall seem best for the prince's profit' and have it 'well prepared'.[118]

104. TNA: PRO SC6/867/13 bailiff's account for Great Munden, 1449/50. This was listed under 'Foreign costs'.

105. TNA: PRO SC6/866/29 manorial accounts for King's Langley, 1324/5; SC6/869/5 minister's account for Standon, 1344/5; HHA Court Rolls 10/16 and 10/19 bailiff's accounts for Bedwell, 1484/5 and 1490/1; HHA Court Rolls 10/16 bailiff's account for Great Munden and Sayes park, 1484/5.

106. HHA Court Rolls 10/16 bailiff's account for Sayes park, 1484/5; 9/25 bailiff's account for Little Hadham, 1435/6.

107. TNA: PRO SC6/864/5 minister's account for Berkhamsted, 1408/9.

108. Birrell, 'Deer and deer farming', p. 118.

109. Dawes, Register of the Black Prince, 4, p. 118.

110. TNA: PRO SC6/863/17, 18, 19 ministers' accounts for Berkhamsted, 1398/9, 1399/1400, 1400/1; SC6/864/5 minister's account for Berkhamsted, 1408/9; HHA Court Rolls 11/4 fo. 35 account of manor of Little Hadham, 1434/5.

111. TNA: PRO SC6/866/20 manorial accounts for Childern Langeleye, 1315–1318; SC6/867/17 bailiff's account for Great Munden, c.1460.

112. TNA: PRO SC6/1090/4 minister's account for Langley, 1296/7.

113. HHA court roll 22/1 account for Hertingfordbury, 1442–3.

114. TNA: PRO SC6/866/26, SC6/866/27 and SC6/866/29 manorial accounts for King's Langley, 1321/2, 1322/3 and 1324/5.

115. TNA: PRO SC6/869/14 minister's account for Standon, 1362/3; HHA Court Roll 22/7 account for Hertingfordbury, 1395/6.

116. Birrell, 'Deer and deer farming', p. 116.

117. Dawes, Register of the Black Prince, 4, p. 82.

118. M.C.B. Dawes, Register of Edward the Black Prince, part 1 A.D. 1346–1348 (London, 1930), pp. 106, 117.

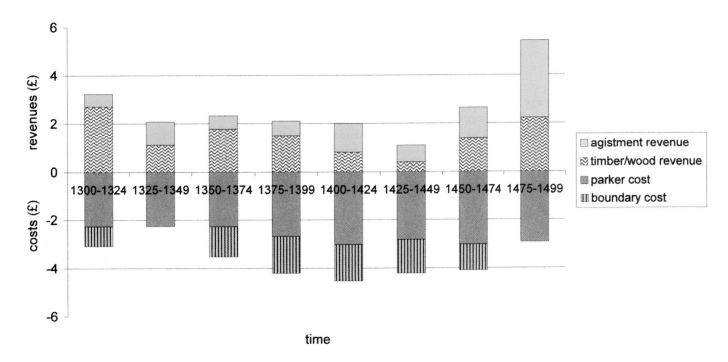

Figure 9. The main revenues and costs of the park of the bishops of Ely at Little Hadham during the fourteenth and fifteenth centuries based on average values calculated from samples of most of the surviving accounts.

Does were usually taken from late November to mid-February.[119] Only once has the killing of a deer been found recorded in the medieval accounts of a Hertfordshire manor – at Little Hadham in 1438 when a doe was killed for the lord for 12d.[120]

Rabbit warrens

Of the other high-status foods which were commonly derived from parks, rabbits seem to have been by far the most common in Hertfordshire. References to warrens have been found in the documentary records of 18 (about 30 per cent) of the manors which had medieval parks. In many cases, however, it is unclear whether or not the warren was located within the park, although this was definitely the case at Little Wymondley, Little Munden and Sayes park (Sawbridgeworth). At Much Hadham the bishops of London had a warren but no park from the thirteenth century and at Flamstead, similarly, there are documentary references to a warren but not to a park. The earliest record of a warren in Hertfordshire was in a Curia Regis Roll of 1226, when it appeared as 'the park and warren of Cheshunt'.[121] There was a warren at Much Hadham by 1273/4 and one at Berkhamsted by the beginning of the fourteenth century, when 'William called Hereford' was given 'custody of the wood of Berchampstede and the park and war-

ren'.[122] Seven warrens made their debuts in the records in the second half of the fourteenth century, another two in the first half of the fifteenth and a further six between 1450 and 1500.

Significant revenues from rabbit warrens started to appear in the accounts from the middle of the fifteenth century. In 1442 the warren at Hertingfordbury was leased for 70 shillings but it was subsequently leased for 60 shillings p.a. from 1480 until the mid-sixteenth century.[123] The sale of rabbits from the warren at Knebworth produced revenue of 37s 6d in 1449/50 and this rose dramatically in 1451/2 to £11 18s 11d from the sale of 1,100 rabbits. The buyer in both years was a London poulterer. From 1481/2 the Knebworth warren was leased for £8 per year.[124] Another lucrative warren was at Bedwell (Essendon). This warren was leased for three years in 1484/5 for 66s 8d a year but within a decade the farm of the warren had increased to £6 13s 4d a year.[125]

Dovecotes

The only known record of a dovecote in a medieval park in Hertfordshire was at Punsho park (Albury) in the late fourteenth century. Here the parker was granted the use of the dovecote (plus the agistment of 12 animals in the park) in return for maintaining the park boundary.[126] It seems

119. Birrell, 'Deer and deer farming', pp. 122–3.

120. This was the year when a new bishop of Ely, Lewis of Luxembourg, was appointed. The account records that the doe was killed for the lord, the 'vicar general', perhaps before the bishop was installed.

121. *Curia Regis Rolls*, p. 486. It is possible that this was a reference to the legal right to hunt small game (free warren) rather than a rabbit warren.

122. Taylor, 'The estates of the bishopric of London', p. 177, citing *Rotuli Hundredorum* (Hundred Rolls (Records Commission)), p. 193a; G.H. Whybrow, *History of Berkhamsted Common* (London, 1934), p. 16.

123. HHA court rolls 22/1, 21/11, 21/10, 22/6, 22/12 accounts, 1442/3, 1480/1, 1495/6, 1518/9, 1554/5.

124. HALS K121, K135, K124 bailiff's accounts, 1449/50, 1451/2, 1481/2.

125. HHA court rolls 10/16, 10/20, 10/21, 10/23 accounts, 1484/5, 1493/4, 1495/6, 1498/9.

126. HALS DE/Ap/M35–9 bailiff's accounts, 1376/7–1385/6.

likely that there was also a dovecote in the park at Kimpton, however, commemorated in the name Dovehouse Wood.

Fishponds

Hertfordshire's medieval records contain several references to ponds in parks, usually as a result of the costs incurred in having them constructed or scoured. For example, a pond in Stortford park was scoured in 1394/5 (8d), as was a pond in the park at Great Munden in 1446/7. A new pond was made in 'the lord's park' at Knebworth in 1412 at a cost of 26s 8d.[127] The accounts do not record whether these ponds contained fish or simply provided a source of water for the deer and livestock in the parks. However, at Knebworth in 1449/50 a fence was made around the lord's fishponds (*stagna and vivar's*) and, perhaps, the presence of fish in the pond in King's Langley park can be inferred, as fencing was erected around it in 1316/7.[128] Parks located close to religious establishments were particularly likely to incorporate water- and fish-management systems and there was certainly a fishpond close to the country house of the abbots of St Albans in the park at Tyttenhanger by the end of the fifteenth century.[129] Chauncy, writing at the end of the seventeenth century, described the 'ancient park' at Ardeley as being 'well water'd with fishponds' and these are also very likely to have originated in the medieval period, when the manor was held by the canons of St Paul's, London.[130]

The economic viability of parks

Medieval parks were multi-functional spaces containing pasture, trees and woodland, providing grazing for the owners' deer, horses and livestock, and fuel and timber for their household needs, as well as a venue for recreation and social display. Surplus grazing, wood and timber might be sold to generate income which could be set against the costs of running the parks. Historians generally agree that establishing and maintaining a park was an expensive enterprise which could be afforded only by the wealthiest members of medieval society and a survey of most of the surviving manorial accounts relating to parks in the county suggests that this was the case in Hertfordshire.[131]

The accounts reveal wide variations in the recorded costs and revenues of parks, both between different parks and within the lifespan of individual parks. The main source of revenue arising from Hertfordshire's parks over both the fourteenth and fifteenth centuries was timber and wood, including faggots and charcoal, but revenue from agistment was also important in some parks. The greatest, and most stable, cost of running a park throughout the period was the wage of the parker, but maintenance of the park boundary was also a substantial, if more variable, expense. Costs were also incurred in providing fodder for the deer in winter but, in Hertfordshire, this practice seems to have been confined almost exclusively to parks held by the crown. The building, or rebuilding, of a park lodge could also add considerably to the costs of a park over a one- or two-year period and, thereafter, at irregular intervals as repairs were needed.

The revenues generated from the county's parks varied enormously. In some cases, notably the royal park at King's Langley in the early fourteenth century, little or no attempt seems to have been made to generate any revenue at all from the park. Similarly, the royal park at Berkhamsted rarely produced much revenue, although there was an exceptional year in 1408/9 when over £15 was generated from sales of wood and a further £4 from pannage of pigs. Neither sum was derived wholly from the park, however, as the account combined the revenues from the park with those from 'the foreign wood' outside the park.[132] Particularly high revenues from sales of wood were also occasionally recorded from other parks: at Weston in 1304/5, 1305/6 and 1396/7 (worth over £12 in each year) and at Knebworth on three occasions in the first quarter of the fifteenth century (worth between £10 and £14). For both of these parks, however, the surviving records are few and, consequently, it is impossible to know whether the high revenues from wood sales were part of a long-term management strategy for the trees and woodland in the parks, or whether the accounts were recording short-term phases of asset-stripping.

The trees and woodland in the great and little parks at Hatfield were probably a major and regular source of revenue for the bishops of Ely but, unfortunately, the records for this manor are also very sparse. The spectacular figure of £64 8s was recorded in the Hatfield account for 1396 from the sale of charcoal in the great park; once costs had been deducted, a profit of over £28 was produced. Whether this was an exceptional event or part of a regular cropping regime in the Hatfield coppices during this period is not clear. The next extant account, from 1428, recorded £10 from charcoal sales, and £5 was received for charcoal sold from the little park in 1436. The bishops' records for their other, much smaller, manor and park at Little Hadham are in marked contrast to the Hatfield records, covering as they do most years in the fourteenth and fifteenth centuries. These manorial accounts provide a comprehensive record of revenues from sales of wood and timber which suggest careful management of resources to generate a regular income. Nevertheless, revenues rarely exceeded the costs of the park – the parker's wage and maintenance of the boundary – until the later fifteenth century, when the rights to manage the woodlands and agistment in the park were leased to tenants. The variations in the revenues and costs of the bishops of Ely's park at Little Hadham are illustrated in Figure 9.[133]

127. TNA: PRO SC6/1140/10 minister's account for Bishop's Stortford, 1394/5; SC6/867/10 bailiff's account for Great Munden, 1446/7; HALS K119 bailiff's account for Knebworth, 1412/13.

128. HALS K121 bailiff's account for Knebworth, 1449/50; TNA: PRO SC6/866/20 manorial accounts for Childern Langeleye, 1315–1318.

129. HALS DE/B2067B/M25 a survey and extent of the manor of Tyttenhanger, 1551, which includes a copy of the extent made in 1500/1.

130. Chauncy, *Historical antiquities*, p. 53.

131. Cantor and Hatherly, 'Medieval parks of England', p. 76; Mileson, 'The importance of parks in fifteenth-century society', p. 31.

132. TNA: PRO SC6/864/5 minister's and receiver's accounts, Berkhamsted, 1408/9.

133. Occasional revenues from pannage, the one-off costs of building the lodge and the subsequent, occasional, costs of repairs have not been included in the chart but can be seen in the Gazetteer entry.

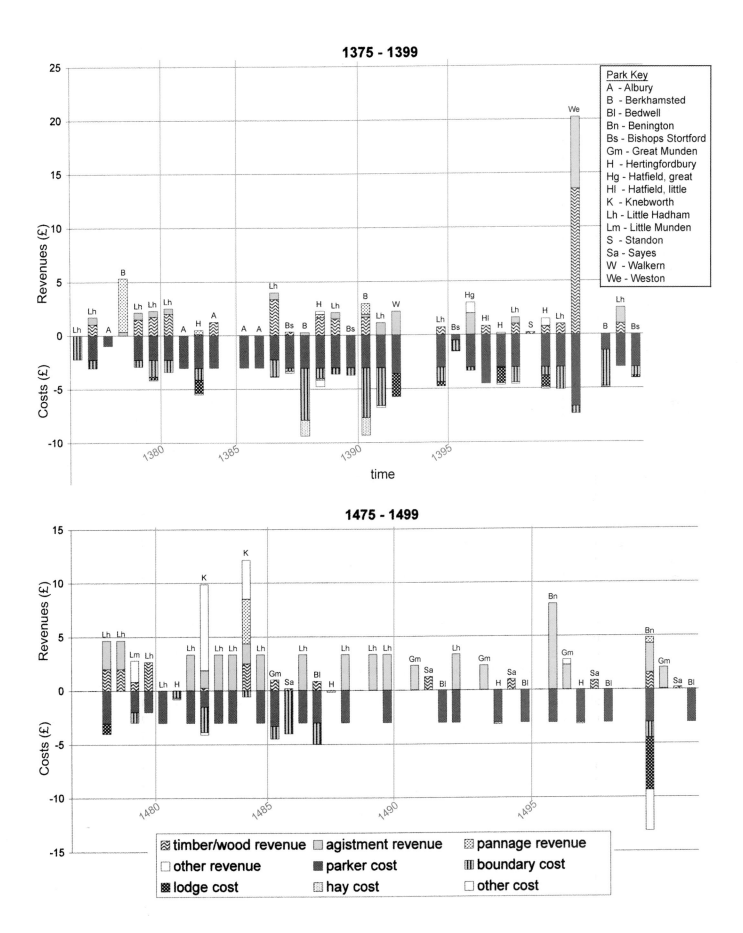

Figure 10. *Some costs and revenues of Hertfordshire parks in the last quarters of the fourteenth and fifteenth centuries.*

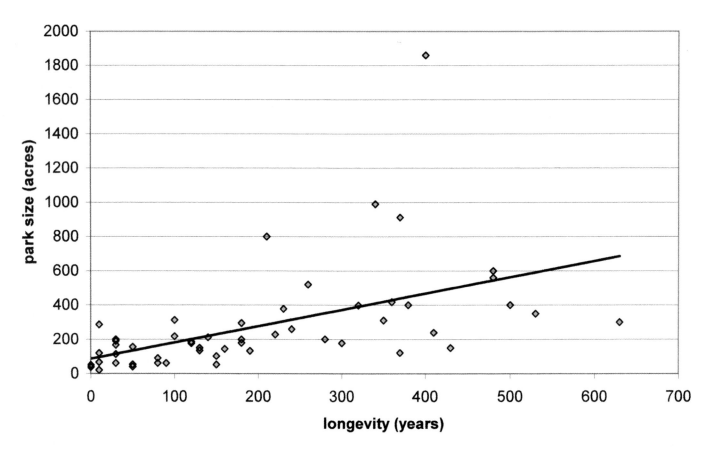

Figure 11. The relationship between the size and longevity of Hertfordshire's parks.

There are no comparably comprehensive records for any other Hertfordshire park – those accounts which do survive are usually sporadic and often lack the relevant details. Wide variations in costs and revenues from year to year also make it difficult to calculate meaningful average values for the county's parks over a period of time: for instance, large revenues from sales of wood from just one or two parks can skew the statistics and give misleading results. Records from the greatest numbers of parks survive, coincidentally, from the last quarter of the fourteenth century and from the last quarter of the fifteenth century, providing the best opportunity to compare general variations in park economics in the county at different periods. The main costs and revenues of ten parks in the late fourteenth century and eight parks in the late fifteenth century are presented in Figure 10. The two sets of records are not directly comparable, however, because only two parks, Hertingfordbury and Little Hadham, feature in both sets.

The revenues and costs of each park are shown on each chart as bars, set out in chronological order. Where the accounts of two or more parks were compiled in the same year, the bars are shown consecutively; consequently, there are more than 25 bars on each chart. The previously mentioned exceptional receipts and production costs for charcoal sold at Hatfield in 1396 have been excluded to avoid distorting the chart.

Comparison of the two charts suggests that revenues from agistment were higher in the late fifteenth century than in the late fourteenth century. Although these figures are dominated by the records from a single park – that of the bishop of Ely at Little Hadham – this apparent increase in revenue from agistment may be part of a more widespread trend which has been noted in other parts of the country.[134] Similarly, the high ('other') revenues received from the rabbit warren at Knebworth in the late fifteenth century were also part of a more general expansion in rabbit farming at that time.[135]

Although the wages paid to parkers changed little between the two periods, the charts appear to show that expenditure on park boundary maintenance was higher in the later fourteenth century, an impression which owes much to the costs recorded for the large park at Berkhamsted. The late fourteenth-century accounts show that most parks were run at a loss and that revenues rarely exceeded expenses. The picture in the late fifteenth century is less clear-cut, with an apparently better match between revenues and costs in several sets of accounts. Here the picture is again dominated by the bishop of Ely's Little Hadham park where, as shown in Figure 9, a profit was indeed being made at this time.

Deficiencies in the documentary record are compounded by the fact that the manorial accounts which survive tend to be those from the most prestigious and, perhaps, better-run manors – those which were held by the crown, the nobility or by religious establishments. This means that the evidence for the financial viability of parks is not only fragmentary but also heavily biased towards the higher end of the social scale. The Hertfordshire evidence suggests that the crown did not

134. Mileson, 'The importance of parks in fifteenth-century society', pp. 20–1.
135. T. Williamson, *Rabbits, Warrens and Archaeology* (Stroud, 2007), p. 17.

manage its parks for economic benefit but that perhaps some bishops of Ely ran their parks more efficiently and sometimes managed to produce a profit. It is possible that some of the less prestigious parks, created and owned by lesser manorial lords, were managed efficiently and produced modest revenues which at least covered their running costs, but this cannot be investigated satisfactorily because the documentary evidence for smaller parks is so scarce.

The size of a park is likely to have been an important factor in its economic viability: lower boundary maintenance costs per acre of park coupled with a greater range and extent of parkland resources gave the owner of a larger park more opportunity to generate a profit from his park than the owner of a smaller park. On the other hand, the owner of a small park might have reduced costs by managing his park without the full-time services of a professional parker. It might be argued that the economic viability of a park would be reflected in the length of time it continued to function and, as Figure 11 shows, there was certainly a tendency for Hertfordshire's larger parks to survive longer than the smaller ones. The average medieval park in Hertfordshire covered about 275 acres (245 acres if Hatfield great park is excluded from the calculation). Of the 18 parks which were above average in size, 83 per cent continued in use for more than two centuries and 33 per cent survived for four centuries or more. Of the 36 parks which were of less than average size, 19 per cent lasted more than two centuries, and only 5.5 per cent lasted four centuries or more. So, smaller parks tended to be more ephemeral features in the county's landscape, but whether or not this was primarily the result of economic factors is open to debate. Perhaps of overriding importance was the willingness (and ability) of the owner to subsidise a loss-making park, whatever its size.

An interesting – and perhaps instructive – case study is provided by one major Hertfordshire landowner in the late fifteenth century. Sir William Say (c.1454–1529) inherited two deer parks, Bedwell (Essendon) and Sayes (Sawbridgeworth) on the death of his father, Sir John Say, in 1478. He subsequently acquired at least another three functioning parks, with their various manors, over the next decade. He seems to have been in control of Little Munden (with its two parks) by 1477, becoming lord of the manor in 1486.[136] By 1484 he was in possession of the neighbouring manor of Great Munden and this was followed by the manor of Benington by 1486. Several sets of bailiff's accounts for Sir William's manors survive, the earliest of which is for Little Munden in 1477, when at least one of the two parks was still operating: a 'custodian of the park' was employed, there was a rabbit warren in the park and the boundary was repaired. Costs exceeded revenues by just 4 shillings but by 1484 both parks at Little Munden had been disparked – the pasture of one was leased to the farmer of the demesne farm for 20 shillings a year and the other was leased

to a number of tenants as parcels of pasture and two crofts for 44 shillings a year, with additional income occasionally arising from the sale of parcels of underwood. A parker was employed at Great Munden in 1484/5 and the net cost of the park was 70 shillings. It appears to have been disparked by 1490, when the farm of agistment and pannage was leased to a tenant for 46 shillings a year. Similarly, Sayes park had a parker in 1484/5 but the recorded net cost of running the park was 77 shillings. It had been disparked within a decade and was added to other manorial lands which were already being leased to a tenant. Sir William continued to receive revenue of up to 20 shillings a year from the wood sold out of the park for fuel (Figure 10).[137]

Sir William Say's principal residence was at Baas manor in Broxbourne and there is no evidence that he resided on his manors at Great and Little Munden, or at Sayes in Sawbridgeworth. He did, however, have a house at Bedwell park by the early sixteenth century, and probably before, and he seems to have maintained the deer park there exclusively for his own use until he died in 1529. Evidence in the accounts suggests that he enlarged the 800-acre park, already one of the largest in the county, around 1492, perhaps to enhance the setting of the house. His park at Benington also remained a deer park throughout his lifetime and beyond. Covering 380 acres, Benington park was also larger than average for Hertfordshire and substantial revenue from agistment (£8) was recorded in 1496. In 1498/9 Sir William made a major investment in the park, spending over £6 on repairing the park pale and rebuilding the lodge (see Figure 10), probably to provide accommodation for himself and his guests whilst hunting in the park.[138]

So, Sir William Say's policy with regard to his deer parks seems to have been one of rationalisation, and the size of the parks does appear to have been a factor in determining which were disparked. The smaller parks were surplus to requirements as status symbols, sources of venison, places of recreation or as settings for grand houses. By disparking them and leasing them to tenants, either in their entirety or divided into parcels, Sir William was able to convert these parks from financial liabilities into economically viable units of his estate. The two larger deer parks, however, were more than just functional economic units: Bedwell park was the setting for one of his main residences and the park and its herd of deer were apparently managed for pleasure and prestige, not as a source of revenue. Benington park, on the other hand, appears to have been managed for both pleasure and as a source of revenue. Those revenues may have been sufficient to at least pay for the normal running costs of the park and perhaps even to make a profit.

The decisions which Sir William Say made regarding his deer parks can be seen as part of a general trend towards a closer association between parks and residences as well as a desire to make his estates as a whole more profitable.[139] Larger parks were usually owned by wealthier men with little concern for costs and the greater longevity of those parks probably had more to do

---

136. TNA: PRO SC6/867/18 account for manor of Little Munden, 1477/8; E210/439 ancient deeds, 1486/7.

137. TNA: PRO SC6/867/18 account for Little Munden, 1477/8; HHA Court Roll 10/16 accounts for Bedwell, Great Munden, Little Munden and Sayesbury, 1484/5; HHA Court Roll 10/19, 10/21 Great Munden, 1490/1, 1495/6; HHA Court Roll 10/20 Sayes park, 1493/4.

138. HHA Court Rolls 10/16 accounts for Bedwell, 1484/5; 10/19, 1490/1; 10/20, 1493/4; 10/21, 1495/5; 10/23, 1498/9; HHA Court Rolls 10/19 accounts for Benington, 1490/1; 10/21, 1495/6; 10/23, 1498/9.

139. Mileson, 'The importance of parks in fifteenth-century society', pp. 23–4.

with social factors than with their economic viability. The costs and revenues were only part of the equation for most park-owners and too much emphasis on the evidence of manorial accounts risks giving a misleading impression of their primary interests, which were probably the social prestige, the supply of venison, the pleasures of hunting and the enjoyment of park landscapes – none of which had a monetary value.

Park management
The park boundaries

Deer are notorious for their ability to escape from their enclosures – either by jumping over, or by squeezing through gaps in, whatever boundary has been erected to keep them in. The height of the barrier was often effectively increased by erecting it on the top of an earth bank, with an internal ditch. Hertfordshire's medieval parks appear to have been enclosed by a combination of hedges, dead hedges and fences, and maintenance of the boundary was a major expense which featured regularly in the manorial accounts.

A characteristic feature of early parks was that their boundaries were maintained by manorial tenants as part of the labour service which they owed to the lord of the manor.[140] Evidence of these customary services has been found for the old park at Cheshunt and for the great park at Hatfield, two of the earliest parks in the county, recorded for the first time in the 1220s, although evidence suggests that the park at Cheshunt was established in the twelfth century. A document of 1323 recorded that 11 perches (c.55m) of the boundary of Cheshunt old park were maintained by the de Bassingbourn family in return for their right to hold the manor of Hoddesdonbury.[141] Free tenants of the manor of Cheshunt were responsible for maintaining 80 perches of hedge around the old park each year (worth 6s 8d) and customary tenants maintained 100 perches worth 8s 4d.[142] The manorial tenants at Hatfield were each responsible for maintaining 120 perches of fence round the bishop's great park.[143] The same practice may also have operated at Ware park (first recorded in 1086) because in 1350 the widow of Geoffrey de Ware died seised of a portion of Ware manor which she held by the service of enclosing 5 perches of the park.[144] At Walkern in 1324/5 the manorial tenants made 435½ perches of new hedge or fence (sepium) around the park and the ox-pasture, which counted as 435½ works, but this was perhaps a single exceptional event, rather than an annual obligation.[145]

A detailed description of the construction of the fence around a Hertfordshire park can be found in the Register of the Black Prince. In February 1353 Prince Edward ordered the sale of beech trees in the 'foreign wood' of Berkhamsted (the wood outside the park) to the value of £20 in order to fund the construction of a new pale around Berkhamsted park. The revenue was to be used to buy oak timber to make the rails and stanchions of the new fence and suitable beeches were to be felled to make the remaining parts.[146] The term 'park pale' is, however, normally taken to include the earth bank (with its internal ditch) upon which the boundary fence or hedge stood. A record of the construction of a new length of park pale can be found recorded in the bailiff's account for the manor of Little Hadham in 1390/1 when the park was enlarged. Enclosing the new land into the park required the construction of 75 perches of new embankment (fossati), on the crest of which was placed a dead hedge (sepe mortua). The cost of the new pale was 5½d per perch and included the erection of a single fence (sepe) 'placed in a double course', which seems to indicate that the dead hedge (a pile of brushwood) was held in place by a double fence.[147]

The scribes who compiled the manorial accounts tended to refer to the park boundary as either a haia or a sepes. A haia was a hedge and a sepes was a hedge or a fence, but the two words seem to have been used interchangeably and it is often not clear whether it was a hedge or a fence that was being made or repaired. A park fence was traditionally said to be constructed with cleft oak pales and yet, amongst all the Hertfordshire documents examined, it was only in the Berkhamsted record just mentioned that the use of oak was specified.[148] Indeed, references to the cleaving of timber to make pales has only been found in the late thirteenth- and early fourteenth-century accounts for the parks at King's Langley, although wood was felled at Hertingfordbury to make the fence of the new park in 1388/9.[149]

More frequently recorded in connection with the making and repairing of park boundaries are thorns (spinis) and thorn-bushes or brambles (dumus), although the exact distinction between the two terms is obscure. The thorns were probably predominantly blackthorn, an abundant species in Hertfordshire hedgerows today, but hawthorn was also plentiful, particularly in the 'Chiltern country' of north-west Hertfordshire.[150] The identification of dumus is less certain but similar words appear to relate to bushes, particularly thorn-

140. Hoppitt, 'Hunting Suffolk's parks', p. 160.

141. Cal. Inq. post mortem, vol. 6, Edward II, no. 400, p. 236. A perch (perticate) was a highly variable linear measure, of between c.10 and 25 feet, dictated by local custom. The equivalent number of metres (given in brackets) is based upon the 'standardised' perch of 16½ feet but, as the length of the local perch is not known, this figure must be taken as very approximate.

142. King's College, Cambridge KCAR/6/2/034 Cheshunt manorial accounts, 1435/6; TNA: PRO SC6/HENVIII/6757 and 6764 reeves' accounts, 1519–21 and 1526–8.

143. HHA Hatfield Manor Papers I, 1392/3, p. 253.

144. Cussans, History of Hertfordshire, 1, p. 133–4 quoting Inq. post mort. 23 Ed. III. No. 91; 1st part.

145. HALS 9325 bailiff's account, 1324/5. The total perimeter of the park was probably c.5950m.

146. Dawes, Register of the Black Prince, 4, p. 81.

147. HHA court rolls 11/4 fo. 68 bailiff's account for Little Hadham, 1390/1. Confusingly, fossa can mean dike, embankment or ditch.

148. Rackham, History of the countryside, p. 125; Cantor and Hatherly, 'Medieval parks of England', p. 72.

149. TNA: PRO SC6/1090/4 and SC6/866/13 accounts for King's Langley, 1296/7 and 1301/2; HHA court rolls 22/8 bailiff's account for Hertingfordbury, 1388/9.

150. J.G. Dony, Flora of Hertfordshire (Hitchin, 1967), p. 73, citing W. Ellis, The timber tree improved (London, 1742).

bushes, brambles and thickets.[151] It had a monetary value, because it was sold at Standon park in 1337/8 (13s 4d) and from le launde of Ipgrave park (Weston) in 1396/7 (13d).[152]

Dead hedges – barriers constructed with cut brushwood – seem to have played a major role in enclosing Hertfordshire's parks. The boundary structures were rarely described as 'dead hedges' but the term (or rather its Latin equivalent) has been found in some manorial accounts, as, for example, at Little Hadham in the late fourteenth century and at Standon in the mid-fifteenth century. As already mentioned, a dead hedge (*sepe mortua*) was part of the new section of park pale constructed at Little Hadham in 1390/1.[153] In 1468/9, 218 perches (*c*.1,100m) of dead hedge (*sepie morte*) around Standon park were 'new made' at a cost of 45s 5d (2½d per perch).[154] A dead hedge may also be what was meant by *cad haye's*, which were repaired with fencing (*claustur'*) and 'rayles' at King's Langley in 1311/12.[155]

There are many references to quite significant lengths of 'new hedge' being made around parks each year. For example, at Standon park in 1354/5, 97 perches of old hedge (*haiarum*) were sold and 97 perches of new hedge (*haie*) were made, presumably a direct replacement for the old hedge which had been removed.[156] Similarly, at Little Hadham park in 1377/8, 35 perches of old hedge were sold and replaced by 35 perches of hedge 'new made'.[157] A 'new hedge' in the modern sense cannot, however, be created instantaneously, but takes several years to become an effective barrier. So the medieval 'hedges' recorded in these manorial accounts must either have been fences or a combination of dead hedges and fencing.

The materials needed to make the new fences were sometimes recorded in the accounts, if somewhat imprecisely. In addition to the timber split to make pales at King's Langley and the wood felled to make the fence at Hertingfordbury mentioned previously, the park at Berkhamsted in 1300/1 was enclosed with fencing (*claustura*) cut and gathered from the park.[158] At Hatfield the cutting and carrying of underwood formed part of the cost of 172 perches of new fence made around the little park in 1395/6.[159] 'Stakes' were provided for

the fence at Bishop's Stortford in 1437/8 and at Knebworth four wagonloads of stakes were carried from Impo wood to make the new fences around the great park in 1481/2.[160] Different styles of fence are revealed in the account for Knebworth in 1449/50: pale with a single rail cost 6d per perch; pale with a double rail cost 8d per perch.[161]

Although not specifically referred to as 'dead hedges' many 'old' park boundaries were repaired using thorns and bushes or brambles cut down elsewhere and carted to the defective stretches of park boundary, as, for example, at Bishop's Stortford in 1351/2, when thorns were carried from the old park to the new park for repairing the hedge or fence. The thorns were used to replace 'old thorns' which had presumably rotted but must have retained some value (perhaps as fuel), because the two men working on the fence kept them as part of their wages.[162] Similarly, at Berkhamsted in 1388/9 thorns were cut and carried to repair parts of the old hedge.[163] At Hertingfordbury in 1480/1 the bailiff divided the costs of mending breaches in the old boundary around the park into three stages: the felling and cutting of bushes/brambles and thorns (two men for eight days); carting the bushes and thorns to where they were needed (one man plus horse and cart for four days); and repairing the breaches (two men for sixteen days), costing a total of 13s 4d.[164]

Another method of repairing an old hedge is indicated in the fifteenth-century manorial accounts for Little Hadham, Knebworth and Pisho (Sawbridgeworth). At Little Hadham between 1404 and 1410 about 60 perches of old hedge were repaired and *barband* each year. The word *barband* appears to refer to the setting of pointed wooden rods, stakes or spikes into the ground and, at Little Hadham, underwood was cut and carted to the boundary for this purpose.[165] At Knebworth a practice called *le Berdynge* was recorded in the account for 1481/2 and, earlier, at Standon in 1461/2 and Pisho park (Sawbridgeworth) in 1421/2.[166] *Berdo* also means 'to set a fence with spikes' and both words seem to relate to replacing a fence, but might also have referred to reinforcing a hedge (living or dead).[167]

151. C.T. Lewis and C. Short, *A Latin dictionary* (Oxford, 1966).

152. TNA: PRO SC6/868/23 manorial account for Standon, 1337/8; SC6/873/25 manorial account for Weston, 1396/7.

153. HHA court rolls 11/4 fo. 68 accounts for the manor of Little Hadham, 1390/1.

154. TNA: PRO SC6/870/6 bailiff's account for Standon, 1468/9.

155. TNA: PRO SC6/866/18 bailiff's account for King's Langley, 1311/12. *Cad* could also mean fallen. *Claustura* also occurs in the Berkhamsted account for 1300/1 and is clearly written. It has not been found in a Latin dictionary but 'fencing' seems the most likely translation.

156. TNA: PRO SC6/869/11 bailiff's account for Standon, 1354/4.

157. HHA court rolls 11/4 fo. 87–8, bailiff's account, 1377/8.

158. TNA: PRO SC6/863/5 bailiff's account for Berkhamsted, 1300/1.

159. HHA Hatfield Manor Papers I, 1396 Michaelmas, p. 265.

160. TNA: PRO SC6/1140/20 parker's account for Stortford park, 1437/8; HALS K124 bailiff's account for Knebworth, 1481/2.

161. HALS K121 bailiff's account for Knebworth, 1449/50.

162. TNA: PRO SC6/1140/5 minister's account for Bishop's Stortford, 1351/2.

163. TNA: PRO SC6/863/14 receiver's account for Berkhamsted, 1388/9.

164. HHA court rolls 21/11 bailiff's account for Hertingfordbury, 1480/1.

165. HHA court rolls 11/4 fos. 54–50, 1404/5–1409/10; also fos. 46 and 43, 1416/7 and 1421/2.

166. HALS K124 bailiff's account for Knebworth, 1481/2; TNA: PRO SC6/870/5 bailiff's account for Standon, 1461/2; TNA: PRO SC6/839/16 parker's account for Pisho park, 1421/2.

167. R.E. Latham, *Revised medieval Latin word-list* (London, 1965). Alternatively, the accounts may be recording the 'trimming' of hedges, but this does not seem compatible with the requirement for underwood recorded at Little Hadham.

The traditional method of managing and strengthening a living hedge in Hertfordshire – at least by the late eighteenth century – was by plashing.[168] Reference to this practice has been found recorded only once in documents relating to the county's medieval parks and that was when defective parts of the park boundary at Bedwell were repaired by 'plasshyng' in 1484/5.[169]

An intriguing practice of daubing the park fence with clay was recorded at two parks, both held by Sir William Say, in the later fifteenth century. At Little Munden in 1477/8 the manorial account recorded 'le dubbing' of the park fence.[170] At Benington in 1498/9, 29s 3½d was spent fencing and daubing (*sepacoe' & dobbyng*) 805 perches (*c.*4,000m) of the park boundary at a cost of 2½d for each 'newly made' perch and 1½d per perch for the daubing.

The costs of maintaining the park boundary rose during the medieval period but varied from park to park. At the turn of the thirteenth and fourteenth centuries it cost 1d to make a perch of new fence (King's Langley) and ¾d to repair a perch of old fence (Berkhamsted). Most of the new fence made at King's Langley still cost 1d per perch in 1324/5. Old fences were sold for ½d per perch at Standon in 1354/5 and new fences were made for 2d per perch. In the early 1360s the price was 2d per perch at both Little Hadham and Standon, but later in the decade it fell to 1½d per perch at Little Hadham then varied between 1½d, 1¾d and 2d per perch of new fence made during the 1370s and 1d per perch of old fence repaired. At the end of the fourteenth century the cost of replacing fences ranged from 1½d (Bishop's Stortford) to 2d per perch (Hatfield great park). In the 1430s the bishop of London was paying 3d for each perch of new fence at Bishop's Stortford and in 1462 it cost 2½d to make a perch of dead hedge at Standon. By the 1480s new fences around the great park at Knebworth cost 2d per perch and it cost 1d per perch for *le Berdynge* of the old fence.

The fine series of manorial accounts for Little Hadham, kept in the archive at Hatfield House, shows that the lengths of new fence made varied considerably from year to year, with a maximum of 310 perches (*c.*1,560m) made in 1367/8, about one-third of the park boundary, which cost 38s 9d. The average total expenditure on maintaining the boundary of Little Hadham park during this period was 33s 7d per annum. At Berkhamsted, where the 975-acre park had a perimeter of about 9,300m, 37s 9d was spent on the park boundary in one year at the start of the fourteenth century, but this rose to 96s 8d in 1388/9 and then settled at 66s 8d per year during the early fifteenth century.

Park gates

All parks must have had at least one gate and many are recorded in the names of fields, places and even people. The village of Newgate Street grew up at the new gate at the eastern end of Hatfield great park, Tyttenhanger park is commemorated at Parkgate Corner on Colney Heath and a Walter de Parkesgate was recorded at Knebworth in the early fourteenth century.[171] Manorial accounts contain references to gates being made and repaired. For example, a carpenter was paid 9d for three days spent making a gate for the great park at King's Langley in 1307/8, while 5 shillings was paid for two carpenters to make a new gate for Little Hadham park in 1368/9 and a new gate was made for Hatfield great park for 2s 11d in 1396.[172] Detailed lists of the wooden components and metalwork required for making gates were recorded in the Little Hadham accounts in 1378/9 and 1409/10.[173] Security of the parks was clearly an issue, and there are several records of new locks and keys being purchased for the gates as, for example, at Hertingfordbury in the 1380s and at Little Hadham in 1390/1. Poachers may also have been deterred by the iron spikes set above the rails of the park gate at Hertingfordbury in 1395/6.[174] A more unusual type of gate – a water gate – was recorded for the parks at King's Langley and Hertingfordbury, both of which lay beside rivers.[175]

The internal components of parks: grass and trees

Medieval parks were essentially enclosed areas of pasture and trees but the density and arrangement of these components varied from park to park. Deer feed mainly on grass but also enjoy tree mast in the autumn and are partial to browsing the foliage on trees and shrubs when the opportunity arises. Areas of mature woodland with grassy glades and well-developed shrub vegetation are their preferred habitat, providing both food and shelter.[176] Rackham proposed two distinct types of park: the 'uncompartmented' and the 'compartmented park'.[177] The uncompartmented park comprised wood-pasture which was accessible to the deer at all times. A proportion of the parkland trees were pollarded each year: that is, cut above the height which could be reached by browsing animals, thus allowing the regrowth of shoots and ensuring a constant supply of wood from the park.

Greater quantities of wood and timber could be obtained from a compartmented park, where there was some separation between trees and grazing and the deer were excluded from compartments of woodland which were coppiced at regular intervals. The records indicate that the parks at Weston and Knebworth, both of which produced substantial quantities of timber and wood, were managed in this way.

The Norman-French word *laund* was presumably introduced to this country from the late eleventh century. It usually referred to an area of grassland or pasture in a compartmented park, typically containing pollarded trees,

168. A. Young, *General view of the agriculture of the county of Hertfordshire* (London, 1804; republished Plymouth, 1971), p. 49.

169. HHA court rolls 10/16 bailiff's account for Bedwell Berkhamsted Lowthes, 1484/5.

170. TNA: PRO SC6/867/18 account for manor of Little Munden, 1477/8.

171. HALS 21870 grant of a messuage 'late of Walter de Parkesgate', 1309.

172. HHA Hatfield Manor Papers I, 1396 Michaelmas, p. 265; TNA: PRO SC6/866/17 bailiff's account for Childelangele, 1307/8.

173. HHA court rolls 11/4 fos. 85–6 and 50.

174. HHA court rolls 19/11 and 22/7 manorial accounts, 1381/2 and 1395/6; 11/4 fo. 67–8.

175. TNA: PRO SC6/866/16 bailiff's account for Langeleye, 1305/6; HHA court roll 19/11 account, 1381/2.

176. J. Langbein and N. Chapman, *Fallow deer* (London, 2003), p. 14.

177. Rackham, *History of the countryside*, p. 125.

which was accessible to the deer at all times.[178] The earliest known use of the word in Hertfordshire was in an extent of the manor of Offley in 1326 which recorded a several pasture called La Launde. No park was recorded, however, and the field-name is the primary evidence that there *may* have been one there previously.[179] A pasture called La Launde was present at Hertingfordbury by 1359, when it was leased for grazing. It is not clear to which of the parks at Hertingfordbury it originally related, but it was certainly part of John of Gaunt's enlarged park by the end of the fourteenth century.[180] Ipgrave Wood, Weston, contained an area called le launde, from which *dumus* worth 13d was sold in 1396/7.[181] The bailiff's account for Knebworth in 1412/13 recorded the cutting of underwood in order to make a laund in the park, and trees and thorns were uprooted from le launde of the park at Great Munden prior to its restocking with deer in 1446/7.[182]

There is insufficient evidence to estimate the relative proportions of compartmented and uncompartmented parks in Hertfordshire but, if the presence of launds and coppiced woodland are reliable indicators of a compartmented park, then at least a quarter of the county's parks were compartmented.

Agistment

Agistment, the leasing of grazing rights, was an important source of revenue for some Hertfordshire park-owners, second only to revenues from sales of timber and wood for most of the medieval period. Based on the limited records available, the average annual value of agistment per park during the fourteenth century was about £1 1s and this rose to £2 during the fifteenth century. The parks which recorded the highest revenues from agistment were Walkern (£8 11s 6½d in 1324/5 and between £5 2s ½d and £7 16s 6d between 1427 and 1432), Weston (£6 13s 4d in 1396/7) and Benington (£7 19s 7d in 1495/6).[183]

Occasionally the kinds of livestock grazing in the park were itemised in the accounts, together with the amounts paid per head for agistment. At Weston in 1275/6 agistment rates per term were 6d for each horse, 4d each for steers and cows, 3d each for young steers and foals and 2d for each calf.[184] At King's Langley, 2d a head was paid for the agistment of 11 calves in the park in the summer of 1322 and 20 calves in the following summer; 4d a head was paid for the summer grazing of 6 young steers in 1323.[185] In Stortford park in 1345/6 agistment of a

shilling per head was paid for 4 young horses and 9 cows.[186] Later in the century, at the bishop of Ely's Little Hadham park, the bailiff recorded simply that 8d per head was paid for 12 'beasts' and 6d per head for 8 'beasts' (cattle).[187]

In the earlier manorial accounts the grazing year was divided into a number of terms which varied between parks. At Weston in 1275/6, for example, there were four terms, each of which was accounted for separately:

Easter (*Pascha*) to 24 June (Feast of St John the Baptist)
24 June to 1 August (*gula augusti*, Lammas day)
1 August to 29 September (Feast of St Michael)
29 September to 30 November (Feast of St Andrew)

At Standon in 1290/1 there were two terms which ran from 3 May (*Inventio sancte crucis*) to 1 August and from 1 August to 29 September. At King's Langley in 1305/6 agistment was also divided into two terms which ran from Easter to 1 August and from 1 August to 29 September.[188]

Levels of agistment were carefully regulated according to the needs of the deer in the park. For example, the account for Bishop's Stortford in 1345/6 recorded revenue of 20s 6d for the agistment of two mares with foals, four young horses, nine cows, one mare, two bulls and six young steers 'and no more because of the deer (*feras*)'.[189] At Berkhamsted in 1408/09 the Prince of Wales ordered that there should be no agistment 'to protect the health of his wild beasts' and at Pisho park (Sawbridgeworth) in 1421/2 no agistment was permitted in the winter because the grazing was reserved for the deer.[190] In 1393/4 and 1396/7 agistment in the park at Little Hadham was forbidden on the orders of the bishop of Ely 'on account of destruction of deer', which suggests that the herd had outgrown the carrying capacity of the park.[191]

Pannage

Pannage was the name given to the practice of putting domestic pigs into woodland and wood-pasture in the autumn so that they could fatten up on acorns and beech mast before slaughter. Pig-owners paid a fee for this privilege and 'pannage of pigs' features frequently in the medieval accounts of manors which had parks. It was, however, a very irregular source of revenue, as it was dependent upon a good crop of acorns or beechnuts,

178. Rackham, *History of the countryside*, p. 126.

179. TNA: PRO C134/101/10 inquisition *post mortem* of John de St Ledger, 1326.

180. TNA: PRO SC6/865/18 accounts for the manor of Hertingfordbury, 1359/60; HHA court rolls 22/7 accounts for the manor of Hertingfordbury, 1395/6.

181. TNA: PRO SC6/873/25 accounts for Weston, 1396/7.

182. HALS K119 bailiff's account for Knebworth, 1412/13; TNA: PRO SC6/867/10 bailiff's account for Great Munden, 1446/7.

183. HALS DE/Hx/Z24 typed translation of account rolls of manor of Walkern, 1324–1432; TNA: PRO SC6/873/25 manorial accounts for Weston, 1396/7; HHA court rolls 10/21 manorial accounts for Benington, 1495/6.

184. TNA: PRO SC6/873/6 manorial account for Weston, 1275/6.

185. TNA: PRO SC6/866/26 and 27 manorial account for King's Langley, 1321/2 and 1322/3.

186. TNA: PRO SC6/1140/1 manorial account for Bishop's Stortford, 1345/6.

187. HHA court rolls 11/4 fo. 99, bailiff's account for Little Hadham, 1370/1.

188. TNA: PRO SC6/873/6 manorial account for Weston, 1275/6; SC6/868/16 manorial account for Standon, 1290/1; SC6/866/16 manorial account for King's Langeleye, 1305/6.

189. TNA: PRO SC6/1140/1 minister's account for Bishop's Stortford, 1345/6.

190. TNA: PRO SC6/864/5 minister's account for Berkhamsted, 1408/9; SC6/839/16 parker's account for Pisho park, 1421/2.

191. HHA court rolls 11/4 fo. 63–4 bailiff's accounts, 1393–7.

an event which is naturally erratic. The abundance of the crop was largely determined by variations in the weather but must also have been affected by the ways in which the trees were managed – oaks which are regularly pollarded or coppiced will not produce acorns. So, good revenues from pannage should indicate parks with an abundance of mature trees capable of producing mast, either growing in wood-pasture or as standards in coppiced compartments within the park.

More often than not, the revenue from pannage was recorded as 'nil because no mast' (*pesona* or *glandis*), as, for example, in 1399/1400, when there was no pannage in the parks at Berkhamsted (*nulla pesona*), Hertingfordbury (*null' glandes*) or Little Hadham, and in 1493/4, when there was no pannage in the parks at Benington, Bedwell or Hertingfordbury.[192] In years with an abundant crop of acorns and beechnuts, however, significant revenues could be recorded. The highest sum found in the medieval Hertfordshire accounts for pannage of pigs was at Weston in 1278/9, when £10 10s 9d was received for pannage in Ipgrave plus 43s 11d for pannage in [the great] park. The next highest sum was also at Weston, when £6 13s 7d was recorded in 1305/6. The number of pigs was rarely stated, but at King's Langley in 1297 12s 4d was received for the pannage of 74 pigs in the park and 'foreign wood' (wood outside the park), at a rate of 2d per pig. If the same rate was applied at Weston in 1278/9, it would indicate an amazing 1,528 pigs!

Unfortunately the documentary record is too sparse to permit any meaningful assessments to be made regarding trends in the frequency or value of pannage but most of the records occur in the last quarter of the thirteenth century and the early fourteenth century and relate to the parks at Weston, Cheshunt old park, Standon, Berkhamsted, King's Langley and Little Hadham. Following a gap in the middle of the fourteenth century, there are a few records for the parks at Berkhamsted and Hertingfordbury in the late fourteenth century and one or two records for each of the parks at Berkhamsted, Walkern, Knebworth and Benington during the fifteenth century. Both agistment and pannage continued to be recorded in Hertfordshire's parks into the sixteenth century – in 1541/2 the bailiff of Knebworth recorded revenue of £3 13s 4d for agistment of the park and £7 10s 4d from pannage.[193]

The sums recorded for pannage of pigs at Berkhamsted were relatively high – 67s 3d in 1296/7, 100 shillings in 1377/8, £4 18d in 1408/9 – but included both the park and the 'foreign wood'. As beech was the tree most frequently recorded in the manorial records at Berkhamsted, it seems likely that the pigs were feeding predominantly on beech mast. In contrast, there are no records of beech at Weston but there are several references to oaks and there must have been a substantial number of mature, acorn-bearing trees in the park at Ipgrave to produce the pannage revenues recorded there in the late thirteenth and early fourteenth centuries.

Production of wood and underwood

Sales of timber, wood, fuel, faggots, charcoal, old hedges and fences formed the major source of revenue from Hertfordshire parks for much of the medieval period. The limited evidence contained in the fragmentary manorial records of 17 parks suggests that average annual revenues per park in the fourteenth century were about £2 7s, rising slightly to about £2 12s in the fifteenth century. It should be remembered, however, that these figures are heavily dependent upon the high values of sales achieved by just a few parks – primarily Weston and Standon in the fourteenth century and Knebworth and Berkhamsted in the fifteenth century.

The records for Weston can be used to illustrate several aspects of wood production in medieval parks. The Weston manorial accounts recorded sales of wood (*bosci*) worth £12 19s 7d and, in Ipgrave park, underwood (*subosc*) worth another £1 12s in 1304/5. The wood was from 'sict' trees sold in both of Weston's parks (Ipgrave and the great park). The abbreviated word 'sict' may mean 'cut' (from the Latin *secare*, to cut), perhaps indicating that the trees had been pollarded. The underwood in Ipgrave park was sold by the acre in two lots: 8 acres of underwood were sold for 2s 6d per acre, while another 4 acres of underwood were sold for 3 shillings per acre. This tells us that the underwood was derived from compartments of coppiced woodland in the park, one of which was worth more than the other, perhaps because it had been growing for a longer period, or perhaps because of better soil or microclimatic conditions. In the following accounting year, £12 was received from the sale of dead wood (*morbosco*) in the park next to the hall and four acres of underwood were sold for 30 shillings (7s 6d per acre), also in the park next to the hall, confirming that Weston's great park was also compartmented. At the end of the fourteenth century prices of underwood sold at Weston ranged from 8 shillings (for underwood and thorns) to 16 shillings per acre; an acre of wood in Ipgrave was sold for £6 and this was presumably mature woodland containing timber trees.[194]

Underwood was also sold by area at Knebworth, as, for example, in 1370/1, when the *cropp'* of one rod in the old park was sold for 2s 6d. One acre of wood was sold in the new park at Knebworth for 13s 4d in 1402/3 and several 'parcels' of wood in the great park were sold for between 14d and 8 shillings in the same year. The same account also recorded numerous sales of 'loppes', presumably the branches cut from pollarded trees. For example, John Dardes paid 5 shillings for 'diverse loppes', Robert Romayn paid 8d for two *lopp'* and John Goderych paid 15d for three *lopp'*.[195]

Some of the wood sold from the parks at the end of the fifteenth century was simply recorded in the manorial accounts as 'fuel', as, for example, at Sir William Say's park at Benington in 1498/9.[196] At Sayes park, another park belonging

192. TNA: PRO SC6/863/18 account for Berkhamsted, 1399/1400; HHA court rolls 20/13 parker's account for Hertingfordbury park, 1399/1400; HHA court rolls 11/4 fo. 59 bailiff's account for Little Hadham, 1399/1400; HHA court rolls 10/20 accounts for Benington and Bedwell, 1493/4; HHA court rolls 22/5 parker's account for Hertingfordbury, 1493/4.

193. HALS K133 bailiff's account for Knebworth, 1541/2.

194. TNA: PRO SC6/873/21, 22 and 25 manorial accounts for Weston, 1304/5, 1305/6 and 1396/7.

195. HALS K100 and K106–7, bailiff's accounts for Knebworth, 1370/1 and 1402/3.

196. HHA court rolls 10/23 bailiff's account for Benington, 1498/9.

to Sir William, underwood and loppings from trees were sold by the cartload for fuel in the 1480s and 90s. Revenues ranged from 3s 8d for 11 cartloads of loppings in 1484/5 to 25s 1½d for 67 cartloads of underwood in 1490/1.[197]

Faggots

Small branches and twigs which were too small for anything else were made up into bundles called faggots which were burnt as fuel. Faggots are recorded in the manorial accounts of the parks at Albury, Berkhamsted, Brantingshay (Cheshunt), Hertingfordbury, Knebworth and Little Hadham. Substantial revenues could be accrued from sales, as, for example, when 2,700 faggots were sold for 108 shillings from Brantingshay park in 1435, but most sales were more modest, raising between 25 shillings and 36 shillings a year from sales of between 1,000 and 1,350 faggots.[198] The earliest record of faggots found in the Hertfordshire manorial accounts was in 1327/8, when 1,000 were sold from the bishop of Ely's park at Little Hadham for 25 shillings.[199] At 40 faggots to the shilling, these were amongst the cheapest recorded in the Hertfordshire accounts; those at Cheshunt, at just 25 faggots to the shilling, were the most expensive. Rackham reckoned that the cost of making faggots was generally 25 per cent of the selling price.[200] Making faggots at Little Hadham in 1327/8 cost 5 shillings, 20 per cent of the selling price. By contrast, 900 faggots made in the new park at Knebworth in 1410/11 cost 9s 9d, 32.5 per cent of the 30-shillings selling price.[201] It is likely that many of the faggots made each year were not destined to be sold but were used on the manor, including, for example, the 3,500 faggots made in Hertingfordbury park in 1396/7 which were all used by John of Gaunt's household at Hertford castle.[202]

Charcoal

Charcoal was another product of medieval parks which features in the manorial accounts from the end of the fourteenth century at Hatfield and during the fifteenth century at Knebworth, Little Hadham and Bedwell (Essendon). The bishop of Ely appears to have instigated large-scale charcoal production in the great park at Hatfield: 3,864 quarters (*qrs*) were made in 1395/6 at a cost of £36 4s 6d; it was sold for £64 8s, giving a profit of £28 3s 6d.[203] In 1427/8 137 cartloads of charcoal were sold for £10 and

40 loads of charcoal were also sold out of the little park for 100 shillings in 1435/6.[204] In other parks, production was on a much more modest scale, as at Knebworth in 1408/9, when 15 quarters of charcoal were made in the old park and sold for 10s 5d, or at Bedwell in 1484/5, when charcoal made from trees felled to repair the park pale was sold for 17s 1½d.[205] In the bishop of Ely's park at Little Hadham in 1462 a ten-year lease for making charcoal was sold to William Valence for £4 a year and in 1467/8 underwood was sold to William Abbott for making charcoal for 53s 4d.[206]

Bark

Oak bark was a regular feature in sales of wood from the bishop of Ely's park at Little Hadham in the early fourteenth century, as, for example, in 1340/1, when the bark (*corticibz*) of seven oaks felled in the park was sold for 7 shillings.[207] In Hatfield great park £10 4s 6d was received for underwood and bark sold in 1286 but no references to sales of bark have been found in the manorial accounts for other parks in the county.[208]

The species of parkland trees

Analysis of references in manorial accounts suggests that oak was the most widespread tree in Hertfordshire's medieval parks, followed by beech and ash, but the records are so scarce and patchy in their coverage, both geographically and chronologically, that it would be unwise to rely on them as a source of evidence for the relative abundance of different tree species in the county during the period. The accounts record only those trees which had an economic value to the manor and there may be some species which were abundant but which never appear in the records.

Amongst the earliest recorded sales of oak was a single tree sold for 5s 4d at Weston in 1294/5, and 66 oaks were sold in the park at Standon for £9 in 1328/9.[209] Oak was the only species recorded in the accounts for Little Hadham in the early fourteenth century – including the pollarding of 112 trees and the felling of 167 others in 1331/2.[210] Although there are few records of oaks in the fifteenth-century accounts, surveys of several Hertfordshire parks in the mid-sixteenth century revealed that oak was abundant (with beech) at Hatfield and was the predominant tree species in Benington park, in the great

197. HHA court rolls 10/16, 10/19, 10/20, 10/21 and 10/23 bailiff's accounts, 1484/5, 1490/1, 1493/4, 1495/6 and 1498/9.

198. King's College, Cambridge KCAR/6/2/034 Cheshunt manorial accounts, 1435/6. See also HALS DE/Ap/M34, 36 and 39 manorial accounts for Albury, 1373/4, 1380/81 and 1385/6; HHA court rolls 22/8, 20/13 and 22/10 manorial accounts for Hertingfordbury, 1388/9, 1399/1400 and 1396/7.

199. HHA court rolls 11/4 fo. 147 manorial account for Little Hadham, 1327/8.

200. Rackham, *Ancient woodland*, p. 142.

201. HALS K117 bailiff's account for Knebworth, 1410/11. See also K108, 114 and 119 for 1403/4, 1408/9 and 1412/13.

202. HHA court rolls 22/10 manorial account for Hertingfordbury, 1396/7.

203. A quarter (*quartarius*) was a fourth part of any measure but presumably a quarter of a hundredweight in the case of charcoal. The scribe noted that 12 qrs made one cartload; each cartload cost 2s 3d.

204. HHA Hatfield Manor Papers I, 1396 Michaelmas, p. 265, 1428 Michaelmas, p. 339 and 1436 Michaelmas, p. 353.

205. HALS K116 manorial account for Knebworth, 1408/9; HHA court rolls 10/16 manorial account for Bedwell, 1484/5.

206. HHA court rolls 11/4 fos. 22 and 21 manorial accounts, 1463/4 and 1467/8.

207. HHA court rolls 11/4 fo. 133–2 manorial accounts for Little Hadham, 1340/1.

208. HHA Hatfield Manor Papers I, 1286 Sep 7, p. 87.

209. TNA: PRO SC6/873/16 reeve's account, 1294/5; SC6/868/20 bailiff's account 1328/9.

210. HHA court rolls 11/4 fo. 141–2.

park at Hunsdon and in the little park at King's Langley.[211]

Records from the mid-fourteenth century indicate that beech was the dominant tree at Berkhamsted – both in the park and in the woods outside the park. Some of the beech wood was used for fuel and charcoal in the castle but most seems to have been used as a source of revenue, as, for example, in 1358, when orders were issued to sell 60 beeches in the park and 100 beeches in the foreign wood to pay for repairs to the park pale and to the castle.[212] Beech may also have been the predominant tree at Knebworth at the beginning of the fifteenth century, as large numbers must have been felled in 1410/11 when income of £8 10s 4d was recorded 'for beech (*fagus*) in the lord's park' and again in 1412/13 when beech worth £10 13s 4d was sold to John Cropper of Stevenage.[213] Beeches worth 68 shillings were sold from the great and little parks at Hatfield in 1428.[214] A mid-sixteenth-century survey of the trees in the great park at King's Langley recorded 1,420 beech, 300 ash and 180 oaks and at Hatfield oak and beech were counted together to give totals of 10,000 trees in the great park and 2,000 trees in the middle park (formerly the little park) in 1538.[215]

The accounts compiled for the bishops of Ely at their park in Little Hadham indicate an interesting shift in the species of tree managed in the park during the mid-fourteenth century. After the felling of seven oaks in 1340/1 there was a lull in tree management which lasted for at least a decade. Then, in 1364/5, hornbeam made its first appearance in the accounts, when the lopps of one hundred trees were sold for 30 shillings. This is the earliest record of hornbeam in any of the Hertfordshire manorial accounts examined to date. Thirteen oaks were pollarded in Little Hadham park in 1368/9, but thereafter the accounts are dominated by regular sales of hornbeam and, occasionally, ash, while oaks were rarely recorded. More than 46 carts of 'cropp de hardebech' (an alternative name for hornbeam) were sold in the park for 17s 1d in 1368/9 and the possibility arises that these trees were being coppiced, rather than pollarded. If this was the case, then it seems likely that fenced compartments of hornbeam saplings had been established in the park a few decades earlier, perhaps after the major felling of oaks in 1331/2. Certainly, by the end of the fourteenth century the 'hernbemcropp' was recorded in the Little Hadham accounts as underwood and was sold by the cart-load, rather than by the tree, but there do seem to have been hornbeam pollards in the park as well because 140 'croppees de hernebemes' (presumably the crowns harvested

from 140 trees) were sold in 1377/8 for the same price per tree (2½d) as 103 'loppes de hernebem' in 1378/9.[216]

Hornbeams were also recorded nearby in the park at Albury, when they were pollarded in 1373/4, but it was to be nearly a century before the tree was recorded at any other parks in the county. '[T]rees called harinebeme' were felled in the park at Great Munden *c.*1460 and then, in 1481/2, 13 'trees called hornebeme' were pollarded in the great park at Knebworth.[217] The way these trees were described in the accounts seems to suggest that, for the scribe at least, the name of the tree was a new word.

It is difficult to draw firm conclusions from such scanty evidence but it does appear that hornbeam was deliberately introduced to some Hertfordshire parks in the fourteenth and fifteenth centuries. This accords with Rackham's view that hornbeam had become established in its Essex–Hertfordshire heartland by AD 1500 at the latest. Although probably native, it seems likely that hornbeam was favoured over other tree species, either deliberately or accidentally, by coppicing and wood-pasture management. It is relatively resistant to browsing and was used as fodder for deer (as recorded at Little Hadham in 1435/6), but its most important use was probably as fuel.[218]

There is no indication in the records that the bishops of Ely also promoted the growth of hornbeam in their parks at Hatfield but, interestingly, Hornbeam Gate was the name of the entrance to the north side of Hatfield great park; the name of the neighbouring manor of 'Herinebemgat' (in Essendon) was recorded in 1367 and is considered to be the earliest place-name which refers to the species.[219] Large quantities of wood were coppiced in the great park for 'firing and for sale' by the late fourteenth century, including the 3,864 quarters of charcoal made and sold in 1396.[220] It is possible that most of the coppiced wood was hornbeam but this was not recorded. In the same year, however, the loppings of 102 hornbeams (herenbemcropp) worth 16s 6d were sold in the little park at Hatfield. By the seventeenth century, at least, there were far more hornbeams (5,227) in Hatfield Great Wood than either beech (520) or oak (227).[221] Further investigation is needed into the estate records of the bishops of Ely to determine whether they may have been instrumental in promoting the species elsewhere.

Park lodges
Records of medieval lodges have been found for 13 (18 per cent) of the county's parks. There are post-medieval records of

211. TNA: PRO LR2/216 Land Revenue Miscellaneous Book 216; TNA: PRO E315/391 survey of manors in the county of Hertford held by King Philip and Queen Mary, 1556.

212. Dawes, *Register of the Black Prince*, 4, pp. 243, 265.

213. HALS K117 and 119 bailiff's accounts, 1410/11 and 1412/13.

214. HHA Hatfield Manor Papers: Summaries I, p. 339.

215. TNA: PRO E315/391 survey of manors in the county of Hertford held by King Philip and Queen Mary, 1556; TNA: PRO LR2/216 Land Revenue Miscellaneous Book 216.

216. HHA court rolls 11/4 fos. 132–3, 108–9, 103–5, 141–2, 87–8, 85–6 Little Hadham accounts.

217. HALS DE/Ap/M34 bailiff's account for Albury, 1373/4; TNA: PRO SC6/867/17 account for Great Munden, *c.*1460; HALS K124 bailiff's account for Knebworth, 1481/2.

218. Rackham, *Ancient woodland*, pp. 221, 223, 224, 235; HHA court rolls 9/25 manorial account for Little Hadham, 1435/6.

219. P. Austin, 'Hatfield Great Wood and its inclosure' *Hertfordshire's Past*, 38 (1995), p. 2, citing TNA: PRO Ancient Deeds E326/4213.

220. HHA Hatfield Manor Papers I, 1396 Michaelmas, p. 265.

221. Austin, 'Hatfield Great Wood and its inclosure', p. 6 citing HHA General 44/1.

lodges at a further 20 medieval parks, some of which may well have originated before 1500. Not surprisingly, the lodges tend to be associated with the larger parks. Eleven of the 13 parks with known medieval lodges were over 200 acres in size; only Sayes park, Sawbridgeworth (c.95 acres) and Rye park, Stanstead Abbots (156 acres) were smaller. Of the 24 Hertfordshire parks containing more than 200 acres, 46 per cent are known to have had a lodge in the medieval period.

The earliest record of a park lodge in the county was in 1290, when the 'old lodge' in Standon park was sold for 3 shillings. The earliest record of the park itself was in 1234, so the earls of Clare, who did not live in Standon, must have had a lodge built during the thirteenth century to provide a base and accommodation for the parker, whose responsibility it was to guard the park and the deer within it. The old lodge was evidently replaced because a wall and roof were repaired in 1335 (12d), but a new lodge was then built in 1337/8 at a cost of 75s 8¹/₂d.[222] The royal park at King's Langley was the only other park with a recorded lodge in the first half of the fourteenth century. In fact there was more than one, the earliest of which may have been the lodge called 'Little London', which was granted to the Dominican friars in 1308 to provide them with accommodation while their house was being built. A new lodge was built in Langley park in 1305/6 (17s 2¹/₄d) and this was probably the same building that was referred to as the 'western new lodge', which was repaired for 3s 1d in 1315/16 – perhaps the earliest lodge to stand on the site indicated on the OS map as Kings Langley Lodge.[223] This is a typical site for a park lodge, as is the site of Standon Lodge Farm in Standon park, both being located on high ground with extensive views of the surrounding parkland. The accounts for Langley indicate there were several thatched outbuildings associated with the lodge (which had a tiled roof), including stables and a longhouse.

The number of manors with recorded park lodges rose to seven during the second half of the fourteenth century. The bishop of Ely had a lodge built in his park at Little Hadham in 1364 at a cost of £3 16s,[224] and other parks, at Berkhamsted, Bishop's Stortford, Hertingfordbury and Walkern, had acquired lodges by the late fourteenth century, when the respective manorial accounts record repairs being made to them. The park on the manor of Hertingfordbury had become a 'royal' park associated with Hertford castle from the middle of the century and the earliest record of a lodge occurred in the 'new' park at Hertingfordbury in 1381. This may, or may not,

be the same as the lodge in the 'little' park which was repaired in 1395 or the lodge in the 'great' park which had a well dug for it in the same year.[225] The lodge in Walkern park appears to have comprised a complex of buildings which included a hall and chambers with a garderobe, a bakehouse and maybe even a chapel.[226]

Another manor which may have had a park lodge by the mid-fifteenth century was Bushey, where a field called 'le logge' was recorded in 1447.[227] At about the same time, in 1446, Sir John Fray embarked upon reinstating the apparently abandoned park at Great Munden. As well as refurbishing the park and restocking it with deer, he spent £6 16¹/₂d on repairs to the lodge and the construction of a new stable for it. Three years later he had fireplaces installed in the lodge at a cost of 33s 4d. The building of the 'parker's howse' was recorded in the account of 1448/9, so the lodge would appear to have been for the use of Fray himself.[228]

The lodge in Benington park was similarly 'new made' for the use of the lord, Sir William Say, in 1498, at a cost of £4 16s 6d.[229] Other lodges recorded for the first time towards the end of the fifteenth century were in the great park at Knebworth in 1483/4, Sayes park (Sawbridgeworth) in 1493 and Rye park (Stanstead Abbots) in the 1470s. Surviving records indicate that there were at least nine functioning park lodges in the county in the second half of the fifteenth century including one in Weston great park which was in need of major repairs when it was first documented in 1507. Some of the other lodges recorded for the first time in the early sixteenth century – in both the Innings and middle parks at Hatfield, in Tyttenhanger park (Ridge), Pisho park (Sawbridgeworth) and Ware park – might also have had medieval origins. At least four of these parks, however, had come into the hands of Henry VIII, a very keen huntsman, and he could have been responsible for a crop of new lodges built in the 1520s and 30s.

Park lodges are sometimes associated with moated sites in medieval parks and in Essex the majority of lodges and manor houses built in parks are reported to have been moated.[230] This does not seem to have been a common phenomenon in Hertfordshire's parks but there is a moat at Little London, the earliest known lodge in the park at King's Langley, and there are moated sites within Hoddesdonpark Wood and Scales Park (Barkway) which may mark the sites of former lodges.[231] Finds from an archaeological excavation of the moated site in Scales Park in the early 1940s dated the earthworks to the second half of the thirteenth century, which corresponds with

222. TNA: PRO SC6/868/16 reeve's account, 1290/1; SC6/1109/6 ministers' and receivers'accounts, 1234/5; SC6/868/21 minister's accounts, 1335/6; SC6/868/23 minister's account, 1337/8.

223. Page, *Hertford*, 2, p. 238 citing Pat. 2 Edw. II, pt. 1, m. 17; TNA: PRO SC6/866/16 bailiff's account for Langeleye, 1305/6; SC6/866/20 manorial accounts for Childern Langeleye, 1315–1318.

224. HHA court rolls 11/4 fos. 108–9 bailiff's accounts between 1322 and 1507.

225. HHA court rolls 19/11 account, 1381/2; court roll 22/7 account, 1395/6.

226. HALS DE/Hx/Z24 typed translation of account rolls of manor of Walkern, 1324–1432, pp. 84–5, quoting HALS 9357 manorial accounts, 1390/1.

227. J.E.B. Gover, A. Mawer and F.M. Stenton, *The place-names of Hertfordshire* (Cambridge, 1938), p. 273.

228. TNA: PRO SC6/867/10, 12 and 13 bailiff's accounts 1446/7, 1448/9 and 1449/50.

229. HHA court rolls 10/23 bailiff's account, 1498/9.

230. Pluskowski, 'The social construction of medieval park ecosystems', p. 65, citing P. Ryan, 'Woodham Walter Hall — its site and setting', *Essex Archaeology and History*, 30 (2000), pp. 178–95.

231. HER I.D. no. 800 – Little London, King's Langley; no. 730 – Hoddesdonpark Wood.

the time that the park is thought to have been created.[232] The lodge in Walkern park was, unusually, described as being located outside the moat in 1429.[233] Another moated site, in Roughground Wood (Little Munden), *may* have been the site of a parker's lodge for the East park of Little Munden.

Apart from the moated site at Scales Park, the only other medieval lodge site known to have been the subject of archaeological investigation in the county was at Stortford park. Stag antlers and pottery fragments dating from the thirteenth to the sixteenth centuries were found in the ditch surrounding the square site of the former lodge during excavations carried out in 1938 and 1958.[234]

Park personnel

Parkers

In 1325 the parker of Walkern park was paid 2d a day; nearly two centuries later, in 1507, the parker at Little Hadham was also paid 2d a day. For most of the fourteenth century, the whole of the fifteenth, and for much of the sixteenth century the standard rate of pay for a parker in Hertfordshire remained constant at this rate (60s 10d p.a.). The earliest records suggest that rates were lower in the thirteenth century: in 1263 the bishop of London's parker at Stortford received a grain livery and a stipend; in 1274 the Earl of Gloucester's parker at Standon was paid 40 shillings for the whole year (*c*.1⅓d per day); in the same year the parker at Stortford received 1½d per day plus a stipend and at Weston in 1279 the Earl of Norfolk's parker took 1d a day plus a robe worth 6s 8d. However, the parker at King's Langley was paid 2d per day (60s 10d) plus 10 shillings for a robe in 1297 and at Berkhamsted, in the same year, the Earl of Cornwall's parker, William de Hockfield, was paid 60s 8d, at 2d per day, and also received 10 shillings for a robe.[235]

The parkers of the bishops of Ely at Little Hadham were poorly paid during the fourteenth century in comparison with the parkers of nine other parks in the county for which records of wages have been found. The Little Hadham parkers were paid just 1½d per day (45s 6d p.a.) until about 1388, when the wage increased to 2d per day.[236] At Stortford in 1345/6 the bishop of London paid two parkers different rates for different periods of the year, presumably indicating seasonal variations in the workload: one parker worked from 29 September to 25 January (118 days) and was paid 2d per day (19s 8d); the other parker worked the remaining 247 days to 29 September 1346 and was paid 1d per day (20s 7d).[237]

The parkers at Albury, Berkhamsted, Bishop's Stortford, Hatfield great park, Hertingfordbury, Standon and Walkern were all paid 2d per day during the fourteenth century, with the following exceptions: in 1337/8 the parker at Standon was paid from 19 February to 30 September only, and received 1½d per day; in 1358/9 the parker at Walkern was paid 3d per day (£4 11s 3d for the year); and at Albury in 1386 the parker had 20 shillings deducted from his usual wage of 60s 8d because he had taken 400 faggots from the park.[238] The parker of the little park at Hatfield was paid 3d per day in the 1380s, 1396, 1436, 1538 and 1593. In contrast, the parker of the great park was paid only 2d per day in 1396 but received the same pay (3d per day) in 1538 and twice as much (6d a day) by 1593.[239] During the fifteenth century the parkers of Bedwell, Benington, Berkhamsted, Bishop's Stortford, Brantingshay (Cheshunt), Great Munden, 'Hertford' (Hertingfordbury), Knebworth, Little Hadham, Standon and Walkern were all paid 2d per day.

A traditional 'perk' of the parker appears to have been the right to collect windblown wood for fuel. This right is explicitly expressed in two formal grants, one from the early fourteenth century, the other from the late fifteenth century: in 1334 the Black Prince granted to Robert le Parker the 'bailiwick of parker of the park of Berkhamstede and the foreign woods there ... with 2d daily for wages and 13s 4d yearly for his robe, and trees and wood [*busca*] blown down by the wind in the park and woods';[240] while in 1483 Sir Thomas Bourghchier granted the office of parker of the great and little parks at Knebworth to Walter Copynger, who was entitled to keep one horse and three cows in the parks and to collect windblown wood and 'browsing' (except good windblown timber (*maeremo habili*)).[241] The value of this perk, in Berkhamsted at least, was brought to light as a result of a severe storm which hit the south of England in January 1362. So great was the devastation to the trees in the park and woods at Berkhamsted that the Black Prince suspended the parker's right to the windblown wood and ordered his steward to enquire what it would be worth in a normal year. The steward reported that the perk was usually worth 'ten marks and more' (about 133s) and the parker was accordingly granted 100 shillings each year from the proceeds of the sale of the storm-felled wood until such time as it had all been sold.[242]

No general conclusions about relative wealth or social status can be drawn from a survey of the 11 men with the occupational name 'le Parker' in the 1307 lay subsidy returns for Hertfordshire. The amounts they paid in tax ranged from the 6¾d paid by Henry le Parker at Baldock to 6s 8d paid by William le Parker of Watford. William le Parker at Eastwick

232. A. Williams, 'A homestead moat at Nuthampstead, Hertfordshire', *The Antiquaries Journal*, 26 (1946), p. 142.

233. HALS DE/Hx/Z24 typed translation of account rolls of manor of Walkern, 1324–1432, pp. 100.

234. T.W. Ellcock, 'The Bishop of London's hall or lodge at Bishops Stortford', *Herts Past and Present*, 5 (1964), p. 33.

235. L.M. Midgley (ed.), *Minister's accounts of the earldom of Cornwall 1296–1297*, vol. 1 (London, 1942), pp. 21, 13.

236. HHA court rolls 11/4 accounts of the manor of Little Hadham, 1322–1507.

237. TNA: PRO SC6/1140/1 minister's account, 1345/6.

238. HALS DE/Hx/Z24 transcript of Walkern manor accounts, p. 41.

239. HHA Hatfield Manor Papers I, 1396, p. 265; 1436, p. 353; 1538, p. 683; 1593, p. 1019.

240. Page, *Hertford*, 2, p. 166; *Cal. Pat. 1334–1338*, p. 550.

241. HALS DE/Z120/44373 confirmation of the earlier grant, 1483.

242. Dawes, *Register of the Black Prince, 4*, p. 464.

paid 3s 1¼d in tax and he and the William le Parker at Watford were the second and third highest taxpayers in their respective vills. William le Parker at Watford paid the same amount as Hugh le Fuller of Watford, perhaps an indication of his relative status in the community, but Henry le Parker at Baldock and John le Parker at Gaddesden paid almost the lowest amounts of tax in their respective vills. The remaining parkers were in the middling ranks of taxpayers, paying between 12d and 21½d in tax. Of course, there were other parkers with different surnames: for example, William de Hereford at Berkhamsted paid 5s 1½d in tax in 1307, but there will be others whose names are simply not known, including perhaps Adam Hunter (*Venatoro*), who was a taxpayer at Hertingfordbury.[243]

Falconers and huntsmen

There are also a few references to falconers in Hertfordshire in the fourteenth century. Edward III is known to have enjoyed the sport of falconry on the banks of the river Lea between Stratford and Hertford, and his sister, Queen Joan of Scotland, had her master falconer with her during her stay at Hertford castle, a residence of their mother, Queen Isabella, in 1346.[244] The abbot of St Albans, Thomas de la Mare, kept falconers as well as huntsmen on his staff in the second half of the fourteenth century and Roger Bigge, the parker at Berkhamsted from 1380, was described as a 'hunter' (*venator*).[245] At a lower social level, Walter de la Lee (whose father had been steward of the royal household) had a falconer at his manor of Albury in the 1380s. The manorial accounts show that the falconer, John Beyford, had the use of two dovecotes on the manor, no doubt a valuable source of food for his falcons.[246]

243. Brooker and Flood, *Hertfordshire lay subsidy rolls*.

244. H.C. Andrews, *The chronicles of Hertford castle* (Hertford, 1947), pp. 22, 24.

245. Page, *Hertford*, 4, p. 396 citing Riley, H.T. (ed.), *Gesta abbatum monasterii Sancti Albani a Thoma Walsingham, vol. 3, AD 1349–1411* (London, 1869; republished Germany, 1965), pp. 390 and 400; Cott. MS. Nero, D vii, fol. 22d.

246. HALS DE/Ap/M37–8 manorial accounts for Albury, 1382/3 and 1384/5; TNA: PRO SC6/863/14 receiver's accounts, 1388/9.

Part Two

Gazetteer of medieval parks in Hertfordshire

Introduction

THE PARKS HAVE BEEN ARRANGED alphabetically in the gazetteer according to the ancient ecclesiastical parish of the manor to which they belonged, and then alphabetically by name of park within each parish. In almost all cases the park was located within the same parish as the manor. The exceptions were the park at Ashridge and perhaps the park belonging to the manor of Broadfield. The account of Ashridge park can be found in the gazetteer under Little Gaddesden, the parish of the parent manor, although the park itself lay in the parishes of Berkhamsted and Pitstone (Buckinghamshire). The location of the park belonging to the manor of Broadfield is not definitely known but it may have been in the parish of Clothall. The reasoning behind this theory can be read in the gazetteer entry for the parish of Broadfield.

Each gazetteer entry is headed with some basic facts and figures about the park, as far as they are known or can be determined. Any uncertain figures are qualified with a question mark. The national grid reference (NGR) identifies a central place within the former park. Geological information has been derived from the maps of the British Geological Survey.[1] For most parks the gazetteer entry consists of a chronological narrative describing all the known sources of documentary evidence, plus any cartographic or field evidence, together with a map showing the likely geographical location and extent of the park in the medieval period.

The base maps used are the first edition Ordnance Survey maps printed at six inches to the mile, most of which were surveyed between 1870 and 1881 and published between 1877 and 1884. These maps were chosen partly because they are out of copyright but mainly because they accurately portray the Hertfordshire countryside as it was before twentieth-century agricultural advances and civil engineering projects eroded much of the county's landscape history, including field boundaries, woods and place-names which had their origins in medieval times. Parkland which existed at the time the maps were surveyed was depicted on the six-inch maps with grey stippling. Individual trees depicted

> ▪ confident that the land was medieval parkland
>
> ⠿ probably medieval parkland but supporting evidence is less certain
>
> ⠿ may have been medieval parkland but supporting evidence is weak

outside woodland on these first edition maps can generally be assumed to have been present in the landscape at the time of the survey. Parish boundaries were marked with a dashed line.

Except where indicated, all maps in the gazetteer are reproduced at the original scale of six inches to the mile. North is always at the top of the page except for Map 36 (King's Langley), Map 46 (The More, Rickmansworth) and Map 55 (Standon). These were big parks and the maps have been turned in order to show them at the largest possible scale.

The extent of former parkland is indicated by green shading superimposed onto the Ordnance Survey map. Three different patterns of shading reflect the degree of confidence with which the land has been identified as former medieval parkland, as shown in the above box.

Where appropriate, the maps have been annotated with field names and other information relating to the location and extent of the former medieval parks. All annotations have been added using Arial font.

Figure 12 shows the parishes which are known to have contained parks in the medieval period and also those parishes for which there is some, inconclusive, evidence for a park. The areas of parkland depicted on this map include all the land covered by the three degrees of confidence listed above.

1. British Geological Survey maps 1:50,000 Series (solid and drift edition) Sheet 221 Hitchin, 1995; Sheet 222 Great Dunmow, 1990; Sheet 238 Aylesbury, 1946 (reprinted 1990); Sheet 239 Hertford, 1978; Sheet 240 Epping, 1981; Sheet 255 Beaconsfield, 2005; Sheet 256 North London, 2006.

x park whose location or boundaries have not been determined

THE WYMONDLEYS

IPPOLLITTS

CLOTHALL

BROADFIELD

BARKWAY

WESTON

GT HORMEAD

HITCHIN

GT OFFLEY

FURNEUX PELHAM

ARDELEY

ALBURY

WALKERN

THE MUNDENS

KNEBWORTH

BENINGTON

LT HADHAM

BISHOPS STORTFORD X

STANDON

MUCH HADHAM

AYOT ST LAWRENCE

KIMPTON

BRAMFIELD

LT GADDESDEN

SAWBRIDGEWORTH

FLAMSTEAD

WARE

TRING

HATFIELD

ALDBURY

GT GADDESDEN

EASTWICK

HUNSDON

STANSTEAD ABBOTS

BERKHAMSTED

ST MICHAELS

HODDESDON

HERTINGFORDBURY

KINGS LANGLEY

ST STEPHENS

RIDGE

XX

CHESHUNT

SHENLEY

ESSENDON

LT BERKHAMSTED

WATFORD

BUSHEY

X ELSTREE

RICKMANSWORTH

X

0   10 miles

0   10 km

Figure 12. Key map showing Hertfordshire's medieval parks with their parishes.

Albury

Punsho park

NGR: TL435241
Date range: before 1336 – not known but after 1386
Size: not known (licence to enclose 300 acres in 1365)
Underlying geology: boulder clay and head gravel

THE EARLIEST KNOWN REFERENCE to a park occurs in the early fourteenth century, when Geoffrey de la Lee gave a gift to Peter, vicar of Albury, and John Vataile of a yearly rent of £10 and 'commoning in the park of Aldebury'. In 1336, after Geoffrey's death, Peter and John Vataile released their claim to the rent and to commoning in the park to Geoffrey's son, John de la Lee.[1] Circumstantial evidence, however, suggests that a park was present at Albury from at least the beginning of the fourteenth century, as a Simon ate Parc was listed in the lay subsidy roll for Albury in 1307.[2] This park was likely to have been created by a member of the Baard family who held the manor of the bishop of London from at least 1166.[3]

In 1316 Robert Baard settled the reversion of the manor on Geoffrey de la Lee and his wife, with successive remainders to their three sons.[4] Geoffrey de la Lee, a royal official and important figure in Hertfordshire, also held the neighbouring manor of Cockhamsted (which lay partly in Braughing), but his main landholding in the county is thought to have been Waterford Hall, Stapleford.[5] Geoffrey died before 1336 and the manor of Albury seems to have passed to his son John. A bailiff's account for that year does not mention a park.[6]

At the time of his father's death John de la Lee was just embarking on a career in administration. He became steward of the household for Queen Isabella until she died in 1358 and then moved to the household of Queen Philippa and became steward of her lands. He also became steward of Edward III's household in 1362 and received a knighthood. As well as his offices at the centre of government, Lee acted on a number of local commissions in Hertfordshire and neighbouring counties. His services were well rewarded and he purchased property near his family holdings in Albury and Clothall, Hertfordshire.[7] In October 1365 John de la Lee and his heirs received a grant 'of free warren in all their demesne lands in the towns of Braghhyng and Aldebury' and a licence 'to impark 300 acres of pasture and wood in his demesne lands, pastures and woods in the towns aforesaid and to hold the park so made to him and his heirs without let or hindrance of the king and his heirs or any their ministers'.[8] Less than three years later, in 1368, Lee was denounced in parliament for various misdeeds, including misuse of his powers as steward and meddling in local courts. He was imprisoned in the Tower of London until he paid a fine and ransom at the king's will. John de la Lee died in January 1370 and the manor passed to his 20-year-old son Walter, who held it for the next 25 years until he died in 1395.[9]

Seven bailiff's accounts which shed some light on the working of the park survive in the Hertfordshire Archives from the period of Walter's tenure.[10] What these accounts do not provide, however, is any evidence for the existence of two parks at Albury: the only park mentioned is the 'park of Punsho'. As the name 'Punsho' also occurred in a bailiff's account of 1335/6, 30 years *before* the licence to impark the 300 acres was granted, it seems likely that Punsho park was the original park recorded in the early fourteenth century. The facts that Geoffrey de la Lee granted out commoning rights in the park and that no park-related activities were recorded in the bailiff's account of 1336 might suggest that the original park had fallen out of use.[11] There are several possible explanations for the licence obtained by John de la Lee in 1366. Firstly, it could represent his attempt to legitimise and/or refurbish and restock the original park with deer. Secondly, he could have been intending to add the 300 acres to the pre-existing park, or, thirdly, his intention may have been to create a new 300-acre park in addition to the pre-existing park. Any of these actions would have been appropriate for Lee at the peak of his career but, if the third scenario was correct, then his intention seems not to have been carried out. Given that there was less than three years between the granting of the licence and Lee's fall from grace, it may simply be that his park-making plans were overtaken by events.

The late fourteenth century accounts show that Walter de la Lee's parker from at least 1374 to 1386 was John Sexteyn. He was paid 2d a day (60s 8d p.a.) and his wage was the only 'cost of the park' recorded in the accounts because of a neat agreement between the two men: John Sexteyn undertook to maintain the boundary of the park in return for the use of the dovecote in the park and for the agistment of 12 animals in the park each year. In 1386 the lord's auditor reduced Sexteyn's wage to 40s 8d 'and no more' because he had been assigned 400 faggots (worth 20 shillings) made in Punsho park.[12] In the 1380s Walter de la Lee also employed a falconer, John Beyford, who was granted the use of two other dovecotes on the manor. Faggots were regularly made in Punsho park and in 1373/4 hornbeams and willows were pollarded and the wood sold for 5 shillings. In 1382/3 five beech trees in the park were sold for 5 shillings each. There was also a warren on the manor but this failed to produce income in any of the accounts as it was used for grazing for the lord's horses and cattle. The last in the series of bailiff's accounts in the Hertfordshire Archives dates from 1394/5, the year of Walter de la Lee's death, and is much shorter than the rest. John atte Parke was the collector of rents and farmer of the manor and he recorded no information relating to the park in the account.[13]

No information has been found about the park in the fifteenth or sixteenth centuries and it is not shown on the county maps by either Saxton (1577) or Norden (1598). It was

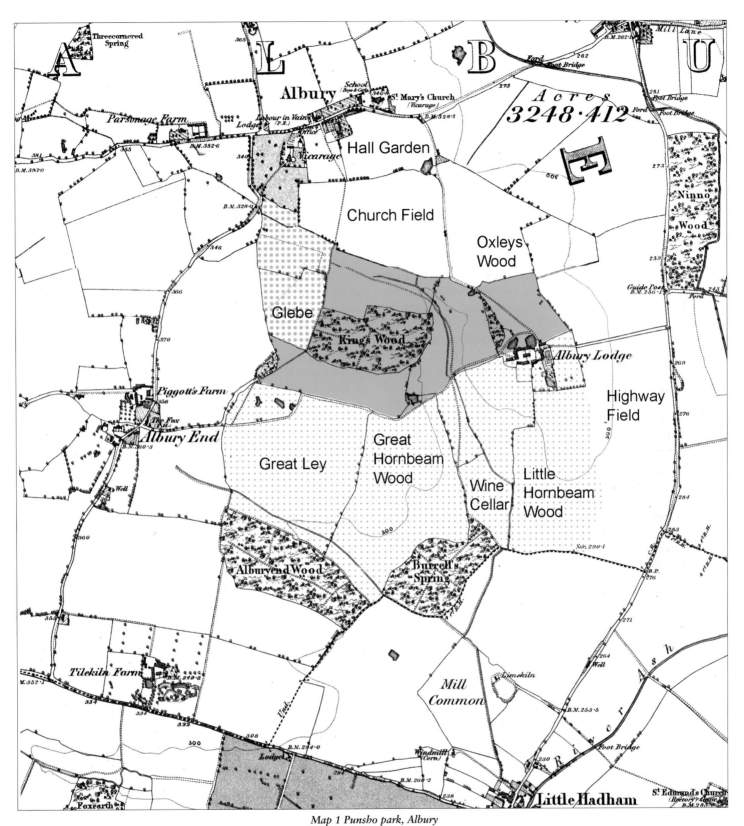

Map 1 Punsho park, Albury

OS 6 inches to the mile map sheets XIV and XXII, surveyed 1876–8, published 1881–3. The shaded area mostly corresponds with land called 'The Park' in 1914 (HALS 64255) but the western end was glebe land in 1842. If this was glebe land in the medieval period, it is unlikely to have been part of the park but it is quite possible that it became glebe land only in the post-medieval period. Field names are derived from the tithe map and award of 1842 (HALS DSA4/1/1 and 2). King's Wood no longer exists.

recorded again, however, in 1601, when the manor of Albury was being divided into four parts. Two of these parts became the Albury Hall estate and a third part became Albury Lodge, described as a capital messuage 'in Punshoe Park or Alburye Parke'. Together with the house went 160 acres of land and 'all the meadows, pastures, woods and grounds commonly called Punshoe Parke or Alburye Parke'.[14] Albury Lodge belonged to the Brograve family throughout the seventeenth century and architectural historian John T. Smith considered that the present-day house called Albury Lodge may have originated as a new house built by the Brograves at the turn of the sixteenth and seventeenth centuries.[15] If so, it presumably replaced an earlier park lodge.

Without further evidence it is impossible to determine the relationship between the original park and the licence to impark 300 acres in 1366: they could have been one and the same park or they could have been two different parks, the later of which may never have been created. The key to locating Punsho park is the 1601 reference to Albury Lodge which lay 'in Punshoe Park' (see Map 1). Unfortunately, the document does not record the size of the park. In the nineteenth century Albury Lodge farm occupied a compact block of land south of the village and church of Albury and extending to the southern boundary of the parish and the south side of Alburyend Wood, with 'the lodge' located on high ground in the middle of it.[16] Most of the nineteenth-century field boundaries of the farm were sinuous and ancient-looking and several of the field- and wood-names recorded on the Albury tithe map and award can be tentatively correlated with fields and woods named in the 1601 document. The latter included Oxlease Wood and Oxlease Close, Vyneseller Mead and Vyneseller Valley and 'twoe greate woodes of hornbeames'. These lands were listed in addition to Punshoe Parke, which indicates that they were not part of the park in 1601, although they could have been in earlier centuries. The land lying adjacent to, and west of, Albury Lodge – including King's Wood – cannot be identified with fields or features named in 1601 and so this seems the likeliest location for the park at that time. This area, covering 56 acres, is indicated on the map by solid shading. The fields immediately to the west were probably also parkland in medieval times but one field had been given to the church by 1842. Just how much of the surrounding land (if any) was also part of the medieval park is open to conjecture, but nineteenth-century field names recalling hornbeam woods to the south and south-east seem suggestive. There was no indication of a park in this area on the tithe map of 1842 but, when Albury Lodge Farm was sold

in 1914, the irregular outline of the fields surrounding the former King's Wood – apparently an area of wood-pasture which covered 67.6 acres – were labelled 'The Park'.[17] The total area shaded on Map 1 covers 230 acres. A bank survives along sections of the west side, which was bounded by a lane for much of its length in the early nineteenth century.

No park was shown at Albury on any seventeenth-century county map, although both Albury Hall and Albury Lodge were named by Seller (1676).[18] The first map to show a park in the parish was Dury and Andrews' county map of 1766, but this park was located north-west of the village, surrounding Albury Hall.

1. Chauncy, *Historical antiquities*, p. 147.
2. J. Brooker and S. Flood (eds), *Hertfordshire lay subsidy rolls 1307 and 1334* (Hertfordshire Record Society, 1998), p. 63. A John atte Park was the bailiff of the manor in the 1370s and (probably) another John atte Parke took over the manor in 1395.
3. Page, *Hertford*, 4, p. 5.
4. Page, *Hertford*, 4, p. 5 citing Feet of Fines Herts. 9 Edw. II, no. 231. Geoffrey de la Lee was holding the manor by 1320 when he received a grant of free warren (*Cal. Chart. 1300–1326*, p. 417).
5. Geoffrey de la Lee was an important royal official under Edward II, including chief taxer for the county for the lay subsidies of 1309, 1313, 1327 and 1332. He also held Queen Hoo in Tewin (Bailey, 'Introduction', citing Page, *Hertford*, 3, pp. 310, 477 and 483).
6. HALS DE/Ap/M33 bailiff's account for Albury, 1335/6.
7. S.L. Waugh, 'Lee, Sir John (*d.* 1370)', *Oxford dictionary of national biography* (Oxford, 2004), accessed online 22 September 2007.
8. *Cal. Chart. 1341–1417*, p. 192.
9. Waugh, 'Lee, Sir John'.
10. HALS DE/Ap/M34–9 bailiff's accounts for Albury, 1373/4, 1376/7, 1380/1, 1382/3, 1384/5, 1385/6.
11. HALS DE/Ap/M33 bailiff's account, 1335/6.
12. HALS DE/Ap/M39 bailiff's account, 1385/6.
13. HALS DE/Ap/M41 bailiff's account, 1394/5.
14. HALS 75037 partition agreement for Albury, 1601. The remaining part was the 'manor or farm of Cockhamsted'.
15. Smith, *Hertfordshire houses*, p. 3.
16. HALS DSA4/1/1 and 2 tithe award and map for Albury, 1842.
17. HALS 64255 sale particulars, 1914.
18. J. Seller, *Hertfordshire actually survey'd and delineated* (1676), republished in D. Hodson, Four county maps of Hertfordshire (Stevenage, 1985).

Parish: Aldbury *see Tring*

Figure 13. *The landscape of the former Punsho park in the middle of the twentieth century. Aerial photograph taken by the RAF 10 October, 1946 (HALS Off Acc 300 CPE/UK/1779, 3346). Reproduced by kind permission of Hertfordshire Archives and Local Studies.*

Ardeley

Ardeley Bury park

NGR: TL302270
Date range: by 1222 – ?pre-sixteenth century
Size: recorded as 60 acres in 1222
Underlying geology: boulder clay

THE CANONS OF ST PAUL'S in London held the manor of Ardeley from pre-Norman times until the early nineteenth century.[1] The manor house and demesne lands were let on lease as early as the twelfth century.[2] By the early thirteenth century it had become customary to lease the manor to one of the canons of St Paul's, which probably accounts for the fact that a park was recorded at Ardeley in an inquisition taken by the Dean of St Paul's, Robert de Watford, in 1222.[3] This states that the manor house of Ardeley was surrounded by a park of 60 acres and that 8 acres of land belonging to the demesne had been exchanged with 8 acres of land held by a tenant.[4] The creator of the park may have been Theobald, Archdeacon of Essex, who was holding the manor in 1222,[5] and the exchange of lands was probably part of the process of establishing the boundaries of the park. A Stephen le Parker was listed as a taxpayer in Ardeley in the 1294 Subsidy Rolls.[6]

According to Salmon the Chauncy family leased the manor house from the early sixteenth century.[7] Sir Henry Chauncy described the manor house as 'situated upon the side of an Hill, distant from the Church above 140 pole, in the Middle of an antient Park, now disparked, well water'd with fish-ponds, and heretofore moated round'.[8] Exactly when the park was disparked is not known, but it was not shown on Saxton's county map of 1577. However, a park *was* depicted at Ardeley by Norden in 1598 but, puzzlingly, the park was located to the east of Ardeley church, whereas Ardeley Bury, and presumably its former medieval park, lay to the west of the church.

A parish map of 1744 shows a cluster of fields adjacent to Ardeley Bury which have 'park' names. Although the more distant fields, such as Gravel-dell Park and Middle Park, appear to have been ploughed, those fields adjacent to the house were under pasture. Avenues of trees were depicted in Great Park to the north-west of the house, indicating a limited area of ornamental landscape within the former parkland.[9] Great Park, however, appears to have been too small to register as parkland on a range of county maps published

during the seventeenth and eighteenth centuries but an Ordnance Survey Drawing dating from 1800 suggests that a larger area of park had been reinstated during the last quarter of the eighteenth century.[10] Consequently, the park field names recorded in 1744 are likely to commemorate the site of the medieval park. The elongated tongue of land which incorporates these fields is not a typical shape for a medieval park, but the area covered – 63 acres – corresponds well with the 60 acres recorded in the survey of 1222.

Apart from the atypical shape, this park does share features in common with many other medieval parks, in that it lay on a ridge of high ground and one side coincided with the parish boundary. Additional supporting evidence is an impressive bank at the south-west corner of the field called Gravel-dell park (see Map 2). At this point the field/park boundary diverges northwards from the parish boundary at almost a right angle and the earth bank is about 0.75m high on its west side. There is no notable earthwork along the former north-east boundary of the field called Great Park and the landscape does not suggest that this was a likely park boundary. It is possible that the medieval park originally formed a more compact area around the manor house and extended further east to the stream, rather than extending south-eastwards along the parish boundary. This would also be more compatible with Chauncy's description of the house sitting in the middle of the ancient park.

1. Page, *Hertford*, 3, pp. 194–5. The canons lost Ardeley for a short period during the Civil War in the seventeenth century but regained their lands on the Restoration.

2. Page, *Hertford*, 3, p. 194, citing Hale, *Domesday of St Paul's*, p. 135.

3. Page, *Hertford*, 3, p. 194, citing MSS of D. and C. of St Paul's, A Boxes 26–40, nos 424, 425, &c.; cf. nos 1411, 1412, and A Box 52, no. 1.

4. Hale, *Domesday of St Paul's*, p. 21.

5. Page, *Hertford*, 3, p. 194, citing Hale, *Domesday of St Paul's*, p. 21.

6. Gover *et al.*, *Place-names of Hertfordshire*, p. 152.

7. Salmon, *Hertfordshire*, p. 323.

8. Chauncy, *Historical antiquities*, p. 53.

9. HALS DE/Z110/P1 map book of Ardeley, 1744.

10. BL Ordnance Survey Drawing 142, 9 (Buntingford sheet), surveyed 1800, published 1805. County maps which did not show a park include those by Seller (1676), Oliver (1695), Warburton (1749) and Dury and Andrews (1766).

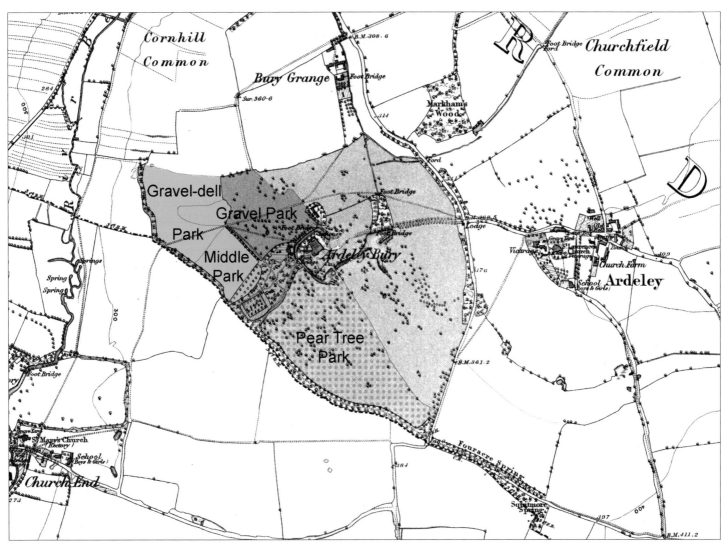

Map 2 The park at Ardeley Bury, Ardeley
OS 6 inches to the mile map sheet XIII, surveyed 1877–8, published 1884. The park field names are derived from
a parish map of 1744 (HALS DE/Z110/P1).

Ayot St Lawrence

No known name

NGR: TL196173
Date range: by 1268 – ?pre-sixteenth century
Size: not known; perhaps c.135 acres
Underlying geology: clay-with-flints

A PARK WAS FIRST RECORDED at Ayot St Lawrence in 1268, when William de Ayot sued Henry, son of Thomas de la Leye, for trespass in it.[1] William held the manor from the earls of Hereford. He was a steward of Henry III and, as lord of the manor, had been granted free warren in 1257 and was probably responsible for creating the park.[2] In 1363 the manor of Ayot St Lawrence was conveyed to Richard de Pembrugge who, in 1367, suffered a serious attack on his property. Seven named men, including a John West of Ayot St Laurence, and others,

> broke his close, houses and park, and entered his free warren, at Ayot Laurence, co. Hertford, hunted in the park and warren, cut down his trees and sold the same, drove away 3 horses, 22 swine, and 200 sheep of his, worth 40 pounds, carried away his goods, a chest, worth 10 shillings with charters, writings, and other muniments in it, and deer from the park, also hares, conies, partridges and pheasants from the warren, and assaulted his men and servants.[3]

The park may not have survived beyond the medieval period. Few relevant documents have been found, but a seventeenth-century copy of a deed dated 1543 at HALS did not mention a park.[4] The former manor house, which lies in the middle of the eighteenth-century park, is thought to date from Tudor times.

The medieval park was most likely to have been located where the landscape park was established around Ayot House in the late eighteenth century. The field to the west of Brimstow Wood was called Lodge Field on an estate map of 1759 and the fields lying west of Lodge Field were called Great and Little Warren (see Map 3).[5] The eastern edge of the estate formed a simple curve bounding three fields named after the Wood. This boundary does not survive today. An alternative eastern boundary for the medieval park, lying closer to the house, corresponds with the early nineteenth-century park boundary shown on Bryant's county map (1822) and is supported by surviving field evidence (see below). To the south the estate was bounded by the lane leading to the Kimpton

Road and to the north it largely followed the parish boundary with Codicote.

The land in this highest corner of the small parish of Ayot St Lawrence rises to 125m OD and the chalk on the plateau here is capped with a layer of infertile clay-with-flints. The topography (high ground with extensive views) and the presence of several lengths of substantial degraded bank support the theory that the medieval park was located here, but conclusive evidence is lacking. The most likely eastern boundary survives today as the east side of Brimstone Wood, where there is a deep ditch; the boundary continues south of the drive as a substantial bank, about 4m wide, down to the lane. This line marks the approximate edge of the plateau and beyond it the land falls away steadily to the river. Similar substantial banks lie along the north side of the lane east and west of the village centre and along the old parish boundaries where they cross the eighteenth-century park. It is possible that the medieval park utilised the parish boundary banks, as there is no bank along the northern boundary of the eighteenth-century park, which lies north of the parish boundary in the parish of Codicote. Along the south side of the park the boundary makes a marked detour northward to form an enclave around the village. There also appears to be a bank along the west side of the churchyard, separating the medieval church from the park. The proximity of the medieval church and park is unusual in Hertfordshire.

Without documentary evidence of the size of the medieval park it is impossible to be confident about its boundaries or its location, so the map here should be considered a 'best guess' based on map and field evidence. The area covered is 135 acres. A possible alternative location is along the south-east parish boundary east of Hill Farm. Here the 1847 tithe map shows an area of large 'planned' fields covering 157 acres and contained within a continuous boundary with lanes on the west and east sides.[6] The only supporting field-name evidence comes from the Ayot St Peter side of the parish boundary, where Lower, Middle and Upper Park Field were recorded on the tithe map for that parish.[7]

1. Page, *Hertford*, 3, p. 61 citing Abbrev. Plac. (Rec. Com.), 163.

2. Page, *Hertford*, 3, p. 61 citing *Cal. Chart. 1226–1257*, p. 474.

3. *Cal. Pat. 1364–1367*, p. 438 and *Cal. Pat. 1367–1370*, p. 354.

4. HALS 27433 copy of deed dated 1543.

5. HALS CV298 Ayot estate map, 1759.

6. HALS DSA4/9/2 Ayot St Lawrence tithe map, 1847.

7. HALS DSA4/10/1 and 2 Ayot St Peter tithe award and map, 1838.

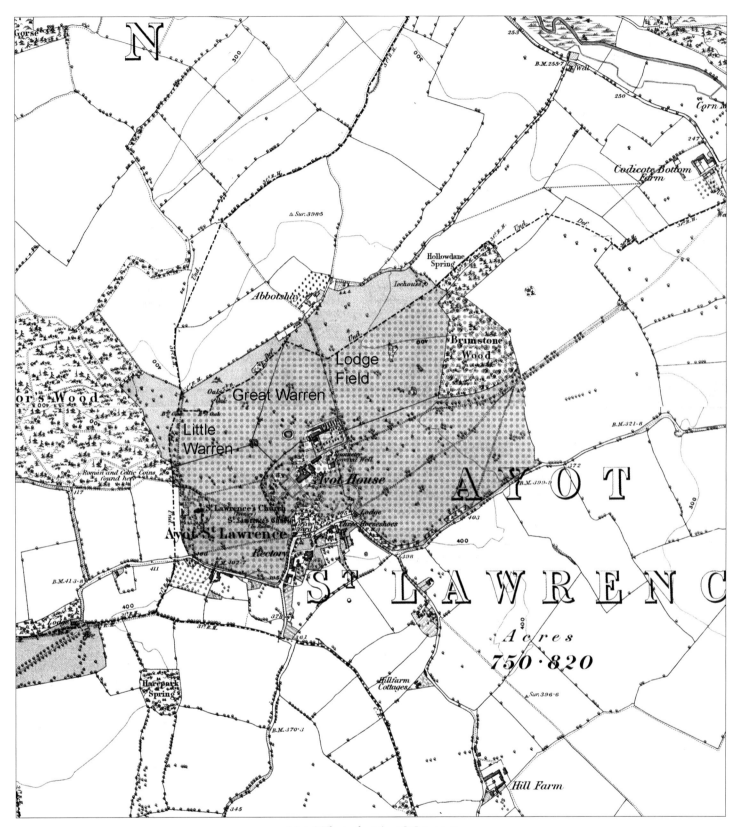

Map 3 The park at Ayot St Lawrence
OS 6 inches to the mile map sheets XX and XXVIII, surveyed 1878–81, published 1884. The field names are derived from an estate map of 1759 (HALS CV298).

Barkway

Scales Park (now in the civil parish of Nuthampstead)
NGR: TL419340
Date range: by 1299 – ?pre-sixteenth century
Size: perhaps c.287 acres
Underlying geology: boulder clay

SCALES PARK IS A WOOD lying in the south-east corner of the ecclesiastical parish of Barkway. The easternmost border of the parish (now the civil parish of Nuthampstead) forms part of the border between Hertfordshire and Essex. It lies on the boulder clay plateau about 135–140m OD with extensive views to the south, west and east and in the 1940s more than a third of the northern part of the wood was felled to create an airfield. Within the remaining woodland are many relics from the Second World War, including Nissen huts and their protective earthworks. Before the 1940s there was a small rectangle of wood adjoining the western side of Scales Park called Jack's Grove with a track along its northern side which entered Scales Park at a point marked 'Park Barrs' on an eighteenth-century estate map.[1] At the north-west corner of Jack's Grove was a moated site which has been identified by Robert Dimsdale as the site of the former Park House, the probable predecessor of the Park Farm which now lies about 500m to the north. Immediately to the north-east of Scales Park on the Essex side of the border was Clavering park, which existed from the twelfth century.

The wood takes its name from the de Scales family who held the manor of Newsells in Barkway from the thirteenth to the fifteenth century. Free warren was granted to Robert, first Lord Scales, in 1270 and in 1299 Lord Scales complained that Walter de Barley and certain others, mainly from Barley, 'broke his houses at Neuseles, co. Hertford, and entred his free warren there, hunted therein and carried away deer'.[2] The description of a 'free warren' rather than a park is a bit puzzling, especially as one *Cecil ate Park* was listed in the Barkway Subsidy Rolls of 1296, and a *Cecil le Parker* in 1307.[3] It is quite possible that the 'houses' and the warren recorded in the Patent Rolls were actually located at Newsells, the manorial centre and just over a mile from Barley, rather than at the outlying Scales Park, which is more than twice the distance from Barley. However, the combined evidence of the 'park' names for the wood and the adjacent house and the personal names recorded in the Lay Subsidies, together with the 'Park Barrs' recorded in 1741 and the topographical characteristics of Scales Park, make it very likely that this was a medieval park.

In 1548 Scales Park was alienated from the manor of Newsells and sold to Robert Chester, who already owned Nuthampstead and Cokenach, and it remained in his family until the mid eighteenth century. A map of 1727 recorded the area as 287 acres.[4] Another map, dated 1741, marked a track winding through the wood between 'Park Barrs' on the west side and 'Measden Gate' on the east side (Figure 14). 'Nuthamsted Gate' was at the north-west corner of the wood and 'Ansty Gate' led onto 'Ansty Common' towards the eastern end of the south side of the park. The area of Scales Park was given as 278a 1r 20p.[5]

Most of the east side of the park coincided with the county boundary, but the north-east corner was bounded by a small lane (Deadman's Lane) leading south-east from the east–west lane between Langley (Essex) and Nuthampstead, and the southern third abutted the boundary of the parish of Meesden in Hertfordshire. The southern boundary of the park also coincided with a parish boundary, with East Wood in the parish of Anstey lying along much of the boundary to the south in 1741, as it still does today. The plan shows a track leading west from the Anstey Gate within the park and a feature called 'The Old Moat' was annotated, perhaps indicating the site of a former hunting or parker's lodge (Figure 14). According to the first edition OS map, the parish boundary from the south-west corner of the wood followed the centre of a ditch running between the two woods with a track running along its north side. The ditch ended at the east end of East Wood and the boundary then crossed to the north side of the track until it reached the south-east corner of Scales Park.[6]

Between Scales Park and East Wood today is a broad grass track created by the Forestry Commission in about 1960.[7] On the north side of this modern track is a well-preserved and substantial earth bank 6–7m wide with a shallow ditch to the south (Figure 15), with the fragmentary remains of the older track leading to the former Anstey Gate running along its north side. The line of this ditch corresponds exactly with the line of the modern parish boundary, which means that the bank was effectively the boundary of the park and the parish.

East of the former Anstey Gate there is no detectable bank, nor is there one northwards from the south-east corner of the wood, where the park/wood boundary coincides with the parish boundary between Nuthampstead and Meesden. At the south-west corner of the wood the bank, with an external ditch, continues north-eastwards to start the western boundary of the park but comes to an abrupt stop after about 100m.

Another earthwork lies on the east side of the modern wood: a substantial broad bank with a ditch on its west side running south-westwards in a straight line for at least 250m from TL42343430. This bank lies 75–80m west of the parish and county boundary, and its straightness suggests that it is more likely to be modern than medieval, but it is nevertheless intriguing. OS map evidence suggests that the wood shrank westwards away from the parish boundary in the late eighteenth century.[8] However, this is not corroborated by either the Barkway Inclosure map of 1808 or an estate survey

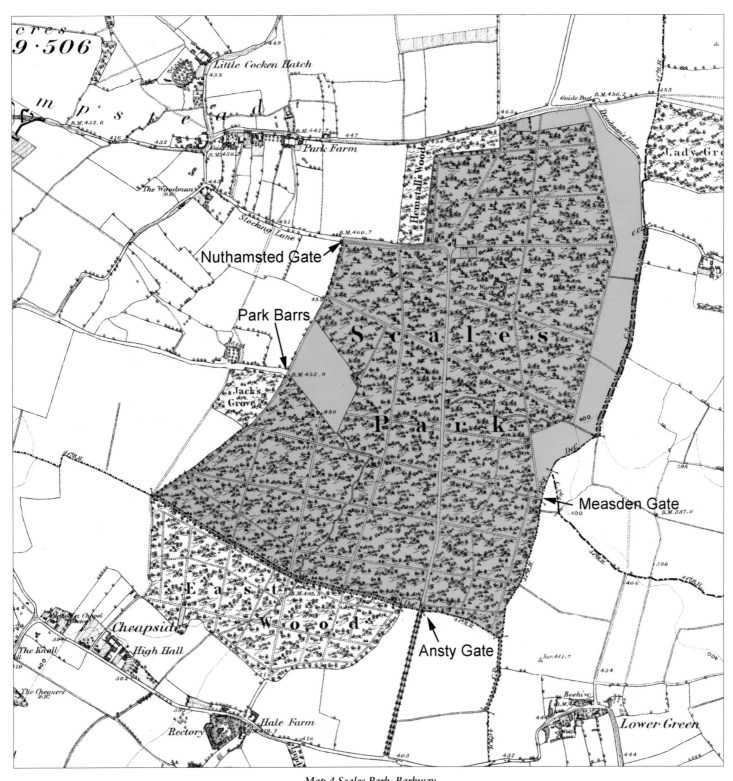

Map 4 Scales Park, Barkway
OS 6 inches to the mile map sheet IX, surveyed 1876–8, published 1880–3. The extent of the park and the names of the gates are taken
from a map of Scales Park of 1741 (HALS D1392).

Figure 14. *Detail of the map of Scales Park, 1741 (HALS D1392) showing wood pasture, the site of the old moat and the track leading to the Meesden Gate. Reproduced by kind permission of Hertfordshire Archives and Local Studies.*

map of 1835.[9] The latter map shows a ride in the wood which corresponds with the location of the bank and Robert Dimsdale considers that the bank is likely to be the remains of this ride, subsequently modified to improve the drainage of the fields lying outside the wood to the east.

The OS Drawing of 1799 is perplexing. The layout of much of the network of lanes appears remarkably accurate when compared with the first edition OS map (1876–8), but the county boundary does not seem to have been plotted accurately in relation to the south-east corner of Scales Park Wood. The outline of the wood suggests that much of the south and west part had been cleared for agriculture. Surviving traces of ridge and furrow noted by the owner within the wood today may support this map evidence, but no other maps show the wood reduced to this extent.[10]

In the middle of the northern half of the wood, about 40m west of the eastern earth bank, the first edition OS map shows a moated site annotated 'The Warren' (see Map 4). This is in a different location from 'The Old Moat' shown on the 1741 plan (which may have been located inaccurately). Before the site was bulldozed *c.*1943 to make the airfield, an archaeological excavation was carried out.[11] The archaeologists concluded that this feature was a small medieval homestead moat which was never completed. Pottery

fragments and an ivory pendant dated the construction of the earthworks to the second half of the thirteenth century, which corresponds with the time that the park is thought to have been created and suggests that this may have been the site of an early park lodge. The name 'The Warren' suggests that rabbits were kept on the island within the moat, or nearby, perhaps during the eighteenth or nineteenth centuries. Soilmarks still identify the site of the former moat.[12]

The wood has clearly undergone massive modification during the twentieth century (if not before), resulting from of the construction of the airfield as well as from modern woodland management practices. However, this remote corner of the county remains relatively undeveloped and undisturbed and what remains of Scales Park contains a wealth of evidence of its history and is also of great ecological interest.

1. HALS D1392 map of Scales Park, 1741.

2. *Cal. Chart. 1257–1300*, p. 146; *Cal. Pat. 1292–1301*, p. 462.

3. Munby, *Hertfordshire Landscape*, p. 131; Brooker and Flood, *Hertfordshire lay subsidy rolls*, p. 57.

4. HALS DE/L/P1 map of Scales Park, 1727.

5. HALS D1392 map of Scales Park, 1741.

6. OS map sheet IX.11, 25 inches to the mile, surveyed 1878.

7. Robert Dimsdale pers. comm.

Figure 15. Looking south-east along the southern boundary of Scales Park. The substantial bank formed the park pale and the ditch marks the boundary between the parish of Barkway to the north (left) and the parish of Anstey to the south.

8. BL Ordnance Survey Drawing 146 (PT1), 2, 2 inches to the mile, Anstey sheet, surveyed 1799, published 1805.

9. HALS DP/13/26/1 Barkway and Reed enclosure award with map annexed, 1808; HALS D1171B estate survey map, 1835.

10. Robert Dimsdale pers. comm

11. A. Williams, 'A homestead moat at Nuthampstead, Hertfordshire', *The Antiquaries Journal*, 26 (1946), pp. 138–44.

12. Robert Dimsdale pers. comm

Benington

Benington park
NGR: TL313236
Date range: by 1086 – late sixteenth century
Size: 400 acres
Underlying geology: mostly derived from boulder clay but there are significant patches of undifferentiated glaciofluvial deposits, Head material and Chalk in the lower parts of the park

BENINGTON IS ONE OF THE THREE Hertfordshire parks recorded in the Domesday Book and it probably survived as a deer park for about 500 years. Most of the boundary of the former park can still be seen on the modern OS map: it filled the north-eastern corner of the parish of Benington, butting up against the parish of Walkern (and its medieval park) to the north-east and the Mundens to the south-east. The park occupied a shallow valley in the boulder clay-covered plateau of east Hertfordshire, the land rising from 85m OD in the valley-bottom to 120m OD in the south-west and about 115m OD along the north-east side (Figure 16).

Before the Norman Conquest Benington was held by Aelmer of Benington, a great local thegn of King Edward, who also had estates in Sacombe, Layston, Ashwell, Hinxworth and Radwell.[1] Aelmer was, therefore, one of the chief English landowners in Hertfordshire in the mid eleventh century and his main residence (as his name suggests) was probably at Benington and probably adjacent to the church. After the battle of Hastings Aelmer's estates were given by King William

to his nephew, a powerful Norman lord called Peter de Valognes. By 1086 de Valognes held over 40 hides of land in Hertfordshire, about half of which were in or near Benington and Sacombe. He was sheriff of Hertfordshire and Essex and his estates extended over six counties in the east of England, but he made Benington the *caput* of his barony and is thought to have been responsible for the substantial defensive earthworks which still survive around the manorial site at Benington (the Lordship and the church).[2] The park, which lay about a mile (1.5km) away to the east, may have been part of the new Norman lordly establishment created by de Valognes between 1066 and 1086, but it might also have originated before the Norman Conquest, under Aelmer of Benington.[3]

There are no known records of the park during the two centuries after the Domesday survey but two park breaks were recorded at the end of the thirteenth century, when Benington was held by Alexander de Balliol.[4] In 1298, while de Balliol was serving the king overseas, Benington park was broken into and the deer hunted and carried away; the same offence was committed in 1300.[5] In 1303 the manor was conveyed to John de Benstede[6] and a major park break was recorded in 1316 when de Benstede was overseas on the king's service.[7] The commission of oyer and terminer issued on 12 August 1316 named 90 men, 'plus others', who were accused of hunting and carrying away deer from the park. Many of the men, such as John le Parker of Walkern and his son, may have been from the local area, but many others came from much further afield,

Figure 16. View across the former Benington park from the eastern boundary looking west. The arrow indicates the likely location of the medieval lodge on a spur of high ground which projects northwards into the valley.

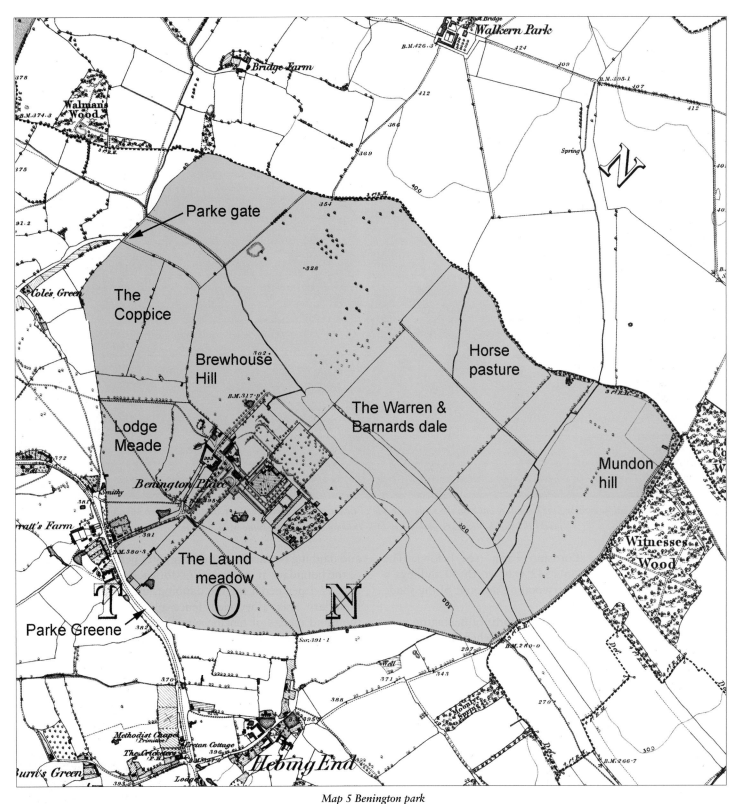

Map 5 Benington park
OS 6 inches to the mile map sheets XIII and XXI, surveyed 1877–8 and 1878–80 respectively, published 1884. Annotated with names as they appear on the estate map of 1628 by Henry Liley (private collection).

ranging from Buntingford and St Albans in Hertfordshire to Suffolk and south Cambridgeshire. The incident may have been related to the great famine which had started two years previously, with harvests ruined by heavy rain and epidemics among livestock, but the number of men involved and the wide area from which they were drawn suggests that the motive may have been personal, aimed specifically at the property of John de Benstede, rather than economic.[8]

The Benstede family continued to hold the manor for most of the fourteenth century and an inquisition taken in 1342 on the death of Petronilla, widow of John de Benstede, recorded two parks at Benington. The inquisition held on the death of her grandson John de Benstede, in January 1359, recorded that among his holdings was a park called 'the great park' and a wood called 'Haylewod'.[9] The second park was known as Hayley Park and lay to the west of Benington Lordship on

Figure 17. Looking south-west along the boundary bank on the south-east side of Benington park with the park to the right of the photograph. The bank also marks the parish boundary, with a row of hornbeam stubs on the Little Munden side.

land now occupied by Lordship Farm (see below). The herbage of the two parks in 1342 was worth 40 shillings a year, 'but there [was] no underwood on account of the shade of the trees'.[10]

There appear to be no surviving records of Benington park for the next 100 years but in 1449/50, when another John Benstede was holding the manor, four deer were taken from the park to restock John Fray's park in the neighbouring parish of Great Munden (see p. 102).[11]

From 1486 the manor of Benington was in the hands of Sir William Say and some accounts compiled for him at the end of the fifteenth century provide a few details of the management of the park in the late medieval period.[12] By 1490 the manor and its rabbit warren were leased for £14 19s 4d and this continued to be the case until at least 1508. The accounts recorded a park keeper, John Feld, who was paid 2d a day (60s 10d p.a.). Agistment in the park was worth an impressive £7 19s 7d in 1495/6 and 54s 2d in 1498/9. There was no pannage of pigs in the park in 1495/6, but in 1498/9 it was worth 11s 3d. The warren was valued at 66s 8d per annum but was leased with the manor. No management of wood or timber was recorded in the park in 1495/6 and nor was there any wind-blown timber to sell.

By 1498/9, however, Sir William Say had evidently decided to make a major investment in the park, spending £4 16s 6d on 'new making' the lodge 'with a roof' (*tectura*) and 29s 3½d on repairing the southern park boundary. This entailed fencing

and daubing (*sepacoe' & dobbyng*) 805 perches (over 4,000m) of the boundary at a cost of 2½d for each 'newly-made' perch, and 1½d per perch for the daubing, indicating that the park boundary was a wooden fence plastered with clay. Four thousand metres of fencing would have enclosed 80 per cent of the park and must have left only the northern boundary (the boundary with the parish of Walkern) unrepaired. Wood was felled in 'le Spayne' and sold for fuel for 17s 9d – a poor return for the 76s 1d it cost to fell and chop the wood. Other trees were sold for 13s 4d, including some ash.[13]

The last account in the series dates from 1508 and recorded agistment in the park worth 51 shillings, but there was no pannage of pigs. Sales of wood amounted to £11 8s. The 'custodian of the park' was still being paid 60s 10d.[14]

On the death of Sir William Say in 1529 the manor of Benington passed to Henry Bourchier, Earl of Essex, the husband of Sir William's daughter, Mary. In 1539 the manor passed to their daughter, Anne Bourchier, and her husband Sir William Parr, from whom she was divorced in 1543.[15] In 1556 the manor was in the hands of the crown and was surveyed for King Philip and Queen Mary.[16] Henry Croxton, appointed by Henry, Earl of Essex, was the custodian of the park, receiving 60s 10d a year plus 'le browse and wyndfalles' and the right to pasture eight cows and two horses in the park. He earned a further 10 shillings for mowing 'les brakes' in the park. Richard Wright received a fee of 40 shillings a year as 'custodian of the capital mansion or place in the park', which

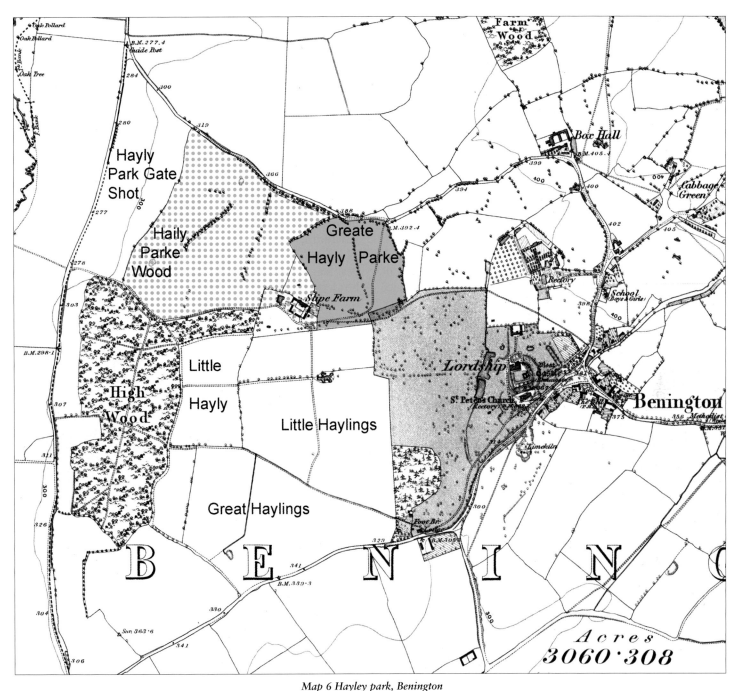

Map 6 Hayley park, Benington

OS 6 inches to the mile map sheets XIII and XXI, surveyed 1877–8 and 1878–80 respectively, published 1884. Annotated with names taken from the estate map of 1628 by Henry Liley (private collection).

was described as being 'in great decaye'. Of the 382 acres of the park (measured at 18 feet to the pole), 60 acres was wood ground 'usually lopped by the keepers of the parke and house for fewell', 200 acres was 'overgrowen with brakes and bushes parkelike' valued at 12d per acre, while the remaining 122 acres was 'laundes and fedinges' valued at 2 shillings per acre, giving a total value for the park of £22. There were 33 deer 'of all sortes' and 160 oaks in the park which were reserved for the park pale and for 'the howsing' in the park. Anne Bourchier appears to have regained her right to the manor and when she died in 1571 she was buried at Benington.[17] The manor was then granted to Walter Devereux, Anne's cousin and nearest heir, who became Earl of Essex in 1572.[18]

Benington was one of the most valuable of the earl's English estates and when he died, in 1576, the manor and park

were left to his widow for her life and then to his ten year old son, Robert Devereux.[19] After two years of widowhood, Lady Essex (née Lettice Knollys) married Robert Dudley, Earl of Leicester, and the couple used Benington as one of their country houses.[20]

In 1580, while Robert Devereux was at Trinity College Cambridge, a letter was sent by two of his guardians to Henry Capel of Hadham Hall, the owner of neighbouring Walkern park, which stated that Benington park had been disparked.[21] Traditionally the joint boundary between the two parks had been maintained by the owner of Benington park and, in return for this service, the owner of Walkern park gave a buck and a doe each year.[22] Once the deer had been removed from Benington park, there was no incentive for the park pale to be maintained on the Benington side and this led to a long-running dispute between the owners of the two parks.[23]

In 1613/4 the third earl of Essex sold the Benington estate to Sir Julius Caesar when it was described as 'a hunting seat and large park of deer'.[24] Whether this was seller's hyperbole or an accurate description of a re-stocked park is not clear. In any event, it appears that the new owners did not want a deer park because in 1616 Caesar's son, Sir Charles Caesar, granted the ownership of the pale between the two parks to Sir Arthur Capel, the then owner of Walkern park, so that Capel could in future maintain it himself.

Twelve years later, in 1628, Sir Charles Caesar commissioned Henry Liley to draw a plan of his lands in the parish of Benington.[25] The park appears at the north-east corner of the parish and the total acreage of its constituent fields and enclosures comes to 380 acres. It was depicted with a fence extending westwards along the northern boundary of Benington park as far as the end of Walkern park. No fence was shown around the remainder of the former park boundary, which clearly stands out as a continuous, sinuous line. Hedgerow trees are indicated along some stretches of the boundary. The park contained no woods in the early seventeenth century although a field on the west side was named The Coppice and did contain scattered trees (see Map 5). Trees were more densely and evenly depicted in two fields named Brewhouse Hill (adjacent to The Coppice) and Mundon hill (far north east of the park) and both were probably surviving areas of medieval wood-pasture. Meadows, named The Laund meadow and Lodge Meade, occupied about 49 acres on the plateau at the south-west side of the park. A fenced enclosure was shown in the centre of the park which incorporated The Warren (35 acres) and fields called Horse pasture and Calves pasture (a further 32 acres).

Very few of the internal park boundaries which were present in 1628 (and possibly originated in medieval times) have survived to the twenty-first century, although several are followed by public footpaths. One which has survived is the eastern boundary of The Coppice, which can be followed as a public footpath along a hedgerow containing old coppice stools and with a marked change in the level of the ground to the east (high) and west (low) of the hedge. 'Parke Greene' survives as a broad verge alongside the Benington road outside the park boundary to the south-west and 'Parke gate' can still be identified (minus the gate) at the western side of the park at the end of an ancient lane from Benington village via the hamlet of Cole's Green. This lane was the most direct route from the medieval manorial centre (beside the church) to the park and may even pre-date the park itself.

The 1628 map shows a substantial house built in the late Tudor or Jacobean style and a large, square, walled garden to the south. A building at the north end of the north-east wall of the garden appears to be two or three storeys high – perhaps a hunting stand or the seventeenth-century park-keeper's lodge. Magnificent earthwork terraces 100m long around three sides of a square survive today on the site of the Jacobean garden and were probably the work of Sir Charles Caesar.[26]

The documentary evidence suggests that it was Sir William Say who first established a lordly residence within the park, probably upgrading a pre-existing lodge. This building was said to be 'in great decaye' by 1556 and must have been substantially renovated, or even rebuilt, by the earl of Essex in

the 1570s. This was, in turn, replaced by a new house built by the Caesars from 1614,[27] which stood in an elevated position on the edge of a spur of high ground projecting into, and providing extensive views of, the park (Figure 16).

The surviving earthwork boundaries around Benington park are very variable, ranging from a broad raised bank with external ditch to nothing more than a ditch. Only one short length of boundary (just south-west of Witnesses Wood) conforms to the 'standard' medieval park boundary of an earthen bank with an internal ditch. Much of the boundary is marked by a hedgerow of variable quality. In many places this is clearly old, containing outgrown coppice stools of ash, hornbeam, beech and oak. Other shrubby species include hawthorn, blackthorn, holly, yew, honeysuckle and spindle. There are also a few old pollards of oak and hornbeam. The best lengths of bank are at the west side adjacent to the verge bordering the Benington Road (c.1m high x 2m wide); along the section running north-east from Park Gate to the stream (c.0.5m high x c.4m wide); between Benington and Walkern parks just east of Park Covert, where the bank is about 5m wide with a hedge on each side of the ditch on the Walkern side; and along the south-east side of the park, where there is a broad bank (c.1m high x c.2.2m wide) ditched on both sides with old coppice stools and bluebells growing on the bank. Both of the last two lengths of bank also define parish boundaries: between Benington and Walkern to the north and between Benington and Little Munden (formerly Great Munden) to the south-east (Figure 17).

The substantial earth bank which marks the south-east section of the park boundary is followed by a public footpath, as is about 600m of the southern boundary which was ploughed out during the twentieth century – the only part of the medieval park boundary to be destroyed. Several ponds survive around the margins of the former park and would, in addition to the stream in the bottom of the valley, have provided sources of water for the animals in the park. The park illustrated on Map 5 covers 400 acres and is enclosed by a boundary 5,000m long.

Hayley park

NGR: TL287239
Date range: by 1342 – pre-1359
Size: not known; perhaps c.66 acres
Underlying geology: a mixture of glaciofluvial deposits and boulder clay

THE ONLY DOCUMENTARY EVIDENCE for a second park in Benington is found in the inquisition *post mortem* of Petronilla de Benstede in 1342. This stated that the herbage of her two parks at Benington was 'worth per annum 40 shillings, but there is no underwood on account of the shade of the trees'.[28] The second park is perhaps most likely to have been established by Petronilla's husband, John de Benstede, a man involved with state and county affairs, who held the manor from 1303 until he died in 1323. It seems to have been disparked before 1359 because the inquisition held on the death of John de Benstede, grandson of John and Petronilla, in January 1359, recorded only the 'great park' and a wood called 'Haylewod'.[29] No other references to this second park are known from the medieval period but a survey of the manor taken in 1556 recorded areas of the demesne lands which were 'parcel of Haylye (or Haylie) Parke'.[30] Henry Liley's parish map of 1628 shows a cluster of 'Hayly' field names west of the church and Lordship of Benington which includes Great Hayly Parke, Haily Parke Wood and Hayly Park Gate Shot (see Map 6).[31] These field names, which had fallen out of use by the time of the 1838 tithe map and award, suggest that the park occupied about 66 acres of the summit of a plateau at 120m OD with extensive views for many miles to the south towards Bramfield Woods.

At the western end of the former park today is a wood called Haily Park Wood. In the early seventeenth century this wood covered 13 acres and the common field lying along its west side was called 'Hayly Park Gate Shot'. The remainder of the former park was divided into fields by 1628, the largest of which (16 acres) was known as Great Hayly Parke. Immediately to the south of Hayly Park the 1628 map showed fields called Little Hayly, Little Haylings and Great Haylings which covered an area of approximately 120 acres and had the same landowner/occupier as the park. These fields were probably part of the 133-acre 'Haylie Filde' recorded on the demesne in 1556 and it is possible that this whole area was, for a time, parkland and then woodland (the 'Haylewod' of 1359), before being cleared for ploughing. However, it is more likely that the park was confined to the higher ground and this is what is shown on Map 6.

A deep hollow-way forms the southern boundary of Haili Park Wood and was perhaps the reason for the park gate recorded in the adjacent seventeenth-century field name. There is also a marked 1.8m-high lynchet along the west side of Haili Park Wood and banks and a ditch (c.7m wide) continue south-eastwards at TL2859723793 for about 40m, then turn 90 degrees to the north-east before petering out.

High Wood, to the south, is abandoned hornbeam coppice with a carpet of bluebells. Haili Park Wood had evidently been felled by 1877 and is now a plantation with no bluebells. A bank, which could have been the southern park boundary, extends along the north side of Hubberts Grove (an extension of the north-east corner of High Wood). The ground flora includes ancient woodland indicator species such as bluebells and yellow archangel (*Lamiastrum galeobdolon*). A group of old oak pollards stands in the field which was once known as Great Hayly Parke.

1. Morris, *Domesday Book: Hertfordshire*, 36,7. See also 4,16; 5,13; 20,4–5, 8; 34,7; 36,1–3, 5, 7, 8, 10–12, 14–18; 37,10; 38,2.

2. Page, *Hertford*, 3, p. 74; Page, *Hertford*, 1, pp. 282–3.

3. For a discussion of the evidence for English deer parks before 1066 see Liddiard, 'Deer parks', pp. 4–23.

4. Page, *Hertford*, 3, p. 74.

5. *Cal. Pat. 1292–1301*, pp. 380 and 553. I am grateful to Twigs Way for these references.

6. Page, *Hertford*, 3, p. 74, citing *Cal. Pat. 1301–1307*, p. 165 (licence for alienation); Charter Roll 32 Edw. I, m. 6 (TNA: PRO C53/90 m.6) (confirmation of grant).

7. *Cal. Pat. 1313–1317*, pp. 588, 592–3.

8. Heather Falvey, pers. comm.

9. Cussans, *History of Hertfordshire*, 2, Broadwater Hundred, p. 126.

10. *Ibid.*

11. TNA: PRO SC6/867/13 bailiff's account for Great Munden, 1449/50.

12. Page, *Hertford*, 3, p. 75; HHA court rolls 10/19, 10/21, 10/23 and 11/5 bailiff's accounts, 1490/1, 1495/6, 1498/9 and 1508.

13. HHA court rolls 10/23 bailiff's account, 1498/9.

14. HHA court rolls 11/5 bailiff's account, 1508.

15. Page, *Hertford*, 3, p. 75.

16. TNA: PRO E315/391 survey of Hertfordshire manors, lands and possessions of King Philip and Queen Mary, 1556.

17. David Perman, pers. comm. (HALS DP/18/1/1 register of baptisms, marriages and deaths, Benington, 1538–1722).

18. Page, *Hertford*, 3, p. 75.

19. *Ibid.*, p. 484.

20. S. Adams (ed.), *Household accounts and disbursement books of Robert Dudley, Earl of Leicester, 1558-1561, 1584-1586* (Cambridge, 1995), p. 26.

21. HALS 9518 letter from T. Sussex and W. Mildmay to Henry Capel Esq, 1580, requesting the giving of a buck and a doe out of Walkern Park to the young earl.

22. The 1556 survey of the manor for the crown recorded that a buck and doe were owed to the king and queen from the park of Walkern each year 'as a rent due' (TNA: PRO E315/391).

23. See surviving correspondence HALS 9518, 9552, 9553, 9555, 9556, 9523, 9524, 9526 and 9601.

24. E. Lodge, *Life of Sir Julius Caesar Knt ... with memoirs of his family & descendants* (London, 1810), p. 32. Sir Julius Caesar (1558–1636) was the most prominent civil lawyer of his generation, Chancellor of the Exchequer (1606) and Master of the Rolls from 1614 (J. Gardiner (ed.), *Who's Who in British History* (London, 2000)).

25. Plan of the 'manor and parish of Benyngton ... part of the possessions of the right worshipfull Sir Charles Caeser Knight', drawn by Henry Liley, 1628 (private ownership); photograph at HALS.

26. For detailed descriptions of the seventeenth- and eighteenth-century gardens at Benington Park based on the 1628 and 1743 maps and other sources, see A. Rowe, *Garden making and the Freman family: a memoir of Hamels 1712–1733* (Hertford, 2001), pp. 49–61.

27. L.M. Hill, 'Caesar, Sir Charles (1590–1642)', *Oxford dictionary of national biography* (Oxford, 2004), accessed online 5 Nov 2007.

28. Cussans, *History of Hertfordshire*, 2, Broadwater Hundred, p. 126.

29. *Ibid.*

30. TNA: PRO E315/391 survey of Hertfordshire manors, lands and possessions of King Philip and Queen Mary, 1556.

31. Plan of the 'manor and parish of Benyngton ... part of the possessions of the right worshipfull Sir Charles Caeser Knight', drawn by Henry Liley, 1628 (private ownership); photograph at HALS.

Berkhamsted

Ashridge park *see Little Gaddesden*

Berkhamsted park
NGR: SP989095
Date range: *c.*1280 – 1627
Size: original size not known; probably expanded to 991 acres before fifteenth century
Underlying geology: clay-with-flints, Upper and Middle Chalk

THIS MUST HAVE BEEN ONE of the county's most beautiful and spectacular medieval parks, set on the rolling Chiltern hills to the north of Berkhamsted with extensive views over the Bulbourne valley to the south. A castle was built at Berkhamsted soon after the Conquest but there is no evidence for a park until two centuries later. Richard, first Earl of Cornwall, King of Germany and brother of Henry III, held Berkhamsted from about 1230 and his first wife, Isabella, died there in 1240. His second wife, Sanchia, was sister to the queen, Eleanor of Provence, and gave birth to their second and only surviving son, Edmund, at Berkhamsted in 1249.[1] Edmund inherited Berkhamsted, as part of his father's vast estates, in 1272. As earl of Cornwall, he was the richest lay baron in England and Berkhamsted castle was the administrative centre of the earldom.[2] Edmund appears to have established a park at Berkhamsted by about 1280.

A substantial series of ministers' and receivers' accounts for the honour and castle of Berkhamsted is preserved in The National Archives at Kew. One undated account for Berkhamsted and Ashridge (*Esserugg*) was probably compiled about 1280 because the Ashridge account details the building of the earl's residence, complete with chapel, where he subsequently established a religious foundation which was completed by 1285 (see Little Gaddesden).[3] The Berkhamsted section of the account included an entry for 'the costs of the park' (*custus parci*). These totalled 33s 11d and included 28s 9d for enclosing 11½ furlongs of the park boundary (*haye*) using old fence. In places the boundary was replaced with a barrier of pointed stakes (*barband*) cut down for 2 shillings. A park gate facing Ashridge was made for 16d. A furlong was 220 yards long, which means that over 2,300m of the park boundary was enclosed – perhaps representing the creation of the park, making use of old hedged boundaries where they already existed.

The account for 1296/7 recorded that William de Hockfield, keeper of the park, was paid 60s 8d a year, at 2d per day, and 10 shillings for a robe. A payment of 67s 3d was received for pannage in the park and 5s 6d for rights of pasture in the park.[4] The accounts also made incidental mention of the park in relation to the maintenance of hedges, one of which extended 'from Cokesgrave as far as the park

beside the wood of the Fryth'.[5] A bailiff's account of 1300/01 recorded the costs of creating 604 perches of new boundary (*haie*) around the park using wood cut down and gathered from the park. This cost ³/₄d per perch 'plus the old hedge/fence', giving a total expenditure of 37s 9d.[6] If converted at 16½ feet per perch, the new boundary was over 3,000m in length – even more than that recorded in the earlier account.

The inquisition held on the death of Edmund, Earl of Cornwall, in 1300 recorded 'a certain park with deer, the pasture with pannage for the support of the deer worth yearly 10s'.[7] Before he died Edmund must have appointed 'William called Hereford of Berchamstede' as parker because in 1302 his appointment was confirmed by Edmund's successor at Berkhamsted, namely his cousin Edward I. William Hereford was given 'custody of the wood of Berchampstede and the park and warren and of 5½d a day, a robe, price 10s a year, and all the wood (*busca*) blown down in that wood and park, and the trunks of the trees thrown down there'.[8]

Numerous park breaks were recorded in the early fourteenth century, when the park was held by Queen Margaret, second wife of Edward I. In 1307, and twice in 1314, Berkhamsted was just one among many of the queen's parks which had been broken into.[9] In August 1316 only Berkhamsted was mentioned in a commission of oyer and terminer

> touching the persons who entered and hunted in her parks, free chases and free warrens at Berkhampstede, co. Hertford, entered her closes and broke her houses, walls and hedges there, felled her trees growing in her woods and gardens, fished in her stews and free fisheries and carried away fish, deer, etc.[10]

However, the same wording was used in previous entries in the Calendar of Patent Rolls relating to the queen's parks and so these details may not relate specifically to Berkhamsted. Margaret died in 1317 and the honour, including the castle and manor, were granted by Edward II to his queen, Isabella.[11] In 1323 the park was again broken into, the deer hunted and carried away.[12] In 1329 Edward III granted the castle and honour to his brother, John de Eltham, and in 1334 Robert le Parker was granted the 'bailiwick of parker of the park of Berkhamstede and the foreign woods there … with 2d daily for wages and 13s 4d yearly for his robe, and trees and wood (*busca*) blown down by the wind in the park and woods'.[13] In 1334 the king's brother complained that several men 'broke his park and entered his free warren … hunted there, fished in his free fishery and carried away deer from the park and hares and partridges from the warren'.[14] On the death of John de Eltham in 1336, the king created his young son Edward (1330–1376) Duke of Cornwall and granted him the honour

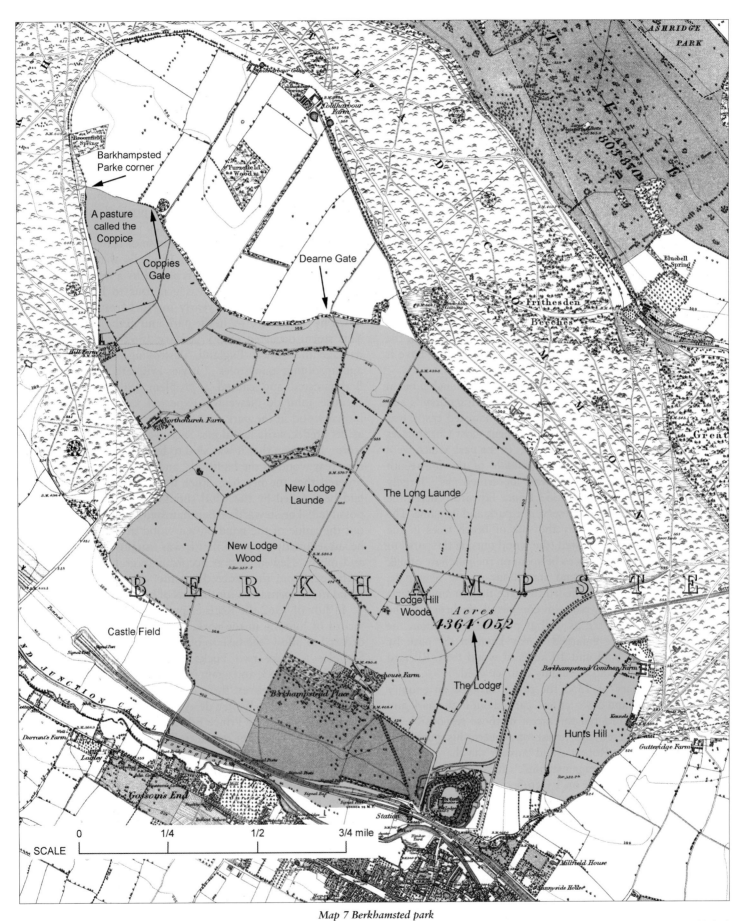

Map 7 Berkhamsted park

OS 6 inches to the mile map sheets XXV, surveyed 1877–9, published 1884; XXVI, surveyed 1877–8, published 1883–4; XXXII, surveyed 1874–7, published 1883–4; and XXXIII, surveyed 1873–8, published 1883 (all reproduced at a reduced scale). Annotated with features as they appear on Norden's plan of the honour of Berkhamsted, c.1612 (TNA: PRO MR1/603), and on a map of Berkhamsted Park c.1638 (HALS 1985). The boundary of the park is that shown as 'the bounds of Old Park' on the Berkhamsted tithe map, 1839 (HALS DSA4/19/2).

of Berkhamsted.[15] A major programme of repairs was undertaken and the castle became 'one of the chief residences of the king and royal family'.[16]

It was perhaps during this period that one of the demesne fields, covering 180 acres, was taken into the park.[17] This significant expansion in the area of parkland is confirmed in the account for 1377/8, which recorded that 180 acres and 3 rods of land in 'Castelfeld' had been enclosed into the lord's park at some (unspecified) time in the past.[18] Seventeenth-century maps indicate that Castle Field probably lay on the west side of the castle and this expansion may have brought the park up to the precincts of the castle for the first time; the earlier park presumably lay a short distance away on the hill to the north-west.[19]

At the age of 16 Edward was fighting with his father in the Crécy campaign in France, returning to England in November 1347.[20] On 1 August 1347 Robert the parker was ordered to take a 'buck of grease' in the park and deliver it to the abbot of St Albans and at the end of the month he and the constable of the castle were ordered to take 'this season's grease' in the park, 'as shall seem best for the prince's profit', and have it 'well prepared'.[21]

Between 1348 and 1354 Prince Edward spent much time on his extensive estates and indulged in the chivalric pursuits and lavish lifestyle of a young nobleman. Berkhamsted castle was one of his principal residences and he spent most Christmases there.[22] He made further improvements to the park which were recorded in his 'Register'. By the middle of the fourteenth century Berkhamsted park was described as 'largely unenclosed', but in February 1353 Prince Edward ordered the construction of a paling to preserve the park and its game. The project was to be funded by the sale of beech trees in the 'foreign wood' of Berkhamsted (the wood outside the park) to the value of £20, which was to be spent on the purchase of oak timber to make the rails and stanchions of the new pale; suitable beeches were to be felled to make the remaining parts of the pale. Until the new pale was completed, the hedges of the park were to be 'repaired as well as possible'.[23] At about the same time, the prince enlarged a new lawn in the park by taking 54 acres of land and 10 acres of wood from Richard Raven and his wife, who were duly compensated.[24]

Also in February of 1353 the prince ordered an enquiry relating to 'wastes and destructions' carried out in the park and foreign wood and ordered the arrest of those responsible. A week later he ordered the arrest of Robert, his parker at Berkhamsted, so that Robert could 'answer the charges which the prince has to bring against him'.[25] It would appear that Robert lost his job because on 1 October 1353 Richard Raven, now described as the prince's yeoman, was appointed keeper of the park 'and the prince's game there', with wages of 2d a day.[26]

In September 1354 the receiver of Berkhamsted was ordered to buy hay to the value of 26s 8d for the sustenance of the deer in the park during the coming winter.[27] Beech timber from the park was delivered to the baker of the prince's household for making three 'gates' for his office; any left-over timber was to be burnt in the baker's ovens.[28] An unusual product of the park was revealed in a grant of 1353 to Robert de Kynebelle, the lessee of the prince's demesne lands at Berkhamsted. He was permitted to collect the fallen leaves and 'other litter of dung in the ditches and elsewhere within the

park' for manuring and improving the demesne lands, provided he did not carry them from the park in the fawning and rutting seasons.[29]

From the autumn of 1354 Prince Edward was at Berkhamsted, 'keeping in touch with his father's court' before leaving to fight in France in September 1355. He returned to England in 1357 at the height of his prestige after a successful military campaign.[30] In January 1358 the prince's council advised that the rabbit warren and 'delles' of the park should be cut and enclosed with a hedge, the work to be supervised by Richard Raven.[31] Two months later the prince ordered the sale of 60 beech trees in the park, the proceeds of which were to be spent on repairing the park pale.[32]

The next (and last) concerted phase of activity in the park recorded in the Register was in 1362. By that time Richard Raven had died and had been replaced by a new parker, John de Newenton. The prince was generous to Raven's widow, granting her five beeches yearly for fuel from wood 'blown down by the last storm' in the park and in the foreign wood.[33] This storm occurred on 15 January 1362 and 'did immense damage' in southern England, 'destroying many tall buildings and uprooting many trees'.[34] It was evidently a major event at Berkhamsted and caused a problem with the new parker because John de Newenton expected to take all the wind-blown wood in the park and foreign wood as part of his fee, as his predecessors had done. Such was the destruction of the storm, however, that it was said to have blown down 'most of the great wood in the bailiwick' and in April 1362 the prince ordered that the beeches, other trees and underwood which had been felled by the wind should be sold as profitably as possible.[35] The steward of Berkhamsted was instructed to find out the value of the wind-blown wood in a normal year and he subsequently reported that it was usually worth 'ten marks and more'. Newenton was accordingly granted 100 shillings each year from the proceeds of the sale of the storm-felled wood in compensation for the loss of his traditional earnings.[36]

In July of 1362 the Register provides the only documented record of hunting in the park, when John de Newenton was ordered to allow 'the bishop of Wircestre and Master John de Stretelee to take two bucks of grease in the park'.[37] In December of 1363, and again in late October 1364, the parker was ordered to deliver 'three does of this season of *fermeson* in the park' to Sir Walter de Aldebury, on the neighbouring manor.[38] By this time Prince Edward had departed for France once again and did not return to England until 1370. In 1372 Edward granted to Thomas de Troghford, for life, the keepership of Berkhamsted park and the venison there with a daily wage of 2d.[39]

On the death of Prince Edward in 1376, Berkhamsted passed to his son, Richard, who became Richard II in 1377. In 1380 Roger Bigge became parker in the place of Thomas Troghford, who had died.[40] In 1381 a 'writ of aid' was issued for Walter Podebat and William Ernald to 'cut a hundred beeches within the king's park of Berkhamsted and the wood outside, by survey of Nicholas Adam'.[41] In 1387 Nicholas Adam was one of the commissioners appointed to enquire who had broken into the king's park and hunted without licence.[42] Richard expanded the park by another 60 acres, taking in land and three small crofts (known as 'Huntsland') belonging to John Hunt at 'le Wodgrene'. This was then leased to the parker, Roger Bigge, described as 'hunter' (*venator*).[43]

There are several accounts surviving from the last quarter of the fourteenth century and first quarter of the fifteenth century which provide interesting details of the park at that time.[44] A regular, and significant, cost of the park was the maintenance of the boundary. In the late 1380s this responsibility was shared by two men: John Chaundeler maintained the boundary from Dernegate to the castle pond (*stagnum*) for 40 shillings p.a. and the boundary between Dernegate and the 'Northcorner' for another 20 shillings p.a., while Henry Phyppes maintained the section from the gate of 'la logge' (the lodge) to 'Le Parkcorner' for 26s 8d p.a. A decade later William Nayll was paid 66s 8d p.a. for maintaining the park boundary, a sum that was shared with another man in subsequent years; but, in 1423/4, the amount paid to the two men employed had been reduced to 64s. Additional lengths of 'old fence' (*haie*) between the gate of 'la logge' and the castle pond were also repaired each year using thorns (*spinis*) cut in the park. For example, in 1388/9 60 perches of old fence were repaired and improved which, including the cost of cutting and carting the thorns, cost 10 shillings. The following year the repair of 30 perches of old fence cost 5s 6d but by 1423/4 10 shillings paid for the repair of just 36 perches of the same stretch of old fence.

Other costs were regularly incurred in caring for the principal inhabitants of the park – the deer. Four carts of hay were bought for the sustenance of the deer in both 1388/9 and 1389/90 which, including carriage, cost 23s 4d and 26s 8d respectively. In 1398/9 just 3 shillings was spent on hay 'above the hay allowed for in the preceding account' but in the following year five cartloads were bought 'for the sustenance of the deer in winter' from 'Lolleseymede' for 29s 10d and in 1400/1 two cartloads were brought from Lolleseymede for 13s 4d. In 1408/9 a meadow called Hogesmore was set aside to produce hay for the lord's deer. Roger Chaundeler was paid for mowing (18d) and lifting (8d) the hay and 12d was spent on carting two loads of hay from the meadow to the park. Lolleseymede was also the source of the two cartloads of hay bought in 1423/4 for 10 shillings, plus 3s 4d for carriage.

At the end of the fourteenth century the accounts reveal that the winter diet of the deer was supplemented with a nutritious fodder crop – pea straw. Two cartloads were purchased for 6s 8d in both 1388/9 and 1389/90. In 1399/1400 one cartload was purchased for 2s 9d and a further two cartloads were bought for 5s 6d, while in 1400/1 just one cartload was bought for 2s 9d. Pea straw does not occur in any of the surviving accounts from the fifteenth century, but another kind of fodder was alluded to in the account of 1408/9 when the scribe mentioned 'wood felled for sustenance of deer there in winter', indicating that trees were being pollarded to produce 'leafy hay' for the deer.

Producing revenue from the park was clearly not a priority in the late fourteenth century and the sums received for agistment of animals each year were relatively modest, ranging from 20d to 6s 8d. In 1408/9 Henry, Prince of Wales, ordered that there should be no agistment in the park in order to ensure the well-being of his deer, but the following year 21 shillings was received for agistment, over and above the 2s 4d paid in tithes. In 1423/4 11s 4d was received for agistment.[45]

The revenue received for the pannage of pigs both in the park and in the 'foreign' woods outside the park (Le Frith) was combined in a single entry in the accounts. In years when there was a plentiful supply of beech mast and acorns, pannage could make a significant contribution to revenues: 100 shillings in 1377/8, 20s 6d in 1389/90 and £4 18d in 1408/9.

Immediately upon the accession of Henry IV in 1399, the castle and honour were granted to his son Henry, Prince of Wales and Duke of Cornwall. The king's knight, Robert Corbet, was granted custody of the park and warren, together with the castle, for 40 marks yearly for life. Roger Bigge was confirmed in his office as parker but, despite this, it was Robert Corbet who was recorded in the accounts receiving 2d per day for the custody of the park and warren.[46] The Prince of Wales was crowned Henry V in 1413 and reigned until 1422, when Henry VI came to the throne. In the same year a new official appeared in the records: Richard Hunte, 'Ferreter of the household', was employed to supply coneys.[47] In 1424 the king granted the office of keeper of the park to John Atkyn 'with the usual fees and wages'.[48]

Henry VI enjoyed hunting but no records have come to light of him using the park at Berkhamsted for that purpose. His queen, Margaret of Anjou, acquired the castle and lordship of Berkhamsted in July 1448, handing it to her son, Edward, Prince of Wales and Duke of Cornwall, in 1459.[49] Accounts for 1449/50 show that the park was no longer under direct management: the farm of the herbage and pannage of the park and foreign wood were leased for 20 shillings a year and the farm of the warren of rabbits 'in the queen's park' was leased for 40 shillings a year. There was still a parker earning 2d per day but no wood, underwood or faggots had been sold.[50]

In 1469 Berkhamsted was granted by Edward IV to his mother, Cicely, Duchess of York. Accounts compiled the following year show that the farm of the agistment of the park, the rabbit warren and pannage were leased to Sir John Pilkington for £12 p.a.[51] The duchess lived at the castle until she died in 1496, when Berkhamsted passed to her granddaughter, Elizabeth, queen of Henry VII.[52] In July 1502 the underkeeper of Berkhamsted park was paid 3s 4d for taking a buck to Queen Elizabeth at Windsor, showing that the deer park was still functioning at the beginning of the sixteenth century.[53]

Although Berkhamsted castle fell into decay after the death of the duchess of York,[54] the park survived and an account compiled for Henry VIII in 1534–6 showed that the farm of agistment was still worth £12 a year and was then leased to John Verney.[55] In the reign of Elizabeth I the park became the setting for a new house, Berkhamsted Place, built by Sir Edward Carey after 1580. Saxton's county map (1577) shows the park lying on the north bank of the river Bulbourn with the castle on its southern margin, while Norden's map (1598) shows a road passing between the park and the river and a house in the middle of the park, suggesting that the southern boundary had perhaps shifted northwards at about the time that Berkhamsted Place was built. This park is shown in greater detail on the earliest-known estate map, which dates from the early seventeenth century and was drawn by John Norden. It shows the very large park forming part of the demesne lands of the manor of Berkhamsted c.1612.[56] The only palings shown were along the south and south-east sides of the park, but various areas of the hills lying north and north-west of the castle were labelled The Long Launde, Lodge Hill Woode (The Lodge is also marked), New Lodge Woode and New Lodge Launde. Norden's survey, which originally accompanied the map, recorded 298 acres of woodland within the park contained in seven parcels, the largest of which was New Lodge Woode (101 acres). There were 441 acres of 'laund and playne [plain] ground' and a piece of pasture ground called the Coppice containing 67 acres. The total acreage of the park recorded by Norden at the beginning of the seventeenth century, including the site of the castle, was 824 acres. He also recorded 107 acres of lands which had lately been taken out of the park in two parcels of 41 acres and 66 acres respectively. Most of the park boundary (1,350 perches) was described as 'very ill fenced and hedges' and a further 378 perches were impaled with beech.[57]

On 14 August 1616 Prince Charles visited Berkhamsted and went hunting. He killed a fat buck which he gave to the men of the town who had attended him.[58] In February 1619 the prince obtained the agreement of the parishioners of Berkhamsted St Peter and Northchurch to enclose 300 acres of 'the waste and common called the Frith' into his park with a pale made from trees felled in the Frith. The pales were initially torn down by rioters protesting at loss of common rights but were later reinstated. This final expansion brought the acreage of the park to 1,132 acres, but it was not to stay that size for long. In 1628 all but 376 acres was disparked and leased as farmland for £46 0s 6d a year.[59]

A map 'made about 1638' showed the boundary of 'Barkhampsted Parke' with a grand house, Berkhamsted Place, sitting in its midst. The short-lived incursion of the park into The Frith was indicated with a dotted line. Two gates were depicted along the northern park boundary: Coppies Gate and Dearne Gate, and 'Barkhampstede Parke Corner' was annotated at the north-western extremity of the park. The park boundary south of the house was not shown.[60] These features can be identified with those recorded in 1388/9, suggesting that the northern boundary of the park, at least, remained unchanged for over two centuries. Hunts Hill was the name given on the c.1612 plan of Berkhamsted to the area of enclosed fields in the south-east of the former park and probably represents the land enclosed into the park by Richard II before 1388.

The Berkhamsted tithe award recorded that a modus was paid in lieu of all tithes of 'lands which formerly constituted the ancient park of Berkhamsted', and the boundary of 'the old park' was shown on the tithe map.[61] This boundary corresponds with the boundary shown on the map of c.1612 but on the southern side it extended as far as the (canalised) river. The area within the boundary covered 991 acres and is shown on Map 7. It does not include the 300 acres added to the park for a short period in 1618.

1. N. Vincent, 'Richard, first earl of Cornwall and king of Germany (1209–1272)', Oxford dictionary of national biography (Oxford, September 2004; online edn, May 2006), accessed online 28 September 2007.

2. Midgley, Ministers' accounts, 1, pp. xx–xxi. An earlier account of the honour of Berkhamsted from 1272/3 contains references to a park but the document is damaged and the name of the manor in which the park was located has been lost (TNA: PRO SC6/863/3).

3. TNA: PRO SC6/863/8 minister's account, 1272–1307. A date within the early part of this range is likely because accounts of 1268/9 and 1272/3 appear to be in the same hand whereas an account of 1299–1301 is in a different hand; N. Vincent, 'Edmund of Almain, second earl of Cornwall (1249–1300)', Oxford dictionary of national biography (Oxford, 2004), accessed online 28 September 2007.

4. Midgley, Ministers' accounts, pp. 21 and 13.

5. Ibid., p. 19.

6. TNA: PRO SC6/863/5 bailiff's account, 1300/01.

7. J.W. Cobb, Two lectures, p. 18, quoting TNA: PRO C133/95 inquisition post mortem of Edmund, earl of Cornwall, 1300.

8. Whybrow, Berkhamsted Common, p. 16.

9. Cal. Pat. 1301–1307, p. 544; 1313–1317, pp. 137 and 228.

10. Ibid., p. 586.

11. Page, Hertford, 2, p. 166.

12. Cal. Pat. 1321–1324, p. 371.

13. Page, Hertford, 2, p. 166; Cal. Pat. 1334–1338, p. 550.

14. Cal. Pat. 1330–1334, p. 583.

15. Page, Hertford, 2, p. 166 citing Rolls of Parliament (Records Commission), iii, 667b.

16. Cobb, Two lectures, p. 19.

17. D. Roden, 'Demesne farming in the Chiltern Hills', Agricultural History Review, 17 (1969), p. 11 n. 2. The source cited is the grant of a lease of the remaining demesne lands in November 1347, so the park expanded before that date (Dawes, Register of Edward the Black Prince, 1, pp. 148–9); the 180-acre field was presumably recorded in the inquisition post mortem of Edmund, earl of Cornwall in 1300 (TNA: PRO C133/95).

18. TNA: PRO SC6/863/12 receiver's account, 1377/8.

19. TNA: PRO MR1/603 plan of the honour of Berkhamsted by John Norden, c.1612; HALS 1985 map of 'Barkhampsted Parke', c.1638.

20. R. Barber, 'Edward, prince of Wales and of Aquitaine (1330–1376)', Oxford dictionary of national biography (Oxford, September 2004; online edn, May 2006), accessed online 28 September 2007.

21. Dawes, Register of the Black Prince, 1, pp. 106, 117. Jean Birrell interprets this as a general cull (Birrell, 'Deer and deer farming', p. 123).

22. Barber, 'Edward, prince of Wales and of Aquitaine'.

23. Dawes, Register of Edward the Black Prince, 4, p. 81.

24. Cal. Pat. 1354–1358, p. 137 confirmation of recompense to Richard Raven and his wife Margery dated 13 November 1354.

25. Dawes, Register of the Black Prince, 4, pp. 81–3.

26. Ibid., p. 106.

27. Ibid., p. 118.

28. Ibid., p. 121.

29. Ibid., p. 82.

30. Barber, 'Edward, prince of Wales and of Aquitaine'.

31. Dawes, Register of the Black Prince, 4, p. 238.

32. Ibid., p. 243.

33. Ibid., p. 423.

34. J.M. Stratton, Agricultural records A.D. 220–1977 (London, 1978), p. 31; G. Manley, Climate and the British scene (London, 1952), p. 237.

35. Dawes, Register of the Black Prince, 4, p. 431. He instructed the bailiff of Gaddesden to do the same.

36. Ibid., p. 464. Ten marks was worth about 133 shillings, so de Newenton was obliged to take a lower, but guaranteed, sum of money.

37. Ibid., p. 458.

38. Ibid., pp. 517 and 536.

39. Cal. Pat. 1377–1381, p. 159.

40. Ibid., p. 446.

41. Ibid., p. 614.

42. Cal. Pat. 1385–1389, p. 390.

43. TNA: PRO SC6/863/14 receiver's accounts, 1388/9; the acreage of the

enclosed land was recorded in the account of 1449–50 (SC6/865/9).

44. TNA: PRO SC6/863/12, 14, 15, 17, 18 and 19, ministers' and receivers' accounts 1377/8, 1388/9, 1389/90, 1398/9, 1399/1400, 1400/1; SC6/864/5, 6 and 20, 1408/9, 1409/10 and 1423/4.

45. TNA: PRO SC6/864/5, 6 and 20 receiver's accounts, 1408/9, 1409/10 and 1423/4.

46. *Cal. Pat. 1399–1401*, pp. 13 and 48; TNA: PRO SC6/863/18 and 19 receiver's accounts for 1399/1400 and 1400/1.

47. The Black Prince had a warren at Berkhamsted by 1356 (Dawes, *Register of the Black Prince, 4*, p. 178). Accounts for the period 1419–56 are at TNA: PRO SC6/867/1.

48. *Cal. Pat. 1422–1429*, pp. 5, 501, 179.

49. R.A. Griffiths, 'Henry VI (1421–1471)', *Oxford dictionary of national biography* (Oxford, September 2004; online edn, May 2006), accessed online 28 November 2007; D.E.S. Dunn, 'Margaret (1430–1482)', *Oxford dictionary of national biography* (Oxford, 2004), accessed online 28 November 2007; Page, *Hertford*, 2, p. 166, citing *Rolls of Parliament* (Records Commission), v, 357b.

50. TNA: PRO SC6/865/9 receiver's account, 1449–50.

51. TNA: PRO SC6/870/7 ministers' and receivers' accounts, 1470–72.

52. Page, *Hertford*, 2, p. 166, citing Patent Roll 9 Edw. IV, pt. 1, m. 19

(TNA: PRO C66/524) and *Rolls of Parliament* (Records Commission), vi, 15a; *Rolls of Parliament* (Records Commission), vi, 462b.

53. Cobb, *Two lectures*, p. 26, citing the privy purse expenses of Queen Elizabeth.

54. H.M. Colvin (ed.), *The history of the king's works*, vol. 2 (London, 1963), p. 563.

55. TNA: PRO SC6/HENVIII/181, minister's account, 1534–6.

56. TNA: PRO MR1/603 plan of the honour of Berkhamsted by John Norden, *c.*1612; a photograph of the plan is at HALS.

57. TNA: PRO Ward 2/61/241/36 'A survey of certain parcels of the honour of Berkhamsted, viz the castle, park, the Frith, the demesnes and landes demised', by John Norden, September 1612. I am grateful to Heather Falvey for bringing this survey to my attention and furnishing me with her transcript.

58. Cobb, *Two lectures*, p. 37.

59. *Ibid.* pp. 34–6; Page, *Hertford*, 2, p. 167, citing Parliamentary Surveys Hertfordshire No. 7 (TNA: PRO E317/Herts/7); H. Falvey, 'Crown policy and local economic context in the Berkhamsted Common enclosure dispute, 1618–42', *Rural History*, 12 (2001), pp. 131–42.

60. HALS 1985 map of 'Barkhampsted Parke', *c.*1638.

61. HALS DSA4/19/1 and 2, Berkhamsted tithe award and map, 1839.

Bishop's Stortford

Stortford park – old, new and great

NGR: TL470212
Date range: old park: by 1263 – ?mid fourteenth century; new (?great) park: 1346/7 – ?mid seventeenth century
Size: old park: not known; new park: 295 acres
Underlying geology: old park: not known; new park: boulder clay

BEFORE THE NORMAN CONQUEST, Stortford was held by Edeva the Fair; it was then sold to the bishop of London by William I and remained part of the lands of the bishopric until 1868.[1] A park had been established at Stortford by 1263, when the parker received a grain livery and stipend.[2] By 1274 the grain livery had been commuted and the parker received 1½d a day and a stipend.[3] In 1282 the park at Stortford was broken into and deer were hunted and carried away.[4]

Several sets of accounts for Stortford compiled for the bishop of London survive from the middle of the fourteenth century and provide some information about the park. Besides deer, the park was grazed in 1345/6 by a variety of livestock, including three mares, foals of various ages, nine cows, two bulls and six young steers, raising 20s 6d in agistment. Interestingly, the job of the parker was split into two periods: one parker worked from 29 September to 25 January (118 days) and was paid 2d per day (19s 8d); the other parker worked the remaining 247 days to 29 September 1346 and was paid 1d per day (20s 7d).[5]

In 1346/7 a new park was established, enclosing an unrecorded area of land which included pasture, 12 acres of meadow, a garden and 7 acres of arable land. Two acres of corn (*fr'*) were destroyed in carrying fencing from the old park to the new and fodder was provided for the deer placed in the new park. The work of the parker during this busy time was shared, consecutively, by three different men: one worked for 31 weeks for 1d per day (18s 1d); one for 13 weeks taking 1½d per day (11s 4½d); the third, William Bedel of Hadham, for 6 weeks taking 1½d per day (5s 3d).[6] The following year there was just one parker, paid 45s 6d (1½d per day) for the whole year, but there was no income from agistment because 'diverse animals' of the bishop were grazing the park.[7] Accounts for 1351/2 record that thorns (*spinis*) were carried from the old park to the new for repairing fences (*sep'm*), and two men worked for 7½ weeks making and repairing the fence around the park, each taking 4d per week 'and old thorns'. A different section of the same account records the cutting of thorn-bushes or brambles in the 'great' park. Four acres of meadow in the park were used to grow hay for the bishop's horses.[8]

In 1354 the bishops' park was again broken into and Master Michael de Northburgh, the bishop elect, complained that evildoers broke the parks and closes of the bishopric of London, while these were in the king's

hands by reason of the voidance of the bishopric, at Storteford, Hadham, Haryngeye and Fulham, hunted therin, felled trees in the same and in other woods of the bishopric, and fished in the stews and free fisheries thereof, and carried away the fish of the same and the said trees, as well as deer from the parks.[9]

Accounts surviving from the late fourteenth century refer to only one park at Stortford. By 1387/8 the manor was at farm for £52 a year and the bishop was paying the parker 2d per day (60s 8d p.a.). Underwood from the park was sold for 6s 8d but 34 perches (*c*.170m) of new fence (*sepis*) was needed around the park, costing 5s 8d (2d per perch).[10] In 1394/5, 120 perches of fence were replaced for 15 shillings (1½d per perch) and a pond called Wygmore was scoured for 8d.[11] The first record of a lodge occurs in the account for 1398/9, when the parker, Richard Panfold, carried out repairs costing 3s 4d. Other costs of the park that year were replacing fences for 16s 7d and carrying hay for winter feed for the foals and deer for 14d.[12]

By 1410 the park seems to have expanded to include lands called Busshylese and Parkfield.[13] From 1437 the park and manor were administered separately and the parker, John Thurkeld, accounted for agistment of horses and cattle worth 55s 6d and sales of underwood worth 11s 4d. The cost of repairs to parts of the park pale totalled 19s 11½d and the wage of the parker was 60s 10d for the year.[14] Parkers continued to be appointed throughout the fifteenth century but in 1515, instead of a parker, there was a 'master of the lord's beasts within his park of Stortford' who received only 20 shillings.[15]

The county map by Saxton (1577) failed to show a park at Stortford, but a park was depicted south-west of the town by Norden in 1598 (Figure 18). In 1647 the park was sold, together with the manor, two watermills, fairs and markets, to Richard Turner, a citizen and merchant taylor of London. It reverted to the bishop of London after the Restoration[16] but it does not appear to have been restocked with deer. In 1667/8

Figure 18. *Detail of Norden's county map, 1598, showing the park established for the bishops of London west of Stortford. Reproduced by kind permission of Hertfordshire Archives and Local Studies.*

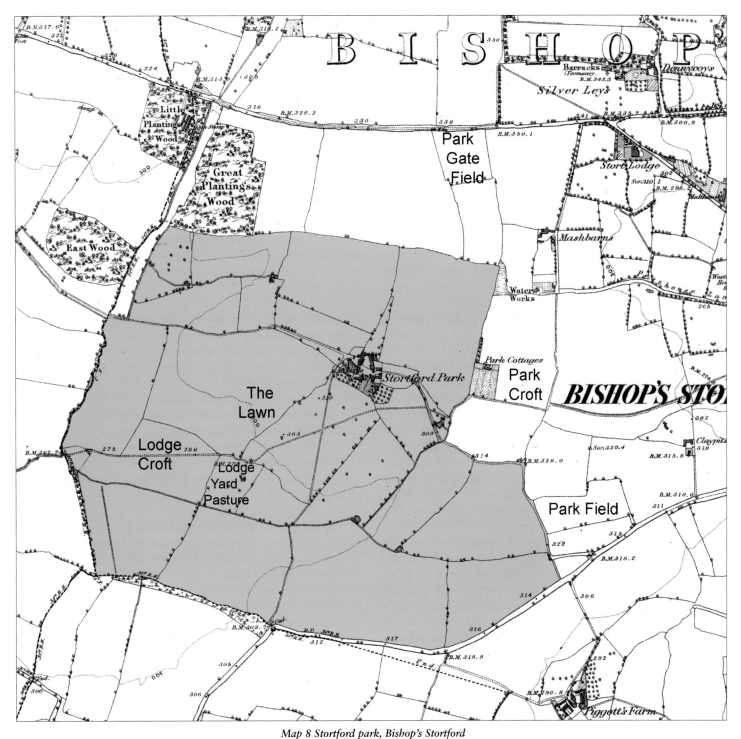

Map 8 Stortford park, Bishop's Stortford
OS 6 inches to the mile map sheet XXIII, surveyed 1874–9, published 1879–83. Field names derived from plan of 1828 (HALS 75989) and the Bishop's Stortford tithe map and award of 1839 (HALS DSA4/21/1 and 2).

the park was leased for 13 years at an annual rent of £145. Included in the lease was the park of about 300 acres, one mansion in the park together with its barns, stables, outhouses, orchards and gardens, a lodge within the park, eight acres of arable land adjoining the park, a small grove and two springs. The tenant was responsible for maintaining and repairing the buildings, including the lodge, and also the hedges, ditches, mounds and fences, gates and stiles. The meadows were not to be ploughed up and planted with corn or woad or madder without special permission from the owner, and 60 acres of pasture was to be left at the end of the term.[17] No park was shown on the seventeenth-century county maps by Seller

(1676) or Oliver (1695).

Chauncy (1700) mentioned 'a great farm called the Park' and in 1728 Salmon recorded that Stortford Park Farm was leased for lives to the Reverend William Stanley, the precentor of St Paul's.[18] In 1812 the Reverend Francis Stanley took out a lease for three lives from the bishop of London on the site of the manor of Stortford, the houses, park and lodge there, two watermills and all the demesne lands.[19] In 1828 William Gorsuch Times, the third of the lives, sold the lease of the site of the manor and Stortford Park Farm, amounting to 295 acres. The lodge was not mentioned, and had perhaps fallen down, but its location can be deduced from the plan accompanying the lease, which reveals a field called Lodge Croft and another called Lodge Yard Pasture. Several field names on the tithe map of 1839 provide additional evidence of the former park: for example, The Lawn, Park Gate Field and Park Croft (see Map 8).[20]

Earthworks at the site of the former lodge were the subject of archaeological investigations in 1938 and again in 1958. Potsherds dated from the thirteenth to the sixteenth centuries were recovered from the ditch surrounding the square site, together with 'bones of ox, boar and sheep, stag antlers, and many types of shell'.[21]

The 300-acre park of the 1667 lease appears to correspond with the 295 acres of Stortford Park Farm in 1828. It occupied the south-west corner of the parish of Bishop's Stortford on the boulder clay plateau at c.95m OD. The boundary of the park has survived almost intact into the twenty-first century as a significant ditch, much of which is bordered on the inside by an old, species-rich, hedge. A common species in the hedge is spindle, an indicator of ancient hedgerows, with a particular concentration along the northern boundary in the vicinity of Great Plantings wood. Occasionally vestiges of a bank inside the ditch have survived, but for much of the boundary this has been ploughed away. The best sections of bank are at the north-west and north-east corners of the former park. A complicated series of banks just outside the north-east corner of the park probably relate to a park gate (note 'Park Gate Field' on the tithe map). From the site of the former lodge there are good all-round views of the surrounding parkland.

The location of the earlier park is a matter for speculation. The two acres of wheat destroyed by the carrying of fences from the old park to the new might suggest that the two were close together, but this was not necessarily the case. The bishops did hold a block of land immediately to the east of the new park (in 1839 at least) around Claypits Farm, so this could have been the location for the earlier park. However, they also held a large area of land on the east side of the Stort in 1839 and may once have held all of that part of the parish which formerly projected eastwards to a point beyond today's M11.[22] This east end of the parish was probably open heath or woodland in medieval times and the regular field boundaries shown on the 1839 tithe map suggest that the land was divided up in a planned fashion at a relatively late date. Much of it is a golf course today, indicating that it is not prime agricultural land, and this area constitutes a plausible alternative location for the bishops' earlier park.

1. Page, *Hertford*, 3, p. 296. The bishops lost the manor temporarily in the mid seventeenth century.
2. P.J. Taylor, 'The estates of the bishopric of London', pp. 179 and 184, citing TNA: PRO E372/108 m.15d.
3. *Ibid.* citing TNA: PRO E372/117 m.7d. The bishop's two parkers in Essex, at Crondon and Clacton respectively, also received 1½d a day and a stipend. In 1304 the bishop's parkers at Stortford and Clacton were still receiving 1½d a day but those at Haringey and Crondon were receiving 2d a day (TNA: PRO E372/149 m.39). Taylor found that, by the late Middle Ages, all but one demesne manor held by the bishop of London had a park or warren or both.
4. *Cal. Pat. 1281–1292*, p. 45.
5. TNA: PRO SC6/1140/1 minister's account, 1345/6.
6. TNA: PRO SC6/1140/2 minister's account, 1346/7.
7. TNA: PRO SC6/1140/3 minister's account, 1347/8.
8. TNA: PRO SC6/1140/5 minister's account, 1351/2.
9. *Cal. Pat. 1354–1358*, p. 127.
10. TNA: PRO SC6/1140/8 minister's account, 1387/8.
11. TNA: PRO SC6/1140/10 minister's account, 1394/5.
12. TNA: PRO SC6/1140/12 minister's account, 1398/9.
13. TNA: PRO SC6/1140/16 minister's account, 1410–12.
14. TNA: PRO SC6/1140/20 parker's account, 1437/8.
15. Taylor, 'Estates of the bishopric of London', pp. 185–6, citing Guildhall MS 10, 123 vol. 1 fo. 6v.
16. Page, *Hertford*, 3, p. 297.
17. HALS 21522 lease of Stortford park, 1667/8.
18. Chauncy, *Historical antiquities*, p. 166; Salmon, *History of Hertfordshire*, p. 271, citing Feet of Fines Herts Easter 5 Geo II (TNA: PRO CP25/2/1136/5GEOIIEASTER).
19. HALS 75989 indenture of 1828.
20. HALS DSA4/21/1 and 2 tithe award and map for Bishop's Stortford, 1839.
21. Ellcock, 'The Bishop of London's hall', p. 33.
22. HALS DSA4/21/1 and 2 tithe award and map, 1839.

Figure 19. *The landscape of Stortford park in the middle of the twentieth century before it was divided into two halves by a ring road and the eastern half became engulfed in housing estates. Aerial photograph taken by the RAF 10 October, 1946 (HALS Off Acc 300 CPE/UK/1779, 4326). Reproduced by kind permission of Hertfordshire Archives and Local Studies.*

Bramfield

Bramfield park

NGR: TL283154
Date range: by early thirteenth century – perhaps disparked by fifteenth century
Size: not known; perhaps *c.*90 acres
Underlying geology: boulder clay

IN 1086 HARDUIN DE SCALERS gave the manor of Bramfield to the abbot and convent of St Albans and in the thirteenth century Abbot John removed the parish from the hundred of Hertford to make it part of the Liberty of St Albans and hundred of Cashio, along with most of the abbey's other estates in Hertfordshire.[1] Although there appear to be no surviving records of a park at Bramfield, it seems very likely that a twelfth- or early thirteenth-century abbot established a deer park about quarter of a mile west of the medieval church of Bramfield, on a piece of land which is marked on the modern OS map as 'Bramfield Park Wood'.

As well as the name Bramfield Park Wood, there are some impressive boundary banks and also various pieces of circumstantial documentary evidence to support this theory. The earliest extant court roll for Bramfield records a juror called Richard de Parco in 1239, perhaps the keeper of the abbot's deer park. Descendents of Richard de Parco appear as jurors in the manor court rolls for the next two centuries.[2] Richard de Park was recorded at Bramfield in 1294 and Richard ate Parc appeared on the 1307 lay subsidy roll.[3]

Unfortunately any records that the abbey must once have kept concerning the revenues from their estate at Bramfield, and the costs of maintaining the presumed deer park, have now been lost. It seems unlikely that the park survived beyond the medieval period because in the fifteenth century one Thomas Glasscocke, who leased the land belonging to Bramfieldbury, was before the manor court more than once for failing to put sufficient cattle into Park Wood to keep the undergrowth down.[4]

The park seems to have covered approximately 90 acres of a clay-covered plateau at about 85m OD with extensive views to the south-west, south and east. The first edition 6-inch OS map (1884) shows a lane bordering the west side of the wood called Park Lane (see Map 9).[5] This lane is now a bridleway which is bordered on its east side by an impressive bank forming the boundary of Park Wood. This bank is about 6m across and, at its highest, rises about 1.8m above the base of the ditch on its west side. Its scale is in marked contrast to the wood-bank on the opposite side of the track, which is just 0.6m high and 2.6m across. The large bank forms a continuous boundary around the southern part of Park Wood.

The boundary around the northern end of the former park is less clear-cut and does not appear to have had the same nice oval shape. The bank along the east side of Park Lane stops where the parish boundary cuts across the lane. The parish boundary heads eastwards into Park Wood, following a ditch. As there are no records of the abbot of St Albans owing land in the neighbouring parish of Tewin, it seems likely that the park boundary also followed this line and a significant bank does indeed border the south side of the ditch. This could be a bank constructed simply to mark the parish boundary, but after about 350m the parish boundary and the bank diverge: the parish boundary turns abruptly north-west while the bank continues to run approximately eastwards to the most easterly point of Park Wood. Up until the 1970s the line of the bank continued south-eastwards as a hedgerow to the lane leading to Bramfieldbury. The hedge was grubbed up and any surviving earthwork bank was ploughed up by 1980.[6]

A fifteenth-century timber-framed house sits in an enclave on the east side of the wood and the boundary bank appears to follow the property boundary on its west side, excluding it from the park.[7] The remains of a possible moat sit nearby to the east, outside the line of the park boundary, perhaps marking the site of an earlier house or a medieval fishpond. The present house is known as Bramfieldbury, and the surviving parts of the original hall-house which it contains may have been built for Robert Ware, the Cellarer of St Albans abbey, in 1420.[8]

In 1540, after the dissolution of the abbey of St Albans, Henry VIII granted Bramfield to Robert Dacres of Cheshunt.[9] The grant records a farm, cottages, a mill, pastures, woods and coppices, but no park. An early nineteenth-century survey shows that Park Farm occupied 84½ acres of land between Park Wood and the village of Bramfield.[10] The northernmost field belonging to the farm bears the name 'Stockings', indicating former woodland,[11] and the earthwork bank which perhaps indicates the former park boundary forms the northern border of this field. Park Wood was in the hands of the lord of the manor and comprised four compartments: Park Wood, Salmon Spring, Cow Wood and Queene Wood.[12] At the time of the 1804 survey Park Wood was said to cover nearly 100 acres and the outline depicted then corresponds with the outline shown on the 1880 OS map.[13] The wood is classified as ancient and semi-natural and there are areas of ancient hornbeam coppice in the west and south, but most of the former park has been replanted by the Forestry Commission.

If the deer park was disparked by the fifteenth century, it is interesting that the name and the boundary banks have survived so well for over 500 years.

1. Page, *Hertford*, 2, p. 343 citing BL Cotton MS. Nero, D. vii, fol. 92b and Assize Roll 323, 325 (TNA: PRO JUST 1/323 and 325).

2. Men appearing as jurors at the manor courts include Richard and Thomas de Parco in the mid thirteenth century, Richard atte Park in the early fourteenth century (HALS 40702), Rogus and Adam atte Park in the mid fourteenth century (HALS 40703), and Johanes Parke, Roger Parke and

Map 9 Bramfield park

OS 6 inches to the mile map sheet XXIX, surveyed 1879–80, published 1884. The field name 'Stockings' was recorded on a map of 1804 (HALS DP/22/29/2 survey of the manors of 'Brantfield and Queenhoo Hall').

Symon Parke in the early fifteenth century (HALS 40705).

3. Munby, *Hertfordshire landscape*, p. 131; Brooker and Flood, *Hertfordshire lay subsidy rolls*, p. 135.

4. HALS O.T. Leslie, 'The history of Bramfield' (unpublished manuscript, 1959), p. 5.

5. OS map sheet XXIX, 6 inches to the mile, surveyed 1879–80, published 1884.

6. HALS Aerial photomaps No. 476 [TL2815/2915] 1972 and 1980.

7. HALS Department of the Environment, List of buildings of special architectural or historic interest, 1986.

8. Page, *Hertford*, 2, p. 343 citing Riley, H.T. (ed.), *Annales monasterii Sancti Albani a Johanne Amundesham, vol. 2* (London, 1871).

9. HALS DE/AS1145 grant of manor by Henry VIII to Robert Dacres, 1540.

10. HALS DP/22/29/2 survey of the manors of 'Brantfield and Queenhoo Hall', 1804.

11. J. Field, *English field names: a dictionary* (Newton Abbot, 1972), p. 220 — from the OE *stoccing*.

12. The divisions between these compartments have not been ascertained.

13. According to the Bramfield tithe award of 1838 Park Wood covered nearly 95 acres (HALS DSA4/23/1).

Broadfield

Broadfield park (possibly in the parish of Clothall)
NGR: ?TL297310
Date range: by 1297 – not known
Size: not known; possibly c.40 acres
Underlying geology: not known but probably boulder clay

THIS PARK SEEMS TO BE RECORDED only once, at the end of the thirteenth century, and locating it is fraught with difficulty. The parish of Broadfield is small but the manor of Broadfield seems to have had a complicated history involving several separate areas of land which lay in the neighbouring parishes of Rushden, Clothall and Cottered as well as Broadfield. In 1297 John de Wengham, Precentor of St Paul's, had deer stolen from his park at Broadfield.[1] John de Wengham was not holding the manor of Broadfield but he was holding the manor of Bygrave from the de Somery family and they appear to have had a park at Broadfield which formed part of his lease. The Victoria County History traces this park back to a virgate of land which was held by Robert Bishop of Chester in 1086 and which, like other lands held by the bishop in Hertfordshire, passed to the Somerys. In 1303 John de Wengham's holding in Broadfield was worth a quarter of a knight's fee, and in 1346 it descended to his nephew, Master Tomas de Wengham, but no further trace could be found of it after that date.[2]

A possible location for this park has been identified at Cumberlow Green in the parish of Clothall by means of a tortuous line of documentary sources combined with some good surviving field evidence. The manor of Cumberlow Green 'appears to have been called the manor of Broadfield in 1346' when 100 acres were 'held of Walter de Mauny, as of the manor of Bradefeld' by service of a quarter of a knight's fee.[3] The manor 'afterwards took the name of Maunseys' and at the end of the fifteenth century it was sold as 'the manor of Broadfield in Cumberlow Green' but was not distinguished from the manor of Cumberlow Green in subsequent transactions.[4]

In 1549 the manor of Cumberlow Green consisted of 300 acres of land, 20 acres of meadow, 60 acres of pasture and 40 acres of wood in the parishes of Rushden, Clothall, Cottered and Wallington. A map of 1729 shows a wood called Munches Wood and fields called Munches Garden and Munches Dell on the Clothall side of the parish boundary at Cumberlow Green.[5] This may indicate the site of the Cumberlow Green manor house which lay in the parish of Clothall.[6] Is it possible that 'Munches' is derived from 'Maunseys' and that these names indicate the land held by Walter de Mauny in the early fourteenth century and by John de Wengham at the end of the thirteenth century? Munches Wood in Clothall probably covered 40 acres prior to 1615 (when it covered just 20 acres)[7] and is a promising location for a medieval park, situated as it is on high ground on the edge of the parish.

Supporting evidence for this hypothesis comes from significant earth banks around the east and north sides of Munches Wood. The banks are relatively low (less than 0.5m) but very broad (5m and as much as 7m in places) and have an external ditch. They are larger than the average wood-bank and are among the broadest banks seen along surviving medieval park boundaries in the county. Along the banks are old coppice stools and the wood itself is clearly ancient coppiced woodland with earthwork compartments and a rich ground flora. The bank continues southwards from Munches Wood alongside Shawgreen Lane, forming the eastern boundary of fields called The Upper and Lower Stocking in 1729. As well as the field names (*stocc* = OE tree-trunk, stump, log), the woodland ground flora surviving on the bank is evidence that Munches Wood formerly extended over these two fields towards Cumberlow Green. Whether the medieval park, if such it was, extended west of Munches Wood to include the field named Knights Wells, or extended south of the modern A507 to include Munches Dell Field, cannot be determined from surviving field evidence.

An alternative location for the medieval park might be the land around Broadfield Hall, where the names Upper Park, Great Park, Little Park and Dial Park were recorded on an eighteenth-century plan of the estate.[8] Running across these enclosures, however, are hollow-ways marking the routes of trackways which fell out of use in the late medieval period. These were associated with the small deserted settlement of Broadfield which lay close to the present-day Broadfield Hall and was the subject of archaeological investigation in the 1960s.[9] The presence of this settlement in medieval times would suggest that the medieval park lay elsewhere. The ornamental park landscape was laid out around the hall from the late seventeenth century.

1. *Cal. Pat. 1292–1301*, p. 316.
2. Page, *Hertford*, 3, p. 211.
3. Page, *Hertford*, 3, p. 268, citing Chan. Inq. p.m. 20 Edw. III (1st nos), no. 51 (TNA: PRO C135/82/1). Roger de Somery was said to be the tenant in chief of the manor of Bradefeld before 1277, but presumably of only a part of the manor (*Cal. Pat. 1272–1281*, p. 193).
4. Page, *Hertford*, 3, p. 268 citing *Feudal Aids, 1284–1481*, ii (HMSO, 1899–1921) 447.
5. HALS 74423 plan annexed to deed showing Munches Wood, 1729.
6. Page, *Hertford*, 3, p. 268.
7. HALS 74380 deeds, 1615.
8. HALS XIII.51 plan of Broadfield Hall and Farm, 1775.
9. E.C. Klingelhofer, *The deserted medieval village of Broadfield, Herts.*, BAR, 2 (1974).

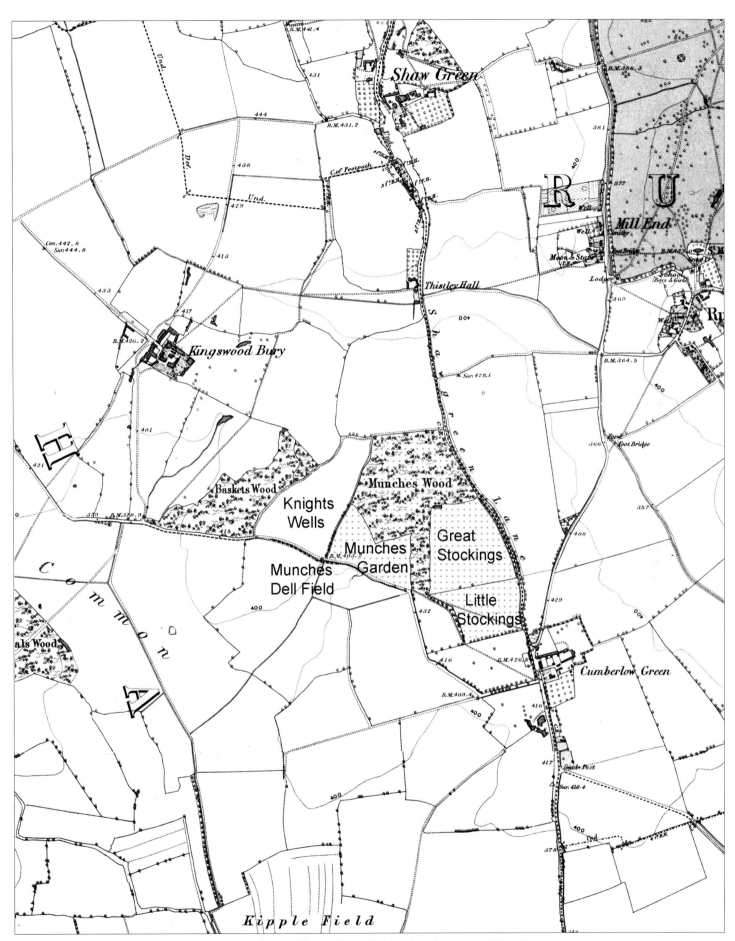

Map 10 The possible site of Broadfield park in the parish of Clothall
OS 6 inches to the mile map sheets VIII, surveyed 1877, published 1883; and XIII, surveyed 1877–8, published 1884. Annotated with field names derived from a map of Munches Wood, 1729 (HALS 74423).

Bushey

No known name

NGR: TQ120976

Date range: c.1427 – perhaps disparked c.1445

Size: not known

Underlying geology: alluvium, chalk, Westmill Gravel

AN EXTENT OF THE MANOR OF BUSHEY taken 1326/7 recorded 'a wood called 'le Park' containing 10 acres, whereof the pasture is worth by the year 9 shillings', perhaps indicating a small area of wood-pasture within which deer had been kept.[1] Manorial accounts from the 1260s and 1270s and from the early 1320s, however, do not appear to contain any references to a park and nor does an extent of the manor of 1314–16.[2] The thirteenth-century lord of the manor, David de Jarpenville, received a grant of free warren in his demesne lands in 1270 but the weight of negative evidence would suggest that he did not establish a park.[3]

A late medieval park is reputed to have been laid out around Bushey Hall (or Bushey Bury), a magnificent house started in 1428 by Thomas, Earl of Salisbury, on low ground east of the river Colne.[4] The earl of Salisbury seems to have spent most of the 1420s on numerous military campaigns in France, returning to England in April 1427. He stayed only until July 1428, when he led a major expeditionary force back to France. He was seriously wounded at the end of October 1428 and died a few days later.[5] Whether he could have established a new deer park at Bushey during the fifteen months that he was in England seems debatable. The estate was inherited, and held for the next 32 years, by his daughter, Alice, and her husband, Richard Nevill, who became the next earl of Salisbury.

The extent of the fifteenth-century park at Bushey is not known; nor is there any evidence that it contained deer. A court roll of 1447 recorded fields called 'le Oldpark' and 'le Logge'.[6] It seems odd that a park established less than 20 years previously should be referred to as the 'old park' but, if the field name did refer to the 1420s park, it must have already been disparked by the Nevills. There are no references to a park at Bushey in documents surviving from the first half of the sixteenth century, although there was a rabbit warren.[7]

An estate map of 1685 shows a series of fields south of Bushey Hall and close to the river Colne called 'The Parks' (see Map 11). There was also a 'Parke Mead' west of the Hall and two 'Lodge Fields' to the south, which suggests that the house

had a grand approach from the south with a lodge at the entrance to the park.[8] These fields could correspond with the 'le Logge' field name recorded in 1447. No park is shown at Bushey on any sixteenth- or seventeenth-century maps, which suggests that these field names recall a park which may have existed for only a short period in the early fifteenth century. Alternatively, they could reflect the park-like appearance of the fields south of Bushey Hall in the late seventeenth century, when there clearly was an extensive ornamental landscape. Both the 1685 estate map and a series of illustrations in Chauncy's county history of 1700 show avenues of trees, lawns and water gardens set amidst arable fields. There does not appear to have been a park there in the late seventeenth century and it may be that there never was a deer park at Bushey.[9]

Suburban sprawl means that surviving field evidence is sparse and unreliable but a possible southern boundary to this park may be preserved in a long property boundary which divides a residential estate to the north from Bushey Hall Golf Course to the south and which is followed by a public footpath (on an intermittent slight bank) and a ditch.

1. G. Montague Hall (rector of Bushey 1898–1937), *A history of Bushey* (Bushey, 1938), p. 19 gives a full transcription of the extent of the manor of Bushey 1326/7 from the inquisition *ad quod damnum* 20 Edward II, No. 34 (TNA: PRO C145/103 No. 34).
2. TNA: PRO ministers' and receivers' accounts: SC6/915/3, 1265–71; SC6/868/10, 1275–77; SC6/868/12, 1278–80; SC6/1145/10, 1321/2; E199/10/4, 1320–23; E199/10/2 extent of the manor of Bushey, 1314–16.
3. Page, *Hertford*, 2, p. 181.
4. Robinson, *Hertfordshire*, p. 43: 'Earl of Salisbury built new hall at Bushey and enclosed large area to make park'. However, neither of the references given, (VCH, and Inventory of Historical Monuments in Herts, Royal Commission on Historical Monuments, 1910) make any mention of a park and the actual source of this statement has yet to be found.
5. A. Curry, 'Montagu, Thomas, fourth earl of Salisbury (1388–1428)', *Oxford dictionary of national biography* (Oxford, September 2004; online edn, May 2006), accessed online 17 August 2007.
6. Gover *et al.*, *Place-names of Hertfordshire*, p. 273.
7. TNA: PRO SC12/8/22 valor of the lordship and manor of Bushey Hall, 1510; E101/459/12 account of repairs at Bushey, 1524–26; SC6/HENVIII/6869 minister's account for Bushey and Ware, 1539/40.
8. HALS DE/Hx/P2 Bushey estate map, 1685.
9. *Ibid.*; Chauncy, *Historical antiquities*, pp. 542–3.

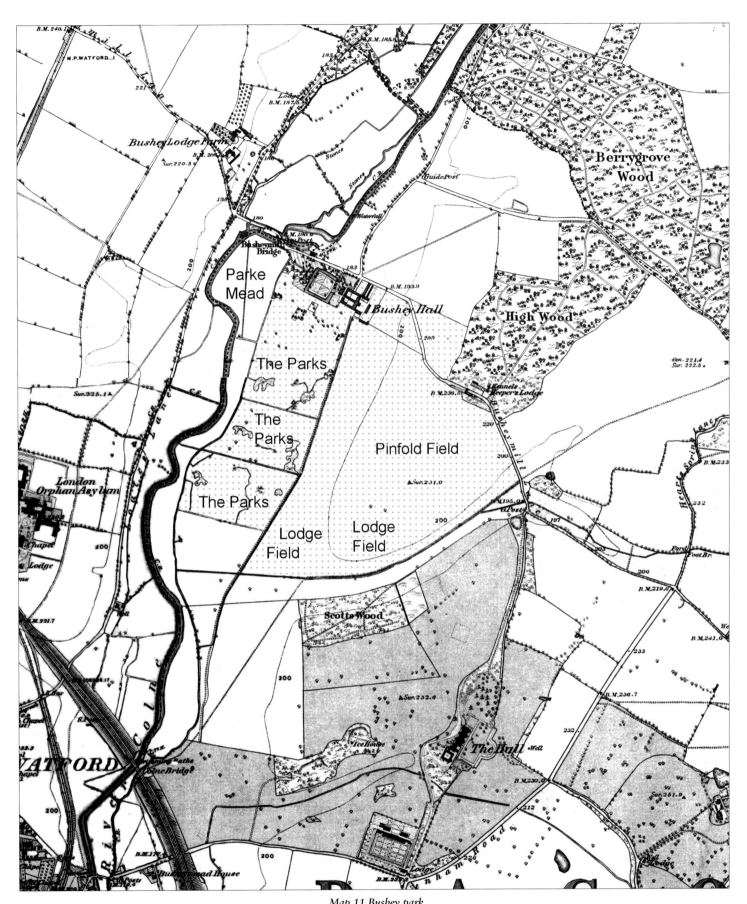

Map 11 Bushey park
OS 6 inches to the mile map sheets XXXIX, surveyed 1871–2, published 1883; and XLIV, surveyed 1871, published 1877. Annotated with field names derived from an estate map of 1685 (HALS DE/Hx/P2).

Cheshunt

Brantingshay or Cheshunt park

NGR: TL350045
Date range: perhaps by 1280 – mid seventeenth century
Size: not known; perhaps c.240 acres
Underlying geology: London Clay, overlain on the higher ground by Pebble Gravel and, on the lower parts, by Taplow Gravel

THE NAME BRANTYNGESHAY was first recorded in 1280 in some accounts detailing the revenues derived from the old park (see p. 80).[1] The 'hay' element of the name could refer to enclosed woodland or even a hunting enclosure.[2] The reference to the 'old' park implies that there was another, more recent, park and it seems quite likely that 'Brantyngeshay' was that other park, because 16 years later it was referred to as 'the park of Brantingshye'. In the account of 1295/6 revenue of £6 was recorded for pasture sold in 'Brantingeshey'.[3] The account of 1435/6 recorded significantly lower receipts of 60s 10d for agistment of animals in the park but the sale of faggots was worth 108 shillings (2,700 faggots at 4s per hundred). As with the old park, the account recorded lands (covering respectively 28 acres and 3 acres) for which rent was no longer due because they had been enclosed within the park, indicating a phase of park expansion during the fourteenth or early fifteenth centuries. Expenses of 14s 10d were incurred in 1435/6 making a park gate and repairing the pales, and the parker, John More, was paid 60s 10d (2d per day).[4]

The keepership of the parks appears to have been held as a rule with the office of bailiff of the manor of Cheshunt and in 1478 John Chapman, king's servitor and a yeoman of the crown, was granted the 'offices of bailiff of Cheston and Waltham crosse and parker of Cheston alias Brantyngeshey' for life. He was to receive '2d daily for the office of bailiff and 2d daily for the office of parker from the issues of the lordship of Cheston'.[5] In 1485 Thomas Sondes was granted the office of parker of Cheshunt Park.[6]

Two accounts from the early sixteenth century, when the manor was in the hands of Henry VIII, record receipts for 'agistment or pannage in the park of Brantyngeshey … lately in the tenure of Thomas Sandes, parker'. Decayed rents were still being recorded for the two pieces of land of 26 and 3 acres respectively which had been enclosed into the park before 1435. However, another three pieces of land had been enclosed into the park by 1519. One in 'lytelstublegh' was worth 9 shillings p.a. and had been enclosed in the time of the Duke of Clarence, who held the manor from 1465 to 1477. The second was 2 acres of land worth 16d p.a. and the third was worth 23d p.a. If we assume that all of this land was worth approximately 8d per acre, then another 18 acres had been added to the park by the early sixteenth century. It was evidently still a fully functioning deer park, because among the

expenses of the steward recorded in both sets of accounts was 20 shillings for four carts of hay bought for the sustenance of the king's deer in the park, at 5 shillings per cart.[7]

In 1538 Anthony Denny and Sir John Henneage were granted the herbage and pannage of the king's park of 'Brantingsley'.[8] By the mid sixteenth century the park had become separated from the manor and in 1567 ownership of 'the park called Brantingsley Parke otherwise Chesthunt Parke' passed from Henry Denny to John Harrington, including the lands 'inclosed within the pales or closures … and also all the Deare and other wild beasts … now in the said park'.[9] In 1570 Harrington sold the park to William Cecil, Lord Burghley, and the park was depicted on the county maps of both Saxton (1577) (Figure 20) and Norden (1598).[10]

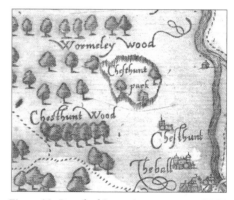

Figure 20. Detail of Saxton's county map, 1577, showing Cheshunt park (HALS CM1). Reproduced by kind permission of Hertfordshire Archives and Local Studies.

A survey by Israel Amyce of the lands held by Burghley's son, Sir Robert Cecil, in 1600/01, recorded an area for the park of 236 acres, with 122 acres 'enclosed with hedge and rail'. The plan which accompanies the survey shows two lodges in the park: the Greate Lodge lying on the north side of the pond shown on the first edition OS map at Park Farm; and the Little Lodge lying to the north-west (see Map 12). Trees were depicted scattered over most of the park with a higher density of them in the north-east corner. The land in the south-east corner of the map was divided into hedged enclosures which probably correspond with the 122 acres 'enclosed with hedge and rail'.[11]

The area of the park was soon to grow to over 669 acres after King James acquired Brantingshay or Cheshunt park, in addition to the Theobalds estate (with its late sixteenth-century park), from Sir Robert Cecil in 1607. Arable land covering 129 acres was enclosed into the park, together with 45 acres of the manor of Periers. Most of this land must have been to the north of the sixteenth-century park and its enclosure meant that the park extended into the parish of

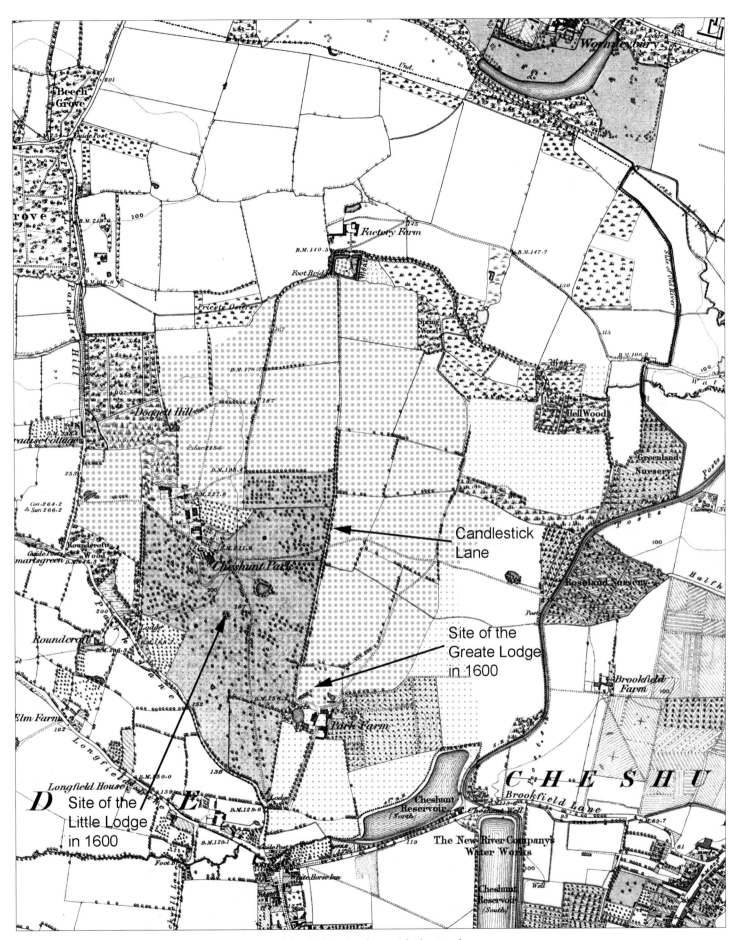

Candlestick
Lane

Site of the
Greate Lodge
in 1600

Site of the
Little Lodge
in 1600

Map 12 Brantingshay or Cheshunt park
OS 6 inches to the mile map sheets XXXVI, surveyed 1873–80, published 1883; and XLI, surveyed 1873, published 1882. The shading represents the
approximate extent of the park in 1600, as shown on the map by Israel Amyce (HHA CP349), and covers about 245 acres. Whether the park had reached
this size before the end of the medieval period is not known.

Wormley in the early seventeenth century.[12] By the time of the parliamentary survey of 1649 the park contained 212 acres of woodland and 459 acres of pasture, and held 200 deer.[13] It was soon disparked and was not shown on the seventeenth-century county maps by Seller or Oliver. In the mid eighteenth century a mansion was built (demolished 1831) and in 1826 the parkland still survived with 658 acres in the parish of Cheshunt and another 11 acres in Wormley. The land has remained largely undeveloped to the present day and is still called Cheshunt Park; it is divided between two farms and a golf club. There are no public rights of way across the former park and a lane (Park Lane) forms its western boundary.

The acreage of the medieval park is not recorded and, as we have seen, it underwent at least two phases of expansion, so any attempt to map its early extent can only be conjectural. In the sixteenth century the park lay across the route of Ermine Street in the north of the parish on the gently rising east-facing slopes of the Lea valley. Much of the park boundary depicted by Amyce in 1600/01 can still be followed on the first edition OS map and it encloses an area of approximately 245 acres. Whether the medieval park occupied the whole of this area, or indeed the additional lands in the enclosures to the south and east of the park in 1600/01, cannot now be determined with certainty.

Some old boundaries still survive as earthworks in today's park, including a 4m-wide bank running almost north–south at the southern end of the track called Candlestick Lane (c.TL3480103851). Another bank, with a ditch to the south, runs east–west to the east of Candlestick Lane at c.TL3506104447, but this may simply be a hedge-bank. A significant boundary, which corresponds with a boundary shown on a 1785 map of the parish, can be detected running north-west to south-east in the south-west corner of the park.[14] The remains of ridge and furrow can be seen at and around TL34660420, and also to the north-east of this position.

The old park

NGR: TL336013
Date range: twelfth century – perhaps early fifteenth century
Size: not known; perhaps c.230 acres
Underlying geology: glacial gravel partially overlying London Clay

CHESHUNT WAS A LARGE AND VALUABLE manor granted after the Conquest to Count Alan, the son of the Duke of Brittany and son-in-law of William the Conqueror. The park and warren 'de Cestrehunt' were first recorded in a Curia Regis Roll of 1226, when it was held by Alan de Bassingeborn by serjeanty (that is, in return for service) and had been so held by his father and antecedents before him.[15] This suggests that the park had been established in the twelfth century and it was presumably this same park which was referred to as the 'old park' in 1280 when it was a source of pannage and wood but also contained some cultivated land. A translation by Cussans of an inquisition taken at Cheshunt in May, 1280, includes the following:

Tilled land within the old park, £2; pasturage in Brantyngeshay, Saryngesmoer and the Marsh, £4 1s 8d;

wood in Cattehall, £1; pannage in the old park, 13s 4d; wood in the old park 13s 4d.[16]

The name suggests that by 1280 there was a 'new' park in Cheshunt in addition to the 'old' one and this is confirmed in account rolls of 1295/6, which refer to the 'park of Brantingshye' as well as to the old park (see p. 78).[17]

Successive dukes of Brittany continued to hold the manor of Cheshunt and also a part of Hoddesdon which was described as an outlier of Cheshunt in Domesday Book. This outlier became the manor of Hoddesdonbury, which was held by the de Bassingbourn family from the late twelfth/early thirteenth century. A document of 1323 recorded that the hedges around the old park in Cheshunt were maintained by customary service, 11 perches (c.55m) of which were the responsibility of the de Bassingbourn family in return for their right to hold the manor of Hoddesdonbury.[18] These customary services were also referred to in manorial accounts from the fifteenth and early sixteenth centuries. Although by 1435 they had evidently lapsed and been replaced by paid labour, these labour services still appeared as an item in the accounts: free tenants had been responsible for maintaining 80 perches (c.400m) of hedge around the old park each year (worth 6s 8d) and customary tenants had maintained 100 perches (c.500m) worth 8s 4d.[19]

In 1339 John, Duke of Brittany and Earl of Richmond, complained that the abbot of Waltham, together with a fellow-canon and several others, 'broke his park at Cheshunt, hunted therein and carried away deer'.[20] Another park break was recorded in 1379, when a subsequent duke of Brittany (John IV) complained that five named men, plus others, had 'hindered his stewards and other ministers from holding their courts at Chesthunt, co. Hertford, broken his park there, hunted therein, taken deer, besides trees and underwood, depastured his corn and grass and assaulted his men'.[21] In neither of these two cases of park breaking is the name of the park specified.

During the last quarter of the fourteenth century there is circumstantial evidence of a substantial manor house at Cheshunt. John IV of Brittany was married to Joan Holland, half-sister of Richard II, and had his main residence at Castle Rising in Norfolk from 1378, although household accounts record that the duke spent the summer of 1378 at Cheshunt.[22] The manor house is thought to have occupied the moated site 300m WNW of the parish church, but it seems to have fallen out of use by the middle of the sixteenth century.[23] In 1383 the duchess appointed Edmund Stokes, esquire, as 'keeper of the parks, woods and warrens of her lordship of Chesthunte, co. Hertford, receiving 6d daily, besides fees'.[24] In 1400 Edmund Stokes vacated 'the office of parker of Chesthunt, worth 12 pounds yearly'.[25]

In 1412 John Norbury esquire was granted the manor of Cheshunt, together with the advowson of the church, knights' fees, parks, warrens, franchises, liberties and other commodities.[26] Norbury died two years later but the manor continued to be held by his widow, Elizabeth (who became Lady Say) until her death in the 1460s. An account compiled in 1435/6 provides some information about the two parks at that time.[27] The account recorded that rent was no longer due on 26 acres of land which had been enclosed to enlarge the old park – but how long ago this had occurred was not stated. Ten

Map 13 The old park, Cheshunt
OS 6 inches to the mile map sheet XLI, surveyed 1873, published 1882. Annotated with field names from a plan of the liberty, manor and parish of Cheshunt, 1785 (HALS DE/Cr/125/2).

shillings was spent on enclosing 60 perches (*c.*300m) of hedge (*haye*) in the old park at 2d per perch. The scribe had initially written *circa* but crossed this out and instead wrote 'in the old park'. This indicates that the old park was being divided up into enclosures or, perhaps, already was. Sale of pasture in the old park was worth 20 shillings, but no revenue was received because it was grazed by the lord's livestock. Nor was there any pannage of pigs in the park that year. One man was paid 16d for cutting eight cartloads of thorns (*spinarum*) in 'le holdpark' which were used to enclose the lord's land called 'lez mores'. Despite the fact that the old park was still being accounted for as a functioning park, the parker's wage recorded in these

accounts was paid to 'John More, parker of the park of Brantynggesey', with no mention of the old park. This probably indicates that the old park was no longer a deer park.

In 1519–21 and 1526–8 the manor was in the hands of Henry VIII. The pasture in the old park was leased for 26s 8d, there was no pannage of pigs and the rabbit warren had ceased to function.[28]

The old park appears to have been located south-west of Bury Green on a spur of ground rising to a ridge over 75m OD about a mile (1.5km) south-west of the medieval parish church of Cheshunt and about quarter of a mile from the southern parish boundary. The park is remembered in the field name

'Old Park Grove' on a map of 1785.[29] The field lay on the east side of Oldpark Wood, which is shown on the first edition OS map along with Oldpark Plantation and Oldpark Farm. These 'old park' names could be interpreted as referring to the early seventeenth-century Theobalds Park but, as we have seen, documentary references to the old park go back to the thirteenth century. As late as the mid sixteenth century the locations of various pieces of land in the parish were being described in relation to the old park: for example, one 5½-acre piece of land was described as 'lying in Brodeffeld on the North part of th'old park'.[30] Broadfield was a common field, its location still indicated on modern OS maps by Broadfield Farm, just to the west of Bury Green (see Map 13). However, no park was shown in the vicinity on the county maps by either Saxton (1577) or Norden (1598).

There is no record of the size of the park in medieval times, but a survey in 1619 recorded that 'The olde Parke in ye tenure of Sir Richard Lucie' covered an area of over 228 acres and comprised a grove of underwood covering 92½ acres, 10¾ acres of 'Good Meadowe called ye Lawns', 30 acres of 'Base or Upland Meadowe', 90½ acres of 'Pasture ye most of it rowghe & bushye' and 2¾ acres of 'flaggie low grownde'. These details were recorded by John Norden as part of a survey he undertook of 'the landes intended by his Majestie to be added to Theobaldes Parke'.[31] A map by Thorpe showing the boundaries of Theobalds park in 1611 demonstrates that the northern boundary at that time ran south of the probable site of the old park.[32] However, subsequent to Norden's survey, the old park did become incorporated into James I's huge, but short-lived, park at Theobalds.[33]

When the royal park was dismantled by parliament in the mid seventeenth century the earlier pattern of landholdings seems not to have survived. A regular pattern of straight-sided fields was established by 1785 and it is difficult now to discern the layout of the enclosures recorded in 1619, or to be confident about the boundaries of the medieval park. The 1785 map does show three long sinuous boundaries which are likely to be relics of an earlier landscape: all run roughly north–south between the long east–west line of the northern boundary of King James' Theobalds Park and 'Old Park Ride' (see Map 13). The medieval park itself appears to have disrupted another long east–west line in the landscape (a characteristic feature of this area of the county), from which Old Park Ride is a diversion around its south side.

The proposed boundaries of the former park are based on a long, sinuous field boundary on the western side which still survives today, and on two watercourses: the Theobalds Brook on the north and another stream on the south, which meet beyond the lane bounding what may be the eastern limit of the park. This encloses an area of 258 acres (30 acres more than the 228 acres recorded in 1619). Moving the proposed southern boundary of the park northwards by one field to the long east–west hedgeline would remove 40 acres from the total. Alternatively, the north-west corner of the former park may have been less extensive than the boundary proposed here. The only significant bank visible from the public footpath survives in vestigial form along the northern half of the east side of Oldpark Wood and is topped by ancient stools of coppiced hornbeam.

Parks belonging to the manor of Periers

NGR: not known
Date range: by 1335 – not known
Size: recorded as 40 acres in 1335
Underlying geology: not known

TWO PARKS BELONGING TO THE MANOR of Periers were recorded only once, in 1335, at the inquisition held on the death of Richard de Periers. He left his Cheshunt lands, including two parks containing 40 acres, held of John Duke of Brittany and Earl of Richmond, to his eldest son, also Richard.[34] The 40 acres was presumably the combined area of the two parks. No subsequent records of the manor contain any references to parks, including a terrier and rental of c.1440 and accounts of 1468/9.[35] At the end of the fifteenth century the manor was leased with its lands, meadows, feedings and pasture for £8 8s per annum.[36]

In 1607 James I acquired the manor of Periers, which included 60 acres of pasture and wood and 129 acres of arable land. The moated site of the Periers manor house and its surrounding fields were subsequently incorporated within Cheshunt park, but there were other lands belonging to the manor in other parts of Cheshunt and Wormley.[37] For example, accounts for 1490/1 included a reference to a 'tenement of the lord in West Wormley called Peryers'.[38] It is now almost impossible to trace some of these parcels of land and no evidence has been found to indicate the locations of the two small parks recorded in the fourteenth century.

1. HALS DP/29/27A/1/11 abstracts of title to Cheshunt Park and Theobalds, 1280, 1485, 1538–1689.

2. Derived from Latin *haia*; Old English *haga*. See D. Hooke, 'Pre-Conquest woodland: its distribution and usage', *Agricultural History Review*, 37, 2 (1989), pp. 113–29; Liddiard, 'Deer parks of Domesday Book', pp. 4–23.

3. TNA: PRO SC6/1116/9 ministers' and receivers' account for Cheshunt, 1295/6.

4. King's College, Cambridge KCAR/6/2/034 Cheshunt manorial accounts, 1435/6.

5. *Cal. Pat. 1476–1485*, p. 68.

6. HALS DP/29/27A/1/11 abstracts of title to Cheshunt Park and Theobalds, 1280, 1485, 1538–1689.

7. TNA: PRO SC6/HENVIII/6757 and 6764, reeves' accounts for 1519–21 and 1526–28.

8. HALS DP/29/27A/1/11 abstracts of title to Cheshunt Park and Theobalds, 1280, 1485, 1538–1689.

9. *Ibid.*

10. Page, *Hertford*, 3, p. 447 quoting Common Pleas Deed Enrolled Trinity Term 12 Eliz (TNA: PRO CP40/1285).

11. HHA CP349 survey of the Hertfordshire estates of Sir Robert Cecil by Israel Amyce, 1600/01.

12. TNA: PRO E178/3900 petition of the inhabitants of Cheshunt as to the assessment of subsidies, and inquisition as to lands taken into Theobalds Park, 1608/9 and 1625/6.

13. HALS DP/29/27A/1/11 abstracts of title to Cheshunt Park and Theobalds, 1280, 1485, 1538–1689; P.C. Archer, *Historic Cheshunt* (Cheshunt, 1923), pp. 138–9 citing Parliamentary Surveys Hertfordshire No. 16 (TNA: PRO E317/Herts/16).

14. HALS DE/Cr/125/2 plan of the liberty, manor and parish of Cheshunt, 1785.

15. *Curia Regis Rolls*, p. 486.

16. Cussans, *History of Hertfordshire*, 2, p. 208. HALS DP/29/27A/1/11 abstracts of title to Cheshunt Park and Theobalds, 1280, 1485, 1538–1689.

17. TNA: PRO SC6/1116/9 ministers' and receivers' account for Cheshunt, 1295/6.

18. *Cal. Inq. post mortem, vol. 6, Edward II*, no. 400, p. 236.

19. King's College, Cambridge KCAR/6/2/034 Cheshunt manorial accounts, 1435/6; TNA: PRO SC6/HENVIII/6757 and 6764 reeves' accounts, 1519–21 and 1526–8.

20. *Cal. Pat. 1338–1340*, p. 285.

21. *Cal. Pat. 1377–1381*, p. 362.

22. Archives Departementales, Loire-Atlantique, Nantes, E206/2 counter-roll of the Duke's household, 1386. I am grateful to Christopher Woolgar for this information.

23. Page, *Hertford*, 3, p. 447.

24. *Cal. Pat. 1381–1385*, p. 308–9.

25. *Cal. Pat. 1399–1401*, p. 386–7.

26. *Cal. Pat. 1408–1413*, p. 404. John Norbury was already in possession of a very large new park at Bedwell for which he had obtained a licence in 1406.

27. King's College, Cambridge KCAR/6/2/034 Cheshunt manorial accounts, 1435/6.

28. TNA: PRO SC6/HENVIII/6757 and 6764 reeves' accounts, 1519–21 and 1526–8. Whether or not the warren was located in the old park is not known; no income was recorded from it in 1435/6 either.

29. HALS DE/Cr/125/2 plan of the liberty, manor and parish of Cheshunt, 1785.

30. HALS DE/Ln/E3 sixteenth-century survey of lands in Cheshunt.

31. HALS 12133 survey by John Norden, 1619.

32. BM Cotton MS, Augustus I, 1/75 Thorpe's map of Cheshunt, 1611.

33. M. Phillips, 'Theobalds Park wall', *East Herts Archaeological Society Transactions*, 5 (1914), pp. 248–62.

34. *Cal. Inq. post mortem, vol. 7, Edward III*, p. 453.

35. HHA court rolls 22/20 terrier and rental of manors of Geddings, Baas, Periers, Hoddesdon, etc., c.1440; court rolls 10/9 accounts of the receiver of Sir John Say for the manors of Baas, Perrers, Geddyngs, Langton, Foxtons, Maryons and Hawes, etc., 1468/9.

36. HHA court rolls 10/16 bailiff's account for Sir William Say, 1484/5; 10/20 bailiff's account for Sir William Say, 1493/4.

37. HHA CP349 survey of the Hertfordshire estates of Sir Robert Cecil by Israel Amyce, 1600/01.

38. HHA court rolls 10/19 bailiff's account, 1490/1.

Clothall (see also *Broadfield*)

Clothall park

NGR: possibly *c.*TL291312
Date range: by mid thirteenth century – not known
Size: not known
Underlying geology: not known but probably boulder clay

THERE IS AN OBLIQUE REFERENCE to a medieval park at Clothall in the Victoria County History, which states that 'there is reason to suppose that Kingswood was identical with the wood called "Socage" in Clothall Park, for which Simon de Clothall owed two pounds of pepper to Adam de Hippegrave'.[1] Simon de Clothall was lord of the manor of Clothall in the mid thirteenth century and died before 1248. A transcript of an early charter states that Adam de Hippegrave was given the 'wood called socage which is within the park of Clohale' by Nicholas de Everesden 'in Kingswood'.[2] The fact that Simon had to pay rent for the wood in the park indicates that it was not part of the demesne of the manor of Clothall and was apparently on land which later became the manor of Kingswood Bury in the parish of Clothall. On Simon's death, the manor was divided among his three daughters and there is no further reference to the park.

The site of the manor of Kingswood Bury survives today to the south-east of Clothallbury (see Map 14) and Kingswood was probably an area of woodland in the south-east of the parish. Significant earth banks, which are very suggestive of a medieval park boundary, survive around the north and east sides of Munches Wood adjoining the eastern parish boundary and also along the southern side of Baskets Wood, to the west. Whether any of these relate to the Clothall park described here or to the Broadfield park linked to Cumberlow Green in the parish of Clothall (see p. 74) – or indeed whether they were the same park – is open to debate. The OS map does show some old field boundaries adjacent to Kingswood Bury which could indicate a former park (shaded on Map 14) but without further evidence it is not possible to offer this site as any more than a possibility.

1. Page, *Hertford*, 3, p. 224, citing Exchequer Transcript of Charter xv, m. 1 d (TNA: PRO E132/2/15).
2. HALS DE/X951/33/11 VCH compiler's notes, *c.*1910.

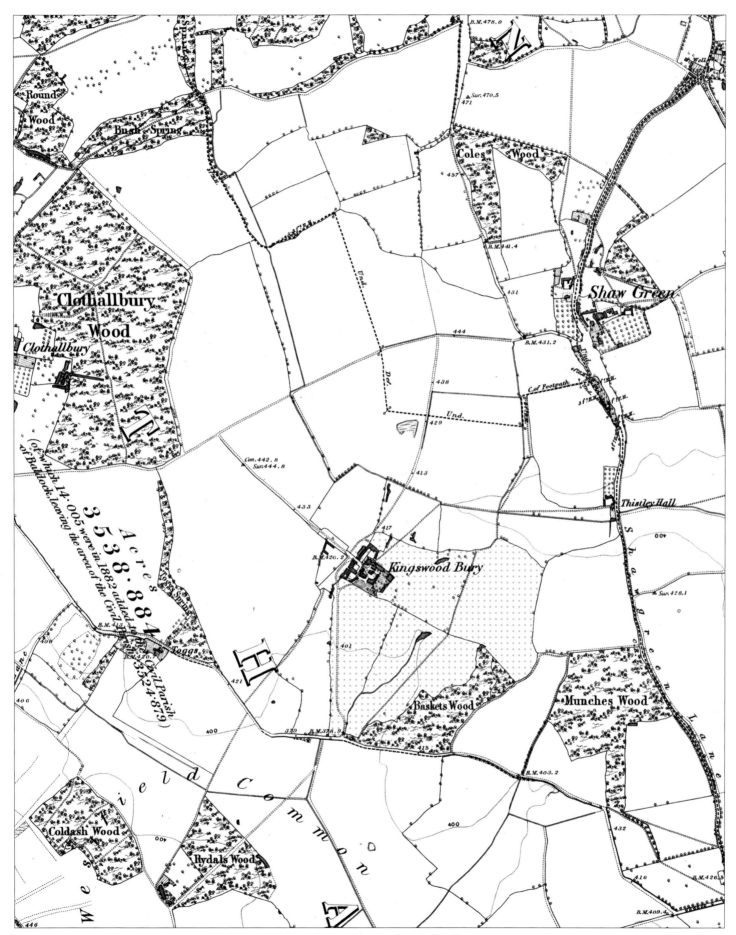

Map 14 A possible site of Clothall park
OS 6 inches to the mile map sheet VIII, surveyed 1877, published 1883.

Eastwick

No known name

NGR: ?TL433150
Date range: by end of thirteenth century – not known
Size: not known but at least 25 acres
Underlying geology: boulder clay

NO DEFINITE RECORD OF A PARK has been found in Eastwick but the accumulated weight of several pieces of circumstantial evidence suggests that there was a park in the parish by the end of the thirteenth century. The de Tany family had held the manor since the twelfth century and in 1253 Henry III granted free warren to Richard de Tany.[1] In 1296/7 a William le Parker 'of Estwyk' was amongst those taking the oath at the Inquisition *post mortem* of John Engayne of Hunsdon and it was probably the same William le Parker who was recorded in the lay subsidy return for Eastwick in 1307.[2] In 1317 one-third of the manor of Estwyke and its gardens were assigned as dower to Margaret, the widow of Laurence de Tany. She was also assigned '25 acres of wood in the wood called 'le Perk', whereof one end abuts upon the way to the wood that belonged to W... le Parker on the south, and the other end abuts upon the field called 'Wydefordeleye' on the north, and one side near the lord's wood on the west'.[3]

Margaret de Tany's 25 acres of wood seem most likely to have been at the northern end of the parish of Eastwick, bordering the parish of Widford and probably, therefore, a field called 'Wydefordeleye'. At *c.*80m OD this was the highest part of this long and narrow parish and also the most wooded part in the early nineteenth century and, quite probably, in earlier centuries. Twenty-five acres fits well into the area of land between the parish boundary and Cockrobin Lane and leaves an area on its western side for 'the lord's wood' – perhaps the enclosure named 'Eastwick Field' in 1845.[4] However, the wording of the 1317 document suggests that Margaret's 25 acres of wood were just part of a larger wood called 'le Perk'. This larger wood (and therefore the possible park) may have extended into one or more of the neighbouring parishes of Hunsdon, Widford and Sawbridgeworth. A very tentative location for Margaret de Tany's wood is indicated on Map 15, in an area where several 'lawn' names were recorded on the Eastwick tithe map and award of 1839 and 1845 (see below).[5]

In 1447 the manor of Eastwick was sold to Sir William Oldhall who, at about the same time, also purchased the neighbouring manor of Hunsdon. For the next two centuries the manors descended together.[6] Hunsdon was the larger and more important of the two, and its expanding parklands probably extended into the parish of Eastwick during the fifteenth and sixteenth centuries (see p. 136). More Eastwick lands, called the Spring, were enclosed into Hunsdon Park in the early seventeenth century and it is possible that the northern end of the parish was also included because land called 'Eastwick Lawn' was reported to have been part of Hunsdon Park in 1684.[7]

On the modern OS map the surviving wood at the north end of the parish of Eastwick is called Lawns Wood. In 1845 it was divided into rectangular enclosures called Lawn Wood, Lawn Field and Lawn Plantation, with the parish boundary along the northern border. Bordering these enclosures to the south was land called 'Newlands', part wood and part arable, with Cockrobin Lane forming its southern boundary. A moat, possibly the remains of the residence of William le Parker, survives on the north side of Cockrobin Lane.

The 'lawn' names at the north end of the parish may well relate to the early seventeenth-century expansion of Hunsdon Park but there could also have been a medieval park in the same location. However, there appears to be little in the way of surviving field evidence. The northern boundary of the wood today (December 2004) is marked by a ditch which ends where the north–south Hunsdon/Eastwick parish boundary meets the west–east boundary with Widford. There is no earthwork along the Hunsdon/Eastwick parish boundary but there is a north–south bank and ditch within the wood at TL4346715039 which marks one of the rectangular enclosures recorded on the tithe map. The bank is about 4m across from the middle of the ditch, which lies on the east side of the bank. Cockrobin Lane survives as a public bridleway, bounded only by ditches as it passes between Lawns Wood to the north and Queen's Wood to the south. Curiously, as the lane continues eastwards in the parish of Sawbridgeworth, it is bounded by a degraded large bank marking the northern end of Battles Wood.

1. Page, *Hertford*, 3, p. 317, citing *Cal. Chart. 1226–1257*, p. 429.

2. Cussans, *History of Hertfordshire*, 1, Braughing Hundred, pp. 42–3, citing Inquisition *post mortem* 25 Ed. I, No. 46 (TNA: PRO C133/80/2); Brooker and Flood, *Hertfordshire lay subsidy rolls*, p. 20.

3. Gover *et al.*, *Place-names of Hertfordshire*, p. 302, citing *Cal. Close 1313–1318*, p. 573. The EPNS volume suggested a link between the fourteenth-century 'le Perk' and a later 'Park Field', but this seems unlikely as Little, Lower and Great Park Field in 1845 were all adjacent to Hunsdon park in the neighbouring parish: this is the likeliest explanation for their park names.

4. HALS DSA4/36/1 and 2 Eastwick tithe award (1845) and map (1839).

5. *Ibid.*

6. Page, *Hertford*, 3, p. 318 citing Feet of Fines Herts, Mich. 26 Hen. VI, no. 139 (TNA: PRO CP25/1/91/115); Close Roll, 37 Hen. VI, m. 9 (TNA: PRO C54/309).

7. Page, *Hertford*, 3, p. 329. 'Spring' indicates coppiced woodland. These fields in Eastwick were still named Hither and Further springs in 1845 (HALS DSA4/36/1 and 2 Eastwick tithe award (1845) and map (1839)); Page, *Hertford*, 3, p. 329, citing Exchequer Depositions Mixed County Mich. 36 Chas. II, no. 22 (TNA).

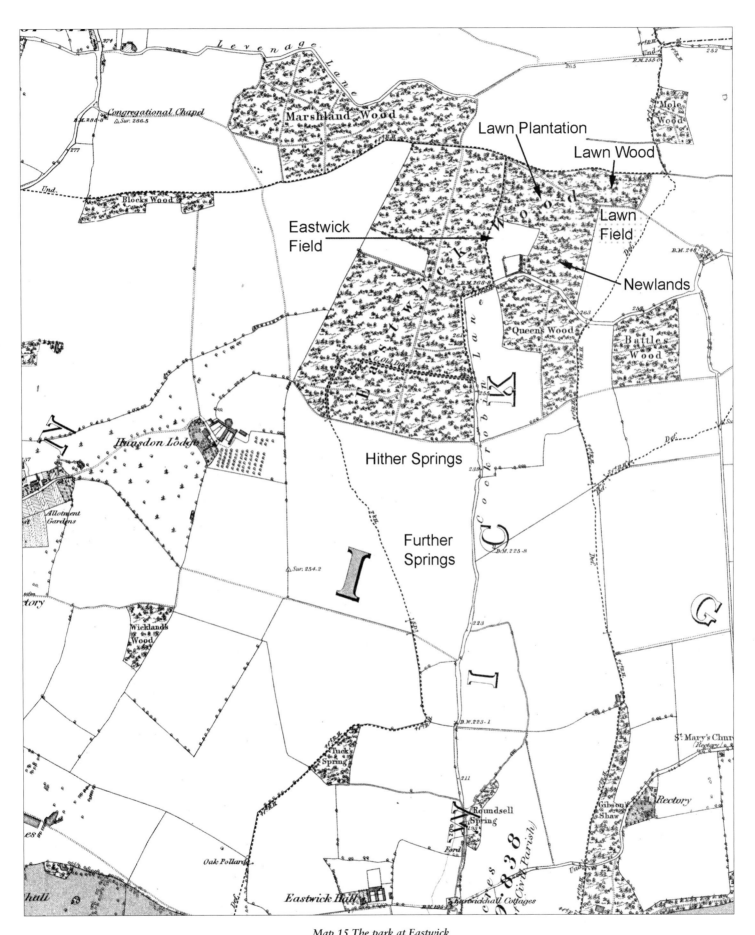

Lawn Plantation

Lawn Wood

Lawn Field

Eastwick Field

Newlands

Map 15 The park at Eastwick
OS 6 inches to the mile map sheet XXX, surveyed 1873–80, published 1881–3. Annotated with field names derived from the Eastwick tithe award and map,
1845 and 1839 (HALS DSA4/36/1 and 2).

Elstree

Boreham (Wood) or Elstree park

NGR: not known
Date range: c.1275 – perhaps late fifteenth century
Size: not known
Underlying geology: London Clay

DESPITE SEVERAL MEDIEVAL REFERENCES, the park in Boreham Wood has remained elusive. According to the Victoria County History the parish of Elstree was granted to the monastery of St Albans in 1188 and the abbey was given the wood of Boreham 'for the feeding of the swine'.[1] In 'about 1275 the abbot appropriated for his own use a park in Boreham Wood and laid claim to free warren there, but by what right was not known'.[2]

In the early fourteenth century, Abbot Richard de Wallingford of St Albans (1327–36) found that certain tenants were bound to find horses for his journey whenever he should visit the Cell of St Mary at Tynemouth, Northumberland. One of those tenants, 'John de London, *in the Park of Idelstre*' (Elstree) was bound to provide one horse.[3] In 1356 the abbot of St Albans complained that several men had broken into his 'park at Borham', 'hunted therein, felled his trees there and carried away those trees as well as deer from the park'.[4]

Over a century later, in 1462, a charter of Edward IV reaffirmed that the wood of Borham, with its park, was confirmed to St Albans Abbey by Henry I and subsequently by Richard I.[5] However, no park was mentioned at Boreham in abbey rentals dated 1504 and 1506, nor in 1541, when Elstree manor and Boreham wood were granted to Sir Anthony Denny after the Dissolution.[6]

An extensive area of woodland survived into the early eighteenth century and is clearly recorded on the county maps by Seller (1676), Oliver (1695) and Morden (1722) (Figure 21). In 1776 a bill for the enclosure of 684 acres of the 'large open common' called Boreham Wood Common was put before parliament, and the common was subsequently enclosed.[7] Dury and Andrews' county map is the only known pre-enclosure map produced at a reasonably large scale (1.95 inches to the mile) but it provides no clues to the site of the medieval park.[8] A lease of 1785 of 'The Manor House' (possibly a spurious name) describes its situation on the north side of Boreham Wood Common and a plan of 1815 shows its modest 'estate' – a rectangular area north of the house.[9] Was the abbot's park created in the demesne land north of the common, or did he appropriate part (or all) of the 684-acre common as his park?

The former common and the manorial estate have been urbanised since the late nineteenth century and, with no record of its size and lacking early maps and field names, it will probably not be possible to locate the medieval park. Curiously, Bryant, on his county map of 1822, marks a house as 'Boreham Park'.[10] This had apparently become Rectory Farm (alias Whitehouse Farm) by 1870. The approximately 200 acres of the farm were enclosed from the common in 1776 and given to the Rectory in lieu of tithe 'so that the whole parish is tithe-free'.[11]

1. Page, *Hertford*, 2, p. 349, citing Matthew Paris, *Chronica Majora* (Rolls Series) vi, 46.

2. *Ibid.*, p. 350, citing *Hundred Rolls* (Records Commission), I, 188 seq.; Assize Roll, 325 (TNA: PRO JUST 1/325); Riley, H.T. (ed.), *Gesta abbatum monasterii Sancti Albani a Thoma Walsingham, vol. 3, AD 1349–1411* (London, 1869; republished Germany, 1965), p. 433.

3. S. Castle and W. Brooks, *The book of Elstree and Boreham Wood* (Buckingham, 1988), p. 23.

4. *Cal. Pat. 1354–1358*, p. 493.

5. Castle and Brooks, *Elstree and Boreham Wood*, p. 25.

6. HALS DE/B2067B/M17–M18 rentals of manor of Boreham 1504–6; Castle and Brooks, *Elstree and Boreham Wood*, p. 25.

7. HALS 5888 bill for 'Inclosing ... Boreham Wood Common, 1776; QS/E/24 enclosure award for Boreham Wood Common, 1776 (no map accompanies the award).

8. A. Dury and J. Andrews, *A topographical map of Hartfordshire* (Hertfordshire Record Society, 2004).

9. HALS 5897 lease, 1785; DE/B818/T2 plans of Barhamwood Lodge estate, 1815.

10. A. Bryant, *The county of Hertford* (London, 1822).

11. HALS DP/36/3/1 plan of 'Rectory Farm at Barham Wood', 1870.

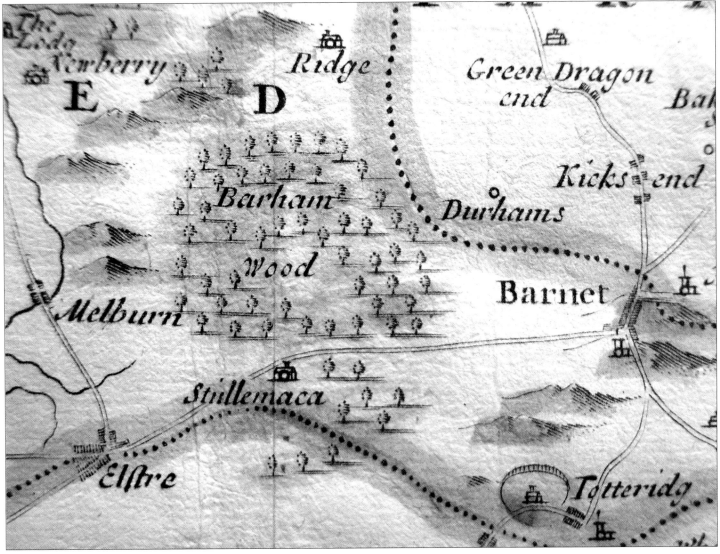

Figure 21. *Detail of Morden's county map, 1722, showing 'Barham Wood' in the early eighteenth century.*

Essendon and Little Berkhamsted

Bedwell park

NGR: TL283075
Date range: 1406 – early seventeenth century
Size: licence to impark 800 acres in 1406
Underlying geology: London Clay partially overlain by Pebble Gravel or boulder clay

THIS WAS A VERY LARGE PARK created at the beginning of the fifteenth century by John Norbury, a man who had progressed from a successful military career to a role at the heart of national political affairs. The park straddled the boundary between the parishes of Essendon and Little Berkhamsted, which follows, for much of its length, a small tributary of the river Lea. On either side of the valley the land rises quite steeply to *c.*110m OD in the west (from where there are very extensive views to the north and north-east) and *c.*120m OD in the south-east.

Norbury came from a Cheshire gentry family and had a successful and very lucrative military career in the Hundred Years War. In 1388 he purchased the manor of Bedwell and by 1402 he had also acquired the neighbouring manor of Little Berkhamsted.[1] He became a major landowner in southern Hertfordshire and was elected to parliament in 1391,[2] rising to become a prominent Lancastrian civil servant. As a permanent member of the royal council, he was at the centre of political affairs and close to Henry IV, which must have been a great advantage when he decided to enclose nearly 20 per cent of the parish of Essendon and a similar proportion of Little Berkhamsted into a park.[3] The licence he obtained in 1406 granted him permission to 'enclose 800 acres of his land belonging to his manors of Bedewell and Little Berkhamstede, with palings, a wall, hedge or ditch, and make a park of the same, and stock the same with deer and other beasts …'.[4] It seems likely that much of the land enclosed into the park was open heath and woodland, as the soils were largely infertile. Nevertheless, the loss of so much land must have had a considerable impact on the local economy and populace.

John Norbury was described as being 'of Hoddesdon and Little Berkhamsted' which suggests that he had a house in Little Berkhamsted (as well as Hoddesdon), perhaps in the park, but evidence is lacking.[5] He died before 1433 and Bedwell was held by his widow, Elizabeth Lady Say, until she died in 1464. The following year, her grandson, John Norbury, conveyed the manor to Sir John Say and when the latter died in 1478 the estate passed to his son, William Say.[6] William Node, who had been appointed custodian of the park in the time of Sir John Say, continued as parker for at least the next 20 years. His wage was 2d a day, amounting to 60s 10d a year. A series of accounts from 1484, compiled by William Say's bailiff, provide some information about the park, which was evidently maintained as a deer park because the meadows and pastures it contained were 'reserved for the deer'.[7] None of the accounts records any revenue from agistment or from pannage of pigs, although Say's own oxen were recorded grazing the park in 1484/5. The account for that year contains the only record of any revenue arising from the park: charcoal, made from trees felled to repair the park pale, was sold for 17s 1½d. Repairs carried out on defective stretches of the park pale in 1484/5 included plashing. In addition to the park, there was also an important warren which, unlike the park, did produce significant revenue for Sir William in the 1490s: it was leased to Thomas Nurse for £6 13s 4d per annum.[8]

Some of the land enclosed into the park had previously been leased to tenants, including one tenement called Quenelles, the rent for which was entered in the accounts as a 'cancelled charge' (*alloc' redditus*) of 6s 4d. From 1493/4 the accounts record a longer list of 'cancelled charges', suggesting that Sir William Say expanded the park around 1492. The newly enclosed lands included a tenement with land called Coupers (worth 4 shillings p.a.) and another parcel of land also called Coupers (4 shillings) which was 'enclosed in the coppice (*copic*) of the park of Bedwell'.

In 1522 Mary Tudor is said to have stayed at Bedwell, which suggests that there was a prestigious residence there even though Sir William's principal house was Baas manor in Broxbourne.[9] Sir William Say died in 1529 and ten years later the manor passed to the crown.[10] Stewardship of the manor and keepership of Bedwell park, of the hunt of deer and of the 'King's mansion of Bedwell with a little garden thereto annexed or adjoining' were granted to Sir Anthony Denny, 'a gentleman of the King's Privy Chamber'.[11] In 1543 the king's park at Waltham was supplied with deer from Bedwell park, and among the privileges granted with the manor of Bedwell were the herbage and pannage of the park and free warren, both within the park and without, in the parishes of Essendon and Little Berkhampstead.[12]

A series of county maps from Saxton (1577) onwards showed the park pales lying well south of the river Lea (Figure 26). Norden (1598) showed the pale extending south to the boundary of Hatfield Wood and this is confirmed by an early seventeenth-century estate map at Hatfield House which shows the pale of Bedwell park bordering the east side of Cucumber Lane and then Hornbeam Lane until it meets the pale of Hatfield Wood.[13] Seller's map (1676) shows the park with an irregular hourglass shape, again with the long axis aligned north–south.

The documentary evidence, however, indicates that the park was broken up in the early seventeenth century with the sale of about 275 acres of the southern end of the park in 1614. This land was divided into seven named closes in Essendon and Berkhamsted, including New lawnefield, Newlodge burrowfield and Posterne Lawne field, which

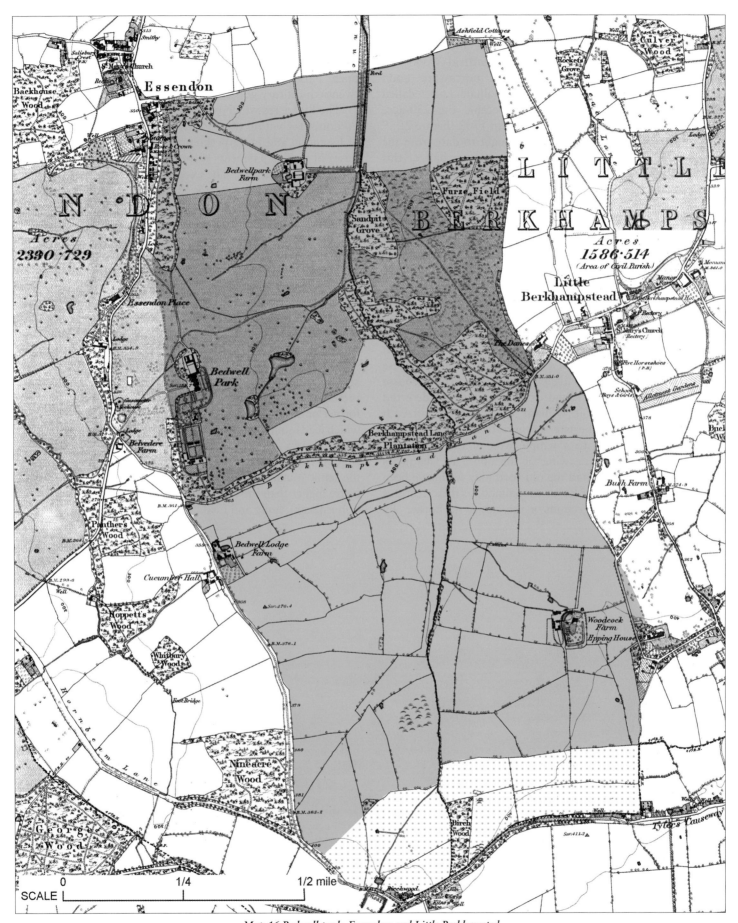

Map 16 Bedwell park, Essendon and Little Berkhamsted
OS 6 inches to the mile map sheet XXXVI (reproduced at a reduced scale), surveyed 1873–80, published 1883.

were 'inclosed with a pale towards the east, south and west and were/are parcel of Bedwell Park and abut eastwards upon Epping Greene, southward upon Hatfield Wood and westward upon Hornebeame lane and northward upon other landes and grounds of the said William Potter called Bedwell Park'.[14] Most of this land became the 230-acre Bedwell Lodge Farm, which was leased in 1702 (Figure 22).[15] Parts of the present farmhouse are thought to date from the early to mid seventeenth century.[16] The eastern half of this south end of the former park had become the estate of Woodcocks Lodge by 1766.[17]

A new house was built about 1630 to stand in the remaining 200-acre Bedwell Park.[18] This seems to have developed into Bedwell Park Farm by 1661 with the addition of further lands. By the early eighteenth century the park was clearly shown as a much smaller rectangular area with the longer axis aligned east–west and extending south from Bedwell Park Farm only as far as Berkhamsted Lane.[19] The mid eighteenth-century park was depicted on a detailed plan of 1765 which showed a much reduced area of parkland, but one embellished with ornamental groves and avenues of trees.[20] The map also showed a drive approaching the house from the north and it seems likely that this followed the course of a previously public road which had been diverted westwards, perhaps by Sir William Say in the late fifteenth century or perhaps in the late seventeenth century. A newly planted avenue leading to a temple west of the house was shown on Drapentier's drawing of the house in Chauncy's county history of 1700, and the old road may well have been rerouted westwards in order to accommodate these features and the new ornamental grounds on this side of the house.[21] By

the early nineteenth century the area of parkland had expanded again to cover the grey-shaded area on the first edition OS map of 1883 (see Map 16).[22] Much remains as open parkland today, although sadly disfigured by late twentieth-century golf course tree planting.

The 800 acres which were licensed to be imparked in 1406 no doubt lay within the 984 acres of land within the parishes of Essendon and Little Berkhamsted which were covered by a series of modus payments recorded in the tithe awards of the two parishes in 1838.[23] The excess of approximately 180 acres was probably at least partly the result of Sir William Say's expansion of the park in 1492 and may include the 94 acres of enclosures (mostly warrens) lying to the north of the proposed original park boundary. A further 30 acres may be accounted for to the west of Bedwell Park mansion, lying between the route of the original road and the new road to the west. The southern boundary of the original 800-acre park is debatable: the boundary proposed on Map 16 was chosen because it brought the total park acreage closest to 800 acres (802 acres), but the park may well have extended all the way to the road called Tyler's Causeway.

Traces of the western park boundary bank can still be seen along the east side of Cucumber Lane today. A much better-preserved length of bank survives along the east side of the former park north of Woodcock Farm and beside the footpath which leads south from Berkhamsted Lane as far as the junction with the track heading north-east at TL293071. This earthwork is about 7m across and incorporates a ditch on the east side of the bank (outside the park). The top of the bank is about a metre higher than the centre of the ditch and old coppice stools of hornbeam, holly and field maple still grow along the bank.

Figure 22. View across the former Bedwell park from the eastern boundary looking south-west towards Bedwell Lodge Farm.

1. Page, *Hertford*, 3, pp. 460, citing Ancient Deeds D448 and B408 (TNA: PRO E210/448 and E326/408).

2. Morgan, 'Norbury, John'.

3. *Ibid*. Norbury witnessed the king's will in 1409 and his eldest son, Henry, was the king's godson.

4. *Cal. Chart. 1341–1417*, p. 430.

5. Roskell *et al.*, *The history of parliament*, p. 843.

6. Page, *Hertford*, 3, p. 460. According to a rental of 1468 for Sir John Say, he enclosed land belonging to the manor of Ponsbourne into Bedwell Park, granting in exchange land called 'Pountesbornesmede' with a rental value of 13s 4d (TNA: PRO SC 11/269)

7. HHA court rolls 10/16 bailiff's account, 1484/5; 10/19 bailiff's account, 1490/1; 10/20 bailiff's account, 1493/4; 10/21 bailiff's account, 1495/6; 10/23 bailiff's account, 1498/9.

8. In 1484/5 John White was granted a three-year lease of the warren for 66s 8d p.a.

9. Page, *Hertford*, 3, p. 460, citing Letters & Papers Hen. VIII, III (2), 3375 (p. 1409) (TNA).

10. *Ibid*., p. 460, citing Chancery Inquisition *post mortem* (Ser. 2), clxxvii, 82 (TNA); Letters & Papers Hen. VIII, xiv (2), g. 780 (27) (TNA).

11. *Ibid*., citing Letters & Papers Hen. VIII, xiv (2), g. 780 (27) (TNA).

12. Page, *Hertford*, 3, p. 461, citing Letters & Papers Hen. VIII, xviii (1), 436 and xiv (2), g. 780 (27) (TNA).

13. HHA CPM Supp. 21 plan of Hatfield estate, *c*.1610; copy at HALS DE/X2/12.

14. HALS 44110 bargain and sale, 1614.

15. HALS F212 lease of Bedwell Lodge Farm, 1702.

16. HALS F409 bargain and sale of Bedwell Park, 1648; DoE List of buildings of special architectural or historic interest.

17. Dury and Andrews, *Hartfordshire*, 1766.

18. HALS 44116 bargain and sale, 1631/2.

19. See the county map by Clark in the front of Salmon, *History of Hertfordshire*.

20. HALS 64333 plan of Bedwell Park, 1765.

21. Chauncy, *Historical antiquities*, pp. 272–3.

22. See also BL Ordnance Survey Drawing 149, 9 (Hatfield sheet), 1805 and Bryant, *Hertford*, 1822.

23. HALS DSA4/37/1 and 2 Essendon tithe award and map, 1838; DSA4/20/1 and 2 Little Berkhamsted tithe award and map, 1838.

Flamstead

No known name (site now in the civil parish of Markyate)
NGR: TL054161
Date range: not known
Size: perhaps *c.*69 acres
Underlying geology: clay-with-flints

THE ONLY KNOWN DOCUMENTARY REFERENCE to a park at Flamstead takes the form of a grant of the manor of Flamstead contained in the Calendar of Patent Rolls for 1397.[1] However, the wording of the grant seems formulaic, including as it does 'the chaces, parks, woods, warrens, [and] fisheries' along with many other rights and privileges appertaining to the manor, and does not constitute secure evidence that there actually was a medieval park at Flamstead. Nevertheless, a combination of good map and field evidence suggests that there was indeed a park. It could have been established by one of several different lords of the manor from the twelfth to the fourteenth centuries, but appears to have been disparked before the end of the fourteenth century.

After the Norman Conquest Flamstead was granted to Ralph de Tosny, a powerful landowner in Normandy who was standard bearer to Duke William at the Battle of Hastings. He was also granted Necton in Norfolk and a handful of other manors in Essex and Hertfordshire, but there is little evidence that he spent much time in England.[2] However, his descendents made Flamstead the capital of the Tosny barony in England and remained the lords of the manor there until the early fourteenth century.[3] The Domesday Book entry suggests that Flamstead was well wooded and therefore a good location for a park. On the death of the last Lord Tosny (or Tony) in 1310, the manor passed to his sister Alice, who subsequently married Guy de Beauchamp, Earl of Warwick, by whom she had a son and heir, Thomas. Guy died in 1315 and Alice then married, as her third husband, William de la Zouche of Mortimer. They appear to have lived at Flamstead because in 1332 William obtained a licence to have a chapel in his manor-house there.[4] The manor then passed into the hands of the Beauchamp and Neville earls of Warwick, but was probably an insignificant part of their vast estates. Accounts from the late fourteenth century make no reference to a park.[5] In 1397 Thomas, Earl of Warwick, forfeited his lands to the king and the manor of Flamstead was granted to the king's brother, the Earl of Rutland. This is the grant recorded in the Calendar of Patent Rolls and quoted above.[6] At the same time, the king granted to one of his yeomen of the chamber the office of warrener of Flamstead, but no parker was appointed.[7]

A bailiff's account from 1480/1 for the manor of Flamstead preserved in the National Archives recorded no evidence of a park. At that time the manor was held by the crown during the minority of the heir and 'the king's warren' at Flamstead, previously leased for 53s 4d p.a., was described as 'totally laid waste'.[8] For the 64 years after 1488 the manor was vested in the crown and bailiffs' accounts from the early sixteenth century show that the warren was not resurrected and there was no park.[9] In 1544 Henry VIII granted the manor to his courtier, Sir Richard Page, and Page may have been at Flamstead when he died in 1548.[10] In 1552 Edward VI granted the manor to George Ferrers, a courtier and poet, and a member of parliament during the 1540s and 50s. Ferrers served as a justice of the peace for Hertfordshire from 1547 to 1554 and died, intestate, at Flamstead in 1579.[11] The manor passed through several generations (more or less illustrious) of the Ferrers family before being sold. No documents have come to light recording a mid sixteenth-century park and no park was depicted on the county maps by either Saxton (1577) or Norden (1598).

However, the tithe map and award for Flamstead of 1838 reveal an interesting group of 'park' field names in an area between Markyatestreet and Roe End to the south-west, concentrated in and around a ridge of high ground surrounded by a sinuous oval boundary close to the parish (and county) boundary.[12] All of the land within the oval boundary, plus some bits outside, had belonged to the lord of the manor of Flamstead, although most of the other manorial lands were elsewhere in the parish. Each of these factors suggests the site of a typical medieval park. In addition, a piece of woodland within the enclosed area was called 'Park Spring' on the first edition OS map (see Map 17). The land was farmed as part of Feverells Farm in 1838 and those fields within the sinuous boundary (as well as some outside) were tithe-free and contained 43½ acres.[13]

Most of the boundary survives today and is followed around its southern half by a public footpath. A significant earth bank marks much of this southern boundary, particularly at its eastern end and there is an abundance of holly in the old hedgerow which grows on it. If the fields along the north and west sides of this 'core' area are included in the area of possible former parkland, the total area could have been 69 acres.

Although the documentary evidence for this park is very weak, the combined map and field evidence provide a strong case for the existence of a park in this location. As it does not appear on any known maps, it is most likely to have been medieval in origin, probably having been disparked by the end of the fourteenth century. If this is the case, then the park-related names have survived for over 600 years.

1. *Cal. Pat. 1396–1399*, p. 201. I am grateful to Twigs Way for this reference.
2. C.P. Lewis, 'Tosny, Ralph de (*d.* 1102?)', *Oxford dictionary of national biography* (Oxford, 2004), accessed online 4 August 2007.
3. Lewis, 'Tosny, Ralph de'; Page, *Hertford*, 2, p. 194.
4. Page, *Hertford*, 2, p. 194, citing Inquisition *post mortem* 9 Edw. II, No.

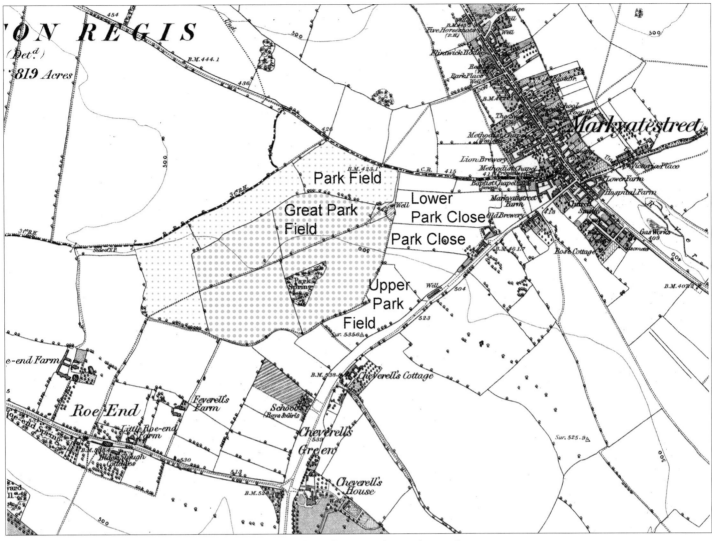

Map 17 The park near Markyate, Flamstead

OS 6 inches to the mile map sheet XXVI, surveyed 1877–8, published 1883–4. Annotated to show the field names recorded on the Flamstead tithe award and map, 1838 (HALS DSA4/38/1 and 2). The core of the possible park covers 43½ acres; it might also have included the fields to the north and west, giving a total of 69 acres.

71 (TNA: PRO C134/49/1) and Lincoln Episcopal Registers Burghersh, 7 Kal. Apr. 1332.

5. TNA: PRO SC6/1123/5 minister's accounts, 1395/6.

6. *Cal. Pat.* 1396–1399, p. 201.

7. *Ibid.*, p. 196.

8. TNA: PRO SC6/1123/6 bailiff's account, 1480/1.

9. TNA: PRO SC6/HENVII/1323 bailiff's account, 1505/6; SC6/HENVIII/6968 bailiff's account 1516/7; SC6/HENVIII/6989 bailiff's account, 1539/40.

10. C. Davies, 'Page, Sir Richard (*d.* 1548)', *Oxford dictionary of national biography* (Oxford, 2004), accessed online 5 August 2007.

11. H.R. Woudhuysen, 'Ferrers, George (*c.*1510–1579)', *Oxford dictionary of national biography* (Oxford, 2004), accessed online 5 August 2007.

12. HALS DSA4/38/1 and 2 tithe award and map for Flamstead, 1838.

13. Most of the other lands which were tithe free in the parish in 1838 (including Feverells) had been the property of Reverend Richard Pearce (deceased), who had purchased the lordship of the manor in 1753, and were 'absolutely exempt from payment of all tithes by prescription or otherwise' (*Ibid.*).

Furneux Pelham

The old park

NGR: TL425285
Date range: by 1274 – ?late fourteenth century. Perhaps re-imparked in fifteenth century
Size: perhaps *c*.186 acres
Underlying geology: boulder clay

A PARK WAS FIRST RECORDED at Furneux Pelham in 1274/5, when it was held by Simon de Furneus, a tenant of the bishop of London.[1] It was recorded again a century later in an inquisition held after the death of Alesia, widow of Hugh le Gros, whose father had been granted the manor in 1309.[2] It was not, however, recorded in a survey of the manor in 1434, which is surprising given that the tenants of Furneux Pelham at the beginning of the fifteenth century were Robert Newport, a member of parliament for Hertfordshire in 1400/01 and 1411, and his (presumed) son, William Newport, who represented Hertfordshire in parliament in 1427 and 1433, either of whom was likely to have aspired to owning a park to complement his elevated social status.[3] William's grandson, Robert Newport, was sheriff of Hertfordshire in 1496 and may well have re-established a park but no evidence for this has been found. There is a lack of documentary evidence for the manor in the late medieval period and it is not until the end of the sixteenth century that there is a record of re-imparking – but unfortunately no evidence for when it took place.

In 1523 Robert Newport's eight-year-old granddaughter was married to Henry Parker, the son and heir of the tenth lord Morley, and the manor passed into the Parker family for the remainder of the sixteenth century. Henry Parker played a prominent role in Hertfordshire affairs, was knighted in 1533, was sheriff of Essex and Hertfordshire in 1536/7, represented the county in parliament and was appointed to most important commissions in the county. He held property in Norfolk but Furneux Pelham appears to have been his Hertfordshire residence. His Hertfordshire lands were valued at £100 a year in 1546, making him one of the county's ten or twelve richest men, and it seems very likely that he would have had a park at Furneux Pelham.[4] He died, before his father, in 1552 and his estates were inherited by his 20-year-old son, also Henry. In 1556 the tenth lord Morley died and Henry inherited the title, Baron Morley, and the family seat at Great Hallingbury in Essex where he entertained Queen Elizabeth for two days in 1561 (Figure 23). He was a catholic and fled the country in 1570, remaining abroad until his death in 1577.[5]

Succeeding barons Morley, with their main residence at Great Hallingbury, can have had little need for Furneux Pelham Hall and in 1600 Sir William Parker, thirteenth Baron Morley and first Baron Mounteagle, sold the hall to Richard Mead, a yeoman of Essex.[6] The sale included 'all those two

several disparked parks or inclosed grounds commonly called the old park and the new park containing by estimation fourteen score and twelve acres' (292 acres) in Furneux Pelham. Also included were 'all those lands ... which were sometimes parcel of the farm called Johns of Pelham and now lie inclosed in the olde park', together with a 'messuage called the old lodge lying within the old park'.[7] These deeds of 1600 show that there were two parks at Furneux Pelham during the sixteenth century, but there is no clear evidence that either of them was created in the medieval period; nor is there any evidence that there was any connection between these parks and the park recorded in the thirteenth and fourteenth centuries.

The new park seems most likely to have been created by Sir Henry Parker, perhaps in the 1530s, and laid out around Furneux Pelham Hall as was fashionable at that time. The old park must, therefore, have been a short distance from the house and its location has been plotted based on the evidence of field names and information contained in seventeenth- and eighteenth-century deeds.[8] It is not clear what the relationship was between the old park and the farm 'called Johns of Pelham'. St Johns Pelham was a moated house, sometimes referred to as a manor, which lay north of the old park and was held by lord Morley in the later sixteenth century in addition to the manor of Furneux Pelham.[9] During the seventeenth century St Johns Pelham was held by the Newport family.

Saxton appears to show a park at Furneux Pelham on his county map of 1577 but whether this was the old park, the new park, or both, is uncertain (Figure 23). No park was shown on the county map by Norden in 1598, which accords with the record of the two disparked parks in 1600. Re-imparkment occurred once again in the mid seventeenth century when, according to Salmon, Edward Cason in 1677 'sold the mansion house and the estate here, with the old and new parks, in his time disparked, but lately paled in, and stocked again with deer' to Felix Calvert.[10]

The most significant field evidence of a former park boundary is a bank about a metre high (more in places) and several metres across along the north side of a pasture field called Aldicke adjacent to the public footpath (TL428283), perhaps marking the south side of part of the old park. The area of park shown on Map 18 relates to the land described as being in the old park in the documents of the seventeenth and eighteenth centuries and covers 186 acres. The field names are derived from those documents and the nineteenth-century tithe map and award. There is no definite evidence, however, that this 'old' park was necessarily the medieval park. The north end of the new park probably butted up to the old park and extended southwards around Furneux Pelham Hall in a roughly rectangular area which mostly survived to be depicted

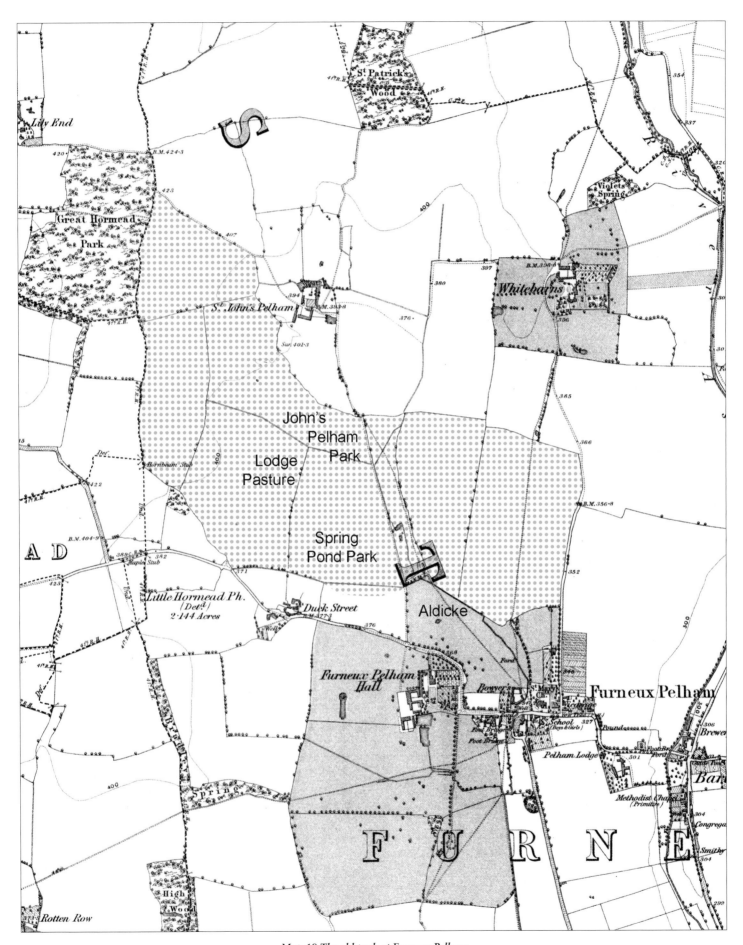

Map 18 The old park at Furneux Pelham
OS 6 inches to the mile map sheet XIV, surveyed 1876–8, published 1881–3. Annotated with field names derived from the Furneux Pelham tithe award and map, 1837 and 1840 (HALS DSA4/76/1 and 2).

as parkland on the first edition OS map. The total area of the two parks, excluding the mansion and its gardens, is about 300 acres, which corresponds well with the 292 acres recorded in 1600.

1. Page, *Hertford*, 4, p. 101, citing *Hundred Rolls* (Records Commission), i, 193.
2. HALS 21347 copy of inquisition *post mortem* of Alesia le Gros, 1367/8.
3. Page, *Hertford*, 4, p. 102, citing Chancery Inquisition *post mortem* 12 Hen. VI, no. 36 (TNA: PRO C139/64/36), taken on the death of William Newport in 1434; D. Warrand (ed.), *Hertfordshire families* (London, 1907), p. 290; Roskell et al., *The history of parliament*, pp. 831–3. Robert Newport, MP 1401 and 1411, was described as 'of Pelham Furneux'.
4. S.T. Bindoff, *The history of parliament: the House of Commons 1509–1558* (London, 1982), p. 58. Parker's entry states that he was 'of Morley Hall and Hingham, Norfolk, and Furneux Pelham, Herts'. He also acquired, through his wife, the manor of Stapleford.
5. J.P. Carley, 'Parker, Henry, eleventh Baron Morley (1531/2–1577)', *Oxford dictionary of national biography* (Oxford, 2004), accessed online 6 November 2007.
6. Page, *Hertford*, 4, p. 102, citing *Visitations of Hertfordshire* (Harleian Society), 79; Warrand, *Hertfordshire families*, p. 283; HALS 21349 bargain and sale of manor house and lands of Furneux Pelham, 1600. At the same time the manor was alienated to Edward Newport.
7. HALS 21349 bargain and sale of manor house and lands of Furneux Pelham, 1600.
8. HALS 21349 bargain and sale of manor house and lands of Furneux Pelham, 1600; 21356 indenture, 1614; 21360 marriage settlement, 1651; 21650 deeds, 1677; 21655 deeds, 1689; 21670 mortgage, 1709; DSA4/76/1 and 2 tithe award and map of Furneux Pelham, 1837.
9. Page, *Hertford*, 4, p. 103–4.
10. Salmon, *History of Hertfordshire*, p. 287.

Figure 23. *Detail of Saxton's county map showing east Hertfordshire and a part of west Essex in the 1570s. This area includes the two parks belonging to Baron Morley: one west of Furneux Pelham in Hertfordshire (centre north of picture) and one at Great Hallingbury in Essex (far right of picture) (HALS CM1). To the centre left of the picture is the park at Standon Lordship, straddling the river Rib. West of Bishop's Stortford is the park at Hadham Hall, Little Hadham. South of Bishop's Stortford and Thorley is the park at Shingle Hall, Sawbridgeworth. Bottom left is Ware park and further east are the three parks at Hunsdon and Pisho park north of Eastwick. All five of these latter parks were in the hands of Henry VIII in the early sixteenth century and two of the three parks which Saxton depicted at Hunsdon were created by him. The park which is partially shown east of Stanstead St Margarets was probably the newly-established park at Stanstead Bury. Reproduced by kind permission of Hertfordshire Archives and Local Studies.*

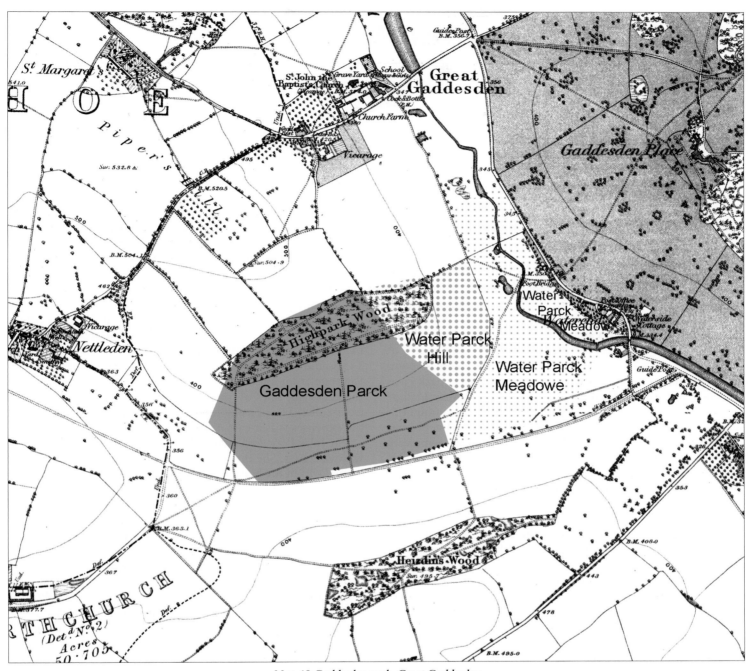

Map 19 Gaddesden park, Great Gaddesden

OS 6 inches to the mile map sheet XXVI, surveyed 1877–8, published 1883–4 and sheet XXXIII, surveyed 1873–8, published 1883. Annotated with field names recorded on a map drawn by Israel Amyce, 1600/01 (HHA CP 349).

Great Munden

Frodgoryshey or Floodgacy park (now Little Munden)
NGR: TL340205
Date range: by 1283 – c.1489
Size: 212 acres
Underlying geology: boulder clay with areas of glaciofluvial deposits

ACCOUNT ROLLS FOR THE MANOR of Walkern show that in 1324/5 two deer (*feris*) were taken for the lord of Walkern manor from Frodgoryshey Park, held by H. de Ossevill of Great Munden.[1] This is presumably the same park which was recorded in 1283 when Gerard de Furnivall complained that certain persons had repeatedly broken into his park at Munden Furnivall (as Great Munden was then known) 'hunted therein and carried away deer'.[2] The park was recorded again in 1302, when the manor was said to include 'a park containing 40 acres wood', a somewhat ambiguous phrase.[3] Apart from the record in 1324/5, no other occurrence of the name Frodgoryshey has been found, but it seems very likely that it was the same park which was called 'Floodgacy' (spelt in various ways) from the late fifteenth century.

The next known reference to a park at Great Munden occurs in some bailiff's accounts of 1446/7.[4] These accounts must have been compiled for John Fray, who became the lord of the manor in 1447.[5] Fray was chief baron of the Exchequer from 1436 until he retired from the post at the age of about 52 in 1448.[6] He already held several properties in Hertfordshire, including the manors of Rushden, Cottered, La More in Sandon and La Mote in Cheshunt, and must also have had a house in London.[7] None of these properties seems to have had a park.

The park at Great Munden had evidently not been stocked with deer for some time prior to 1446 because the accounts show that Fray spent large sums of money bringing it back into working order over the next few years. Costs of £14 7s 7d were incurred in 1446/7 when the boundary earthwork of the park was redug, trees and thorns in 'le launde' were uprooted and a pond was scoured. A further £6 16s 5d was spent on upgrading the lodge – a new stable was built and repairs were made to the outhouses – and deer were obtained to restock the park. These costs were partially offset by the 100 shillings received from the sale of underwood felled in the park.[8] Between 1448 and 1451 the parker's house was repaired, fireplaces were added to the lodge, bushes were 'tidied' in the park and a park gate was installed.[9] An interesting item of expenditure during this period was the capture of four deer in the parks of Weston (see p. 228), Knebworth (p.154), Hallingbury (Essex, see Figure 23) and Benington (p.56), presumably to help restock the park at Great Munden, at a cost of 16d.[10] This not only provides a useful record of parks which were active in the mid fifteenth century, but also indicates John Fray's social network.

No parker was employed when Fray acquired Great Munden in 1447 and the accounts suggest that the park had previously been rented out for grazing. However, between at least 1446 and 1451, the bailiff was unable to lease the park because it was occupied by the prioress of Rowney. Rowney Priory, a house of Benedictine nuns, lay adjacent to the east side of the park and the prioress claimed that the park was necessary for the support of the priory church: the priory was very poor and unable to pay for the repairs needed to its house and church. It was finally closed and handed over to John Fray, who held the advowson of the church, in 1457.[11] Perhaps coincidentally, the wage of a parker was first accounted for in the year 1456/7 but, as there is a gap in the accounts between 1451 and 1456, he could have been employed earlier.[12] Revenue from agistment was also recorded from this period, together with sales of 'parcels of lopp and cropp' and 'diverse trees called Hornbeams felled in the park this year'. Among the expenses was a cart of hay for the deer.[13]

Sir John Fray died in 1461 and Great Munden passed to his widow, Agnes. She then married Sir John Say and by 1484 the manor was in the hands of Sir John's son, Sir William Say, who had married John Fray's daughter in 1480 and held extensive estates elsewhere in Hertfordshire.[14] The bailiff's account of 1484/5, compiled for Sir William Say, shows that the park was still functioning: underwood was felled 'for the sustenance of the wild animals in the park' and a parker was paid 66s 8d. Revenue from agistment, pannage and the lease of the rabbit warren in the park came to just 20 shillings; the cost of maintaining the park boundary was 23s 4d.[15] By 1490 Sir William appears to have stopped managing the park directly and it seems to have been disparked: neither the warren, the deer nor the parker was mentioned in the accounts during the following decade. Instead, Sir William leased the farm of agistment and pannage of pigs to John Colt for 46 shillings a year, an arrangement which continued throughout the 1490s.[16] In 1495 Colt also paid 10 shillings for the rent of wildfowling for two years but this was not continued in 1498/9. Sir William retained control of the wood and timber resources in the park but seems to have done little to manage them effectively: the only record of wood sold in the surviving accounts was one cartload of sallows sold for 8d in 1498/9.[17] In 1493/4 repairs were made to the roof of the lodge in Flodgaise park, also referred to as Flodgarsey park elsewhere in the account.[18] Sir William Say died in 1529 and the manor of Great Munden descended to Henry, Earl of Essex, husband of his daughter Mary.[19]

An area totalling 130 acres of the southern part of the park was immediately divided up into copyhold tenures: six of the eight tenants held about 10 acres each but there were two larger holdings of 28 and 42 acres respectively. The rental income from these tenancies in 1556 was £8 8s 4d. The

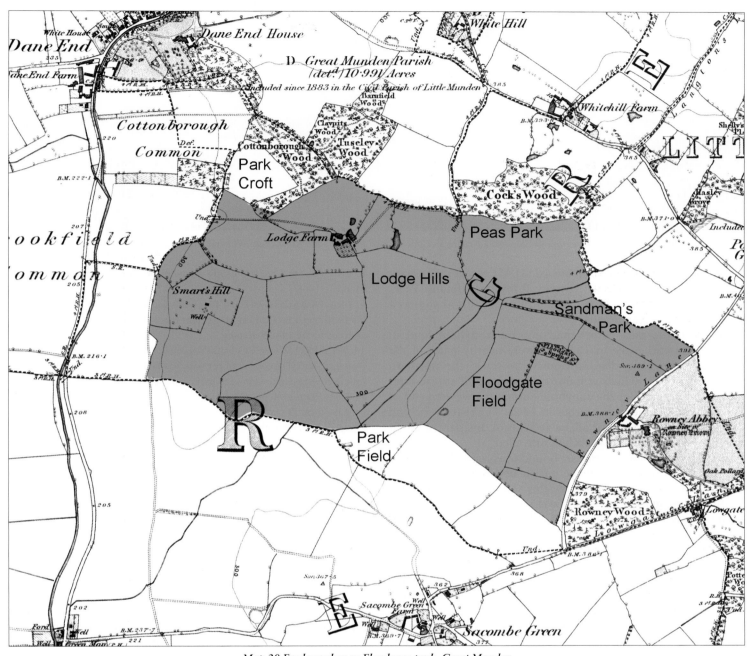

Map 20 Frodgoryshey or Floodgacy park, Great Munden
*OS 6 inches to the mile map sheet XXI, surveyed 1878–80, published 1884. Annotated with field names recorded
on the Great Munden tithe award and map, 1841 (HALS DSA4/70/1 and 2).*

remaining 71 acres of the park – comprising arable land, meadow and pasture – were leased, with its lodge, and were held by Margaret Roche in 1556 for 78s 9d p.a. The combined area of the lands described as being part of Flodgacye park in 1556 was 202 acres.[20]

Upon the death of Lady Anne Parr (granddaughter of Sir William Say) in 1571, the manor reverted to the crown and in 1573 William, lord Burghley, took out a lease on 'lands called Fludgates alias Fludgacie Parke, parcel of the demesne lands of Munden Magna'.[21] His son, Robert Cecil, had the park surveyed and drawn by Israel Amyce c.1600. The plan shows the park divided between the copyhold tenants much as described in 1556; just 69 acres in the north of the park remained demesne land at the end of the sixteenth century.[22] By Amyce's measurements, the former park covered 185 acres.

The lodge was again recorded in the park from 1606 (when the park was said to cover 71 acres) but was not shown on Amyce's plan five years earlier, although three other buildings were shown: 'Rowney Nunnery' to the east of the park and two houses on the copyhold lands.[23]

No park was shown at Great Munden on sixteenth-century county maps but Seller's map (1676) annotates an area north of Sacombe Green as 'the Park', as does Dury and Andrews' map of 1766, although no palings were depicted on either map. By the end of the eighteenth century a messuage called Floodgates or Floodgacy Park and several pieces of land described as 'part of', or 'adjoining', Floodgacy park were laid into a farm called 'the Park'.[24] A document of 1800 recorded that land copyhold of the manor of Great Munden abutting Rowney Lane was 'formerly parcel of Fludgate Park'.[25] The

Figure 24. View across the former Floodgacy park from Cock's Wood looking south-west (now Whitehills Golf Course, Little Munden).

Great Munden tithe map and award (1841) reveal many park field names to the west of Rowney Priory: Sandman's Park, Park Field, Park Croft, Peas Park and Lodge Hills as well as a field called Floodgate Field.[26]

Most of the park which had become copyhold land in 1529/30 was tithe-free in 1841, as were nearby parts of the parish of Little Munden. Curiously, however, the northern part of the park, which remained demesne land in the later sixteenth century, plus the copyhold land at the western end of the park, *was* liable to pay tithes in 1841. The reasons behind the differing tithe status of adjacent fields in this part of Great and Little Munden remain to be unravelled.[27]

At the time that the parish boundaries were established, this southern projection of the parish of Great Munden, on relatively high ground with heavy clay soils, probably retained a covering of woodland which was subsequently enclosed to create the deer park (Figure 24). Much of the former park boundary can be traced in today's landscape. The western boundary is still marked by a fine lynchet (only part of which is also the parish boundary) which continues northwards before making a 90-degree turn to the east. A good 5m-wide bank survives in parts along the south side of Cock's Wood (the north side of the park and not part of the parish boundary) and there are two oak pollards marking the park and parish boundary about 50m west of Cock's Wood. The park boundary coincides with the parish boundary along the northern part of its west side and also along three other sections of its length: on the north, north-east and south sides of the park. Rowney Lane runs along the eastern boundary and a public footpath follows the north side. The boundaries shown on Map 20 enclose an area of 212 acres.

1. HALS 9325 bailiff's account, 1324/5; Henry de Osevill held the manor in the early fourteenth century according to the VCH.

2. *Cal. Pat. 1281–1292*, p. 94.

3. *Cal. Inq. post mortem, vol. 4, Edward I*, p. 56.

4. TNA: PRO SC6/867/10 bailiff's account for the manor of Great Munden, 1446/7.

5. Page, *Hertford*, 3, p. 126, citing Ancient Deeds, D 465 (TNA: PRO E210/465).

6. S. Alsford, information about the husbands of Lady Agnes Say on a website about medieval towns, www.trytel.com/~tristan/towns/florilegium/lifecycle/lcdth18.html; John Fray was knighted before 1459.

7. He was buried in 1461 at St Bartholomew the Less in London (*ibid.*).

8. TNA: PRO SC6/867/10 bailiff's accounts for the manor of Great Munden, 1446/7.

9. TNA: PRO SC6/867/12 and 13 bailiff's accounts, 1448/9 and 1449/50. A bill providing a detailed list of expenses for repairing the parker's house is attached to the 1448/9 account.

10. TNA: PRO SC6/867/13 bailiff's account, 1449/50. This was listed under 'Foreign costs'. The cost of 4d per park has been interpreted to mean that four deer were captured in each park, rather than a single deer in each.

11. Page, *Hertford*, 4, pp. 434–5, citing Feet of Fines Hertfordshire 26 Hen. VI, no. 138 (TNA: PRO CP25/1/91/115). Fray continued to maintain the church and a perpetual chantry with a chaplain 'to celebrate for the good estate of the king and himself, and for the souls of the founder and benefactors of the late nunnery' (Page, *Hertford*, 4, pp. 434–5, citing Dugdale, *Monasticon* iv, 343, no. ii.).

12. TNA: PRO SC6/867/16 bailiff's accounts, 1456/7. He was paid 60s 10d a year at a rate of 2d per day.

13. TNA: PRO SC6/867/17 bailiff's accounts, date missing but probably *c.*1460. 12s was the price of the 'lopp, cropp and underwood'; 13s 4d was received from 'diverse persons for agistament of diverse animals' in the park; the cart of hay cost 4s.

14. Page, *Hertford*, 3, p. 126, citing Chancery Inquisition *post mortem* 18 Edw IV no. 43 (TNA: PRO C140/67/43); J.G. Nichols (ed.), 'Will of Sir William Say, knt, 1529', *The topographer and genealogist*, 1 (London, 1846), p. 412.

15. HHA 10/16 bailiff's account, 1484/5. The wage of the 'custodian of the park' also included collecting rents and farms of the land for the lord.

16. Although Colt paid only 40s rent in 1498/9.

17. HHA court rolls 10/21 bailiff's account, 1495/6; 10/23 bailiff's account, 1498/9.

18. HHA court rolls 10/20 bailiff's account, 1493/4.

19. Page, *Hertford*, 3, p. 126, citing Chancery Inquisition *post mortem* (Ser. 2), li, 50 (TNA: PRO C142/51/50); Court of Wards, Misc. Bks. 578, fol. 372a (TNA); Feet of Fines Hertfordshire Hil. 33 Hen. VIII (TNA: PRO CP25/2/17/97/33HENVIIIHIL); Patent Roll 3 & 4 Phil. and Mary, pt. xii (TNA: PRO C66/917).

20. TNA: PRO E315/391 survey of manors in Hertfordshire, lands and possessions of King Philip and Queen Mary, 1556.

21. *Cal. Pat. 1572–1575*, p. 3.

22. There are three versions of this plan in the Hatfield House Archive, all drawn by Amyce: HHA Box T/38 and CP349, 1600/01.

23. HHA deeds 198/28 (1606), 190/12 (1609), 58/1 (1612).

24. HALS DE/L/5258 draft admission out of court to the manor of Great Munden, 1848.

25. HALS DE/L/5320 surrender of copyhold land, 1800.

26. HALS DSA4/70/1 and 2 Great Munden tithe award and map, 1841.

27. The neighbouring Rowney Priory may be a factor.

Figure 25. *The landscape of the former Floodgacy park in the middle of the twentieth century. The village of Dane End is at the top left of the photograph, Rowney Priory is bottom right. Aerial photograph taken by the RAF 10 October, 1946 (HALS Off Acc 300 CPE/UK/1779, 4306). Reproduced by kind permission of Hertfordshire Archives and Local Studies.*

Great Offley

No known name
NGR: ?TL148271 ?TL142266
Date range: not known – perhaps thirteenth century
Size: not known
Underlying geology: clay-with flints and/or boulder clay

AN EXTENT OF THE MANOR OF OFFLEY compiled on the death of John de St Ledger in 1326 suggests that there may have been an earlier park at Offley, although it was not recorded as such by that time. On the manor in 1326 was a several pasture called La Launde, a name which is normally associated with a deer park. The pasture was valued at 6s 8d per annum, as was the 41 acres of wood on the manor which contained 'underwood with herbage' and was used for pannage.[1] It is possible that a park was established by Geoffrey de St Ledger, who received a grant of free warren on his demesne lands at Offley in 1265, but the earliest known confirmation of a park does not appear until 1451 when Sir Thomas Hoo, Lord Hastings and Alianora his wife granted to Nicholas Mattok of Hitchin and John Colyn of Welwyn 'all wood and underwood in the park of Offley'.[2] No park was mentioned in an account of 1540/1, when the manor was in the hands of Henry VIII, and no park was shown on the sixteenth-century county maps by Saxton (1577) and Norden (1598).[3]

Despite the meagre documentary evidence, the field evidence for a medieval park is good; however, the picture is confused by the park which was established at Great Offley before 1676, when it was depicted on the county map by Seller, and which still exists today. It sits on the edge of a plateau at about 155m OD with extensive views to the north-east towards Hitchin, and around the eastern end of the park is a substantial bank (see Map 21). The south side of the park is bounded by a deep ditch or hollow-way (over 1m deep) with a slight bank on the outside.

The topographical location of this park and the surviving boundary earthworks suggest that this could have been the site of a medieval park which was abandoned during the medieval period and then subsequently reinstated. The presence of the medieval church within or adjacent to the park would, however, be slightly unusual, and it is also possible that the boundary earthworks were created around an entirely new park in the seventeenth century.

An alternative site for the possible medieval park lies immediately to the south-west on the opposite side of the village street from the church. Here there is a larger block of land which was also held by the lord of the manor in the early nineteenth century and which is bounded almost entirely by lanes and public footpaths and, in places, by a substantial bank and ditch. The land was called The Lawns in 1807 and the name may preserve the memory of the pasture called La Launde in 1326.[4] A house built in the northern corner of the land later in the nineteenth century was given the same name.

It is also possible that the seventeenth-century park and the land called The Lawns to the south-west once formed a single enclosure which *could* have been a medieval park and this is the area tentatively indicated on Map 21.

1. TNA: PRO C134/101/10 inquisition *post mortem* of John de St Ledger, 1326. I am grateful to Janet Holt for drawing my attention to this source.
2. Page, *Hertford*, 3, p. 40, citing Charter Roll 49 Hen. III, m. 4 (TNA: PRO C53/54); an extent of the manor of Offley taken in 1337/8 is, unfortunately, virtually illegible (TNA: PRO E199/10/10); BL Add Ch 28868 grant, 28 May, 1451 (I am indebted to Bridget Howlett for this information, derived from BL Add Ch 28680–28997, 1261–1777).
3. TNA: PRO SC6/HENVIII/6222 ministers' account for Great Offley, 1540/1.
4. HALS QS/E/55 and 56 enclosure award and map for Great Offley, 1819 and 1807, respectively.

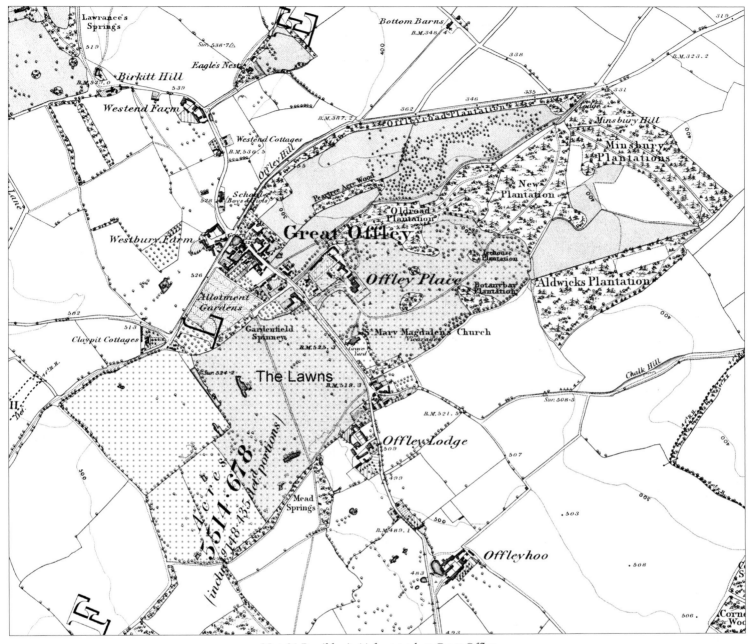

Map 21 Possible site(s) for a park at Great Offley

OS 6 inches to the mile map sheet XI, surveyed 1880, published 1884. Annotated with a field name recorded on the enclosure award and map for Great Offley, 1819 and 1807, respectively (HALS QS/E/55 and 56).

Hatfield

Gacelyn(s) park

NGR: ?c.TL301061
Date range: by 1300 – not known
Size: recorded as 60 acres in 1324
Underlying geology: Pebble Gravel over London Clay

GEOFFREY GASCELIN WAS HOLDING LAND in Hatfield by 1255 and in 1268 he and his wife conveyed their manor to William de Valence, Earl of Pembroke. The manor, which was held partly of the manor of Hatfield and partly of the manor of Bayford, was described as a messuage and two carucates of land, with no mention of a park.[1] Geoffrey Gascelin was recorded as a knight in the royal household in 1241 and acquired a substantial estate in Wiltshire when he married c.1247. Shortly afterwards he was recruited to the household of William de Valence, half-brother of Henry III, who held the castle at Hertford.[2]

In 1296 William's estates were inherited by his son, Aymer de Valence, who complained in 1300 that, while he was in Scotland on the king's service, certain persons had broken into his park at Hatfield Gacelyn, 'hunted therein, and carried away deer'.[3] The likelihood is, then, that a park was created by either William or Aymer de Valence at the end of the thirteenth century. The inquisition *post mortem* taken at Aymer's death in 1324 reveals that he held 104 acres of arable and a park containing 60 acres of woodland at Gacelyns. The woodland was said to contain no underwood and the pasture of it was worth 8s 4d a year, indicating that it was wood-pasture.[4] The manor at this time is thought to have occupied land at the eastern end of Hatfield parish, beyond the great park of the bishops of Ely, and extending northwards into Bayford parish. The manor is not mentioned after the middle of the fifteenth century and it seems likely that it became absorbed into the Ponsbourne estate.

A park was shown at Ponsbourne by both Saxton (1577) and Norden (1598) but whether either corresponded with the fourteenth-century Gacelyn park cannot be determined. Saxton depicted Ponsbourne Park lying some distance away from Hatfield Wood (the great park) and nearer to Bayford (Figure 26), whereas Norden showed it adjoining the eastern end of Hatfield Wood with a north–south road running between the two sets of palings. Whether or not these maps reflect a real change in the location of the park in the late sixteenth century is difficult to establish but it is tempting to conclude that Saxton was depicting the medieval park and Norden a new park created to embellish the grand mansion of Ponsbourne which was certainly standing 'below the high road from Cheshunt through Newgate Street to Hatfield' by the early seventeenth century.[5] Accompanying the mansion at this time was a 'park or land disparked' and, indeed, no park was shown by either Seller (1676) or Oliver (1695) on their county maps.

By 1718 Ponsbourne House had a park once more and field names recorded in deeds provide circumstantial evidence for at least two phases of park history, with a Lodge Orchard and an Old Lodge Field.[6] No park was depicted by either Warburton (1749) or Dury and Andrews (1766). The Hatfield tithe map and award reveal a cluster of 'park' names north of the late nineteenth-century park and warren (see Map 22).[7] However, field evidence, in the form of a 5m-wide bank bordering the east side of the Ashendene Road just west of Ashendene Farm, suggests that the medieval park may have lain in the north-west corner of the estate in the parish of Bayford, which would correspond with the placing of the park shown by Saxton. But this conflicts with the documentary evidence, all of which states that the Earl of Pembroke's park was in Hatfield rather than Bayford.

Further fieldwork may reveal more earthwork evidence of a medieval park boundary, but a succession of parks which came and went over many centuries in the Ponsbourne area has left a complex array of very fragmentary evidence. The accompanying map shows a speculative location for the medieval park, based upon the evidence of nineteenth-century field names and boundaries, which covers approximately 60 acres.

The great park

NGR: TL268061
Date range: by 1222 – early seventeenth century
Size: recorded as 'one thousand acres' in 1251; probably c.1,860 acres
Underlying geology: London Clay overlain in places by Pebble Gravel or boulder clay

ACCORDING TO A MONK OF ELY ABBEY writing in the late twelfth century, 40 hides of well-wooded land in Hatfield were given by King Edgar to the monastery at Ely so that 'the brothers would be able to have timber from it for the building of the church and enough firewood to satisfy their needs'. After King Edgar died, there was a dispute over his right to grant the land to the monastery and it was seized by the claimants. The brothers, having no woodland elsewhere to supply their needs, were forced to buy the land back.[8] This probably all took place in the late tenth century and the brothers' land in Hatfield became a long easterly extension of the parish reaching from Millwards Park in the west to Newgate Street in the east. It encompassed a tract of high, wooded ground with intractable clay and gravel soils which subsequently became known as the great park.

In 1109 the abbey's holdings were transferred to the bishopric of Ely.[9] The earliest indication of a park appears in a

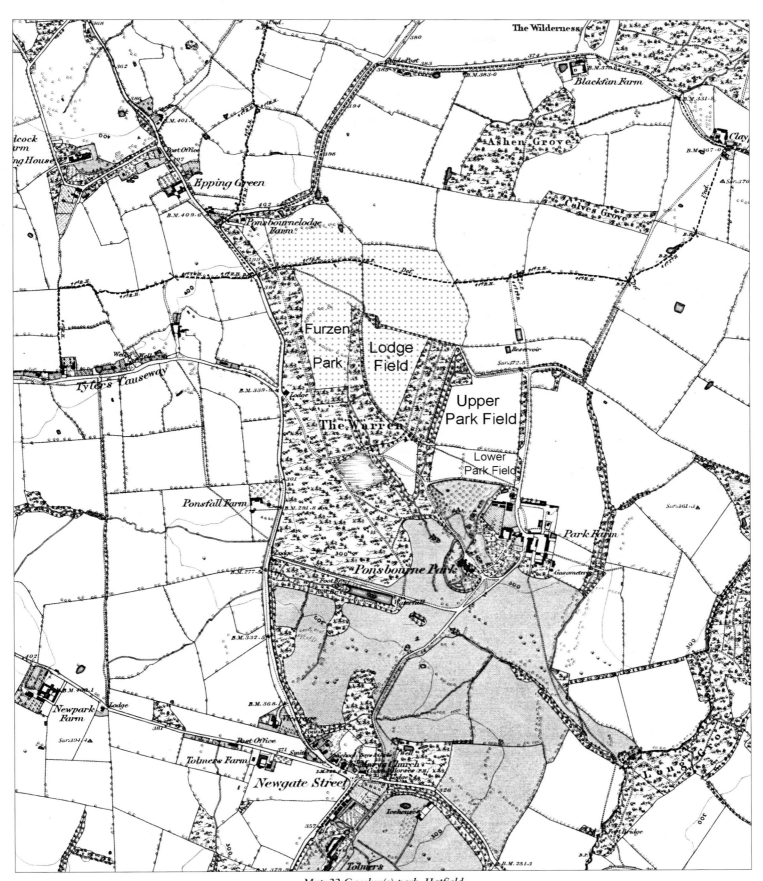

***Map 22** Gacelyn(s) park, Hatfield*
OS 6 inches to the mile map sheet XXXVI, surveyed 1873–80, published 1883. Annotated with field names derived from the Hatfield tithe award and map,
1839 (HALS DSA4/47/1 and 2).

Map 23 The great park, Hatfield
OS 6 inches to the mile map sheets
XXXV, surveyed 1873–9, published
1883; XXXVI, surveyed 1873–80,
published 1883; XL, surveyed
1870–3, published 1877; and XLI,
surveyed 1873, published 1882
(reproduced at a reduced scale).
Location of Hornbeam Gate after P.
Austin (1995).

list of tenants and their holdings compiled in 1222 which included Ralph le Parker and Walter le Parker.[10] In 1229 Henry III instructed the keeper of the bishop of Ely to let Nicholas de Molis have six beeches and six oaks from the park at Hatfield.[11]

A survey of the property of the bishop of Ely in 1251 stated that the demesne included among its woodland a great park of about 1,000 acres and a little park containing about 350 acres (see p. 114).[12] The great park was not for the exclusive use of the bishop, as his tenants in chief had rights of common and 'woderight' in it. The Old Coucher Book of Ely also contains descriptions of the manors belonging to the bishopric in 1251. It recorded a great wood at Hatfield (*unus magn[u]s* [with *boscus* struck through]), estimated at 1,000 acres, within which tenants were able to put their horses, livestock and pigs for pannage. There was also a little park of 350 acres.[13] The estimate of 1,000 acres for the great park seems a remarkably round number and was perhaps intended to convey the impression of a very large area rather than being a genuine estimate of size. Measurement of the likely former area of the great park using modern GIS technology gives an area of 1,860 acres (see Map 23).

Despite the common rights of the tenants, the bishops of Ely were sometimes able to obtain considerable revenues from the sale of agistment, pannage and wood in the great park. Accounts for 1286 show that £6 1s 3½d was received for 'herbage in the park and pasture' and £10 4s 6d for underwood and bark.[14] At the end of the thirteenth century 35 shillings was recorded 'for pasture in the two parks [great and little] sold; 2 shillings for pannage of 393 pigs, [and] agistment from the Feast of St Martin'.[15] At the end of the fourteenth century agistment and pannage in the great park were leased to John Garlyk for six years at 60 shillings a year, although in 1396 he only paid 40 shillings.[16] In 1428 the 'rent of the vaccarie' was worth 100 shillings 'for 20 cows calved there at 5s' and pannage of pigs in the great park was worth 6s 8d.[17]

Manorial documents in the Hatfield House Archive reveal several other ways in which resources within the park were exploited. There was evidently clay suitable for pottery-making because, in 1396, John Pottere of Essendon paid 6 shillings and John Gynne, Robert Pottere and John Wylmyn, potter, each paid 3s 4d for licences to dig clay in the great park; William Basely paid 4s 6d for the same, 'for making tiles'.[18] Similar entries in the accounts for 1428, 1436 and 1437 reveal reduced revenues from the 'rent of the pottery': two men paid 3s 4d for licences to dig clay in 1428 and one man paid 3s 4d in 1436 and 1437.[19]

Wood was coppiced for 'firing and for sale' and, in 1396, 322 cartloads (3,864 *qrs*) of charcoal were made and sold for the huge sum of £64 8s. The charcoal cost 2s 3d per cartload to make, giving a profit of £28 3s 6d.[20] In 1428 137 cartloads of charcoal were sold for £10.[21] The park was also a major source of timber: 68 shillings was received for 'divers beeches in both parks [great and little] in 1428' and 'sawing pits' were recorded 'next Ruddyswykes Lade' in 1507, when they needed mending.[22] In addition, labourers holding Cottier tenements could be licensed to 'collect branches in the park and woods of the lord' on payment of a fee.[23] Hay was sold in 1436 and 1437: it was worth just 8 shillings in 1436 'and not more on account of the increase of rain in the summer and hay time', while the following year it was worth 17 shillings, '16 acres

sold and not more, because of the great rain in the summer'.[24]

The bishops' expenses for maintaining the park included the wages of the parker and the repair of parts of the park pale and the gates at the entrances into the park. In 1396 the following costs were recorded:[25]

Wages of Walter Olyve, Parker of the great park	60s 8d
20 perches of new fence made round the park	3s 4d
Gate of the same park called New Gate made anew	2s 11d
Plate and pik [*sic*] of iron for the same	3d

The manorial tenants were responsible for maintaining much of the park pale: a document of 1392 recorded that one of the services required for a tenant's holding was to make 120 perches of fence round the bishop's park.[26] In 1482 the court roll recorded that 'John Fysshe does not repair the Lord's pales towards the great park at Potwellgrove, containing 42 roods, and is order[ed] to repair the same before Easter under a penalty of 40d'.[27]

As well as the New Gate mentioned previously, other park gates are thought to have been located at Bell Bar in the south and Hornbeamgate on the north of the park.[28] The New Gate was at the eastern end of the park and gave its name to the settlement of Newgate Street which developed there. In the sixteenth century a house was purchased in the hamlet and made into a lodge.[29] Tolls were collected from loaded carts and horses passing through the park and in 1348 the tolls were granted by Queen Isabella to Reginald de Newport, yeoman of the king's chamber and custodian of the two parks of Hatfield.[30]

Some of the animals inhabiting the park were recorded in a survey of 1358: two stray bulls were valued at 10 shillings; one stray boar was valued at 2s 6d and three mares with three foals were valued at 6 shillings and were said to be 'in the custody of the parker'.[31]

In 1514 Hannibal Zenzano, farrier to Henry VIII, became the lessee of the manor of Hatfield and keeper of its three parks (great, middle (formerly little) and Innings). From this time the king appears to have used Hatfield almost as his own property although he did not become the legal owner until 1538, when the bishop of Ely accepted other properties in exchange for it.[32] The king had a survey and valuation of his new estate carried out in 1538 and appointed Anthony Denny Esq as Master of the game. The survey recorded that the great park contained 10,000 oaks and beeches valued at 8d each. It had a 'Circuit of 7 miles, extending from Fisshes Grove to Hansmeregate' and it contained '18 deer of antlers and 62 raskells'.[33] Another survey in 1551 for Princess Elizabeth recorded 120 deer and two lodges, 'somewhat dekayd'.[34] In 1591 the park fence was in need of repair and the queen's Woodward in Hertfordshire, Barnard Dewhurst, was instructed to fell 50 trees in 'hir majesties Midlepark and Great Park called hatfeld woode' for new fencing'.[35]

On the death of the queen in 1603, ownership of the manor of Hatfield with its palace and parks passed to James I. He, however, preferred the magnificent (and much newer) house built by William Cecil at Theobalds in Cheshunt. Cecil's son, Robert, was made first Earl of Salisbury in 1605 and in 1607 was persuaded to accept various royal properties,

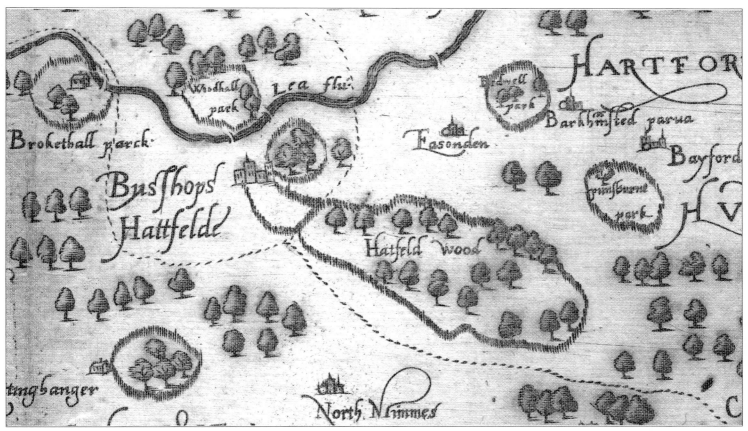

Figure 26. *Detail of Saxton's county map showing the parks in the Hatfield area, 1577 (HALS CM1). At the western end of Hatfield Wood (the great park) is the little or middle park (Millwards park) and adjacent to the town symbol, on its north-east side, is Innings park. The other parks in the parish are Woodhall park, on the north bank of the river Lea, Brocket park and Ponsbourne park. Brocket park appears to have been created in the sixteenth century but Ponsbourne park may have evolved from, or incorporated the site of, the medieval Gacelyn park. Also shown are Bedwell park to the west of Little Berkhamsted and Tyttenhanger park to the south-west of Hatfield. Reproduced by kind permission of Hertfordshire Archives and Local Studies.*

including Hatfield, in exchange for Theobalds. The old palace at Hatfield was soon largely demolished and a grand new house built in its place between 1608 and 1611. At the same time, Lord Salisbury set about transforming the landscape around Hatfield House. The great park, lying over a mile from the house, did not become part of Cecil's 'designed' landscape and was surplus to requirements as a deer park. In 1611 it was enclosed at the request of the commoners, with 883 acres at the western and eastern ends of the Great Wood, as it then became known, being divided among them. The remaining 560 acres in the middle of the Wood were made into New Park by Lord Salisbury. The park was stocked with deer and conies and leased to a series of tenants but it was not a success. Much timber was felled for sale and the park was divided up to make three farms in about 1630.[36]

Innings park (now part of Home Park)

NGR: TL238093
Date range: by 1468 – present
Size: recorded as *c.*100 acres in 1538
Underlying geology: glacial gravel over Upper Chalk

THE EARLIEST REFERENCE TO INNINGS PARK is in a rental of 1468 which records lands in Hatfield's common fields which had been granted in exchange 'for certain lands late Robert Louthe's' lying within the Bishop of Ely's park 'called Innyngesparke'. In 1508 Roger Nott was fined for stealing an oak tree 'in the little park called Innings', together with a sapling from the park pale.[37] A reference to 'Hatfield smaller park' in 1388 and to 'both parks' in 1428 implies that there were then only two parks, namely the great park and the little park (subsequently known as the middle, then Millwards Park).[38] Innings park was therefore established in the mid fifteenth century on land which had, at least in part, been arable farmland. It lay adjacent to the Bishops' palace on land rising to about 80m OD and had a central keeper's lodge. In the seventeenth century it became part of the Home Park and is still parkland today.

The survey undertaken in 1538, when the manor of Hatfield was acquired by Henry VIII, recorded '5 deer of antlers and 35 raskells' in Innings park, which was estimated to contain 100 acres. In the park were eight acres of great timber in two places which, although valued at 60 shillings per acre, could not be sold as they provided essential cover for the deer. There was also 'a warren of coneys conveniently stored with game, and most part of the game black'. The pasture was described as 'very bare and mossy, and scarcely enough to feed the deer' and there was a lodge for a deer-keeper.[39] The Lodge House, still standing in Home Park, remained the home of the head gamekeeper until the early twentieth century and still has outbuildings for the hanging of venison.[40]

A survey in 1551 recorded just 34 deer in Innings park and in 1578 the park was found to be so much overgrown with moss that the deer 'had been corrupted and wanted sufficient feeding whereby many had died'.[41] The park was shown on the county maps by both Saxton (1577) (Figure 26) and Norden (1598) and also on early seventeenth-century estate maps in the Hatfield House Archive, and the cartographic evidence suggests that the park covered about 150 acres by the end of the sixteenth century.[42] A smaller area of about 100 acres is shown on Map 24 to correspond with the acreage recorded in 1538 but there is little in the way of field evidence to indicate where the earlier boundaries actually lay.

The estate map of *c*.1610 shows Innings park being crossed by the new carriage drive, created as part of the grand, formal landscape being laid out around the Earl of Salisbury's magnificent Hatfield House, which was then nearing completion. The new Hatfield House Park was established on former common fields farmed by the tenants of the manor and filled the space between the Innings or Home Park in the north and the middle park to the south. The county maps by Seller and Oliver show the new park and do not distinguish the former Innings Park.

In 1610 Robert Cecil paid £21 to have 14 red deer brought from Tattershall Park, Lincolnshire to stock his new park, and in 1624 a count of the deer in the two parks (Hatfield House and middle) recorded 626 fallow deer.[43] In 1700 Chauncy described 'two large parks, one for fallow- the other for red-deer' and in 1734 a newspaper reported that Lord Salisbury had given George II 80 red deer to stock Windsor Great Park.[44] Subsequently, only fallow deer seem to have been kept at Hatfield. In 1804 the park was said to cover 1,050 acres.[45] In 1867 Evelyn Shirley recorded that Hatfield Park comprised 314 acres, a much reduced area which presumably excluded all plantations and other areas of parkland which were inaccessible to the herd of 360 fallow deer.[46] By 1892 this herd had decreased to an estimated 200 fallow deer, by 1903 there were just 150 deer and in 1916/7 most of the remaining deer were culled and no deer were kept in the park until 1997, when the beginnings of a new herd of fallow deer was re-introduced.[47]

The little park (middle park from the sixteenth century, now Millwards Park)

NGR: TL238067
Date range: by 1248 – ?late eighteenth century
Size: recorded as 350 acres in 1248/9
Underlying geology: glacial Pebble Gravel partially overlying London Clay and Reading Beds

THIS PARK, KNOWN ORIGINALLY as the little park, then the middle park and, latterly, Millwards Park, has the longest and most interesting history of the medieval parks belonging to the manor of Hatfield. It was first recorded in 1248[48] and lies on gentle south-west-facing slopes, rising from marshy ground in the west to a plateau about 117m OD along its north-east border. The south-west side of the park adjoins the parish boundary and, although the other boundaries appear to have fluctuated slightly over the centuries, the core of the park has remained intact and lies about half a mile south of the site of the medieval manor house of the bishops of Ely, to whom the park belonged (Map 25). The fact that most of the park

remains woodland today is perhaps an indication of the poor quality of the soil for agriculture.

A survey of the manor of Hatfield for the bishop of Ely in 1222 did not record any parks but, significantly, there were park-related names among the tenants, including Ralph le Parker and Walter le Parker, indicating that at least one park had been established by this date.[49] The earliest reference to this park in the Hatfield House Archive, dating from 1248/9, recorded 'a little park which contains 350 acres by estimation, where no-one has right of common'.[50] The same document contains details which suggest that the park had only recently been established – or enlarged: it recorded two acres lying in the little park belonging to a messuage which was now in the hands of the lord, plus a widow's cottage, with eight acres belonging to it, in the hands of the lord which also lay in the little park, as well as half a virgate of land with two acres 'which William Ordgar held, the lord took into his own hands and enclosed within the little park for pasture'. A virgate is a variable measure but is generally taken to equate to 30 acres, so this record suggests that roughly 27 acres of tilled land were taken by the bishop and incorporated into his park. A little park of 350 acres with no common rights, in addition to the great park of 1,000 acres, was also recorded in 1251.[51] The two parks shared a boundary at the eastern end of the little park and one theory is that deer were bred in the little park and released into the great park when needed for hunting.[52]

It may have been the little park in which William de Valence, half-brother of the king and custodian of Hertford castle, hunted without permission in 1252. He and his retinue then went to the bishop's house at Hatfield and indulged in some outrageous drunken behaviour in the wine cellar, which was described by the St Albans monk Matthew Paris.[53]

A survey of 1356/7 recorded 'a certain park [probably the little park], whose pasture is worth two shillings per annum and no more, on account of the shade of the trees'.[54] In the 1380s custody of the little park was granted by the prior and chapter of Ely to John de Ake, a household servant, together with the warren and all the deer in the park, for which he received 3d a day with 'the usual fees and profits'.[55] The wages of the parker, John de la Panetrye, in 1396 were also 3d a day, amounting to £4 11s a year. Agistment should have brought in 20 shillings and pannage another 20 shillings but there was no revenue from either that year. However, the sale of the loppings of 102 hornbeams (herenbemcropp) in the little park was worth 16s 6d. Thirty-two shillings was spent on 172 perches of new fence made around the park at 2d per perch, plus the cost of cutting and carrying the underwood used to make the fence (8s 8d).[56]

Around the turn of the fourteenth and fifteenth centuries a tenant with a messuage and two acres of land in the little park relinquished his holding so that the park could be enlarged.[57] In 1428 agistment in the little park was worth 30 shillings but there was no revenue from pannage. In 1436 40 loads of charcoal were sold out of the little park for 100 shillings; agistment brought in a further 26s 8d. In the following two years no wood or underwood from the park was sold, 'except four shillings received by the parker and expended in the fence of the said park' in 1437. In both 1437 and 1438 13s 4d was taken for agistment.[58]

By the sixteenth century, a third, even smaller, park had been established on the manor, adjacent to the bishops' manor

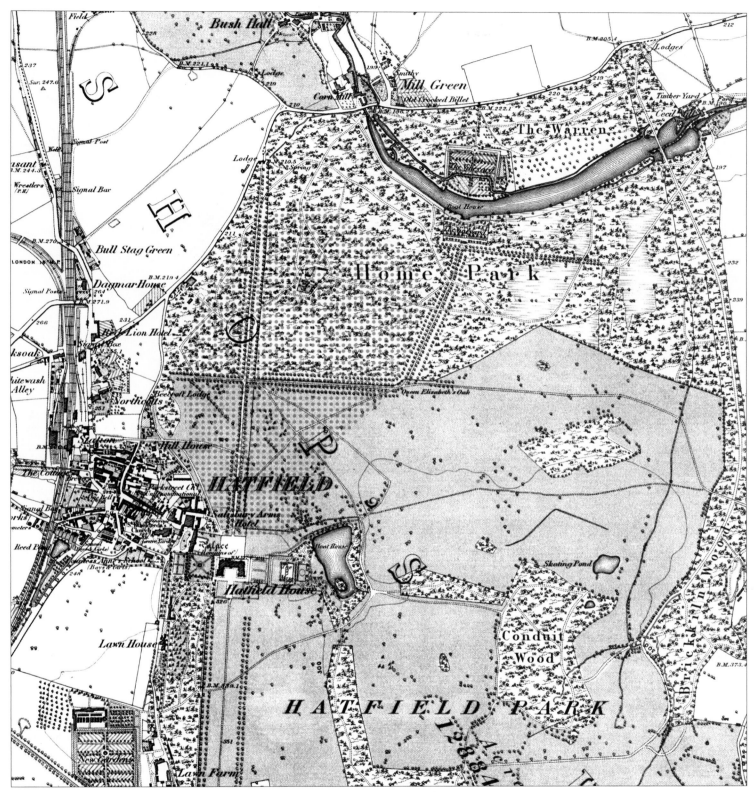

Map 24 Innings park, Hatfield
OS 6 inches to the mile map sheet XXXV, surveyed 1873–9, published 1883.

Figure 27. View of the Halfwayoak Pond in Millwards Park (the medieval little park).

house. This was known as the Innings park and the former little park then became known as the middle park. The survey carried out in 1538, when Henry VIII acquired the manor of Hatfield, recorded that the 350-acre middle park was enclosed with a pale and the farm of the herbage was worth £2; that year it was let to John Kechyn for £3 6s 8d. Two thousand oaks and beeches were valued at 8d each (£80) and were worth 33s 4d yearly to sell. The pasture was described as 'scant sufficient for the deer there', which comprised '7 deer of antler and 73 raskell' and the little lodge was in need of repair.[59] Another survey, undertaken when Princess Elizabeth became the owner in 1551, recorded 111 deer in the middle park, of which 16 were 'of antler'. There were two lodges in the park in the custody of a gentleman, Simon Clare, and these may be the buildings depicted on an estate plan drawn before 1608.[60] One of the lodges shown on the plan appears to have been a substantial house and was perhaps occupied by Clare himself. In the early seventeenth century the park became incorporated in the new 'designed' landscape around the Earl of Salisbury's magnificent Hatfield House. It was extended northwards to surround the south side of the house and its gardens and was embellished with walks and a 'riding' – a formal approach to Hatfield House from the south. A substantial new lodge was built within the park in 1612. However, by the early eighteenth century the park had contracted back to its medieval proportions, and it was

probably disparked by the end of the eighteenth century. It has been managed as woodland ever since and should be of great ecological and archaeological importance.

Establishing the boundary of the 350-acre medieval park is not straightforward. The late sixteenth-/early seventeenth-century park pale shown on the estate plan enclosed an area of approximately 510 acres, significantly more than the recorded medieval acreage.[61] Parts of that boundary are now difficult to trace. Construction of the Great Northern Railway in the mid nineteenth century prompted the second Marquess of Salisbury to re-route the London road which, until then, had passed through his estate close to the west side of Hatfield House. He closed the old road and replaced it with a road running along the western border of his estate, which was also the west side of the park (Map 25). Construction of the road (now the A1000) will have damaged much of the medieval boundary of the park, although parts may have survived. The railway and the road crossed the north-west end of the former late sixteenth-century park, an area which had been disparked by about 1720. The former parkland to the west of the railway line was developed as part of Hatfield New Town in the twentieth century and is now a residential area. Whether or not this was part of the medieval park is not clear.

The south-east side of the former park is bounded by a lane with a well-preserved, substantial bank running the width of the wood on the west side of the lane. There appears to be a

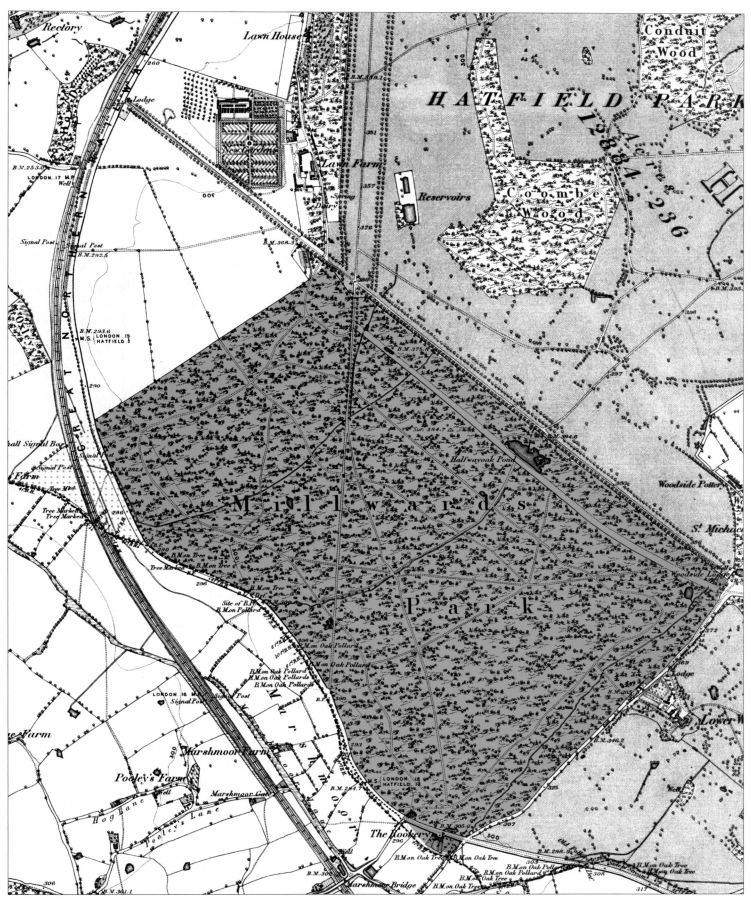

Map 25 The little park, Hatfield (later known as the middle park, now Millwards Park)
OS 6 inches to the mile map sheet XXXV, surveyed 1873–9, published 1883.

substantial bank and ditch along almost the whole of the north-east side of the present woodland, about 27m south-west of the modern tarmac drive. The combined width of the bank and ditch is about 6–7.5m, with the ditch lying on the north side of the bank. Several old pollards, mostly hornbeam and with bluebells beneath, grow on and adjacent to the bank and also around the Halfwayoak Pond at approximately TL242069 (Figure 27). An unexpected finding was that there was also a broad shallow bank, about 5m wide, along the north-west side of the present Millwards Park woodland. This forms a suspiciously straight line, suggesting that it is relatively recent in date, and yet the fact that this boundary encloses 360 acres of woodland to the south-east – very close to the medieval measurement of 350 acres – suggests that it may be the medieval park boundary, or perhaps a 'tidied-up' version of the original. Alternative explanations are that the earthwork bank was a compartment boundary within the medieval park or that it was created as the new park boundary in the early eighteenth century.

The woodland today consists of plantations of various species and ages of tree and appears to contain very few old trees. A long straight drive extends through the wood from a lodge on the south-west side, heading for Hatfield House. At its northern end, before it leaves Millwards Park, the drive is lined by an avenue of pollarded limes. Most of these appear to date from the nineteenth century, but some are clearly much older.

Symondshyde park

NGR: TL195110
Date range: not known – perhaps sixteenth century
Size: 167 acres
Underlying geology: boulder clay

THE EARLIEST KNOWN REFERENCE to a park on the manor of Symondshyde, a sub-manor belonging to the bishops of Ely, is in a rental of the manor dating from 1478 which recorded 'two gardens next the park called Potterys'.[62] Whether the name 'Potterys' related to the gardens or to the park is not clear but no subsequent record of the name has been found. A court roll of 1493 recorded that 'Richard Beche has two gates lying open at Symonds Side Parke, to the injury of his neighbours', which confirms that there was a park in the medieval period, and a survey of the manor of Symondshyde dating from about 1600 recorded a 'wood called Simonshide parke conteyning 166 acres 3r 17p'.[63] No park was depicted on the county map by Saxton in 1577, which suggests that it had ceased to be a deer park by that date. The tithe map and award for Hatfield show a field lying adjacent to the north-east side of Symondshyde Great Wood called Park Field, and another called Penley park lies close by.[64]

The area of 166a 3r 7p corresponds with the area of Symondshyde Great Wood shown on the first edition OS map, plus the land and Chalkdell Wood to the north and the land to the east, all of which is enclosed within the old lane on the north and east sides and the parish boundary on the west side (see Map 26). The land rises westwards to about 105m OD and is today completely covered in woodland (albeit mostly plantations). A bank topped with overgrown hornbeam coppice and with a ditch on its north side forms the southern

boundary of the wood and former park. From the point where this bank meets the lane at the south-east corner of the wood, the bank heads straight northwards before turning to rejoin the lane about 110m to the north-east, suggesting that this small corner of the wood lay outside the park. A boundary earthwork can be seen around most of the east and north sides of the wood, adjacent to the lane. In places it takes the form of a double bank with old hornbeam coppice or hedge on the inner bank.

The shape and location of this park are typical for an early medieval park and it seems likely that it was established significantly earlier than the documentary record would suggest.

Woodhall park

NGR: ?TL236108
Date range: before 1470 – perhaps late sixteenth century
Size: not known; up to 566 acres
Underlying geology: glacial gravel over Upper Chalk

THE EARLIEST KNOWN RECORD of this park is a deleted entry in an account for the manor of Astwick of 1470, which states that A. Haverley was allowed 13s 4d 'for the custody of the game within the park of Wodham Hall' for four years, 'besides 53s 4d allowed to William Haverley for the like, for the same time'. This entry is in a document entitled 'Farmers' accounts of Wodehall, Anstewik and Manewdon', which has been transcribed by a former archivist at Hatfield House. The account for the manor of Woodhall included an allowance of 26s 8d to William Haverley, farmer, 'for his wages for the custody of the park there' and John Budder was paid 66s 8d for 'mending the pales of the park there in divers places'.[65]

The manor of Woodhall was held by the Bassingburn family from the twelfth century until 1535, together with the nearby manor of Astwick.[66] No park was recorded at the inquisition *post mortem* of John Bassingburn in 1276/7 but in 1299/1300 another John Bassingburn was granted free warren in his manors of Hatfield and Redbourn in Hertfordshire and Manuden and Rettenden in Essex. He was sheriff of Hertfordshire and Essex in 1303/4 and again in 1306.[67] A man of his status is very likely to have aspired to owning a deer park and the park at Woodhall is, therefore, likely to date from the beginning of the fourteenth century. A subsequent John Bassingburn was sheriff of Hertfordshire and Essex in 1371/2 and served in two parliaments.[68] At the end of the fifteenth century the manor was held by Thomas Bassingburn, who was married to Katherine, sister of Sir William Say.

Woodhall park was shown on the north bank of the river Lea on Saxton's county map of 1577 (Figure 26), but not on Norden's map of 1598, suggesting that it was disparked before the end of the sixteenth century. No park was depicted around the house named Wood Hall on Seller's map of 1676, but there was a paled park on the county map by Oliver of 1695, so it seems likely that the medieval park was reincarnated during the later seventeenth century, perhaps by Sir Francis Boteler, who died in 1690.[69] This park appears to have survived into the second half of the eighteenth century but was not shown as parkland on the Ordnance Survey Drawing of 1805.[70]

Map 26 Symondshyde park, Hatfield
OS 6 inches to the mile map sheets XXVIII, surveyed 1878–81, published 1884; and XXXV, surveyed 1873–9, published 1883. Annotated with field names from the Hatfield tithe award and map, 1838–9 (HALS DSA4/47/1 and 2).

Several park-related features and field names were recorded on the Hatfield tithe map and award of 1838/9 but these probably related to the park which existed from the seventeenth century rather than to the medieval park. The lane heading north-east from Stanborough appears to follow the curving boundary of a large enclosure, possibly a park. The eastern limit of the former parkland is likely to have been determined by a common arable field shown on a late eighteenth-century map (see Map 27).[71] With the limited

information found for the park in the medieval period, it is impossible to know whether the medieval park filled the area shaded on this map (about 500 acres), or whether it covered a smaller area within it.

A railway line was constructed across the former park in the nineteenth century and much of the land disappeared under Welwyn Garden City during the twentieth century. The south end of the former park remains arable farmland but field evidence is sadly lacking.

119

1. Page, *Hertford*, 3, p. 102, citing Feet of Fines Hertfordshire Hil. 39 Hen. III, no. 458 (TNA: PRO CP25/1/85/26); Feet of Fines Hertfordshire Trin. 52 Hen. III, no. 599 (TNA: PRO CP25/1/85/31).

2. H. Ridgeway, 'William de Valence and his *familiares* 1247–72', *Historical Research*, 65 (1992), pp. 246–7.

3. *Cal. Pat. 1292–1301*, p. 552.

4. Cussans, *History of Hertfordshire*, 2, Broadwater Hundred, p. 275, citing Chancery Inquisition *post mortem* 17 Edw. II. No. 75 (TNA: PRO C134/83/1).

5. HALS DE/X2/14 *The Cosmopolitan*, May 1888, p. 30.

6. HALS DE/B1727/T2, deeds of 1718.

7. HALS DSA4/47/1 and 2 Hatfield tithe award and map, 1839.

8. J. Fairweather, *Liber Eliensis translated from the Latin* (Woodbridge, 2005), pp. 103–4.

9. Williamson, *Origins of Hertfordshire*, p. 128.

10. BL Cotton MS, Tiberius Bii, fo. 140–1 survey of manors of the bishopric of Ely, 1222.

11. HHA Hatfield Manor Papers I, 1229 Feb, p. 41; see also *Cal. Close. 1227–1231*, pp. 149 and 155 — this states four oaks.

12. BL Cotton MS, Claudius C.xi.

13. CUL EDR G/3/27 Old Coucher Book of Ely, fo. 80.

14. HHA Hatfield Manor Papers I, 1286 Sep 7, p. 87.

15. HHA Hatfield Manor Papers I, 1297–1300, p. 107.

16. HHA Hatfield Manor Papers I, 1396, p. 265.

17. HHA Hatfield Manor Papers I, 1428, p. 339.

18. HHA Hatfield Manor Papers I, 1396 Michaelmas, p. 265.

19. HHA Hatfield Manor Papers I, 1428, 1436 and 1437, pp. 339, 352 and 366.

20. HHA Hatfield Manor Papers I, 1396 Michaelmas, p. 265–71. The charcoal appears to have been measured in 'quarters' (Latin *quartarius*), presumably a fourth part of a hundredweight.

21. HHA Hatfield Manor Papers I, 1428 Michaelmas, p. 339.

22. *Ibid.*, 1507 17 May p. 673.

23. HHA Hatfield Manor Papers I, 1436 Michaelmas, p. 356. A Cottier was an annual tenure of land let direct to the labourer who made the highest public bid for it.

24. HHA Hatfield Manor Papers I, 1436 Michaelmas, p. 352; 1437 Michaelmas, p. 367.

25. HHA Hatfield Manor Papers I, 1396 Michaelmas, p. 265.

26. HHA Hatfield Manor Papers I, 1392/3, p. 253.

27. HHA Hatfield Manor Papers I, 1482 6 Jan, p. 423.

28. Austin, 'Hatfield Great Wood', p. 2. It is not clear whether the park boundary lay along the parish boundary at Bell Bar, or along the field boundary just to the north.

29. Page, *Hertford*, 3, p. 99 citing Land Revenue Miscellaneous Book 16 (6).

30. *Cal. Pat. 1348–1350*, p. 184.

31. HHA Hatfield Manor Papers I, 1358, p. 205.

32. Page, *Hertford*, 3, p. 92.

33. TNA: PRO LR2/216 Land Revenue Miscellaneous Book 216. Rascal deer were those, such as young males, which were considered unsuitable for hunting.

34. TNA: PRO LR2/216 Land Revenue Miscellaneous Book 216, p. 7.

35. Austin, 'Hatfield Great Wood', p. 4, citing HHA Accounts 5/5.

36. Austin, 'Hatfield Great Wood', pp. 4–7.

37. TNA: PRO SC 11/269 rental of Sir John Say, 1468. HHA Hatfield Manor Papers II, Nov 1508, p. 587.

38. HHA Hatfield Manor Papers I, 1388 12 June, p. 239; 1428 Michaelmas, p. 339.

39. TNA: PRO LR2/216 Land Revenue Miscellaneous Books 216, p. 5.

40. HHA R. Harcourt Williams, 'Deer at Hatfield', Hatfield Estate Newsletter, February 1997.

41. TNA: PRO LR2/216 Land Revenue Miscellaneous Books 216, p. 7; Page, *Hertford*, 3, p. 100, quoting Exchequer Special Commissions Eliz. no. 1026 (TNA: PRO E178/1026).

42. HHA CPM Supp. 23 & 24, both pre-1608; CPM Supp. 21 *c*.1610.

43. HHA Williams, 'Deer at Hatfield'.

44. Chauncy, *Historical antiquities*, p. 308; HHA Williams, 'Deer at Hatfield'.

45. Young, *General view*, p. 24.

46. Shirley, *English deer parks*, p. 79.

47. HHA Williams, 'Deer at Hatfield'.

48. HHA Hatfield Manor Papers I, 1248–9, p. 47.

49. BL Cotton MS, Tiberius B. ii.

50. HHA Hatfield Manor Papers I, 1248–9, p. 47.

51. BL Cotton MS, Claudius C.xi and CUL EDR G/3/27 Old Coucher Book of Ely, fo. 80.

52. Workers' Educational Association, *Hatfield and its people: A thousand years of history, 1* (1959), p. 15.

53. Page, *Hertford*, 3, p. 100, quoting M. Paris, *Chronica Majora* (Rolls Ser.), v, 344.

54. HHA Hatfield Manor Papers I, 1356/7.

55. HHA Hatfield Manor Papers I, 1388 12 June, p. 239.

56. HHA Hatfield Manor Papers I, 1396 Michaelmas, p. 265.

57. HHA Hatfield Manor Papers I, p. 303 citing HHA court rolls 9/20, 1406.

58. HHA Hatfield Manor Papers I, 1436 Michaelmas, p. 353 and 1437 Michaelmas, p. 367.

59. HHA Hatfield Manor Papers II, 1538 Feb, p. 683 & Nov, Dec, p. 703; TNA: PRO LR2/216 Land Revenue Miscellaneous Books 216, p. 4; Page, *Hertford*, 3, p. 99, citing Rentals and Surveys Roll Hertfordshire 276 (TNA: PRO SC11/276).

60. HHA Hatfield Manor Papers II, 1551 25 April, p. 807; CPM Supp. 24 plan of Hatfield estate, pre-1608.

61. HHA CPM Supp. 24 plan of Hatfield estate, pre-1608.

62. HHA Hatfield Manor Papers I, p. 415.

63. Ibid. p. 497; HALS DE/X265/Z1 survey of the manor of Simonshyde, *c*.1600.

64. HALS DSA4/47/1 and 2 tithe award and map for Hatfield, 1839 and 1838.

65. HHA Hatfield Manor Papers I, pp. 399–400.

66. Page, *Hertford*, 3, p. 100, citing Feet of Fines, Hertfordshire, 9 Ric. I, no. 21 (TNA: PRO CP25/1/84/1); p. 107 citing Chancery Inquisition *post mortem* (Ser. 2), lxii, 64 (TNA: PRO C142/62/64).

67. Clutterbuck, *History and antiquities*, 2, p. 344.

68. *Ibid.*

69. Salmon, *History of Hertfordshire*, p. 213.

70. Dury and Andrews, *Hartfordshire*; BL Ordnance Survey Drawing 149, 9 (Hatfield sheet).

71. Workers' Educational Association, *Hatfield and its people: farming yesterday and today, 9* (Hatfield, 1962), p. 8.

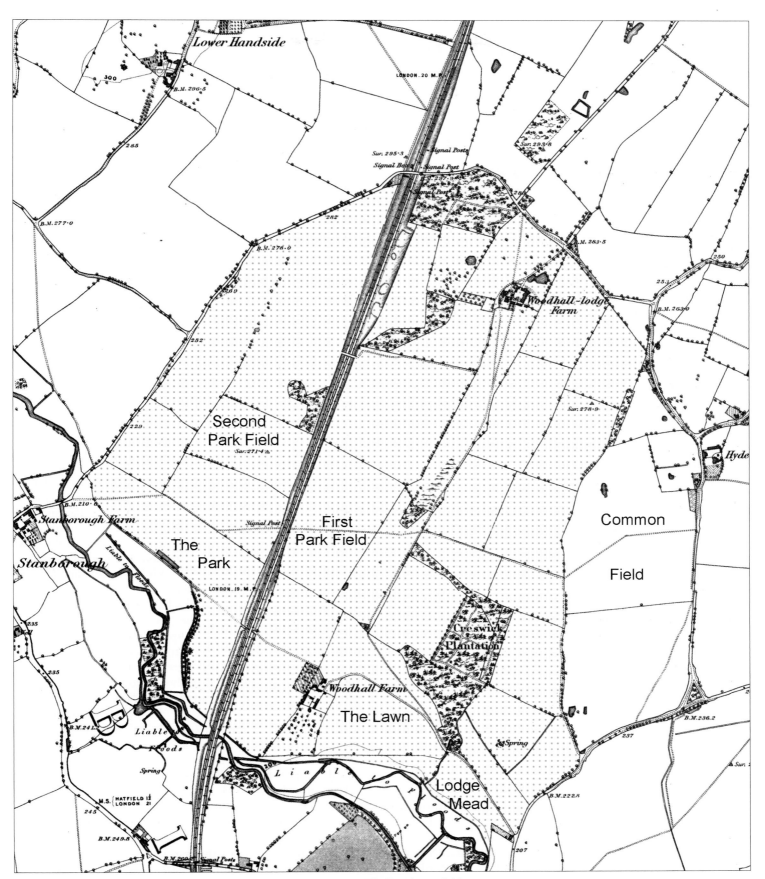

Map 27 Woodhall park, Hatfield
OS map sheet XXVIII, 6 inches to the mile, surveyed 1878–81, published 1884; and sheet XXXV, surveyed 1873–9, published 1883. Annotated with field names from the Hatfield tithe award and map, 1838–9 (HALS DSA4/47/1 and 2), which probably related to the post-medieval park. The Common Field was shown on a map of Hatfield Hyde, 1796 (HHA CPM Supp. 66).

Hertingfordbury

Old, new, great, little, Hertingfordbury or Hertford park
NGR: TL315117
Date range: by 1285 – early seventeenth century
Size: not known
Underlying geology: ?great park: glacial gravel, boulder clay and Laminated Clay (brickearth) over Upper Chalk; ?little park: glacial gravel and Upper Chalk

HERTINGFORDBURY WAS HELD by Christina de Valognes from the mid thirteenth century. She was married to Peter de Maune before 1247 and they had a household in the manor.[1] Christina claimed free warren in 1273/4 but no park was recorded in an inquisition of the manor compiled in 1279 and the first record of the park dates from 1285.[2]

The manor passed to Christina's son, Henry de Maune, before 1294 and he granted his lands to Agnes de Valence, the daughter of William de Valence (half brother of Henry III) who held nearby Hertford castle from 1247 until his death in 1296. It was perhaps from the 1290s that the park at Hertingfordbury first became linked with Hertford castle. In October 1295 William's wife, Joan de Valence, Countess of Pembroke, was at Hertford and was joined there by her pack of hunting dogs – the closest we come to a record of hunting taking place at Hertingfordbury in medieval times.[3]

On the death of William de Valence Hertford castle reverted to the crown but was granted to his son, Aymer de Valence, from 1299. William's daughter, Agnes, must have maintained a high-status household at Hertingfordbury, accommodating her newly widowed mother, the dowager countess of Pembroke, for two months in the summer of 1296. Agnes' sister, Isabella de Hastings, also joined them for a week, being fetched there in the countess's coach.[4] An inquisition taken after the death of Agnes in 1309/10 shows that she held the manor of Hertingfordbury of the king in chief by homage only and that her heir was her brother Aymer de Valence, Earl of Pembroke, who was already holding Hertford castle.[5] Unfortunately, the document is in a poor condition and reveals no information about the park at Hertingfordbury.[6] On the death of Aymer de Valence in 1323 the park and castle became separated as Hertingfordbury passed to his niece, Elizabeth Comyn, and Hertford castle was surrendered to the crown.[7]

Within a few days of his accession in 1327, Edward III granted Hertford castle to his mother, Queen Isabella, for life and it became one of her main residences where she received frequent visits from the king. It was to be another 18 years before Isabella also acquired the manor of Hertingfordbury and its park: in 1345, they were surrendered to the king by Elizabeth Comyn and her husband, Richard Talbot, in exchange for lands in Herefordshire. Edward granted the manor to his mother and she then held it, together with Hertford castle and other nearby manors, until she died.[8]

Accounts for the manor of Hertingfordbury compiled in 1355 record the receipt of 12d for the pannage of pigs in the park during the preceding year. No payments were recorded to a parker or for repairs to the park boundary but a wage of 60s 8d was paid to a warrener.[9] In July 1358 the queen appointed Robert de Louthe as:

> keeper of the castle of Hertford and surveyor of the town of Hertford and the manors of Esynden [Essendon], Bayford and Hertfordyngbury and the parks and warren there, for life, with 12d daily for his wages by the hands of the bailiffs and reeves of the town and manors, and a robe yearly or twenty shillings for the same, wood for his fuel by view of the steward in the outwoods of the manor, without [outside] the parks.[10]

There is no known record of Queen Isabella using the park but her daughter, Queen Joan of Scotland, had her master falconer with her when she was at Hertford castle from 1346 and Edward III also enjoyed the sport of falconry on the banks of the river Lea between Stratford and Hertford.[11] Just a month before she died in August 1358, Isabella and her daughter visited the parks at Almshoe and Maydencroft, near Hitchin (see p. 142–5), so it seems very likely that Hertingfordbury park would also have been enjoyed by the royal family.[12] Indeed, the reference to 'parks' in the plural in the grant of the keepership of the castle to Robert de Louthe suggests that a second park had been established at Hertingfordbury by 1358. The presence of two parks is confirmed in accounts drawn up by William de Louth in 1359/60 which recorded repairs to the boundary of the little park using wood lopped in the great park and carried to the little park using a cart and three horses for four days.[13]

In 1377 Edward III granted the castle, town and honour of Hertford and 'the towns of Beyford, Esendon and Hertfordyngbury' to John of Gaunt.[14] He seems to have been in possession of the castle and park for a few years before this, however, because in correspondence recorded in his Register, John of Gaunt refers to 'our castle of Hertford' and 'our park of Hertingfordbury' in 1373 and 1376 respectively. The letter of March 1376 was addressed to John Halstead, parker of Hertingfordbury park, and requested timber from the park to repair buildings at the castle.[15] Two accounts from the 1380s show that at least one of the parks contained deer and that John of Gaunt was investing in park maintenance.[16] He spent 77s 1d on the parks in 1381/2, including 24s 3d on repairs to a lodge in the 'new' park. The park gates were repaired and furnished with a new lock and key and references to a 'watergate' and to gates 'beyond the river bank' suggest that the park bordered either the river Mimram or Lea, or both. A

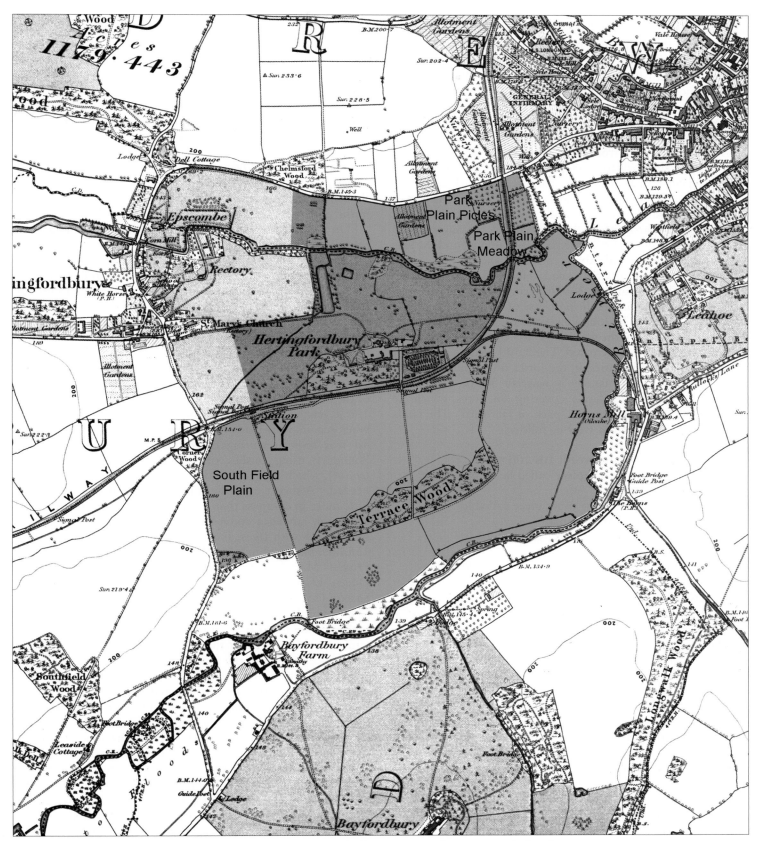

Map 28 The park at Hertingfordbury, sometimes known as Hertford park
OS 6 inches to the mile map sheets XXIX, surveyed 1879–80, published 1884; and XXXVI, surveyed 1873–80, published 1883. Park boundary and field names are derived from an estate map of 1732 (HALS DE/P/P7).

new hedge, 172 perches (*c*.865m) long, was made between the old park and the lawn and a new cart road was constructed to facilitate the transport of wood to Hertford castle. In 1388/9 a new gate (with lock and key) was made for the old park, within which wood was felled and 1,350 faggots were made. A carter was paid to carry wood from the old park to the new park where it was used to make a hedge from the water gate. A hedge was also made around the new park and rabbits were taken to the new park from the warren in the wintertime. The total costs of the park for 1388/9 were 34s 8½d, including 3 shillings spent on hay for the deer in the new park in winter, but this did not include the wages of John Halstead, parker and warrener, who earned 60s 10d a year at 2d per day. These expenses were partly offset by the sale of the faggots (33 shillings), pannage of pigs in the park (6 shillings) and the sale of partridges (3s 4d) and rabbits (3 shillings).

From 1396 John of Gaunt made Hertford castle his chief residence.[17] The account for 1395/6 records repairs to a lodge in the little park, including the purchase of reeds for part of the roof (5 shillings).[18] The following year a well was dug in the garden of the lodge in the great park at a cost of 21s 5d and a garden (*herbarium*) was created. The 3,500 faggots made that year were not sold but used in the lord's own household.[19] In 1397 John of Gaunt issued a warrant to the bailiff of Hertingfordbury listing lands covering 88 acres which he wanted enclosed to enlarge his 'park of Hertford'. The lands listed in the 1397 warrant were as follows:

36 acres of arable land worth 10s 10d of rent p.a.
9 acres of pasture in one piece called la chapelle croft worth 5s 4d p.a.
18 acres of pasture in one other piece called le Smythesmede worth 18s p.a.
9 acres of meadow in one other piece called le Brodemede worth 30s p.a.
5 acres of meadow in one other piece called le Castelhoke worth 10s p.a.
11 acres of meadow in one other piece called le Stywardesmede worth 14s 8d p.a.[20]

The 36 acres of arable land were to be enclosed from the common field called Southfield but the remaining 27 acres of pasture and 25 acres of meadow seem most likely to have been closes on the north bank of the Mimram (in the parish of St Andrews, Hertford) and on the west bank of the Lea.

The last account for the fourteenth century showed an unusually healthy income from the park, but did not record any 'costs of the park' beside the 60s 10d paid to the parker and warrener, John Bolowe:

Agistment of animals	38s	2d
Sale of 48 ash trees	19s	3d
Sale of wood		14d
Sale of 1,200 faggots	36s	
Total £4	14s	7d

However, the enclosure of the meadows into the park resulted in a marked fall in manorial income and must have had a considerable impact on the local tenantry. In the 1390s, before the park expanded, 30 acres of meadow in

Stewardsmead, Hassokmead, Broadmead, Castlehoke and Fernhern, plus 30 acres of 'winter herbage', were rented out for 72 shillings a year.[21] In 1442/3 just one acre of meadow was available for rent and that was leased to the parker for two shillings. Fifty-one acres of meadow were inside the park and even the small areas remaining outside the park were not available for rent: six acres in Smallmead and Castlehoke were mowed to make hay to feed the king's deer in the park during the winter and a further five acres provided winter grazing for the king's rabbits.[22] Over a century later, in the mid sixteenth century, little had changed: just three shillings was received for the rent of the meadow in Stewardsmead and all the meadows in the park were used to feed the deer and rabbits.[23]

On the death of John of Gaunt in 1399 the park and castle reverted to the crown and remained in royal hands throughout the fifteenth and sixteenth centuries. There was a reference to the great park in 1462/3 but later records refer only to a single park.[24] The few surviving accounts from 1442 until 1554/5 do not record any income from pannage or agistment in the park, nor was there any income from pollarding or felling trees in the park or in the woods on the manor. The deer were present throughout this time, grazing a 35-acre meadow in the park and provided with hay made in Smalemede each winter at a cost of 3s 4d.[25] A parker was employed at least until the end of the fifteenth century, still receiving the standard wage of 60s 10d a year. Additional expenditure was recorded in 1462/3, when repairs were made to the lodge, and in 1480/1, when 13s 4d was spent repairing defects and breaches in the park boundary using bushes or brambles (*dumus*) and thorns (*spinis*), which were cut and then carried to where they were needed.[26] A survey carried out in 1523 recorded 'a small park, little more in compass than a mile, distant from the castle not a quarter, having a convenient lodge built with timber; it is well stored with trees, fuel, wood, and coal' [charcoal].[27] In 1553 the park and manor of Hertingfordbury were granted to Princess Mary by Edward VI and they subsequently passed to Queen Elizabeth.[28] The sixteenth-century county maps by Saxton (1577) and Norden (1598) both show the park at the east end of the parish of Hertingfordbury, occupying a ridge of higher ground which separated the rivers Lea and Mimram and extending north of the Mimram, as it had presumably done since the end of the fourteenth century.

A survey in November 1604 found that Hertingfordbury park contained 201 acres 'as appeared by a survey taken some 14 years since'. The soil was found to be 'very hard, after the manor [*sic*] of Harts' and the park was considered capable of supporting no more than 150 deer. It was reported to the surveyors that 200 deer had been kept in the park one year but 160 of them had died within the year. The surveyors did not think 'it would keep 150 fair game without an addition of 3 acres called the Deer Meadow, which now is and alwaies was allowed to the Park for the maintenance of the deer'.[29]

In the same year, 1604, the keeper of the park for James I was commanded to forbear killing any deer there for three years.[30] Four years later another survey recorded 1,126 oaks, 3,311 hornbeams and other trees in the park.[31] In 1623 the king gave a buck from Hertingfordbury to a judge of the Admiralty Court.[32] Free chase and free warren were granted in the park in 1627 and in the same year the park was said to contain 237 acres besides a meadow of 3 acres called 'le deere meadowe',

Figure 28. *Detail of a 'map of Hertingfordbury Farm' by A. Griffin, 1732 (HALS DE/P/P7) showing the lands which were probably once part of the medieval great park. NB the map was drawn with north at bottom. Reproduced by kind permission of Hertfordshire Archives and Local Studies.*

and 1 acre of osier woods.[33] Deer were caught and taken to Hatfield park in 1632 at a cost of £7 3s 9d for carriage.[34]

Also at the beginning of the seventeenth century, Sir William Harrington 'converted the Lodge into a good house for his own habitation'.[35] No park was shown by either Seller (1676) or Oliver (1695), but both show 'Park House'. A small park was depicted south of the Mimram by Warburton (1749) which probably corresponds with the new 136-acre park, the pales of which were plotted onto an estate map by Griffin in 1732 and annotated as 'the Bounds of the intended Park'.[36]

Griffin's map provides the earliest known plan of the park, and shows it as it was after a century of transformation from medieval hunting park to early eighteenth-century ornamental park complete with gentleman's residence, formal gardens, ornamental canal and avenues of trees (Figure 28). It nevertheless shows boundaries which may well date from the medieval period and these have been used to reconstruct the possible extent of the late medieval park shown on Map 28. The

map suggests that the park boundary on the western side was composed of a series of field boundaries, evidence of its late fourteenth-century expansion onto arable land. The acreage of the estate as shown on Griffin's map was approximately 246 acres, very close to the acreage given for the park in 1627. The field names 'Park Plain Meadow' (field P) and 'Park Plain Picles' [pightles] (fields labelled R) shown on this map lying between the river and the main road heading west from Hertford (see Map 28) provide further evidence for the late fourteenth-century expansion of the park north of the Mimram.

This, then, was the park enlarged by John of Gaunt at the end of the fourteenth century. What is less clear is whether the park which he enlarged was the old, new, little or great park recorded in the decades preceding this expansion. Nor can we be sure where the earliest park lay. It is possible that the thirteenth-century park was located on the extensive gravelly heathland which extended westwards from Hertingfordbury towards Birch Green south of the river Mimram, which was still apparently largely unenclosed in 1732. There is certainly evidence to suggest that the little park lay to the west of the village of Hertingfordbury, in an area occupied by extensive rabbit warrens in the post-medieval period.

A warrener was employed at Hertingfordbury by 1354 and by the mid fifteenth century the lease of the warren was providing significant revenues for the manor (70 shillings in 1442/3 and 60 shillings p.a. in later accounts) which suggests that it covered an extensive area and was not part of the fifteenth- and sixteenth-century park. In 1623/4 the 'warren of conies' was leased by those holding the manor on behalf of Charles, Prince of Wales, to Periam Docwra of Putteridge, Hertfordshire.[37] He sub-let it in 1634 to Reynold and James Pace, yeomen of Hertingfordbury, who were to manage the rabbits in the warren. The lease included the warren and lodge 'together with one greate Close neere adjoyninge to the said lodge called the little Park'.[38] According to a later lease, the warren held by Reynold and James Pace covered 16½ acres and was part of the land surrendered by Queen Elizabeth to William Kempton in 1566/7.[39] Part of Kempton's land subsequently become Place Farm and a list of lands belonging to Place Farm (now Bury Farm) in 1693 included The Warren, which had formerly covered 67 acres but was 'now divided into 5 arable fields'. The next field on the list was 'Oakleys Warren alias little park', 20 acres, followed by an enclosed arable field of 4 acres called Little park. A field of 24 acres was still part of Place Farm and known as Oakley Warren in 1838, when it was shown on the Hertingfordbury tithe map (see Map 29).[40]

In order to follow this thread of evidence, we have to assume that the little park recalled in the late seventeenth-century field name corresponds with the little park recorded three centuries earlier which, although quite possible, is by no means certain. The 1693 field-name evidence suggests that the little park formerly covered at least 24 acres but, as it lay adjacent to further extensive warrens, it seems likely that at least some of those warrens were also once part of the former medieval deer park. The soil of the field named Merry Boys Warren in 1838 is very stony and cannot have been conducive to ploughing in medieval times, and a steep scarp, marked as Chisel Shelf on the OS map, must have remained woodland through the centuries, as it does today. Both of these areas were likely to have been imparked in the thirteenth century. The *possible* extent of this park could have been as much as 130 acres and is indicated by the shading on Map 29.

1. Page, *Hertford*, 3, p. 465.

2. Page, *Hertford*, 3, p. 464, citing *Placita de Quo Warranto* (Record Commission), 281, 290; TNA: PRO C145/37 (6) miscellaneous inquisitions (7 Edw. I, no. 42); Page, *Hertford*, 3, p. 464, citing Coram Rege Rolls 92, m. 2 (TNA: PRO KB27/92).

3. Woolgar, *The great household*, p. 193.

4. *Ibid.*, pp. 46, 49, 53.

5. Andrews, *Hertford castle*, pp. 18–19.

6. TNA: PRO C134/15 (8) inquisition *post mortem*, Agnes de Valence, 1309/10 (3 Edw. II, no. 37).

7. Page, *Hertford*, 3, pp. 464, 501.

8. Page, *Hertford*, 3, p. 464.

9. TNA: PRO SC6/865/17 ministers' and receivers' accounts for Hertingfordbury, 1354/5.

10. *Cal. Pat. 1358–1361*, p. 97.

11. Andrews, *Hertford castle*, pp. 22, 24.

12. Bond, 'Notices of the last days of Isabella, Queen of Edward the second', p. 462.

13. TNA: PRO SC6/865/18 ministers' and receivers' accounts for Hertingfordbury, 1359/60. The total cost of the work recorded in the parks was 7s 8d.

14. *Cal. Pat. 1377–1381*, p. 26.

15. S. Armitage-Smith (ed.), *John of Gaunt's register*, 2 (London, 1911), p. 28.

16. HHA court rolls 19/11 account, 1381/2; court rolls 22/8 account, 1388/9.

17. Page, *Hertford*, 3, p. 505.

18. HHA court rolls 22/7 account, 1395/6.

19. HHA court rolls 22/10 account, 1396/7.

20. HHA court rolls 22/7 account, 1395/6.

21. HHA court rolls 22/10 account, 1396/7; 20/13 account, 1399/1400.

22. HHA court rolls 22/1 account, 1442/3.

23. HHA court rolls 22/12 account, 1554/5.

24. HALS DE/P/T638 bailiff's account, 1462/3.

25. HHA court rolls 22/1 account, 1442/3; 21/11 account, 1480/1; 21/18 account, 1485/6; 22/5 account, 1493/4; 21/10 account, 1495/6; 21/17 account, 1513/14; 22/6 account, 1518/19; 22/12 account, 1554/5.

26. HHA court rolls 22/10 accounts 1396–7; HALS DE/P/T638 bailiff's account, 1462/3; HHA court rolls 21/11 account, 1480/1.

27. Page, *Hertford*, 3, p. 464.

28. Andrews, Hertford castle, p. 62.

29. Clutterbuck, *History and antiquities*, 2, p. 202, citing the archives of the Duchy of Lancaster.

30. Page, *Hertford*, 3, p. 464 citing *Calendar of State Papers Domestic* 1603–10, p. 141.

31. Cussans, *History of Hertfordshire*, 2, p. 104.

32. Page, *Hertford*, 3, p. 464 citing *Calendar of State Papers Domestic* 1623–5, p. 46.

33. Page, *Hertford*, 3, p. 464.

34. HHA Hatfield Manor Papers: Summaries I, p. 198.

35. Chauncy, *Historical antiquities*, p. 272.

36. HALS DE/P/P7 map of Hertingfordbury Farm by A. Griffin, 1732.

37. HALS DE/P/T263 deeds, 1623/4.

38. HALS DE/P/T264 lease of Hertingfordbury warren, 1634.

39. HALS DE/P/T262 deeds, 1651.

40. HALS DE/P/T283 deeds, 1693 (see also DE/P/T840, 1639); DSA4/51/1 and 2 Hertingfordbury tithe award and map, 1838.

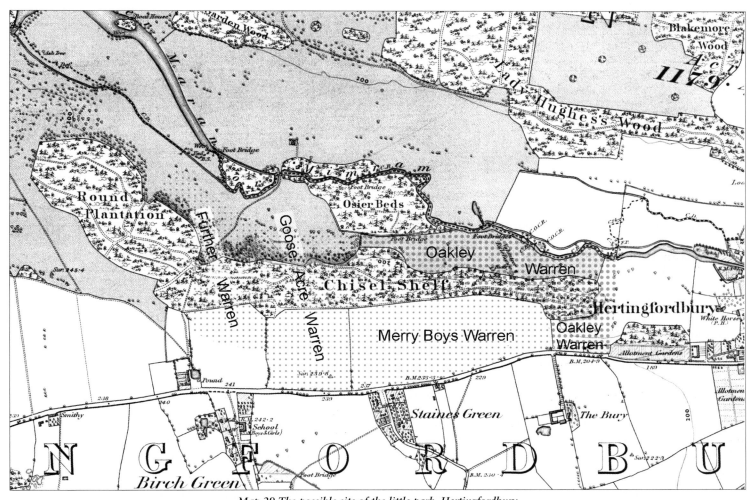

Map 29 The possible site of the little park, Hertingfordbury

OS 6 inches to the mile map sheet XXIX, surveyed 1879–80, published 1884. Annotated with warren field names from the Hertingfordbury tithe award and map, 1838 (HALS DSA4/51/1 and 2), and from a map of the Cole Green Park estate, 1704 (HALS DE/P/P4), which may provide evidence of the location of the former little park (see text) and, perhaps, the earliest park at Hertingfordbury.

Hitchin

Punfold park

NGR: TL178294
Date range: by 1380 – not known
Size: perhaps c.48 acres
Underlying geology: glaciofluvial deposits and Middle Chalk

A GRANT OF THE MANOR OF HITCHIN to Sir Hugh Segrave in 1380 concluded with the statement, 'there are there certain void pieces of land within the site of the manor, and a park called Punfold which remain in common because they may not be divided'.[1] No park was mentioned in the inquisition *post mortem* of John de Balliol, lord of the manor and father of the Scottish king, in 1269.[2] Unfortunately the manuscript recording the inquisition held on the death of Edward de Kendale in 1373 is in poor condition and does not provide evidence for either the presence or absence of a park.[3]

A map of 1818 shows many park field names, including Pain's Park, Park Piece and Little Park Piece, in an area west of the town centre now bounded by roads called Paynes Park, Tilehouse Street, Grays Lane, Lucas Lane, Oughtonhead Way

and Bedford Road.[4] This area, identified by Bridget Howlett, covers about 48 acres and, lying close to the market place and church, it would have made an unusual location for a medieval park. By the seventeenth century the area had been converted to copyhold land[5] and part of it was depicted on a bird's-eye view of the town drawn at the end of the century by J. Drapentier for Sir Henry Chauncy's county history. The large fields rising up the hill beyond the town in Figure 29 were perhaps the eastern end of the fourteenth-century Punfold Park – located on an east-facing slope and rising almost to the summit of the hill where it is bounded today by Lucas Lane. The first edition OS map shows that the eastern end of the potential parkland was crossed by a road called Old Park Road (see Map 30) and this road could have formed an alternative eastern boundary to the park.

Possible fragments of surviving boundary identified by Bridget Howlett include a hedge-bank at the corner of Grays Lane and Lucas Lane and another short section near the junction of Lucas Lane and West Hill.[6] Any other earthworks will have disappeared under the urban sprawl of Hitchin long

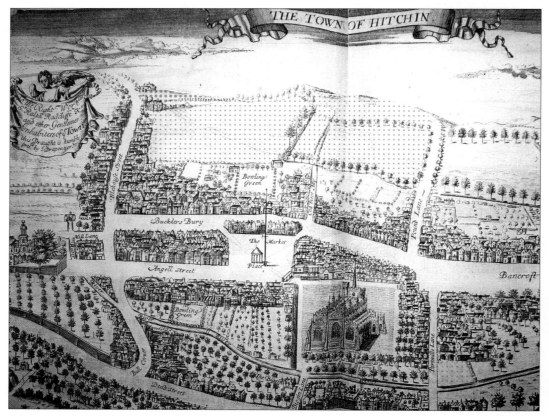

Figure 29. Detail of the bird's-eye view of Hitchin (looking west) by J. Drapentier published in Sir Henry Chauncy's Historical Antiquities
of Hertfordshire *(1700) showing the possible locations of two parks for which documentary evidence has been found.*
Reproduced by kind permission of Hertfordshire Archives and Local Studies.

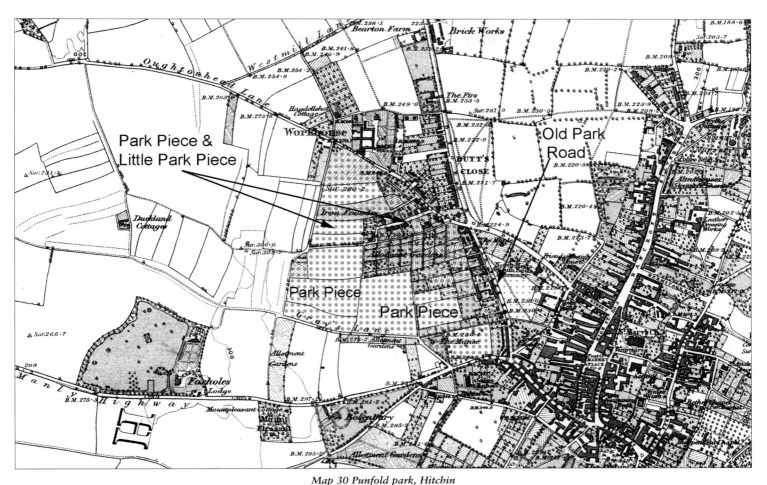

Map 30 Punfold park, Hitchin

OS 6 inches to the mile map sheet XII, surveyed 1878–81, published 1884. Annotated with field names from an early eighteenth-century map (HALS PC160) and from the Hitchin tithe award and map, 1841 (HALS DSA4/53/1 and 2). The road 'Old Park Road' is named on the OS map itself. The likely extent of the park has been determined by Bridget Howlett, as has the location of the small plot north-east of St Mary's church identified as the 'lady's park' in sixteenth-century documents.

ago. It is possible, however, that the park once extended further westwards. An early eighteenth-century map at Hitchin Museum shows a large open area of land west of the town labelled 'Park Piece' with just a few rectangular enclosures at the south-eastern and western peripheries.[7] The land is still open farmland today and rights of way enclose a large elliptical area which does have a vestigial bank surviving along short stretches of the boundary (most notably at the western end north-west of Oughton Head Farm and alongside Oughtonhead Lane just west of the nature reserve). However, these banks may simply be surviving field hedge-banks and do not constitute good evidence for a medieval park.

Further research by Bridget Howlett into the development of the town of Hitchin has identified a small plot of land on the west bank of the Hiz and on the north side of Port Mill Lane which was described in a series of entries in the manor court rolls dating from the mid sixteenth century onwards as lying 'where the lady's park used to be situated'.[8] The lady in question was probably one (or both) of Henry VIII's queens: Katherine of Aragon, who held the manor from 1509, or Anne Boleyn, who held it from 1534 to 1536.[9] Given the size of the plot and its location in the town this is a puzzling reference to a park and one possibility is that this was the site of the pinfold recorded in

the fourteenth-century name 'Punfold Park', but how this might relate to the evidence for the park west of the town is not clear.

1. *Cal. Close 1377–1381*, p. 507.

2. R.L. Hine, *The history of Hitchin*, 1 (London, 1927), pp. 33–4, citing Chancery Inquisition *post mortem* 53 Hen. III, no. 43 (TNA: PRO C132/36/5).

3. TNA: PRO C135/232 (11) inquisition *post mortem* of Edward de Kendale, 1373.

4. B. Howlett, *Hitchin Priory Park* (Hitchin Historical Society, 2004), pp. ix and 1–3, citing a plan of the township of Hitchin by Henry Merrett, 1818.

5. Howlett, *Hitchin Priory Park*, p. 2.

6. *Ibid*., p. 3.

7. Hitchin Museum, map of the town of Hitchin and Ippollitts, *c*.early eighteenth century; photograph at HALS PC160.

8. HALS 60313 copy of court roll manor of Hitchin Foreign, 1555; 60353–60365 copies of court rolls manor of Hitchin Foreign, 1559–1657. I am grateful to Bridget Howlett for bringing these references to my attention. See her chapter on Hitchin in T. Slater and N. Goose (eds), *A county of small towns: the development of Hertfordshire's urban landscape to 1800* (Hatfield, 2008).

9. Page, *Hertford*, 3, p. 9, citing Letters & Papers Henry VIII, i, 155 and vii, 352.

Hoddesdon

Bassingbourne's park and William of Louth's park; Hoddesdon park

NGR: TL351085
Date range: perhaps early thirteenth century – pre-1323, perhaps a second park by 1290 – not known
Size: recorded as 91 acres in 1573; perhaps *c.*150 acres
Underlying geology: London Clay overlain in places by Pebble Gravel or boulder clay

RECORDS SUGGEST THAT THERE may have been two medieval parks in Hoddesdon. The first park was probably established in the early thirteenth century because in 1277 Stephen de Bassingburn 'claimed a park in Hoddesdon of ancient custom'.[1] Members of the Bassingbourne family were recorded in Hoddesdon from the beginning of the thirteenth century and held two manors: Hoddesdonbury, the larger of the two, was held from the dukes of Brittany as an outlier of their Cheshunt manor; and Bassingbourne manor, which was held from the de Mandeville and then the de Bohun families. Of the two, Hoddesdonbury seems the most likely location for the park because at Domesday it had woodland for 260 pigs, compared with just 50 pigs on the land destined to become Bassingbourne manor.[2]

Further evidence for the park comes in 1313, when John de Bassyngburne complained 'that Roger Chauntecler of the suburb of London, Reginald Brangor, John Fraunk of Brokesburne, and Walter Fraunk of Brokesburn with others felled his trees in his park at Hoddeston, co. Hertford, and carried them away'.[3] According to Tregelles, there is also a reference in a deed of 1355 or 1357 to 'Bassingbourne's Park', but he does not give any information about the deed or its whereabouts.[4] The theory that the park was part of the Bassingbournes' Hoddesdonbury manor is severely weakened, however, by an inquisition taken in 1323 on the death of Agnes de Bassingbourne, which failed to record a park. Indeed, it specifically stated that there was no grazing in the 120 acres of woodland and that the underwood was worth 6s 8d a year; that is, the woodland was coppiced and consequently not compatible with deer-keeping. The 120 acres of grazing and heath which were also recorded on the manor were said 'at times to be worth nothing for lack of cattle', reflecting perhaps the widespread shortage of cattle after several years of bad weather and epidemics of disease in livestock.[5] So, it would appear that the Bassingbournes had no park in 1323. If Tregelles' record of a park in a deed of 1355 or 1357 can be relied upon, then it may have been only a temporary disparkment (perhaps also related to the livestock epidemics).

A second park seems to have been established in Hoddesdon in the late thirteenth century, because in January 1290 William of Louth was permitted to have two bucks and two does from the king's Forest of Essex to help stock 'his

park of Hoddesdon'.[6] William had worked as a royal administrator from about 1270 and in 1283 he became dean of the collegiate church of St Martin's-le-Grand, London. The canons of St Martin's held land in Hoddesdon, probably in the wooded west of the parish, from before the Domesday survey until the late fifteenth century.[7] Presumably William of Louth enclosed (or perhaps intended to enclose) some of the woodland belonging to the canons in order to make a park and his long working relationship with the king resulted in the gift of the deer. However, in May 1290, shortly after obtaining the grant of the deer, William of Louth was elected bishop of Ely.[8] As there is no further record of the park, it seems possible that William, having gained access to the extensive parks belonging to the bishopric of Ely in Hertfordshire and elsewhere, decided that an additional park in Hoddesdon was no longer required.[9] This park may then have existed for only a short time, if indeed it was ever created.

There is one obvious location for a medieval park in Hoddesdon, namely Hoddesdonpark Wood, lying just north of Hoddesdonbury. Whether it originated as the park of the Bassingbourne family or as the park created by William of Louth or as another, as yet unidentified, park is open to debate. The histories of the holdings of the numerous Hoddesdon manors were complex and it may not now be possible to determine which thirteenth-century manor held the land which later became known as Hoddesdonpark Wood. By the 1570s the wood, along with the lands of the manor of Hoddesdonbury, was part of the estate of William Cecil and was annotated on his estate map, dated 1573, as 'Hoddesdon burye Parke 91 acres'.[10] However, bailiff's accounts for the manor of Hoddesdonbury in the second half of the fifteenth century contain no evidence that there was a park on the manor at that time.[11]

Despite the name, there is no evidence that Hoddesdonpark Wood was a park in the sixteenth century either. A Schedule of Felling of 1595 in the Hatfield House Archives shows that 'Hoddesdon Park' was woodland which was coppiced in two halves (46 and 47 acres respectively) in consecutive years.[12] Just five years later, a map surveyed by Israel Amyce gave an area of 176 acres for the wood, almost twice the acreage given in 1573 and 1595. Comparison of Amyce's map with the map of 1573 is difficult because the earlier map is very schematic, but most of the boundary on both maps seems to be fixed: on the west by the Roman road (Elbow Lane), on the south by the Spital Brook and on the north by Goose Green. This leaves only the eastern boundary with the potential to move and the 1600/01 map does indeed indicate that the wood had expanded eastwards, but not to the extent of doubling the size of the wood. It shows that the south-east corner of the wood extended to the course of a stream flowing into the Spital Brook, a boundary which has

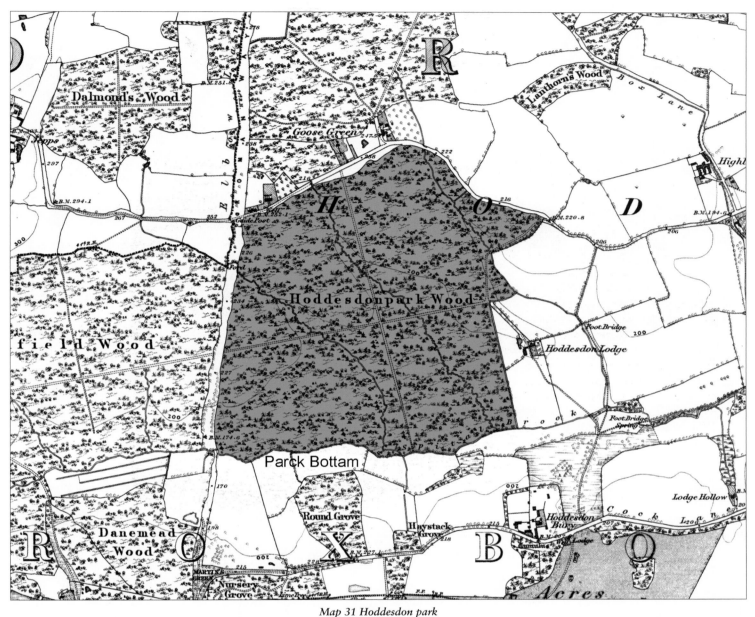

Map 31 Hoddesdon park

OS 6 inches to the mile map sheet XXXVI, surveyed 1873–80, published 1883. Annotated with field name from a survey of 1600/01 (HHA 349). The extent of the park shown is about 150 acres and is based largely on field evidence – the boundary around the west, north and most of the east sides is marked by substantial banks.

now been lost under the A10 dual carriageway.

No lodge was marked on the 1600/01 map but in 1792 a house called 'The Lodge Farm' occupied the south-east corner of the wood, which had by then been cleared of trees and divided into fields.[13] This house still stands and has been dated to the mid seventeenth century.[14] On nineteenth-century maps the house was labelled 'Hoddesdon Lodge'.[15] Close to the south boundary in the middle of Hoddesdonpark Wood is a moated site, a Scheduled Ancient Monument, which may represent the site of a medieval park-keeper's lodge.

The development of the names of the fields lying immediately south of Hoddesdonpark Wood can also be traced on various maps. On the 1573 map they were West and East Pond Meadowe but on the estate map of 1600/01 the two fields had been divided into three, called (from west to east) Parck Bottam, Wignolls Leaz and Ponde Meadowe.[16] On a map of Hoddesdonbury Farm dated 1792, and on a map of

Hoddesdon of 1819, more 'park' field names had appeared, including Further Park Bottom and Long Park Bottom.[17]

All the documentary and cartographic evidence suggests that Sir Robert Cecil expanded the area of Hoddesdonpark Wood at the end of the sixteenth century and perhaps that he and his successors hunted in the wood during the seventeenth and subsequent centuries. The nineteenth-century marquess of Salisbury owned, in addition to Hoddesdonpark Wood, several other woods in the parish, all of which were exempt from payment of tithes by prescription according to the tithe award in 1841.[18]

Hoddesdonpark Wood lies on a south-facing slope and forms part of an extensive area of woodland which lies on relatively high ground west of the Lea Valley. It is a Site of Special Scientific Interest as it is one of the best-preserved and most ecologically important woodlands in Hertfordshire, and is also a National Nature Reserve owned by The Woodland

Figure 30. *The boundary bank around the north-east side of Hoddesdonpark Wood.*

Figure 31. *Hornbeams on the north bank of the Spital Brook forming the southern boundary of Hoddesdonpark Wood, with the field previously known as Parck Bottam beyond.*

Trust. A well-preserved section of the roman Ermine Street forms the west side of the wood, with substantial earthwork banks between the road and the park. There are also good banks around the northern side of the wood and along much of the east side which, in places, are 4–6m wide and 1–1.5m high, topped in places with old laid hornbeams (Figure 30). Along the south side of the wood, bounded by the Spital Brook, remnants of an old laid hornbeam hedge survive along the north bank of the stream (Figure 31). These boundaries form the basis of the park shown in Map 31, which covers an area of 152 acres.

The record of 'Hoddesdon burye Parke' on the 1573 map and the impressive boundary earthworks are the best evidence we have that Hoddesdonpark Wood was the site of one of the medieval parks recorded at Hoddesdon, but that evidence is not entirely conclusive. A thorough search for earthworks in the still-extensive woodlands of western Hoddesdon – Box Wood to the north of Hoddesdonpark Wood, and Cowheath, Brambles or Highfield Woods to the west – may well reveal other potential sites for one or more of Hoddesdon's medieval parks.

1. Page, *Hertford*, 3, p. 435, citing *Placita de Quo Warranto* (Record Commission) 276.
2. Morris, *Domesday Book: Hertfordshire*, p. 16,10; 33,13. For an analysis of how the medieval manors developed from the holdings recorded in Domesday see S. Garside, *Hoddesdon: a history* (Chichester, 2002), pp. 7–11, or J.A. Tregelles, *A history of Hoddesdon* (Hertford, 1908).
3. *Cal. Pat. 1307–1313*, p. 603.
4. Tregelles, *Hoddesdon*, pp. 50, 66.
5. Page, *Hertford*, 4, p. 187.
6. *Cal. Close 1288–1296*, p. 64.
7. Page, *Hertford*, 3, p. 435, citing Dugdale, *Monasticon* viii, p. 1324 and Tregelles, *Hoddesdon*, p. 66; Garside, *Hoddesdon*, pp. 7–9 (after Tregelles).
8. G.H. Martin, 'Louth, William of (*c*.1240–1298)', *Oxford dictionary of national biography* (Oxford, 2004), accessed online 20 July 2007.
9. According to the VCH, the canons' lands were leased to tenants and gradually evolved into separate manors bearing the names of those tenants. Late fifteenth-century bailiffs' accounts in the Hatfield House archive compiled for Sir William Say, which included these manors, contain no evidence of a park.
10. HHA CPM Supp. 20 map of lands between Hoddesdon and Cheshunt, *c*.1573.
11. HHA court rolls 10/9 accounts of the receiver of Sir John Say, 1468/9; 10/21 bailiff's account for Sir William Say, 1495/6; 10/23 bailiff's account for Sir William Say, 1498/9.
12. HHA Deeds 198/38, relating to Hoddesdon woodlands, 1595. For an account of the management of Cecil's woodlands see P. Austin, 'The leasing of Lord Burghley's Hoddesdon woodlands in 1595', *Hertfordshire's Past*, 41 (1996), pp. 11–21.
13. HALS B1444 plan of Hodsdon Burry Farm, 1792.
14. HALS Department of the Environment, List of Buildings.
15. HALS DSA4/54/1 and 2 Hoddesdon tithe award and map, 1841; first edition OS map sheet XXXVI, 6 inches to the mile, surveyed 1873–80, published 1883.
16. HHA CPM Supp. 20 map of lands between Hoddesdon and Cheshunt, *c*.1573; CP349 survey of the Hertfordshire estates of Sir Robert Cecil by Israel Amyce, 1600/01.
17. HALS B1444 plan of Hodsdon Burry Farm, 1792; UDC11 51/1 map of Hamlet of Hoddesdon, 1819.
18. HALS DSA4/54/1 and 2 Hoddesdon tithe award and map, 1841.

Hormead

Hormead park

NGR: ?c.TL418293
Date range: perhaps by 1325 – not known
Size: not known
Underlying geology: boulder clay

A PARK MAY HAVE BEEN RECORDED at Hormead in 1325 in a 'Grant for life to Mary, late wife of Aymer de Valencia, Earl of Pembroke, of the manors of Anesty, Mesedene, Hormad and Westmylne in the county of Hertford ... to hold with knights' fees, advowsons ... chaces, warrens, parks, woods, stanks, stews, fisheries ...'.[1] This might have been a standard administrative phrase of the time, however, and is not, by itself, good evidence for a park at Hormead.

Supporting documentary evidence is almost completely lacking. Two sets of accounts compiled by the reeve of the manor in the 1260s and another two compiled in the 1320s contain no references to a park.[2] The last of these accounts dates from 1326–8, immediately after the grant of 1325, which could be taken as conclusive proof that there was no park in Hormead at the time the grant was made. However, a 'Parkfeld' was recorded in a court roll of 1477.[3]

No park was shown on any county maps published from the sixteenth century onwards, but a wood named Great Hormead Park filled the south-east corner of the parish of Great Hormead on the first edition OS map.[4] The boundary of the woodland has remained almost unchanged into the early twenty-first century and encloses an area of 37 acres. It is ancient woodland which has been designated a Site of Special Scientific Interest because of its range of tree species and rich ground flora, which have resulted from many centuries of management as coppice with standards.[5]

South of the wood, in the parish of Little Hormead, a cluster of field names provides supporting evidence for a park: three fields called Park Leys lay at the eastern end of a common field called Park Field in 1839 (see Map 32).[6] An alternative explanation for these park names, however, could be the medieval park of Furneux Pelham, which probably lay on the far side of the parish boundary just to the east of Great Hormead Park Wood and the Park Leys (see p. 96). The evidence for a medieval park in Hormead is, therefore, at best, inconclusive.

1. *Cal. Pat. 1324–1327*, p. 153.
2. TNA: PRO SC6/866/1, 2, 3 and 4 accounts of the reeve for the manor of Hormead, 1260–2, 1263–5, 1323–5 and 1326–8.
3. Gover *et al.*, *Place-names of Hertfordshire*, p. 299.
4. OS map sheet XIV, 6 inches to the mile, surveyed 1876–8, published 1881–3.
5. www.english-nature.org.uk, accessed 11 August 2007.
6. HALS DSA4/55/1 and 2 Little Hormead tithe award and map, 1839.

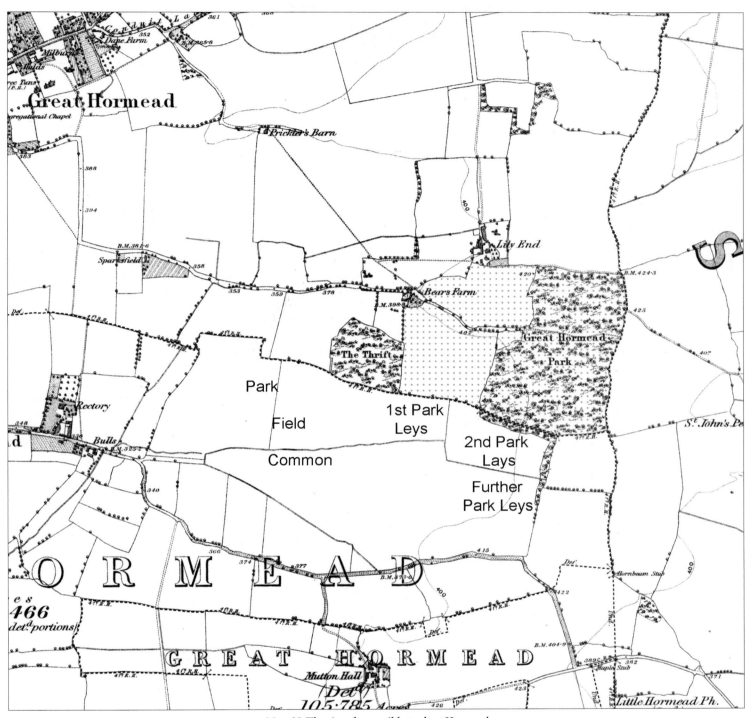

Map 32 The site of a possible park at Hormead
OS 6 inches to the mile map sheet XIV, surveyed 1876–8, published 1881–3. Annotated with field names derived from the Little Hormead tithe award and map, 1839 (HALS DSA4/55/1 and 2).

Hunsdon

The old park

NGR: TL426140
Date range: by 1296 – mid seventeenth century
Size: not known; perhaps *c.*400 acres
Underlying geology: boulder clay

THE PARK AT HUNSDON WAS probably created in the second half of the thirteenth century, after Henry Engayne, the lord of the manor, received a grant of free warren in his demesne lands in 1253 and before 1296, when the first documentary reference to the park occurs, recording a commission appointed 'touching the persons who entered the park of John Engayne at Hunsdon, hunted therein, and carried away deer'.[1] Within a few weeks of the park break John Engayne had died and one of the oath-takers at the inquisition *post mortem* held early in February of 1297 was a William le Parker of Honnesdone.[2] The manor descended to four further generations of Engaynes before passing to a sister on the death of Thomas Engayne in 1367/8. The sister was married to John Goldington and Hunsdon was inherited by two further generations of Goldingtons before passing out of the family in 1423.[3] Unfortunately there appears to be no record of the size of this first park and, as a result of subsequent enlargements, the creation of additional parks at Hunsdon by Henry VIII in the early sixteenth century and changes in the names used for the parks over time, it is difficult now to determine the boundaries of the medieval park with any confidence. However, a few clues in later documents suggest that the earliest park lay to the east and south-east of the village of Hunsdon. This was where the World War II airfield was established and the consequent loss of possible field evidence has further added to the confusion. In order to gain some understanding of the location of the medieval park we first need to examine the evidence for the later parks which existed in and around the parish of Hunsdon.

The first recorded expansion of the park appears to have occurred in 1445, when Richard Duke of York was permitted to 'inclose a way (100 virgates long and 16 feet wide) called Jermynslane leading from Eastwick to Hunsdon, in his park of Hunsdon, making another road on the south of the park'.[4] Exactly how or why Richard acquired the manor of Hunsdon does not appear to be known. In September of 1445 he returned to England after four years in France governing military activities in Normandy during the Hundred Years War.[5] He held vast estates in other counties and it is interesting that he should have chosen to add Hunsdon to his possessions and then set about enlarging the park.[6] Over the next four years he was to take an active part in the government of the nation and in October 1446 he was granted the abbey and town of Waltham because 'he will come often to London for the king's business and his own'.[7] Perhaps it was the greater

convenience of Waltham Abbey that led him to sell Hunsdon to his chamberlain, Sir William Oldhall, in 1447. In the same year Oldhall also purchased the neighbouring manor of Eastwick and over the next few years he set about building a fine house at Hunsdon.[8] Oldhall sat as MP for Hertfordshire in the parliament of November 1450 and was elected speaker but a year later his fortunes took a marked turn for the worse and he was held prisoner until 1455.[9] His estate, like his fortunes, ebbed and flowed during the Wars of the Roses but he died in possession of Hunsdon and Eastwick in 1460. The two manors descended together for the next two centuries. Edward IV was holding them by 1478 and they then passed to Richard III, who granted them to Sir William Stanley. By 1495 Hunsdon and Eastwick were once more in the hands of the crown.[10]

Although he enlarged and established parks elsewhere, there is no record of Henry VII increasing the parkland at Hunsdon and in 1503 he granted the manor with its park to his mother, Margaret Countess of Richmond, for life.[11] She died in 1509 and Hunsdon was just one of 30 manors granted by Henry VIII to Thomas Howard, Earl of Surrey, when he was made Duke of Norfolk in 1514.[12] However, the grant did *not* include the park, which was retained by the crown.[13] The manor was inherited in 1524 by the duke's son, another Thomas Duke of Norfolk, and the Howard household moved between the family mansions at Lambeth and Tendring Hall, Suffolk in the summers and Hunsdon for the winters.[14] From 1526 the manor came back under the control of Henry VIII and in 1529 he granted it to Henry Norris, but this time he reserved for his own use both the house and the *parks*, plural.[15]

Hunsdon became a favourite residence of the king and he spent thousands of pounds on improving the house from about 1525 to 1536.[16] In 1532 he created the honour of Hunsdon, which included not only the manor of Hunsdon but also Eastwick, Stanstead and Roydon.[17] Each of his children lived at Hunsdon at various times and Henry escaped to the relative safety of Hunsdon in 1528 when the 'sweating sickness' was raging in London.[18] But his primary reason for coming to Hunsdon was for the hunting: in August 1532 Stephen Gardiner wrote to Wolsey from Hunsdon: 'I have been hunting from morn till night by the king's commandment'.[19] In 1537 Henry had mews built at Hunsdon for his hawks.[20]

Henry VIII's parks at Hunsdon

In order to improve the opportunities for hunting in the area, Henry VIII appears to have made some important changes to the landscape of Hunsdon. Three parks were recorded in 1529: the 'old park', the 'new park' and 'Goodmanneshyde park'.[21] The latter two were apparently established by Henry VIII at some time during the previous 20 years, but perhaps most probably in the three years after 1526. The new parks seem to

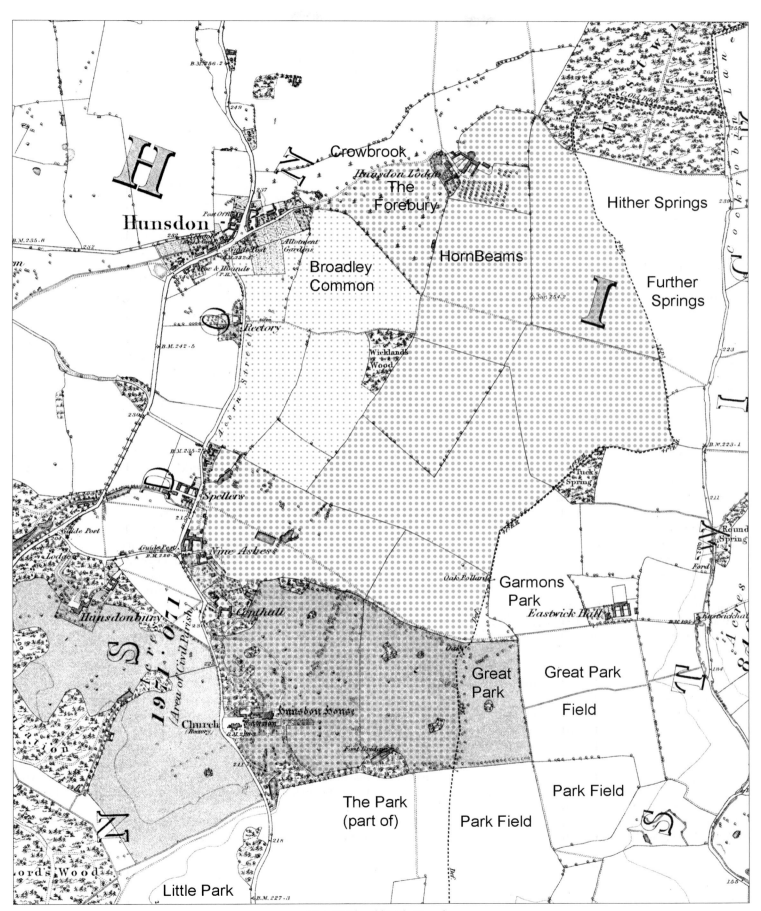

Map 33 The old park, Hunsdon

OS 6 inches to the mile map sheet XXX, surveyed 1873–80, published 1881–3. Annotated with field names derived from the Hunsdon tithe award and map, 1837 (HALS DSA4/56/1 and 2), and the Eastwick tithe award and map, 1845 and 1839 (HALS DSA4/36/1 and 2).

Figure 32. Hunsdon's parks as depicted by Norden on his county map of 1598. Reproduced by kind permission of Hertfordshire Archives and Local Studies.

Figure 33. The parks at Hunsdon as depicted on Saxton's county map of 1577 (HALS CM1). Reproduced by kind permission of Hertfordshire Archives and Local Studies.

have occupied most of the parish around Hunsdon House and southwards as far as the Stanstead to Sawbridgeworth road. What the land had been used for previously is not easy to ascertain but a field called Godmundeshyde was recorded at the inquisition *post mortem* of John Engayne in 1297, when it was being rented for half a mark yearly from Humphrey, Earl of Hereford, who was overlord of Gilston.[22] The fact that John Engayne was paying rent for the field suggests that it formed part of the demesne lands of his manor of Hunsdon rather than being a common arable field. Ministers' accounts for 1536/7 held in The National Archives do not record whether lands were exchanged to make the new parks but they do show that the rector of Hunsdon church was to be paid 25s 4d a year and the rector of Eastwick 5s 8d a year in tithes for lands enclosed in the 'new park'. This indicates that one of the new parks was on the east side of Hunsdon parish and extended into Eastwick but, as the accountant did not write 'le Newpark' as he did elsewhere in the account, we cannot be sure to which new park he was referring. These accounts also show that, in addition to the three parks – all of which contained deer – a substantial acreage of meadow was allocated to produce hay for the deer.[23]

Another clue to the location of one of the parks is in a portrait of Prince Edward dating from about 1546 which shows deer grazing in a park lying south-west of the church and Hunsdon House – the park pale is clearly shown on the west side of the track which heads south-east from the church.[24] As the old and the new parks were under the care of a single keeper it seems most likely that their lands were contiguous and lay on the east side of the parish of Hunsdon, extending into the parish of Eastwick. Goodmanshyde park had its own keeper and may have been the park shown lying south-west of Hunsdon House in the portrait. This seems to be the arrangement of parks depicted by Norden in his county map of 1598 (Figure 32). However, as the name Goodmanshyde does

not recur in the records after 1536 and different names were used for the parks over the succeeding centuries, it is very difficult to be sure exactly where each of Henry VIII's parks lay.

A survey undertaken in 1556 for King Philip and Queen Mary recorded three parks, all of which contained deer: the great park adjoining the house, the little park and the pond park. The information contained in the survey is presented in Table 1 (below).[25]

The trees growing in the parks were overwhelmingly oaks – 750 in the great park, 140 in the little park and 60 in the pond park – with 60 ash, 4 'wyches' (presumably wych elm) and woodgrounds 'set with maple, thornes, hasell, hornebeame and oke'. The surveyors recommended that the little park and the pond park should be disparked but the great park should 'be kepte as a parke for the stateliness[s] of the house'.

A further important source of information about Henry's parks are the tithe maps and awards of Hunsdon and its neighbouring parishes, all dating from c.1840. Although drawn up more than three centuries after Henry VIII re-arranged the landscape, they appear to indicate the extent of his parks because at some time after 1536 the tithe payment on 775 acres of parkland 'formerly known as the three parks' was replaced by a modus payment of fifteen shillings and four pence per annum.[26] This area of 775 acres represents just over 40 per cent of the parish of Hunsdon. Interestingly, only one field in Eastwick parish was covered by a modus payment and that was the field called 'Great Park' (21.5 acres), land which was still shown as the eastern end of the late nineteenth-century Hunsdon Park on the first edition OS map (see Map 33).[27]

The subsequent history of the parks in brief

In 1557 the keeper of the Old Park wrote his will and left to his son 'two crossbows and their rack, three long bows with whatever belonged to them ... and all his hounds'.[28] In 1559

Park	Laundes & feedings	Wood ground	Ponds	Total area	Number of deer 'of all sortes'
Great park	262a 3r	82a 2r		345a 1r	150
Little park	201a	21a		222a	100
Pond park	181a 2r	35a	12a	228a 2r	80
Totals	645a 1r	138a 2r	12a	795a 3r	330

Table 1

Figure 34. *View looking north-east along the likely northern boundary of the medieval park at Hunsdon, with the former park to the right. The boundary is marked by a track on a raised bank which leads to the site of Hunsdon Lodge, now replaced by the distant buildings on the right of the photograph.*

the three parks of Hunsdon were granted by Queen Elizabeth to her cousin Sir Henry Carey, Lord Hunsdon, and his successors.[29]

How long Henry VIII's three parks survived intact is not known. Saxton's county map of 1577 showed three parks at Hunsdon, the largest of which was depicted to the north of Hunsdon House and was probably the great park (Figure 33). In his will of 1591 James Gray described himself as 'keeper of the Great Park', and he is commemorated by a striking brass in the church at Hunsdon.[30]

The estate remained in the Carey family during the first half of the seventeenth century. Some time after 1628 Henry Carey, fourth baron and Earl of Dover, extended the great park eastwards as far as Cockrobin Lane when he purchased 'certain lands called the Spring … in the parish of Eastwick'.[31] He may also have added other lands because Brick Hills, the Nursery, Eastwick Lawn and Edward's Downs were all recorded as having been part of the park in 1684/5, but were not included in the lands covered by the modus payments.[32] In 1637 the Earl of Dover conveyed the manor of Eastwick to trustees and it was sold shortly afterwards.[33] He was a prominent royalist during the Civil War and his estates were sequestrated by parliament. He must have compounded for

them and subsequently sold Hunsdon in 1653 to William Willoughby.[34]

Hunsdon's parks were probably disparked during the Civil War: in 1636 the 'parkes and warren or enclosed grounds' were known as 'Greate parke, Little parke and warren' but by 1653 all three had been disparked 'and laid into farmes and converted into Tillage and pasture and soe now used and enjoyed by diverse severall tenants and farmers thereof …'.[35] Lord Willoughby (as he became in 1666) appears to have reinstated much of the parkland in the south of the parish between 1653 and 1671, when he sold the estate to Matthew Bluck. Bluck's descendents held the manor until the mid eighteenth century. Seller's county map of 1675 shows two parks lying south of Hunsdon church: the one east of the lane contained a house labelled 'the Warren House'. Oliver's county map of 1695 also shows the same two parks, but they were not shown on Warburton's map of *c.*1720 nor on Dury and Andrews' map of 1766, which suggests that there were no deer parks in Hunsdon after the early eighteenth century. Several ornamental parks were established around the residences of various branches of the Calvert family during the eighteenth and early nineteenth centuries, most on land which had been parkland for centuries, but there is no evidence that they contained deer.

Locating the medieval park

Assuming that the medieval park can be equated with Henry VIII's 'old park', then the earliest park in Hunsdon lay to the east and south-east of today's village. Evidence for this statement appears in the record of a court baron of 1770, which mentions 'a parcel of pasture land of 4 acres formerly described to lye betweene a place called the Old Park and Hookfield'.[36] Hook Field Lane lay on the south side of the common field called Broad Ley, which lay to the south-east of the village (see Map 33).

The northern boundary of the medieval park may have been marked by the bank which bears a track leading north-east from the village to the site of the former Hunsdon Lodge (Figure 34). The boundary of the lands covered by the modus payment lies along this bank and a document from 1672 mentions 'the pale of Crowbrooke', the name of the field lying north of the bank.[37] Another plausible park boundary could be the stream – the Crow Brook – which flows approximately parallel to this bank but slightly further north.

To the east, the parish boundary may well have formed the park boundary, at least until the mid fifteenth century, when Hunsdon and Eastwick came under joint ownership. The southern boundary of the medieval park is much more difficult to determine. We know that until 1445 the park was bounded to the south by a lane called Jermynslane which connected Hunsdon with Eastwick and that the lane was then moved further south to form a new boundary to the park. With some detailed fieldwork it might be possible to find evidence of one or both of these lanes but repeated phases of park-making, disparkment, landscaping and agricultural activity over the succeeding centuries will make this a challenge. However, the grand new house which was built shortly after the lane was diverted in 1445 is likely to have been set within parkland, which means that the replacement lane and park boundary probably lay to the south of Hunsdon House. The boundary proposed for the late medieval park on Map 33 encloses an area of about 400 acres, but the southern boundary is merely a best guess, with no firm evidence.

A curious feature of the lands covered by the modus payment in the nineteenth century is an enclave of fields on the west side of the former park, including Broadley Common, which were excluded from the payment (lighter shading on map). It seems much more likely that the original park boundary reached westwards to Acorn Street and filled the corner between Acorn Street and the main street at the heart of today's village. Indeed, these streets probably developed around the outside of the park. It may be that Henry VIII gave this western part of the old medieval park to his tenants in exchange for lands which they had previously farmed further south in the parish and which he wished to impark. The village of Hunsdon as we know it today may, consequently, have become a focus for settlement in the parish only after the king had reorganised the local landscape in the early sixteenth century.

1. *Cal. Pat. 1292–1301*, p. 220.

2. Cussans, *History of Hertfordshire*, 1, Braughing Hundred, pp. 42–3, citing Inquisition *post mortem* 25 Ed. I, no. 46 (TNA: PRO C133/80/2). Curiously, the inquisition did not record a park.

3. Page, *Hertford*, 3, p. 327.

4. Page, *Hertford*, 3, p. 329; TNA: PRO C143/450/32 inquisition *ad quod damnum*, 1445/6. A virgate is a (variable) measurement of area, so cannot be converted into a reliable distance.

5. J. Watts, 'Richard of York, third duke of York (1411–1460)', *Oxford dictionary of national biography* (Oxford, 2004), accessed online 27 July 2007.

6. He had also held the manor of Standon in Hertfordshire, with its large park, since 1425 and had granted it to Sir William Oldhall for life in 1441 (Page, *Hertford*, 3, p. 353).

7. Watts, 'Richard of York', citing *Cal. Pat. 1446–1452*, p. 43.

8. Page, *Hertford*, 3, p. 232.

9. A. Curry, 'Oldhall, Sir William (d. 1460)', *Oxford dictionary of national biography* (Oxford, 2004), accessed online 27 July 2007.

10. Page, *Hertford*, 3, p. 328.

11. S. Thurley, *The royal palaces of Tudor England: architecture and court life, 1460–1547* (New Haven, 1993), p. 68. Henry VII enlarged the medieval park at Sheen, Surrey and created a new one at Greenwich. Page, *Hertford*, 3, p. 328, citing Close Roll, 18 Hen. VII, no. 28 (TNA: PRO C54/363).

12. D.M. Head, 'Howard, Thomas, second duke of Norfolk (1443–1524)', *Oxford dictionary of national biography* (Oxford, 2004; online edn, May 2005), accessed online 27 July 2007.

13. Page, *Hertford*, 3, p. 329 citing Letters & Papers Henry VIII, I, 4694 (TNA).

14. S. Brigden, 'Howard, Henry, earl of Surrey (1516/17–1547)', *Oxford dictionary of national biography* (Oxford, September 2004; online edn, January 2007), accessed online 27 July 2007.

15. Page, *Hertford*, 3, p. 328, citing Feet of Fines Herts Trin. 18 Hen. VIII (TNA: PRO CP25/2/16/92/18HENVIIITRIN) — the manor was conveyed in 1526 'to Sir Henry Wyatt and others evidently in trust for the king'; Letters & Papers Henry VIII, iv (3), 5336 (10) (TNA).

16. Hunsdon Local History and Preservation Society, *Hunsdon and Widford: a local history* (1979; reprinted 2002), p. 9.

17. TNA: PRO SC6/HENVIII/6012 ministers' accounts, 1536/7, which describe the manors of Roydon and Stanstead as being 'parcel of the honour of Hunsdon'.

18. Mary was visited there by Henry and his new (third) queen, Jane Seymour, in July 1536 (A. Weikel, 'Mary I (1516–1558)', *Oxford dictionary of national biography* (Oxford, September 2004; online edn, May 2006), accessed online 28 July 2007; Page, *Hertford*, 3, p. 324, citing Letters & Papers Henry VIII, iv, 4403, 4408 (TNA).

19. Page, *Hertford*, 3, p. 329 citing Letters & Papers Henry VIII, iv, 5831 (TNA).

20. Thurley, *Royal palaces*, p. 193.

21. Page, *Hertford*, 3, p. 329 citing Letters & Papers Henry VIII iv, g. 5336 (10) (TNA).

22. *Cal. Inq. post mortem, vol. 3, Edward I*, p. 279. The field was part of the manor of Hunsdon held of Humphrey Earl of Hereford (overlord of the manor of Gilston); the remainder of the manor of Hunsdon was held of Roger Lestrange by service of 1/6 knight's fee.

23. TNA: PRO SC6/HENVIII/6012 ministers' and receivers' accounts, 1536/7. The parks were under the care of two parkers and 22s 2d was expended in making and carting two crops of hay from about 12 acres of meadow.

24. Portrait of Prince Edward by an unknown artist c.1546 in the Royal Collection, reproduced in Thurley, *Royal palaces*, figures 106 and 107.

25. TNA: PRO E315/391 survey of manors in Hertfordshire, lands and possessions of King Philip and Queen Mary, 1556.

26. HALS DSA4/56/1 Hunsdon tithe award, 1837. The total acreage of the fields listed in the award as being covered by the modus only amounts to 674 acres but woodlands may have been listed separately and ponds were not assessed for tithe.

27. HALS DSA4/36/1 and 2 Eastwick tithe award (1845) and map (1839); OS map sheet XXX, 6 inches to the mile, 1881–3. The modus payment did not include the lands in Eastwick taken into Hunsdon Great Park by the Earl of Dover after 1628.

28. Hunsdon Local History and Preservation Society, *Hunsdon and Widford*, p. 12.

29. Page, *Hertford*, 3, p. 329.

30. H. Prince, *Parks in Hertfordshire since 1500* (Hatfield, 2008), p. 20.

31. Page, *Hertford*, 3, p. 329. These fields in Eastwick were still named Hither and Further Springs in 1845 (HALS DSA4/36/1 and 2 Eastwick tithe award (1845) and map (1839)).

32. Page, *Hertford*, 3, p. 329 citing Exchequer Depositions Mixed County Mich. 36 Chas. II, no. 22 (TNA).

33. Page, *Hertford*, 3, p. 318 citing Feet of Fines Div. County Mich. 13 Chas. I. (TNA: PRO CP25/2) and Close Roll, 17 Chas. I, pt. xxiii, no. 20.

34. Page, *Hertford*, 3, p. 328; HALS DE/B1630/T4 deeds, 1634–1730, including sale agreement, 1653.

35. HALS DE/B1630/T4 deeds, 1634–1730, including sale agreement, 1653.

36. HALS DE/B1630/T11 deeds of Nine Ashes, 1671–1837 including a Court Baron and Court of Survey, 1770.

37. HALS DE/B1630/T11 deeds of Nine Ashes, 1671–1837.

Ippollitts

Almshoe park
NGR: TL207253
Date range: perhaps *c*.1240 and certainly by 1358 – not known
Size: not known
Underlying geology: Upper Chalk, glaciofluvial deposits and boulder clay

THERE APPEARS TO BE JUST ONE SURVIVING medieval reference to two parks in the parish of Ippollitts: notes written in the margin of her daily household accounts reveal that on 26 July 1358, Queen Isabella and her daughter the Queen of Scotland 'spent the day at Almesho Park; on the following day at Madecroft Park'.[1]

No other records have come to light and it is not known when Almshoe park was established, or by whom. The manor became part of the Valognes barony in 1120 through the wife (or widow) of Peter de Valognes. Valognes' descendents may have created the park during the twelfth century but it seems unlikely given their extensive estates elsewhere, which included a park at Benington. The manor passed by marriage to the Fitz Walter family who remained the overlords until the fifteenth century but sub-enfeoffed the manor from the early thirteenth century. The present house called Almshoe Bury incorporates the timber frame of an aisled hall house which has been dated to the mid thirteenth century. The dog-tooth ornament on an arch-brace, together with records of a chapel on the manor, indicates a high-status residence, and architectural historian John Smith believes it was built by Simon Fitz Adam, a sub-tenant of the manor, who settled the house on his wife at their marriage in 1241.[2] The family subsequently adopted Fitz Simon as the surname and it was either Hugh Fitz Simon or his son, Edward, who was lord of the manor at the time of the visit of the two queens.[3] It seems very likely that Simon Fitz Adam could have established Almshoe park in the middle of the thirteenth century and fragmentary documentary and field evidence suggests that the park may have surrounded his grand new manor house (Figure 35).

Enclosures partly encircling Almshoe Bury in 1816 had park names – Little Park and Great Park – but were very small: 6a 3r 1p and 5a 3r 13p respectively. An even smaller field lying in the south-east corner of the adjacent Coneydell Wood was named The Lawn.[4] Taken in isolation, these field names are insufficient evidence to locate the medieval park here, but 'three closes of pasture called the Parkes containing 18 acres' were recorded in 1672 and, assuming the field names do recall an earlier park, then that park must pre-date 1672.[5] No park was mentioned in an indenture of 1625 and no park was shown on the county maps by either Saxton (1577) or Norden (1598) in the second half of the sixteenth century, which suggests that the park being commemorated by these field names existed before 1577 and was therefore most likely to be medieval in origin.[6]

Supposing that these field names do commemorate the medieval park, the 18 acres recorded in 1672 would hardly be sufficient to provide entertainment for the two queens in 1358. These 'three closes' form a striking enclosure around the Bury on the first edition OS map, and the sinuous, ancient-looking, boundary still largely survives today. This may be the result of the underlying geology, as a thin band of hard Chalk Rock encircles the Bury on the north, west and south sides in a position which correlates with the old field boundaries.

Figure 35. The house called Almshoe Bury occupies a prominent position in the landscape, as can be seen in this view from the north-east (the house itself is now obscured by modern farm buildings on the skyline). The clump of shrubs on the right marks the site of a pond.

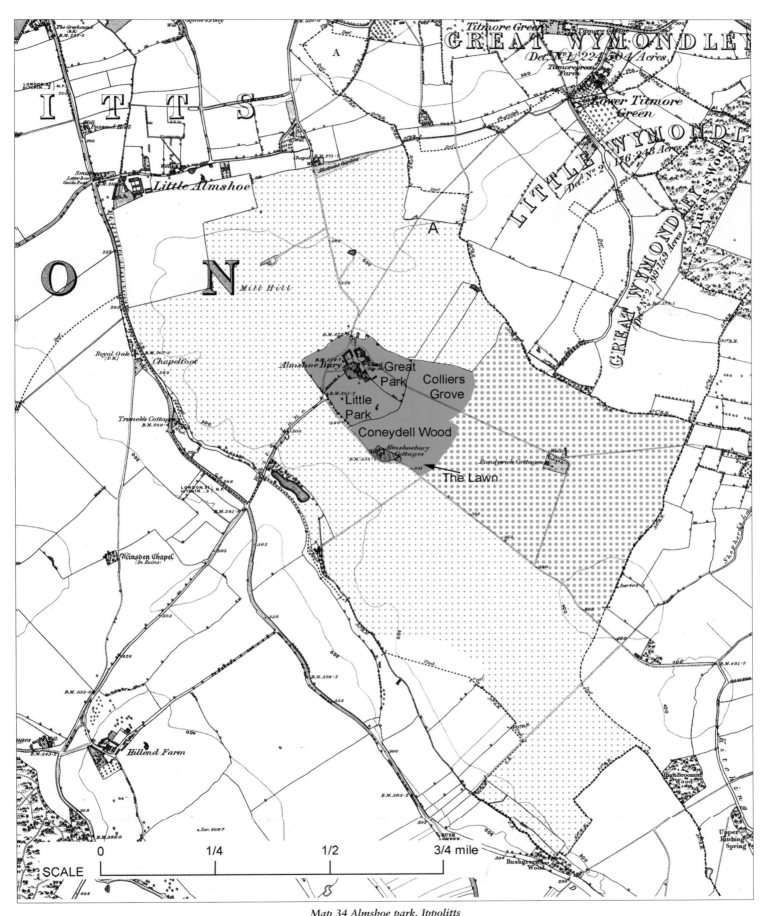

Map 34 Almshoe park, Ippolitts
OS 6 inches to the mile map sheets XII, surveyed 1878–81, published 1884; and XX, surveyed 1881, published 1884 (both reproduced at a reduced scale).
Annotated with field names derived from the Ippollitts enclosure award and map, 1818 and 1816 (HALS QS/E/44 and 45).

Figure 36. View looking west along the possible park boundary at A on Map 34. This section of boundary, together with the adjoining section heading north on the right side of the photograph, does not follow the parish boundary and is marked by a significant lynchet. The inside of the proposed park (to the left) is about 2m higher than the land to the north (right).

Nevertheless, it seems likely that this enclosure was an inner, or 'little', park around the house and circumstantial topographical evidence suggests that it lay within a much more extensive area of parkland. The estate in the early nineteenth century was a compact area of about 550 acres of enclosed fields filling the south-eastern projection of the parish of Ippollitts, indicated by the lightest shading on Map 34. It occupied a ridge of high ground with land rising from 80 to 120m OD and it was the most wooded part of the parish. This is a typical situation for a medieval park and it may be that the whole estate (*c*.550 acres) was once the park but became the 'great farm called Almshoebury' (recalled in the deed of 1672) at a relatively early date.[7] Alternatively, the park may have been an enclosed area of unrecorded size and location within the estate.

A substantial bank with a ditch on its north side (*c*.6m wide in total) survives along what may have been the northern boundary of the park just east of Little Almshoe Cottage (TL204260). This boundary continues ENE, becoming a marked lynchet of a metre or more (higher ground to south) and developing into a very significant boundary earthwork (a bank about 1.5m high) which turns southwards through 90 degrees to follow the parish boundary at what may have been the north-east corner of the park. Most other parts of the possible park boundary accessible from rights of way are also parish boundaries and earth banks survive in good condition in the vicinity of TL214253 and TL218251. One section of the boundary, however, does not follow the parish boundary but is also marked by a significant earthwork (see Figure 36). A hollow trench at TL214250 marks the site of a former pond close to the summit of the ridge and another pond survives at the northern end of the park (Figure 35), both of which will have been dug to provide a source of water for deer and other livestock on the dry chalk hill.

Maydencroft park

NGR: not known
Date range: by 1358 – probably disparked by 1482
Size: not known
Underlying geology: not known

AS WITH ALMSHOE PARK, the only known medieval reference to this park is in a note written in the margin of the daily household accounts of Queen Isabella, who spent a day with her daughter, the Queen of Scotland, at 'Madecroft park' on 27 July 1358.[8] One post-medieval reference to this park has been found in a set of accounts for the manor from 1507/8. By this time it was evidently no longer a functioning deer park and the account recorded that in a rental of 1482/3 the 'site of the manor with the park' was leased for 10 shillings a year.[9] No other evidence for this park has been found and its location remains unknown.[10]

This manor lay mostly in the parish of Ippollitts but also extended into Hitchin. According to the Victoria County History, the manor of Maydencroft was the part of the manor of Dinsley in Hitchin thought to have been granted by William Rufus to Richard de Loveceft in the thirteenth century. In the later thirteenth century the manor was in the tenure of the de Furnival family (hence the manor's alternative name of Dinsley Furnival), and was in the hands of Gerard de Eylesford, grandson of Gerard de Furnival, in 1315–16. Soon afterwards the manor came into the hands of the overlord, Robert Kendale, who was granted free warren in his demesne lands at Maydencroft in 1317–18. The Kendale family were still lords of the manor at the time of the visit by the two queens.[11] The park may have been created by any of the above holders of the manor but perhaps Robert Kendale, who received the grant of free warren, is the most likely candidate.

A 'Survey of the Township of Hitchin' dated 1676 covered only part of the manor and did not record any evidence of a park.[12] The 1816 enclosure award recorded a group of park-related names just north-east of the village of Ippollitts:

Lodges Farm, Lodges Mead and Hunting Gate close.[13] No record has been found of a park in this vicinity, or any connection with the manor of Maydencroft.

1. Bond, 'Notices of the last days of Isabella, Queen of Edward the second', p. 462.
2. J.T. Smith, *English houses 1200–1800: The Hertfordshire evidence* (London, 1992), pp. 12–15.
3. Page, *Hertford*, 3, p. 26.
4. HALS QS/E/44 enclosure award for Ippollitts, 1818; QS/E/45 enclosure map, 1816.
5. HALS DE/B686/T1 deeds of Almshoebury manor and estate, 1625 and 1672.
6. *Ibid.*
7. *Ibid.*
8. Bond, 'Notices of the last days of Isabella, Queen of Edward the second', p. 462.
9. TNA: PRO SC6/HENVII/1238 minister's account, 1507/8.
10. Bond, 'Notices of the last days of Isabella, Queen of Edward the second', p. 462. Medieval spellings included Medcroft, Madecroft and Maidecroft.
11. Page, *Hertford*, 3, pp. 10–11.
12. B. Howlett (ed.), *Survey of the royal manor of Hitchin, 1676* (Hertfordshire Record Society, 2000). 'Maydencroft Gate' was recorded, but there is no indication that it was a park gate.
13. HALS QS/E/44 enclosure award for Ippollitts, 1818; QS/E/45 enclosure map, 1816.

Kimpton

No known name

NGR: TL174187
Date range: 1366 – not known
Size: not known
Underlying geology: Upper Chalk

DOCUMENTARY EVIDENCE FOR A medieval park at Kimpton rests on the interpretation of an entry in the Calendar of Charter Rolls for 1366 recording a licence granted to Nigel Loring 'to impark his woods of Porlok (co. Somerset), Chalgrave (co. Bedfordshire), Conyngton (co. Hereford), Kystemelebrugg and Beworthy' (both co. Devon).[1] 'Conyngton, co. Hereford' was taken to be Kimpton, Hertfordshire by the compilers of the Calendar. Other fourteenth-century spellings of Kimpton include Kemynton and Kumynton, which makes Conyngton a more plausible variant than would at first

appear.[2] Herefordshire and Hertfordshire have long been mistranslated and there does not appear to be a Conington in Herefordshire, so the Calendar may well be correct.

Sir Nigel Loring had a successful career as a soldier. He was one of the founding Knights of the Garter in 1348/9 and was chamberlain to the Black Prince by 1351.[3] His family estate was at Chalgrave in Bedfordshire and he held one of the three manors in Kimpton from before 1346 until his death in 1386. This manor was subsequently (in 1436) referred to as the manor of Parkbury.[4] Although no further documentary evidence has been found, the map and field evidence for a park at Park Farm, formerly Parkbury, Kimpton, is strong.

No park is shown at Kimpton on any county map, which suggests that it had been disparked before the 1570s. Seventeenth-century documents do not mention a park and there is a lease of the 240-acre Parke Farm from 1748.[5] An

Figure 37. View of Kimpton from the Park by J.C. Buckler, 1840 (HALS D/EBg/4, p. 169). Reproduced by kind permission of Hertfordshire Archives and Local Studies.

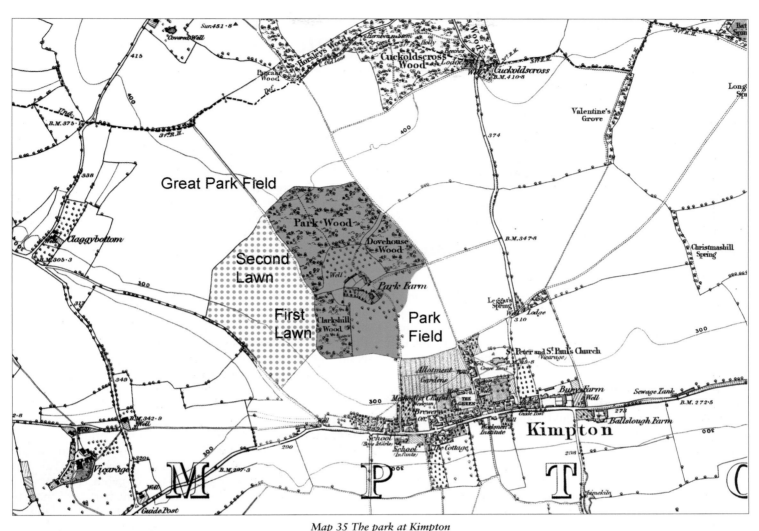

Map 35 The park at Kimpton
OS 6 inches to the mile map sheets XIX and XX, surveyed 1878–81, published 1884. Field names derived from the Kimpton tithe award and map, 1837–8 (HALS DSA4/61/1 and 2). NB some field boundaries recorded in 1837–8 had been removed by 1881.

early–mid eighteenth-century map of The Hoo estate shows a continuous enclosure around the Park Farmhouse covering approximately 34 acres and consisting of three woods – Park Great Wood, Dove House Wood and Clarks Hill Wood – around the central clearing containing the farmhouse. The two fields to the west were labelled 'Lawns'.

The Kimpton tithe map and award of 1837 recorded a total acreage for Park Farm of 232 acres, which included the following park-related field names shown on the accompanying map: Great Park Field (32 acres), Park Field (23 acres), First (10 acres) and Second Lawn (9 acres).[6] The wood named Park Great Wood in the mid eighteenth century was called Great Lawn Wood in 1837 and Park Wood on the first edition OS map.

A site visit in August 2004 revealed a substantial degraded earthwork – perhaps a double bank with ditches – about 10m across, along the line of the former south-east boundary of Dovehouse Wood (see Map 35). There was also a substantial bank along the north-east side of Dovehouse wood, measuring *c*.0.9m vertically from the bottom of the outer ditch to the top of the bank, and *c*.4m horizontally from the bottom of the ditch to the inside of the bank. Another substantial bank bounds the north-east side of Park Wood and turns beautifully around the north-east corner of the wood to head westwards. The total

width of the ditch and bank is *c*.10m and the base of the ditch is *c*.0.6m below the top of the bank. There are also good banks between Park and Dovehouse Woods alongside the track.

The field evidence suggests that the northern and eastern sides of Park Wood and the eastern sides of Dovehouse Wood were also the park boundary. The Lawn field names to the west of the farmhouse suggest that these areas were open grassy spaces within the park, but where the boundary lay on this, and on the south, side of the park is less certain.

Considering the lack of documentary evidence and the apparent absence of a functioning deer park by the mid sixteenth century, it is surprising that the park names have survived for so long. However, an attractive watercolour entitled 'View of Kimpton from the Park' and painted by J.C. Buckler in 1840 is evidence that the area was still regarded as parkland as late as the mid nineteenth century (Figure 37).[7]

1. *Cal. Chart. 1341–1417*, p. 193–4.

2. *Cal. Chart. 1327–1341*, p. 192; Page, *Hertford*, 3, p. 29.

3. C.L. Kingsford, 'Loring, Sir Neil'.

4. Page, *Hertford*, 3, pp. 29–30.

5. HALS 57588 lease of Kimpton Park Farm, 1748.

6. HALS DSA4/61/1 and 2 Kimpton tithe award, 1837 and map, 1838.

7. HALS DE/Bg/4, p. 169, painting by J.C. Buckler, 1840.

King's Langley

Langley park, great park and little park

NGR: great park: TL065018; little park: TL077016
Date range: by 1276 – mid seventeenth century
Size: probably 913 acres at its greatest extent
Underlying geology: great park: Upper Chalk partially overlain by glacial gravel or Pebbly Clay and sand; little park: valley gravel and alluvium

THE MANOR OF LANGLEY formed part of the honour of Berkhamsted and was acquired by Eleanor of Castile, queen consort of Edward I, in the years following their coronation in 1274. By the mid 1280s a residence fit for the king had been established and this developed into a royal palace which became the favourite residence of Edward II and was much used by subsequent kings and queens during the medieval period. Records in the thirteenth and fourteenth century refer to the manor as Childerlangley (or some variant); it was not until the end of the fourteenth century that it became known as Langley Regis or King's Langley.[1] The first record of a park at Langley was in November 1276, when Edward I made a part payment towards the sum of £60 which he owed to Roger and Philippa de Lancastre 'for the vesture of 60 acres of wood within the park of Langley'.[2] In the same year 30 does were requested from Odiham, Hampshire, to stock the queen's new park and in 1282 a white roe doe and five white roe bucks were sent from the king's chase at Rugeley (Staffordshire), or the chace of Longboys.[3]

A survey made on the death of Queen Eleanor in 1290 recorded that land enclosed in the new park included 120 acres of arable land and 8 acres of 'meadow which used to be mowed before deer were placed therein'.[4] This statement, together with the record of 60 acres of wood in the park in 1276, suggests that the queen's park covered at least 188 acres by 1290. The extent also recorded a pasture for 'plough-beasts' (*stots*) and cows which was worth 16 shillings if there were no deer.

Within six years of the queen's death there were two, and possibly three, parks at Langley. Accounts for 1296/7 recorded a great park and a little park. There was also a reference to 'the park called little London' (*parva London*) which was probably an alternative name for the little park but may have been a third park. A new fence, 213 perches (over 1,000m) long, was made around 'the park' at a cost of 17s 9d, and a further 6s 6d was spent on felling and splitting timber to make pales which were erected in places around the little park. The pasture in both the great and the little park was grazed solely by the deer and was valued at 46 shillings in the great park and 10 shillings in the little park. Eight acres of meadow was used to grow hay, valued at 20s 2d, to feed the deer in winter. Seventy-four pigs were allowed pannage 'in the park and foreign woods' that year, producing revenue for the manor of

12s 4d (2d per pig). The hall and chamber in the park called little London underwent major repairs and were re-roofed with tiles brought from St Albans. The parker was paid 60s 10d (2d per day), plus a robe worth 10 shillings.[5]

In 1301 and (perhaps) again the following year 'the king's park of Langeleye' was broken into and deer were hunted and carried away.[6] In 1302 Edward I granted Langley to his son, Edward Prince of Wales, just before his eighteenth birthday.[7] The bailiff, Robert Parker, recorded a payment of 13s 2d for agistment of 'beasts' pasturing in the great park, repairs were made to the pales of the little park and a carpenter worked for three days to make a new back gate (*posternam*) for the park beside the church. Robert Parker received 2d a day in wages.[8]

The account for 1305/6 reveals much expenditure on the parks. A new lodge was built for 17s 2¼d and a great gate and a water gate were made for the great park, indicating that the great park bordered the river Gade. New gates were also made for the little park and the vineyard and a new bridge was made at little London. Over 20 shillings was spent on fencing the parks, including 16s 4d on 4 furlongs 36 perches (c.1,000m) of fence around the great park at 1d per perch. Thorns were cut to reinforce a hedge between the great park and the hay meadow (*falcabile*) to preserve the hay for the deer, and thorns were also cut to enclose parts of the boundary of the little park. These costs were offset by revenue from the agistment of livestock in the great park, which was worth 42s 4d between Easter and 1 August (the feast of St Peter ad vincula) and a further 6s 3d for the months of August and September. Oats were also grown in the park for use on the manor but extra hay, costing 10s 8d, had to be bought for the deer in winter.[9]

The prince became King Edward II in 1307 and a great deal of building work was recorded at Langley in the accounts for the year 1307/8. Once again significant costs were incurred in fencing the parks: 14s 2d was spent on 4 furlongs 10 perches (c.855m) of new fence around the great park, two men spent 4 days repairing the hedge (*haye*) around parts of the great park (16d) and one man spent 25 days felling and cleaving (*scindend*) timber to repair the pales of the little park (4s 2d). A carpenter worked for three days to make a gate between the great park and la Northgrove (9d). Robert le Parker remained the bailiff of the manor and one Elye Parkar' was also recorded in the account; they were each paid £4 11s for the year. Thirty shillings was received for the agistment of livestock in the great park in summer and pannage of pigs in the same park was worth 7s 6d.[10]

By 1312 Robert Parcar', bailiff, had received a pay rise and was earning £6 2s p.a. (4d per day); Elye the parker was earning £4 11s 6d p.a. (3d per day). In contrast to the earlier accounts, no revenue from agistment or pannage was recorded for 1311/12 and it appears to have been a difficult year, with dead livestock recorded in the account. The costs of the great

Map 36 The great and little parks, King's Langley

OS 6 inches to the mile map sheets XXXVIII, surveyed 1873–7, published 1882–3; and XXXIX, surveyed 1871–2, published 1883 (both reproduced at a reduced scale). Locations of park gates after Munby (1963).

park totalled 31s 8d and included over 8 furlongs of new fence and one man working for 12 days to repair sections of dead or fallen hedge (*haye*) with fence and 'rayles' (4 shillings).[11]

In 1308 the lodge called Little London was granted to the Dominican Friars while the king had a new house built for them, also in the park.[12] It seems that he also granted them the little park itself because subsequent accounts record the costs of maintaining only the great park. A series of three accounts between 1315 and 1318 recorded expenditure on the great park under 'Foreign expenses'. Elie the parker was described as the custodian of the great park. The length of fence made around the great park was 175 perches (*c*.880m) in 1315/16, 9 furlongs 7 perches (*c*.1,850m) in 1316/17 and 4 furlongs 12 perches (*c*.860m) in 1317/18, costing a total of £3 8s 4d over the three years. An additional 9s 6d was spent on erecting a fence around 25 acres of oats grown in the park in 1315/16 and 6 shillings was spent on fencing a pond in the park the following year. Lodges in the park also needed repairs: 3s 1d was spent on the 'western new lodge' in 1315/16; 9s 8d was spent repairing the roof of a lodge with tiles and the roof of its outbuilding with straw in 1316/17; 18s 9½d was spent on repairs to a long house and other buildings, including a stable, associated with a lodge in 1317/18. Hay was purchased to feed the deer in winter: this cost 13s 3d in 1315/16 and 12s the following year.[13]

Other details relating to the park have been found in the accounts from this period: one of the king's hunting dogs worried a sick sheep that had been put in the park, resulting in a payment in compensation by the kennel-keeper; a local man was hired to drive wild beasts into the meadow from the park; and the carpenter was employed making wolf traps.[14]

By 1321 a new man was compiling the manorial accounts and it is less clear which expenses related to the park(s). One man was paid 5s 8d for 34 days spent making hedges around the park and a carpenter and his assistant spent three days repairing the lodge (le Logge) in the park for 15d in 1321/2. In the same year work was carried out on the boundary between the park and a field of the abbot of St Albans. The boundary seems to have been a ditch (or maybe a bank, *fossati*') and, after the underwood had been cleared (and sold for 2 shillings), 24 perches (*c*.120m) of ditch was made (6 perches of which was planted (*plantand*) and turfed (*turband*)) and 24 perches of hedge (*haie*) was made above the ditch. Significantly more of the boundary of the great park received attention in 1324/5: 274 perches plus two other sections totalling 14 perches were 'made new' for 1d per perch but 12 perches made new between the park and 'Le Northgrove' cost 2d per perch and 60 perches of hedge for the pasture which was leased in the park cost just ½d per perch. A further 6d was spent repairing the hedge around the lodge (La Looge). In 1324/5 repairs were carried out on the roof of the lodge and on the deerhouse (Le Derhows) using 'fern' gathered by the roofer's assistant.[15]

Income from the park in the early 1320s was produced by leasing pasture in winter – worth 5 shillings in 1321/2 and 3s 9d in the following year – and from agistment of calves in the summer – 21d for 11 calves in 1321/2 and 3s 4d for 20 calves the following year. Pigs were allowed in the park after the feast of St Michael (29 September) – earning ?2 shillings for 12 pigs for four weeks in 1321/2 and 18d for 9 pigs for six weeks the

following year. In the account for 1324/5 the names of ten individuals paying agistment for their cows, steers and calves, were listed, raising 4 shillings in total. However, what appears to be a later insertion into the account states that no herbage was sold in the park (presumably in the winter) because there was 'hardly sufficient to sustain the deer'. This shortage of grass was the result of a summer drought which affected much of England in 1324.[16]

On the death of Edward II in 1327 'the manor of Chirder Langeleye, with the park' (together with many manors and parks in other counties) was granted to his widow, Queen Isabella, for life. It was said to have been worth £38 a year.[17] However, 16 years later in 1343, Edward III changed his mind and made a

> grant to the prior and Friars Preachers dwelling within [his] manor of Childerlangele of the issues and profits of the manor ... on condition that thereout they repair and maintain all houses and buildings of the manor and of Little London, pay the usual wages and enclose his park there when necessary and that they apply the balance on the building of their church and of other works which they are to make there.[18]

Queen Isabella was granted £100 a year in compensation for surrendering her life interest in the manors of Childer langele and Eltham.[19] The Friars complained in 1345 of suffering delays in obtaining the annual payment due to them from the exchequer and, as a result, 'the new work begun there and the enclosure of the King's park are in many ways retarded'.[20] Whether the Friars were being asked to enclose the existing park, perhaps as repairs became necessary, or whether they were enclosing additional land into the park, is not made clear.

In 1358 the king made a grant to the prior and Friars 'in aid of their sustenance, of the fishery of the King's water of Childerlangele', and he also gave them a licence to

> have a weir in the said water by the King's park of Childerlangele and free entrance and exit through the middle of the park in going from their manse to the water and weir, and returning, and beyond this another way 40 feet wide through the middle of the park for them and their men on foot, horses and carts, from their manse to their garden and meadow by the parish church of Childerlangele, to bring victuals, fuel and other things to their said manse and elsewhere as they will.[21]

The Friars appear not to have repaired the buildings, however, because in 1360 the king lost patience with them and took back the issues of the manor.[22] A year later he gave them a grant 'in aid of their new work at the manor of Langeley and the enclosure of his park there' and later the same year he appointed John Marche and John le Forester 'to take sufficient masons, carpenters and other workmen for the King's works in the manors of Childerlangele and Little London and for the enclosure of the park of the first named manor'.[23]

This expansion of the park resulted in the enclosure of 160 acres of arable land, for which Edward III gave the parson four marks a year in compensation for lost tithes.[24] The works appear to have continued for a few years and part of an account from February 1359 to November 1361 is 'concerned almost exclusively with the enlargement and enclosure of the park', recording a total expenditure of nearly £110.[25] It records the felling, purchase, donation and carriage of hundreds of oaks from Hertfordshire and beyond, and the making of 150 perches (c.750m) of paling (*palicii*) and 97 perches of the park hedge using thorns. The cost of the pales and hedge alone came to £86 12s 8d.[26]

Other lands incorporated into the enlarged park and purchased from the abbot of St Albans in 1364 comprised:

> certain land in Abbot's Langele – viz. the ditch and hedges between the king's park of Langeleye and the fields of the said Abbot and convent called 'Wodefeld' and 'Whippenden,' also all the land in Langeleye newly enclosed by the king, the enclosure beginning at the water of Gateseye and stretching to a marlpit in the field called 'Waterfeld' and to a croft called Bricescroft, in length 224 perches, croft on West to Gateseye in length 40 perches 11 ft.[27]

The royal family were still spending much time at King's Langley in the 1360s and surviving accounts for the period record the provision of hay and thorn branches 'for the wild animals in the park' during the winter.[28]

In 1373 William Strete was granted for life the 'keeping of the park of Childernelangele and of the lodge of Little London in the said park'. He was to take a wage of 4d daily plus a tun of Gascon wine each year.[29] This grant was confirmed by Richard II when he came to the throne in 1377/8.[30] In 1378 Richard appointed a clerk of works to look after his numerous palaces, castles and manors. Among the clerk's responsibilities was the care of the lodges in various royal parks, including 'Childernelangeley'.[31] Accounting records in 1384–88 contain references to the queen's garden, the 'lodge called Little London in the park', and to three park gates called 'Pyngelsgate, Abbottesgate and Courtegate'.[32] In 1389 Richard II stayed at Langley himself and in 1392 he and the royal court spent Christmas and New Year at the palace. The lodges continue to appear in the Patent Rolls up to 1423. Henry IV's queen, Joan of Navarre (widowed in 1413), used the palace at King's Langley (having exchanged it for Hertford castle), together with Berkhamsted, as one of her residences at least until 1431, when it was damaged by fire.[33]

In 1466 Edward IV granted the Holme Park, together with 'le Freres Wode', trees, branches and 'agistements for their cattle in it', to a convent in Kent which was under the jurisdiction of the Friary at Langley.[34] The king granted the palace and manor to his mother, Cicely, Duchess of York, and she held them until her death in 1495 when they passed to her granddaughter, the queen of Henry VII. The estate subsequently passed to three of Henry VIII's queens in succession: Katherine of Aragon, Anne Boleyn and Jane Seymour. Nevertheless, the palace probably fell into decay during the last quarter of the fifteenth century and was in ruins by the late sixteenth century.[35]

The park, however, survived into the seventeenth century. John Verney was the steward and custodian of the parks in 1534/5 for Henry VIII, earning a fee of £15 2s 6d p.a. The farm of agistment and pannage of the park was worth £18 13s 4d p.a.[36] On the death of Lady Jane Seymour, all the agistment and pannage of the park and the conies were leased to Lord Russell, keeper of the privy seal.[37] A survey in 1556 recorded a park of 697 acres which included three meadows covering 51 acres and 646 acres of 'parke like ground'.[38] The survey reveals that the little park lay in one corner of the great park and contained two acres of underwood and 790 oak trees, in all worth £74 13s 4d. Growing dispersed in the great park were 180 oaks, 300 ash and 1,420 beech trees, valued at nearly £180. The surveyors recommended that the park be disparked. Two years later in 1558, the first year of Elizabeth's reign, a survey was made of the park pale which described the park boundary and calculated how much of the pale needed repairing. This was quoted in full by Clutterbuck and included the following sections of boundary:

> the pale from the ryver-syde, on the North side of the said parke, up to the old Manor corner (175 pole); From the Manor corner to Maple style, and so along to Whippenden botome, beyinge also on the North parte of the said parke, and adjoyninge upon a highwaye (230 pole); From Whippenden Bottom to Pyngell Gate, and so to Bury Bushes, beyinge the West side of the parke (449 pole); From Bury Bushes, and unto Abbots Gate, and from thence to the river, beyinge the South side of the parke (406 pole); From the river on the Sowth side of the said parke, and so along by London higher waye on the East parte unto the river side on the North parte (300 pole); Summe of the hole number of poles about the said parke, besyd the circuyte of the Old Manor and the Friars Orchards, there conteyne 1560 pole.[39]

Having calculated the cost of repairs needed to the pale, the surveyors recommended that the 'park may well be disparked'. This does not appear to have been done, however, as Saxton's county map of 1577 showed the park lying west of the river Gade and south of the town, and Norden's map (1598) clearly showed the park crossing to the east side of the river and bordered to the east by a road between Hemel Hempstead and Watford.

In 1608 a survey of the woods in Langley park recorded a total of 3,727 trees, of which 567 were in the little park and 782 were listed as 'beech and ash'.[40] In 1610 James I gave the park and chase to his son Henry, Prince of Wales, and then to his younger son Charles. In 1626 Charles I leased the park to Sir Charles Morrison of Cassiobury for 99 years together with 'all the deer, marsh, grass, wood and all trees' for £37 6s 8d per annum. The park was then estimated to contain 667 acres and was 'parcel of the Dutchy of Lancaster'.[41] It subsequently became part of the Cassiobury estate and was disparked by the Earl of Essex. Munby states that in 1652 ten tenants were leasing land in the park, and by the eighteenth century two large farms took up the whole area of former parkland.[42]

Map 36 shows the park boundary as it was recorded in the mid sixteenth century, presumed to be its greatest extent, enclosing an area of 913 acres. The park ranged from the flood plain of the Gade, at just under 70m OD, to over 120m

OD. In the south-west quarter, close to the highest part of the park, was one of the park lodges. At about 118m OD this lodge would have enjoyed good views of the park to the east and north-east. Significant lynchets mark the western boundary of the park and the site of Pingels Gate can be clearly identified where the public footpath enters the park.

A large bank survives in the middle of the park on the south side of the footpath that crosses the park from Pingels Gate towards the site of the palace (see Map 36). This may mark an early boundary of the great park and forms part of a continuous field boundary shown on the first edition OS map which appears to enclose a quasi-rectangular area with the Kings Langley Lodge close to its centre and the long southern border following the parish boundary. However, several other field boundaries within the former park also display marked lynchets which could be interpreted as former park boundaries at different stages of its enlargement, or could simply be the result of ploughing and erosion in the long periods before and after the park was in existence. The little park, which also seems to have been called the Home or Holme park, probably lay south-east of the church – extending eastwards to the river and southwards to include the moated site identified as Little London.

1. Variations include Chiltern Langley, Childes Langley, Langley Regina.
2. *Cal. Pat. 1272–1281*, p. 166. Vesture was a legal term meaning 'all that grows upon or covers the land, with the exception of trees'. In this case it must refer to grass growing beneath the trees in the wood.
3. *Cal. Close 1279–1288*, p. 148. Odiham castle (and presumably its park) was assigned to Queen Eleanor in 1275 (Page, *Hampshire*, 4, pp. 87–98); Rugeley was part of the king's forest of Cannock (Midgley, *Stafford*, 5, pp. 49–63).
4. Munby, *King's Langley*, p. 11, quoting TNA: PRO SC11/279 extent of the manors late of Queen Eleanor, 1290/01.
5. TNA: PRO SC6/1090/4 minister's account, 1296/7.
6. *Cal. Pat. 1301–1307*, pp. 80 and 82.
7. *Ibid.*, p. 31.
8. TNA: PRO SC6/866/13 minister's account, 1301/2.
9. TNA: PRO SC6/866/16 bailiff's account for Langeleye, 1305/6.
10. TNA: PRO SC6/866/17 bailiff's account for Childelangele, 1307/8.
11. TNA: PRO SC6/866/18 bailiff's account for Langley, 1311/12.
12. Page, *Hertford*, 2, p. 238 citing Patent Roll 2 Edw. II, pt. 1, m. 17 (TNA: PRO C66/131).
13. TNA: PRO SC6/866/20 manorial accounts for Childern Langeleye, 1315–1318.
14. Munby, *King's Langley*, p. 14.
15. TNA: PRO SC6/866/26, SC6/866/27 and SC6/866/29 manorial accounts for 1321/2, 1322/3 and 1324/5.
16. Stratton, *Agricultural records*, p. 28.
17. *Cal. Pat. 1327–1330*, p. 67.
18. *Cal. Pat. 1343–1345*, p. 135.
19. *Ibid.*, p. 263.
20. *Ibid.*, p. 547.
21. *Cal. Pat. 1358–1361*, p. 34.
22. *Ibid.*, p. 337.
23. *Cal. Pat. 1361–1364*, p. 93.
24. *Cal. Close 1396–1399*, p. 107. This payment was still being recorded in the accounts in 1535, when 53s 4d was paid to the vicar of Kings Langley in exchange for the lost tithes.
25. *Cal. Pat. 1358–1361*, p. 578–9; *Cal. Pat. 1361–1364*, pp. 93, 330 and 353; Colvin, *The king's works*, 1, p. 259, citing TNA: PRO E101/676/4.
26. TNA: PRO E101/676/4 account, 1359–61.
27. Munby, *King's Langley*, p. 16.
28. *Ibid.*, p. 18.
29. *Cal. Pat. 1370–1374*, p. 237.
30. *Ibid.*, p. 277.
31. *Cal. Pat. 1377–1381*, p. 197.
32. Colvin, *The king's works*, 2, p. 976.
33. Page, *Hertford*, 2, p. 237 citing Riley, *Annales monasterii, vol. 1*, pp. 28, 61.
34. Munby, *King's Langley*, p. 33.
35. Page, *Hertford*, 2, p. 237.
36. TNA: PRO SC6/HENVIII/181 minister's account, 1534/5.
37. Cussans, *History of Hertfordshire*, 3, p. 194.
38. TNA: PRO E315/391 survey of Hertfordshire manors, lands and possessions of King Philip and Queen Mary, 1556.
39. Clutterbuck, *History and antiquities*, 1, pp. 43–4.
40. Cussans, *History of Hertfordshire*, 3, p. 195 quoting TNA: PRO DL 44/741 Hertfordshire: survey and valuation of the woods belonging to the duchy of Lancaster, 1607–8.
41. Clutterbuck, *History and antiquities*, 1, pp. 43–4.
42. Munby, *Hertfordshire landscape*, p. 152.

Figure 38. *Aerial view of the former park at King's Langley prepared from air photos taken by the RAF in August 1947 (HALS RAF photo No. 75). Most of the park boundary is clearly visible in the field-scape of the mid-twentieth century. Reproduced by kind permission of Hertfordshire Archives and Local Studies. Location of Pingels Gate after Munby (1963).*

Knebworth

The old, new, great and little parks

NGR: old park ?TL239210; great park TL240200; little park
TL231206
Date range: by late thirteenth century – perhaps disparked
in sixteenth century
Size: great park: perhaps 340 acres; little park: 37 acres
Underlying geology: mostly clay-with-flints over chalk; also
areas of boulder clay and undifferentiated glaciofluvial
deposits

THE EARLIEST RECORD OF A PARK at Knebworth found so far dates from 1334, but surname evidence strongly suggests that a park existed by at least the late thirteenth century. Walter le Parker was a witness to a grant to the church 'before 1294'; Thomas le Parker was listed as a tax-payer in the lay subsidy of 1307; and his son, William le Parker, was recorded in a document of 1321.[1] In addition, a Walter de Parkesgate held a messuage in the town of Knebworth before 1309.[2] The park may have been established by Robert de Hoo, who obtained a patent for a weekly market and an annual fair in Knebworth in 1292 and was granted free warren there by Edward I.[3] By 1316 the manor had been conveyed to Richard and Joan de Perers (Joan was probably the daughter of Robert de Hoo) and it was in a grant of the manor by Richard de Perers to his son Edmund in 1334 that the park was mentioned for the first time.[4]

A bailiff's account of 1370/1 reveals that by that time there was already an 'old park'. This was evidently an important source of coppiced wood which was sold in lots of one acre for 10 shillings each.[5] Income of 8s 5d was also received from the agistment of 'diverse beasts going in the park', presumably another park and not the old park. This is the only known bailiff's account for Knebworth from the fourteenth century, but many more survive from the early fifteenth century with a smattering from later in the century and two from the sixteenth century.

The accounts from the first decade of the fifteenth century recorded a confusing array of parks, with references to the old park, the new park, the great park, the lord's park and, simply, the park. The account of 1401/2 referred to a bridge being made at 'Newparkponde' and in the following year one acre of wood was sold in the new park for 13s 4d.[6] The new park was also a source of faggots, underwood and *lopp'*. In 1410/11 900 faggots were made in the new park at a cost of 9s 9d; they were sold for 30 shillings, giving a profit of 20s 3d.[7] The great park was recorded in 1402/3, when eight oaks and a beech were felled there for use on the new bridge and several parcels of wood were also sold in the great park.[8] The old park was the source of 15 loads of charcoal sold for 10s 5d in 1408/9 and was mentioned again in 1412/3 in conjunction with the new park, when trees were felled in both parks.

Wood sales were a significant source of income in the early fifteenth century and the accounts include detailed lists of purchasers. In 1403/4 John Horewode paid 18d for four parcels of *lopp'* sold in the park of Knebworth, and 17 others bought *lopp'* in the park for between 12d and 16 shillings – the highest price being paid by Robert Colyer, probably a charcoal-burner. In 1407/8 22 named individuals bought wood lopped from trees in the lord's park. The prices paid ranged from 15d to 12 shillings, with two of the purchasers travelling from Ippollitts and Hitchin and paying 3s 4d and 3s respectively.[9] Trees felled and sold as timber in 1410/11 included ash, beech, oak and *wiche*. In the same year three beech trees were felled in the lord's park for making *palisbord*.[10] In 1412/13 'diverse' beech trees in the park were sold to John Cropper of Stevenage for £10 13s 4d, a huge sum of money indicating a great number of trees felled.[11]

Agistment of animals in the park (which one was not specified) was also recorded in detail, with lists of named graziers, the amounts they paid, the animals which they put in the park and the number of weeks they were there. Income from agistment rose from 6 shillings in 1402/3 to about 30 shillings a year between 1407 and 1413.[12]

In 1412 John Hotoft became lord of the manor of Knebworth and a major programme of repairs and improvements was recorded in the accounts for that year. These included the making of a new pond in the lord's park (cost 26s 8d) and the cutting down of underwood in the park in order to make a *launde* (16s 6½d). The boundary of the new park received some attention: 120 perches of new hedge (*haie*) were made (at 2d per perch) and 40 perches of hedge were repaired (1d per perch). Thirty-eight man-days were spent making a new fence (*sep'*) around the park 'in diverse locations' at 4d per day, with a total cost of 12s 8d.[13] These expenses were perhaps funded by the massive sale of beech trees mentioned previously.

Hotoft was controller of the household of the Prince of Wales (soon to become Henry V) and Knebworth was his country seat. Henry V granted him several lucrative posts and he was elected a knight of the shire on four occasions. As keeper of the great wardrobe from 1423 he had an official residence in London and appears to have made useful contacts with architects and builders who subsequently worked for him embellishing the parish church at Knebworth.[14] As well as his work for the crown, Hotoft also acted as a justice of the peace for Hertfordshire and was sheriff in 1428. In 1427 he was appointed keeper of Walkern park (see p. 218), an administrative post which entitled him to pasture his own beasts there. He died in 1443 and his will revealed his 'profound love of Knebworth', where he was buried.[15] The manor passed to his daughter Idonea and her husband, Sir John Barre of Ayot St Lawrence.[16]

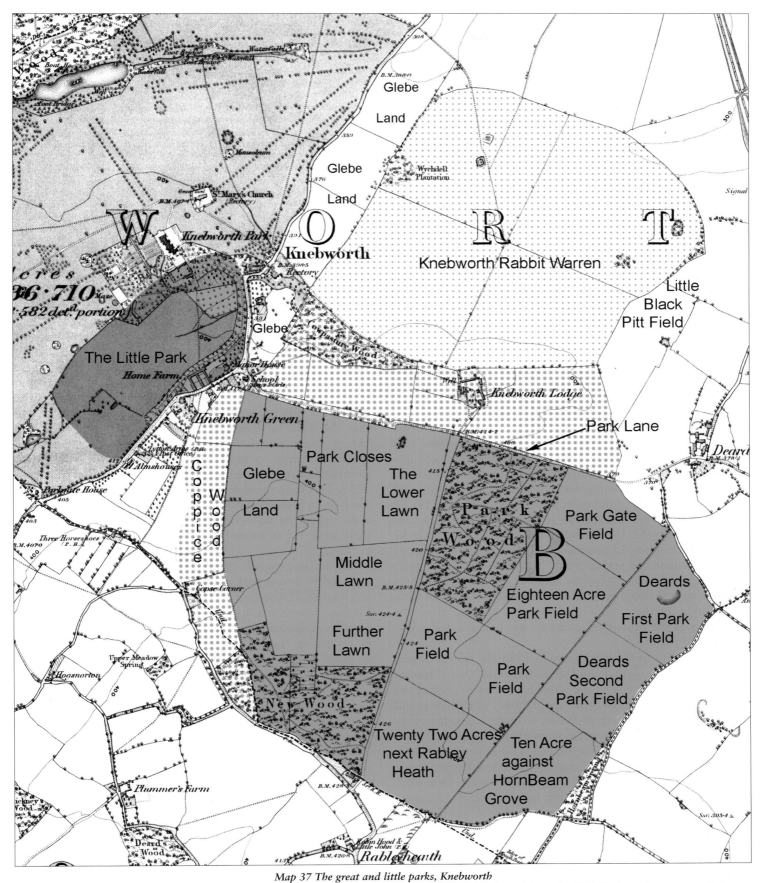

Map 37 The great and little parks, Knebworth
OS 6 inches to the mile map sheet XX, surveyed 1881, published 1884. Annotated with field names derived from the 1731 Knebworth estate map (private collection) indicating the extent of the great park, which probably included lands to the north of Park Lane.

By the middle of the fifteenth century there was a substantial rabbit warren at Knebworth. John Sexton, who was the custodian of the great park and warren, received pay of 60s 8d a year. The warren was a major source of income: John Kelet of London, poulterer (*pulter*), paid 37s 6d for an unspecified number of rabbits in 1449/50 and £11 18s 11d for 1,100 rabbits in 1451/2. In addition, the lord of the manor took two dozen rabbits for his own use in London that year. It is possible that the warren occupied the site of the old park, which does not feature in the accounts after 1413. In addition to the wages of John Sexton, the accounts reveal that John Perceval was paid 26s 8d a year to maintain the boundary of the great park and, in 1449/50, 9 shillings was spent on making 18 perches of pale with a single rail (at 6d per perch) and 19 shillings on making 28½ perches of pale with a double rail (at 8d per perch) around parts of the park.[17] Although deer were never mentioned in the Knebworth accounts, their presence is confirmed in a record from 1449/50, when four deer were taken from Knebworth park to restock Sir John Fray's park at Great Munden (see p. 102).[18]

Sir John Barre held Knebworth until he died in 1483. Accounts compiled for 1481/2 show that income from agistment of animals in the great park (in the summertime) was 32s 4d, much the same as 70 years previously. Income from sales of wood was, however, much reduced: just 12d from the sale of *loppes* of three hornbeams and 4 shillings for the *loppes* of ten hornbeams, all in the great park. The scribe wrote 'trees called hornebeme', as though the name was new to him and, indeed, the tree is not recorded in earlier accounts at Knebworth. Sir John had leased the rabbit warren to Thomas Hyde for £8 for a term of five years. The cost of maintaining the pale of the great park came to 27s 5d: 19s 2d paid to two men for making 115 poles of new fence (*sepis*) at 2d per pole; 6s 11d for setting spikes (*le berdynge*) into 83 poles of old fence at 1d per pole; and 16d for the carriage of four wagon-loads of stakes from 'Ympo' to the lord's great park for making the new fences. Another 5 shillings was spent on scouring and flooding a ditch on the south side of the little park and a further major expense was the wage of the 'custodian of the great park', one Richard Sexton, who was paid 30s 4d p.a.[19]

On the death of Sir John Barre in 1483 the manor passed to his daughter Isabel and her husband, Sir Thomas Bourghchier. Bourghchier took immediate steps to control the park finances. He granted the office of Parker of the Great and Little Parks at Knebworth to Walter Copynger, together with all the profits, products and emoluments of the office, for an annual rent of £6 20d. Walter was entitled to keep one horse and three cows in the parks and to collect windblown wood and 'browsing' (except good windblown timber (*maeremo habili*)).[20] During Bourghchier's first year as lord of the manor income from the great park increased markedly: agistment (in both winter and summer) brought in 37s 5d and pannage of pigs was worth £4 2s 8d. Three parcels of wood in the park were sold for 26s 8d, 12s and 4s 8d respectively. In addition, broken branches were sold from 8 virgates in le Nywparke at 3d per virgate. A lodge in the great park was recorded for the first time in 1483/4 and the cost of repairing both the lodge and the pales of the great and little parks and the making of two gates came to just 11s 8d.[21]

A very different picture is revealed in the account compiled by Robert Hoggekyns, bailiff and rent collector for the manor, in 1511. He recorded that there was no income from agistment because the great park was reserved for the lord's horses and the little park was reserved for the use of the reeve. No wood or underwood was sold. On the death of Sir Thomas Bourghchier in 1492 two-thirds of the manor had passed to William Lytton but one-third remained in the hands of Bourghchier's second wife, who was still living at this time, and the efficient management of the manorial resources does not appear to have been a priority. William Lytton died in 1517 leaving his young son Robert as his heir. Robert finally came of age in 1533/4[22] and the next surviving bailiff's account, compiled in 1541/2, shows that the great park was producing income again: £3 13s 4d for agistment and £7 10s 4d for pannage. The Lyttel Parke was leased, along with the mansion and other lands, for £20 p.a. The warren was also leased, with Dardes, to Edward Foster for £12 p.a.[23] In 1561 one tenant paid 13s 4d for a tenement called Le Parkgate and the agistment of two cows and a horse in the great park and another paid 6s 6d for a tenement called Naylers and the agistment of one cow in the great park.[24]

Given that the great park was evidently still functioning in the 1560s, it is puzzling that Saxton did not show a park at Knebworth on his 1577 map of the county. Norden's map of 1598 also fails to show a park and the explanation may be that the park no longer contained deer. In 1563 Rowland Lytton (who inherited the estate in 1551) built a new courtyard house to replace the medieval house and Queen Elizabeth stayed at Knebworth in 1571 and perhaps again in 1588. This shows that in the mid sixteenth century the Lyttons were of high social status and could be expected to have had a deer park but no evidence has been found to confirm that there were deer in either the great or little park in the sixteenth century.[25]

In the seventeenth century the medieval great park was replaced by a new park created by Sir William Lytton around Knebworth House and the parish church. The first evidence for this survives in a document of 1641 confirming Sir William Lytton's acquisition of common rights over Winter Green, described as 'newly inclosed into Knebworth Park'. Also included were a piece of land 'called Knebworth Green in Knebworth and Codicote and also of and in all the lane and other grounds now lately inclosed within the new made park of Sir William and Rowland Lytton in Knebworth and Codicote'.[26] The new park incorporated the medieval little park but not the great park. The primary function of the new park, created just before the outbreak of the English Civil War in 1642, was to provide an ornamental setting for Knebworth House. The seventeenth-century county maps by Seller (1676) and Oliver (1695) show the new park but not the medieval great park.

An early eighteenth-century estate map shows that the little park lay immediately south of Knebworth House and its walled gardens; it covered 37 acres.[27] Field-name evidence shows that the great park covered about 313 acres which lay south of the modern Park Lane between Knebworth Green and Deard's End (see Map 37 and Figure 39).[28] However, a field lying north of the lane was also considered part of the 'old' park in 1732 so the total acreage of the great park could

Figure 39. View across the former Knebworth great park from the south-east corner. Park Wood is on the right of the photograph, New Wood is to the left.

have been about 340 acres. To the north of the great park lay an extensive rabbit warren, first documented in 1449/50, covering a further 150 acres.[29]

The boundary of the former great park is revealed on maps as a long, sinuous line, parts of which can still be traced on the ground today. The line of the boundary around the west of the park appears to continue north of Park Lane to also encompass the warren, which was itself enclosed within a distinctive oval-shaped boundary. It is possible that this oval area may have been the original 'old' park created in the late thirteenth century and that this had become the warren by the mid fifteenth century. The great park was recorded from 1402 and it seems likely that the park and the warren became one large enclosure (c.500 acres).

The western boundary of the great park is tracked by public footpaths and, north of Park Lane, was bordered on its west side by four closes of arable land belonging to the church. The 1638 glebe terrier described these closes as 'butting south east upon Knebworth Parke, north west upon the highway leading from Knebworth to Steavenage [sic]'.[30] It is possible that the boundary south of Park Lane lay further to the west, following the lane to the south-west of New Wood then continuing northwards as a field boundary shown on the 1731 estate map. This would mean that a part of the parish of Codicote was included within the park, a theory that is supported by a mid sixteenth-century grant of land in Codicote described as being 'part of Knebworth Park'.[31] Most of the southern boundary of the great park followed the parish boundary between Knebworth and Codicote to the south and Datchworth to the east. A significant earth bank survives in New Wood marking the parish and park boundary. This continues eastwards along the north side of the lane to Rabley Heath before leaving the lane to form the rear boundary of a row of houses in Rabley Heath. About 200m further east the parish and park boundaries part company and the park boundary, still marked by a ditch and bank and an ancient hedgerow, continues eastwards towards Hornbeam Spring. The eastern park boundary is bounded in the south by Gypsy Lane before heading north-westwards towards Deards End. Its course then becomes less well defined, but the 'park pale' was said to

abut Black Pitt Field in 1650 (see Map 37).[32] The northern boundary has now been lost under a golf course.

The present Park Lane runs east–west along a low ridge of land which separates the fairly steep northward-facing slopes of the warren from the more gentle undulations of the park to the south. At the highpoint of the ridge lies Lodge Farm (Knebworth Lodge on Map 37). This was probably the location of the park lodge recorded in 1483/4, from which the parker or warrener would have had excellent views over both the warren to the north and the park to the south, with a particularly clear view along the track towards Rabley Heath, which survives as a footpath to this day. Several gates provided access to or through the medieval deer park: the 'great park gate' was recorded in 1526, Dardesende gate and Bobleyheyth gate in 1542.[33]

Park Wood has survived to the present day on the south side of Park Lane (see Map 37) and seems to have existed since at least the fifteenth century, when two cottages were recorded as standing between 'the wood called le Park and the way leading to the middle of the town' [of Knebworth].[34] In 1731 it was called Old Park Wood. Another feature of the medieval park can be deduced from several 'lawn' field names lying west of Park Wood, first recorded on the estate map of 1731. Lawn (originally *launde*) suggests an open grassy area within the park but by 1731 these fields had all been ploughed.

Most of the large original enclosure containing the medieval park and warren is underlain by relatively infertile soils – mostly clay-with-flints over chalk – but there are also areas of glacial till and undifferentiated glaciofluvial deposits. This land was probably better-suited to management as wood-pasture rather than arable cultivation in medieval times and the great park and the warren, in particular, were an important source of revenue for the manor.

The location of the new park recorded in the fifteenth century is open to conjecture and it may have been incorporated into the seventeenth-century park – it is difficult to determine the previous use of the land which became incorporated into the latter park. An unknown proportion was already in Lytton hands, some appears to have been glebe land and other parts could have been one or more of the numerous common fields of Knebworth.

Figure 40. *A grove of pollarded hornbeams in the present-day deer park at Knebworth. The tree in the foreground has recently been re-pollarded – in full leaf – and the lopped branches left on the ground to provide browse for the deer during a period of drought when there was little grass available in the park, a practice which was doubtless common in the medieval period. The crown of this tree started to regrow the following spring.*

1. HALS K149d grant to church 'before 1294'; Brooker and Flood, *Hertfordshire lay subsidy rolls*, p. 82; HALS 21833 grant by William le Parker to his son, 1321.

2. HALS 21870 grant of a messuage 'late of Walter de Parkesgate', 1309.

3. Salmon, *History of Hertfordshire*, p. 200.

4. HALS 21843 grant of manor of Knebworth, 1334.

5. HALS K100 bailiff's account, 1370/1. Up to five 'cropp' of one acre were sold from the old park at 10s each, together with the 'cropp' of diverse branches from 1½ acres for 15s and the 'cropp' of one rod for 2s 6d. Underwood was also sold by the acre from 'Ymphoe' for significantly lower sums of money. Impo Wood was shown on the 1731 Knebworth estate map (see below for reference).

6. HALS K102 bailiff's account, 1401/2; K106 bailiff's account, 1402/3.

7. HALS K108, 114, 117 and 119 bailiff's accounts, 1403/4, 1407/8, 1410/11 and 1412/13. Two hundred faggots were sold for 6s 4d in 1403/4 and 300 were sold in 1407/8 for 9s 6d.

8. HALS K106 bailiff's account, 1402/3.

9. HALS K108 and K114 bailiff's accounts, 1403/4 and 1407/8.

10. HALS K117 bailiff's account, 1410/11. *Wiche* was presumably wych elm; *palisbord* were perhaps boards for the park pale.

11. HALS K119 bailiff's account, 1412/13.

12. HALS K106, K108, K114, K116, K117 and K119 bailiff's accounts, 1402/3, 1403/4, 1407/8, 1408/9, 1410/11 and 1412/13.

13. HALS K119 bailiff's account, 1412/3; 160 perches is approximately 800 metres.

14. E. Roberts, *A school of masons in 15th century north Hertfordshire*

(Hertfordshire Library Service and Hertfordshire Local History Council, 1979), pp. 3–4.

15. *Ibid.*, p. 6.

16. *Ibid.*, p. 22.

17. HALS K121 bailiff's account, 1449/50; K135 bailiff's account, 1451/2.

18. TNA: PRO SC6/867/13 bailiff's account for Great Munden, 1449/50. Sir John Fray, Baron of the Exchequer and close associate of John Hotoft, was bequeathed a gilt cup in Hotoft's will of 1439 and was responsible for the sale of his goods after his death in 1443 (Roberts, *A school of masons*, p. 6.)

19. HALS K124 bailiff's account, 1481/2. See also fn. 5.

20. HALS DE/Z120/44373 confirmation of the earlier grant, 1483.

21. HALS K126 bailiff's account, 1483/4.

22. Page, *Hertford*, 3, p. 116, citing Court of Ward Books clxxiii, fo. 73 (TNA).

23. HALS K133 bailiff's account, 1541/2. Foster was leasing the warren as early as 1526 and, in 1544, he was supplying a 'weekly couple of fat conies' to Hogekyn the manor bailiff in addition to his rent for the warren; he also had conies in the great park (HALS 79547 and 79548 rentals of the manor of Knebworth, 1526 and 1543/4).

24. HALS 26565 rental of the manor, 1561.

25. Rowland Lytton was county sheriff in 1567/8 and his son (also Rowland) was lieutenant of the county in 1588, knighted and made sheriff in 1593/4, and one of the two knights of the shire in 1596/7 and 1603/4 (Salmon, *History of Hertfordshire*, pp. 200 and 360–4).

26. HALS 46572 quit claim by William Adye alias Gynn of Knebworth, yeoman, and Judith his wife, 18 August 1641.

27. Knebworth House 'Plan of the north part of the manor & parish of Knebworth … the estate of William Robinson Lytton Esq, surveyed by Augustine Hale, new drawn & examined by Thomas Browne, gent, 1731'. Photocopy at HALS 47259.

28. Many park-related field names were recorded in the estate survey of 1731 (HALS 47259 and 46655B) and in the Knebworth tithe award and map, 1845 (HALS Acc 2643/1/3).

29. Twenty-eight pairs of rabbits were, however, sold in 1408/9 for 5d per pair (HALS K116 bailiff's account).

30. HALS 47132 'A terrier of the glebe land and houses belonging to the rectory of Knebworth made the 11th day of April 1638'. The 'park pale' abutting Black Pitt Field on the north-east side of the warren/park was also mentioned in 1650 (HALS DE/B987/T1 deeds of Deards End Farm).

31. HALS 22850 grant of land, 1569.

32. HALS DE/B987/T1 deeds of Deards End Farm, 1650.

33. HALS 79547 rental, 1526. The great park gate was perhaps at 'parkegate green' recorded in 1553 (HALS 22844); HALS 22834 grant of annuity, 1542.

34. HALS 21901 grant of two cottages by Richard Schyrlock to his son, 1430.

Little Berkhamsted

Bedwell park *see Essendon*

No known name
NGR: not known
Date range: by 1337 – not known
Size: not known
Underlying geology: not known but probably Pebble Gravel
on London Clay

A PARK WAS RECORDED at Little Berkhamsted in 1337 on the death of John de Moels. An extent of the manor included 'a park, 8 acres of which he held of the bishop of Ely by service of 4s 8d yearly'.[1] The manor had been granted to John's ancestor, Nicholas de Moels, by the king in 1226 and had then passed down through three generations of the family. John's grandfather, Roger, received a grant of free warren in 1290 but no park was recorded in the extent made at his death.[2] Roger's son, another John, was summoned to parliament as Lord Moels, so he may have established the park, but he died in 1310 and any of the three sons who, in turn, subsequently inherited the manor are equally plausible contenders, including the John who died in 1337. Apart from the manorial extent of 1337, no other reference to this park is known. By 1402 the manor of Little Berkhamsted was held by John Norbury, who previously, in 1388, had acquired the neighbouring manor of Bedwell in Essendon with lands and tenements in Little Berkhamsted.[3] In 1406 he obtained a licence to enclose 800 acres of land to make a park in the two manors. Bedwell Park occupied approximately 350 acres of the west and south-west side of the parish of Little Berkhamsted, extending towards (and perhaps butting up to)

Hatfield great park (Hatfield Wood) on the south, land held by the bishops of Ely.

Given a lack of evidence for a park elsewhere in the parish, the most likely location for the early fourteenth-century park was on land which became subsumed within the new Bedwell Park from 1406 (see Map 16). As part of the fourteenth-century park was held of the bishop of Ely, it probably lay at the southern end of the parish (Map 38), perhaps where the parish of Hatfield extends north of Tylers Causeway south of Epping Green (the land to the south of Tylers Causeway was part of Hatfield great park (see Map 23)).

Most of the 1337 park probably occupied land which, by the early nineteenth century, was known as Woodcock Lodge Farm. No evidence has been found to show when the lands of Woodcock Lodge became separated from the Bedwell park estate but it may have been as early as the sixteenth century and certainly before Dury and Andrews' county map was published in 1766.

There are no good alternative locations for the earlier medieval park on lands which were still held by the lord of the manor, the Honourable Baron Dimsdale, in the early nineteenth century. In 1838 Baron Dimsdale was holding three collections of fields in different parts of the parish. The most northerly of these included Culver Wood and a field of under two acres called Penley Park.[4] A small field with a 'park' name is more likely to have been given the name in an ironical sense, rather than having once been a park but it is, nevertheless, one of the few park-related names in the parish.

1. *Cal. Inq. post mortem, vol. 8, Edward III*, p. 83, no. 139.

2. *Cal. Inq. post mortem, vol. 3, Edward. I*, p. 181.

3. Page, *Hertford*, 3, p. 428.

4. HALS DSA4/20/1 and 2 Little Berkhampsted tithe award and map, 1838.

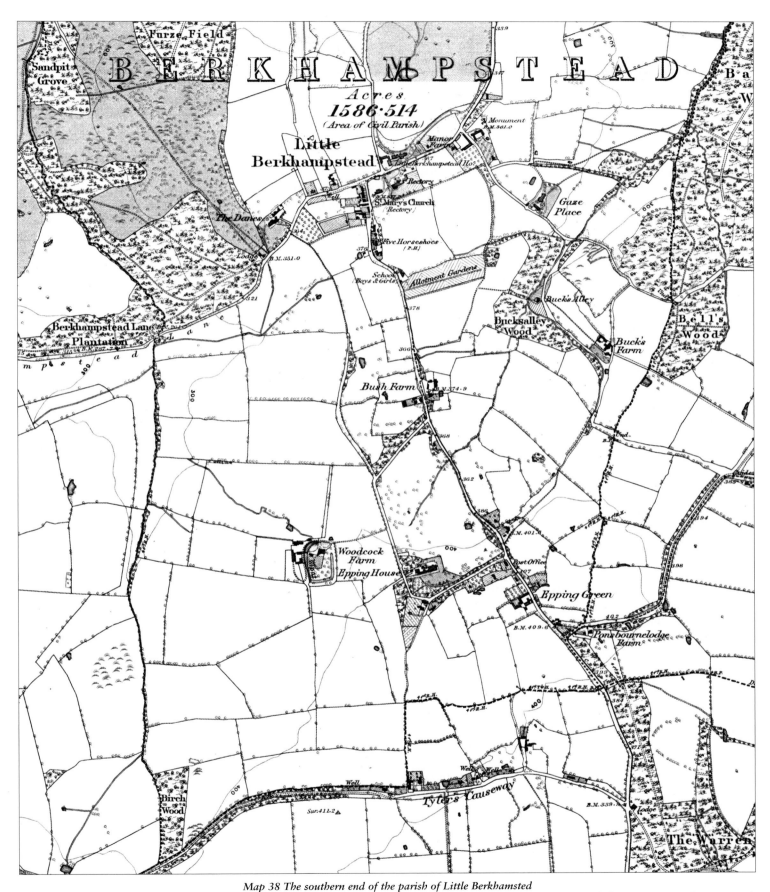

Map 38 The southern end of the parish of Little Berkhamsted

OS 6 inches to the mile map sheet XXXVI, surveyed 1873–80, published 1883. The most likely location for the park recorded in 1337 was in the vicinity of Woodcock Farm but lack of information makes it impossible to plot its extent. In 1406 this park probably became part of Bedwell park (see Map 16). Culver Wood and the small field named Penley Park are in the north of the parish and are not shown on this map.

Little Gaddesden

Ashridge park (park formerly in Berkhamsted, Hertfordshire and Pitstone, Buckinghamshire)

NGR: SP992121
Date range: by 1280 – not known
Size: *c*.200 acres
Underlying geology: clay-with-flints

THIS IS PERHAPS THE longest-surviving area of park-like land in the county, established by 1280 and still roamed by deer today, although no longer strictly a park, as it is not enclosed. It was probably created by Edmund, Earl of Cornwall, during the 1270s. Ashridge, a manor in Little Gaddesden, lay next to Edmund's manor of Berkhamsted and was given to him by Ulian Chenduit.[1] Although Edmund's main seat was nearby at Berkhamsted castle, he appears to have been very fond of Ashridge and built himself a residence there, complete with gardens and a chapel, set within a park.[2] The building of this establishment – and the existence of the park – is recorded in a manorial account at The National Archives which is, unfortunately, undated.[3] It appears to have been written, however, by the same hand as two other surviving accounts dating from 1269 and 1273.[4] By 1285 Edmund had established a religious foundation at Ashridge which was placed under the care of secular priests later recognised as an independent order of English Augustinian Bonhommes.[5] Among the properties granted by Edmund to the rector and brothers in his foundation charter was the 'manor of Ashridge cum Pitstone with the park of Ashridge in the parishes of Berkhamsted and Pitstone'.[6]

Edmund's charter granted the brothers the right of common pasture for their 'beasts' in his wood of Berkhamsted known as 'Le Fryth', the right to put their pigs in the wood 'in the time of mast' without paying pannage, and the rights of 'housbote and heybote and fencing of the said park of Esserugge in the said Frith wood'. In January 1286 the rector of Pitstone granted the rector and brothers of Ashridge the right of common pasture and housebote in 'the park and new close of Ashridge and its ditches and hedges old and new'. The grant also stated that they 'may widen and enlarge the ditch of the said park and new close as they wish by a space of twelve feet on all sides'.[7] In April 1286 Edmund obtained a licence

> to enclose the king's highway leading through his wood of Esserugge and Berchamstede with a dike and hedge for the enlargement of his park there, and to make another road of the same length and breadth, safer, smoother, and clearer, on his own ground adjoining the hedge of his said park.[8]

Edmund entertained Edward I and his court at Ashridge at Christmas 1290 and for the first two weeks of January 1291,

and a parliament was held there.[9] One of the charters issued during the king's stay at Ashridge was an *inspeximus* and confirmation of Edmund's grant of lands to the rector and brethren at Ashridge which recorded details relating to the boundary of the land and the park. The grant included:

> the wood and all the lands which lie between the heath of Aldebur' on the east within the manor of Berchamstede and the wood of Pichelesthorne on the north, and are bounded in length and breadth on the south by a way (*itineris*) which runs through the middle of a valley called Twyselden eastwards to the park of Asserugge and so stretches on the east of the said park to a valley called 'Frithesden', and along the middle of that valley to a way called 'Keneswey' opposite a tenement late of John Spramich, and all the wood to the east of that way within the manor of Berchamstede, which way runs through the middle of the Frith to a channel (*wayera*) called 'La Swylye' and thence to a dike called 'Grymesdich, …'.[10]

After Edmund's death at Ashridge in 1300, Edward I confirmed his foundation charter to the brothers.[11] No further information relating to the park in medieval times has been found and the Bonhommes continued to hold the manor until 1538/9, when it was surrendered to Henry VIII.[12]

Detailed research and fieldwork by Angus Wainwright, an archaeologist working for the National Trust, led him to conclude that 'little remains on the ground of the medieval park and much of what can be found is open to alternative interpretation'. Nevertheless, his identification of sections of the medieval park boundary enabled him to reconstruct a probable outline for the park (see Map 39). The southern park boundary survives as a substantial 5m-wide bank which has been levelled in places. A smaller bank runs on a parallel course outside the main bank and between the two banks is an abandoned track. Wainwright considered that 'this part of the park would have acted as an extended deer leap. The deer being able to jump from the higher ground of the common into the lower ground within the park, once inside they would have found it impossible to escape' (Figure 41). Tracks from Northchurch and Berkhamsted, surviving today as linear earthworks, converged on two breaks in the park boundary, one at the south-west corner and the other in the middle of the south side. The western boundary follows a curving course about 500m from the present house and is marked by an earthwork (a series of linear mounds about 8m wide and 80cm high) and a soil mark across the ploughed field to the north. The northern boundary is thought to have followed the Pitstone parish boundary, which can be traced as a slight earthwork through Golden Valley, but the

Map 39 Ashridge park
OS 6 inches to the mile map sheet XXVI, surveyed 1877–8, published 1883–4. Conjectural park boundary after Angus Wainwright.

south-eastern boundary is largely conjectural with no surviving evidence on the ground except for a pronounced lynchet at its south-west end.[13]

Wainwright concluded that the medieval park covered about 200 acres. It lay on a ridge of high ground (*c*.180m OD) on land which had formerly been used for common grazing by four different parishes in the counties of Hertfordshire and Buckinghamshire. The surviving park pale has a curving boundary to the north and west, indicating that it was probably carved out of common land; to the south and east the straight boundaries probably abutted earlier fields.[14]

Henry VIII used Ashridge as a royal nursery. Princess Elizabeth retired to Ashridge after the coronation of her sister, Mary, and it was there that she was arrested and taken to London to face charges of involvement in Wyatt's rebellion in

1554. Wainwright suggests that the Tudor park consisted of only the western two-thirds of the medieval park; the land to the east of the former college of the Bonhommes was disparked and divided into fields.[15] The mansion was leased to tenants by Princess Elizabeth from 1556 and a list of fields at Ashridge in 1575 included Ash park (8 acres), Bush park (83 acres) and Hudnall park (8 acres), as well as a Park field (40 acres) and Connyger field (40 acres).[16] The acreages of the fields are derived from an inquisition into the value of the estate, also compiled in 1575, which recorded that all the lands were leased out, except for the 'parks called the Bush Park and Hudnall Park', and also informs us that all the lands lay in the county of Buckinghamshire, except for 40 acres of Bush Park.[17] Although this survey recorded the value of some of the wood in the parks, it made no mention of deer and no evidence has been found for

Figure 41. Earthworks at Ashridge which may have formed part of the southern boundary of the medieval park. The park lay to the right of the picture.

a functioning deer park in the sixteenth century (or, indeed, in the previous two centuries).[18] Furthermore, no park was depicted at Ashridge on Saxton's county map of 1577, or on the map by Norden of 1598, which also weakens the case for the survival of the medieval deer park into the early modern period. However, as the park lay only partly in Hertfordshire, it is possible that it was simply overlooked by the map surveyors.

By the early seventeenth century the manor was owned by Thomas Egerton, Baron Ellesmere, lord keeper to Queen Elizabeth and Lord Chancellor to James I. His main residence was at Harefield, Middlesex, however, and it may have been his son, John, who took up residence at Ashridge and presumably converted the monastic buildings and set about expanding the area of parkland and, perhaps, restocking it with deer.[19] It was, nevertheless, Lord Ellesmere who was granted a licence by James I to enclose 400 acres for a park and this seems to have incorporated the former medieval park plus a large area of fields to the south of it.[20] The park at Ashridge underwent another major phase of expansion in the later seventeenth century, when the second Earl of Bridgewater (grandson of Lord Ellesmere) enclosed another 400 acres to the north-west of the house in two phases during the 1660s, creating a park of nearly 1,000 acres.[21] Part of the newly enclosed land was to be used to form another park, presumably the red deer park recorded in 1664.[22] Thomas Baskerville visited Ashridge in 1681 and remarked on the herds of red and fallow deer, and on the 'lofty groves of trees, so thick set together that the like is scarce anywhere else to be seen'.[23] Separate compartments for fallow and red deer were subsequently recorded. The park at its full extent was shown on the county map by Seller (1676) and on later maps.

Formal rides were established through the park in the late seventeenth or early eighteenth century and Capability Brown worked at Ashridge for the third Duke of Bridgewater from 1759 to 1768.[24] Information about the management of the deer in the first half of the nineteenth century, including the provision of beans, acorns and the cutting of browse, was recorded in the countess of Bridgewater's Establishment books.[25] Harting recorded that the park in 1881 was about five miles in length by more than two in breadth, and was well timbered. It contained some red deer as well as a herd of fallow.[26] Map 39 shows the outline of the medieval park, as proposed by Wainwright, sitting within the extensive parkland of the late nineteenth century.

At the beginning of the twentieth century the park of 986 acres was said to be stocked with about 100 red deer and 300 fallow deer and was described as 'a considerable stretch of wild and forest-like ground, [with] an abundance of fine timber, chiefly oak, beech and ash.'[27] Most of the red deer were caught and taken to Richmond Park in 1920, but about 800 fallow deer remained at Ashridge. The National Trust took over the management of the estate from the 1920s and threw down the park pale, allowing the deer to go free.[28] Fallow deer continue to inhabit the estate, however, and, despite the lack of a park pale, the area of the original medieval park to the north and west of the present mansion must represent one of the oldest park landscapes in the county.

1. Page, *Hertford*, 2, p. 209; *Cal. Chart. 1257–1300*, pp. 324–5.

2. He died at Ashridge and his heart was buried there.

3. TNA: PRO SC6/863/8 minister's account for the honour of Berkhamsted, 1272–1307.

4. TNA: PRO SC6/863/2 and 3 minister's accounts for the honour of Berkhamsted, 1268/9 and 1272/3.

5. Vincent, 'Edmund of Almain'.

6. *Cal. Chart. 1257–1300*, p. 324; HALS AH916 catalogue entry describing a late fifteenth- or early sixteenth-century copy of the confirmation by Edward I, after Edmund's death in 1300, of the foundation charter.

7. HALS AH918, release, 25 January 1286. I am grateful to Lee Prosser for this translation.

8. *Cal. Pat. 1281–1292*, p. 231.

9. Vincent, 'Edmund of Almain'; charters issued at Ashridge are recorded in *Cal. Chart. 1257–1300*, pp. 382–8.

10. *Cal. Chart. 1257–1300*, p. 385.

11. HALS AH916 late fifteenth- or early sixteenth-century copy of the confirmation by Edward I.

12. Page, *Hertford*, 2, p. 209, citing Letters and Papers Hen. VIII, xiv (2), 261 (TNA).

13. A. Wainwright, 'Ashridge park survey', unpublished report for the National Trust, 1989, pp. 13–14.

14. *Ibid.*, p. 15.

15. *Ibid.*, plan between pp. 16 and 17.

16. Page, *Hertford*, 2, p. 209, citing Patent Roll 17 Eliz. pt. 5, No. 1 (TNA: PRO C66/1127); HALS AH943b grants of lands, 1545–1609.

17. Wainwright, 'Ashridge park survey', pp. 10–11, citing Buckinghamshire Record Office I 72/2.

18. A manorial account of 1540 makes no reference to a park (TNA: PRO SC6/HENVIII/238).

19. L.A. Knafla, 'Egerton, John, first earl of Bridgewater (1579–1649)', *Oxford dictionary of national biography* (Oxford, September 2004; online edn, May 2007), accessed online 22 October 2007.

20. Wainwright, 'Ashridge park survey', p. 22.

21. Page, *Hertford*, 2 p. 210, citing *Calendar of State Papers Domestic 1660–1*, p. 578 and 1664–5, pp. 47–8.

22. HALS AH1181 marriage settlement, 1664.

23. Page, *Hertford*, 2, p. 210, citing *Welbeck Abbey MSS.* (Historical MSS. Commission), ii, 306.

24. T. Williamson and the Hertfordshire Gardens Trust, *The parks and gardens of west Hertfordshire* (Hertford, 2000), pp. 44–5.

25. HALS AH2478 and AH2481 countess of Bridgewater's Establishment books, 1830 and 1832.

26. Harting, 'Hertfordshire deer-parks', p. 103.

27. Page, *Hertford*, 4, p. 277.

28. Wainwright, 'Ashridge park survey', p. 42.

Little Hadham

No known name

NGR: TL426227

Date range: by 1285 – sixteenth century

Size: perhaps 260 acres

Underlying geology: Head Gravel and Kesgrave Sands and Gravels

THE MANOR OF LITTLE HADHAM belonged to the church of Ely in Saxon times and was retained by the abbot of Ely after the Conquest, despite a claim by the bishop of London.[1] Free warren was granted in 1251 and a park was first recorded in an account of 1285/6, when the estates of the (by then) bishopric of Ely were in the hands of the king following the death of Bishop Hugh de Balsham.[2] A remarkable series of accounts compiled for the bishops of Ely is preserved in the Hatfield House Archive and records the management of the park from the early fourteenth century to the beginning of the sixteenth century.[3]

The deer themselves rarely feature in the accounts because expenditure which was directly related to the animals was incurred only irregularly. Occasionally deer were brought to the park: for example, one doe was brought in 1340/1 (origin unknown), and 13 deer came from Walkern park (see p. 218) in 1367/8 when the park at Little Hadham needed restocking.[4] Sometimes the cost of catching deer, perhaps for gifts, was recorded: two bucks were caught in 1368/9 and three deer were taken in the park and transported to London at the request of the lord, Bishop John Fordham, in 1395/6. In 1437/8 a doe was killed for the lord for 12d.[5] In 1393/4 and 1396/7 agistment (grazing by livestock) was forbidden on the orders of the lord 'on account of destruction of deer', which suggests that the herd had grown to a size which the park's pasture could barely sustain. In 1404/5 a cart of straw was bought for 'the deer keeper in wintertime' at a cost of 16d and in 1434/5 a cart of white straw was bought for the deer for 2 shillings. In 1435/6 'hornbeam *cropp*' was used to feed the deer in wintertime.

Maintenance of the park boundary was a regular 'cost of the park' recorded from 1365 until 1458. New hedge (*haie*) was made at a cost which usually varied between 1d and 2d per perch, rising to 2½d per perch in 1435 and 1438. The lengths of new hedge made varied considerably from year to year, the greatest length being 310 perches (*c*.1,560m), made in 1367/8. This must have been about one-third of the park boundary and cost 38s 9d. A period of sustained hedge maintenance occurred between 1404 and 1410 and is recorded by an almost complete run of accounts. An average of 176 perches (*c*.885m) was made new each year and, in addition, an average of 60 perches of old hedge were repaired and *barband* – a word which appears to refer to the setting of pointed wooden rods, or spikes, into the ground, either to protect or

reinforce the hedge. This required the carting of cut underwood to the hedge at a cost of between 5 shillings and 8 shillings a year. The average total expenditure on maintaining the boundary hedge of the park during this period was 33s 7d p.a. Hedges disappear from the accounts after 1456: from 1463 agistment of the park was farmed out and maintenance of the park boundary was made part of the requirements of the farmer's lease.

In 1390/1 the park was enlarged by taking in parcels of customary land on its east side. Seventy-five perches of new embankment were made to enclose the new land in the park and a dead hedge (*sepe mortua*) was constructed on the crest of the bank at a cost of 5½d per perch, a total of 34s 4d. This cost included erecting '1 single fence placed in a double course', which suggests that the dead hedge, presumably a linear heap of brushwood, was contained within a double fence.

Park gates featured regularly in the accounts from the later fourteenth century. In 1368/9 5 shillings was paid for two carpenters making a new gate on the north side of the park. In 1378/9 three oaks were sawn for boards and for other timber for two pairs of gates (3d) and a sawpit was made in the park for the sawyer (2 shillings). The wage of 'two sawyers sawing boards and timber for gastaples, spores, grundsell, logges, 2 posts and for ligaments for [the] two pairs of gates of the park for 5 days' was 5 shillings. A 'posterngate to the east' was also repaired. In 1390/1 a carpenter was paid 15d for three days' work making one gate and repairing another. Materials purchased for the gates included 30 nails (2d), 2 hooks and hinges (6d), a lock and key (6d) and packed (*ramand*) clay (4d). In addition, 2 iron bands were bought for one other park gate (6d). In 1404/5 the posterngate 'facing the lodge' was repaired again (12d), requiring the purchase of a hook, hinge and 2 iron keys (6d). Another new gate was constructed in 1409/10 'next to the king's highway', and a detailed list of the component parts was again recorded in the account. One gate was repaired in 1426/7 and another in 1427/8, each costing 8d, and in 1437/8 4d was spent on 'hokes and iron staples' for a park gate.

The early medieval accounts recorded regular income from agistment of livestock in the park. The amounts received varied considerably, ranging from 4s 1d in 1323/4 to 35s 5d in 1337/8, but the average for 18 years of accounts between 1316 and 1350 was 18s 2d. Neither the number nor the species of the animals grazing in the park each year was recorded. On the rare occasions that it occurred, pannage of pigs in the park provided a significant additional source of income: for example, 8s 8d in 1322/3, 14s 4d in 1332/3 and 5s 2d in 1345/6.

Revenue was also provided by the oak trees in the park – no other species was mentioned until the second half of the fourteenth century. The bark and branches of the trees were

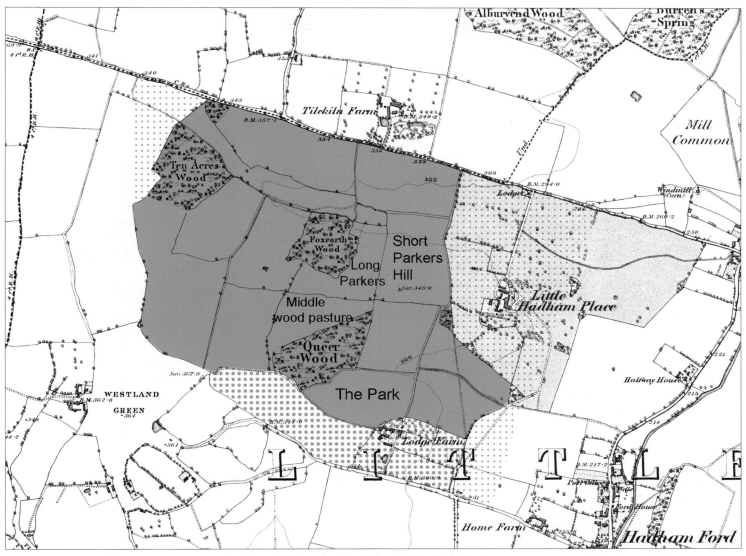

Map 40 The park of the bishops of Ely, Little Hadham
OS 6 inches to the mile map sheet XXII, surveyed 1878, published 1883. Annotated with field names recorded on the Little Hadham tithe award and map, 1843 and 1844 (HALS DSA4/45/1 and 2).

regularly sold but the timber was usually used on the manor. For example, 12 oaks were felled for a new building in 1330/1 and the bark and branches were sold for 5 shillings, and in 1337/8 one oak was felled 'for the windmill' and the branches and bark were sold for 10d. In 1331/2 112 oaks were pollarded and the bark of 167 oaks felled for building a new 'chamber for the lord' was sold for 100 shillings. The bark of 60 oaks and saplings was sold for 19s 6d in 1333/4 and in 1340/1 seven oaks in the park were felled and the bark sold for 7 shillings and the branches for 9 shillings.

Faggots do not generally appear in the accounts but 1,000 were sold for 25 shillings in 1327/8. Another product of the park was thorns or brambles (*dumus*): in 1325/6 4s 6d was received for *dumus* sold in the park at the empty pasture (*ad pastur' vacuend*); in 1326/7 2s 1d was received for *dumus* sold in the park at the empty pasture (*pastur' vacuanda*) 'by tally of the parker'; the following year *dumus* was sold for 3s 5d.

The effects of the Black Death in 1349 can be detected in the accounts: a new bailiff was appointed in 1349/50 and only two sets of accounts survive from the 1350s, compared with annual returns in the 1340s. As far as the running of the park

was concerned, the accounts suggest that income from agistment fell to 5s 6d (1350/1) and 5s (1351/2) from an average of 16s 2d during the decade before the Black Death. This reduction in grazing may have been related to the quality of the pasture, which, in a survey of 1356, was valued at only 3s 4d as a result of heavy shading by large trees.[6] While there may well have been a reduction in the manpower available for pollarding the trees, it seems unlikely that the shading problem had arisen in just seven years and it may be that the reduction in revenue from grazing was because cheaper pastures had become available elsewhere in the neighbourhood.

From 1364 the management of the park, as revealed by the accounts, seems to have moved into a higher gear. This may be related to the bishopric of Simon Langham, who became bishop of Ely in 1362 and was known to be an excellent administrator.[7] The period of greatest investment in the park appears to start in 1364/5 and lasts until the death of Bishop Philip Morgan in 1435. A lodge was built in the park from 1364 on the orders of Bishop Simon Langham: it had a tiled roof and a solar and cost £3 16s.[8] The cost of maintaining the park boundary was recorded in the accounts from Langham's

167

Figure 42. Aerial photograph showing the landscape of the former park of the bishops of Ely at Little Hadham in the middle of the twentieth century. Photograph taken by the RAF 10 October, 1946 (HALS Off Acc 300 CPE/UK/1779, 3320). Reproduced by kind permission of Hertfordshire Archives and Local Studies.

time but his interest in the park must have been continued by his successor, Bishop John Barnet, who had the park restocked with the 13 deer from Walkern in 1367/8. Perhaps the bishop who had the most (and certainly the longest) influence on the management of the park during this period was John Fordham, who was bishop of Ely from 1388 until 1426 and lived almost permanently on his episcopal manor of Downham, Cambridge.[9] From 1393/4 the bishop relinquished direct control of the manor of Little Hadham and the farm was leased to a tenant for £23 a year. From 1416 until 1436 the manor was leased to John Kirkby, a relative of Bishop John Fordham, and he appointed himself as parker from 1424 (his predecessor, William Otes, had been parker since 1375–48 years' service!)

Sales of wood from the park from the later fourteenth century were markedly different from those of the early medieval period. Oaks were rarely recorded: in 1368/9 four were lopped and sold for 4 shillings and the lopps of nine others were cut into lathes and sold for 20 shillings, and in

1379/80, four *croppys* of oak were cut into lathes and sold for 4 shillings. Most of the wood sold in the later fourteenth century was hornbeam (*hardebech* or *hernebeme*), apparently harvested from pollards in the park. In 1375/6 90 *cropp' de hernebem* were sold for 18s 9d and in 1377/8 140 *croppees de hernebemes* were sold, at 2¹/₂d per crop, for 29s 2d. In 1378/9 103 *loppes* of hornbeam were sold for 21s 5¹/₂d and 100 faggots of hornbeam crops for 4 shillings. Forty carts of hornbeam crops were sold for 20 shillings in each of three years between 1395/6 and 1398/9 but the numbers of trees were not recorded and it may be that these entries related to hornbeam coppice rather than pollarded trees. Records of hornbeam sales appear throughout the early fifteenth-century accounts: in 1416/17 30 *hernbemcroppes* were sold (6s 3d) and between 1428 and 1430 120 *hernbemcroppes* were sold (for 14s 8d), with another 40 crops of 'wood' sold ten years later. The only other trees mentioned in the accounts were 15 ash trees and a single maple. Wood sales appear to have ceased from 1440; then, in 1462, a ten-year lease for making charcoal was sold to William Valence for £4 a year. A year later the farm of 'agistment of beasts in the lord's park' was leased to William Abbot for a period of ten years for 46s 8d a year. In 1467/8 underwood was sold to William Abbott for making charcoal for 53s 4d. In 1476/7 John Ramssey took out a 24-year lease of the sale of 'cropporum and lopporum in the wood there' at 40 shillings a year and a 24-year lease of the agistment in the park for 53s 4d a year, thus providing the bishop of Ely with a regular income of £4 13s 4d from his park at Little Hadham for the rest of the fifteenth century. An investment of 19s 10d in repairs made to the lodge in 1476/7 suggests that he was still intending to use it.

In 1536 the bishop of Ely entered into a 99-year lease of the park which included a 'house or tenement called a lodge'.[10] The lessee, one William Pattmer, was to pay £14 a year in rent. In 1600 the bishop of Ely gave the manor to Queen Elizabeth in exchange for some other lands and in 1602 the queen granted it to Thomas Bellot and Richard Langley in trust for Sir Robert Cecil, principal Secretary of State, who in 1605 was created Earl of Salisbury.[11] A lease of the park by the Earl of Salisbury from 1634 recorded that the 'premises' comprised one messuage, one barn, one garden, one orchard, 120 acres of land, 30 acres of meadow, 80 acres of pasture and 30 acres of wood: a total of 260 acres.[12]

The manor descended to subsequent earls and marquesses of Salisbury and in 1843 the Little Hadham tithe award recorded that the Marquess of Salisbury was the owner of Bury Green Farm and also a parcel of land over a mile away near the north-west corner of the parish known as Lodge Farm.[13] The farmhouse was annotated on the tithe map as 'The Lodge' and there were fields named 'The Park', 'Long Parkers' and 'Short Parkers Hill'. The total area given for Bury Green Farm was 320 acres and Lodge Farm covered 197 acres (63 acres less than in 1634).

The compact nature of this farm, its name and its location alongside the parish boundary at perhaps the highest part of the parish (over 110m OD) all support the theory that this was the site of the medieval park of the manor of Little Hadham. In addition, earth banks survive along Chapel Lane south of Lodge Farm (TL430220) and along the track heading north from Chapel Lane at TL43152200. A public footpath traces the line of much of what may have been the eastern boundary of the former park and large earth banks survive along much of its length, particularly where it borders or passes through small patches of woodland. The bank disappears north of the stream at TL432228 and there is no bank westwards where the footpath meets the A120 (Stane Street) which suggests that the park may have ended at the stream. However, the fields are ploughed, centuries of road-making and repairing will have altered any boundary between the park and the road, and a bank does seem to appear in stretches along the south side of the A120 further west from Kiln Dairy with a significant bank heading south-west from the road at the end of the Marquess of Salisbury's land – suggesting that the park originally did indeed reach to the Roman road. This theory is supported by the documentary reference to the park gate made at the king's highway in 1411.

A very substantial but degraded bank several metres wide which looks more like a park boundary than a wood-bank survives along the south-west side of Queer (formerly Quarry) Wood. This, rather than the lane, therefore, may have been the southern boundary of the park – placing the lodge at the park boundary and perhaps leaving the intervening land to sustain the parker and his family (Figure 42).

In the absence of a medieval acreage for the park, the best guide we have is the 260 acres leased in 1634. The whole of the shaded area on Map 40 covers 260 acres but whether or not this was ever all parkland is debatable. With the exception of the southernmost fields, all of the 197 acres of Lodge Farm in 1843 can confidently be assumed to have been part of the medieval park and is, therefore, indicated with the solid green shading. The earthwork evidence supports a concave boundary on the east side of the park but there are possible traces of a straighter boundary further east detectable on an aerial photograph.[14] Fieldwork in the land around Little Hadham Place may reveal further clues to the landscape history of this area.

The woodlands which have survived on the farm provide an indication of the relatively poor quality of the soils for cultivation, and are all ancient and semi-natural woodlands of significant ecological value.

Hadham park (Hadham Hall)
NGR: TL458227
Date range: by 1275 – late seventeenth century
Size: perhaps 240 acres
Underlying geology: boulder clay

WILLIAM BAUD HAD A PARK at his manor of Hadham Hall or Baud's Manor in 1275.[15] He was dead by 1278 and was succeeded by his son, Walter, who was sheriff of Hertfordshire and Essex in 1307.[16] It was probably Walter's son, William, who was holding the manor in 1323 when the park was broken into by Thomas de Bassele, master of the nearby hospital of Standon, and several others, who 'hunted therein and carried away deer'. They were also accused of breaking into Baud's other park on his manor of Milkley in Standon (see p. 208).[17] At the time of the break-ins, both parks had been confiscated by the king as a result of William Baud's involvement in the rebellion by Thomas Earl of Lancaster, but they were restored to him on the accession of Edward III in 1327.[18]

The first of the family to take up residence at Little Hadham was said to be William Baud's grandson, another William, in the mid fourteenth century, and the family continued to live there throughout the fifteenth century until the manor was sold in 1504. The Bauds were prominent in county affairs during their time at Little Hadham: William Baud was sheriff for Hertfordshire and Essex in 1371 and a member of parliament in 1373, Thomas Baud sat in parliament in 1432 and was sheriff for Hertfordshire in 1446–7, Ralph Baud was sheriff in 1469 and his son, Thomas, was made a knight of the Bath in 1494.[19] Archaeological investigations and documentary research by William Minet, the owner of Hadham Hall at the beginning of the twentieth century, led him to conclude that Thomas Baud built a substantial house with a chapel around 1440, which stood on the same site as the house built c.1572, much of which remains today.[20] There are no further records of the park although, given the social status of the owners, it seems very likely to have continued until at least the end of the medieval period.

The new owners of the manor from 1505 were the Capel family, who lived elsewhere. It was probably Henry Capel who built a new house, Hadham Hall, in the 1570s, in which he entertained Queen Elizabeth in 1578.[21] His park, which is assumed to be that of the Bauds, was depicted on the county maps by Saxton (1577) (see Figure 23) and Norden (1598). At the beginning of the seventeenth century, it contained 240 acres. This is the area shown on Map 41, which is based on research by Minet.[22] While neither the area nor, indeed, the location of the medieval park are known for certain, the area delineated by Minet is a typical site for a medieval park, located as it is on some of the highest ground in the parish (c.90m OD) and bounded on two sides by the parish boundary. The Roman road, Stane Street, which continued to be used in medieval times, would have made a convenient southern boundary to the park. It seems very likely, therefore, that the medieval park did occupy some or all of this area.

In 1635 Sir Arthur Capel of Hadham Hall received a licence to add 501 acres to his existing park, expanding it eastwards and slightly northwards to incorporate the Wickham Hall estate, which he had recently purchased, and which included land in the neighbouring parishes of Bishop's Stortford, Farnham and Albury.[23] This additional 500 acres was known as Hadham New Park; the original 240 acres was Hadham Old Park. The combined areas of the two parks were depicted on the county maps by Seller (1676) and Oliver (1695). Capel was executed during the Civil War but his son and heir, another Arthur, was created Earl of Essex in 1661 on the restoration of the monarchy.[24] In 1669 he moved the Capel family seat from Hadham Hall to the seat of his mother's family, the Morrisons, at Cassiobury near Watford.[25] The park at Hadham Hall was subsequently disparked and in 1686 the red deer were removed to Epping Forest and Bagshot Park. By the early eighteenth century the park was divided into three farms: Hadham Hall farm, Hadham old park lodge farm and Wickham Hall farm.[26]

1. Page, *Hertford*, 4, p. 53.

2. Page, *Hertford*, 4, p. 54, citing *Cal. Chart. 1226–1257*, p. 367; TNA: PRO SC6/1132/9 accounts of the manors held by the bishops of Ely, 1285/6. There are also accounts for 1298/9, 1301/2 and 1315/6 (SC6/1132/10, 11 and 13). From 1300 the tithes of the Bishop of Ely's deer were to be divided equally between the church of Ely and the rector of Hadham (Page, *Hertford*, 4, p. 58).

3. HHA court rolls 11/4 bailiff's accounts between 1322 and 1507; 9/27 bailiff's accounts 1424/5, 1425/6, 1440/1; 9/25 bailiff's accounts 1435/6, 1436/7, 1437/8.

4. It would be interesting to learn the connection between John Barnet, the then bishop of Ely, and William, third lord Morley, the owner of Walkern park. Walkern was certainly nearer to Little Hadham and presumably a more convenient source of deer than the bishop's own parks at Hatfield. But there were, in theory at least, two sources of deer just a short distance away at Hadham Hall or Stortford parks.

5. This was the year when a new bishop of Ely, Lewis of Luxembourg, was appointed. The account records the doe was killed for the lord, the 'vicar general', perhaps before the bishop was installed.

6. Page, *Hertford*, 4, p. 54, citing BL Add. MS. 6165, fo. 231.

7. As abbot of Westminster between 1349 and 1362 he reformed the management of the abbey's estates and transformed the abbey's financial state from one of heavy debt to one of prosperity. W.J. Dohar, 'Langham, Simon (d. 1376)', *Oxford dictionary of national biography* (Oxford, 2004), accessed online 24 August 2007.

8. Repairs to the lodge were recorded in 1378/9, 1393/4, 1404/5, 1426/7, 1427/8 and in 1476/7 and detailed lists of materials and costs are preserved in the accounts in Hatfield House Archive.

9. R.G. Davies, 'Fordham, John (c.1340–1425)', rev., *Oxford dictionary of national biography* (Oxford, 2004), accessed online 24 August 2007.

10. HHA Deeds 188/8 lease of the park in 1620 reciting an earlier lease. Subsequent leases were cited in the VCH, as follows: Page, *Hertford*, 4, p. 54, Court of Req. bdle 44, no. 44; Patent Roll 44 Eliz pt. ii, m. 29 (TNA: PRO C66/1571); 5 Jas I, pt. xvii (TNA: PRO C66/1737).

11. Page, *Hertford*, 4, p. 54.

12. HHA Deeds 188/8 lease of the park to Dr Theophilus Ailmer, Archdeacon of London, 1620.

13. HALS DSA4/44/1 and 2 Little Hadham tithe award and map, 1843 and 1844.

14. http://earth.google.com, accessed 24 August 2007.

15. Page, *Hertford*, 4, p. 53, citing *Hundred Rolls* (Records Commission), i, 193.

16. Page, *Hertford*, 4, p. 52.

17. *Cal. Pat. 1321–1324*, p. 383.

18. Page, *Hertford*, 4, p. 52.

19. *Ibid*.

20. Minet, *Hadham Hall*, pp. 60–2.

21. Page, *Hertford*, 4, p. 52.

22. Minet, *Hadham Hall*, pp. 28–32.

23. Minet, *Hadham Hall*, p. 28, citing a writ of *ad quod damnum*, 1635. The writ was required because enlarging the park necessitated the rerouting of some local roads.

24. R. Hutton, 'Capel, Arthur, first Baron Capel of Hadham (1604–1649)', *Oxford dictionary of national biography* (Oxford, September 2004; online edn, October 2006), accessed online 22 July 2007.

25. R.L. Greaves, 'Capel, Arthur, first earl of Essex (bap. 1632, d. 1683)', *Oxford dictionary of national biography* (Oxford, 2004), accessed online 22 July 2007.

26. Minet, *Hadham Hall*, p. 31, citing Camden Society, O.S., vol. lii, p. 135.

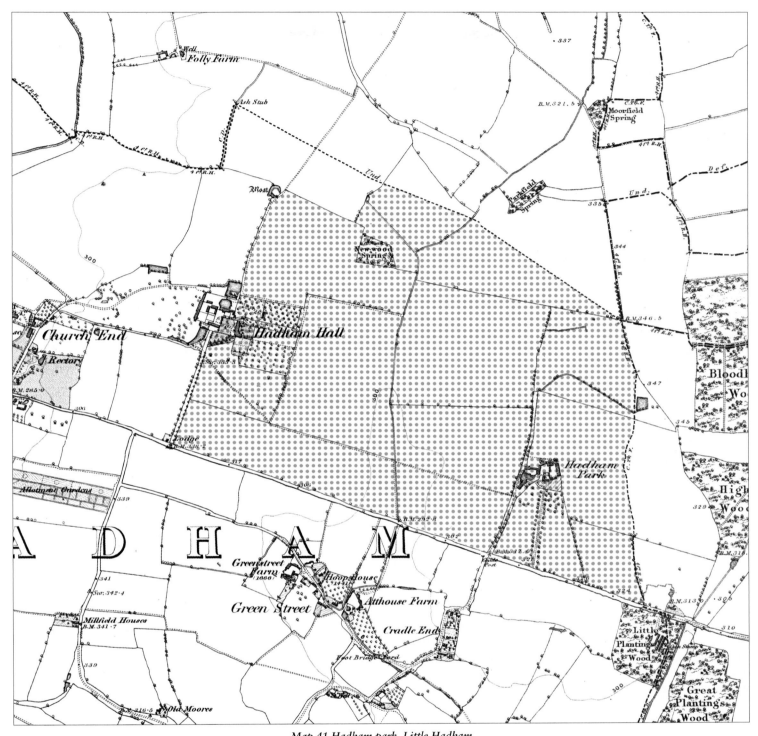

Map 41 Hadham park, Little Hadham
OS 6 inches to the mile map sheets XXII and XXIII, surveyed 1878 and 1874–9 respectively, published 1883 and 1879–83. Park extent determined by W. Minet (1916).

Little Munden

Munden park and East park(s)

NGR: Munden park TL335227; East park(s) TL355213
Date range: by 1299 – fifteenth century
Size: East park: perhaps *c.*144 acres; Munden park: perhaps *c.*60 acres
Underlying geology: East park: boulder clay; Munden park: undifferentiated glaciofluvial deposits, a mixture of chalky sand and gravel

TWO PARKS WERE RECORDED at Little Munden at the end of the thirteenth century. The inquisition *post mortem* held after the death of Richard de Frevill in 1299 recorded one park of 60 acres which produced a profit of half a mark a year and another of 20 acres 'of which may be taken 5 shillings a year'.[1] One (and perhaps both) of these two parks can be assumed to have been the 'East parks of Munden' recorded in 1324/5, held by Lady de Fryvill, from which two wild beasts (*feris*) were taken for the lord of the nearby manor of Walkern, probably to help stock his new park there (see p. 218).[2] The East park(s) was located in a detached part of the parish of Little Munden on the watershed between the valleys of the Dane End tributary and the river Rib, a typical location for an early medieval park. However, the name of the park suggests that there was another, more westerly, park in the parish from which it needed to be distinguished.

In 1379/80 the manor of Little Munden was conveyed to Sir John Thornbury who, in 1383, also acquired the manor of Bygrave. Sir John was active in public service and was licensed to crenellate his two houses at Bygrave in 1386, 'a mark of royal trust and favour'.[3] He was, nevertheless, buried at Little Munden and his tomb, complete with carved stone effigies of himself and his wife, is in the choir of Little Munden church. This suggests that Sir John Thornbury had a high-status manor house at Little Munden in the late fourteenth century which was inherited by his son, Philip, in 1396.[4]

Sir Philip Thornbury was a member of the household of Thomas Beaufort, Duke of Exeter, and accompanied him on a military mission on behalf of the king in 1404. He was also a member of parliament on two occasions during the reign of Henry V and was a Justice of the Peace for many years. He employed skilled craftsmen to improve the churches at both Bygrave and at Little Munden, where he had a wonderfully elaborate tomb carved for himself and his wife.[5] It is entirely plausible that a man of Sir Philip's status might have created a new park as a setting for his house at Little Munden and there is good circumstantial evidence that a park was established in the vicinity of the former manor house, but no clear evidence of when this occurred. In 1448 Thornbury employed a new 'lardyner, catour and cook' who was permitted to collect 'reasonable fuel in the east park',[6] and in 1455/6 he granted the keepership of the park of Little Munden and the warren to

Thomas Averell and his wife.[7] As he did not feel it was necessary to specify *which* park Averell was to manage, we have to conclude there was only one functioning deer park in Little Munden in 1455: either the East park or a park which was subsequently referred to as Munden park.[8] Sir Philip died in 1457 and 20 years later the manor passed from his descendents to Sir William Say.[9]

Thomas Averell was still the custodian of the park in 1477 when he drew up an account of the manor for Sir William which revealed that the rabbit warren was in the park and was leased for 40 shillings a year, and that repairs had been made to the park boundary.[10] These repairs had required the daubing ('dubbing') of the park fence and making pales for the pinfold (*pinfaldi*).[11] The account also shows that a pasture within 'le Estparke' was being leased to a tenant and underwood from 'le Estparke' was sold for 16 shillings. Interestingly, there was still a connection with Walkern park, as one fallow buck was rendered by Lord Morley from his park at Walkern to the manor of Little Munden. This appears to have been a payment made annually from 1425 in exchange for four pieces of land in Munden called Oldelaunde below Walkern park.[12]

More information about the parks at Little Munden can be gleaned from a series of accounts compiled for Sir William Say between 1484 and 1498.[13] It would appear that by 1484 Sir William had disparked Munden park – Thomas Averell had been replaced by a bailiff, a parker was no longer employed and 'all the pasture in the park there' was leased to John Chapman for 20 shillings.[14] Although there was still a rabbit warren, it was no longer described as being in the park. Chapman was also leasing the 'long house' with its gardens and barns on the site of the manor and most of the demesne lands, all of which lay in the vicinity of today's Lordship Farm (Figure 43).[15]

A survey of the manor in 1556 revealed that among the demesne lands of the manor leased to John Colte from 1541/2 was a field called 'Neither Parke' containing 40 acres and a 'Brome filde' containing 32 acres. There was also a 9½-acre wood on the manor called Munden Park.[16] Two 'park' field names were recorded on a plan of Lordship Farm in 1814:[17] Nether Park (23 acres) and Broom Park (19½ acres) were located at opposite ends of an oblong-shaped area, bounded by long, sinuous boundaries which enclosed about 60 acres, heading north-west from just north of the farmhouse (see Map 42). The north-eastern side of the enclosure is contiguous with an ancient boundary running between the Old Bourne and the Dane End Tributary. There was no wood called Munden Park on the 1814 plan but it can probably be identified with the 29-acre Lordship Wood, which lay at the south-east end of the oblong-shaped enclosure. At the south-west end of the wood were two small fields called Old Lordship and Old Wood, perhaps indicating the site of the fifteenth-century manor house.

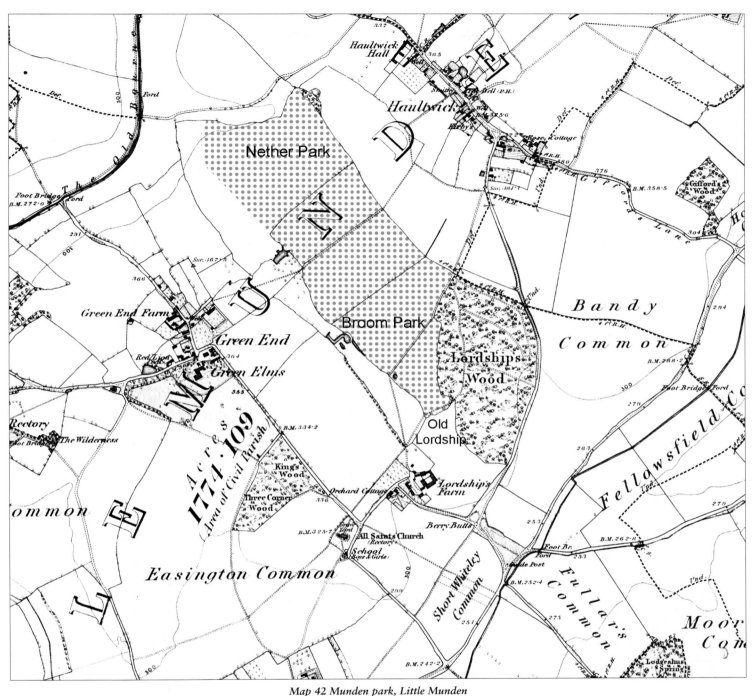

Map 42 Munden park, Little Munden
OS 6 inches to the mile map sheet XXI, surveyed 1878–80, published 1884. Annotated with field names recorded on a farm plan of 1814 (HALS 81751).

Also recorded in the bailiff's accounts at the end of the fifteenth century were references to the East park. This appears to have been partially divided into closes which were leased to a variety of tenants. The highest rent, 20 shillings, was paid for a 'pasture called Estparke'; 14 shillings was paid for 'two crofts in Estparke called Potters Hill and Clerkesgrove'; and 10 shillings was paid for a pasture called 'le Copy parcel of Estparke'.[18] In addition, a 'parcel of underwood in Estpark' was sold in 1498/9. This evidence suggests that the East park had also been disparked, probably before 1455. By the mid sixteenth century the East park had been divided into at least nine parcels, all held by different tenants on copyhold leases. The parcels ranged in size from 7

to 40 acres and covered a total area of over 144 acres.[19] This is the area covered by the proposed park shown on Map 43, which incorporates several 'park' field names recorded near Potters Green in the seventeenth, eighteenth and nineteenth centuries, including Benns Parks (1658), Shellys Park (1730), Andrews Parks (1730) and East Park (1840).[20]

The area indicated represents a 'best guess' at the location of the park: further field work might result in amendments to the boundary proposed here. The first edition OS map shows a mixture of sinuous, ancient-looking boundaries and straight-sided fields which appear to have been laid out in a planned way from a previously unenclosed area of land. The older boundaries may relate to one or both of the two earlier parks

(60 and 20 acres) recorded at the end of the thirteenth century, which may subsequently have been subsumed within a single, larger park. Two areas of woodland within the former park – Shelley's Wood and Roughground Wood – have been classified as ancient or semi-natural woodland and are of significant ecological importance. Earthworks of unknown date or origin are preserved within Roughground Wood, some of which *might* relate to a medieval parker's lodge.[21]

Munden park was recorded as late as 1594 but no park was shown at Little Munden on the earliest county maps by Saxton (1577) or Norden (1598) and it seems unlikely that there was a functioning deer park in the parish after the fifteenth century.[22] Repairs to a 'lodge at Munden' were mentioned in the accounts for 1490/1 but it is not clear whether these occurred at Little or Great Munden (see p. 102).[23] No other reference to a lodge at Little Munden has been found.

1. Cussans, *History of Hertfordshire*, 2, p. 148, citing Chancery Inquisition *post mortem* 27 Edw. I no. 16 (TNA: PRO C133/87/15).
2. HALS 9325 bailiff's account for the manor of Walkern, 1324/5; see also DE/Hx/Z24 typed translation of account rolls of manor of Walkern, 1324–1432, translated by Rev. F.A.W. Gibbs, 1939.

Figure 43. *Aerial view of the landscape of the former Munden park in the middle of the twentieth century. Photograph taken by the RAF 10 October, 1946 (HALS Off Acc 300 CPE/UK/1779, 3305). Reproduced by kind permission of Hertfordshire Archives and Local Studies.*

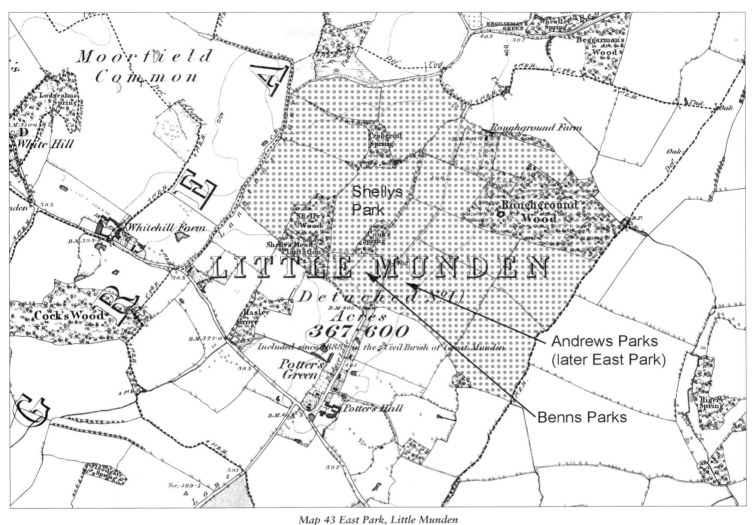

Map 43 East Park, Little Munden
OS 6 inches to the mile map sheet XXI, surveyed 1878–80, published 1884. Annotated with field names recorded from the seventeenth to the nineteenth centuries (see text).

3. Roberts, *A school of masons*, p. 8.

4. Page, *Hertford*, 3, p. 130, citing TNA: PRO Ancient Deeds B 2576 and 2574 (TNA: PRO E326/2576 and 2574).

5. Roberts, *A school of masons*, pp. 8–9; A. Rowe, *The protected valley: a history of Little Munden* (1999), p. 56.

6. Page, *Hertford*, 3, p. 130, citing TNA: PRO Ancient Deeds D 1172 (TNA: PRO E210/1172).

7. TNA: PRO E210/1576 ancient deeds, 1455/6.

8. A single 'Munden park' was recorded in 1480 (Page, *Hertford*, 3, p. 133 citing Ancient Deeds B 2562 (TNA: PRO E326/2562)) and in 1594 (*Ibid.*, Patent Roll 37 Eliz. pt. x (TNA: PRO C66/1434)).

9. William Say acquired the manor in 1486 (TNA: PRO E210/439 ancient deeds, 1486/7) but appears to have been running the manor from 1477.

10. TNA: PRO SC6/867/18 account for manor of Little Munden, 1477/8.

11. For another reference to daubing the park fence, see Benington park, p. 58.

12. HALS 9559 item from a bundle of letters concerning requests for deer out of Walkern and Hadham parks. This annual render of one buck by Lord Morley to the manor of Little Munden is also recorded in each of the accounts seen for the 1480s and 1490s (see references below).

13. HHA court rolls 10/16 bailiff's account, 1484/5; 10/19 bailiff's account,

1490/1; 10/20 bailiff's account, 1493/4; 10/21 bailiff's account, 1495/6; 10/23 bailiff's account, 1498/9.

14. The warren was leased for 53s 4d in 1477–9; this had increased to 60s p.a. by 1490.

15. John Chapman was also leasing land in 1477, but not the site of the manor.

16. TNA: PRO E315/391 survey of manors in Hertfordshire, lands and possessions of King Philip and Queen Mary, 1556.

17. HALS 81751 plan of Lordship Farm, 1814.

18. HHA court rolls 10/21 bailiff's account, 1495/6; 10/23 bailiff's account, 1498/9.

19. TNA: PRO E315/391 survey of manors in Hertfordshire, lands and possessions of King Philip and Queen Mary, 1556.

20. Rowe, *The protected valley*, p. 13 citing HALS PC630 extracts from the Little Munden court rolls; DP/71/3/1 field book of the manor of Mundane Parva, 1730; DSA4/71/1 and 2 Little Munden tithe award and map, 1840.

21. H.C. Andrews, 'An unknown earthwork at Old Hall Green', *Transactions of the East Herts Archaeological Society*, 7 (1926), pp. 105–8.

22. Page, *Hertford*, 3, p. 130, citing Patent Roll 37 Eliz. pt. x (TNA: PRO C66/1434).

23. HHA court rolls 10/19 bailiff's account, 1490/1.

Little Wymondley

The great park and little park

NGR: TL217268
Date range: by 1299 – not known
Size: *c*.50 acres
Underlying geology: boulder clay with some glaciofluvial deposits comprising chalky sand and gravel

RECORDS OF TWO MEDIEVAL PARKS were discovered as a result of research by the late Noel Farris into the history of the Wymondleys. No record of imparkment was found, but a licence of free warren was granted to Reginald de Argentein 'in all his demesne lands in Wymondley' in 1285.[1] Reginald was the son of Sir Giles d'Argentein of Great Wymondley, a baronial leader whose own father had been a knight of the royal household and crusader of the 1230s, and came from a line of sheriffs of Hertfordshire, Essex and Cambridgeshire.[2] The medieval manor court rolls contain several references to a park: for example, in 1299 John le Wyte damaged the grass in the lord's park, in 1351 Alice Man broke into the lord's park within the lord's demesne and in 1370 William Pride broke down the hedges of the park and warren.[3] The manorial account rolls also contain some interesting records: in 1366 underwood and thorns were taken down to make fences round the park for 73 perches (about 370m) at a cost of 15s 2d and in 1369 one man was paid 5s 10d 'for seventeen days making the fence anew between the park and the lord's hall, on the orders of the lord'.[4]

The last of these records indicates that the park was adjacent to the manor house in 1369. Wymondley Bury, a timber-framed building dated to before 1400, occupies a moated site adjoining the south side of Little Wymondley churchyard and is considered to be the medieval manor house of Great and Little Wymondley.[5] A Chancery Inquisition of 1423 into the dower holdings of Margaret, widow of John de Argentein (who died in 1419) showed that she was entitled to a third share (17$\frac{1}{6}$ acres) of the 51$\frac{1}{2}$ acres of the great park and the little park.[6] The document also revealed that the parks lay between Hay Field and Broad Field which, in addition to some park field names, were recorded on an estate map of 1803.[7] Park field names were also preserved in the enclosure map and award of Great and Little Wymondley in 1811 in the 'old enclosure' fields lying immediately south of Wymondley Bury in Little Wymondley.[8]

The east, west and south boundaries of the park can be readily identified on the first edition OS map of 1884 (see Map 44). A lane curves around the boundary on the south-east and south sides and this is followed by the parish boundary between Little Wymondley to the north and a detached part of Great Wymondley to the south. This suggests that Wymondley was separated into two parishes after the park had been established. Noel Farris, writing in 1989, recorded a surviving 'high bank' along the western edge of Lawn Park and a former bank and deep ditch on the east side of Ploughed Park, which was destroyed in the 1930s.[9] These boundaries marked the west and east sides of the park respectively. A site visit in January 2005 revealed only a ditch and unremarkable hedge-bank along the western boundary (north of the A602).

Farris also recorded an earthwork running south-west – north-east through Bury Wood along its northern boundary, which he described as 'a hollow way with a bank on one side'. Just 100m of the earthwork was said to survive in the remaining remnant of the wood in 1989.[10] Perhaps this latter earthwork marked the boundary between the park and the warren, or between the great and little parks. Farris considered that the park terminated south of the Bury and the ditch along the western boundary does end at about this point today. It is possible that the park once continued up to the church, thereby enclosing an area of nearly 67 acres, but there is no field evidence today to support this theory.

Documentary evidence therefore confirms the rather unusual position of this modest park adjacent to the medieval manor house, although how it was subdivided into a great and little park is uncertain. Topographically, the park is more typical: at 95m OD, the park site is elevated above the surrounding landscape and does have extensive views to the south-east, south-west and north. The Little Wymondley bypass, the A602 connecting Hitchin with the A1(M), was cut through the middle of the former park in the late twentieth century.

1. *Cal. Chart. 1257-1300*, p. 285.

2. Ridgeway, 'Argentine, Sir Giles d".

3. Farris, *The Wymondleys*, p. 189, citing HALS 57485, 57489 and 57492 manor court rolls, 1299, 1351 and 1370.

4. *Ibid.*, citing HALS 57532/4 account rolls, 1366 and 1369.

5. Smith, *English houses*, p. 24; Page, *Hertford*, 3, p. 189.

6. *Ibid.*, citing HALS 59336 inquisition *post mortem* of John de Argentein setting out the dower of his widow, 1423.

7. HALS 44216 plan of parish of Much Wymondley and part of Little Wymondley, 1803.

8. HALS QS/E/80 and 81 enclosure award and map for Great and Little Wymondley, 1811.

9. Farris, *The Wymondleys*, p. 189.

10. *Ibid.*

Parish: Markyate *see Flamstead*

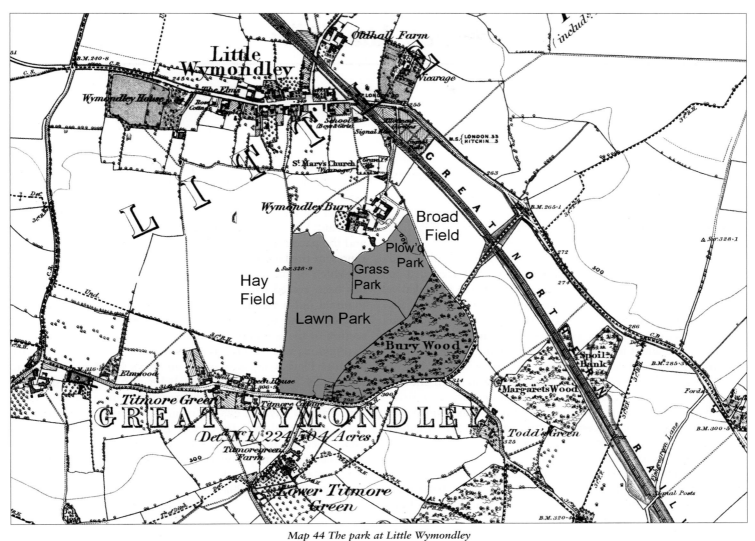

Map 44 The park at Little Wymondley
OS 6 inches to the mile map sheet XII, surveyed 1878–81, published 1884. Annotated with field names recorded on a Wymondley estate map of 1803 (HALS 44216). The shaded area covers 49$\frac{1}{2}$ acres (20ha).

Much Hadham

The old park

NGR: TL445165
Date range: before 1199
Size: 190 acres
Underlying geology: boulder clay

THIS EARLY PARK BELONGED to the bishops of London and was called the old park when it was first recorded in 1199, when bishop William de Ste. Mere-Eglise founded a chantry for the souls of the bishops in the lower chapel of his London palace and endowed it with rents which included those from two parts of the old park at Hadham.[1] Nothing is known about when it was established but the name suggests that it had either fallen out of use as a park and/or that a newer park had been established within the bishop's manor at Much Hadham by the end of the twelfth century. Manorial records show that the pasture in the old park was farmed out by the bishops in the fifteenth century and 'the wood called Oldeparke' was farmed for 8d in 1458–9.[2]

The bishops of London had held the manor of Much Hadham since before the Norman Conquest and they had a residence on the manor next to the church. After 1066 they also held the manor of Stortford, with its castle, about four miles to the east. They had established a park at Stortford by 1263 (see p. 68), which may help explain why the old park at Hadham fell out of use.

Despite its early demise as a park, both the name and the land which it encompassed have survived as a remarkably intact unit into the early twenty-first century. It lay some distance from the bishops' residence in Much Hadham, in the extreme south-east corner of the parish, and was bounded for much of its length by the Fiddler's Brook, which formed the parish boundary. The land of the former park slopes up from the brook to the north and west to a summit of 80m OD.

In 1838 the bishop of London still owned several parcels of land in Much Hadham, including a discrete 190-acre block of fields belonging to Old Park Farm which was leased to a Robert Elliott. The long continuous boundaries of this farm, its location on the margin of the parish and the survival (in 1838) of a 25-acre wood called Old Parkwood (Map 45) leave little doubt that the entire farm was formed from the early medieval park of the bishops. Four narrow fields (numbered 146, 147, 148 and 179 on the tithe map) lie between the bishop's land and the parish boundary at the south end of the park and *may* represent the land given up in 1199 to found the chantry.[3]

Much of the south-western boundary of the former park has been erased by ploughing and surviving field evidence is minimal but a public footpath follows the boundary around the north end of the park and another traces the surviving section of the southern boundary.

Previous writers have assumed that the post-medieval park at Moor Place, lying west of the village of Much Hadham, had its origins in a medieval park belonging to the bishops of London but there is no evidence to support this theory.[4] In fact, Pamela Taylor's examination of the medieval records of the bishops led her to conclude that no later park was established to replace the old park. In 1273–4 the bishop apparently had only a warren at Much Hadham. It lay with the orchards and gardens near the house and was still operating in 1399/1400.[5]

1. Taylor, 'The estates of the bishopric of London', p. 177, citing W. Dugdale (ed.), The history of St Paul's Cathedral ... (London, 1818), p. 94; Page, *Hertford*, 4, p. 60.
2. Page, *Hertford*, 4, p. 60, quoting Ministers' Accounts Bdle 1139 no. 14 (TNA: PRO SC6/1139/14); Taylor, 'Estates of the bishopric of London', p. 182, citing TNA: PRO SC6/1140/23m. 1d.
3. HALS DSA4/45/1 and 2 Much Hadham tithe award and map, 1838.
4. See Page, *Hertford*, 4, p. 60.
5. Taylor, 'Estates of the bishopric of London', p. 177, citing *Rotuli Hundredorum* (*Hundred Rolls* (Records Commission)), p. 193a; *Ibid.*, p. 186, citing TNA: PRO SC6/1140/12.

Parish: Nuthampstead *see Barkway*

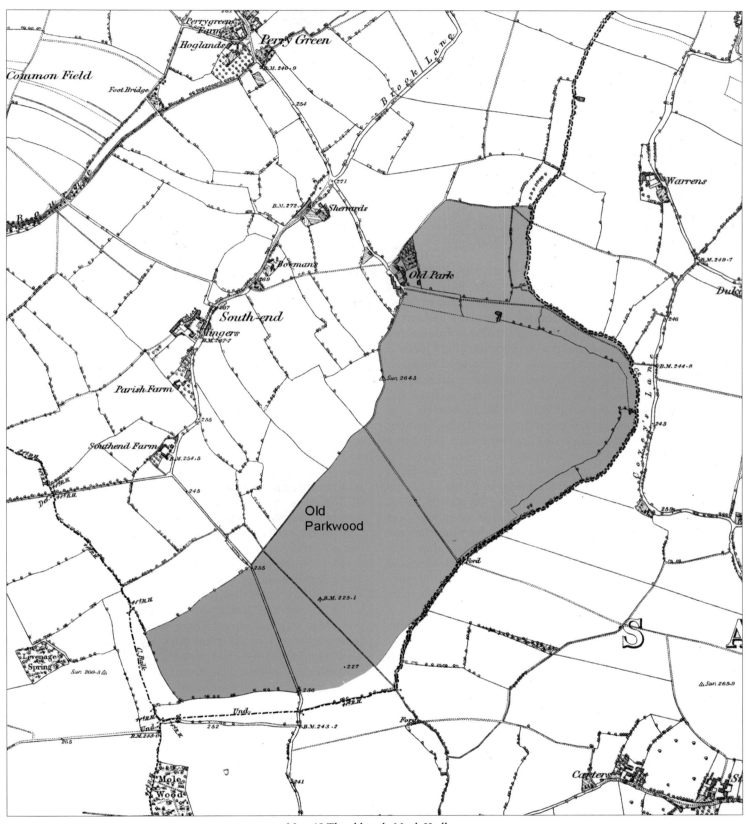

Map 45 The old park, Much Hadham

OS 6 inches to the mile map sheet XXX, surveyed 1873–80, published 1881–3. Almost all the field boundaries within the former park, which were shown on the tithe map of 1838, had been removed by 1880. Old Parkwood was a rectangular area of woodland bordering the west side of the former park in 1838 (HALS DSA4/45/1 and 2).

Rickmansworth and Watford

The More or Moor park

NGR: TQ090933
Date range: c.1426 – perhaps early twentieth century
Size: licence to impark 600 acres in 1426
Underlying geology: Shepperton Gravel, Chalk, Upnor, Woolwich & Reading Formations, London Clay

ON 28 JULY 1426 HENRY VI granted a charter licensing William Flete and others to 'enclose, crenellate, enturret and embattle, with stones, lime and brik their manor of More in Rykmersworth, and also to impark 600 acres of land in wood in Rikmersworth and Watford; grant also of free warren there, unless the land be within the metes of the king's forest'.[1] Flete was a rich London mercer and an influential figure in Hertfordshire but it seems he may not have carried out the permitted works on the manor house (or perhaps did not complete them) because in 1458 Sir Ralph Boteler, lord of Sudeley, was granted a pardon for crenellating without licence his manors of Sudeley in Gloucestershire and More in Hertfordshire.[2] No clear evidence has been found to show which of the two men enclosed the park but Flete, who represented the county in parliament in 1414, 1423 and 1433 and held the manor from 1416 until he died in 1444, seems the more likely candidate.[3] The bones of fallow deer appear in the archaeological record from the time that the brick-faced house was constructed – whether that was from 1426 or a few decades later.[4] Virtually no information about the park during the remainder of the fifteenth century has been found but it is possible to deduce some details from sixteenth-century records.

The manor of More was subsequently sold to George Neville, chancellor of England, who used the house from at least 1462.[5] He became archbishop of York in 1465 but was embroiled in the political turmoil of the Wars of the Roses and was imprisoned by Edward IV in 1472 charged with treasonable activities.[6] The king seized The More with goods allegedly worth £20,000. State papers show that the king stayed at The More on occasion and the manor and the park were granted separately to different people during his reign.[7] In 1475 he granted the custody of the park to John Hawdeles.[8] In 1483 both manor and park were returned to the king. In 1486 Henry VII granted the manor to John de Vere who remained the tenant until his death in 1513, upon which the manor again reverted to the crown.[9]

By 1520 the manor had come into the possession of the abbot of St Albans and when, the following year, Cardinal Thomas Wolsey became the abbot he took up residence at The More. He made major alterations to the building which, when the work was completed, would have been similar to Hampton Court, and Henry VIII was a frequent visitor. Wolsey also extended the park by seizing nearly 200 acres of land from a tenant called Tolpott and redirecting the road towards Watford.[10] Fields enclosed into the park included Le Westfeld, Hokefeld, Myddelfeld and Bryckecrofte.[11] Wolsey lost The More to the king when he failed to obtain the annulment of Henry's marriage to Katherine of Aragon.

In 1529 Sir John Russell was granted custody of the manor and acted as a sort of 'caretaker' for the king, who resided there periodically from 1530 onwards. The queen was ordered to retire to The More in 1531 and appears to have spent much of the year there. Sir John Russell wrote to Henry's chief minister Thomas Cromwell concerning the state of the park paling in the spring of 1532[12] and again in 1533: 'Sir, the Park palings at The More are decaying and the deer are escaping, many are killed daily', and it was subsequently reported that 'only 100 deer of the original 500 remained'.[13]

In the following year Henry VIII appears to have decided to make improvements to the park, including the creation of 'a great plain for the King's Course' and the building of a standing in 1538.[14] Accounts for the manor compiled in 1536/7 and 1539/41 show that the king was receiving £4 a year for the farm of herbage and pannage in the park, together with a further £5 for the farm of the warren of rabbits. Tithes of 26s 8d were paid to the vicar of Rickmansworth for the park and warren and John Clement was paid 6d per day to care for the garden, ponds, orchard and 'les sluces' of the king, but no parker appeared in the accounts.[15]

In 1556 the estate was annexed to the duchy of Lancaster and a detailed survey was made of The More and its parks.[16] From this we learn that there was a great park of 830 acres and a little park of 208 acres, each of which contained at least one lodge in good repair. There were 'deare of all sortes' in both parks: 415 in the great park and 90 in the little park. Over a quarter of the great park (225 acres) was taken up with 'parockes and courses', described by the surveyors as 'newlie taken in' to the park although they probably dated from Henry VIII's improvements of the 1530s.[17] The remainder of the park was described as 'la[u]nds and feedings' (300 acres), 'wood set with very little timber, well stored with pollards', namely wood-pasture (261 acres), and 44 acres of 'woods set with young timber of one hundred and [?] three hundred years' growth. The trees in both the wood-pasture and the woods were hornbeams and maples. The little park was almost entirely 'laundes and fedinges much growen with ferne' (197 acres), plus 5 acres of wood set with oak and beech of two hundred years' growth and 6 acres of coppice wood called Pypers and Bakers. The keeper was allowed £7 10s to purchase 30 loads of hay for the deer each year, but the surveyors considered that it would be more economical to use hay which was being mown in the park.[18]

From the evidence provided in this survey, it would appear that the original 600-acre medieval park underwent two

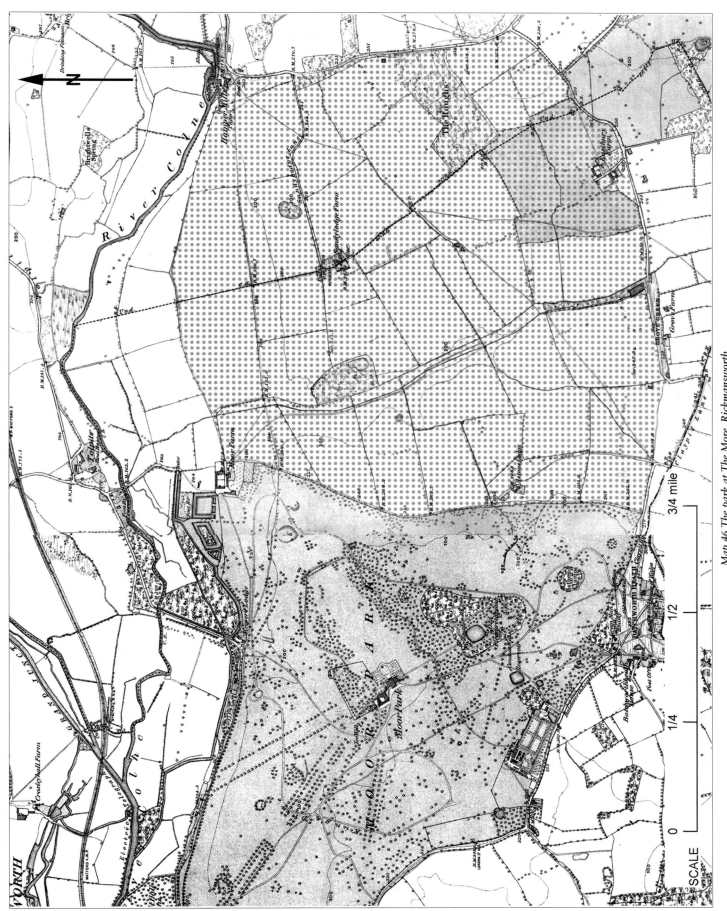

Map 46 The park at The More, Rickmansworth

OS 6 inches to the mile map sheets XLIII, surveyed 1864–76, published 1868–83; and XLIV surveyed 1871, published 1877 (both reproduced at a reduced scale).

Figure 44. *View from the footpath crossing the east side of Sandy Lodge Golf Course – the probable site of the fifteenth-century park of The More – looking west towards the higher ground of the present-day Moor Park. A long bank crosses the view behind the bunker in the middle-ground of the photograph. How, or whether, this related to the medieval park is not known.*

phases of expansion in the early sixteenth century: the first in the 1520s, when Cardinal Wolsey added 200 acres, and the second in the 1530s, when Henry VIII added a further 225 acres for 'parockes and courses'.

No park was depicted by Saxton on his county map (1577) but the south-west extremity of the county, where The More lies, appears to be outside the frame of the map. Norden (1598) shows Morehouse lying just outside the northern boundary of the park, which extended southwards to the top of a hill with a road running north–south through the middle of it. The shape depicted by Norden suggests that in Tudor times the park extended further east than it does today, crossing over the parish boundary into Watford and including Sandy Lodge Farm and probably Astons Lodge. This would fit the terms of the 1426 licence to enclose land in Rickmansworth *and* Watford. It may not have extended as far to the west as the present park. Norden was presumably showing the great park of 830 acres recorded in 1568; the original fifteenth-century park should have contained only 600 acres.

Both Seller (1676) and Oliver (1695) showed a squarish park lying further to the west than the park depicted by Norden and with perhaps the eastern boundary lying further west than today as Moor House was shown some distance east of the park. Dury and Andrews depicted the park in great detail in 1766 and also showed the area to the east, which had formerly been park, divided into fields around Sandy Lodge and Parson's Lodge (later called Astons Lodge). The Rickmansworth tithe map and award of 1838 recorded the area of the park as 416 acres.[19] By the late nineteenth century the park contained *c.*466 acres; Harting, writing in 1881, stated that it then covered 500 acres and that when it was sold to the Earl of Monmouth, in the time of Charles I, it was '400 acres or thereabouts'. In 1881 it contained about 250 fallow deer.[20]

An approximately square area containing mostly straight-sided fields and delineated by roads and tracks lay directly to the east of the nineteenth-century Moor Park on the first edition OS map (see Map 46). This area contains about 590 acres, an area which corresponds closely with the 600 acres licensed for enclosure into a park in 1426. Cardinal Wolsey's 200-acre extension (probably the little park) is likely to have surrounded the moated site of Moor Place (lying north-west of the buildings labelled Moor Farm on the OS map), perhaps extending eastwards to fill the area between the great park and the river Colne and also extending southwards into what became the late nineteenth-century park. The additional 225 acres which were added by Henry VIII must also have been south-west of The More, so that the western park boundary by the mid sixteenth century must have lain north–south across the approximate mid-point of the late nineteenth-century park depicted on the first edition OS map. This corresponds with the park outline depicted by Norden in 1598.

Little in the way of field evidence has survived in the area east of today's Moor Park and, indeed, boundary banks may never have been constructed. Sandy Lodge Farm is now a golf course and, as the name implies, the soils are very sandy and this was probably an area of open heath and woodland in the early fifteenth century. The most obvious earthwork is a large bank running NNW from TQ0944893459 (Figure 44); this is the line of a former field boundary but seems too big an earthwork for this purpose alone. There is also a modest bank bounding the hollow-way of the original Sandy Lodge Lane at its eastern end. Other possible boundaries to the south and west are inaccessible because of housing development. Despite the lack of field evidence, the site of Sandy Lodge (and Astons Lodge to the west) and the rolling, open landscape of the present golf course, make a convincing location for the medieval park.

1. H. Falvey, 'The More: Rickmansworth's lost palace', *Hertfordshire's Past*, 34 (1993), p. 3; *Cal. Pat. 1422–1429*, p. 351.

2. *Cal. Pat. 1452–1461*, p. 422. I am grateful to Heather Falvey for sharing this information with me.

3. Roskell *et al.*, *History of parliament*, pp. 88–91.

4. M. Biddle, L. Barfield and A. Millard, 'The excavation of the manor of The More, Rickmansworth, Hertfordshire', *The Archaeological Journal*, 116 (1959), p. 193.

5. Falvey, 'The More', p. 8.

6. M. Hicks, 'Neville, George (1432–1476)', *Oxford dictionary of national biography* (Oxford, 2004), accessed online 15 October 2007.

7. Falvey, 'The More', p. 9.

8. Page, *Hertford*, 2, p. 376 citing Patent Roll 15 Edw. IV. pt. 1, m. 6 (TNA: PRO C66/535).

9. Page, *Hertford*, 2, p. 376.

10. *Ibid.*; M. Pedrick, *Moor Park: The Grosvenor legacy* (Rickmansworth, 1989), p. 8.

11. TNA: PRO SC6/HENVIII/6012 ministers' and receivers' account, 1536/7.

12. Falvey, 'The More', p. 13, citing Letters & Papers, Henry VIII, vol. 6, entry 426 (TNA).

13. Pedrick, *Moor Park*, p. 10.

14. Thurley, *Royal palaces*, p. 192.

15. TNA: PRO SC6/HENVIII/6012 and 1016 ministers' and receivers' accounts, 1536/7 and 1539/41.

16. TNA: PRO E315/391, fo. 8v survey of manors in the county of Hertford, possessions of King Philip & Queen Mary, 1556.

17. A parrock is an enclosure or paddock, perhaps for coursing deer.

18. I am grateful to Heather Falvey for permitting me to use her transcription of this survey.

19. HALS DSA4/80/1 and 2 Rickmansworth tithe award and map, 1838.

20. Harting, 'Hertfordshire deer-parks', p. 103.

Ridge

Tyttenhanger park

NGR: TL193047
Date range: c.1427 – perhaps eighteenth century
Size: recorded as 311 acres in 1500/01
Underlying geology: glacial gravel, valley gravel and boulder clay

A PARK WAS ESTABLISHED at Tyttenhanger by John of Wheathampstead, the abbot of St Albans, around 1427–8. The manor formed part of the estates of the abbey and a manor house had been built there by Abbot Richard in the early fourteenth century. His successor, Abbot Michael, found that the proximity of the house to the high road from London resulted in too many guests and so he had the house pulled down. However, the landscape beside the river Colne proved so attractive that Abbot John de la Moot (1396–1401) started to rebuild the house at the end of the fourteenth century. The next abbot, William Heyworth (1402–20), completed the work in 1411 and the house became a favourite resort of his successors and their guests for the next 128 years.[1]

During Heyworth's abbacy a dispute – which continued under Abbot John of Wheathampstead (1420–40) – arose with Thomas Knollys, lord of the neighbouring manor of North Mymms, over the right of chase on Tyttenhanger Heath. As part of the resolution of this dispute, it was agreed in 1427/8 that the abbot could enclose 30 acres of the 'more or pasture' called Colney or Tyttenhanger heath 'lying near a grove called le Conyngere'.[2] In addition, Abbot John created a park (of unknown size) in the meadows and pastures adjacent to the manor house which he stocked with both red and fallow deer. In order to do this he had to persuade the manorial tenants to surrender their rights to the land and they received due compensation for their shortened tenancies. A barricade of fences and ditches was speedily erected to create a secure and secluded area for the abbot to walk in and he appointed a keeper to guard his deer from thieves.[3]

The main source of information about the medieval park is an extent of the manor compiled in 1500/01 for Abbot Thomas Ramryge (1492–1520(?)) which shows that by the end of the fifteenth century the park had expanded to cover an area of 311 acres.[4] The park incorporated the manor house with its stables, barns, moat and fishpond and included a wood of 42½ acres and a grove called Perygrove 'lying next le park pale' containing 18 acres. The remainder of the park was recorded as a series of 13 parcels which ranged in size from 3a 3r to 46a 3r.

In December 1532 Abbot Robert Catton granted the office of 'Parker or Keeper of the Parke of Tittenhanger' to Richard Ives for life. His wage was 2d a day plus an allowance for his board when the abbot was absent of 12d per week. He was permitted to pasture eight cattle (keyne) and one horse in the park and was entitled to 'all the wyndfall and browsing within the said parke together with sufficient ffewell to be spente in the lodge of the said park'.[5] The abbey was suppressed in 1539 and in 1543 Henry VIII granted the office of keeper of the manor-house and park to Nicholas Briscowe.[6] It was not until 1547, however, when Edward VI granted the manor to Sir Thomas Pope and his wife, Elizabeth, that Richard Ives released his life interest in the office of parker.[7]

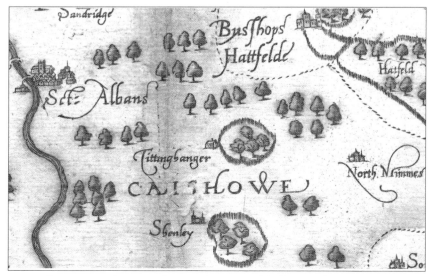

Figure 45. *Detail of Saxton's county map showing Tyttenhanger park, 1577, lying east of the house and perhaps already much reduced from its early sixteenth-century extent (HALS CM1). Reproduced by kind permission of Hertfordshire Archives and Local Studies.*

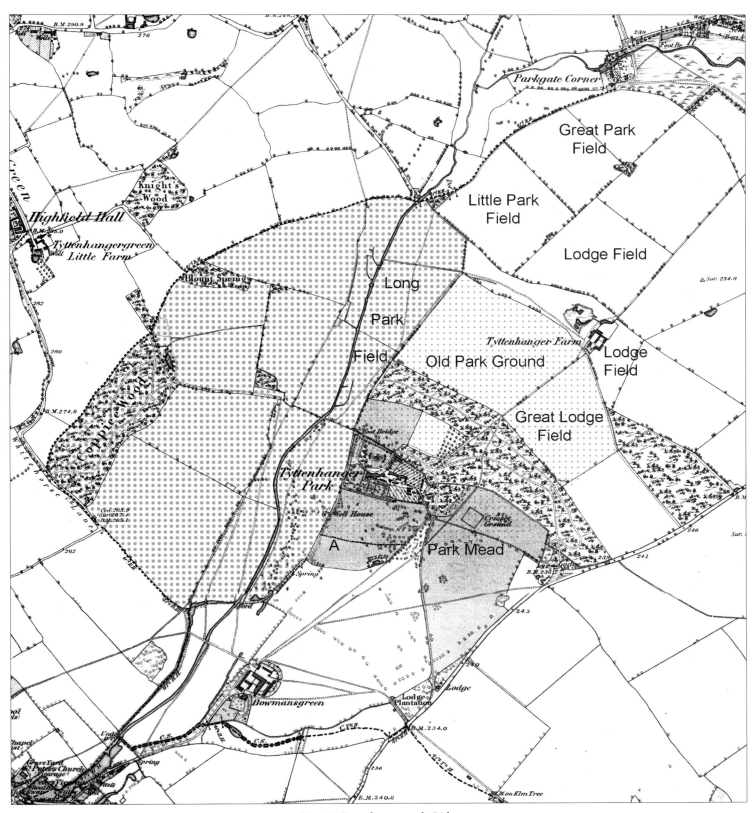

Map 47 Tyttenhanger park, Ridge

OS 6 inches to the mile map sheets XXXV, surveyed 1873–9, published 1883; and XL, surveyed 1870–3, published 1877. Annotated with field names derived from a map and field book of the Tyttenhanger estate, 1777 (HALS PC484 and DE/B2067 B/E26). The dotted line at A marks the approximate line of the ditch discovered by archaeological excavation.

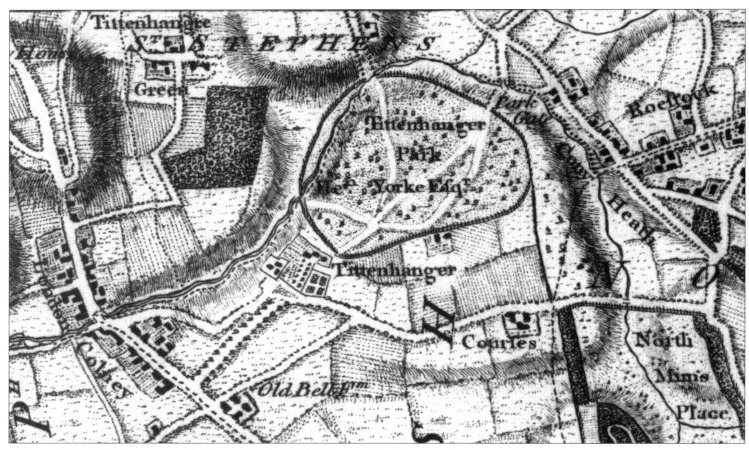

Figure 46. *Detail of the county map by Dury and Andrews, 1766, showing Tyttenhanger park as it was in the mid eighteenth century. Note the river Colne flowing through the west side of the park and the Park Gate to the north-east.*

The manor descended in the family of Sir Thomas Pope for the next two centuries.[8] Dury and Andrews' county map (1766) provides much information about the eighteenth-century park, indicating the Park Gate at the north-east end and what was probably a lodge on the south side of the park, as well as the mansion just outside the park to the south-west (Figure 46). The approximate area of the park depicted by Dury and Andrews is 185 acres, considerably smaller than the 311 acres recorded in 1500. Numerous field names shown on a map of the Tyttenhanger Estate from 1777 might help to locate the late medieval park (see Map 47): these include Old Park Ground, Great Lodge field, Little Park Field, Great Park Field and Lodge Field.[9] Parkgate Corner was marked on the first edition OS map itself. Many of these names, however, are more likely to reflect the post-medieval landscape and it is difficult now to reconstruct the pattern of fields listed in the extent of 1500/01. The wood named 'Coppice Wood' on the OS map is an area of ancient and semi-natural woodland which covers 18 acres. It has been identified by Hunn as the Perygrove 'lying next le park pale' recorded in 1500 and, if correct, suggests that the park extended up to the parish boundary. A substantial ditch, with a vestigial bank on its west side, can still be traced along the curving boundary running east and south-east from Parkgate Corner, but whether the park extended this far in medieval times is debatable (Figure 47).

An archaeological survey south of Tyttenhanger House in 1999 revealed a large ditch, originally over 2m deep, with a smaller ditch or palisade trench running along its southern side (see A on Map 47). This was interpreted as a substantial park boundary consisting of an internal ditch and an external bank retained by a palisade.[10] The archaeological evidence therefore suggests that the medieval park extended south of the manor house. Map and fragmentary field evidence suggests a park-like enclosure of 206 acres straddling the river west of the house (darker shading on map). A further, conjectural, 100 acres has been shown (lighter shading) to the east of this but where the boundaries lay is not known. The land of the former park rises from the floodplain of the river Colne to a height of about 80m OD in the west. Much of it is underlain by glacial gravels which have been, and continue to be, commercially extracted and replaced by extensive water-filled pits.

1. *Page*, Hertford, 2, p. 387.

2. Riley, *Annales Monasterii*, p. 257. Translations of this passage vary: Koughnet says the heath near Coursers was enclosed plus 30 acres of land and pasture (J.C.E. Van Koughnet, *A history of Tyttenhanger* (London, 1895), p. 13); the VCH states that 'a corner of the heath near the mansion of Tyttenhanger called le Conyngere containing thirty acres' was enclosed (Page, *Hertford*, 2, p. 387).

3. Riley, *Annales Monasterii, vol. 1*, p. 261. I am grateful to Kate Banister for her translation of this passage.

4. HALS DE/B2067B/M25 a survey and extent of the manor of 1551 which includes a copy of the extent made in 1500/01.

5. HALS DE/B2067B/E34 release by Richard Ives of office of parkership of Tyttenhanger, 1547.

6. Page, *Hertford*, 2, p. 388, citing Letters and Papers Hen. VIII, xviii (1), 545 (TNA).

Figure 47. *View looking north-west along the boundary between the eighteenth-century Tyttenhanger park (left) and Colney Heath (right). Was this also the boundary of the medieval park?*

7. *Ibid.*, p. 388, citing Patent Roll 1 Edw. VI, pt. 4, m. 19 (TNA: PRO C66/802); HALS DE/B2067B/E34 release by Richard Ives of office of parkership of Tyttenhanger, 1547.

8. Page, *Hertford*, 2, p. 388.

9. HALS PC484 Tyttenhanger estate map, 1777.

10. J. Hunn, 'Tyttenhanger Park. The rise and fall of a manorial estate', *Hertfordshire's Past*, 52 (2002), p. 10.

St Michael's, St Albans

Childwick park
NGR: *c.*TL143105
Date range: fourteenth century – perhaps fifteenth century
Size: not known
Underlying geology: clay-with-flints

A LATE FOURTEENTH-CENTURY ACCOUNT recorded a field in the manor of Batchworth which butted up to 'Childwyk park'.[1] The manor of Childwick was given to the abbot and monks of St Albans Abbey in the tenth century, and abbey records suggest that in the fourteenth century it was a reasonably high-status part of the abbey's establishment as Thomas, prior of Tynemouth, was entertained at the manor of Childwick when he came to take part in the election of the abbacy in 1346.[2] At the end of the fourteenth century abbot John de la Moote (1396–1401) invested in the construction of 'a large barn and other necessary buildings' on the manor.[3] No park was recorded on any early maps and, in the absence of any further documentary evidence, it seems likely that the park had decayed before the Dissolution (1536–9).[4]

Located on a 130m-high plateau east of the Ver, within a northerly extension of the parish of St Michael, the Childwickbury estate does form a typical setting for a medieval park and, indeed, for the landscape park which was laid out in the eighteenth century and which largely remains today. The boundary between the Childwickbury and Batchwood estates in the nineteenth century ran on a south-west – north-east alignment along the north-west side of Batch Wood (see Map 48).[5] If this was also the boundary between the two manors in medieval times, Childwick park presumably lay somewhere along that boundary. There is a substantial bank along the north-west side of Green Wood at Childwick Green which *may* represent the west side of the medieval park (Figure 48). No ancient-looking boundaries appear to have survived to the east of Green Wood by the late nineteenth century, however, so the shading in Map 48 is simply meant to indicate a possible location for the park, extending east from the bank to the presumed approximate boundary of the medieval manor. The size of the park is not known so it may have sat within the shaded area or, conversely, the shaded area may represent the core of a larger area of parkland. Further fieldwork may reveal other possible boundary earthworks and, perhaps, an alternative site for the medieval park.

Figure 48. The bank bounding the west side of Green Wood at Childwick Green.

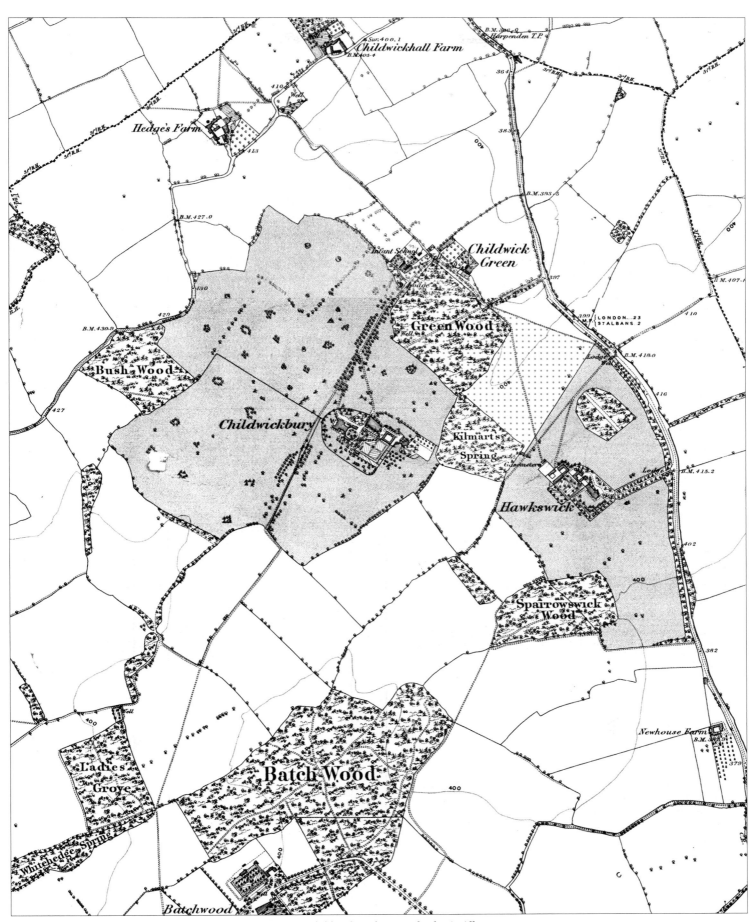

Map 48 Childwick park, St Michael's, St Albans
OS 6 inches to the mile map sheets XXVII, surveyed 1877–8, published 1884; and XXXIV, surveyed 1872–8, published 1883.

Derefold

NGR: TL136069
Date range: perhaps early thirteenth century – perhaps later fourteenth century
Size: perhaps c.120 acres
Underlying geology: Upper Chalk and valley gravel

A POSSIBLE MEDIEVAL PARK has been identified at St Albans by Dr Jonathan Hunn.[6] During his research into former land-use in the area, he found several field and wood names containing the name 'Derefold' – suggesting an enclosure for deer. Derefold Wood is recorded as early as 1235–60 by Thomas Walsingham in his fourteenth-century history of the abbey, the *Gesta Abbatum*.[7] It also occurs in fourteenth-century court rolls for the manor of Kingsbury, along with Derefoldland.[8] Another important medieval reference comes in the account of the Peasants' Revolt of 1381, which mentions a '*campum de Derefolde*' and a '*sylva de Derfold*': that is, a field and a wood called Derefold.[9]

Lands recorded with a property called St Jermans in early seventeenth-century deeds included 'all those eight severall closes or fields of land and wood ground called Dorvold Feildes or Dorvold woods alias Verulam, containing 120 acres'.[10] This land had formerly belonged to the monastery of St Albans[11] and Dr Hunn has concluded that an early medieval park known as Derefold Wood, which may have survived into the later fourteenth century, covered at least 120 acres of the southern part of the old Roman town of Verulamium. He gives the following description of the boundaries of the medieval 'Deer-fold', which (as indicated on Map 49)

> can be broadly defined on its western side by the
> Roman defences and King Harry Lane; to the north by
> what is now the A414 road to St Michaels; on its
> eastern side by the River Ver and the Roman defences,
> parts of which still stand today; and its southern side
> by what may have been irregularly routed park pales,
> possibly reflecting fields or secondary woodland.[12]

Dr Hunn further suggests that the creation of the park may have been partly responsible for the diversion of the Roman road, Watling Street, from its original north-westerly course through the Roman town of Verulamium to a north-easterly course over the river Ver and up the hill to the east of Verulamium. The other reason for this diversion was the need to persuade traffic to pass through the new town founded at the top of the hill by the abbot of St Albans in the early eleventh century. If this scenario is accepted, then this park in Derefold Wood at St Albans could have been one of the three Hertfordshire parks recorded in the Domesday survey of 1086.

The evidence for an early medieval park is, however, very slight. No surviving traces of a park, or the exact location of Derefold Wood, have been identified on the ground.[13] While it seems entirely feasible that the steep banks of the former walls of the Roman town could have been used to enclose deer, the location of the site, close to the medieval town, is not typical for a medieval park, and particularly for a very early one. The word 'fold' seems to suggest a relatively small enclosure for holding a few deer and this may well have lain within the shaded area on the map but perhaps did not cover the whole area as indicated.

1. BL Harley MS, 602, fo. 42. This reference was found by Jonathan Hunn (Hunn, *Reconstruction and measurement*, p. 178). On fo. 38 is the start of an account dated 1386–90.

2. Page, *Hertford*, 2, p. 397–8, citing H.T. Riley, *Gesta abbatum monasterii Sancti Albani a Thoma Walsingham, vol. 2, AD 1290–1349* (London, 1867; republished Germany, 1965), p. 381.

3. *Ibid.*, citing Riley, *Gesta abbatum, vol. 3*, p. 445.

4. Hunn, *Reconstruction and measurement of landscape change*, pp. 178–9.

5. HALS DSA4/87/1 and 2 tithe award and map for St Michael's, 1843 and 1840 respectively.

6. Hunn, *Reconstruction and measurement of landscape change*, pp. 178–9.

7. Riley, *Gesta abbatum, vol. 1*, p. 319.

8. HALS X.D.O.A Gorhambury Deeds, court rolls, 1269–1332. See, for example, fo. 76.

9. Riley, *Gesta abbatum, vol. 3*, , p. 336.

10. HALS 26624 deeds of St Jermans, 1636.

11. HALS DE/X438/T5 title deeds of a capital messuage called Mary Magdalen and St Germains, 1779/80.

12. Hunn, *Reconstruction and measurement of landscape change*, pp. 178–9.

13. Isobel Thompson pers. comm.

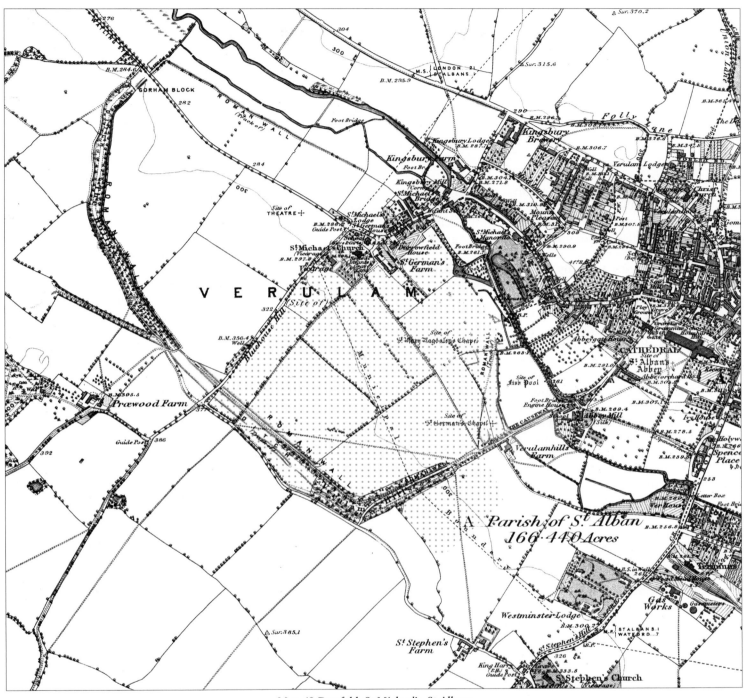

Map 49 Derefold, St Michael's, St Albans

OS 6 inches to the mile map sheet XXXIV, surveyed 1872–8, published 1883. Shaded area represents extent of the possible 'Deer-fold' (based on the work of J. Hunn, 1994).

St Stephen's, St Albans

Eywood park
NGR: TL150055
Date range: probably by 1086 – perhaps fifteenth century
Size: perhaps c.418 acres
Underlying geology: Upper Chalk capped with glacial gravel on the higher ground; valley gravel on the lower ground

AMONG THE LANDS HELD by the abbot of St Albans and associated with the town in the Domesday survey of 1086 was a park for woodland beasts.[1] It is possible that the park was established before the Norman Conquest, perhaps by Abbot Leofstan (c.1048–66), who presided over a period of prosperity for the abbey, or by Abbot Frederic (1066–77). Both abbots had close connections with the crown and could have enclosed a park as part of their improvements to the abbey's estates. Abbot Frederic, however, had to contend with the difficulties of the new Norman rule and he and many of the aristocratic English inmates of his wealthy abbey were seen as a threat by William I, who sought to lessen the abbey's power and influence by confiscating some of its lands. The first Norman abbot, Paul de Caen (1077–93), supported by his kinsman Archbishop Lanfranc, recovered some of these lands, including a wood called *Eiwoda*.[2] Eywood was an extensive area of woodland which lay in a bend of the river Ver south of the town and has been identified as the most likely location for the Domesday park.[3] If this identification is correct, then the fact that Eywood was not described as a park when recovered by Paul de Caen suggests that, of the three abbots, he is the most likely to have created the park recorded at the time of Domesday.

There is little doubt that there was a park in Eywood in medieval times: a document of 1440 refers to the '*parco de Eywode*' and an earlier reference to the '*portas warrennae*' of Sopwellbury in 1381 may relate to a gate at the northern end of the park.[4] Watling Street appears to have formed the western boundary of the wood and the settlement of Park Street, together with a field known in medieval times as 'La Parkmede', appear to mark the southern limit of the medieval park (see Map 50).[5] Jonathan Hunn estimates that the early medieval wood would have covered at least 418 acres but how much of the wood was enclosed in the park is not recorded.[6]

It seems likely that this park was the source of various park names which were recorded in the area from the thirteenth century. The Hertfordshire volume of the English Place-Names Society recorded *campis de Parco* (1239), *villa de Parco* (1294), *La Parcsokne* (1255), *Park Sokene* (1275), *Parcbiri* (1260) and *Parkesbur'* (1291), as well as *le Parkstret* from the early fourteenth century.[7]

St Albans was the premier English abbey in the twelfth and thirteenth centuries and ample stocks of venison would have been required for entertaining and for gifts. There are no known records of any of the abbots hunting for sport but the imposition of a rule in the early fourteenth century which permitted only the cellarer and kitchener of the abbey to keep a dog for coursing suggests that some of the monks did indulge.[8] Later in the fourteenth century Abbot Thomas de la Mare (1349–96) was known as a generous host and provided hospitality for many noble guests, some of whom would have been keen on hunting. He maintained a staff of huntsmen and falconers who no doubt helped to provide entertainment for the visitors as well as providing venison and other game for the abbey's kitchens.[9]

There is no known reference to the park of Eywood after 1440 and it may have been superseded by the new park created at Tyttenhanger by Abbot John of Wheathampstead in the 1420s. It may well have been disparked after the second battle of St Albans in 1461, when both town and monastery were sacked and suffered severe hardship. No monastic parks existed close to St Albans by the early sixteenth century[10] and no park was depicted at Eywood on the county maps by Saxton (1577) and Norden (1598). The wood itself survived into the seventeenth century and was recorded on a plan of c. 1600, when it was estimated to contain 343 acres.[11] The plan shows that a portion of the southern end of the wood had been felled and made into two fields. These were annotated 'last called the lodge ground', providing further evidence of the former park. The approximate location of the fields (but not their boundary) is indicated by the annotation transcribed onto Map 50.

1. Morris, *Domesday Book: Hertfordshire*, 10,5.
2. Riley, *Gesta abbatum, vol. 1*, p. 53.
3. Hunn, *Reconstruction and measurement of landscape change*, p. 176.
4. Riley, *Gesta abbatum, vol. 3*, p. 288; Hunn, *Reconstruction and measurement of landscape change*, p. 178.
5. Hunn, *Reconstruction and measurement of landscape change*, p. 89.
6. *Ibid.*, p. 176.
7. Gover *et al.*, *Place-names of Hertfordshire*, p. 98 citing *Gesta abbatum*, lay subsidy rolls, Feet of fines, Taxatio ecclesiastica and Cartulary of St Albans abbey.
8. Page, *Hertford*, 4, 'Houses of Benedictine monks: St Albans Abbey — after the Conquest', p. 385, citing Riley, *Gesta abbatum, vol. 2*, pp. 95–106.
9. *Ibid.*, p. 396, citing Riley, *Gesta abbatum, vol. 3*, pp. 390 and 400; BL Cotton MS. Nero, D vii, fo. 22d.
10. Hunn, *Reconstruction and measurement of landscape change*, p. 178.
11. HALS IV.A.25 plan of Aye Wood, c.1600.

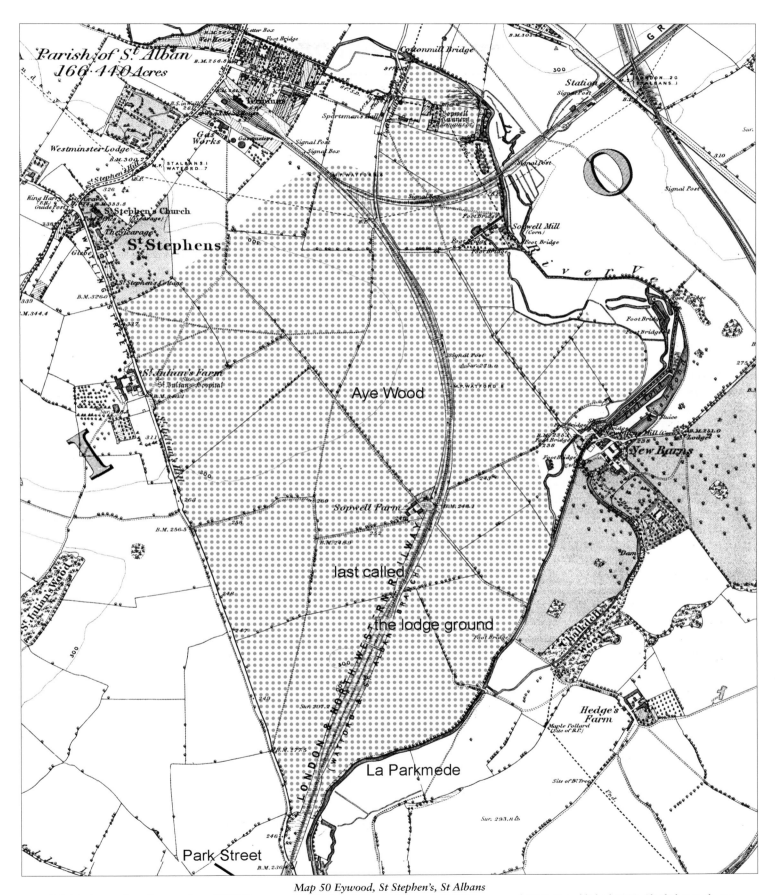

Map 50 Eywood, St Stephen's, St Albans

OS 6 inches to the mile map sheets XXXIV, surveyed 1872–8, published 1883; and XXXIX, surveyed 1871–2, published 1883. Shaded area shows the likely extent of the medieval wood based on the boundary of 'Aye Wood' depicted on an early seventeenth-century map, from which the note about the 'lodge ground' was also taken (HALS IV.A.25). The field name 'La Parkmede' was found and located by J. Hunn (1994). Whether or not the park occupied the entire wood is not known.

Sawbridgeworth

Pisho park

NGR: TL443120
Date range: by 1294 – late sixteenth century
Size: 156 acres recorded in 1294; modern estimate 178 acres
Underlying geology: boulder clay with some Head deposits along the south and east margins of the former park

WHEN THE PARISH OF GILSTON was formed out of the south-west corner of the large parent parish of Sawbridgeworth, 275 acres of the south-westernmost corner of the new parish was retained as a detached part of Sawbridgeworth. This 275-acre block of land seems to have belonged to the manor of Pishobury in Sawbridgeworth, the manor itself having been created in the early twelfth century from a part of the parent manor of Sawbridgeworth. This detached piece of land lay about three miles south-west of the town of Sawbridgeworth and comprised steeply sloping ground which had probably retained much of its woodland cover: the ideal landscape for a medieval park. The park was established in the second half of the thirteenth century probably by a descendent of Baldwin de Redvers, Earl of Cornwall. No park was mentioned in 1248 when Margaret, Baldwin's widow, was granted the right of free hunting on her own estate with dogs, birds or nets, and free fishing in the river where it joined her lands.[1] The park was first recorded in a rental of 1294, which included '242 acres of arable land, 29 acres of meadow, 27 acres of several pasture, an inclosed wood of 156 acres called the Park, where was both several and common pasture, and a water-mill'.[2] The reference to pasture indicates that the 'wood' was in fact wood-pasture. An account roll of 1295/6 mentioned underwood sold in the park, evidence that there was a mosaic of wood-pasture and coppiced woodland.[3] By this time the manor had passed into the hands of the Lisle family and they continued to hold it for most of the fourteenth century.

Where the manor house lay at this time is not known. It may have been the moated site in the former park just west of Pye Corner but is more likely to have been in or near the town of Sawbridgeworth on land bordering the river Stort which was still part of the Pishobury estate in the nineteenth century. In the early fourteenth century it had an outer and inner court with hall and chapel.[4] In 1337 the park was broken into, the deer hunted and taken away.[5] A document of 1343 referred to the 'park of Gedelesho' and 'the keeper of Gedelesho Wood'.[6] In 1394 Robert de Lisle released all right in the manor of Pisho to Richard, first Baron Scrope of Bolton. Baron Scrope (c.1327–1403) had a successful military career followed by many years in government administration and his principal residence was Bolton castle in Wensleydale, West Yorkshire, which he built from 1378. According to his biography, however, he 'seems to have spent his later years mostly at his manor of Pishiobury, Hertfordshire, which he bought in 1394, and where he drew up his will on 2 August 1400'.[7]

The manor was held by Baron Scrope's descendents throughout the fifteenth century, although it was in the hands of mortgagees on the death of Richard, third Lord Scrope in 1420.[8] Accounts for the manor and park were compiled for Richard de Neville for the period 1421/2. The account prepared by the parker, William del Chambre, in 1422 reveals that deer were present in the park and no agistment was permitted in order to preserve the grazing for them.[9] No record of the park has been found from the later fifteenth century. It re-emerges in the 1530s when Henry VIII obtained the manor of Pisho from John, eighth Lord Scrope, in 1534 in order to annex the manor to his honour of Hunsdon.[10] An extent of the manor was compiled at about this time and describes 'a park nearly 2 miles in circumference, well wooded, with game, deer and coneys, and a lodge on one side for the keeper, a moated house within the park, then somewhat fallen into decay, and a stable in good repair, with room for twenty horses'.[11]

In 1536/7 the king's bailiff, Oliver Rigby, was 'custodian of the king's park' in the manor of 'Pyshoo'. His account included an allowance for the mowing, spreading and carriage of hay for the lord's deer in the park during the winter.[12] Hay was also bought for the deer the following year and improvements and repairs were made to Le Fludgate in the park pale and to other parts of the pale which had been damaged by strong winds.[13] Repairs to the fence or hedge 'above the park pale' were also recorded in 1539/40 which, together with the scouring of four big ponds in the park, cost 21s 6d.[14]

In 1547 Edward VI granted the manor with Sawbridgeworth mill and Pisho Park to Sir Thomas Cawarden, Gentleman of the Privy Chamber, who a few months later alienated it to Sir Wimund Carew of Blechingley.[15] His son conveyed it in 1555 to Thomas Mildmay, from whom it passed to Walter Mildmay, who was holding in 1576.[16] The park is depicted on Saxton's county map (1577) (Figure 49) but not by Norden (1598) or Seller (1676), which suggests that it was disparked in the late sixteenth century, probably by Walter Mildmay who, in 1585, built a new house called Pishobury south of the town of Sawbridgeworth and bordered by the river Stort to the east. He laid out ornamental grounds with avenues of trees around his new house together with a 'paddock' of 20 acres for deer.[17] The medieval park was no longer required.

During the late seventeenth century a new park was developed around a house called New Place by Sir Humphrey Gore. It lay to the north of the medieval park of Pisho, in the parish of Gilston, and extended southwards into the detached portion of Sawbridgeworth. His father, Sir John Gore, had bought land in adjacent parishes in order to beautify and

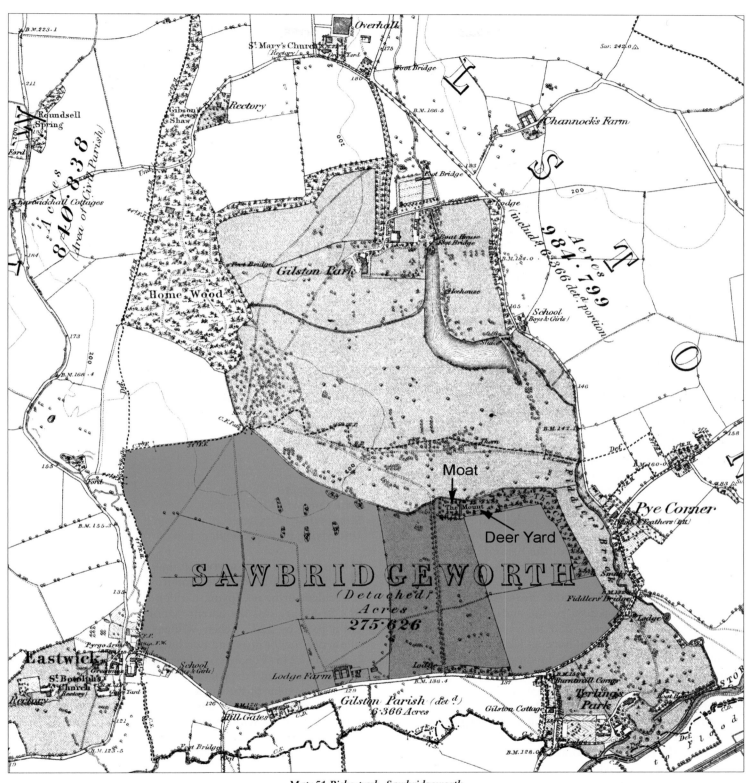

Map 51 Pisho park, Sawbridgeworth
OS 6 inches to the mile map sheet XXX, surveyed 1873–80, published 1881–3. Annotated with features recorded on the Sawbridgeworth tithe award and map, 1838 and 1839 (HALS DSA4/93/1 and 2).

Figure 49. Detail of Saxton's county map showing a park, probably Pisho, lying closer to Eastwick than to Gilston (Geldesden), 1577 (HALS CM1). The park lying west of the town of Sawbridgeworth is probably the one at Shingle Hall. Reproduced by kind permission of Hertfordshire Archives and Local Studies.

enlarge New Place and this land must have included at least part of the medieval Pisho park.[18] An indenture of 1694 recorded lands belonging to Sir Humphrey Gore's estate at Gilston, which included

> all that land and pasture in Pishoe Parke in the parish of Sabridgeworth … containing by estimation three score acres and all those parcels of woodgrounds and those Coppices or underwoods in Gilston and Sawbridgeworth … containing by estimation forty and four acres and all that house or Lodge and the lands and grounds thereunto belonging … in the parish of Sawbridgeworth being part of the Parke or late Parke or inclosed ground called Pishoe Parke …[19]

So, it would appear that the medieval Pisho park had survived, albeit without deer, to the end of the seventeenth century. Whether or not it had survived in its entirety is difficult to say but it did still have its lodge. The Lodge Farm of 1699 can be identified as the Sawbridgeworth Lodge Farm recorded on the tithe award in 1838.[20] During the eighteenth century the park at New Place expanded further southwards and became known as Gilston Park. The old lodge was demolished and a new one built about 100m further east at the new entrance to the estate, with a tree-lined drive heading north from the road. In addition, a new farmyard was laid out to the west of the old lodge; this was labelled 'Lodge Farm' on the first edition OS map, but is now known as Eastwick Lodge Farm. By the mid nineteenth century Gilston Park was stocked with fallow deer, which are beautifully illustrated in paintings by J.C. Buckler in 1834.[21] In 1838/9 the Sawbridgeworth tithe award and map recorded an enclosure known as the 'Deer Yard' lying east of the moat near Gilston (TL444122), which was presumably in use in the nineteenth century but which may have originated in a much earlier period.[22]

The medieval park lay on the gently rising slopes of the north side of the Stort valley, reaching 65m OD towards the north-west, and enjoying extensive views of the south side of the valley

(including, today, much of modern Harlow). A slight bank still survives at the western parish boundary where the public footpath enters the former park but most of the east–west parish boundary bank which may once have marked the north side of the detached area of Sawbridgeworth has been obliterated, although some parts can still be detected as cropmarks on aerial photographs. However, at the point at the top of the hill where the footpath enters Gilston Park (as shown on the first edition OS map) there is a marked earthwork – a hollow-way with banks on either side. This may well mark the northern boundary of the medieval park, re-used perhaps in the seventeenth century when the new park was created around New Place. The earthwork appears to continue to the NNW, forming the southern boundary of Home Wood and meeting the public footpath and parish boundary at TL435127. This raises the possibility that the medieval park extended into the parish of Gilston, explaining perhaps the origin of the name 'Gedelesho Wood' recorded in the fourteenth century. On the east side of the park any bank which may once have marked the parish boundary has been ploughed out but a boundary can be detected extending eastwards from the north side of the woodland which contains the moat and nineteenth-century deer yard.

The extent of the park shown on Map 50 is a best guess based upon a combination of documentary, map and field evidence. It covers an area of 178 acres, rather more than the 156 acres of wood called the park recorded at the end of the thirteenth century.

Sayes park
NGR: TL453140
Date range: by 1237 – c.1490
Size: perhaps c.95 acres
Underlying geology: boulder clay

SAYES PARK LAY ON THE EDGE of the parish two miles west and slightly south of the town and manor house of Sawbridgeworth, occupying a ridge of high ground 65–75m OD. Sayesbury was the parent manor of Sawbridgeworth and had a park by 1237, when William de Say was granted ten fallow deer (eight does and two bucks) from the royal forest of Essex.[23] In 1245 William got a licence for free warren.[24] In 1283 poachers broke into the park, 'hunted therein and carried away deer'.[25] An extent of the manor taken in 1295 on the death of William's son, another William, recorded 'forty acres of wood in which there are wild animals'.[26]

The largest recorded extent of the park was in 1359 on the death of Geoffrey, second Lord de Say, when there was said to be 'a park of sixty acres with great trees and deer in it'.[27] An extent taken in 1375 on the death of William de Say, son of Geoffrey, did not record the park but there were '100 acres of wood', which probably included the park.[28] The main landholdings of the de Say family were in Kent and it appears that they did not reside on their Sawbridgeworth manor during the later fourteenth century because an extent taken in 1404 recorded that the capital messuage, which stood in the town of Sawbridgeworth, was ruinous.[29]

In 1478 Sir William Say inherited the manor (along with many others) from his father and remained lord of the manor until his death in 1529.[30] He did not live on the manor but

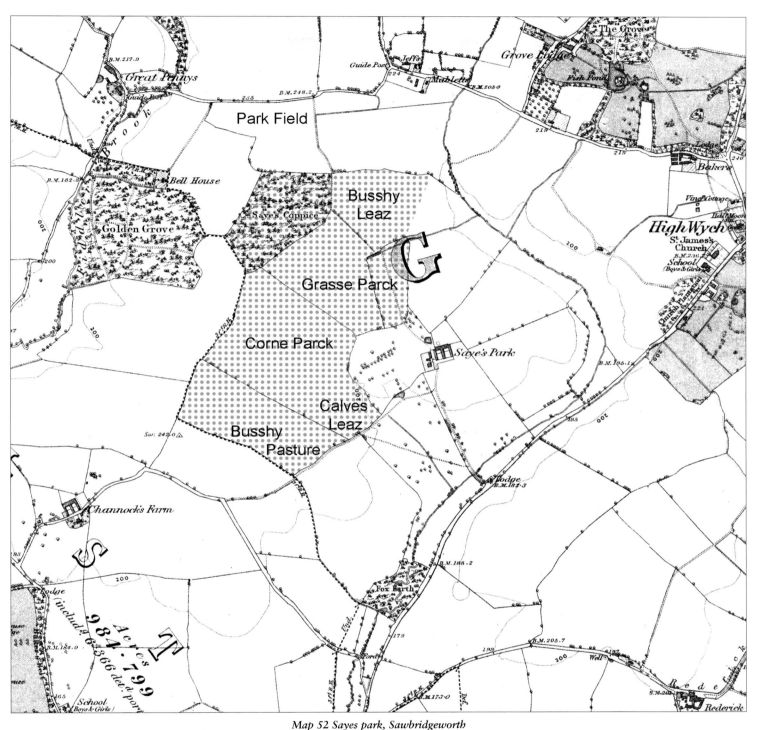

Map 52 Sayes park, Sawbridgeworth
OS 6 inches to the mile map sheets XXX, surveyed 1873–80, published 1881–3; and XXXI, surveyed 1873–9, published 1880–4. Annotated with field names from a map drawn by Israel Amyce, 1600/01 (HHA CP 349). NB the field boundaries on the OS map bear little resemblance to the field boundaries shown in 1600/01.

appears initially to have maintained the deer park, as the bailiff's account for 1484/5 recorded that the grazing was reserved for the lord's deer (*feris*) and animals and mention was made of 'underwood felled for sustenance of the deer in the park'.[31] The park also contained a rabbit warren but there is no record of the size of either warren or park. The parker was paid 60s 10d and 20 shillings was spent on maintaining the park boundary.[32] Various fields and meadows on the manor were leased for £6 3s 4d for the year, including a large barn in the park.[33] In 1490/1 these same lands and barn were

leased to new tenants, John Grave and his son John, on a 12-year lease for £6 13s 4d.[34] However, by the time of the next surviving bailiff's account in 1493/4, the fourth year of their lease, John Grave and his son were paying £10 to lease 'the park called Sayes park with a lodge and other houses' in addition to the lands in their original lease.[35]

So, by 1493, Sir William Say appears to have relinquished his deer park in Sawbridgeworth. Instead, he gained a regular income by leasing the park pasture to tenants and, by retaining the right to manage and sell the wood and timber, he remained

197

in control of a resource which produced significant revenues. The accounts record the following receipts: 3s 8d for 11 cartloads of loppings from trees in 1484/5; 25s 1½d for 67 cartloads of underwood in 1490/1; 20 shillings for wood felled in 1493/4; 17s 4d from the sale of 52 cartloads of wood felled in 1495/6 (a further 6 carts of fuel were delivered to the vicar as tithe); and 4 shillings for 12 cartloads of fuel sold in 1498/9.[36]

In 1573 the park was referred to as 'a farm called Sayes Park' when William, Lord Burghley, took a 31-year lease on the property.[37] The total area of the farm was given as about 293 acres in a survey carried out in 1600/01.[38] At that time the farm, with a substantial house in its midst, was leased to a widow and her son and comprised 119 acres of pasture, 142 acres of arable land, 17 acres of meadow and 14 acres of wood (the grove called the Coppice). The names of the fields to the east and south of Saye's Coppice all indicate pasture and two had 'park' names (see Map 52). Several of these fields are depicted with common external boundaries and with interlocking internal boundaries on the map of 1600/01 (only some of which survived to the late nineteenth century), suggesting that they may once have formed an area of parkland covering about 95 acres.

No park was depicted on either of the sixteenth-century county maps (1577 and 1598). But at least a part of it appears to have been subsequently reinstated as parkland because in 1614 'the manor and park' were granted in fee to Lionel Cranfield and in 1633 'the manor with the inclosed park called Sayesbury Park' was granted by royal charter to trustees for Lord Cranfield.[39] The county maps by both Seller (1676) and Oliver (1695) depict a house called Sayes Park (but no park pale), which suggests that a replacement manor house had been built in the former park in the early seventeenth century. The site appears to have fallen in social status before 1766 as Dury and Andrews do not indicate the name of the owner, as they do with other gentry houses.[40] The 1601 field names 'Corn Park' and 'Bushey Leys' survived to be recorded on the Sawbridgeworth tithe map and award in 1838; 'Grass Park' had become 'Park Field'. Another 'Park Field', belonging to the neighbouring farm, bordered Saye's Coppice to the north.[41]

Surviving field evidence in this area of intense arable farming is, however, disappointing. Sayes Coppice remains an area of semi-natural and ancient woodland, although partly replanted. Significant boundaries surround it on its north and east sides, that on the latter comprising a bank with an external ditch. A deep ditch extends south-eastwards from the wood towards the farmhouse and is followed by a public footpath on its east side, but this was not marked as a field boundary in 1600/01 and probably does not relate to the former park. Another public footpath, however, follows the possible southern boundary of the park south-westwards from the farmhouse to the parish boundary.

The apparent 95-acre core of the medieval park illustrated in Map 52 is based primarily on the evidence of the map of 1600/01. The configuration of the parish boundary and the local topography makes it tempting to speculate that the park may once have extended eastwards at least as far as the stream but there is no historical evidence to support this.

Shingle Hall park

NGR: TL465182
Date range: 1447 – perhaps late seventeenth century
Size: licence to impark 520 acres in 1447
Underlying geology: boulder clay

THE MANORS OF SHINGLE HALL and Mathams in Sawbridgeworth were joined about 1301 and were acquired by the Leventhorpe family in 1414.[42] A few years later John Leventhorpe also obtained the neighbouring manor of Thorley.[43] In 1439 Leventhorpe's son, another John, obtained a grant of free warren in Sawbridgeworth, Thorley and Stortford.[44] In 1447 he obtained a licence to 'impark 400 acres of land, 40 acres of meadow and 80 acres of wood in Sawbridgeworth and Thorley and surround them with dikes, hays, hedges palings and stakes (*pilis*)'.[45] John Leventhorpe was member of parliament for Hertfordshire in 1467 and succeeding generations of Leventhorpes enjoyed high social status – his grandson, another John, was sheriff of Hertfordshire in 1509 and, a century later, another John Leventhorpe was knighted, was twice sheriff of Hertfordshire and was created a baronet in 1622.[46] The park at Shingle Hall was shown on the sixteenth-century county maps by Saxton (1577) and by Norden (1598) (Figures 49 and 50).

Sir Thomas Leventhorpe sold the manor of Thorley, and perhaps a part of the park, in 1672.[47] He died without male heirs in 1679 and the manor of Shingle Hall passed to a niece who was married to John Coke of Melbourne, Derbyshire. Presumably Shingle Hall was leased to tenants during the later seventeenth century, but whether as a country house set within a park or as a farm is not known. Neither house nor park was shown on Seller's county map of 1676 but both were depicted on Oliver's map of 1695.[48]

In 1706 the son of John and Mary Coke sold Shingle Hall and Mathams to Ralph Freman, member of parliament for

Figure 50. Detail of Norden's county map, 1598, showing the parks between Bishop's Stortford and Hunsdon at the end of the sixteenth century. Pisho park is not shown but Shingle Hall is marked in the middle of its park. Reproduced by kind permission of Hertfordshire Archives and Local Studies.

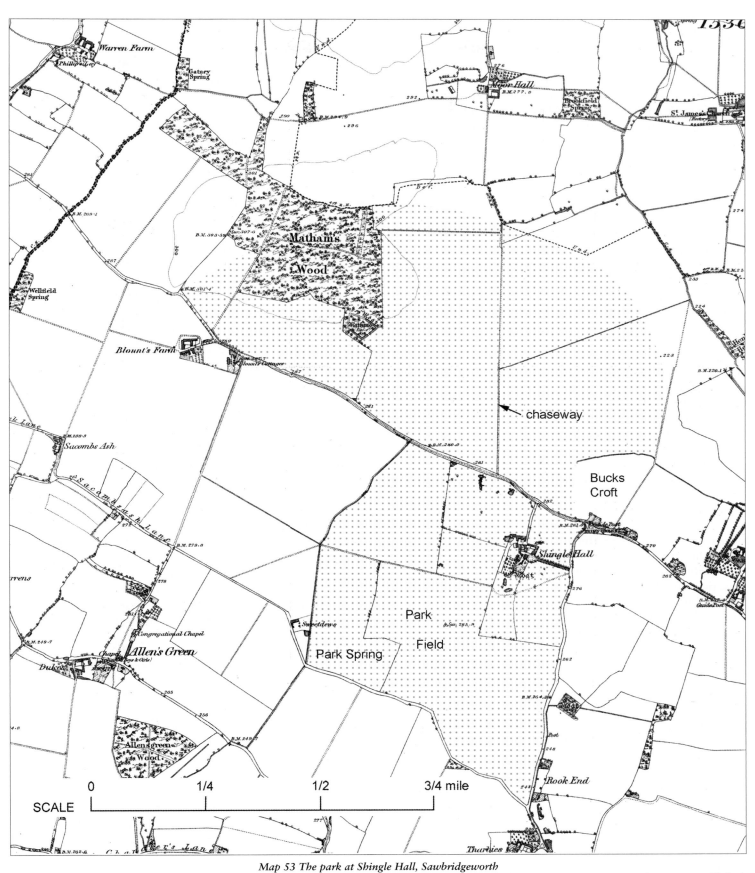

Map 53 The park at Shingle Hall, Sawbridgeworth
OS 6 inches to the mile map sheets XXII, surveyed 1878, published 1883; XXIII, surveyed 1874–9, published 1879–83; XXX, surveyed 1873–80, published 1881–3; XXXI, surveyed 1873–9, published 1880–4 (all reproduced at a reduced scale). Annotated with features from the Sawbridgeworth tithe award and map, 1838 and 1839 (HALS DSA4/93/1 and 2).

Hertfordshire since 1697.[49] The sale documents make no reference to a park so it must have been dismantled by the end of the seventeenth century. Freman's family seat was at Aspenden Hall, where his parents were both still living in 1706. It is possible that he purchased Shingle Hall with a view to living there and he may indeed have done so for a few years, but he went on to acquire the Hamels estate near Braughing in 1713 and made his permanent home there instead.[50] Nearly 50 years later, in 1754, the Sawbridgeworth property was referred to as 'Yardley's Farm alias Shingle Hall', confirming the decline in social status.[51] In the 1830s the manor of Shingle Hall was joined with Sayesbury and Pishobury under a single owner, Rowland Alston.[52]

The total area of the park licensed in 1447 was 520 acres but whether or not a park of this area was ever enclosed is uncertain. It would have lain on a boulder clay-covered plateau at about 85–95m OD between the valleys of Fiddlers' Brook to the west and the Stort to the east. In 1845 Rowland Alston owned just 17½ acres in Thorley parish enclosed in small, and apparently old, closes which did not appear to have been part of a former park.[53] Within the parish of Sawbridgeworth, many of the fields lying to the north, west and south of Shingle Hall had rectilinear boundaries in 1839 and may well have been created from former parkland but no long, outer boundary can be detected.[54] As the wording of the fifteenth-century licence suggests that 400 acres of the park was to be created from farmland, this is perhaps not surprising: the park would have been fitted into the pre-existing fieldscape.

The lands sold with Shingle Hall and Mathams in 1706 included Blunts Farm and Sweat Dews Farm, but no acreages were given in the sale document.[55] In 1754 the estate comprised Yardleys Farm alias Shingle Hall (340 acres) and Blunts Farm (270 acres) plus Mathams Wood, which covered nearly 47 acres. By 1838 Shingle Hall Farm covered 366 acres and included a 42-acre field called Park Field, lying south-west of the Hall, and Park Spring, adjacent (see Map 53). By the time the first edition OS map was surveyed many of the earlier field boundaries had already been obliterated and, without further evidence, it has not proved possible to plot the boundaries of this park. The accompanying map attempts to show where the park is most likely to have been located, based upon the evidence of earlier maps and recorded field names, but is not intended to indicate the boundaries of the park. The shaded area covers about 470 acres.

1. Page, *Hertford*, 3, p. 337, citing Feet of Fines Hertfordshire 32 Hen. III no. 385.

2. *Cal. Close 1288–1296*, p. 236.

3. TNA: PRO SC6/868/6 ministers' and receivers' accounts, Pisho, 1295/6. The roll is in poor condition.

4. Page, *Hertford*, 3, p. 337 fn. 80, citing Rentals and Surveys portf. 8, no. 43 (TNA: PRO SC12/8/43).

5. *Cal. Pat. 1334–1338*, p. 44.

6. Page, *Hertford*, 3, p. 337, citing *Cal. Close 1343–1346*, p. 119. Clutterbuck, *County of Hertford*, 3, Braughing Hundred, p. 200. Clutterbuck transcribed the name of the park as 'Gedeseshe' and cited the source as Claus. 17 E. III. p. 1. m. 9.

7. B. Vale, 'Scrope, Richard, first Baron Scrope of Bolton (*c*.1327–1403)', *Oxford dictionary of national biography* (Oxford, 2004), accessed online 19 August 2007.

8. Page, *Hertford*, 3, p. 337, citing Chan. Inq. p.m. 9 Hen. V, no. 27 (*Cal. Inq. post mortem, vol. 21, Henry V*, p. 251).

9. TNA: PRO SC6/839/16 account of the parker, 1421/2.

10. Page, *Hertford*, 3, p. 338, citing Letters and Papers Hen. VIII, v, 916; vi, 43, 348, 383 (TNA); *The statutes of the realm*, iii (London, 1810-28), 488.

11. Page, *Hertford*, 3, p. 338, citing Rentals and Surveys portf. 8, no. 35 (TNA: PRO SC12/8/35).

12. TNA: PRO SC6/HENVIII/6443 bailiff's account for Pishoo, 1534/5.

13. TNA: PRO SC6/HENVIII/6012 bailiff's account for Pyshoo, 1536/7.

14. TNA: PRO SC6/HENVIII/6016 bailiff's account for Pysho, 1539/40.

15. Page, *Hertford*, 3, p. 338, citing Patent Roll 1 Edw. VI, pt. i, m. 37 and pt. iii, m. 41 (TNA: PRO C66/799 and 801).

16. Page, *Hertford*, 3, p. 338, citing Recovery Rolls Easter Term 1576, rot. 155.

17. Chauncy, *Historical antiquities*, p. 178.

18. *Ibid*., p. 190.

19. HALS DE/Bo/T14/1 indenture, 1694.

20. HALS DE/Bo/E1 'Particular of an estate purchased of Henry Gore', surveyed 1699/1700; DSA4/93/1 Sawbridgeworth tithe award, 1838.

21. HALS DE/Bg/2, p. 74, paintings of Gilston by J.C. Buckler, 1834.

22. HALS DSA4/93/1 and 2 Sawbridgeworth tithe award and map, 1838 and 1839.

23. *Cal. Close 1234–1237*, p. 445.

24. *Cal. Chart. 1226–1257*, p. 282.

25. *Cal. Pat. 1281–1292*, p. 105.

26. *Cal. Inq. post mortem, vol. 3, Edward I*, p. 170.

27. *Cal. Inq. post mortem, vol. 10, 33 Edward III*, p. 403.

28. *Cal. Inq. post mortem, vol. 14, 49 Edward III*, p. 212.

29. P. Fleming, 'Say, Geoffrey de, second Lord de Say (1304/5–1359)', *Oxford dictionary of national biography* (Oxford, 2004), accessed online 17 July 2007; Page, *Hertford*, 3, pp. 335, quoting Chancery Inquisition *post mortem* 6 Hen. IV. No. 21 (TNA: PRO C137/48/21); According to Chauncy, parts of the foundations could still be seen at the end of the sixteenth century in a field called 'Sayes Garden' between the church and the river (Salmon, *History of Hertfordshire*, p. 260).

30. Page, *Hertford*, 3, pp. 335; Sir William Say held the Hertfordshire manors of Baas, Periers, Geddings, Langtons, Foxtons, Halles, Hokys, Hoddesdonbury, Wykeham Hall, Bedwell, Little Berkhamsted, Benington and Great and Little Munden [HHA court rolls bailiffs' accounts 10/16, 10/19–23].

31. HHA court rolls 10/16 bailiff's accounts, 1484/5.

32. In addition to his duties as 'custodian of the park' he also collected rents for the lord.

33. HHA court rolls 10/16 bailiff's accounts, 1484/5.

34. HHA court rolls 10/19 bailiff's accounts, 1490/1.

35. HHA court rolls 10/20 bailiff's accounts, 1493/4.

36. HHA court rolls 10/16 bailiff's accounts, 1484/5; 10/19 bailiff's accounts, 1490/1; 10/20 bailiff's accounts, 1493/4; 10/21 bailiff's accounts, 1495/6; 10/23 bailiff's accounts, 1498/9.

37. *Cal. Pat. 1572–1575*, p. 25.

38. HHA CP349 survey of the estates of Robert Cecil carried out by Israel Amyce, 1600/01.

39. Page, *Hertford*, 3, p. 336 quoting Patent Roll 11 Jas I. pt. xiii (TNA: PRO C66/1990); Harting, 'Hertfordshire deer-parks', p. 106.

40. HALS DSA4/93/1 and 2, tithe map and award for Sawbridgeworth, 1838.

41. *Ibid*.

42. Page, *Hertford*, 3, p. 340, citing Feet of Fines Hertfordshire Hil. 1 Hen. V (TNA: PRO CP25/1/91/108).

43. Page, *Hertford*, 3, pp. 374–5, citing Feet of Fines Hertfordshire Mich. 24 Chas II (TNA: PRO CP25/2/622/24CHASIIMICH).

Figure 51. *An ancient pollard, sole survivor from the former Pisho park, Sawbridgeworth.*

44. Page, *Hertford*, 3, p. 340, citing Charter Roll 1–20 Hen. VI, no. 41 (TNA: PRO C53/187).

45. *Cal. Chart. 1427–1516*, p. 98. This grant was re-confirmed to his great-grandson, Thomas, in 1517 (Page, *Hertford*, 3, p. 340 citing Letters and Papers Hen. VIII, ii (2), 3730) (TNA).

46. Page, *Hertford*, 3, p. 340.

47. Page, *Hertford*, 3, p. 375 citing Feet of Fines Hertfordshire Mich. 24 Chas. II (TNA: PRO CP25/2/622/24CHASIIMICH).

48. Hugh Prince lists a Philip Halton at Shingle Hall in 1695 but this name does not appear on the 'Table of the nobility and gentry' accompanying

Oliver's county map (Prince, *Parks in Hertfordshire*, p. 46).

49. HALS DE/Cd/T36 deeds, 1706.

50. Rowe, *Garden making*, pp. xx–xxi.

51. HALS DE/Cd/T36 deed to produce title deeds, 1754.

52. Page, *Hertford*, 3, p. 340, citing Cussans, *History of Hertfordshire*, 1, Braughing Hundred, p. 82.

53. HALS DE/X52/P4 and P4A Thorley tithe map and award, 1845.

54. HALS DSA4/93/1 and 2 Sawbridgeworth tithe award and map, 1838 and 1839.

55. HALS DE/Cd/T36 deeds, 1706.

Shenley

Salisbury Park

NGR: TL198023
Date range: not known – perhaps early seventeenth century
Size: not known; perhaps *c.*218 acres
Underlying geology: Upper Chalk on the lower ground with Reading Beds and London Clay capped with Pebble Gravel on the highest ground

NO CLEAR DOCUMENTARY EVIDENCE for a medieval park at Shenley has been found. A field called '*Parkefeld*' was recorded in a rental of the manor of Holmes alias Cannons of 1386.[1] This manor had been granted early in the thirteenth century to the prior and canons of St Bartholomew, of West Smithfield, London.[2] The field name, by itself, does not constitute evidence of a deer park.

A park was shown at Shenley by Saxton on his county map of 1577 and Norden seems to have shown the same park in 1598 and labelled it 'Salsebery'. This house was the home of John Montagu, third Earl of Salisbury, at the end of the fourteenth century.[3] The property belonged to his wife, Maud, and she continued to live there until she died in 1424. Their descendants included the next earl of Salisbury and, subsequently, John, Earl of Northumberland and Marquess of Montagu, but it seems unlikely that they took much interest in the manor.

Perhaps the strongest evidence for a medieval park lies in a comment written by the traveller John Leland about Sir John Cuttes who owned the Salisbury estate in the early sixteenth century and died in 1521. He recorded that 'Old Cutte' had married an heiress who brought him land worth £200 a year. 'He built at Childerley in Cambridgeshire, Salisbury Park near

St Albans, and Horham Hall ... near Thaxted in Essex'.[4] If Cuttes built a house 'at Salisbury Park' it suggests that the park was already there and that it had been created (or at least owned) by an earl of Salisbury, either at the end of the fourteenth century or during the fifteenth century. This must be the park depicted by Saxton in 1577. No park was shown on seventeenth-century county maps, by which time it had presumably been disparked.

The area of parkland shown on Map 54 is purely conjectural and assumes that the park *was* medieval in origin and incorporated Salisbury Hall and a cluster of early nineteenth-century park field names around Shenley Lodge – a part of the estate which became separated in the late nineteenth century.[5] The field names are most likely to relate to the post-medieval parkland developed around Shenley Lodge but the same land would also have made a good park in earlier centuries. The area which has been shaded as possible parkland covers 218 acres.

1. Gover *et al.*, *Place-names of Hertfordshire*, p. 274. See TNA: PRO SC11/297 detailed rental of the manor of Shenley Holmes (alias Cannons), 1385/6.

2. Page, *Hertford*, 2, p. 271, citing Charter Roll 6 Ric. II, No. 7 (TNA: PRO C53/159).

3. S. O'Connor, 'Montagu, Maud, countess of Salisbury (*d.* 1424)', *Oxford dictionary of national biography* (Oxford, 2004), accessed online 7 November 2007.

4. Chandler, *John Leland's itinerary*, pp. 245–6. The comment is not dated but was probably written in the 1530s.

5. HALS DE/Bn/P44 map of Shenley Lodge estate, 1829.

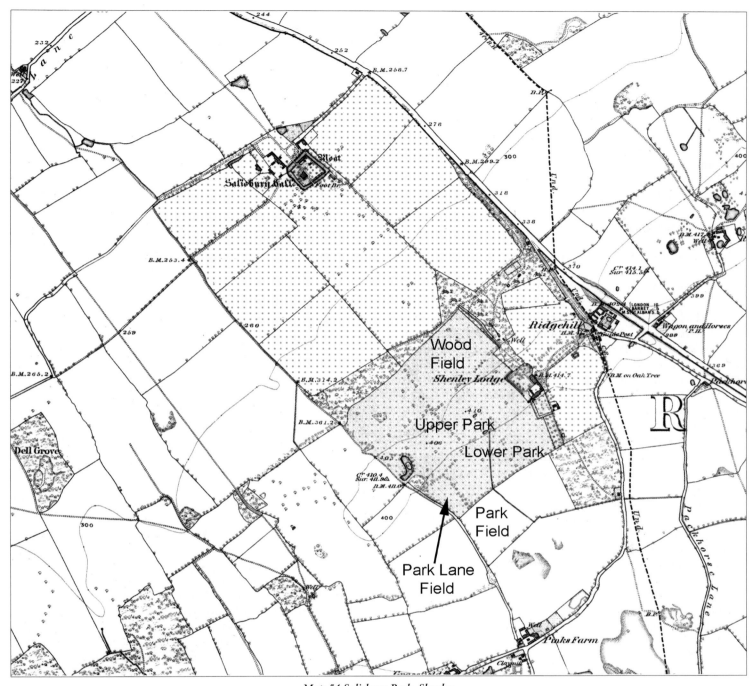

Map 54 Salisbury Park, Shenley
OS 6 inches to the mile map sheet XL, surveyed 1870–3, published 1877. Annotated with field names derived from a map of the Shenley Lodge estate, 1829
(HALS DE/Bn/P44).

203

Standon

Standon park

NGR: TL405206
Date range: by 1234 – early eighteenth century
Size: c.560 acres
Underlying geology: boulder clay

THE MANOR OF STANDON was held by the de Clare family after the Norman Conquest. The *caput* of their barony was at Clare in Suffolk but they also had extensive estates elsewhere. Gilbert de Clare became Earl of Gloucester *c.*1218 and died in 1230.[1] His vast estates were inherited by his young son, Richard (born 1222), and Standon was granted to Gilbert Marshal, Earl of Pembroke, during Richard's minority.[2] Richard came of age in 1243[3], after the first record of the park which occurs in the manorial account for 1234/5, so it seems likely that Richard's father, Gilbert de Clare, or his grandfather, Richard de Clare, created the park at Standon in the late twelfth or early thirteenth century.[4] In 1262, when Earl Richard died, the park was said to be about two leagues in circumference (about six miles) and was valued for its pannage (3 shillings), pasture (30 shillings), underwood and deadwood (two marks (26s 8d)).[5] The park was to survive, apparently with little or no change to its boundaries, for 500 years.

There are many references to the medieval park in royal and manorial records. The account for 1234/5 recorded 'payment to a certain servant for keeping the park and crops in the fields for 7 weeks and 1 day, 6s 8d, at 3 halfpennies per day'.[6] The manor descended to Earl Richard's son, Gilbert Earl of Gloucester, and in 1273/4 Philip Midday, who received 40 shillings a year, was his parker.[7] In 1290/1 agistment of animals in the park was worth 41s 3d, 4s 8d was received for pannage of pigs and 7s 6d for *loppes* and fallen wood (*escaeta*) from 13 oaks pollarded in the park. This timber was used to repair the bridge in Standon. A further 3 shillings was received for the sale of the old lodge (*veter' Logge*), the earliest reference to a park lodge in the county.[8] Gilbert died in 1295 and his son, also Gilbert, inherited the manor and park at the age of four. He was granted seisin of the Clare estates by Edward II on the death of his mother in 1307 and was styled earl of Gloucester and Hertford when only sixteen.[9] Two sets of manorial accounts survive from Gilbert's lifetime, one from the period before the death of his mother and the other from when he was in his early twenties. These reveal little about the park apart from revenue of between 14 and 15 shillings in both years from the agistment of young steers and foals.[10]

Gilbert de Clare died at the battle of Bannockburn in 1314 and his estates were subsequently divided between his three sisters. Standon passed to Elizabeth, widow of John de Burgh, in 1317 after a period in the hands of the king while the partition of the Clare estates was finalised.[11] During this period Edward II sent his professional huntsmen with their dogs to take deer in the park at Standon to provide venison for the next sitting of parliament at Westminster.[12] Elizabeth de Burgh was widowed for the third and final time in 1322 and held Standon as part of her Clare inheritance until she died in 1360. There is an excellent run of accounts for the whole of this period, and beyond, which reveal regular revenues from agistment of animals, usually young steers and foals. The numbers of animals grazing in the park for which agistment was paid were not large and the sums recorded in the accounts examined between 1305 and 1363 ranged from 3s 4d (1358) to 22s (1336), significantly less than the 41s 3d received from agistment in 1291.[13] Pannage of pigs rarely produced any income – usually because of a lack of acorns or beech mast – but 1322 must have been a good mast year, as 15s 2d was recorded in the accounts.[14]

The park was a significant source of timber and wood, and sales were recorded in the accounts up to the end of the fourteenth century. Oak was by far the commonest species mentioned and was used for repairing buildings on the manor or the bridges at Standon. For example, eight oaks were taken from the park for the watermill at Latchford in 1328/9 and five oaks were felled for the 'great bridge' in 1335/6.[15] Much felling of timber occurred in 1328/9 when 66 oaks in the park were sold for £9. Another three oaks were sold for 26 shillings and 18d was received for 'one old oak and dobit'. Beside the eight oaks felled for Latchford mill, a further ten oaks were lopped and coppiced (*copic*') and five beech trees were also felled 'for the said works'.[16]

The hedges around and within the park were also a source of revenue during the middle years of the fourteenth century, presumably being sold for fuel. The selling price of the hedges ranged from ½d and 1d per perch for 'old hedge' (*haie*) to 2d per perch for (?overgrown) hedge. This produced revenue of 4s 6d (at ½d per perch) in both 1337/8 and 1354/5 and 3s 4d in 1362/3 at 1d per perch. In 1357/8 303 perches (about 1,500m) of old hedge were sold at ½d per perch (12s 7½d) and a further 71 perches of (?overgrown) hedge were sold for 2d per perch (11s 10d) some of which was used by Elizabeth de Burgh when she was at Standon. The majority of these hedges were 'in' rather than 'around' the park, indicating that the park was subdivided into compartments. It cost 2d per perch to make a new hedge: 97 perches were made around the park in 1354/5, 362 perches in 1357/8 and 264 perches in 1362/3.[17]

The old lodge sold in 1290/1 must have been replaced because the wall and roof were repaired in 1335/6 for 12d. Just two years later a new lodge was built, requiring eight oaks from the park. A marginal note in the accounts indicates that the total cost of the new lodge was 75s 8½d.[18]

On the death of Elizabeth de Burgh in 1360 Standon passed to her granddaughter and then to her great-granddaughter,

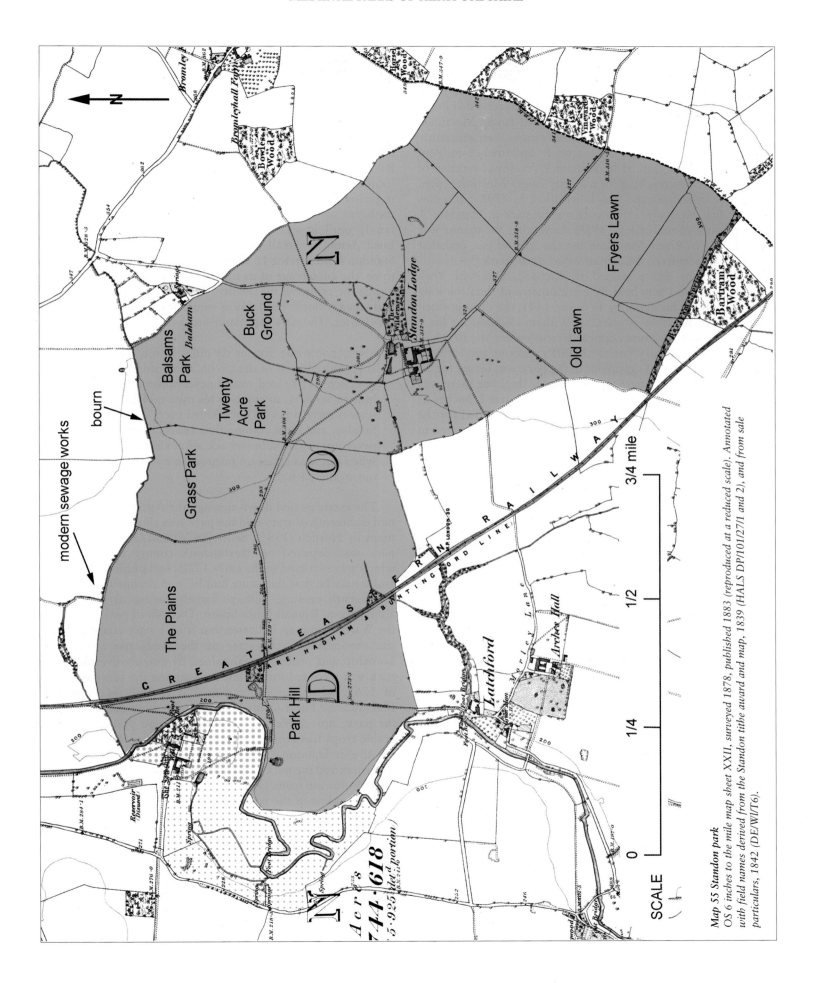

Map 55 Standon park
OS 6 inches to the mile map sheet XXII, surveyed 1878, published 1883 (reproduced at a reduced scale). Annotated with field names derived from the Standon tithe award and map, 1839 (HALS DP/101/27/1 and 2), and from sale particulars, 1842 (DE/Vl/T6).

Philippa, in 1369/70. Philippa was married to Edmund Mortimer, Earl of March, who died in 1381. During their tenure the demesne lands were farmed out to a Collector of Rents and little activity relating to the park was recorded in the account of 1372/3.[19] During the minority of Roger Mortimer, son and heir of Edmund, the Mortimer estates were efficiently run by a council headed by his uncle and the custody of Standon park was granted to William Wynselowe, yeoman of the chamber.[20] On reaching his majority Roger Mortimer spent much time in Ireland and was killed there in 1398.[21] It seems unlikely that he made any impact on the park at Standon. A short account compiled for 1395/6 shows that the manor was being leased to Roger Marescall for £66 13s 4d p.a. and that 4s 4d was raised from the sale of wood in the park.[22]

In 1425 the estate passed to Richard, Duke of York (1411–1460), and was held by his mother and then the king until he attained his majority. In about 1441, the duke granted the manor to his close adviser, Sir William Oldhall, for life.[23] Unfortunately no accounts appear to survive for the first half of the fifteenth century but the bailiff's account for 1459/60 shows that the farm of agistment in the park was leased for 24 shillings. There was a parker (paid 2d per day) but there was no pannage and no sale of wood, underwood, tree branches or 'brusshett' in the park. A rabbit warren was recorded for the first time but it is not clear whether or not this was located in the park.[24] On the death of the duke in 1460, the manor descended to his son, who became Edward IV the following year and granted Standon to his mother Cicely, Duchess of York.[25] In 1461/2 the farm of agistment had risen to 40 shillings and covered both the summer and wintertime. The park boundary received some attention: 5 shillings was paid for 'berdyng' 60 perches (c.300m) of fence or hedge (sepis) in those places where it most needed repair.[26] Repairs were still ongoing a decade later but in 1468/9 218 perches of dead hedge (sepie morte) were 'new made' on the northern side of the park at a cost of 45s 5d (2½d per perch).[27]

In 1476 Cicely granted to 'her servant John Felde, squire, the office of keeping her park of Standon, taking the accustomed fees with all other profits'.[28] This was a new breed of parker, who was granted the position as a financial perk but did not engage in the hands-on park management of his predecessors. The earliest recorded 'servant' with responsibility for Standon park in 1235 was paid ¾d per day; a century later this had risen to 1½d per day; by 1358 (after the Black Death) it was 2d per day (60s 8d p.a.) and it was to stay at this rate for at least the next 175 years![29]

The duchess of York died in 1495 and in 1504 Henry VII's servant Francis Marzen, groom of the chamber, was granted

the office of bailiff of the lordship of Standon, … and of the keeping of the manor and park of Standon for life, with the usual fees and the profits of the coneys, the herbage and pannage and other emoluments, in as full a manner as John Flygh, late yeoman of the robes, held the same.[30]

In the early sixteenth century the manor of Standon was held in turn by Henry VIII's queens, Katherine of Aragon and Jane Seymour. An account from 1533/4 records that 89 rods of pale were 'new made' in the west part of Standon park at a

cost of 4½d per rod plus 2 shillings for the carriage of six wagon-loads of pales (35s 4½d in total). In addition, 10 shillings was spent on providing hay as winter feed for the deer from a meadow in the park.[31] In 1539 Ralph Sadleir was appointed 'parker' and the following year obtained a 'grant of the manor with the park and warren'.[32] In 1546 he began building a grand house in the park on the west side of the river Rib. The earliest county maps give conflicting evidence on the location of the house in relation to the park (see Figure 23) but it seems most likely that Sadleir's house stood within the medieval park. The estate passed down through the Sadleir family until it was inherited, through marriage, by Walter Lord Aston of Tixall in Staffordshire in 1660. He lived at Standon Lordship for 18 years, a period which was considered to be 'the golden age of its history, during which it became for a time the centre of the county'.[33] Every evening, between five and seven o'clock, Lord Aston would 'stroll about the park' in his chariot. The park was described as

a very noble one, five or six miles about, with five or six hundred head of deer, with about thirty or forty red deer. … My lord would never suffer any but hunted venison, to come to his own table: for all the season there was one buck killed every day but Sunday, and most commonly a brace, though my lord never appeared on horseback a-buckhunting, unless when one was taken on purpose in a toil and turned out of the park.[34]

The estate passed down through the Aston family until the mid eighteenth century and the park was shown on the county maps by Norden (1595), Seller (1676) and Oliver (1695). No park was depicted on Warburton's county map, however, which was surveyed in the early 1720s and published in 1749, and it may be that the estate had been in decline from the late seventeenth century, perhaps largely owing to the Astons' adherence to Roman Catholicism. The lack of park palings on the Warburton map indicates that it no longer contained deer but the park-like character of the landscape around the Lordship was probably maintained by grazing livestock. The park was recorded for the last time among the sale particulars of 1767, when the estate was sold to William Plumer of Blakesware,[35] but it seems likely that the more distant parts of the park, not visible from the house, were ploughed up for arable crops from the early eighteenth century. Mr Plumer did not live at Standon Lordship: the house was allowed to fall into ruins and the park was presumably turned over entirely to agricultural use from 1767.[36]

The outline of the park proposed in Map 55 is based on a combination of documentary, cartographic and field evidence. The length of the boundary is about five miles, rather less than the two leagues (approximately six miles) recorded in 1262. It encloses an area of about 560 acres, making it the sixth-largest medieval park in Hertfordshire. For much of its length the proposed park boundary follows the boundary of the Lordship estate as indicated on the Standon enclosure map of 1835.[37] The eastern boundary also runs along the parish boundary between Standon and Much Hadham. The southern boundary is marked by Bartrams Spring – a narrow strip of woodland with a deep, modern ditch on its north side and a degraded

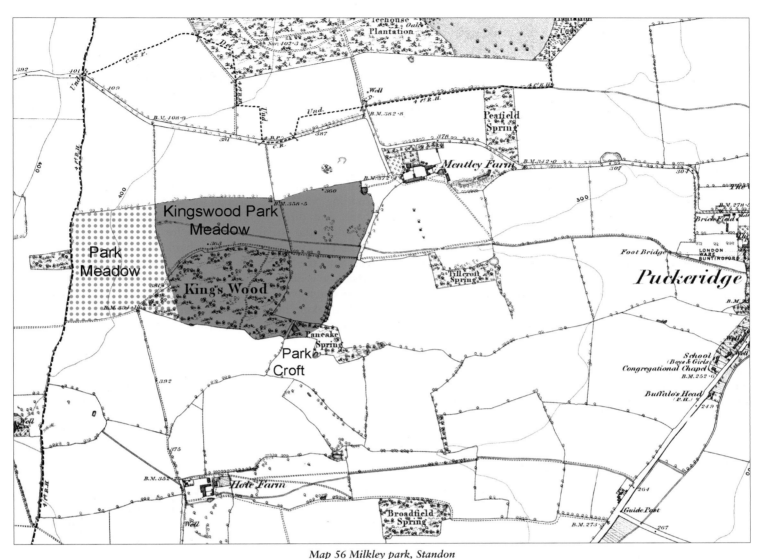

Map 56 Milkley park, Standon

OS 6 inches to the mile map sheet XXII, surveyed 1878, published 1883. Annotated with field names from the Standon tithe award and map, 1839 (HALS DP/101/27/1 and 2).

bank to the south of that and perhaps a further bank along the south side of the wood. A deep bourn formed the northern park boundary westwards from Balsams as far as what is now the sewage works, where the bourn turns sharply northwards. The park boundary, however, continued westwards and one of the best surviving stretches of bank can be seen just beyond the northward turn in the footpath at the sewage works, where it is topped by old hornbeam coppice stools. The bank is about 5m across and up to 1m high. Further west the line of the boundary has been lost between the former railway line and the river Rib. Two possible courses are suggested by map and field evidence: the first (shown on Map 55) follows the line of a drainage channel to the river; the second heads slightly north of west to join up with the remains of a hedge-bank which rises up the steep slope on the west side of the river. A lack of good field evidence on the west side of the river means that the boundary is plotted with less confidence here than on the east.

Field names shown on the tithe map and award of 1839, and elsewhere, which indicate former parkland have been added to the map.[38] One park field name, Stags Park (not shown), lies some distance west of The Lordship, perhaps indicating that the park once extended further west than shown in Map 55.

However, this field lay partly on what had previously been a common field, Stanborough Common, before enclosure. The park is unlikely to have contained a common field and, therefore, most probably did not extend this far west.

A park of Standon's longevity could be expected to have had an effect on the local network of roads and tracks and today the entire eastern half of the park boundary is followed by public footpaths. East of the Rib the land in the park rises fairly rapidly to a boulder clay plateau about 80m OD but then rises further to the east and south to 90–110m OD, with lovely views of the surrounding landscape. Standon Lodge Farm occupies a good vantage point in the centre of the park. It probably marks the site of former medieval lodges and lay adjacent to a series of ponds (joined to form a lake in recent years) which would have formed an important source of water for the deer and livestock in this higher part of the park. The oldest part of the present building is thought to date from the seventeenth century.[39]

The first edition OS map of 1883 shows there were still a few trees remaining in the fields to the north of Standon Lodge Farm in the late nineteenth century (Map 55), but the former park is virtually devoid of old trees today. The only tree which may have been growing in the park is an old ash pollard on the valley side about 500m west of The Lordship Cottages. In 1751 the last Lord Aston left the estate to his two daughters.[40] A local tradition relates how one sister inherited the house and estate, the other all the timber on the estate. A quarrel ensued and the owner of the timber had it all felled, which may explain the lack of trees today.

Milkley park

NGR: TL372234
Date range: by 1323 – perhaps early fifteenth century
Size: perhaps 53 – 75 acres
Underlying geology: boulder clay

THIS RELATIVELY SMALL PARK belonged to the manor of Milkley (later Mentley) and lay in the vicinity of King's Wood on high ground at *c.*115m OD, about three-quarters of a mile west of the village of Puckeridge. This is the north-west corner of the parish of Standon and the park may have abutted (or at least come very close to) the parish boundary with Great Munden, which runs north–south along the watershed. The park occupied the valley of a small stream (the northern Puckeridge Tributary) and the pasture fields lying north and south of this stream at the eastern end of King's Wood retain a park-like appearance even today. They contain some quite steep slopes and appear not to have been ploughed, preserving some interesting earthworks and several old trees. King's Wood is ancient bluebell woodland on boulder clay soils with old hornbeam coppice stools and oak standards.

In 1311 Robert de Milkley, together with William le Baud and his wife and heirs, received a grant of free warren in all their demesne lands in Standon, Braughing and Much Hadham.[41] William le Baud was holding the manor when his lands were forfeited in the rebellion of Thomas Earl of Lancaster in 1321 and Milkley was still being held by the crown when the park was broken into in 1323.[42] In November 1323 a commission of oyer and terminer heard that Thomas de Bassele, master of the hospital of Standon, and more than 14 other men, 'broke the king's parks of Little Hadham and Melkeleye, co. Hertford, hunted therein and carried away deer'.[43] This is the only known medieval reference to the park at Milkley, but in 1345 a William le Parker was constable of Puckeridge and Standon. The constable was normally resident in the village of Puckeridge and William was, therefore, perhaps more likely to have been the parker of Milkley park than Standon park to the south.[44]

Milkley park was documented again in the middle of the sixteenth century, when the manor was again being held by the crown. A survey of 1556 recorded that there were 24$^1/_2$ acres of woods over and above what was needed by the lessee of the manor. Two parts of that woodland were in 'Milkeley parke': one of 3$^1/_2$ acres and 22 years' growth, worth 40 shillings per acre and ready to be sold; the other of 8 acres, which had been sold three years previously for 40 shillings per acre and was now worth 6 shillings per acre.[45] Although no longer functioning as a deer park, Milkley park evidently continued to be a recognisable feature in the landscape and was generating valuable revenue for the manor from sales of wood.

A number of 'park' field names survived into the nineteenth century in the vicinity of King's Wood and were recorded on the Standon tithe map and award in 1839.[46] These include Park Meadow, Kingswood Park Meadow and Park Croft (see Map 56). There is a major field boundary along the north side of Kingswood Park Meadow, extending eastwards as a broad, very slight, bank (approximately 4m across) towards Mentley Farmhouse in the field to the east. Unfortunately many of the field boundary ditches have been mechanically excavated and probably over-deepened, making it difficult to assess their historic importance. Banks run along the northern and southern boundaries of King's Wood and a broad shallow bank running NNW–SSE through the wood continues the line of the bank and ditch forming the west side of Kingswood Park Meadow and possibly marks the former park boundary on the west. The area enclosed by this bank and the hollow-way to the east and the boundary on the north side of Kingswood Park Meadow is about 53 acres. However, the park could have been more extensive than this and if, for example, Park Meadow is added, taking the park westwards to the parish boundary, then the area would have been nearer 75 acres.

Besides possible boundary banks, there are other interesting earthworks preserved in the area of the former park. In the field east of Kingswood Park Meadow are the remains of pits dug into the valley sides, together with platforms for buildings and a trackway. There are also apparent trackways continuing eastwards into the next field, heading towards Puckeridge. These earthworks may relate to a tile-works recorded at Milkley in 1422, when Thomas Baud made a grant of the tile-house with land and a pasture and 'free entrance and exit for carrying tiles by three ways'.[47] Thomas Baud was sheriff of Hertfordshire in 1446/7 but his main residence was at Hadham Hall, where he had a park which was probably considerably larger than the one at Milkley (see p. 169).[48] The presence of the tile-works in 1422 suggests that Milkley park had fallen out of use as an enclosure for deer by the early fifteenth century.

1. T.A. Archer, 'Clare, Gilbert de, fifth earl of Gloucester and fourth earl of Hertford (*c.*1180–1230)', rev. Michael Altschul, *Oxford dictionary of national biography* (Oxford, 2004; online edn, Oct 2005), accessed 2 October 2007.

2. Page, *Hertford*, 3, p. 352, citing *Cal. Close 1231–1234*, p. 482.

3. M. Altschul, 'Clare, Richard de, sixth earl of Gloucester and fifth earl of Hertford (1222–1262)', *Oxford dictionary of national biography* (Oxford, 2004), accessed online 2 October 2007.

4. TNA: PRO SC6/1109/6 ministers' and receivers' accounts, 1233–37.

5. Page, *Hertford*, 3, p. 353, citing Chancery Inquisition *post mortem* Hen. III, file 27, no. 5 (TNA: PRO C132/27/5); Clutterbuck, *History of Hertfordshire*, 3, p. 224.

6. TNA: PRO SC6/1109/6 ministers' and receivers' accounts, 1233–37. I am grateful to Dr Jonathan Mackman at The National Archives for this translation.

7. TNA: PRO SC6/1109/12 ministers' and receivers' accounts, 1273/4. Philip Midday (or his descendent) was still the parker forty years later.

8. TNA: PRO SC6/868/16 reeve's account, 1290/1.

9. M. Altschul, 'Clare, Gilbert de, eighth earl of Gloucester and seventh earl of Hertford (1291–1314)', *Oxford dictionary of national biography* (Oxford, 2004), accessed online 3 October 2007.

10. TNA: PRO SC6/868/17 and 18 ministers' accounts for Standon, 1304/5 and 1312/13.

11. J.C. Ward, 'Clare, Elizabeth de (1294/5–1360)', *Oxford dictionary of national biography* (Oxford, 2004), accessed online 3 October 2007.

12. *Cal. Close 1313–1318*, pp. 140–1; the huntsmen were also sent to the dead earl's parks at Hundon in Suffolk and Great Bardfield, Essex. The keeper of Standon's park at this time was Philip Middey (*Ibid.*, p. 411).

13. TNA: PRO SC6/868/17, 18 and 21 minister's accounts, 1304/5, 1312/3 and 1335/6; SC6/869/11, 12 and 14 minister's accounts 1354/5, 1357/8 and 1362/3. NB there are several accounts which have not been examined.

14. TNA: PRO SC6/1147/9 minister's account, 1322/3.

15. TNA: PRO SC6/868/20 and 21 ministers' accounts, 1328/9 and 1335/6.

16. TNA: PRO SC6/868/20 minister's account, 1328/9.

17. TNA: PRO SC6/868/23 minister's account, 1337/8; SC6/869/11, 12 and 14 minister's accounts 1354/5, 1357/8 and 1362/3.

18. TNA: PRO SC6/868/23 minister's account, 1337/8.

19. Page, *Hertford*, 3, p. 353; TNA: PRO SC6/869/15 minister's account, 1372/3.

20. *Cal. Pat. 1381–1385*, p. 93.

21. R.R. Davies, 'Mortimer, Roger (VII), fourth earl of March and sixth earl of Ulster (1374–1398)', *Oxford dictionary of national biography* (Oxford, September 2004; online edn, May 2006), accessed online 3 October 2007.

22. TNA: PRO SC6/870/1 account of Roger Marescall, farmer of the manor, 1395/6.

23. Page, *Hertford*, 3, p. 353, citing *Cal. Pat. 1436–1441*, p. 473; Curry, 'Oldhall, Sir William'.

24. TNA: PRO SC6/870/4 bailiff's account, 1459/60.

25. Page, *Hertford*, 3, p. 353.

26. TNA: PRO SC6/870/5 bailiff's account, 1461/2.

27. TNA: PRO SC6/870/6 bailiff's account, 1468/9.

28. *Cal. Pat. 1476–1485*, p. 599.

29. TNA: PRO ministers' and receivers' accounts: SC6/1109/6, 1233–37; SC6/868/21, 1335/6; SC6/869/12, 1357/8; SC6/HENVIII/6629, 1533/4.

30. *Cal. Pat. 1494–1509*, p. 356. For John Flygh's appointment see *Ibid.*, p. 111.

31. TNA: PRO SC6/HENVIII/6629 bailiff's account, 1533/4.

32. Page, *Hertford*, 3, p. 353 — Sadleir had been appointed keeper of the site, parker, bailiff of the manor and steward of the lordship the previous year.

33. C. Perowne, *A history of the parish of Standon* (Hertford, 1967), p. 89.

34. J. Morris, *Troubles of our Catholic forefathers* (London, 1872), pp. 403–4, quoting Sir Edward Southcote, grandson of Lord Aston.

35. Page, *Hertford*, 3, p. 354.

36. See painting by J.C. Buckler, 1834, at HALS DE/Bg/2, p. 83.

37. HALS QS/E/61 Standon enclosure map, 1835.

38. HALS DP/101/27/1 and 2 tithe award and map, 1839; also DE/Wl/T6 sale particulars, 1842.

39. HALS Department of the Environment, List of Buildings.

40. Page, *Hertford*, 3, p. 354.

41. *Cal. Chart. 1300–1326*, p. 183.

42. Page, *Hertford*, 3, p. 360, citing *Parliamentary Writs* (Records Commission), ii, App. 178.

43. *Cal. Pat. 1321–1324*, p. 383. Hadham Hall at Little Hadham was another of William le Baud's manors, where he also had a park. His lands were restored to him on the accession of Edward III in 1327.

44. I am grateful to Kathryn Shreeve for this information.

45. TNA: PRO E315/391 survey of Hertfordshire manors, lands and possessions of King Philip and Queen Mary, 1556.

46. HALS DP/101/27/1 and 2 Standon tithe award and map, 1839.

47. Page, *Hertford*, 3, p. 360, citing Ancient Deeds, D 407 (TNA: PRO E210/407).

48. Salmon, *History of Hertfordshire*, p. 363.

Stanstead Abbots

Easneye park

NGR: TL381134
Date range: 1332 – perhaps early sixteenth century
Size: not known; possibly up to 200 acres
Underlying geology: valley sides: Upper Chalk; plateau: glacial gravel over Reading Beds

THE ABBEY OF WALTHAM HOLY CROSS held the manor of Stanstead Abbots from the thirteenth century, paying rent to the earls of Pembroke.[1] In 1253 the abbey obtained a grant of free warren in their demesne lands and also a licence 'to close two roads through their wood of Isneye and to make two other roads without the said wood'.[2] Nearly 80 years later, in 1332, the abbot was granted a licence 'to impark his wood of Isneye' after an inquisition *ad quod damnum*.[3] No further records of the medieval park have been found and its size is not known.[4]

In 1522 the abbey leased the manor for 61 years (reserving manorial rights) to John Rodes of London and in 1526 Rodes was granted a lease of the lodge in the park 'with the lands belonging' for 57 years.[5] The presence of a lodge in 1526 suggests that the deer park continued in use throughout the fifteenth century and perhaps into the sixteenth. The manor was obtained from the abbey by Henry VIII in 1531 and accounts compiled by John Rodes in 1536/7 record that he was paying rent of 106s 8d for the lodge in Isney Park together with meadows, pastures, 'Lez Laundes' and woods.[6] In Elizabeth's reign John Raymond had a lease of Isney Park together with the Great Farm of Stanstead.[7] There is, however, no evidence that Isney Park was still being used as a deer park in the sixteenth century and no park was shown on the sixteenth-century county maps by Saxton (1577) or Norden (1598), so it is likely that it had been disparked before John Rodes acquired it in 1522.

The 1840 tithe award and map of Stanstead Abbots recorded Henry Wilkinson Esq as the owner and occupier of the wood named 'Easney Park and Cottage', which covered 133a 1r 3p.[8] The 'cottage' was sited on top of the hill, where a large house was later built, and was approached by a track from the north. It presumably originated as the lodge within the medieval park. The park boundary in 1840 was set slightly back from the rivers (the Ash and the Lea) which flowed along its north and west sides but much of the meadow land between the park's northern boundary and the river Ash was also owned by Mr Wilkinson, suggesting that the river Ash had formed the northern boundary of the park in earlier times.

The land lying south of the Easeney Park woodland in 1840 was occupied by Warren Farm and Halving Farm, both of which were also owned by Mr Wilkinson. Field names suggest that Warren Farm was a rabbit warren. The estate was acquired by Thomas Buxton in 1866, when 'Isney was still a thick wood'.[9] He built the present house in 1869 and it was described as standing in a park of 133 acres, approached from the south by an avenue of trees nearly a mile long.[10] Buxton's new park incorporated land belonging to Warren and Halving Farms, with extensive woodland to the north.

The wood, known as Easeney Park Wood in the nineteenth century and Easneye Wood today, still exists in the north-west corner of the parish of Stanstead Abbots near the confluence of the river Ash with the Lea. On the north and west sides of the wood the land rises steeply from the rivers, reaching a plateau at about 65m OD, from which there are extensive views reaching southwards down the Lea valley as far as the city of London. The wood is a mixture of ancient and semi-natural woodland with areas of old hornbeam coppice, some fine specimen trees, including beech, and some replanted areas.[11] The ground flora includes extensive spreads of snowdrops, daffodils and bluebells.

A public footpath follows the eastern side of the nineteenth-century park northwards, then continues around the eastern end of Easneye Wood. The degraded remains of a possible park boundary bank can be seen running parallel with this footpath on its west side. There is a substantial bank along the north-east side of the wood at *c*.TL387137 but this may be marking the parish boundary rather than the boundary of the medieval park. On the north side of the wood a pasture field slopes down to the river Ash and a marked lynchet follows the contour part-way down the slope for several hundred metres. This may also mark a former park boundary.

Within the wood are the remains of old trackways: one is marked on the first edition OS as a track running east of, and parallel with, the Hollycross Road; another, also marked on the OS map, runs down to the north-east side of the wood in a hollow-way about 3m deep. These may be the roads which were closed to the public in the mid thirteenth century. Their replacements, re-routed outside the wood, are quite likely to have been the footpath which bounds the east side of the nineteenth-century park and wood and the Hollycross Road, running around the west side of the park. The Hollycross Road was diverted westwards at the beginning of the twentieth century but its original route can still be traced within the wood. The east side of the road is bounded by a significant bank at TL377134, topped with hornbeam stubbs, which may well have formed the western boundary of the medieval deer park.[12]

If the medieval park occupied the whole of the area between these two routes, with the river Ash forming the northern boundary, it would have covered approximately 200 acres.

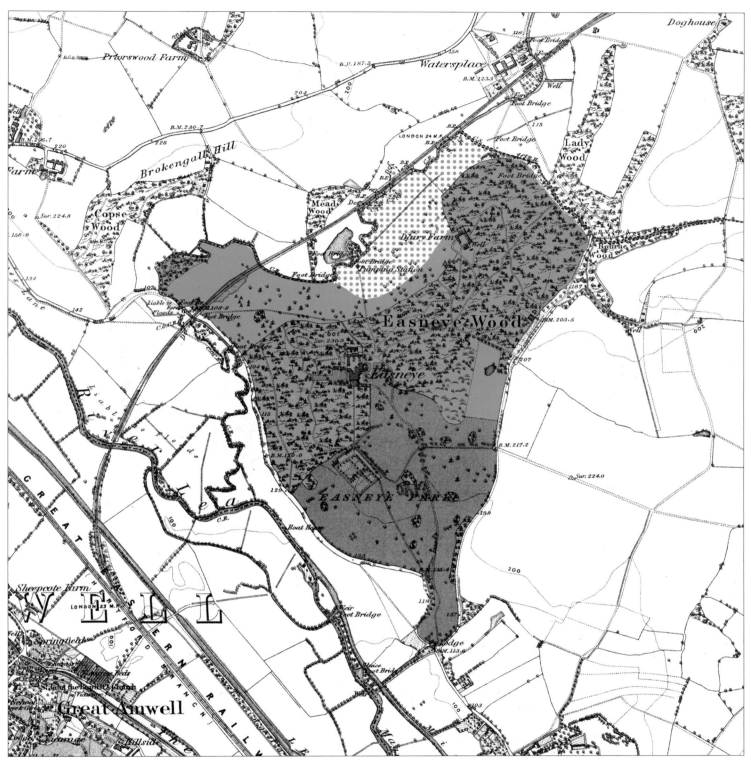

Map 57 Easneye park, Stanstead Abbots
OS 6 inches to the mile map sheet XXX, surveyed 1873–80, published 1881–3.

Rye park

NGR: TL387100
Date range: 1443 – perhaps sixteenth century
Size: c.157 acres
Underlying geology: flood plain gravel and alluvium

In 1443 SIR ANDREW OGARD obtained a licence to inclose the site of his manor of Rye alias the Island of Rye and 50 acres of land, 10 acres of meadow, 80 acres of pasture and 16 acres of wood within the island, to make a park and have free warren, and to crenellate the house.[13] The low-lying Isle of Rye, on the flood plain between the rivers Lea and Stort, was an unusual location for a medieval park but presumably came with ready-made watery barriers to help keep any deer within the park. The park was bounded by the river Lea on the west and a ditch running from the Lea to the Stort on the east and covered about 157 acres. The boundary of the park shown in Map 58 is based on a map published in 1902 by R.T. Andrews, who researched the extent of the manor.[14]

Andrew Ogard was born in Denmark of a distinguished family and was naturalised in England in 1433.[15] He was chamberlain to the Duke of Bedford in 1435 and was a wealthy man with lands in Norfolk as well as Hertfordshire, where he served as a Justice of the Peace on several occasions in the 1440s.[16] He built an ornate and substantial fortified manor house on the 'island of Rye' and surrounded it with a park to enhance its setting and prestige. R.T. Andrews quoted an extract from the itinerary of the fifteenth-century traveller William of Worcester, which provides a detailed description of the moated manor house in the 1470s. One clause states: 'From ye utter gate to ye logge paled and parked yn every side, ys yn length 360 tayllors yards.'[17] This confirms that a park was established by Ogard and indicates that there was also a lodge. Only the gatehouse remains standing, but it is considered to be one of the finest examples of early English brickwork in the country. Ogard's favoured residence, however, seems to have been at Bradenham in Norfolk. He was patron of Wymondham Priory and was instrumental in having the priory converted into an abbey in 1449.[18] He died 'at Bockenham' (there is a farm of that name in Bradenham) in 1454 and was buried in Wymondham Abbey church; his widow, Alice, was also buried in Wymondham, in 1460.[19]

Sir Andrew Ogard left his estates to his four-year-old son, Henry. During Henry's minority the manor of Rye was granted to the king's brother, George, Duke of Clarence. The manor subsequently passed down through two further generations of the Ogard family before being sold in 1559. No further record of the park has come to light and there is no good evidence that it ever contained deer. No park was shown on Saxton's county map (1577), but Norden (1598) did depict a park between Stanstead church and Roydon on the banks of the river Stort which may have been Rye Park; if so, it was plotted very inaccurately.

A number of 'park' field names did survive long enough to be recorded in seventeenth- and eighteenth-century documents. In 1619 the land of the former park was sold to Edward Baesh, the owner of the neighbouring estate of Stanstead Bury. Field names recorded included Little or Hither Park and the Further Park.[20] Late eighteenth-century deeds include a reference to a four-acre Parke Mead.[21] A field name recorded on the Stanstead Abbots tithe map and award suggests that 48 acres of the former park were subsequently used as a rabbit warren (see Map 57).[22]

1. Page, *Hertford*, 3, p. 369.
2. *Cal. Chart. 1226–1257*, p. 427.
3. *Cal. Pat. 1330–1334*, p. 259.
4. Manorial records of the abbey of Waltham Holy Cross, which may hold details of the medieval park, are held in a private archive and have not been accessed (National Register of Archives ref. 23254).
5. Page, *Hertford*, 3, p. 369, citing BL Harley MS. 303, fo. 10 and Ancient Deeds A 640 (TNA: PRO E40/640).
6. TNA: PRO SC6/HENVIII/6012 ministers' accounts, 1536/7.
7. Page, *Hertford*, 3, p. 367, citing Chancery Proceedings (ser. 2), bdle 113, no. 47 (TNA).
8. HALS DSA4/97/1 and 2 Stanstead Abbots tithe award and map, 1840.
9. Page, *Hertford*, 3, pp. 367–8.
10. Cussans, *History of Hertfordshire*, 1, p. 31.
11. www.magic.gov.uk
12. I am grateful to Nicholas Buxton for showing me around the wood early in 2008.
13. Page, *Hertford*, 3, p. 367, citing Charter Rolls 21–4 Hen. VI, no. 44 (TNA: PRO C53/188).
14. R.T. Andrews, 'The Rye House castle and manor of Rye', *East Herts Archaeological Society Transactions*, 2 (1902), pp. 32–6.
15. D. Dawson Haggard, 'History of the Haggard family in England and America: 1433–1899', www.surnames.com, accessed 26 August 2007, citing Paston Letters, vol. 1, p. 224. Ogard received 'letters of denization' in 1436 (*Cal. Pat. 1429–1436*, p. 288).
16. Page, *Hertford*, 3, p. 370, citing *Cal. Pat. 1446–1452*, pp. 382, 388 and 537; *1441–1445*, p. 471. According to William of Worcester, Ogard left with Robert Whittingham, receiver-general of the Duke of Bedford, a chest with about 7000 marks in 'French gold' (see Pendley park, Tring).
17. Andrews, 'The Rye House', p. 37, quoting William of Worcester, *Itineraries*, ?1478 or '79.
18. Page, *Norfolk*, 2, pp. 336–43, 'The abbey of Wymondham'.
19. Haggard, 'History of the Haggard family'.
20. Page, *Hertford*, 3, p. 370, citing Common Pleas Deed Enrolled Trin. 17 Jas I, m. 34 (TNA); Mich. 17 Jas I, m. 47 (TNA); Feet of Fines Hertfordshire Easter 18 Jas I (TNA: PRO CP25/2/347/18JASIEASTER). His father Ralph Frankland joined in the sale (Common Pleas Deed Enrolled Mich. 17 Jas I, m. 47) (TNA).
21. HALS DE/Z100/T2 deeds, 1764–91.
22. HALS DSA4/97/1 and 2 Stanstead Abbots tithe award and map, 1839 and 1840.

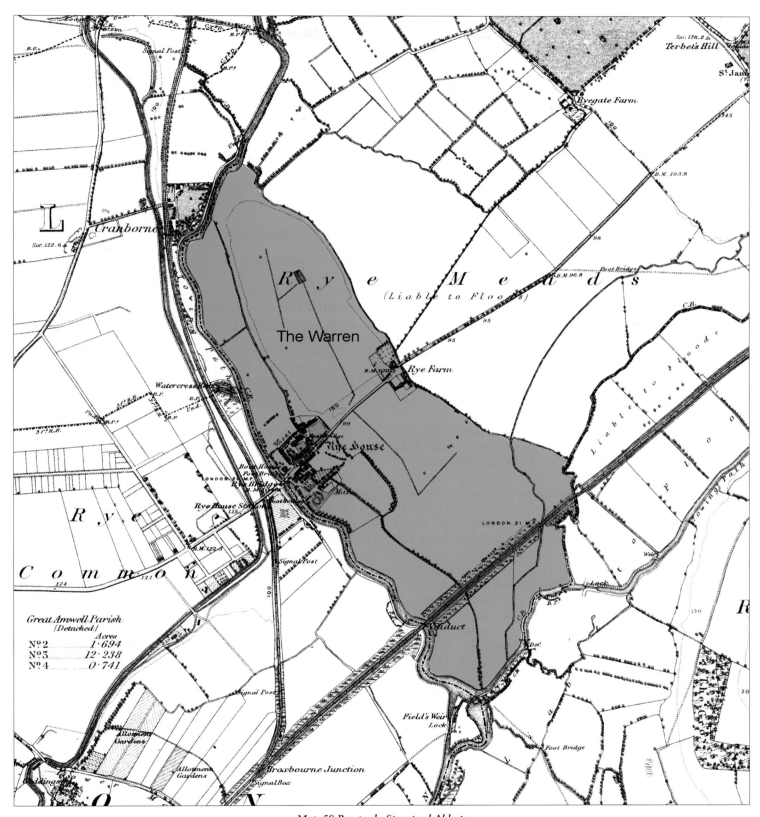

Map 58 Rye park, Stanstead Abbots
OS 6 inches to the mile map sheet XXXVII, surveyed 1870–80, published 1880–2. Field name derived from Stanstead Abbots tithe award and map, 1840
(HALS DSA4/97/1 and 2). Extent of park after R.T. Andrews (1902).

Tring and Aldbury

Pendley park

NGR: SP945115
Date range: 1440 – perhaps early seventeenth century
Size: licence to impark 200 acres in 1440
Underlying geology: Lower and Middle Chalk overlain with valley gravel in the northern part

IN JUNE 1440 KING HENRY VI made a grant, of special grace, to Robert Whityngham and Agnes his wife, and their heirs, of free warren for deer (*damis*) and rabbits in all their demesne lands within their manor of Pendeley *alias* Pendele within the parishes of Tryng and Aldebury, co. Hertford; grant also to the same that they may enclose 200 acres of land within the said parishes with a paling and dike and hold them so enclosed to them and their heirs, so that no one shall enter the said lands to hunt or take aught therein which pertains to a park, without the leave of the said Robert and Alice.[1]

Lionel Munby described Pendley as the 'most outstanding example in Hertfordshire of turning arable and pasture land into a park' and stated that by 1448 the tenants were prevented from exercising their common grazing rights over 80 acres.[2] A sworn statement from a man born over 80 years previously in Pendley was recorded in the court rolls of Aldbury in 1506 and reveals that in the 1420s there was a 'greate towne' at Pendley, lying in the parishes of Tring and Aldbury. At that time there was no

> greate mancion place ther[e] buylded but there was in the said towne above thirteen ploes [ploughs] besydes divers handcrafte men … as taylors, shoemakers and cardmakers with divers others. Thys sayd towne afterward was keste [cast] downe and leyde to pastur[e] by Sir Robert Whittingham, wheche buylded the said place at the weste end ther[e] as the towne some tyme stode, for the towne was in the e[a]st and south parte of the same place.[3]

Subsequent proceedings show that Sir Robert Whittingham also ploughed up a common way, and that in 1491–2 vestiges of the hedges still remained.[4]

Robert Whittingham was a merchant and financier who had a leading role in trade with the continent at the time he was granted permission to enclose his park at Pendley. He had started out as a draper in London by 1407 and inherited city property in 1413 from his uncle, a wealthy London tailor of the same name. He rose through trade and was elected member of parliament for London in 1416 and was sheriff of London in 1419–20. In the 1420s he was appointed receiver-general in England for John, Duke of Bedford, brother of Henry V and regent of France. In 1435 Whittingham was appointed executor of Bedford's estates; he was also trustee of

the estates of several magnates and acted as banker to others, including Sir Andrew Ogard (see Stanstead Abbots, Rye park). In 1436 he became treasurer of Calais and master of the Calais mint; by 1439 he was mayor of the Calais staple and was appointed ambassador on a series of missions on the continent in 1438–41.[5]

At the end of 1441 Whittingham left his post as treasurer of Calais amid a scandal and presumably then had more time to devote to his own properties. As well as owning a substantial house in London, Whittingham had become a country gentleman with properties in Hertfordshire, Buckinghamshire and Berkshire. He was active in Hertfordshire during the 1430s: he was member of parliament for the county in 1432 and sheriff of Essex and Hertfordshire in 1433–4 and 1438–9. His main manor was Pendley and he had built a chapel there by 1442. He died in 1452 and Pendley was inherited by his son, another Sir Robert Whittingham,[6] who held the manor until 1461, when he was attainted for treason; in 1472 it was returned to his daughter, wife of John Verney, and subsequently passed down through several generations before being sold out of the family at the beginning of the seventeenth century.[7]

A park was shown at Pendley by both Saxton (1577) (Figure 52) and Norden (1598) and the latter depicted an east–west road, linking Northchurch and Tring, passing through the south of the park (Figure 53). This suggests that the medieval park had spread southwards into the parish of Wigginton as the road – Akeman Street – was the parish boundary. No park was shown by Seller in 1676 or by Oliver in 1695, so it would seem that the medieval park was disparked by the mid seventeenth century.

The fifteenth-century Pendley Hall lay north-east of the present Pendley Manor, on the site now occupied by Pendley Farm, and was still marked as Pendley Hall on Bryant's county map of 1822. However, the same map also shows a house called 'Park House', which appears to be the forerunner of today's Pendley Manor. Parkland had been reinstated around

Figure 52. *Detail of Saxton's county map showing Pendley park, 1577. Reproduced by kind permission of Hertfordshire Archives and Local Studies.*

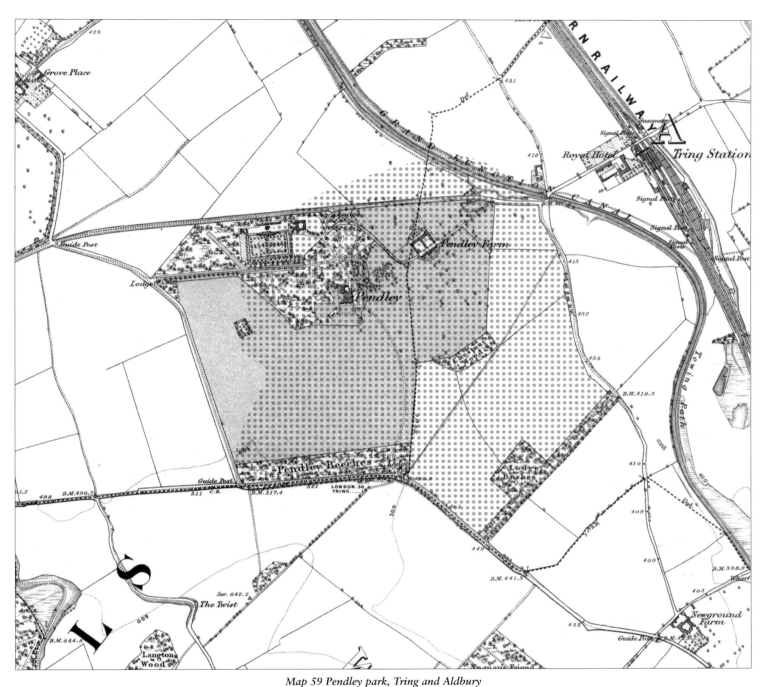

Map 59 Pendley park, Tring and Aldbury
OS 6 inches to the mile map sheet XXV, surveyed 1877–9, published 1884. Showing a conjectural boundary for the medieval park deduced from a number of different maps (see text).

this Park House by the end of the eighteenth century, but not around the house called Pendley Hall.[8] During the nineteenth century the area of park expanded to the extent indicated by the grey shading on the first edition OS map surveyed in 1877–9 (see Map 59).[9] During the twentieth century the area of park contracted once more but the fields south of Pendley Manor retain a park-like appearance today.

A thorough earthwork survey of the area might reveal surviving remnants of the ditch which may have been constructed when the park was established in the mid fifteenth century. From public rights of way it is possible to see a bank bordering the lane at the northern end of the belt of woodland called Lodge Bushes and then continuing northwards along the west side of the lane. It would appear from the map

evidence that there was a gently curving drive which extended south and eastwards from the site of the fifteenth-century mansion (the site of Pendley Farm on the first edition OS, and still so today) and through Lodge Bushes, the name of which suggests a lodge at the entrance to the park. The drive passed close to the highest part of the park, at just over 150m OD, and followed a slight ridge south-eastwards. The remnants of an avenue of trees are shown on the first edition OS map heading south-east from the farm house. Earthworks are visible in the pasture lying between the public footpath and Pendley Farm house at *c*.SP946118, which may relate to the cleared village and/or the medieval park.

The combined evidence of the former lodge, the avenue and the earthworks strongly suggests that the medieval park

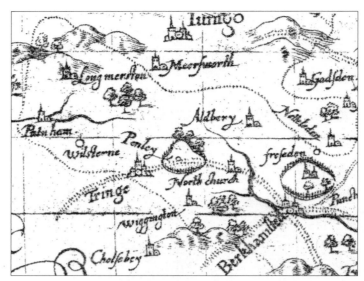

Figure 53. Detail of Norden's county map, 1598, showing the road from Northchurch to Tring passing through the south side of Pendley park. To the east is the sixteenth-century park around Berkhamsted Place, a surviving part of the much larger medieval Berkhamsted park. Reproduced by kind permission of Hertfordshire Archives and Local Studies.

was laid out around the site of the present farmhouse, and a conjectural boundary, enclosing approximately 200 acres, is shown on Map 59. The licence to impark included land in Tring and Aldbury and, indeed, the parish boundary does run north–south through the likely site of the park. The lane running south-eastwards towards Newground Farm (Beggars Lane) appears sinuous and ancient, and is likely to have formed the eastern park boundary. Akerman Street, a roman road, probably formed the original southern boundary. The suggested western park boundary is based on the layout of old enclosed land belonging to Richard Bard Harcourt Esq, the owner of Pendley, in 1799.[10] The northern boundary of the park is even less certain and, given the huge changes made to the landscape during the eighteenth and nineteenth centuries with the construction of the Grand Junction Canal, the London & North Western Railway and a new road linking the town of Tring with its new station, any surviving traces of the fifteenth-century landscape pattern will be very difficult to find. However, the county maps by both Dury and Andrews

(1766 and pre-canal) and Bryant (1822, post-canal and pre-railway), as well as the Ordnance Survey Drawing of 1806 (post-canal), all show an east–west lane which curved northwards at the north end of the proposed medieval park, possibly following the park boundary.[11]

1. *Cal. Chart. 1427–1516*, p. 8.
2. Munby, *Hertfordshire landscape*, p. 133.
3. TNA: PRO SC2/176/120 Aldbury court roll, 1506.
4. Page, *Hertford*, 2, p. 285.
5. Stratford, 'Whittingham, Sir Robert'.
6. *Ibid.*
7. Page, *Hertford*, 2, p. 285.
8. BL Ordnance Survey Drawing 150, 9 (Hemel Hempstead sheet), surveyed 1806, published 1822–34.
9. OS map sheet XXV, 6 inches to the mile, surveyed 1877–79, published 1884.
10. HALS DE/X234/P11 map of the parish of Tring, 1799.
11. BL Ordnance Survey Drawing 150, 9 (Hemel Hempstead sheet).

Figure 54. *Aerial view of Pendley park prepared from air photos taken by the RAF in September 1947 (HALS RAF photo No. 51(detail)). The area of parkland in the mid twentieth century incorporated much of the park created in the fifteenth century. Reproduced by kind permission of Hertfordshire Archives and Local Studies.*

Walkern

Walkern park
NGR: TL320244
Date range: by 1324 – mid seventeenth century
Size: *c.*400 acres
Underlying geology: boulder clay

THE EARLIEST DOCUMENTARY REFERENCE to this park is in the manorial accounts of 1324/5.[1] The park occupied the eastern extremity of the parish of Walkern and lay about a mile south-east of the manorial centre, now known as Walkern Bury Farm, on the watershed between the valleys of the Beane and the Old Bourne. It was bounded on three sides by the parish boundary and Benington park lay immediately to the south. The manorial centre itself was also located on high ground, about half a mile east of the church and village of Walkern, and is marked by the earthwork remains of a fortified enclosure at Walkern Bury Farm.

From 1316/17 the manor was held by Robert, second Lord Morley, and, as no park was recorded in the numerous preceding transfers of ownership, it seems likely that he created the park.[2] Indeed, the manorial accounts compiled in 1325 may have recorded the actual creation of the park, including as they do the making of an impressive length of new boundary fence and the acquisition of deer from neighbouring parks. On the other hand, a John le Parker of Walkern was recorded breaking into Benington park in 1316 and sections of the park boundary and two gates were repaired rather than new-made, so there may have been an earlier park at Walkern which Lord Morley set about refurbishing in 1324.[3]

Lord Morley had a 'long, varied and distinguished' career as a soldier and administrator. He held estates in Norfolk and Essex as well as in Hertfordshire, and there appears to be little record of him spending much time in this county.[4] Nevertheless, he was clearly keen to have a deer park at Walkern and, at about 400 acres, it was one of the largest in Hertfordshire.[5] A rent payment recorded in the manorial accounts of 'two leashes for the lord's dogs for coursing' suggests that Lord Morley took a personal interest in hunting.[6]

A few sets of accounts have survived in the manorial records of Walkern.[7] These show that in 1324/5 the manorial tenants were put to work repairing the hedge or fence (*sep'm*) around the park to enclose the deer (*feris'*), and made 435½ perches of new fence or hedge around the ox-pasture and elsewhere around the said park (435½ works).[8] This equates to approximately 2,000m of new boundary, about one-third of the likely perimeter of the park. In addition to the 'free' labour provided by the tenants of the manor, another man was paid 14d for making 56 perches of fence around the park at ¼d per perch plus the old hedge/fence. A carpenter was paid 2s 1d to repair two gates in the park and make one paling (*palys*) beside the gate of the manor. Old hedges or fences in the park were

sold for 8d, presumably for fuel. Incidental costs included bread and ale provided for some manorial tenants who, as part of their boon-work, were sent to capture deer in the nearby parks of Great and Little Munden: two deer from the park of 'Frodgoryshey' were given by H. de Ossevill of Great Munden (see p. 102), and another two were taken from the 'East Parks of Munden' belonging to Lady de Fryvill (see p. 172).[9]

The deer herd must have grown because in 1367/8 13 deer were taken from Walkern to help restock the bishop of Ely's park at Little Hadham (see p. 166).[10] Gifts of deer were also recorded in 1390/1, when William Holm was paid 5d for 'drawing 1 slaughtered deer up to Cambridge of the lord's gift to the Augustinian Friars there', and in 1431/2, when one deer each was delivered 'to Clement Clyffyn and the Abbess of Berkyng by order of the lord', as well as two 'to the lord in Holborn being there for the King's Council' (2s 7d).

The park was a significant source of revenue for the manor, mainly from renting grazing for cattle (agistment), which amounted to £8 11s 6½d in 1324/5. A century later, most revenue was still from 'agistment of beasts' (worth £7 22d in 1427/8), but by 1435 the value of the agistment had fallen dramatically to just '26s 8d beyond the sustentation of the wild animals'.[11] Sales of underwood were sometimes significant (51s 4d in 1428/9) and in 1431/2 men were hired 'to lop and cut the underwood and branches of trees in the park'. Pannage of pigs was worth 16 shillings in 1428/9.

In 1358/9 the wage of the park-keeper, John Basset, was £4 11s 3d (3d per day), significantly more than the bailiff, who earned 60s 8d (2d per day). In 1390/1 two men shared the duties of park-keeper: William Holm was paid 42s 8d for the year and John Skot was paid 29s 2d for 25 weeks' work from 7 April. In 1427 the fifth Lord Morley appointed John Hotoft as master and keeper of Walkern and Hallingbury parks for life at five marks a year. Hotoft's job was presumably to oversee the management of the two parks, while the person responsible for day-to-day work in Walkern park was John Humberston, who was given the office of keeper of Walkern park and warren for life with wages of 2d a day.[12]

The other regular 'cost of the park' was maintaining the boundary. In the 1420s 'the making and keeping of hedges around the park' cost 13s 4d p.a. Larger sums were expended on the lodge in the park. This had a bakehouse, which needed repairs costing 32s 10½d in 1390/1. The account also records that a lock and key were purchased for 'fastening the gardrobe of the Lodge' (6d), 'burnt limes [were] bought for divers houses within the Lodge' (4s 2d), tiles were bought for the chapel and repairs were needed to 'divers defects in the hall and chambers' (6d).[13] Whether these last entries related to the lodge or to the manor house is not clear. Repairs were also recorded in 1428/9 'upon a certain house called le Lodge outside the moat within the park' (22s 8d).[14] The site of the

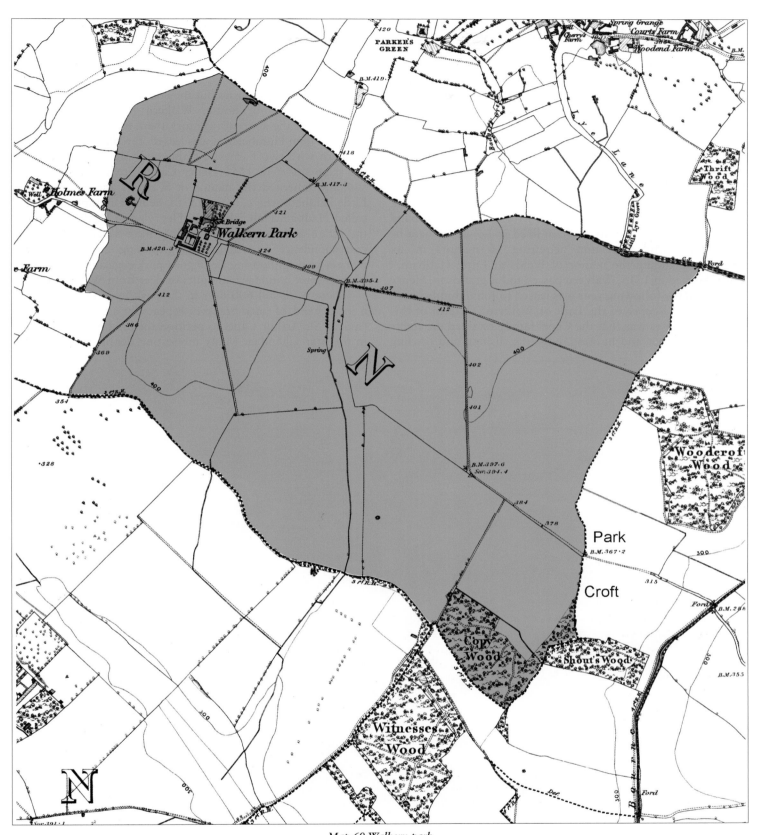

Map 60 Walkern park
OS 6 inches to the mile map sheets XIII and XXI, surveyed 1877–8 and 1878–80 respectively, published 1884. The field name Park Croft was recorded on the tithe award and map for Great Munden, 1841 (HALS DSA4/70/1 and 2).

lodge is now marked by the moated farmhouse of Walkern Park Farm ('Walkern Park' on Map 60), which stands at the highest point (130m OD) of the former park. Harting, writing in 1881, reported that 'a vast number of antlers were brought up' when the moat was dredged a few years previously.[15]

Bailiff's accounts for the manor of Little Munden in the late fifteenth century show that Lord Morley rendered a buck from his park at Walkern every year to the lord of Little Munden.[16] This appears to have been a payment made from 1425 in exchange for land in Munden called Oldelaunde below Walkern park.[17]

In 1506 the manor of Walkern, including 'warrens, park and fishings', was sold by Lady Alice Morley and her husband to Sir William Capel.[18] Sir William lived in London where he was a successful merchant, acquiring 16 manors in six counties, including the manor of Bauds at Little Hadham.[19] When he died in 1515, Walkern passed to his grandson, Henry Capel, and the following year was leased to John Humberston, described as 'Keeper of the Park of Walkern'. A term of this and future leases was that the Capel family retained the rights to the park, deer and hunting, hawking, fishing and fowling

on the land.[20] The bailiff's account of 1532 records the making of a new pond (10 shillings) and a new pale in the park, as well as continued payments for 'hedging the park' (10 shillings).[21]

The manor of Walkern descended through the Capel family for the next four centuries but they do not appear to have ever lived at the manor house, Walkern Bury. Indeed, at the beginning of the sixteenth century there may not have been a house as John Humberston was leased 'the *site* of the manor of Walkern with two barns, a stable and another house within the same site'.[22] In 1556 Henry Capel, great-grandson of Sir William, inherited the manor of Walkern and the manor in Little Hadham where, in the 1570s, he built a grand new house called Hadham Hall.[23] In 1588 Henry's son, Arthur, inherited the estate and many of his records have survived, including correspondence regarding a long-running dispute with the owners of neighbouring Benington park regarding the upkeep of their joint boundary and gifts of deer from Walkern park.[24]

There were still 600 deer in the park in 1611 but in 1613 a local band of park-breakers repeatedly attacked the park, causing Sir Arthur Capel to petition the king for legal remedy in the Star Chamber. Many interesting details of the attacks

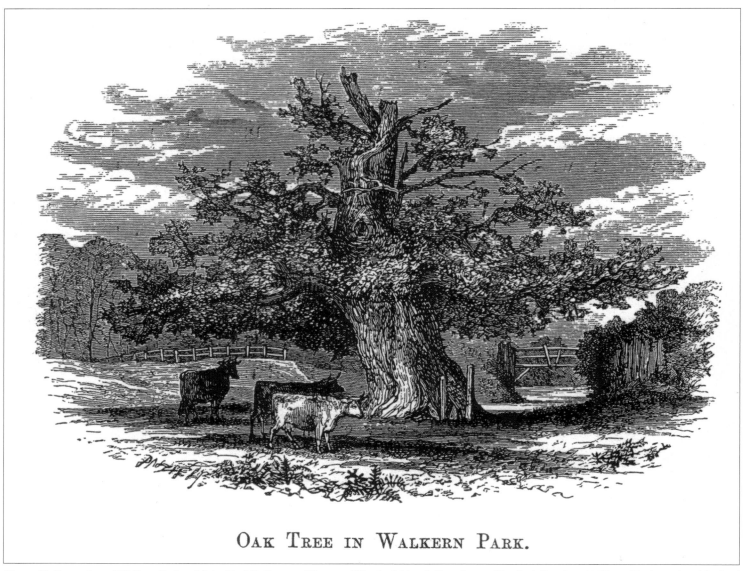

OAK TREE IN WALKERN PARK.

Figure 55. Engraving of Walkern Park published in J.E. Cussans, History of Hertfordshire, 2, Broadwater Hundred *(London, 1878), p. 85. Reproduced by kind permission of Hertfordshire Archives and Local Studies.*

are recorded in a draft petition in the Cassiobury papers.[25] Sir Arthur also kept detailed accounts relating to the management of his estates, including sales of wood and timber from the park, the building of a deerhouse in 1603 and the scouring of a pond in 1624. The renting of grazing appears to have ceased by the seventeenth century but, in addition to maintaining a herd of deer, Arthur Capel was using the park for breeding horses and for keeping swans.[26]

In 1632 Sir Arthur Capel died and the manors of Walkern and Hadham Hall were inherited by his grandson, Arthur first Baron Capel, a royalist whose estates were sequestrated by parliament in 1643 during the Civil War. Baron Capel was executed in 1649 but the Capel estates were restored to his son, also Arthur. On the restoration of the monarchy this next Arthur Capel was made Earl of Essex and, in a strange twist of history, the title skipped over the park boundary – from the Devereux earls of Essex of Benington Park in the sixteenth century to the Capel earls of Essex, owners of Walkern Park, in the seventeenth. However, it seems likely that Walkern was disparked in the mid seventeenth century. Seller's map of 1676 included the words 'Walkern Park' (and Walkern Lodge and Walkern Bury), but did not show any park palings. In 1685 the former park was leased as 'a farmhouse called Walkern Lodge together with the barns, stables, buildings, lands, meadows and pastures' to Phillip Adams, a yeoman of North Mymms. The area of the farm was said to be 408 acres, an area very similar to the 398 acres recorded in 1379.[27] The farm subsequently became Walkern Park Farm.

Evidence for the eastern boundary of the park is found in a survey of lands belonging to the manor of Great Munden in 1600/01 which recorded a wood called Woodcrofte which butted upon 'Wayon Parck' (Walkern Park) towards the WNW.[28] Woodcroft Wood was shown on the late nineteenth-century OS maps adjoining the parish boundary between Great Munden and Walkern (see Map 60), but was subsequently felled. The field lying between Woodcroft Wood and Shout's Wood along the eastern boundary of Walkern park was still called Park Croft on the Great Munden tithe map and award of 1841.[29] The contrasting pattern of field boundaries shown on nineteenth-century maps also helps to reveal the extent of the former park: the fields of Holmes Farm and Bridge Farm to the west, and around Parker's Green and Wood End to the north, were small, with wiggly boundaries; the fields created within the former park were large and straight-sided. Holmes Farm (see Map 60) probably commemorates William Holm who, in 1358, paid rent for two acres of land 'at the gates of the park'.

Although the former park boundary appears to survive almost intact, the field evidence is a little disappointing, with only vestigial banks and ditches along much of the north and east sides. However, a deep ditch, lying west of a hedge-bank, marks a significant lynchet along the west side of the park, with the higher ground lying inside the former park. The most impressive earthworks survive along the southern boundary, between the two parks of Walkern and Benington.

1. HALS 9325 bailiff's account, 1324/5; see also DE/Hx/Z24 typed translation of account rolls of manor of Walkern, 1324–1432, translated by Rev. F.A.W. Gibbs, 1939.
2. Page, *Hertford*, 3, p. 154; the manor of Walkern came to Lord Morley through his wife, Hawise.
3. *Cal. Pat. 1313–1317*, pp. 588, 592–3.
4. A. Ayton, 'Morley, Robert, second Lord Morley (*b.* in or before 1295, *d.* 1360)', *Oxford dictionary of national biography* (Oxford, 2004) accessed online 2 September 2007.
5. *Cal. Inq. post mortem*, vol. 15, Richard II, p. 48 inquisition held after the death of William Morley (son of Robert), 1379.
6. HALS DE/Hx/Z24 typed translation of account rolls of manor of Walkern, 1324–1432, p. 32.
7. HALS 9325, 9345, 9357, 9378, 9379 and 9380 bailiff's accounts for 1324/5, 1358/9, 1390/1, 1427–9, 1431/2 and 1436/7. See also DE/Hx/Z24 typed translation of account rolls of manor of Walkern, 1324–1432, translated by Rev. F.A.W. Gibbs, 1939.
8. A 'standardised' perch was 16½ feet; 435½ p = 7,186 feet = 2190m. The total perimeter of the park was probably *c*.5950m.
9. Henry de Osevill was under-tenant of the lord of Munden Furnivall (Great Munden). The de Frevill family were lords of the manor of Little Munden until 1377.
10. HHA court rolls 11/4 fos. 103–5 bailiff's account, 1367/8.
11. HALS 9325 and 9378 bailiff's accounts, 1324/5 and 1427–9; Page, *Hertford*, 3, p. 154, citing Chancery Inquisition *post mortem* 14 Hen. VI, no. 20 (TNA: PRO C139/74/20); Cussans, *History of Hertfordshire*, 2, Broadwater Hundred, p. 73, provides a transcript of the inquisition *post mortem* of Thomas, fifth Lord Morley, 1435/6.
12. HALS DE/Hx/Z24 H.C. Andrews' introduction to Gibbs' translation of account rolls of manor of Walkern 1324–1432. According to Andrews, the Humberstone family can be traced through the Walkern parish registers to 1679, 'the main family living at Walkern Park'. A brass memorial can be seen in Walkern church.
13. HALS DE/Hx/Z24 typed translation of account rolls of manor of Walkern, 1324–1432, pp. 84–5, quoting HALS 9357 manorial accounts, 1390/1.
14. *Ibid.*, pp. 99–102, quoting HALS 9378 manorial accounts, 1427–9.
15. Harting, 'Hertfordshire deer-parks', p. 109.
16. TNA: PRO SC6/867/18 bailiff's account for Little Munden 1477/8; HHA court rolls 10/16, 1484/5; 10/19 1490/1; 10/22 1495/6; 10/23 1498/9.
17. See HALS 9559 correspondence relating to gifts of deer.
18. HALS 9505 bargain and sale of manor of Walkern, 1506; Page, *Hertford*, 4, p. 52.
19. Bindoff, *The history of parliament*, pp. 569–70.
20. HALS 9508, 9510, 9513 leases to John Humberstone of Walkern, yeoman, 1516, 1547 and 1555.
21. HALS 9509 bailiff's account, 1532.
22. HALS 9508 lease of 1516 by the executors of Sir William Capel's will; see also Inquisition *post mortem* of Thomas, fifth Lord Morley, 1435/6 (TNA: PRO C139/74/20) transcribed by Cussans, *History of Hertfordshire*, 2, Broadwater Hundred, p. 73 which states that within the manor 'is a certain site of the same worth nothing beyond reprises'.
23. Page, *Hertford*, 4, p. 52.
24. See surviving correspondence HALS 9518, 9552, 9553, 9555, 9556, 9523, 9524, 9526 and 9601.
25. HALS 9533 draft petition to the King, 1613/4.
26. HALS 9607 bundle of estate accounts for Hadham and Walkern, 1591–1640.
27. HALS 9669 Lease of Walkern Lodge and farm, 1685; *Cal. Inq. post mortem*, vol. 15, Richard II, p. 48 inquisition held after the death of William Morley, 1379.
28. HHA CP349 survey of the lands of Robert Cecil by Israel Amyce, 1600/01, p. 202.
29. HALS DSA4/70/1 and 2 Great Munden tithe award and map, 1841.

Ware

Ware park

NGR: TL335146
Date range: by 1086 – perhaps eighteenth century
Size: *c.*325 acres
Underlying geology: mix of boulder clay and glacial gravel over Upper Chalk

WARE PARK WAS ONE of the three Hertfordshire parks recorded in Domesday Book in 1086, when it was described as a park for woodland beasts (*parcus bestiaru' silvaticar'*).[1] It is shown as a park on maps from the sixteenth to the twentieth century and fragments of the early park landscape, complete with ancient hornbeam and oak pollards, still survive today. It lay about three-quarters of a mile west of the town of Ware, on a spur of high ground (rising to about 70m OD) between the valleys of the Rib and the Lea, and probably filled the western corner of the parish.

In 1086 Ware was held by Hugh de Grandmesnil, a Norman lord who had fought alongside William the Conqueror at the battle of Hastings and was one of his most trusted followers.[2] Twenty years later Hugh was castellan and sheriff of Leicestershire, where he held 67 manors, and he also held extensive property in five other counties.[3] It appears that immediately after the Conquest the manor of Ware was granted to Ralph Taillebois, but it was subsequently acquired by Hugh de Grandmesnil in exchange for lands in Bedfordshire.[4] Domesday Book recorded that Ware was of exceptional value and importance but Hugh was already very wealthy and gave some of Ware's assets – the church and some land – to endow his abbey at Saint-Evroul in Normandy.[5] He also founded an 'alien house' at Ware – a cell to the abbey of Saint Evroul.[6] As well as the deer park, Domesday Book also recorded a newly planted vineyard and commentators have interpreted this as strong evidence that Hugh de Grandmesnil had a residence at Ware.[7] By the end of the twelfth century it was the home of the last representative of this great Norman aristocratic family, Petronilla de Grandmesnil, who died in 1212.[8]

Whether or not Hugh was responsible for creating the park is a matter for debate: it is possible that a pre-existing park was one of the reasons behind his acquisition of the manor of Ware from Ralph Taillebois. While Ralph *could* have established the park, it is also possible that it was created by the erstwhile Saxon lord of the manor *before* the Norman Conquest. Domesday Book recorded that this Saxon lord was Askell of Ware, a thegn of Edward the Confessor. To be known by a place-name was highly unusual in the late Saxon period and almost certainly means that Askell lived in Ware.[9] Domesday Book shows that many parcels of land in the Ware area were held by individuals described as 'men of Askell of Ware'.[10] This indicates that he was an important person in east Hertfordshire, with many men who were in his service or

owed allegiance to him. Askell's sphere of influence, however, spread well beyond east Hertfordshire: he (or in some cases his men) also held land in 20 Bedfordshire manors and a further two in Huntingdonshire.[11] Ware was by far his most valuable manor, however, and a man of his rank in Saxon society may well have aspired to a deer park. In any event, the natural geography of the land between the two rivers would have encouraged the establishment of a regular hunting ground in Saxon times, if not an enclosed park *per se*.

A limited amount of information about the medieval park is contained in a variety of state records from the thirteenth century onwards. The earliest reference to its size is in 1284, when it was described as 'containing in circuit one league', probably about three miles, and the park 'with the herbage' was worth 20 shillings per annum.[12] In 1350 Beatrice, widow of Geoffrey de Ware, died seised of a portion of the manor which she held from Thomas Wake de Lydell by the service of enclosing five perches (about 25m) of the manorial park.[13] On the death of Blanche, widow of Thomas Wake, in 1381, the manor of Ware was held of Henry Ferrers, lord of Groby in Leicestershire, by the service of 6s 8d per annum and included '40 acres of meadow within the enclosure of the manor park [worth] 12d p.a.' and '36 acres of wood, within and without the park', worth '20s beyond reprisals'.[14] The presence of meadow within the park suggests that one of the rivers, probably the Rib to the south-west, formed part of the park boundary at this time.

From the late fourteenth century the manor was held by successive earls of Kent and then, in 1408, passed by marriage to Thomas de Montagu, Earl of Salisbury. On his death in 1428 the park was said to be 'worth nothing beyond the keeper's fee, the sustenance of the animals therein, and other reprisals'.[15] The earl's daughter was married to Richard Neville and Neville became the next earl of Salisbury through her. An undated letter written by Queen Margaret of Anjou to 'the Parker of Ware' suggests that Ware park was used as a royal hunting park in the middle of the fifteenth century. Henry VI and his queen both enjoyed hunting and Richard Neville was a kinsman of the king (both were descended from John of Gaunt). Queen Margaret's letter states that 'our cousin the Earl of Salisbury will be right well content and pleased that, at our resorting unto our castle of Hertford, we take our disport and recreation in his park of Ware'. She asks the parker to ensure that 'the game there be spared, kept and cherished' and to ensure that no other persons should 'hunt or have shot, course or other disport' which would harm the game in the park.[16]

Later in the fifteenth century the manor came to the crown and in 1487 Henry VII granted it to his mother, Margaret Countess of Richmond. In 1509 William Compton, 'page of the stole', was appointed 'bailiff of the town and manor, keeper of the fishery, truncagium, two mills and the park and

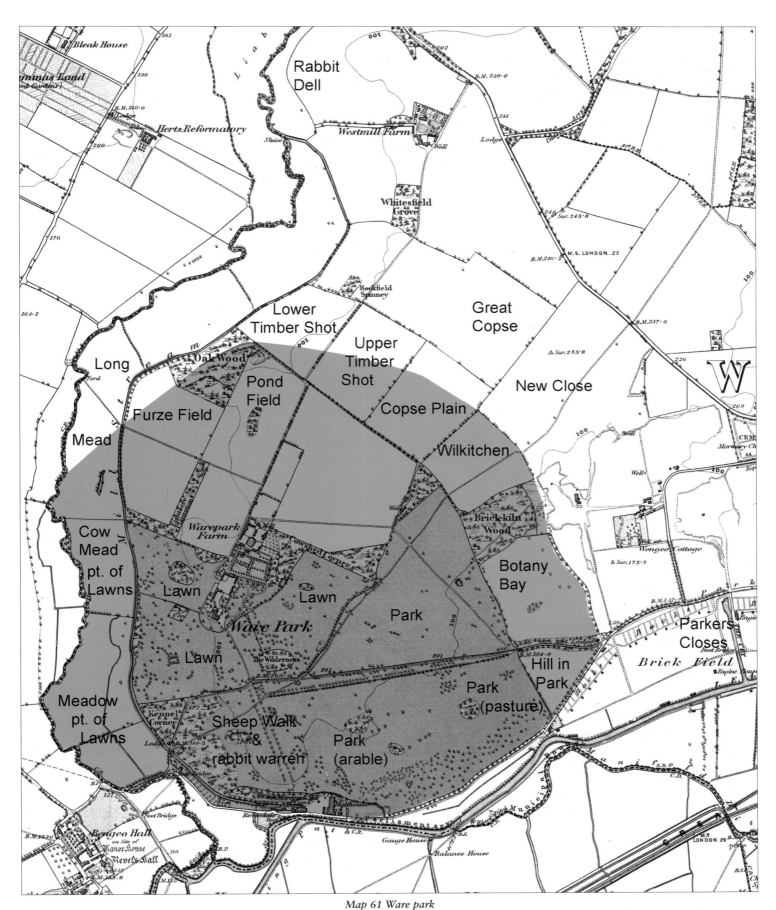

Map 61 Ware park

OS 6 inches to the mile map sheet XXIX, surveyed 1879–80, published 1884. Annotated with field names from the Ware and Thundridge tithe map and book of reference of 1803 (CUL MS Plans 632–3; S696.a.80.1). The boundary on the north side of the park is conjectural and not as definite as it appears on this map.

meadows,' which were kept for the use of the countess 'for livery of her horses'.[17] Compton was still the bailiff in 1513/4 and received 60s 8d for his role as parker. Revenue from the 'farm of the fishery with agistment of the park' were entered as a combined sum of £8 13s 4d in the account for that year.[18]

In 1539 the manor returned to the crown and the account for that year has survived. The pasture in the park was reserved exclusively for the deer and eight acres of a 21-acre meadow called Closelaunde in the park was reserved to grow hay for the deer. Oliver Frankelyn was bailiff and custodian of the park, receiving 4d per day in wages (£6 20d p.a.). Repairs were made to the lodge in the park (£3 4s 7d), a new barn was built (7 shillings) to store hay for the deer and a new pinfold was constructed (12d). Thirty-one perches of new pales were erected (15s 6d) and a further 15 perches of old pales were repaired (5s 10d).[19]

This account may also contain an important clue to the location of the medieval manor house of Ware, as it mentions the 'site of the manor called le Bury', which was leased to a tenant. The name 'Bury' usually indicates the manor house in this part of the county and a tithe map of 1803 recorded fields called The Bury at the eastern end of a tongue of land which also included fields called Parkers Closes and extended westwards to meet Ware park. All these fields were owned by the early nineteenth-century owner of Ware park, who was also the lord of the manor of Ware.[20] The field was still marked as 'Bury Field' on the first edition OS map in 1884 when it lay on the western outskirts of the town. Could this have been the location of the Grandmesnil residence from the eleventh to the early thirteenth century?

In 1548 the manor and park were granted by King Edward VI to his sister, the Lady Mary, for life. When she became queen, Mary granted them to Francis, Earl of Huntingdon, and his wife Katherine.[21] In the early 1570s Thomas Fanshawe purchased the manor from the countess of Huntingdon and acquired the park and mills in 1575, having gained considerable wealth in his office as Queen's Remembrancer in the Exchequer.[22] He is thought to have built, in the late 1580s, the first substantial house in the park.[23] His grandson, Thomas Fanshawe, a high-ranking royalist, seems to have been responsible for the enlargement of the estate and the park during the seventeenth century, perhaps initially after being made a Knight of the Bath in 1625/6 on the coronation of Charles I. However, the Civil War was very costly for the Fanshawes and parts of the estate were mortgaged in 1649 towards payment of debts.[24] An indenture of 1649 mentions the mansion house in the park, a warren adjoining the park, lawns and meadows outside the park pale and a 'close called new close taken and impaled into the saide parke'.[25] This 20-acre field, still called New Close in 1803, lay to the north-east of the park and seems to have been enclosed out of Wengeo open field by private agreement (see Map 61).[26] A further 80 acres, known as the warren, had been 'lately purchased of George Bromley' from the manor of Westmill, which adjoined the estate to the north, and this land was also impaled within the park.[27] Mid seventeenth-century documents record 60 acres of meadow, known as the Park Lawn, lying west of the park between the river and the park pale, which suggests that by then the meadows were outside the park.[28] By 1668 Parke Lawne meadow had grown to 80 acres, 'lately divided into several parcells'.[29]

Leases of 1656 and 1668 record 'all that parke or impaled ground wherein the said Capitall Messuage standeth and all those *two other parkes* or impaled grounds all of them being commonly called Ware Parke' (my italics).[30] The boundary of the 'core' park surrounding the mansion is probably marked on its east and south sides by a surviving earthwork in the form of a broad, shallow ditch. The other two parks, lying north, east and south of the core, may have been divided by the avenues and drive shown on later maps.

On the restoration of the monarchy Sir Thomas Fanshawe became Baron Fanshawe and Viscount Fanshawe of Dromore in Ireland, but the sequestration of his property by parliament had nearly ruined him and he died intestate in 1665.[31] His son Thomas, the second Viscount, succeeded to his father's 'heavily encumbered estates' and to his office of Remembrancer of the Exchequer.[32] In May 1667 there were stated to be '500 acres within the park pale', which probably represents the park at its greatest extent and must include the 80-acre warren purchased from the manor of Westmill earlier in the century.[33] By March of the following year the combined acreage of the three parks 'commonly called Ware Parke' was stated to be just 390 acres. Following the death of his mother in 1668, the second viscount Fanshawe sold Ware Park for £26,000 to Sir Thomas Byde, a high sheriff of the county in 1669 and a wealthy London brewer.[34]

The two county maps published in the last quarter of the seventeenth century both appear to show the park at its maximum extent (500 acres), with the north-eastern boundary running along the Westmill road.[35] Having expanded during the seventeenth century, the area of the park contracted again in the early eighteenth century and it seems to have lost its deer before 1713.[36] Although the deer had gone, the park pale continued to be shown on eighteenth-century maps. The Ware Park estate was inherited in 1789 by Thomas Hope Byde and in 1803 it was mapped for the Master, Fellows and Scholars of Trinity College, Cambridge, impropriators of the parish.[37] The area that could be described as 'park' had now been reduced to 224 acres (40 acres of which was listed as arable). A significant area of the park was retained as an ornamental landscape around the mansion throughout the nineteenth century and into the twentieth century before being divided up between two farms.

Exactly where the park boundaries lay in medieval times is impossible to determine, the best indications being provided by the earliest county maps by Saxton (1577) (see Figure 23) and Norden (1598). Both show a park with a nearly circular outline which almost reaches the river Rib on its south-west side; Norden shows the road from Ware to Westmill adjacent to the north-east side of the park. Any boundary banks have been lost to later major construction or destruction projects: the construction of a mill leat around the west side of the former park in the early eighteenth century and of a dual carriageway and extensive gravel workings on the east and northern sides of the park respectively in the twentieth century. However, the boundary circuit of one league (about three miles) recorded in 1284 corresponds reasonably well with the park outline shown by Dury and Andrews in 1766 and the acreage of the medieval park can be estimated at about 325 acres. The boundaries shown on Map 61 are largely conjectural and, especially on the north side, are not as definite as the map suggests. An earthwork can be detected at one of the highest parts of the former park – a large oval depression, with its long axis running east–west. This may represent a former pond constructed to provide water for the deer.[38]

Although most of the parkland pasture has been ploughed up, the south-west quarter of the park appears to have escaped because of its steep terrain. The field lying west of today's mansion (Wilderness Field) is grazed by cattle (2002) and still retains vestiges of its wood-pasture character, with a handful of ancient hollow hornbeam pollards still standing.[39] Most have already collapsed or are in the final stages of senescence but a couple still retain healthy crowns of foliage. South of this field the relatively steep, sandy slopes have been planted with a mixed plantation of broad-leaved trees in the latter part of the twentieth century. This area was listed as 'Sheep Walk and Rabbit Warren' in the Reference book accompanying the 1803 map and remnants of heath-like vegetation can still be found. Scattered around the remainder of the former park are about a dozen ancient pollarded oak trees (*Quercus robur*). Most are still alive, albeit at an advanced stage of senescence, and the largest has a girth of approximately 10–11m.

1. Morris, *Domesday Book: Hertfordshire*, pp. 138 c, d.

2. K.S.B. Keats-Rohan, 'Grandmesnil, Hugh de (*d.* 1098)', *Oxford dictionary of national biography* (Oxford, 2004), accessed online 14 October 2007.

3. *Ibid.*; K.S.B. Keats-Rohan, *Domesday People: a prosopography of persons occurring in English documents, 1066–1166, I Domesday Book* (Woodbridge, 1999), pp. 262–3.

4. J.H. Round, 'Introduction to the Hertfordshire Domesday' in Page, *Hertford*, 1 (London, 1971), p. 284.

5. Ware had a total value of £45 in Domesday book (Morris, *Domesday Book: Hertfordshire*); Keats-Rohan, *Domesday People*, p. 262: Hugh and his brother Robert founded the monastery around 1050.

6. Page, *Hertford*, 3, p. 382.

7. Page, *Hertford*, 1, p. 283; Williamson, *Origins of Hertfordshire*, p. 177. Two other vineyards were recorded in the county in Domesday Book: at Berkhamsted and Standon. It seems there may not have been a manor house in the thirteenth century as Joan de Bohun had a house built for herself in the close of the priory (Page, *Hertford*, 3, p. 382).

8. D. Crouch, 'Grandmesnil, Petronilla de, countess of Leicester (*d.* 1212)', *Oxford dictionary of national biography* (Oxford, 2004) accessed online 14 Oct 2007.

9. R. Liddiard pers. comm.

10. One of his thanes held part of the manor of Pelham and a second thane held part of another manor in Pelham; a freeman in Westmill, four freemen at Stanstead, one in Ware and another two in Sacombe were all described as 'Askell of Ware's men'; a woman in Sacombe also held land from Askell (Morris, *Domesday Book: Hertfordshire*).

11. I am indebted to David Perman for alerting me to Askell's land-holdings outside Hertfordshire.

12. Page, *Hertford*, 3, p. 386, citing Chancery Inquisition *post mortem* Joan de Bohun 12 Edw. I, no. 27 (TNA: PRO C133/39/10); *Cal. Close 1279–1288*, p. 250; Cussans, *History of Hertfordshire*, 1, pp. 133–4.

13. Cussans, *History of Hertfordshire*, 1, pp. 133–4, quoting Inquisition *post mortem* 23 Edw. III. No. 91; 1st part (TNA: PRO C135/99/4). Thomas Wake (1298–1349) was a nobleman who founded a Franciscan house at Ware in 1338 (*Oxford dictionary of national biography*).

14. Cussans, *History of Hertfordshire*, 1, pp. 133–4, quoting Inquisition *post mortem*, 4 R. II., Rot. 59, No. 7 (TNA: PRO C136/17/3).

15. *Ibid.*, quoting Inquisition *post mortem* 7 Hen. VI., Rot. 57, No. 27

16. Monro, *Letters of Queen Margaret of Anjou*, p. 91.

17. Cussans, *History of Hertfordshire*, 1, p. 137, quoting Patent Roll 1, Hen. VIII., pars. 1 mem. 27 (TNA: PRO C66/610).

18. TNA: PRO SC6/HENVIII/1593 bailiff's account, 1513/4.

19. TNA: PRO SC6/HENVIII/6869 minister's account, 1539/40.

20. CUL MS Plans 632–3 tithe map drawn up for Trinity College, 1803; S696.a.80.1 book of reference.

21. Page, *Hertford*, 3, p. 387, citing Patent Roll 2 Edw. VI, pt. v, m. 32 (TNA: PRO C66/812); Patent Roll 1 Mary, pt. vii, m. 20 (TNA: PRO C66/870).

22. S.M. Jack, 'Fanshawe, Thomas (*c.*1533–1601)', *Oxford dictionary of national biography* (Oxford, 2004; online edn, May 2005), accessed online 14 October 2007. He succeeded to this office on the death of his uncle in 1568 and owned other estates, including Jenkins in Barking, Essex and Fanshawe Gate, the family seat in Derbyshire which he let to his brother.

23. L. and J.C. Stone, *An Open Elite? England 1540–1880* (Oxford, 1995), p. 117. This is substantiated by a line of poetry brought to my attention by David Perman. It was written by William Vallans *c.*1590 and entitled 'A Tale of Two Swannes': '... Fetch me (saith she) two Cignets of the best / And in the Laund, hard by the parke of Ware / Where Fanshawe buildes for his succeeding race / Thy speedie coming I will there await.'

24. HALS 82949 release upon trusts, 11 November 1649.

25. *Ibid.*

26. HALS DE/Z53/Z3 undated terrier listing tithes due from Sir Thomas Fanshaw of Ware Parke.

27. HALS 38050 lease of 1649 included a 'close of pasture called new close taken and impaled into the park' and excluded 80 acres 'now lying within the pale of the parke lately purchased of George Bromley and known by the name of the Warren'. George Bromley was lord of the neighbouring manor of Halfhide or Westmill.

28. HALS 70613 indenture of 1634 records 'meadowe ground ... by the name of the Parke Laune adioyninge to the said Parke'; 81045 lease of 1653 describes Park Laund lying 'upon Ware Parke pale on the East and upon the River and Ozier grounds there on the West'.

29. HALS 82955 possession lease, 26 March 1668.

30. HALS 82954, 1656 and 82955, 1668.

31. Page, *Hertford*, 3, p. 388; HALS D/Z119/9 Knowsley Clutterbuck vol. 9, p. 296.

32. S.M. Jack, 'Fanshawe, Thomas, first Viscount Fanshawe of Dromore (1596–1665)', *Oxford dictionary of national biography* (Oxford, 2004), accessed online 14 October 2007.

33. HALS DE/X150/Z1 copy of 'A Particular of Ware Parke given by Sr John Evelin, Hertford, May 1667'.

34. Jack, 'Fanshawe, Thomas, first Viscount Fanshawe of Dromore'; B.D. Henning, *The history of parliament: the House of Commons 1660–1690* (London, 1983), p. 758.

35. County maps by Seller (1676); Oliver (1695, surveyed *c.*1675). The course of the river Rib on both these maps (the origins of which are probably linked as Seller and Oliver worked together in the 1670s and 80s) appears to be inaccurate, which makes it difficult to translate the park they depict onto later maps.

36. HALS DE/Lm/T12/4 assignment of the estate of 1834 recites this clause from a document dated March 1713.

37. CUL MS Plans 632–3 tithe map drawn up for Trinity College, 1803.

38. The depression is located at grid reference TL3389114632; it has been ploughed and its rim is most pronounced along the south side.

39. The only two hornbeams which are still in a condition to permit measurement have girths of 595cm and 685cm. As they are hollow, it is impossible to determine an accurate age but they have probably been growing there since at least the early seventeenth century.

Watford

Moor park *see Rickmansworth*

Oxhey park

NGR: ?TQ113938
Date range: 1360 – perhaps early seventeenth century
Size: not known
Underlying geology: Upnor, Woolwich & Reading Formations; London Clay to the south

A WILLIAM LE PARKER WAS listed on the lay subsidy roll for Watford in 1307 but the first clear record of a park dates from 1360, when Roger de Louthe was granted free warren in his demesne lands of Oxeye and a further grant to 'impark his woods of Gippes and Edeswyk'.[1] Roger de Louthe appears to have held half of the manor of Oxhey.[2] The manor house was probably located at the moated site just east of the river Colne, which is still known as Oxhey Hall, and the demesne lands of the manor appear to have extended south and eastwards from Oxhey Hall. The land rises from c.58m OD on the flood plain near Oxhey Hall to c.70m OD at Oxhey Warren and continues rising to 132m OD in Oxhey Woods, to the south. The soils on this higher ground are derived from London Clay and are poorly draining and infertile. Even today, there is no agriculture in this part of the parish and Oxhey Woods continue to extend over the land which has not been covered by twentieth-century housing developments. In the fourteenth century this would have been an area of extensive woods and heathland and a suitable location in which to establish a medieval park, especially given the reduced pressure on land resources in the decades after the Black Death.[3] Unfortunately, there is no record of the size of Roger de Louthe's park.

No park was depicted by either Saxton (1577) or Norden (1598), probably because it had been disparked and no longer contained deer. However, the medieval park itself does appear to have survived up to the end of the sixteenth century because 'In July 1598 the Royal licence was granted to Francis Heidon, of Watford, to cut timber in the park of Oxey, and to convert pasture-land into tillage'.[4] Shortly afterwards, in 1601, Heidon sold to Henry Fleetwood of Grays Inn esq land covering about 500 acres:[5]

> The mansion called St Cleeres, otherwise St Clowes, together with all that ympaled or warren ground lying near to the said mansion house, through which the way leadeth from the said mansion-house towards the town of Watford, and also all the warren-house or lodge commonly called Edeswick, otherwise Oxey Lodge; also, the grounds, pastures, etc lying on the backside of the said mansion-house, called the Great Parke, etc; and also, all that part of the old Parke, called Oxey Parke, to hold to him and his heirs and assignes for ever.[6]

So, at some point, probably during the sixteenth century, a mansion house had been built and a new park, the Great Park, was created to provide an ornamental landscape setting for the house. According to Cussans, St Cleeres was the 'old mansion' which was pulled down in 1688 and replaced by a new house called Oxhey Place.[7] This, in turn, was demolished by Sir William Bucknall in 1799, rebuilt in the late nineteenth century and subsequently also demolished.[8] Today, only the early seventeenth-century chapel remains.

The older of the two parks recorded in 1601, Oxey Parke, was presumably the medieval park. No park was depicted on the seventeenth-century county maps by Seller and Oliver. Dury and Andrews (1766) showed park-like ground around Oxhey Place but only a small part of the boundary on the south was impaled. This corresponds with a field named Black Park on the tithe map and award of 1844.[9] In the absence of further evidence, we cannot tell whether this was part of the medieval Oxhey Park or the later Great Park. The only clue available from the 1601 document is that the lodge associated with the warren was 'commonly called Edeswick, otherwise Oxey Lodge'. This may indicate the approximate location of the wood called Edeswyk which was imparked in 1360. Oxhey Lodge and the warren are both shown on the tithe map lying north of Oxhey Place and its church (see Map 62) but no attempt has been made to suggest the extent of the medieval park.

There are some significant earth banks in Oxhey Woods which *may* have been related to a former park. The first edition OS map also indicated two lodges on the lane forming the west side of the Woods. The more northerly of these (c.TQ104925) is traditionally believed to have been an early hunting lodge. As it is located close to the highest point of Oxhey Woods, there may well be some truth in this tradition.

1. Brooker and Flood, *Hertfordshire lay subsidy rolls*, p. 123; *Cal. Chart. 1341–1417*, p. 167.

2. Page, *Hertford*, 2, p. 456.

3. A grant of 1354 mentions 'Gyppisheth', perhaps heathland adjacent to Gippes Wood (HALS DE/Z120/44973).

4. Cussans, *History of Hertfordshire*, 3, pp. 174–5, quoting State Papers Domestic Ser., Elizab. vol. 268 (TNA). Heidon had held the manor of Oxhey Hall c.1570 but had sold it (Page, *Hertford*, 2, p. 456).

5. Page, *Hertford*, 2, p. 456, citing Close Roll, 43 Eliz. pt. 24 (TNA: PRO C54/1701).

6. Clutterbuck, *History and antiquities*, 1, p. 248, quoting Cart. Penes Hon. et Rev. Harbottellum Bucknall.

7. Cussans, *History of Hertfordshire*, 3, p. 175.

8. Page, *Hertford*, 2, p. 457.

9. HALS DSA4/111/1 and 2 Watford tithe award and map, 1844.

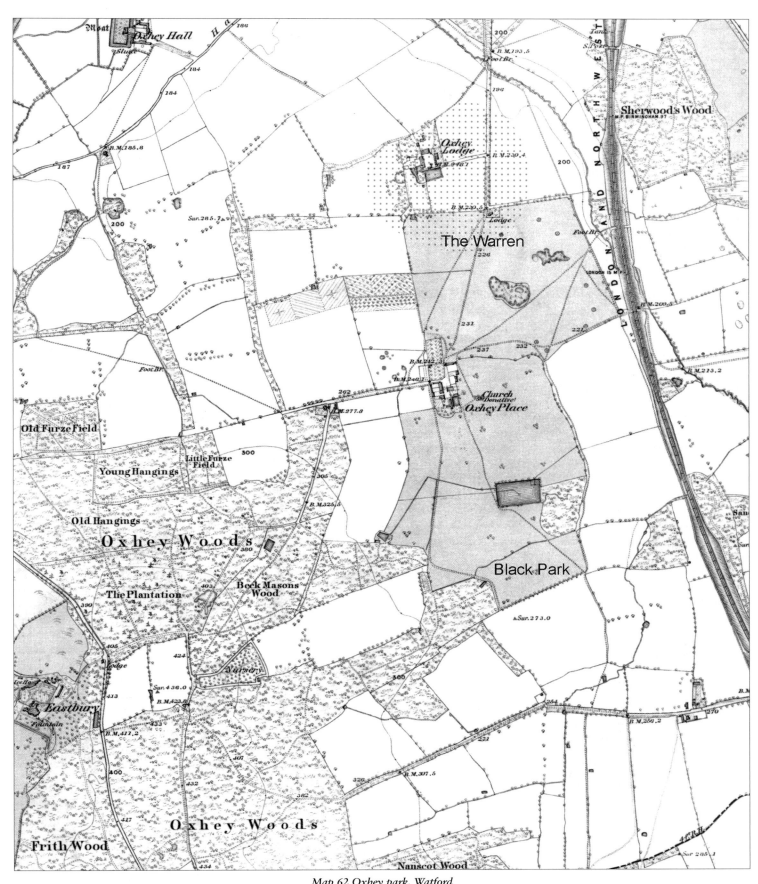

Map 62 Oxhey park, Watford
OS 6 inches to the mile map sheet XLIV, surveyed 1871, published 1877. Annotated with field names derived from the Watford tithe award and map, 1844 (HALS DSA4/111/1 and 2). The shaded area was probably part of the medieval park but its boundaries are not known.

Weston

The great park and Ipgrave park

NGR: great park: TL270295; Ipgrave park: TL253319
Date range: by 1231 – early sixteenth century
Size: great park: *c.*380 acres; Ipgrave park: *c.*179 acres
Underlying geology: great park: boulder clay with clay-with-flints and Chalk in the valleys; Ipgrave park: clay-with-flints, boulder clay and glaciofluvial deposits

THE EARLIEST RECORD OF A PARK at Weston dates from 1231, when Ranulf Briton claimed 15 does (*damas*) and 5 bucks (*damos*) from it, which he stated had been given to him by Earl William Marshal before he died and which had not been delivered.[1] It was the second William Marshal, fifth Earl of Pembroke, who died in 1231 and the park is likely to have been established by him or by his father, the first William Marshal, Earl of Pembroke and regent of England, who held the manor from 1189 until his death in 1219.[2] From 1231 until 1275 the manor was held by the second William Marshal's widow, Eleanor, sister to Henry III.[3] It was perhaps during this period that a second park was established at Weston.

For the last quarter of the thirteenth century, and until his death in 1306, the manor was held by Roger le Bigod, fifth Earl of Norfolk, a magnate and soldier.[4] There is no evidence that the earl ever resided at Weston, but five sets of accounts compiled by his reeve survive from this period and provide information about the two parks which then existed in the manor – the great park and Ipgrave park.[5] The manor house appears to have sat within, or on the boundary of, the great park, as there are references to the sale of dead wood (*morbosco*) and underwood 'in the park beside the house' in 1305/6 and in 1275/6 pales were repaired at the great park 'around the garden'. A parker was paid for 38 weeks in 1278/9, taking 7d per week and a robe worth 6s 8d (29s 3d in total).

Grazing (agistment) was rented in the great park for a wide variety of animals during three terms of the year. For example, between Easter and the feast of St John the Baptist (24 June) in 1276 there were 13 horses grazing in the park for 6d a head, 23 oxen and cows (4d per head), 59 young steers, mares and foals (3d per head) and 49 calves (2d per head), providing a total of 37s 1d in rent. Rent of 17 shillings was received between 25 June and 1 August and 10s 9d between 2 August and 29 September. Income from agistment in the park was much lower in subsequent accounts, as, for example, in 1304/5, when 4s 10d was received for the period from Easter to 24 June, 4s 5d for the period to 1 August and 2s 6d for the period to 29 September.

Grazing was also leased on pasture in Yppegrave, an area of wood-pasture,[6] at the end of the year: three young horses were grazed there for 8d between the feasts of St Michael and

St Andrew in 1275 and 3s 2d was received for the agistment of 'beasts' in 'le clos' of Yppegrave up to Christmas in 1294/5. In the accounts of 1278/9 a combined total of 23s 10d was received for the agistment of animals both in Yppegrave and in the park. Another, very similar, name was recorded in the account for 1304/5, when no income was received from the sale of pasture in Ympeye because it was grazed by deer. The scribe was clearly confused by the two names because he had initially written 'Yppegrave' then crossed it out. Even more confusing is the account for the following year, when the pasture, this time spelt 'Yppehey', was again grazed by deer. The two names, Yppegrave and Ympehey (spelt in various ways), both appear in an account at the end of the fourteenth century and were clearly used deliberately. Despite Ympehey being grazed by deer in 1304/5, there were references in 1306 and 1398 to the 'park called Yppegrave', so perhaps Ympehey was the name given to a particular area of pasture, or lawn, within Yppegrave wood (but see below).

Pannage could also be very lucrative in good mast years: £10 10s 9d was received for pannage in Yppegrave in 1278/9, with a further 43s 11d for pannage in the park. A total of 45s 4d was received for pannage to 11 November for the years 1294/5 and £6 13s 7d in 1305/6.

Sales of wood, timber and thorns (*spinis*) also made significant contributions to the accounts: one oak (worth 5s 4d) and 6 'diverse' trees were sold for 9s 4d in 1294/5; in 1304/5 unspecified trees 'in the two parks' were sold for £12 19s 7d; and the following year two oaks were sold for 8 shillings. Dead wood 'in the park beside the house' was sold for £12 in 1305/6. Eight acres of underwood were sold in Yppegrave for 20 shillings (2s 6d per acre) and another four acres in the same wood were sold for 12 shillings (3s per acre) in 1304/5. The following year four acres of underwood were sold in the park for 30 shillings. Thorns worth 7 shillings were sold in Yppegrave in 1277–9 and in 1294/5 thorns in the park were sold in parcels for a total of 14s 5d.

Two parks were recorded at Weston in the extent made on the death of Roger le Bigod in 1306: 'a park called Yppegrave in which there are no deer and another park in which there are deer'.[7] Two parks were also mentioned in documents of 1366.[8] In 1384 Margaret Mareschall, Countess of Norfolk and kinswoman of the king, granted to her butler, John Ethom, for life, 'the custody of her park, warren and game (*deduit*) appurtenant to her manor of Weston'.[9] The grant was reconfirmed to John Ethom in 1399 after the death of the duchess and he was recorded in the accounts of 1396/7 as receiving payment of £6 13s 4d as parker for the two-year period.[10] These accounts also provide much interesting detail about the parks at the end of the fourteenth century.

Income from 'agistment of the park' came to £6 13s 4d, comprising £4 for pasture in the park for the whole year with

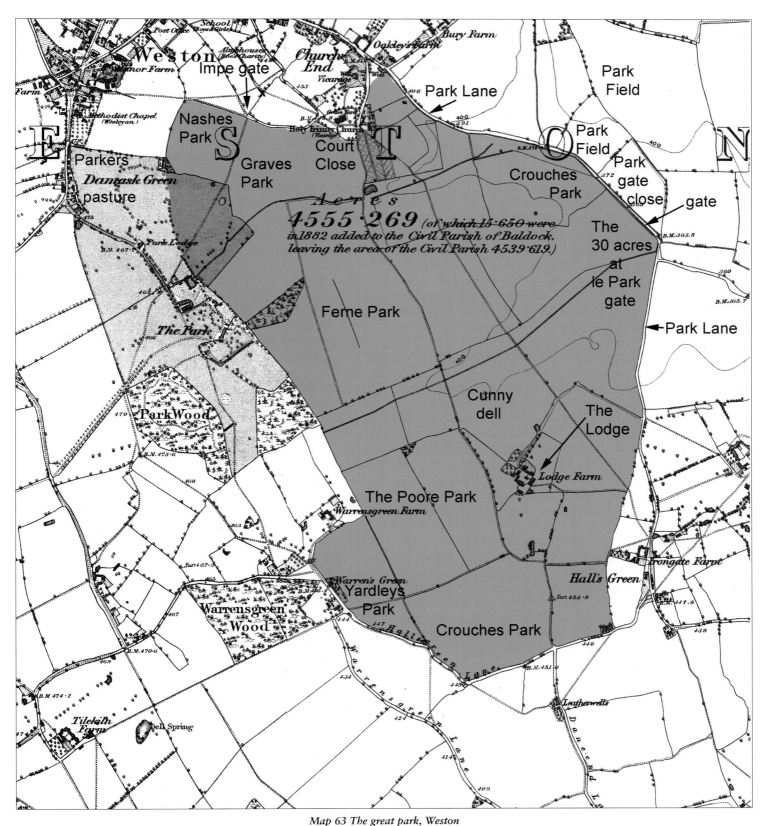

Map 63 The great park, Weston

OS 6 inches to the mile map sheets XII and XIII, surveyed 1878–81 and 1877–8, respectively, published 1884. Annotated field names and features are derived from a plan of the township and parish of Weston by Henry Lily, 1633 (HALS Acc 4283), drawn about a century after the deer park had fallen out of use.

all the pasture in the wood of Ipgrave leased to William Polyti, plus 53s 4d for a 'parcel of pasture in the park of Ipgrave'. Sales of wood and underwood totalled £12 14s ³/₄d and included underwood sold in the park at 13s 4d per acre; 224s ³/₄d for 3 acres and 3 perches of underwood and thorns sold in

le Netherwoode of Ipgrave (8s per acre); £6 for one acre of wood in Ipgrave; and 20 shillings for the underwood of one bank or ditch on the east side of Ipgrave. A further 70s 10d was received from the pollarding (*cropp'* and *eschaet*) of eight oaks in 'le Ympehey', five oaks in Ipgrave and four ash trees in the park, in addition to the sale of one oak in le Ympehey and one ash, and for the sale of bushes and scrub (*dumis*) in 'le launde' of Ipgrave. Repairs were made to the boundaries of the park, le Ympehey and the wood of Ipgrave.

In 1405 the manor was confiscated by Henry IV following the insurrection of the earl Marshall and the office of 'parker of the park of Weston' was granted to the king's esquire, Robert Scot.[11] In 1437 the park was stated to be 'worth nothing beyond the profit of the deer'.[12] In 1449/50, when the manor was held by John Mowbray, Duke of Norfolk, four deer were taken from Weston to help restock Sir John Fray's park at Great Munden (see p. 102).[13] The duke granted custody of the park 'with the custody of the coneys in it' to the king's esquire Laurence Fairclough and the office was confirmed to him in 1476 after the duke's death.[14] By the end of the fifteenth century the manor was back in the hands of the crown and a survey carried out for Henry VII in 1507 recorded that the park contained 160 deer but that the lodge and the hedge of the park were 'in decay'; the lodge would cost 40 marks to repair and 400 poles of hedge would cost 3d per pole 'and the old wood'.[15]

In 1532 Henry VIII granted the manor to Anne Boleyn and her bailiff compiled an account for the years 1534/5.[16] The grazing of pasture in the park and the pannage of pigs were both leased but few details were given except for one reference to the rent of wood-pasture (*herbag' silue*) called Ipgrave Wood. The 8 shillings formerly received in rent from John Isode for placing 'foals and animals' in the wood-pasture was not answered for by the bailiff because of 'destruction of the wood and the regrowth of buds'. The warren was leased for 15 shillings. No parker was recorded in the account and no repairs were made to the park boundary so it is likely that it was no longer being maintained as a deer park. In 1541 a messuage called the Lodge and certain lands 'parcel of the late park of the manor of Weston' were leased to Edmund Kympton.[17]

The site of the former great park has been identified using a combination of map and field evidence (see Map 63). It covered about 380 acres of beautiful rolling countryside butting right up to the south side of the churchyard and rising to 140m OD at its north and south ends. The manor house recorded in the early fourteenth-century accounts probably lay close to the church at the north end of the park – perhaps in the field named Court Close on a map of the parish of 1633. As well as the numerous park field names recorded on the map, there are several other interesting features including the park boundary, park gates, the location of the warren (Cunny dell) and the lodge.[18] Old lanes, some now only footpaths, follow much of the perimeter of the park. Lodge Farm sits on the site of the former lodge on high ground in the south-east quadrant of the park; from it there are extensive views across the park to the north and north-west, with Weston church on the distant skyline. Good banks survive along parts of the eastern boundary. The course of the boundary on the north-west side of the park can still be traced as an earthwork crossing the nineteenth-century park which extends into the former medieval park at this point. Curiously, most of the nineteenth-century park extends westwards from the western boundary of the medieval park.

Another intriguing piece of evidence has been preserved on the 1633 map concerning the location of 'le Ympehey'. Outside the north-west corner of the great park was a crossing point of two tracks marked 'Impe Cross', and 200m eastwards along the track bounding the north side of the park, on the north side of the track, was 'Impe gate'. This suggests that le Ympehey was an adjunct to the great park rather than Ipgrave park, which lay a mile away to the north-west.

The location of Ipgrave Park is revealed on the 1633 map as a large woodland called 'Ibgrove al[ia]s Weston Wood' in the north of the parish (see Map 64).[19] It was a spectacular site covering 179 acres on a high plateau at *c*.145m OD in the Weston Hills, with a steep valley to the north-east and very extensive views in most directions. Whether this park was established before or after the great park will probably never be known. 'Weston Wood with a warren' was recorded in 1557,[20] which suggests that when disparked it continued to be managed as wood-pasture. Much of the boundary can still be traced and stretches of bank survive along the north-west side of the former park and alongside the lane to Weston towards its southern end. Sadly, the Baldock bypass has recently ripped through the heart of this former park.

1. Page, *Hertford*, 3, p. 173, quoting *Cal. Close 1227–1231*, p. 489.

2. D. Crouch, 'Marshal, William (I), fourth earl of Pembroke (*c*.1146–1219)', *Oxford dictionary of national biography* (Oxford, September 2004; online edn, May 2007), accessed online 27 September 2007.

3. Page, *Hertford*, 3, p. 171, citing Chancery Inquisition *post mortem* 40 Edw. III (2nd nos.), no. 53 (TNA).

4. M. Prestwich, 'Bigod, Roger (IV), fifth earl of Norfolk (*c*.1245–1306)', *Oxford dictionary of national biography* (Oxford, 2004), accessed online 27 September 2007.

5. TNA: PRO SC6/873/6, 7, 16, 21 and 22 ministers' accounts, 1275/6, 1278/9, 1294/5, 1304/5 and 1305/6.

6. In 1534/5 rent was received for wood-pasture (*herbag' silue*) called Ipgrave Wode (TNA: PRO SC6/HENVIII/6443).

7. *Cal. Inq. post mortem, vol. 4, Edward I*, p. 291.

8. Page, *Hertford*, 3, p. 173, citing Feet of Fines Hertfordshire 8 Edw. II, no. 190 (TNA: PRO CP25/1/87/58); Chancery Inquisition *post mortem* 40 Edw. III (2nd nos.), no. 53 (TNA).

9. *Cal. Pat. 1381–1385*, p. 482.

10. *Cal. Pat. 1399–1401*, p. 77; TNA: PRO SC6/873/25 manorial account, 1396/7.

11. *Cal. Pat. 1405–1408*, p. 24.

12. Page, *Hertford*, 3, p. 173, citing Chancery Inquisition *post mortem* 16 Hen. VI, no. 60 (TNA: PRO C139/89/60).

13. TNA: PRO SC6/867/13 bailiff's account for Great Munden, 1449/50.

14. Page, *Hertford*, 3, p. 173, quoting *Cal. Pat. 1467–1477*, p. 599.

15. P. Bliss (ed.), *Reliquiae Hearnianae*, 3 (London, 1869), pp. 51-2. One of the witnesses to the survey was 'Rawff Farclow, gentylman' who was probably a descendant of Laurence Fairclough, the fifteenth-century custodian of the park.

16. Page, *Hertford*, 3, p. 172 citing Letters & Papers Hen. VIII, iii (I), g. 1499 (23), p. 634 (TNA); TNA: PRO SC6/HENVIII/6443 bailiff's account, 1534/5.

17. Page, *Hertford*, 3, p. 173 quoting Letters and Papers Hen. VIII, ii, 621 (TNA).

18. HALS Acc 4283 plan by Henry Lily of the Township and Parish of Weston together with the Manor of Weston Argentines and Newberry, 1633. Many of the park field-names survived to be recorded on the 1801 enclosure

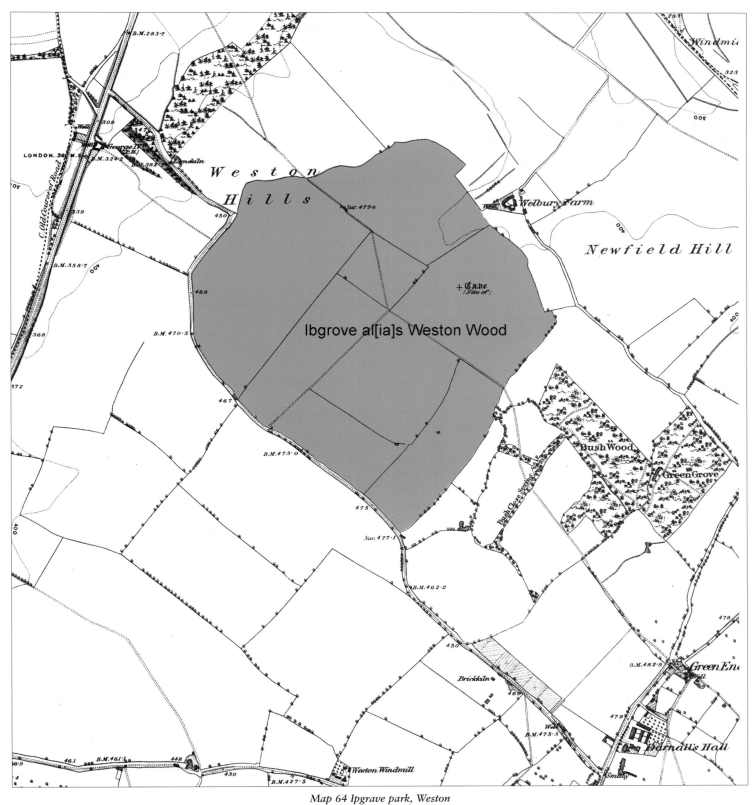

Map 64 Ipgrave park, Weston

OS 6 inches to the mile map sheet VII, surveyed 1880, published 1884. The park has been identified as an area of enclosed woodland depicted on a plan of the township and parish of Weston by Henry Lily, 1633 (HALS Acc 4283). None of the woodland survived to be recorded in 1880.

award and map (HALS QS/E/73 and 78430).

19. HALS Acc 4283 plan by Henry Lily of the Township and Parish of Weston together with the Manor of Weston Argentines and Newberry, 1633.

20. Page, *Hertford*, 3, p. 173 quoting Patent Roll 4&5 Phil. & Mary, pt. xi, m. 25 (TNA: PRO C66/928).

Parish: Wymondley *see Little Wymondley*

Glossary

Aestivalis (estivalis)	summer
Agistment (Agistamentum)	payment for grazing of beasts
Amputatio	a pruning, lopping off of branches
Aquarius	pond, watercourse
Aucupatio (Aucupacio)	wildfowling, profits from wildfowling
Averium	cattle, livestock
Barbare, berdare	to point, set a fence with spikes
Bestia	farm animal, beast of the chase
Boscus	wood
Bovettus	young steer
Bovicolus	bullock
Brusca	brushwood, scrub, thicket
Carpentarius	carpenter
Claudere	to close, enclose
Clausura	enclosure
clausur' parcii	enclosure of the park
Cortex	bark
Crescentia	growth, production
Croppa	clippings from trees or hedges, crop, harvest, harvest of trees felled for timber
Cunicularium	rabbit warren
Cuniculus	rabbit
Custus parci	costs of the park
Dama (damma)	doe
Damus (dammus)	buck (fallow)
Daubere, dobare	to daub
Depassare, depascere	to graze, depasture
Depastatio	depasturing/depastured, grazing down/grazed down
Dobbing – see Daubere	daubing, plastering, filling with clay
Dumetum	scrub
Dumus	thorn-bush, thorn-hedge, thicket, brambles, bushes
Emendare	to repair
Equus	horse
Esca	fuel for fire, tinder
Escaeta (escheat)	wood fallen from tree (?pollarded branches)
Escorchiare	to strip a tree of bark
Escurare	to scour, to clean (ponds/ditches)
Estivalis, estivatio	summer, pasturing of beasts in summer
Factura	a making, manufacture
Fagotare	to split wood
Fagotus	faggot – bundle of rods, twigs or split wood used for fuel
Fagus	beech tree
Falcatio	mowing, measure mown in one day
Fenum (faenum)	hay
Ferus, ferinus	wild animals – usually, in a park context, meaning deer
Fermesona (fermiso)	close season for hunting
Findere	to cleave/split
Focale	fuel
Fossura	a digging
Fossa/fossatum/fossus	ditch, dike, moat, embankment
Fraxinus	ash tree
Free warren	the right to hunt small animals such as hares, foxes and wild cats, and sometimes rabbits and game birds
Frondicus/frondeus	covered with leaves, leafy
Frumentum	wheat
Glans	an acorn, beechmast, chestnut, mast
Grava	grove, wood
Grease – 'in grease', 'a buck of grease'	a description of deer in the summer months when carrying the most venison and fat in preparation for the autumn rut and the winter
Haia	hedge
Hardbeam/harinebem/hernbemis	early modern English for hornbeam
Herbagium/herbage	right to cut grass or to pasture/payment for pasture
Herbarium	arbour, garden
Heybote (haibota)	right to take wood to make or repair fences
Hiemalis (yemalis)	wintry
Hiems	winter
Housbote (husbota)	wood for repairing houses, the right to take such wood
Includunt infra parcum	they enclose in the park
Inventio sancte crucis', Feast of	Feast of the Invention of the Holy Cross, 3 May
Jumentum	mare, draught animal
Landa	open grassland, especially in parks or woodland clearings
Laund	Norman French word for open unwooded field, pasture. Origin of modern English word 'lawn'.
Logia	lodge
Custus logi'	costs of the lodge
Loppa	twigs
Loppare	to cut off, trim; pollarding; lopping or cutting branches off a tree
Magnus parcus	great park
Marc	mark, sum of money (13s 4d)
Meremium (maeremium)	timber
Morbosium	dead wood
Palicii parci	park pales
Palicium	fence, palings
Palus	pale, stake
Pannagium	pannage (payment for or right to pasture pigs)
Parcarius	parker, park keeper
Parcus	park, pound, pinfold
Parrock	an enclosure or paddock, perhaps for coursing deer
Parvus parcus	little park
Pascere	to feed, graze
Pascua	feedings, pastures

Pastura	pasture; right of pasture
Perch (pole or rod)	a highly variable linear measure of between 9 and 26 feet but when standardised measured 16½ feet
Perdix	partridge
Pertica	a perch (see Perch)
Pessona (nulla pessona)	acorn and beechmast crop (no acorn or beechmast crop)
Pindfalda, pinedfalda	pound, pinfold
Plashing	laying a hedge
Porcus	pig
Porta	gate
Posterna	postern (back) gate
Prati	meadowland, grassland
Prosternere	to fell, cut down
Prostratio	felling, felled
Pullanus	colt, foal
Querculus	young oak, oak sapling
Quercus	oak tree
Rakk/rakkes	rack, racks
Ramus	branch, bough
Rascal deer	those not considered suitable for hunting, including immature males
Re-ficere	to make again/repair
Salix (salics)	willow tree
Sarratio	sawing
Sarrator	sawyer
Savagnie	beasts of the forest [Norman or Old French]
Scapulatio	the squaring of logs with an adze (scappling)
Scindere	to split, cleave
Scurant'/scurand	see Escurare
Secare	to cut
Sepes, sepus (sepum)	hedge, fence
Sepe mortua/sepie morte	dead hedge
Serjeanty	tenure in return for service
Several	separate
Spinus	a blackthorn, sloe-tree, thorns
Splentare	to fit with laths (split timbers used to repair park pales)
Staca (staka, stakis)	stake – used to make new fences
Stagnum	pond
Stokko	to stub up
Stot(t)	plough-beast, draught horse
Stramen	straw

Stramen pisae (straminis pis)	pea straw
Subboscus	underwood, undergrowth, brushwood
Succidere (succindere)	to cut down (trees, etc)
Terra	land
Tinare	to tine, furnish with spikes (as in a new park fence)
Turba	turf, peat
Turbare	to turf
Vacca	cow
Vadire	to pay wages to
Venatio	hunting
Venator	a hunter
Vepres	a thorn bush, brier-bush, bramble-bush
Vetus	old, ancient
Virgata/verga	a linear measure of three feet
Virga (virge)	rod (rods or coppice poles)
Virgultum	brushwood/cuttings of trees, small rod, withy
Vitulus	calf
Vivarius	fish-pond, stew
Warecta	fallow (land)
Warennarius	warrener
Yemalis (hiemalis)	of or for winter

Sources

J.L. Fisher, *A medieval farming glossary of Latin and English words* (London, 1966)

D.R. Howlett, *Dictionary of medieval Latin from British sources* (Oxford, 1989)

R.E. Latham, *Revised medieval Latin work-list* (London, 1965)

C.T. Lewis and C. Short, *A Latin dictionary* (Oxford, 1966)

J. Morris, *A Latin glossary for family and local historians* (Birmingham, 1989, reprinted 1997)

O. Rackham, *Ancient Woodland* (London, 1980; republished Dalbeattie, 2003)

J. Richardson, *The local historian's encyclopedia* (New Barnet, 1974, second edition 1986)

W. Smith and J. Lockwood, *Chambers Murray Latin–English dictionary* (Edinburgh, 1933, reprinted 2001)

L.W. Stone, W. Rothwell and T.B.W. Reid, *Anglo-Norman Dictionary* (London, 1983)

D. Yaxley, *A researcher's glossary of words found in historical documents of East Anglia* (Dereham, 2003)

Bibliography

Primary sources

Manuscript sources

Archives Departementales, Loire-Atlantique, Nantes
E206/2 counter-roll of the Duke of Brittany's household, 1386

British Library (BL)
Cotton MS, Augustus I, 1/75 Thorpe's map of Cheshunt, 1611
Cotton MS, Tiberius Bii, fo. 140–1 survey of manors of the
    bishopric of Ely, 1222
Cotton MS, Claudius C.xi survey of manors of bishopric of Ely, 1251
Harley MS, 602, fo. 42
Ordnance Survey Drawing 142, 9 (Buntingford sheet), surveyed
    1800, published 1805
Ordnance Survey Drawing 146 (PT1), 2 (Anstey sheet), surveyed
    1799, published 1805
Ordnance Survey Drawing 149, 9 (Hatfield sheet), surveyed 1805,
    published 1805–34
Ordnance Survey Drawing 150, 9 (Hemel Hempstead sheet),
    surveyed 1806, published 1822–34

Cambridge University Library (CUL)
EDR G/3/27, f.80, Old Coucher Book of Ely
MS Plans 632–3 Ware and Thundridge tithe map drawn up for
    Trinity College, 1803
S696.a.80.1 book of reference to accompany Ware and Thundridge
    tithe map, 1803

Hatfield House Archives (HHA)
Box T/38 map of Great Munden estate of Sir Robert Cecil by Israel
    Amyce, *c*.1600
Court rolls 9/25 bailiff's accounts for the bishop of Ely for Little
    Hadham 1435/6, 1436/7 and 1437/8
Court rolls 9/27 bailiff's accounts for the bishop of Ely for Little
    Hadham 1424/5, 1425/6 and 1440/1
Court rolls 10/9 accounts of the receiver of Sir John Say for the
    manors of Baas, Perrers, Geddyngs, Langton, Foxtons, Maryons
    and Hawes, tenement called Sewelles and piscaries in Nasyng
    and Holyfelde, and the manors of Hoddesdonbury and
    Wormleybury, 1468/9
Court rolls 10/16 bailiff's account for Sir William Say for the
    manors of Baas, Periers, Geddings, Langtons, Foxtons,
    Maryons, Halles, Hokes, Hoddesdonbury, Bedwell, Sayesbury,
    Benington, Munden magna and parva, 1484/5
Court rolls 10/19 bailiff's account for Sir William Say for various
    manors including Periers, Hoddesdonbury, Bedwell, Saysbury,
    Benington, Munden magna and parva, 1490/1
Court rolls 10/20 bailiff's account for Sir William Say for various
    manors including Periers, Hoddesdonbury, Bedwell, Saysbury,
    Benington, Munden magna and parva, 1493/4
Court rolls 10/21 and 22 bailiff's account for Sir William Say for
    the manors of Periers, Hoddesdonbury, Bedwell, Saysbury,

Benington, Munden magna and parva, and others, 1495/6
Court rolls 10/23 accounts of the collector for Sir William Say for
    his manors of Baas, Periers, Geddings, Langtons, Foxtons,
    Halles, Hokys, tenement called Sewalls, piscaries in Nasyng and
    Holyfeld, manors of Hoddesdonbury, Wykeham Hall, Bedwell
    Berkhamsted and Lowthes, Sayesbury, Benington, Munden
    Magna and Parva, 1498/9
Court rolls 11/4 bailiff's accounts for the bishops of Ely for Little
    Hadham, 1322–1507
Court rolls 11/5 bailiff's account for Sir William Say for the manors
    of Baas, Hoddesdonbury, Sayesbury, Bedwell Berkhamsted and
    Lowthes, Benington, Great and Little Munden, 1508
Court rolls 19/11 account for Hertingfordbury, 1381/2
Court rolls 20/13 account for Hertingfordbury, 1399/1400
Court rolls 21/10 account for Hertingfordbury, 1495/6
Court rolls 21/11 account for Hertingfordbury, 1480/1
Court rolls 21/17 account for Hertingfordbury, 1513/14
Court rolls 21/18 account for Hertingfordbury, 1485/6
Court rolls 22/1 account for Hertingfordbury, 1442/3
Court rolls 22/5 account for Hertingfordbury, 1493/4
Court rolls 22/6 account for Hertingfordbury, 1518/19
Court rolls 22/7 account for Hertingfordbury, 1395/6
Court rolls 22/8 account for Hertingfordbury, 1388/9
Court rolls 22/10 account for Hertingfordbury, 1396/7
Court rolls 22/12 account for Hertingfordbury, 1554/5
Court rolls 22/20 terrier and rental of manors of Geddings, Baas,
    Periers, Hoddesdon, etc., *c*.1440
CP349 survey of the Hertfordshire estates of Sir Robert Cecil by
    Israel Amyce, 1600/01
CPM Supp. 20 map of lands between Hoddesdon and Cheshunt,
    c.1573
CPM Supp. 21 plan of Hatfield estate, *c*.1610 (copy at HALS
    DE/X2/12)
CPM Supp. 23 & 24 plans of Hatfield estate, both pre-1608
CPM Supp. 66 map of Hatfield Hyde, 1796
Deeds 188/8 lease of the park of Little Hadham, 1620 reciting an
    earlier lease
Deeds of Great Munden 198/28 (1606), 190/12 (1609), 58/1 (1612)
Deeds 198/38 relating to Hoddesdon woodlands, 1595
Hatfield Manor Papers I A.D. 970–1493
Hatfield Manor Papers II A.D. 1493–1589
Hatfield Manor Papers: Summaries I
R. Harcourt Williams, 'Deer at Hatfield', Hatfield Estate
Newsletter, February 1997

Hertfordshire Archives and Local Studies (HALS), Hertford
Acc 2643/1/3 Knebworth tithe award and map, 1845
Acc 4283 plan by Henry Lily of the Township and Parish of Weston
    together with the Manor of Weston Argentines and Newberry,
    1633
AH916 catalogue entry describing a late fifteenth- or early

sixteenth-century copy of the confirmation by Edward I of the foundation charter of Ashridge

AH918 release, Ashridge, 1286

AH943b grants of lands, 1545–1609

AH1181 marriage settlement, Ashridge, 1664

AH2478 and AH2481 countess of Bridgewater's Establishment books, 1830 and 1832

AH2771 estate map of the Duke of Bridgewater, 1729

B1444 plan of Hodsdon Burry Farm, 1792

CM1 county map by C. Saxton, 1577

CV298 Ayot estate map, 1759

D1392 map of Scales Park, 1741

D1171B estate survey map of Scales Park, 1835

DE/Ap/M33 bailiff's account for Albury, 1335/6

DE/Ap/M34–9 bailiff's accounts for Albury, 1373/4, 1376/7, 1380/1, 1382/3, 1384/5, 1385/6

DE/Ap/M41 bailiff's account, 1394/5

DE/AS1145 grant of manor of Bramfield by Henry VIII to Robert Dacres, 1540

DE/B686/T1 deeds of Almshoebury manor and estate 1625 and 1672

DE/B818/T2 plans of Barhamwood Lodge estate, 1815

DE/B987/T1 deeds of Deards End Farm, 1650

DE/B1630/T4 Hunsdon deeds, 1634–1730, including sale agreement, 1653

DE/B1630/T11 deeds of Nine Ashes, Hunsdon, 1671–1837 including a Court Baron and Court of Survey, 1770

DE/B1727/T2 deeds of Ponsbourne Estate, 1718

DE/B2067B/E26 field book to accompany Tyttenhanger estate map, 1777

DE/B2067B/E34 release by Richard Ives of office of parkership of Tyttenhanger, 1547

DE/B2067B/M17–M18 rentals of manor of Boreham 1504–6

DE/B2067B/M25 survey and extent of the manor of Tyttenhanger, 1551 (includes copy of extent made in 1500/01)

DE/Bg/2 paintings by J.C. Buckler

DE/Bg/4 paintings by J.C. Buckler

DE/Bn/P44 Shenley Lodge estate map, 1829

DE/Bo/E1 'Particular of an estate purchased of Henry Gore', surveyed 1699/1700

DE/Bo/T14/1 indenture, Gilston estate, 1694

DE/Cd/T36 deeds of Shingle Hall, 1706, 1754

DE/Cr/125/2 plan of the liberty, manor and parish of Cheshunt, 1785

DE/Gm/350 photographic reproduction of a plan of the honour of Berkhamsted, *c*.1612, held at The National Archives [MR1/603]

DE/Hx/P2 Bushey estate map, 1685

DE/Hx/Z24 typed translation of account rolls of manor of Walkern, 1324–1432, translated by Rev. F.A.W. Gibbs, 1939

DE/L/5258 draft admission out of court to the manor of Great Munden, 1848

DE/L/5320 surrender of copyhold land at Great Munden, 1800

DE/L/P1 map of Scales Park, 1727

DE/Lm/T12/4 assignment of Ware Park estate, 1834

DE/Ln/E3 sixteenth-century survey of lands in Cheshunt

DE/P/P4 map of the Cole Green Park estate, 1704

DE/P/P7 map of Hertingfordbury Farm by A. Griffin, 1732

DE/P/T262 Hertingfordbury deeds, 1651

DE/P/T263 Hertingfordbury deeds, 1623/4

DE/P/T264 lease of Hertingfordbury warren, 1634

DE/P/T638 bailiff's account for Hertingfordbury, 1462/3

DE/P/T283 Hertingfordbury deeds, 1693

DE/P/T840 Hertingfordbury deeds, 1639

DE/Wl/T6 sale particulars, Standon, 1842

DE/X2/12 copy of plan of Hatfield estate, *c*.1610 (HHA CPM supp 21)

DE/X2/14 *The Cosmopolitan*, May 1888

DE/X52/P4 and P4A Thorley tithe map and award, 1845

DE/X150/Z1 copy of 'A Particular of Ware Parke by Sr John Evelin, 1667'

DE/X234/P11 map of the parish of Tring, 1799

DE/X265/Z1 survey of the manor of Simonshyde, *c*.1600

DE/X438/T5 title deeds of a capital messuage called Mary Magdalen and St Germains, 1779/80

DE/X951/33/11 VCH compiler's notes for Clothall, *c*.1910

DE/Z53/Z3 undated terrier listing tithes due from Sir Thomas Fanshaw of Ware Parke

DE/Z100/T2 deeds, Stanstead Abbots, 1764–91

DE/Z110/P1 map book of Ardeley, 1744

DE/Z120/44373 confirmation of grant of parkership, Knebworth, 1483

DE/Z120/44973 grant of land in Watford, 1354

DP/18/1/1 register of baptisms, marriages and deaths, Benington, 1538–1722

DP/13/26/1 Barkway and Reed inclosure award with map annexed, 1808

DP/22/29/2 survey of the manors of 'Brantfield and Queenhoo Hall', 1804

DP/29/27A/1/11 abstracts of title to Cheshunt Park and Theobalds, 1280, 1485, 1538–1689

DP/36/3/1 plan of 'Rectory Farm at Barham Wood', 1870

DP/71/3/1 field book of the manor of Mundane Parva, 1730

DP/101/27/1 and 2 Standon tithe award and map, 1839

DSA4/1/1 and 2 Albury tithe award and map, 1842

DSA4/9/2 Ayot St Lawrence tithe map, 1847

DSA4/10/1 and 2 Ayot St Peter tithe award and map, 1838

DSA4/19/1 and 2 Berkhamsted tithe award and map, 1839

DSA4/20/1 and 2 Little Berkhamsted tithe award and map, 1838

DSA4/21/1 and 2 Bishop's Stortford tithe award and map, 1839

DSA4/23/1 Bramfield tithe award, 1838

DSA4/36/1 and 2 Eastwick tithe award (1845) and map (1839)

DSA4/37/1 and 2 Essendon tithe award and map, 1838

DSA4/38/1 and 2 Flamstead tithe award and map, 1838

DSA4/40/1 and 2 Great Gaddesden tithe award and map, 1839 and 1838

DSA4/44/1 and 2 Little Hadham tithe award and map, 1843 and 1844

DSA4/45/1 and 2 Much Hadham tithe award and map, 1838

DSA4/47/1 and 2 Hatfield tithe award and map, 1839 and 1838

DSA4/51/1 and 2 Hertingfordbury tithe award and map, 1838

DSA4/54/1 and 2 Hoddesdon tithe award and map, 1841

DSA4/55/1 and 2 Little Hormead tithe award and map, 1839

DSA4/56/1 and 2 Hunsdon tithe award and map, 1837 and 1842

DSA4/61/1 and 2 Kimpton tithe award and map, 1837 and 1838

DSA4/70/1 and 2 Great Munden tithe award and map, 1841

DSA4/71/1 and 2 Little Munden tithe award and map, 1840

DSA4/76/1 and 2 Furneux Pelham tithe award and map, 1837 and 1840

DSA4/80/1 and 2 Rickmansworth tithe award and map, 1838

DSA4/87/1 and 2 St Michael's, St Albans, tithe award and map, 1843 and 1840

DSA4/93/1 and 2 Sawbridgeworth tithe award and map, 1838 and 1839

DSA4/97/1 and 2 Stanstead Abbots tithe award and map, 1840

DSA4/111/1 and 2 Watford tithe award and map, 1844

D/Z119/9 Knowsley Clutterbuck (grangerised copy of R. Clutterbuck's *History and antiquities of the county of Hertfordshire*) vol. 9 of 10

F212 lease of Bedwell Lodge Farm, 1702

F409 bargain and sale of Bedwell Park, 1648

K100 bailiff's account for manor of Knebworth, 1370/1

K102 bailiff's account for manor of Knebworth, 1401/2

K106–7 bailiff's account for manor of Knebworth, 1402/3

K108 bailiff's account for manor of Knebworth, 1403/4

K114 bailiff's account for manor of Knebworth, 1407/8

K116 bailiff's account for manor of Knebworth, 1408/9

K117 bailiff's account for manor of Knebworth, 1410/11

K119 bailiff's account for manor of Knebworth, 1412/13

K121 bailiff's account for manor of Knebworth, 1449/50

K124 bailiff's account for manor of Knebworth, 1481/2

K126 bailiff's account for manor of Knebworth, 1483/4

K133 bailiff's account for manor of Knebworth, 1541/2

K135 bailiff's account for manor of Knebworth, 1451/2

K149d grant to Knebworth church 'before 1294'

Off Acc 216 (part) Hertford Borough Charter, 1605

Off Acc 300 RAF aerial photographs, 1940s

PC160 photograph of a map of Hitchin and Ippollitts in Hitchin Museum, *c.*early eighteenth century

PC484 Tyttenhanger estate map, 1777

PC630 extracts from the Little Munden court rolls

QS/E/24 enclosure award for Boreham Wood Common, 1776

QS/E/44 enclosure award for Ippollitts, 1818

QS/E/45 enclosure map for Ippollitts, 1816

QS/E/55 enclosure award for Great Offley, 1819

QS/E/56 enclosure map for Great Offley, 1807

QS/E/61 enclosure map for Standon, 1835

QS/E/73 enclosure award for Weston, 1801

QS/E/80 and 81 enclosure award and map for Great and Little Wymondley, 1811

UDC11 51/1 map of Hamlet of Hoddesdon, 1819

IV.A.25 plan of Aye Wood, *c.*1600

X.D.O.A Gorhambury Deeds, court rolls, 1269–1332

XIII.51 plan of Broadfield Hall and Farm, 1775

1985 map of 'Barkhampsted Parke', *c.*1638

5888 bill for 'Inclosing ... Boreham Wood Common', 1776

5897 lease of the Manor House, Boreham Wood, 1785

9325 bailiff's account for the manor of Walkern, 1324/5

9345 bailiff's account for the manor of Walkern, 1358/9

9357 bailiff's account for the manor of Walkern, 1390/1

9378 bailiff's account for the manor of Walkern, 1427–9

9379 bailiff's account for the manor of Walkern, 1431/2

9380 bailiff's account for the manor of Walkern, 1436/7

9505 bargain and sale of manor of Walkern, 1506

9508 lease to John Humberstone of Walkern, yeoman, 1507

9509 bailiff's account for Walkern, 1532

9510 and 9513 leases to John Humberstone of Walkern, yeoman, 1547 and 1555

9518 letter from T. Sussex and W. Mildmay to Henry Capel Esq re Walkern Park, 1580

9518, 9552, 9553, 9555, 9556, 9523, 9524, 9526 and 9601 correspondence relating to shared boundary between Walkern and Benington parks

9533 draft petition to the King, Walkern park 1613/4

9559 item from a bundle of letters concerning requests for deer out of Walkern and Hadham parks

9607 bundle of estate accounts for Hadham and Walkern, 1591–1640

9669 lease of Walkern Lodge and farm, 1685

12133 survey by John Norden, 1619

21347 copy of inquisition *post mortem* of Alesia le Gros, 1367/8

21349 bargain and sale of manor house and lands of Furneux Pelham, 1600

21356 indenture, Furneux Pelham, 1614

21360 marriage settlement, Furneux Pelham, 1651

21522 lease of Stortford park, 1667/8

21650 deeds, Furneux Pelham, 1677

21655 deeds, Furneux Pelham, 1689

21670 mortgage, Furneux Pelham, 1709

21833 grant by William le Parker of Knebworth to his son, 1321

21843 grant of manor of Knebworth, 1334

21870 grant of a messuage 'late of Walter de Parkesgate' of Knebworth, 1309

21901 grant of two cottages in Knebworth by Richard Schyrlock to his son, 1430

22834 grant of annuity, Knebworth, 1542

22844 grant of property in Knebworth, 1553

22850 grant of land in Knebworth, 1569

26565 rental of the manor of Knebworth, 1561

26624 deeds of St Jermans, 1636

27433 copy of deed relating to Ayot St Lawrence, 1543

38050 lease of Ware Park, 1649

40702–5 court rolls manor of Bramfield, 1236–1378, 1422–60

44110 bargain and sale, Bedwell Park estate, 1614

44116 bargain and sale, Bedwell Park estate, 1631/2

44216 plan of parish of Much Wymondley and part of Little Wymondley, 1803

46572 quit claim by William Adye alias Gynn of Knebworth, 1641

46655B Knebworth estate survey, 1731

47132 'A terrier of the glebe land and houses belonging to the rectory of Knebworth made the 11th day of April 1638'

47259 photograph of 'Plan of the north part of the manor & parish of Knebworth ... the estate of William Robinson Lytton Esq', 1731

57588 lease of Kimpton Park Farm, 1748

59336 inquisition *post mortem* of John de Argentein, 1423

60313 copy of court roll manor of Hitchin Foreign, 1555

60353–60365 copies of court rolls manor of Hitchin Foreign, 1559–1657

64255 sale particulars of Albury Lodge Farm, 1914

64333 plan of Bedwell Park, 1765

70613 indenture of Ware Park, 1634

74380 Clothall deeds, 1615

74423 plan annexed to deed showing Munches Wood, Clothall, 1729

75037 partition agreement for manor of Albury, 1601

75989 indenture, Bishop's Stortford, 1828

78430 enclosure map for Weston, 1801

79547 rental of manor of Knebworth, 1526

79548 rental of manor of Knebworth, 1543/4

81045 lease of Ware Park, 1653

81751 plan of Lordship Farm, Little Munden, 1814

82949 release upon trusts, Ware, 1649

82954 lease of Ware Park, 1656

82955 possession lease, Ware Park, 1668

O.T. Leslie, 'The history of Bramfield' (unpublished manuscript, 1959)

Department of the Environment, List of Buildings of Special

Architectural or Historic Interest, 1986
Aerial photomaps No. 476 [TL2815/2915] 1972 and 1980

Hertfordshire Biological Records Centre
Site report for Highpark Wood, file code 53/008

Hertfordshire County Council, Historic Environment Record (HER)
HER I.D. no. 800 – Little London, King's Langley; no. 730 –
    Hoddesdonpark Wood

Hitchin Museum
Map of the town of Hitchin and Ippollitts, *c.*early eighteenth
century (photograph at HALS PC160)

King's College, Cambridge
KCAR/6/2/034 Cheshunt manorial accounts, 1435/6

The National Archives: Public Record Office (TNA: PRO), Kew
C134/15 (8) inquisition *post mortem* of Agnes de Valence, 1309/10
    (3 Edw. II, no. 37)
C134/101/10 inquisition *post mortem* of John de St Ledger, 1326
C135/232 (11) inquisition *post mortem* of Edward de Kendale, 1373
C143/450/32 inquisition *ad quod damnum*, Hunsdon, 1445/6
C145/37 (6) miscellaneous inquisitions (7 Edw. I, no. 42)
E101/459/12 account of repairs at Bushey, 1524–26
E101/676/4 account for King's Langley, 1359–61
E178/3900 petition of the inhabitants of Cheshunt as to the
    assessment of subsidies, and inquisition as to lands taken into
    Theobalds Park, 1608/9 and 1625/6
E199/10/2 extent of the manor of Bushey, 1314–16
E199/10/4 accounts of the manor of Bushey, 1320–3
E210/439 ancient deeds, Little Munden, 1486/7
E210/1576 ancient deeds, Little Munden, 1455/6
E315/391 survey of Hertfordshire manors, lands and possessions of
    King Philip and Queen Mary, 1556
LR2/216 Land Revenue Miscellaneous Book 216
MR1/603 plan of the honour of Berkhamsted, *c.*1612
SC2/176/120 Aldbury court roll, 1506
SC6/839/16 account of the parker of Pisho, 1421/2
SC6/863/2 minister's accounts for the honour of Berkhamsted, 1268/9
SC6/863/3 account for the honour of Berkhamsted, 1272/3
SC6/863/5 bailiff's account for Berkhamsted, 1300/01
SC6/863/8 minister's account for Berkhamsted, 1272–1307
SC6/863/12 receiver's account for Berkhamsted, 1377/8
SC6/863/14 receiver's account for Berkhamsted, 1388/9
SC6/863/15 ministers' and receivers' accounts, Berkhamsted, 1389/90
SC6/863/17 ministers' and receivers' accounts, Berkhamsted, 1398/9
SC6/863/18 ministers' and receivers' accounts, Berkhamsted, 1399/1400
SC6/863/19 ministers' and receivers' accounts, Berkhamsted, 1400/1
SC6/864/5 ministers' and receivers' accounts, Berkhamsted, 1408/9
SC6/864/6 ministers' and receivers' accounts, Berkhamsted, 1409/10
SC6/864/20 ministers' and receivers' accounts, Berkhamsted, 1423/4
SC6/865/9 receiver's account for Berkhamsted, 1449–50
SC6/865/17 ministers' and receivers' accounts for
    Hertingfordbury, 1354/5
SC6/865/18 ministers' and receivers' accounts, Hertingfordbury, 1359/60
SC6/866/1 accounts of the reeve for the manor of Hormead, 1260–2
SC6/866/2 accounts of the reeve for the manor of Hormead, 1263–5
SC6/866/3 accounts of the reeve for the manor of Hormead, 1323–5
SC6/866/4 accounts of the reeve for the manor of Hormead, 1326–8

SC6/866/13 minister's account for King's Langley, 1301/2
SC6/866/16 bailiff's account for Langeleye, 1305/6
SC6/866/17 bailiff's account for Childelangele, 1307/8
SC6/866/18 bailiff's account for Langley, 1311/12
SC6/866/20 manorial accounts for Childern Langeleye, 1315–1318
SC6/866/26 manorial accounts for King's Langley, 1321/2
SC6/866/27 manorial accounts for King's Langley, 1322/3
SC6/866/29 manorial accounts for King's Langley, 1324/5
SC6/867/1 accounts of the Berkhamsted warren, 1419–56
SC6/867/10 bailiff's account for Great Munden, 1446/7
SC6/867/12 bailiff's account for Great Munden, 1448/9
SC6/867/13 bailiff's account for Great Munden, 1449/50
SC6/867/16 bailiff's account for Great Munden, 1456/7
SC6/867/17 bailiff's account for Great Munden, date missing but
    probably *c.*1460
SC6/867/18 account for manor of Little Munden, 1477/8
SC6/868/6 ministers' and receivers' accounts, Pisho, 1295/6
SC6/868/10 ministers' and receivers' accounts, Bushey, 1275–7
SC6/868/12 ministers' and receivers' accounts, Bushey, 1278–80
SC6/868/16 reeve's account for Standon, 1290/1
SC6/868/17 minister's account for Standon, 1304/5
SC6/868/18 minister's account for Standon, 1312/13
SC6/868/20 minister's account for Standon, 1328/9
SC6/868/21 minister's account for Standon, 1335/6
SC6/868/23 minister's account for Standon, 1337/8
SC6/869/5 minister's account for Standon, 1344/5
SC6/869/11 minister's account for Standon, 1354/5
SC6/869/12 minister's account for Standon, 1357/8
SC6/869/14 minister's account for Standon, 1362/3
SC6/869/15 minister's account for Standon, 1372/3
SC6/870/1 account of Roger Marescall, farmer of the manor of
    Standon, 1395/6
SC6/870/4 bailiff's account for Standon, 1459/60
SC6/870/5 bailiff's account for Standon, 1461/2
SC6/870/6 bailiff's account for Standon, 1468/9
SC6/870/7 ministers' and receivers' accounts, Berkhamsted,
    1470–72
SC6/873/6 minister's account for Weston, 1275/6
SC6/873/7 minister's account for Weston, 1278/9
SC6/873/16 minister's account for Weston, 1294/5
SC6/873/21 minister's account for Weston, 1304/5
SC6/873/22 minister's account for Weston, 1305/6
SC6/873/25 minister's account for Weston, 1396/7
SC6/915/3 ministers' and receivers' accounts, Bushey, 1265–71
SC6/1090/4 minister's account for King's Langley, 1296/7
SC6/1109/6 ministers' and receivers' accounts, Standon, 1233–7
SC6/1109/12 ministers' and receivers' accounts, Standon, 1273/4
SC6/1116/9 ministers' and receivers' accounts, Cheshunt, 1295/6
SC6/1123/5 minister's account for Flamstead, 1395/6
SC6/1123/6 bailiff's account for Flamstead, 1480/1
SC6/1132/9 accounts of the manors held by the bishops of Ely, 1285/6
SC6/1132/10 accounts of the manors held by the bishops of Ely, 1298/9
SC6/1132/11 accounts of the manors held by the bishops of
    Ely, 1301/2
SC6/1132/13 accounts of the manors held by the bishops of
    Ely, 1315/6
SC6/1140/1 minister's account for Bishop's Stortford, 1345/6
SC6/1140/2 minister's account for Bishop's Stortford, 1346/7
SC6/1140/3 minister's account for Bishop's Stortford, 1347/8
SC6/1140/5 minister's account for Bishop's Stortford, 1351/2

SC6/1140/8 minister's account for Bishop's Stortford, 1387/8

SC6/1140/10 minister's account for Bishop's Stortford, 1394/5

SC6/1140/12 minister's account for Bishop's Stortford, 1398/9

SC6/1140/16 minister's account for Bishop's Stortford, 1410–12

SC6/1140/20 parker's account for Bishop's Stortford, 1437/8

SC6/1145/10 ministers' and receivers' accounts, Bushey, 1321/2

SC6/1147/9 minister's account for Standon, 1322/3

SC6/HENVII/1238 minister's account for Maydencroft manor, 1507/8

SC6/HENVII/1323 bailiff's account for Flamstead, 1505/6

SC6/HENVIII/181 minister's account for Berkhamsted, 1534–6

SC6/HENVIII/238 collector's account for Ashridge, 1539/40

SC6/HENVIII/1016 ministers' and receivers' accounts for The More, 1539/41

SC6/HENVIII/1593 bailiff's account for Ware, 1513/4

SC6/HENVIII/6012 ministers' accounts for The More, Pisho, Stanstead and Hunsdon, 1536/7

SC6/HENVIII/6016 bailiff's account for Pisho, 1539/40

SC6/HENVIII/6146 ministers' and receivers' accounts, Great Gaddesden, 1528/9

SC6/HENVIII/6222 ministers' account for Great Offley, 1540/1

SC6/HENVIII/6443 bailiff's account for Weston, Hunsdon and Pishobury, 1534/5

SC6/HENVIII/6629 minister's account for Standon, 1533/4

SC6/HENVIII/6757 and 6764 reeves' accounts for Cheshunt, 1519–21 and 1526–8

SC6/HENVIII/6869 minister's account for Bushey and Ware, 1539/40

SC6/HENVIII/6968 bailiff's account for Flamstead, 1516/7

SC6/HENVIII/6989 bailiff's account for Flamstead, 1539/40

SC11/297 rental of the manor of Shenley Holmes (alias Cannons), 1385/6

SC12/8/22 valor of the lordship and manor of Bushey Hall, 1510

Ward 2/61/241/36 'A survey of certain parcels of the honour of Berkhamsted, viz the castle, park, the Frith, the demesnes and landes demised', by John Norden, September 1612

Private collections

Plan of the 'manor and parish of Benyngton … part of the possessions of the right worshipfull Sir Charles Caeser Knight', drawn by Henry Liley, 1628

'Plan of the north part of the manor & parish of Knebworth … the estate of William Robinson Lytton Esq, surveyed by Augustine Hale, new drawn & examined by Thomas Browne, gent, 1731' (photograph at HALS)

Printed primary sources: Calendars of Rolls

Calendars of Charter Rolls (Cal. Chart.)

Calendar of Charter Rolls, vol. 1, Henry III, 1226–1257 (London, 1903)

Calendar of Charter Rolls, vol. 2, Henry III, 1257–1300 (London, 1906)

Calendar of Charter Rolls, vol. 3, Edward I, Edward II, 1300–1326 (London, 1908)

Calendar of Charter Rolls, vol. 4, Edward III, 1327–1341 (London, 1912)

Calendar of Charter Rolls, vol. 5, Edward III–Henry V, 1341–1417 (London, 1916)

Calendar of Charter Rolls, vol. 6, Henry VI–Henry VIII, 1427–1516 (London, 1927)

Calendars of Close Rolls (Cal. Close)

Calendar of Close Rolls, Henry III, 1227–1231 (London, 1902)

Calendar of Close Rolls, Henry III, 1234–1237 (London, 1909)

Calendar of Close Rolls, Henry III, 1237–1242 (London, 1911)

Calendar of Close Rolls, Edward I, 1279–1288 (London, 1902)

Calendar of Close Rolls, Edward I, 1288–1296 (London, 1904)

Calendar of Close Rolls, Edward I, 1296-1302 (London, 1906)

Calendar of Close Rolls, Edward II, 1313–1318 (London, 1893)

Calendar of Close Rolls, Richard II, 1377–1381 (London, 1914)

Calendar of Close Rolls, Richard II, 1396–1399 (London, 1927)

Calendars of Inquisitions (Cal. Inq. post mortem)

Calendar of Inquisitions Post Mortem, vol. 3, Edward I, 1290–1300 (London, 1912)

Calendar of Inquisitions Post Mortem, vol. 4, Edward I, 1300–1307 (London, 1913)

Calendar of Inquisitions Post Mortem, vol. 6, Edward II, 1316–1327 (London, 1910)

Calendar of Inquisitions Post Mortem, vol. 7, Edward III, 1327–1336 (London, 1909)

Calendar of Inquisitions Post Mortem, vol. 8, Edward III, 1336–1347 (London, 1913)

Calendar of Inquisitions Post Mortem, vol. 10, Edward III, 1352–1361 (London, 1921)

Calendar of Inquisitions Post Mortem, vol. 14, Edward III, 1374–1377 (London, 1952)

Calendar of Inquisitions Post Mortem, vol. 15, Richard II, 1377–1384 (London, 1970)

Calendar of Inquisitions Post Mortem, vol. 21, Henry V, 1418–1422 (Woodbridge, 2002)

Calendars of Patent Rolls (Cal. Pat.)

Calendar of Patent Rolls, Edward I, 1272–1281 (London, 1901)

Calendar of Patent Rolls, Edward I, 1281–1292 (London, 1893)

Calendar of Patent Rolls, Edward I, 1292–1301 (London, 1895)

Calendar of Patent Rolls, Edward I, 1301–1307 (London, 1898)

Calendar of Patent Rolls, Edward II, 1307–1313 (London, 1894)

Calendar of Patent Rolls, Edward II, 1313–1317 (London, 1898)

Calendar of Patent Rolls, Edward II, 1321–1324 (London, 1904)

Calendar of Patent Rolls, Edward II, 1324–1327 (London, 1904)

Calendar of Patent Rolls, Edward III, 1327–1330 (London, 1891)

Calendar of Patent Rolls, Edward III, 1330–1334 (London, 1893)

Calendar of Patent Rolls, Edward III, 1334–1338 (London, 1895)

Calendar of Patent Rolls, Edward III, 1338–1340 (London, 1898)

Calendar of Patent Rolls, Edward III, 1343–1345 (London, 1902)

Calendar of Patent Rolls, Edward III, 1348–1350 (London, 1905)

Calendar of Patent Rolls, Edward III, 1354–1358 (London, 1909)

Calendar of Patent Rolls, Edward III, 1358–1361 (London, 1911)

Calendar of Patent Rolls, Edward III, 1361–1364 (London, 1912)

Calendar of Patent Rolls, Edward III, 1364–1367 (London, 1912)

Calendar of Patent Rolls, Edward III, 1367–1370 (London, 1913)

Calendar of Patent Rolls, Edward III, 1370–1374 (London, 1914)

Calendar of Patent Rolls, Richard II, 1377–1381 (London, 1895)

Calendar of Patent Rolls, Richard II, 1381–1385 (London, 1897)

Calendar of Patent Rolls, Richard II, 1385–1389 (London, 1900)

Calendar of Patent Rolls, Richard II, 1396–1399 (London, 1909)

Calendar of Patent Rolls, Henry IV, 1399–1401 (London, 1903)

Calendar of Patent Rolls, Henry IV, 1405–1408 (London, 1907)

Calendar of Patent Rolls, Henry IV, 1408–1413 (London, 1909)

Calendar of Patent Rolls, Henry VI, 1422–1429 (London, 1901)

Calendar of Patent Rolls, Henry VI, 1429–1436 (London, 1907)
Calendar of Patent Rolls, Henry VI, 1452–1461 (London, 1910)
Calendar of Patent Rolls, Edward IV–Edward V–Richard III, 1476–1485 (London, 1901)
Calendar of Patent Rolls, Henry VII, 1494–1509 (London, 1916)
Calendar of Patent Rolls, Elizabeth I, 1572–1575 (London, 1973)
Many of the references in the Patent Rolls up to 1452 were checked online using the website of the Calendar of Patent Rolls project of Professor G.R. Boynton and the University of Iowa Libraries; http://sdrc.lib.uiowa.edu/patentrolls/ [last accessed March 2008].
Curia Regis Rolls of the reign of Henry III vol. XII 1225–1226 (London, 1957)

Printed maps

Bryant, A., *The county of Hertford* (London, 1822), reprinted by Hertfordshire Record Society (2003)
Dury, A. and Andrews, J., *A topographical map of Hartfordshire* (London, 1766), reprinted by Hertfordshire Record Society (2004)
Morden, R., *Hertfordshire* (1722)
Norden, J., *Hartford Shire* (1598)
Oliver, J., *The actual survey of the county of Hertford* (1695), republished in D. Hodson, *Four county maps of Hertfordshire* (Stevenage, 1985)
Saxton, C., *Hartfordiae Comitatus* (1577), published in V.G. Scott and T. Rook, *County maps and histories: Hertfordshire* (London, 1989)
Seller, J., *Hertfordshire actually survey'd and delineated* (1676), republished in D. Hodson, *Four county maps of Hertfordshire* (Stevenage, 1985)
Warburton, J., county map (surveyed 1720–3, published 1749), republished in D. Hodson, *Four county maps of Hertfordshire* (Stevenage, 1985)

Ordnance Survey maps, 6 inches to the mile

Sheet VII, surveyed 1880, published 1884
Sheet VIII, surveyed 1877, published 1883
Sheet IX, surveyed 1876–8, published 1880–3
Sheet XI, surveyed 1880, published 1884
Sheet XII, surveyed 1878–81, published 1884
Sheet XIII, surveyed 1877–8, published 1884
Sheet XIV, surveyed 1876–8, published 1881–3
Sheet XIX, surveyed 1878–81, published 1884
Sheet XX, surveyed 1881, published 1884
Sheet XXI, surveyed 1878–80, published 1884
Sheet XXII, surveyed 1878, published 1883
Sheet XXIII, surveyed 1874–9, published 1879–83
Sheet XXV, surveyed 1877–9, published 1884
Sheet XXVI, surveyed 1877–8, published 1883–4
Sheet XXVII, surveyed 1877–8, published 1884
Sheet XXVIII, surveyed 1878–81, published 1884
Sheet XXIX, surveyed 1879–80, published 1884
Sheet XXX, surveyed 1873–80, published 1881–3
Sheet XXXI, surveyed 1873–9, published 1880–84
Sheet XXXII, surveyed 1874–7, published 1883–4
Sheet XXXIII, surveyed 1873–8, published 1883
Sheet XXXIV, surveyed 1872–8, published 1883
Sheet XXXV, surveyed 1873–9, published 1883
Sheet XXXVI, surveyed 1873–80, published 1883
Sheet XXXVII, surveyed 1870–80, published 1880–82
Sheet XXXVIII, surveyed 1873–7, published 1882–3
Sheet XXXIX, surveyed 1871–2, published 1883

Sheet XL, surveyed 1870–73, published 1877
Sheet XLI, surveyed 1873, published 1882
Sheet XLIII, surveyed 1864–76, published 1868–83
Sheet XLIV, surveyed 1871, published 1877

Ordnance Survey maps, 25 inches to the mile
Sheet IX.11, surveyed 1878

British Geological Survey maps 1:50,000 Series (solid and drift edition)
Sheet 221 Hitchin, 1995
Sheet 222 Great Dunmow, 1990
Sheet 238 Aylesbury, 1946 (reprinted 1990)
Sheet 239 Hertford, 1978
Sheet 240 Epping, 1981
Sheet 255 Beaconsfield, 2005
Sheet 256 North London, 2006

Secondary sources

Adams, S. (ed.), *Household accounts and disbursement books of Robert Dudley, Earl of Leicester, 1558-1561, 1584-1586* (Cambridge, 1995)
Almond, R., *Medieval hunting* (Stroud, 2003)
Altschul, M., 'Clare, Gilbert de, eighth earl of Gloucester and seventh earl of Hertford (1291–1314)', *Oxford dictionary of national biography* (Oxford, 2004), accessed online 3 October 2007
Altschul, M., 'Clare, Richard de, sixth earl of Gloucester and fifth earl of Hertford (1222–1262)', *Oxford dictionary of national biography* (Oxford, 2004), accessed online 2 October 2007
Andrews, H.C., 'An unknown earthwork at Old Hall Green', *Transactions of the East Herts Archaeological Society*, 7 (1926)
Andrews, H.C., *The chronicles of Hertford castle* (Hertford, 1947)
Andrews, R.T., 'The Rye House castle and manor of Rye', *East Herts Archaeological Society Transactions*, 2 (1902)
Archer, P.C., *Historic Cheshunt* (Cheshunt, 1923)
Archer, T.A., 'Clare, Gilbert de, fifth earl of Gloucester and fourth earl of Hertford (c.1180–1230)', rev. Michael Altschul, *Oxford dictionary of national biography* (Oxford, 2004; online edn, Oct 2005), accessed 2 October 2007
Armitage-Smith, S. (ed.), *John of Gaunt's register*, 2 (London, 1911)
Austin, P., 'Hatfield Great Wood and its inclosure', *Hertfordshire's Past*, 38 (1995)
Austin, P., 'The leasing of Lord Burghley's Hoddesdon woodlands in 1595', *Hertfordshire's Past*, 41 (1996)
Ayton, A., 'Morley, Robert, second Lord Morley (b. in or before 1295, d. 1360)', *Oxford dictionary of national biography* (Oxford, 2004) accessed online 2 September 2007
Bailey, M., 'Introduction', in J. Brooker and S. Flood (eds), *Hertfordshire lay subsidy rolls 1307 and 1334* (Hertfordshire Record Society, 1998)
Barber, R., 'Edward, prince of Wales and of Aquitaine (1330–1376)', *Oxford dictionary of national biography* (Oxford, September 2004; online edn, May 2006), accessed online 28 September 2007
Biddle, M., Barfield, L. and Millard, A., 'The excavation of the manor of The More, Rickmansworth, Hertfordshire', *The Archaeological Journal*, 116 (1959)
Bilikowski, K., *Hampshire's countryside heritage: historic parks and gardens* (Winchester, 1983)

Bindoff, S.T., *The history of parliament, the House of Commons 1509–1558* (London, 1982)

Birch, W. De Gray, *Cartularium Saxonicum: A collection of charters relating to Anglo-Saxon history*, 1 (London, 1885, reprinted 1964)

Birrell, J., 'Deer and deer farming in medieval England', *Agricultural History Review*, 40, (1993)

Bliss, P. (ed.), *Reliquiae Hearnianae*, 3 (London, 1869)

Bond, E.A., 'Notices of the last days of Isabella, Queen of Edward the second, drawn from an account of the expenses of her household', *Archaeologia*, 35 (1853)

Brigden, S., 'Howard, Henry, earl of Surrey (1516/17–1547)', *Oxford dictionary of national biography* (Oxford, September 2004; online edn, January 2007), accessed online 27 July 2007

Brooker, J. and Flood, S. (eds), *Hertfordshire lay subsidy rolls 1307 and 1334* (Hertfordshire Record Society, 1998)

Bryant, A., *The county of Hertford* (London, 1822), reprinted by Hertfordshire Record Society (2003)

Campbell, E.M.J., 'Hertfordshire', in Darby, H.C. and Campbell, E.M.J. (eds), *The Domesday geography of south-east England* (Cambridge, 1962)

Cantor, L.M., 'Forests, chases, parks and warrens', in Cantor, L.M. (ed.), *The English Medieval Landscape* (London, 1982)

Cantor, L.M., *The medieval parks of England: a gazetteer* (Loughborough, 1983)

Cantor, L.M. and Hatherly, J., 'The medieval parks of England', *Geography*, 64 (1979)

Carley, J.P., 'Parker, Henry, eleventh Baron Morley (1531/2–1577)', *Oxford dictionary of national biography* (Oxford, 2004), accessed online 6 November 2007

Castle, S. and Brooks, W., *The book of Elstree and Boreham Wood* (Buckingham, 1988)

Chandler, J., *John Leland's itinerary: travels in Tudor England* (Stroud, 1998)

Chauncy, H., *The historical antiquities of Hertfordshire* (London, 1700)

Clutterbuck, R., *The history and antiquities of the county of Hertford*, 1–3 (London, 1815–27)

Cobb, J.W., *Two lectures on the history and antiquities of Berkhamsted* (London, 1883)

Colvin, H.M. (ed.), *The history of the king's works*, vols. 1 and 2 (London, 1963)

Crouch, D., 'Grandmesnil, Petronilla de, countess of Leicester (d. 1212)', *Oxford dictionary of national biography* (Oxford, 2004) accessed online 14 Oct 2007

Crouch, D., 'Marshal, William (I), fourth earl of Pembroke (c.1146–1219)', *Oxford dictionary of national biography* (Oxford, September 2004; online edn, May 2007), accessed online 27 September 2007

Curry, A., 'Montagu, Thomas, fourth earl of Salisbury (1388–1428)', *Oxford dictionary of national biography* (Oxford, September 2004; online edn, May 2006), accessed online 17 August 2007

Curry, A., 'Oldhall, Sir William (d. 1460)', *Oxford dictionary of national biography* (Oxford, 2004), accessed online 27 July 2007

Cussans, J.E., *History of Hertfordshire*, 1–3 (London, 1870–81)

Davies, C., 'Page, Sir Richard (d. 1548)', *Oxford dictionary of national biography* (Oxford, 2004), accessed online 5 August 2007

Davies, R.G., 'Fordham, John (c.1340–1425)', rev., *Oxford dictionary of national biography* (Oxford, 2004), accessed online 24 August 2007

Davies, R.R., 'Mortimer, Roger (VII), fourth earl of March and sixth earl of Ulster (1374–1398)', *Oxford dictionary of national biography* (Oxford, September 2004; online edn, May 2006), accessed online 3 October 2007

Dawes, M.C.B., *Register of Edward the Black Prince, part 1 A.D. 1346–1348* (London, 1930)

Dawes, M.C.B., *Register of Edward the Black Prince, part 4 (England) 1351–1365* (London, 1933)

Dohar, W.J., 'Langham, Simon (d. 1376)', *Oxford dictionary of national biography* (Oxford, 2004), accessed online 24 August 2007

Dony, J.G., *Flora of Hertfordshire* (Hitchin, 1967)

Dunn, D.E.S., 'Margaret (1430–1482)', *Oxford dictionary of national biography* (Oxford, 2004), accessed online 28 November 2007

Dury, A. and Andrews, J., *A topographical map of Hartfordshire* (London, 1766), reprinted by Hertfordshire Record Society (2004)

Ellcock, T.W., 'The Bishop of London's hall or lodge at Bishops Stortford', *Herts Past and Present*, 5 (1964)

Ellis, W., *The timber tree improved* (London, 1742)

Fairweather, J., *Liber Eliensis translated from the Latin* (Woodbridge, 2005)

Falvey, H., 'The More: Rickmansworth's lost palace', *Hertfordshire's Past*, 34 (1993)

Falvey, H., 'Crown policy and local economic context in the Berkhamsted Common enclosure dispute, 1618–42', *Rural History*, 12 (2001)

Farris, N., *The Wymondleys* (Hertfordshire Publications, 1989)

Field, J., *English field names: a dictionary* (Newton Abbot, 1972)

Fisher, J.L., *A medieval farming glossary of Latin and English words* (London, 1968)

Fleming, P., 'Say, Geoffrey de, second Lord de Say (1304/5–1359)', *Oxford dictionary of national biography* (Oxford, 2004), accessed online 17 July 2007

Gardiner, J. (ed.), *Who's who in British history* (London, 2000)

Garside, S., *Hoddesdon: a history* (Chichester, 2002)

Gover, J.E.B., Mawer, A. and Stenton, F.M., *The place-names of Hertfordshire* (Cambridge, 1938)

Greaves, R.L., 'Capel, Arthur, first earl of Essex (bap. 1632, d. 1683)', *Oxford dictionary of national biography* (Oxford, 2004), accessed online 22 July 2007

Griffiths, R.A., 'Henry VI (1421–1471)', *Oxford dictionary of national biography* (Oxford, September 2004; online edn, May 2006), accessed online 28 November 2007

Haggard, D. Dawson, 'History of the Haggard family in England and America: 1433–1899', www.surnames.com, accessed 26 August 2007

Hale, W.H., *The Domesday of St Paul's of 1222* (Camden Society, 1858)

Hall, G. Montague, *A history of Bushey* (Bushey, 1938)

Harting, J.E., 'Hertfordshire deer-parks', *Transactions of the Hertfordshire Natural History Society*, 2 (1881)

Head, D.M., 'Howard, Thomas, second duke of Norfolk (1443–1524)', *Oxford dictionary of national biography* (Oxford, 2004; online edn, May 2005), accessed online 27 July 2007

Henning, B.D., *The history of parliament: the House of Commons*

1660–1690 (London, 1983)

Hicks, M., 'Neville, George (1432–1476)', *Oxford dictionary of national biography* (Oxford, 2004), accessed online 15 October 2007

Hill, L.M., 'Caesar, Sir Charles (1590–1642)', *Oxford dictionary of national biography* (Oxford, 2004), accessed online 5 November 2007

Hine, R.L., *The History of Hitchin*, 1 (London, 1927)

Hodson, D., *Four county maps of Hertfordshire* (Stevenage, 1985)

Hooke, D., 'Pre-Conquest woodland: its distribution and usage', *Agricultural History Review*, 37, 2 (1989)

Hoppitt, R., 'Hunting Suffolk's parks: towards a reliable chronology of imparkment', in Liddiard, R. (ed.), *The medieval park: new perspectives* (Macclesfield, 2007)

Howlett, B. (ed.), *Survey of the royal manor of Hitchin, 1676* (Hertfordshire Record Society, 2000)

Howlett, B., *Hitchin Priory Park* (Hitchin Historical Society, 2004)

Howlett, D.R., *Dictionary of medieval Latin from British sources* (Oxford, 1989)

Hunn, J., *Reconstruction and measurement of landscape change: a study of six parishes in the St Albans area*, BAR British Series, 236 (1994)

Hunn, J., 'Tyttenhanger Park. The rise and fall of a manorial estate', *Hertfordshire's Past*, 52 (2002)

Hunsdon Local History and Preservation Society, *Hunsdon and Widford: a local history* (1979; reprinted 2002)

Hutton, R., 'Capel, Arthur, first Baron Capel of Hadham (1604–1649)', *Oxford dictionary of national biography* (Oxford, September 2004; online edn, October 2006), accessed online 22 July 2007

Jack, S.M., 'Fanshawe, Thomas (c.1533–1601)', *Oxford dictionary of national biography* (Oxford, 2004; online edn, May 2005), accessed online 14 October 2007

Jack, S.M., 'Fanshawe, Thomas, first Viscount Fanshawe of Dromore (1596–1665)', *Oxford dictionary of national biography* (Oxford, 2004), accessed online 14 October 2007

Keats-Rohan, K.S.B., *Domesday people: a prosopography of persons occurring in English documents, 1066–1166, I Domesday Book* (Woodbridge, 1999)

Keats-Rohan, K.S.B., 'Grandmesnil, Hugh de (d. 1098)', *Oxford dictionary of national biography* (Oxford, 2004), accessed online 14 October 2007

Kingsford, C.L., 'Loring, Sir Neil (c.1315–1386)', rev. Richard Barber, *Oxford dictionary of national biography* (Oxford, 2004; online edn, October 2005), accessed online 18 July 2007

Klingelhofer, E.C., *The deserted medieval village of Broadfield, Herts.*, BAR, 2 (1974)

Knafla, L.A., 'Egerton, John, first earl of Bridgewater (1579–1649)', *Oxford dictionary of national biography* (Oxford, September 2004; online edn, May 2007), accessed online 22 October 2007

Langbein, J. and Chapman, N., *Fallow deer* (London, 2003)

Lasdun, S., *The English park: royal, private and public* (London, 1991)

Latham, R.E., *Revised medieval Latin word-list* (London, 1965)

Levett, A.E., *Studies in manorial history* (Oxford, 1938)

Lewis, C.P., 'Tosny, Ralph de (d. 1102?)', *Oxford dictionary of national biography* (Oxford, 2004), accessed online 4 August 2007

Lewis, C.T. and Short, C., *A Latin dictionary* (Oxford, 1966)

Liddiard, R., 'The deer parks of Domesday Book', *Landscapes*, 4, 1 (2003)

Liddiard, R. (ed.), *The medieval park: new perspectives* (Macclesfield, 2007)

Lodge, E., *Life of Sir Julius Caesar Knt … with memoirs of his family & descendants* (London, 1810)

Manley, G., *Climate and the British scene* (London, 1952)

Martin, G.H., 'Louth, William of (c.1240–1298)', *Oxford dictionary of national biography* (Oxford, 2004), accessed online 20 July 2007

Midgley, L.M. (ed.), *Ministers' accounts of the earldom of Cornwall 1296–1297*, vol. 1 (London, 1942)

Midgley, L.M. (ed.), *A history of the county of Stafford*, 5 (VCH, 1959)

Mileson, S.A., 'The importance of parks in fifteenth-century society', in L. Clark (ed.), *The fifteenth century V* (Woodbridge, 2005)

Mileson, S.A., 'The sociology of park creation in medieval England', in R. Liddiard (ed.), *The medieval park: new perspectives* (Macclesfield, 2007)

Minet, W., *Hadham Hall and the manor of Bawdes alias Hadham Parva* (1914)

Monro, C., *Letters of Queen Margaret of Anjou* (London, 1863)

Morgan, P., 'Norbury, John (d. 1414)', *Oxford dictionary of national biography* (Oxford, 2004; online edn, May 2006), accessed online 9 July 2007

Morris, J., *Troubles of our catholic forefathers* (London, 1872)

Morris, J. (ed.), *Domesday Book: Hertfordshire* (Chichester, 1976)

Morris, J., *A Latin glossary for family and local historians* (Birmingham, 1989, reprinted 1997)

Munby, L.M. (ed.), *The history of King's Langley* (Workers' Educational Association, 1963)

Munby, L.M., *The Hertfordshire landscape* (London, 1977)

Neave, S., *Medieval parks of East Yorkshire* (Beverley, 1991)

Norden, J., *A description of Hertfordshire* (Ware, 1598, reprinted 1903)

O'Connor, S., 'Montagu, Maud, countess of Salisbury (d. 1424)', *Oxford dictionary of national biography* (Oxford, 2004), accessed online 7 November 2007

Page, W. (ed.), *A history of the county of Norfolk*, 2 (Victoria County History (hereafter VCH), 1906)

Page, W. (ed.), *A history of the county of Hertford*, 2 (VCH, 1908)

Page, W. (ed.), *A history of the county of Hampshire*, 4 (VCH, 1911)

Page, W. (ed.), *A history of the county of Hertford*, 3 (VCH, 1912)

Page, W. (ed.), *A history of the county of Hertford*, 4 (VCH, 1971)

Pedrick, M., *Moor Park: The Grosvenor legacy* (Rickmansworth, 1989)

Perowne, C., *A history of the parish of Standon* (Hertford, 1967)

Phillips, M., 'Theobalds Park wall', *East Herts Archaeological Society Transactions*, 5 (1914)

Pluskowski, A., 'The social construction of medieval park ecosystems: an interdisciplinary perspective', in R. Liddiard (ed.), *The medieval park: new perspectives* (Macclesfield, 2007)

Prestwich, M., 'Bigod, Roger (IV), fifth earl of Norfolk (c.1245–1306)', *Oxford dictionary of national biography* (Oxford, 2004), accessed online 27 September 2007

Prince, H., *Parks in Hertfordshire since 1500* (Hatfield, 2008)

Rackham, O., *Ancient woodland* (London, 1980; republished Dalbeattie, 2003)

Rackham, O., *The history of the countryside* (1986; republished London, 1997)

Richardson, A., '"The king's chief delights": a landscape approach to the royal parks of post-Conquest England', in R. Liddiard (ed.), *The medieval park: new perspectives* (Macclesfield, 2007)

Richardson, J., *The local historian's encyclopedia* (New Barnet, 1974, second edition 1986)

Ridgeway, H., 'William de Valence and his *familiares* 1247–72', *Historical Research*, 65 (1992)

Ridgeway, H.W., 'Argentine, Sir Giles d' (*c*.1210–1282)', *Oxford dictionary of national biography* (Oxford, September 2004; online edn, May 2007), accessed online 29 November 2007

Riley, H.T. (ed.), *Gesta abbatum monasterii Sancti Albani a Thoma Walsingham, vol. 1, AD 793–1290* (London, 1867; republished Germany, 1965)

Riley, H.T. (ed.), *Gesta abbatum monasterii Sancti Albani a Thoma Walsingham, vol. 3, AD 1349–1411* (London, 1869; republished Germany, 1965)

Riley, H.T. (ed.), *Annales monasterii Sancti Albani a Johanne Amundesham, vol. 1* (London, 1870)

Roberts, E., *A school of masons in 15th century north Hertfordshire* (Hertfordshire Library Service and Hertfordshire Local History Council, 1979)

Robinson, G., *Hertfordshire*, Barracuda Guide to County History, 3 (Chesham, 1978)

Roden, D., 'Demesne farming in the Chiltern hills', *Agricultural History Review*, 17 (1969)

Roskell, J.S., Clark, L. and Rawcliffe, C., *The history of parliament: the House of Commons 1386–1421* (Stroud, 1992)

Rotherham, I.D., 'The historical ecology of medieval parks and the implications for conservation', in R. Liddiard (ed.), *The medieval park: new perspectives* (Macclesfield, 2007)

Round, J.H., 'Introduction to the Hertfordshire Domesday', in W. Page (ed.), *The Victoria history of the county of Hertford*, 1 (London, 1971)

Rowe, A., *The protected valley: a history of Little Munden* (1999)

Rowe, A., *Garden making and the Freman family: a memoir of Hamels, 1713–1733* (Hertford, 2001)

Rowe, A., 'The distribution of parks in Hertfordshire: landscape, lordship and woodland', in R. Liddiard (ed.), *The medieval park: new perspectives* (Macclesfield, 2007)

Ryan, P., 'Woodham Walter Hall – its site and setting', *Essex Archaeology and History*, 30 (2000)

Salmon, N., *The history of Hertfordshire* (London, 1728)

Shirley, E., *English deer parks* (London, 1867)

Slater, T. and Goose, N. (eds), *A county of small towns: the development of Hertfordshire's urban landscape to 1800* (Hatfield, 2008)

Smith, J.T., *English houses 1200–1800: the Hertfordshire evidence* (London, 1992)

Smith, J.T., *Hertfordshire houses: selective inventory* (London, 1993)

Smith, W. and Lockwood, J., *Chambers Murray Latin–English dictionary* (Edinburgh, 1933, reprinted 2001)

Stone, L. and J.C., *An open elite? England 1540–1880* (Oxford, 1995)

Stone, L.W., Rothwell, W. and Reid, T.B.W., *Anglo-Norman Dictionary* (London, 1983)

Stratford, J., 'Whittingham, Sir Robert (*d*. 1452)', *Oxford dictionary of national biography* (Oxford, 2004), accessed online 29 August 2007

Stratton, J.M., *Agricultural records A.D. 220–1977* (London, 1978)

Taylor, C., 'Medieval ornamental landscapes', *Landscapes*, 1 (2000)

Taylor, P.J., 'The estates of the bishopric of London from the seventh century to the early sixteenth century', (PhD thesis, London, 1976)

Thurley, S., *The royal palaces of Tudor England: architecture and court life, 1460–1547* (New Haven, 1993)

Tregelles, J.A., *A history of Hoddesdon* (Hertford, 1908)

Vale, B., 'Scrope, Richard, first Baron Scrope of Bolton (*c*.1327–1403)', *Oxford dictionary of national biography* (Oxford, 2004), accessed online 19 August 2007

Van Koughnet, J.C.E., *A history of Tyttenhanger* (London, 1895)

Vincent, N., 'Richard, first earl of Cornwall and king of Germany (1209–1272)', *Oxford dictionary of national biography* (Oxford, September 2004; online edn, May 2006), accessed online 28 September 2007

Vincent, N., 'Edmund of Almain, second earl of Cornwall (1249–1300)', *Oxford dictionary of national biography* (Oxford, 2004), accessed online 21 October 2007

Wainwright, A., 'Ashridge park survey', unpublished report for the National Trust (1989)

Ward, J.C., 'Clare, Elizabeth de (1294/5–1360)', *Oxford dictionary of national biography* (Oxford, 2004), accessed online 3 October 2007

Warrand, D. (ed.), *Hertfordshire families* (London, 1907)

Watts, J., 'Richard of York, third duke of York (1411–1460)', *Oxford dictionary of national biography* (Oxford, 2004), accessed online 27 July 2007

Waugh, S.L., 'Lee, Sir John (*d*. 1370)', *Oxford dictionary of national biography* (Oxford, 2004), accessed online 22 September 2007

Way, T., *A study of the impact of imparkment on the social landscape of Cambridgeshire and Huntingdonshire from c.1080 to 1760*, BAR British Series, 258 (1997)

Weikel, A., 'Mary I (1516–1558)', *Oxford dictionary of national biography* (Oxford, September 2004; online edn, May 2006), accessed online 28 July 2007

Whybrow, G.H., *History of Berkhamsted Common* (London, 1934)

Williams, A., 'A homestead moat at Nuthampstead, Hertfordshire', *The Antiquaries Journal*, 26 (1946)

Williamson, T., 'Fish, fur and feather: Man and nature in the post-medieval landscape', in K. Barker and T. Darvill (eds), *Making English landscapes* (Bournemouth, 1999)

Williamson, T. and the Hertfordshire Gardens Trust, *The parks and gardens of west Hertfordshire* (Hertford, 2000)

Williamson, T., *The origins of Hertfordshire* (Manchester, 2000)

Williamson, T., *Rabbits, Warrens and Archaeology* (Stroud, 2007)

Workers' Educational Association, *Hatfield and its people: a thousand years of history*, 1 (1959)

Workers' Educational Association, *Hatfield and its people: farming yesterday and today*, 9 (1962)

Woolgar, C.M., *The great household in late medieval England* (New Haven & London, 1999)

Woudhuysen, H.R., 'Ferrers, George (*c*.1510–1579)', *Oxford dictionary of national biography* (Oxford, 2004), accessed online 5 August 2007

Yaxley, D., *A researcher's glossary of words found in historical documents of East Anglia* (Dereham, 2003)

Young, A., *General view of the agriculture of the county of Hertfordshire* (London, 1804; republished Plymouth, 1971)

Websites

http://earth.google.com (Google Earth)

www.british-history.ac.uk (Victoria County History)

www.english-nature.org.uk

www.magic.gov.uk

www.oxforddnb.com (*Oxford dictionary of national biography*)

www.trytel.com/~tristan/towns/florilegium/lifecycle/lcdth18.html

Index

Page numbers in **bold** indicate the main reference to a subject.
Page numbers in *italic* refer to the map of the park in the Gazetteer.
Page numbers followed by 'n' refer to footnotes.

Abbot, William 169
Abbott, William, charcoal-maker 33
Adam, Nicholas 64
Adams, Phillip 221
Adye alias Gynn, William, of Knebworth 158
Aelmer of Benington 10, 56
Agistment 3, 4, 6, 22, 24, 26, **31**, 32, 232
    Albury 23, 44
    Benington 27, 31, 58
    Berkhamsted 31, 65
    Bishop's Stortford 31, 68
    Cheshunt 78
    Essendon 90
    Great Munden 27, 102
    Hatfield 112, 114
    Hertingfordbury 124
    King's Langley 31, 148, 150, 151
    Knebworth 32, 154, 156
    Little Hadham 31, 166, 167, 169
    Sawbridgeworth 31, 194
    Standon 31, 204, 206
    Walkern 31, 218
    Ware 224
    Weston 31, 228
Ailmer, Dr Theophilus 170n
Ake, John de 114
Albury 5, 7, 8, 9, 37, 44–7, 170
    Albury Hall 46
    Albury Lodge 46
    Punsho park 23, 33, 34, 36, **44–7**, *45*
    vicar of 44
Aldbury 8, 214
    Aldbury heath 162
    Pendley Farm 214, 215–16
    Pendley Hall 214–15
    Pendley park **214–17**, *215 see also* Tring
Aldebury, Walter de 6, 64
Aldenham 14, 17
Almshoe *see* Ippollitts
Alstan, thane of King Edward 10
Alston, Rowland 200
Amyce, Israel 78, 80, 100, 103, 130
Andrews, H.C. 221n
Andrews, R.T. 212, 213
Anne Boleyn, Queen 129, 151, 230
Anstey 52, 134
Ardeley 7, 11, 12, 48–9

Ardeley Bury park **48–9**, *49*
    fishponds 24, 48
    Parker's Green 221
    Wood End 221
Argentein/Argentine, Sir Giles d' 13, 176
    John de 176
    Margaret de 176
    Reginald de 11, 13, 176
Ashridge park 7, 11, 12, 17, 18, 19, 42, **162–5**, *163*
Ashwell 15, 56
Askell of Ware 10, 222
Aspenden Hall 200
Aston, Walter, Lord, of Tixall 206, 208
Atkyn, John, park keeper at Berkhamsted 65
Augustinian Friars, Cambridge 218
Averell, Thomas 172
Aylesbury 17
Ayot St Lawrence 7, 8, 11, 12, 14, 50–1, 154
    Hill Farm 50
    park 13, **50–1**, *51*
Ayot St Peter 50
Ayot, William de 11, 13, 50

Baard family 44
Baard, Robert 44
Baesh, Edward 212
Bagshot Park 170
Baldock 8, 36–7, 230
Balliol, Alexander de 56
    John de 128
Bannockburn, battle of 204
Barband 29, 62, 166
Bark **33**, 112, 166–7
Barking/Berkyng, Abbess of 218
Barkway 5, 52–5
    Cokenach 52
    Newsells manor 52
    Scales park 7, 11, 20, 35, 36, **52–5**, *53*
Barley 52
Barley, Walter de 52
Barre, Idonea 154
    Sir John 14, 154, 156
Basely, William 112
Baskerville, Thomas 164
Bassele, Thomas de 169, 208
Basset, John, parker at Walkern 218
Bassingbourn, Alan de 7
    family, de 28, 80
Bassingbourne family 130
    Agnes de 130
Bassingbourne's park 7, 130

Bassingburn family 118
 John (d. 1276/7) 118
 John, sheriff of Hertfordshire and Essex 118
 Katherine née Say 118
 Stephen de 130
 Thomas 118
Bassingeborn, Alan de 80
Bassyngburne, John de 130
Baud, Ralph 169
 Thomas 14, 169, 208
 Walter 169
 William 169
 William le 208, 209n
Bayford 108, 122
 Ashendene Farm 108
Beauchamp, Alice de (née Tosny/Tony) 94
 Guy de, Earl of Warwick 94
 Thomas de 94
Beaufort, Thomas, Duke of Exeter 172
Beche, Richard 118
Bedel, William 68
Bedford, duke of 11, 12, 212
 John, Duke of 214
Bedfordshire 9, 14, 15, 17, 222
 Chalgrave 146
Bedwell see Essendon
Bellot, Thomas 169
Benington viii, 7, 56–61
 Aelmer of 10
 Cole's Green 60
 Hailey Park Wood 6, 59, 61
 Hayley park 7, 57, 59, 60–1
 Lordship 57, 61
 manor 10–11, 27, 56, 57, 58, 59
 park 6, 10, 22, 27, 30, 31, 32, 33, 35, 36, 56–60, 57, 102, 142,
  175n, 218, 220, 221
Benstede, John de 56, 60
 John de, grandson of John 57, 60
 Petronilla de 57, 60
Berding, lelle berdynge 29, 30, 156, 206
Berkhamsted 7, 37, 42, 62–7, 162, 225n
 castle 9, 12, 13, 64, 65, 162
 honour 148
 park 3, 6, 7, 8, 9, 17, 18, 19, 21, 22, 24, 26, 31, 32, 33, 34, 35,
  36, 62–7, 63, 216
 park pale 28, 29, 30, 62, 64, 65, 66
 Place 65, 66, 216
 St Peter 66
Berkshire 214
 Windsor 65
Bernwood, Buckinghamshire 21, 100
Beyford, John, falconer 37, 44
Bigge, Roger, parker at Berkhamsted 37, 64–5
Bigod, Roger le, fifth Earl of Norfolk 228
Bishop's Stortford 7, 68–71, 99, 198 see also Stortford
 Claypits Farm 70
 park 29, 30, 31, 35, 68–71, 69
 Stortford Park Farm see Stortford
 Wickham Hall estate 170
 Wickham Hall farm 170

Black Death 7, 8, 9, 167, 206, 226
Black Prince see Edward, the Black Prince
Blakesware 206
Bluck, Matthew 139
Bohun, de, family 130
 Joan de 225n
Boleyn, Anne, Queen 129, 151, 230
Bolowe, John 124
Bolton castle, Wensleydale 194
Bonhommes 162
Boreham Wood 7, 11, 21 see also Elstree
Boteler, Sir Francis 118
 Sir Ralph, Lord of Sudeley 13, 180
Bourchier, Anne 58, 59
 Henry, Earl of Essex 58, 102
 Mary née Say 58, 102
Bourghchier, Isabel née Barre 156
 Sir Thomas 36, 156
Bramfield 7, 11, 72–3
 park 72–3, 73
 Park Wood 6, 72, 73
 Woods 61
Brangor, Reginald 130
Braughing 8, 44, 208
 Cockhamsted manor 44
 Hamels estate 200
Bridgewater, Countess of 164
 Duke of 100, 164
 Earl(s) of 100, 164
Briscowe, Nicholas 184
British Geological Survey 42
Briton, Ranulf 21, 228
Brittany, Count Alan of 10, 80
 Duke of 10, 12, 80, 130
 John IV, Duke of 80
 John, Duke of, and Earl of Richmond 80, 82
Broadfield 42, 74–5
 Hall 74
 park 7, 42, 74–5, 75, 84
Brograve family 46
Bromley, George 224, 225
Brown, Capability 164
Browne, Thomas 159n
Broxbourne 27, 130
 Baas manor 27, 90
Bryant, A., mapmaker 50, 88, 214, 216
Buckinghamshire 9, 14, 21, 42, 100, 214
 Bernwood 21, 100
 Pitstone 42, 162
 Whaddon Chase 21, 100
Buckler, J.C. 146, 147, 196
Bucknall, Sir William 226
Budder, John 118
Buntingford 15, 57
Burgh, Elizabeth de 204
 John de 204
Bushey 7, 8, 76–7
 Hall or Bury 13, 76
 Hall Golf Course 76
 manor 35

park **76–7**, *77*
Buxton, Thomas 210
Byde, Sir Thomas 224
    Thomas Hope 224
Bygrave manor 74, 172

Caesar, Sir Charles 60
    Sir Julius 60
Calais 214
Calvert family 139
Calvert, Felix 96
Cambridge:
    Augustinian Friars 218
    Downham manor 168
    Trinity College 59, 224
Cambridgeshire 5, 13, 15, 57, 176
    Childerley 202
Cannock forest, Staffordshire 21
Cantor, Leonard 4, 5, 9
Capel earls of Essex 221
Capel family 170, 220
Capel, Sir Arthur 60, 170, 220
    Arthur, first Baron 221
    Arthur, Earl of Essex 170, 221
    Henry 59, 170, 220
    Sir William 220
Carew, Sir Wimund 194
Carey, Sir Edward 65
    Henry, Baron Hunsdon and Earl of Dover 139
    Sir Henry, Lord Hunsdon 139
Cashio hundred 72
Cason, Edward 96
Cawarden, Sir Thomas 194
Cecil, Sir Robert 78, 100, 103, 112, 114, 131, 169 *see also*
Salisbury, Earl of/Lord
    William, Lord Burghley 78, 103, 112, 130, 198
Chambre, William del, parker at Pisho 194
Chapman, John 172, 175n
Chapman, John, parker at Cheshunt 78
Charcoal 24, 26, 32, **33**, 33n, 34, 90, 112, 114, 120n, 124, 154, 168–9
Charles I 151, 182, 224
Charles, Prince 66, 151
Charles, Prince of Wales 126
Chauncy family 48
Chauncy, Sir Henry 4, 24, 48, 69, 76, 92, 114, 128, 201n
Chaundeler, John 65
    Roger 65
Chauntecler, Roger 130
Chenduit, Ulian 162
Cheshire 90
Cheshunt 6, 7, 12, 20, 72, 78–83, 112
    Brantingshay park 7, 33, 36, **78–80**, *79*
    Bury Green 81
    La Mote manor 102
    manor 10–11, 28, 78, 80, 130
    old park 7, 8, 28, 32, **80–2**, *81*
    Periers manor 7, 12, 78, **82**
Chester, Robert 52
Chester, Robert, Bishop of 74

Childwick *see* St Michael's
Chilterns 14, 17, 18, 19, 28
Civil War 48n, 139, 156, 170, 221, 224
Clare, earls of 35
Clare and Pembroke, Gilbert, Earl of 10
Clare, de, family 204
    Gilbert de, Earl of Gloucester (d. 1230) 10, 204
    Gilbert de, Earl of Gloucester (d. 1295) 204
    Gilbert de, Earl of Gloucester and Hertford (d. 1314) 21, 204
    Richard de (1222-1262) 204
    Richard de (d. 1217) 204
Clare, Simon 116
Clarence, George, Duke of 78, 212
Clement, John 180
Clothall 42, 44, 74, 84–5
    Kingswood Bury manor 84
    park 7, **84–5**, *85*
    Simon de 84
Clutterbuck, R. 151
Clyffyn, Clement 218
Cockhamsted manor 44
Codicote 50, 156, 157
Coke, John of Melbourne 198
    Mary 198
Colney Heath 30, 184, 187
Colt, John 102
Colte, John 172
Colyer, Robert 154
Compartmented park 30–1, 32, 204
Compton, William 222, 224
Comyn, Elizabeth 122
Coney 50, 65, 113, 126, 142, 151, 158n, 194, 206, 230
    see also Rabbit
Copynger, Walter, parker 36, 156
Corbet, Robert 65
Cornwall, Earl of 11, 36, 62, 194
    Edmund, Earl of 9, 12, 13, 62, 162
    Edward, Duke of 62
    Richard, first Earl of, King of Germany 62
    Sanchia of Provence, Countess of 62
Cottered 74, 102
Cranfield, Lionel Lord 198
Cromwell, Thomas 180
Cropper, John 34, 154
Croxton, Henry 58
Cumberlow Green 74, 84
Cussans, J.E. 80, 220, 226
Cuttes, Sir John 14, 202

Dacres, Robert 72
Dardes, John 32
Datchworth 157
Deer 3–4, 6, 8, **21–3**, 44, 60, 62, 65, 78, 90, 96, 102, 113, 122, 124, 125, 138, 148, 151, 156, 162, 164, 166, 172, 184, 190, 194, 218, 221, 228
    counts of 59, 80, 112, 113, 114, 116, 124, 138, 164, 180, 182, 194, 206, 220, 230
    fallow 3, 21, 100, 114, 164, 172, 180, 182, 184, 196
    fodder 6, 22, 24, 34, 64, 65, 68, 78, 102, 124, 138, 148, 150, 158, 166, 180, 194, 197, 206, 224

gifts of 6, 21–2, 58, 102, 130, 156, 166, 218, 220, 230
management 27, 30–1, 35, 65, 68, 114, 124, 158, 162, 164, 166, 194, 197
red 21, 114, 164, 170, 184, 206
roe 21, 148
stealing 5, 50, 52, 56, 62, 68, 74, 80, 88, 102, 108, 136, 148, 169, 196, 208
wild 4
Denmark 212
Denny, Sir Anthony 78, 88, 90, 112
Henry 78
Derby, Earl of 100
Derbyshire:
Fanshawe Gate 225n
Melbourne 198
Derefold *see* St Michael's
Devereux, earls of Essex 221
Lettice, Lady Essex née Knollys 59
Robert 59
Walter, Earl of Essex 59, 60
Devon 146
Dewhurst, Barnard, woodward 112
Dimsdale, Baron 160
Robert 52, 54
Dissolution (of the monasteries) 72, 88, 188
Docwra, Periam 126
Domesday Book 5, 7, 10, 11, 14, 15, 16, 17, 56, 80, 94, 130, 190, 192, 222
population distribution 18
woodland 16
Dominican Friars 150
Dovecotes **23–4**, 37, 44
Drapentier, Jan 92, 128
Dudley, Robert, Earl of Leicester 59
Dury and Andrews, mapmakers 46, 88, 103, 108, 139, 160, 182, 186, 198, 216, 224, 226

Easneye park 11, 19, *211 see also* Stanstead Abbots
East Anglian Heights 15
Eastwick 7, 17, 36, 86–7, 99, 136, 138, 140, 141n, 196
Lodge Farm 196
park **86–7**, *87*
Edeva the Fair 10, 68
Edgar, King 17, 108
Edward The Confessor 11, 56, *222*
Edward I 3, 9, 12, 62, 148, 154, 162
Edward II 4, 13, 21, 62, 148, 150, 204
Edward III 8, 13, 37, 44, 62, 150, 169, 209n
Edward IV 65, 88, 136, 151, 180, 206
Edward VI 94, 124, 184, 194, 224
Edward, the Black Prince 3, 6, 8, 11, 22, 28, 36, 64, 146
Edward, Prince 138
Edward, Prince of Wales 148
Edward, Prince of Wales and Duke of Cornwall 65
Egerton, John 164
Thomas, Baron Ellesmere 164
Eleanor of Castile, Queen 9, 13, 21, 148
Eleanor of Provence, Queen 62
Elizabeth I 65, 96, 124, 126, 139, 151, 156, 163, 164, 169, 170, 210
Elizabeth, Princess 112, 116, 163

Elizabeth of York, Queen 65, 151
Elliott, Robert 178
Elstree 21, 88–9
Boreham Wood 7, 11, 21, **88–9**
Rectory Farm alias Whitehouse Farm 88
Eltham manor 150
Eltham, John de 62
Ely abbey 17
abbots of 11, 17, 166
Ely, bishop of 8, 12, 14, 21, 24, 26, 27, 31, 33, 34, 35, 36, 108, 112, 114, 118, 160, 166, 169, 218
Bishop Hugh de Balsham 166
Bishop John Barnet 168, 170n
Bishop John Fordham 166, 168
Bishop Simon Langham 167
Bishop Lewis of Luxembourg 23n, 170n
Bishop William of Louth 21, 130
Bishop Philip Morgan 167
bishopric of 4, 108
monk of 108
Engayne, Henry 136
John 86, 136, 138
Thomas 136
Epping Forest 170
Ermine Street 80
Ernald, William 64
Essendon 19, 21, 23, 27, 33, 90–3, 122
Bedwell 5, 7, 8, 11, 160
Bedwell park 13, 19, 22, 27, 30, 32, 33, 36, 83n, **90–3**, *91*, 160
Bedwell Park Farm 92
Bedwell warren 23, 90, 92, 93n
Herinebemgat/Hornbeamgate manor 34
Essex 13, 22, 52, 94, 96, 169, 176, 214, 218
Barking, Jenkins estate 225n
Clavering park 52
Farnham 170
forest of 21, 130, 196
Great Bardfield 209n
Great Hallingbury 96, 99
Hallingbury park 22, 99, 102, 218
Horham Hall, Thaxted 202
Langley 52
lodges 35
Manuden 118
Rettenden 118
Roydon 136
Essex, Earl of 60, 151, 221
Essex, Theobald, Archdeacon of 48
Ethom, John, parker at Weston 228
Everesden, Nicholas de 84
Eylesford, Gerard de 144
Eywood park 6, 11, *193 see also* St Stephen's

Faggots 24, 32, **33**, 36, 44, 65, 78, 124, 154, 158n, 167, 168, 232
Fairclough, Laurence 230
Fanshawe, Sir Thomas, Baron and Viscount 224
Thomas 224, 225n
Thomas, second Viscount 224
Farris, Noel 176
Feld, John, parker at Benington 58

Felde, John, parker at Standon 206
Ferrers, George 94
    Henry, lord of Groby 222
Fish, fisheries, fishing 62, 68, 94, 134, 150, 194, 220, 222, 224
Fishponds **24**, 48, 72, 184 *see also* ponds
Fitz Adam, Simon 13, 142
Fitz Simon, Edward 142
    Hugh 142
Fitz Walter family 142
Flamstead 6, 7, 8, 18, 94–5
    Feverells Farm 94
    park **94–5**, *95*
    Roe End 94
Fleetwood, Henry 226
Flete, William 12, 13, 180
Flygh, John 206
Forester, John le 150
Forestry Commission 52, 72
Foster, Edward 156, 158n
France 12, 64, 76, 136
Francis, Earl of Huntingdon
Frankelyn, Oliver 224
Fraunk, John 130
    Walter 130
Fray, Agnes 102
    Sir John 21, 35, 58, 102, 156, 158n, 230
Free warren 23n, 44, 46n, 50, 52, 62, 76, 86, 88, 90, 106, 118,
    122, 124, 136, 144, 154, 160, 166, 176, 180, 196, 198, 208,
    210, 212, 214, 226, **232**
Freman, Ralph MP 198
Frevill/Fryvill, de, family 221n
    Lady de 172, 218
    Richard de 11, 12, 172
Frodgoryshey park *see* Great Munden
Fulham 68
Fuller, Hugh le, of Watford 37
Furneus, Simon de 11, 96
Furneux Pelham 7, 8, 9, 11, 96–8
    old park **96–9**, *97, 134*
    St Johns Pelham 96
Furnival, de, family 144
Furnival/Furnivall, Gerard de 11, 102, 144
Fysshe, John 112

Gacelyn park *see* Hatfield
Gaddesden (Great) 37, 100–1
    Hall 100
    park 7, 21, **100–1**, *101*
    South Hall 100
Gardiner, Stephen 136
Garlyk, John 112
Gascelin, Geoffrey 108
Gaunt, John of 22, 31, 33, 122, 124, 125, 222
George II 114
Gilston 138, 140n, 194, 196
    New Place 194, 196
    Gilston Park 196
Glasscocke, Thomas 72
Gloucester, earl of 36
Gloucestershire:

Sudeley manor 180
Goderych, John 32,
Goldington, John 136
Gore, Sir Humphrey 194, 196
    Sir John 194
Grand Junction Canal 216
Grandmesnil, Hugh de 10, 222
    Petronilla 222
    residence 224
Grave, John 197
Gray, James 139
Great Gaddesden park *see* Gaddesden
Great Munden 11, 102–5, 156, 174, 208, 219, 230
    Floodgacy park 6, 7, 8, 11, 21, 22, 27, 31, 34, 35, 36, **102–5**, *103*
    Frodgoryshey park 102, 218
    manor 27, 102, 103, 221
    parish 20, 58, 60
    pond 24, 102
Great Offley 106–7
    park at **106–7**, *107*
Great Wymondley 13, 176
Griffin, A. 125
Gros, Alesia de 96
    Hugh le 96
Gynne, John 112

Hadham 68 *see also* Little and Much Hadham
Hadham Hall *see* Little Hadham
Hale, Augustine 159n
Hallingbury park *see* Essex
Halstead, John, parker at Hertingfordbury 122, 124
Halton, Philip 201n
Hamels estate *see* Braughing
Hampshire 5, 21
    Odiham (castle) 21, 148, 152n
Hampton Court 180
Harcourt, Richard Bard 216
Haringey/Haryngeye 68
Harpenden 17
Harrington, John 78
    Sir William 125
Harting, James E. 4, 164, 182, 220
Hastings, Isabella de 122
Hatfield 12, 17, 20, 21, 108–21
    Astwick manor 118
    Bell Bar 112
    charcoal sales 24, 112, 114
    Gacelyn park 5, 7, 11, 21, **108**, *109*
    great park 7, 11, 24, 27, 28, 30, 33, 34, 36, **108–13**, *110–11*,
        114, 160
    Great Wood 34, 113 *see also* Hatfield Wood
    Home/House Park 113
    Hornbeam Gate 34, 111, 112
    Innings park 11, 14, 35, **113–14**, *115*, 116
    little park 7, 11, 24, 29, 33, 34, 36, **114–18**, *117 see also*
        Hatfield middle park
    manor 112
    middle park 34, 35, 114, 116, 117 *see also* Hatfield little park
    Millwards Park 108, 118
    New Park 113

New Town 116
parks 4, 14, 114, 125, 170n
'Potterys' 118
Symondshyde 8, 11, 21
Symondshyde park **118**, *119*
Woodhall 8, 21, 118
Woodhall park **118–19**, *121*
Hatfield House 113, 116, 118
Archive 8, 30, 90, 112, 113, 114, 130, 166
Hatfield Wood 90, 92 *see also* Hatfield Great Wood
Haverley, A. 118
William 118
Hawdeles, John 180
Hayley park *see* Benington
Heidon, Francis 226
Hemel Hempstead 151
Henneage, Sir John 78
Henry I 88
Henry II 100
Henry III 13, 21, 50, 62, 86, 100, 108, 112, 122, 228
Henry IV 65, 151, 230
Henry V 65, 154, 172, 214
Henry VI 65, 214, 222
Henry VII 65, 136, 180, 206, 222, 230
Henry VIII 35, 72, 78, 81, 94, 99, 100, 106, 112, 113, 116, 129, 136, 139, 140, 151, 162, 163, 180, 182, 184, 194, 206, 210, 230
Henry, Prince of Wales 31, 151, 154
Henry, Prince of Wales and Duke of Cornwall 65
Hereford, earls of 50
Humphry, Earl of 138, 140n
Hereford, William de 23, 37, 62
Hertford 37, 122
castle 3, 10, 12, 33, 35, 37, 108, 114, 122, 124, 151, 222
park 36, *123*, 124 *see also* Hertingfordbury park
St Andrew's parish 124
Hertingfordbury/Hertfordyngbury 9, 10, 12, 37, 122–7
Birch Green 126
great park 122
little park 122, *127*
new park 8, 28, 122
old park 7, 21
park 18, 22, 26, 29, 30, 31, 32, 33, 35, 36, **122–6**, *123 see also* Hertford park
Place Farm or Bury Farm 126
warren 23, 122, 124, 126, 127
water gate 30, 122
Hinxworth 56
Hippegrave, Adam de 84
Hitchin 8, 106, 128–9, 144, 154, 176
Dinsley manor 144
Museum 129
Oughton Head Farm 129
Punfold park **128–9**, *129*
Hockfield, William de, parker 36, 62
Hoddesdon 7, 11, 80, 90, 130–3
Bassingbourne manor 130
Bassingbourne's park 7, 130
Goose Green 130
Hoddesdonbury manor 28, 80, 130

Spital Brook 130, 133
William of Louth's park 7, 21, 130
Hoddesdonpark Wood 6, 35, **130–3**, *131*
Hoggekyns, Robert 156
Holland, Joan 80
Holm, William, parker at Walkern 6, 218, 221
Hoo, Robert de 154
Hoppitt, Rosemary 5
Horewode, John 154
Hormead 134–5
park 7, **134–5**, *135*
Hornbeam 22, 34, 46, 90, 102, 110, 112, 124, 132, 133, 157, 166, 180, 225n *see also* Trees
coppice 60, 61, 72, 82, 92, 118, 168, 207, 208, 210
pollard 4, 44, 60, 114, 118, 156, 158, 168, 222, 225
stub 58, 210
Hotoft, John 154, 158n, 218
Howard, Thomas, Earl of Surrey and Duke of Norfolk 136
Howlett, Bridget 128, 129
Humberston, John, parker at Walkern 218, 220
Humberstone family 221n
Hundred Years' War 90, 136
Hunn, Jonathan 186, 190, 192, 193
Hunsdon 86, 136–41, 198
Crow Brook 140
park(s) 5, 6, 7, 14, 17, 34, 86, 99, **136–40**, *137*
honour of 136, 194
Hunsdon House 138, 140
Hunt, John 64
Hunte, Richard, ferreter 65
Hunter, Adam of Hertingfordbury 37
Huntingdon, Francis, Earl of 224
Katherine, Countess of 224
Huntingdonshire 222
Hyde, Thomas 156

Ippollitts 8, 12, 142–5, 154
Almshoe Bury 12
Almshoe park 3, 8, 13, 122, **142–4**, *143*
Maydencroft park 3, 8, 122, **144–5**
Ireland 206, 224
Isabella of France, Queen 3, 12, 13, 37, 44, 62, 112, 122, 142, 144, 150
Isabella, Countess of Cornwall 62
Isneye *see* Easneye
Isode, John 230
Ives, Richard, parker of Tyttenhanger 184

James I 78, 82, 112, 151, 164
Jane Seymour, Queen 151, 206
Jarpenville, David de 76
Joan of Navarre, Queen 151
Joan, Queen of Scotland 3, 37, 122, 142, 144

Katherine of Aragon, Queen 129, 151, 180, 206
Kechyn, John 116
Kelet, John, poulterer of London 156
Kempton, William 126
Kendale, Edward de 128
Robert 144

Kent 151, 196
    earls of 222
Kimpton 5, 8, 11, 146–7
    park 24, **146–7**, *147*
    Parkbury manor 146
    The Hoo estate 147
King's Langley viii, 9, 12, 148–53
    great park 7, 8, 30, 34, 148
    Little London 35, 148, 150, 151
    little park 7, 34, 148
    Lodge 35, 148, 150, 152
    park 13, 18, 21, 22, 24, 31, 32, 35, 36, **148–53**, *149*
    park pale 28, 29, 30, 148, 150, 151
    water gate 30, 148
King's Walden 8, 16
Kirkby, John, parker at Little Hadham 168
Knebworth 6, 7, 12, 16, 21, 29, 30, 154–9
    great park 19, 29, 30, 34, 35, 36, 154, *155*, 156, 157
    Impo/Ympo Wood 29, 156
    little park 8, 14, 36, *155*, 156
    Lodge Farm 157
    new park 8, 33, 154, 156
    old park 7, 33, 154, 156, 157
    park(s) 4, 22, 31, 32, 33, 34, 36, 102, **154–9**
    warren 23, 26, 155, 156, 157
    wood sales 24, 154, 156
Knebworth House 156
Knight of the Garter 146
Knollys, Thomas 184
Kympton, Edmund 230
Kynebelle, Robert de 64

Lancaster, duchy of 180
Lancaster, Thomas, Earl of 169, 208
Lancastre, Philippa de 148
    Roger de 148
Lanfranc, Archbishop 192
Langley manor 12, 13, 148 *see also* King's Langley
    palace 13
    park 21
Langley Regis *see* King's Langley
Langley, Richard 169
Laund(e) 7, 29, 30–1, 59, 60, 66, 102, 106, 138, 154, 157, 172, 180, 210, 220, 224, 225n, 230, **232**
Layston 56
Lee, Geoffrey de la 44
    John de la 8, 44
    Walter de la 37, 44
Leicestershire 9, 222
Leland, John 202
Lestrange, Roger 140n
Leventhorpe family 198
Leventhorpe, John 13, 198
    John, sheriff of Hertfordshire 198
    Sir John 198
    Sir Thomas 198
Leye, Henry de la, son of Thomas 50
Licence to impark **5**, 7, 8, 11, 44, 90, 146, 160, 164, 170, 180, 198, 210, 212, 214
Liley/Lily, Henry 60, 61, 229, 231

Lincolnshire:
    Tattershall Park 114
Lisle family 194
Lisle, Robert de 194
Little Berkhamsted 7, 13, 90–3, 160–1
    Epping Green 92, 160
    park at **160–1**
    Woodcock Lodge Farm 160
    Woodcocks Lodge 92
Little Gaddesden 7, 42, 162–5 *see also* Ashridge park
Little Hadham 7, 14, 166–71 *see also* Hadham
    Baud's manor or Hadham Hall 7, 8, 14, *59*, 99, 169, 170, 208, 220, 221
    Bury Green Farm 169
    Hadham Hall *see* Little Hadham, Baud's manor
    Hadham Hall Farm 170
    Hadham old park lodge farm 170
    Hadham park **169–71**, *171*
    Little Hadham Place 169
    Lodge Farm 169
    manorial accounts 23, 30, 166
    park 4, 7, 11, 21, 22, 26, 31, 32, 33, 34, 35, 36, **166–9**, *167*, 218
    park gate 30, 166
    park pale 28, 29, 30, 166, 167
    wood sales 24, 166, 167, 168-9
Little Munden 7, 11, 12, 60, 104, 172–5
    East park(s) 21, 36, **172–5**, *175*, 218
    Lordship Farm 172
    manor 27, 172, 220
    Munden park **172–4**, *173*
    park 23, 30, **172–4**
    Potters Green 173
Little parks **12**
    Broadfield 74
    Hatfield 7, 11, 12, 24, 29, 33, 34, 36, 112, 113, 114, 116, 117
    Hertingfordbury 122, 124, 126, 127
    Hunsdon 138, 139
    Ippollitts 142, 144
    King's Langley 7, 34, 148, 149, 150, 151, 152
    Knebworth 8, 12, 14, 154, 155, 156
    Little Wymondley 176
    Rickmansworth 180, 182
Little Wymondley 7, 11, 12, 176–7
    park 13, 23, **176–7**, *177*
    Wymondley Bury 176
Lodge 6–7, 24, **34–6**
    Albury 46
    Ayot St Lawrence 50
    Barkway 52, 54
    Benington 27, 56, 58, 60
    Berkhamsted 65, 66
    Bishop's Stortford 68, 69, 70
    Bushey 76
    Cheshunt 78
    Elstree 88
    Essendon 90, 92
    Furneux Pelham 96
    Great Munden102, 103, 104
    Hatfield 108, 112, 113, 116, 118
    Hertingfordbury 122, 124, 125, 126

Hoddesdon 131
Hunsdon 139, 140
Ippollitts 145
King's Langley 148, 150, 151, 152
Knebworth 156, 157
Little Berkhamsted 160
Little Hadham 166, 167, 169, 170, 170n
Little Munden 174
Rickmansworth 180, 182, 183
Ridge 184, 186
Sawbridgeworth 194, 196, 197
Shenley 202, 203
St Stephen's 192, 193
Standon 204, 207
Stanstead Abbots 210, 212
Tring 215
Walkern 218, 220, 221
Ware 224
Watford 226
Weston 230
London 14, 17, 116, 130, 136, 151, 154, 156, 166, 184, 210, 214
    bishop of 7, 11, 23, 36, 68, 69, 96, 166, 178
        Bishop (elect) Master Michael de Northburgh 68
        Bishop William de Ste. Mere-Eglise 178
    citizen and merchant/tradesman 12, 68, 156, 180, 220, 224
    city of 210
    draper 214
    Holborn 218
    Lambeth 136
    Priory of St Bartholomew, West Smithfield 202
    St Martin's-le-Grand 11, 130
    St Paul's 48 see also St Paul's
    Stratford 37, 122
    Tower of 44
    Westminster 4, 204
    Westminster abbey 14, 17, 170n
London, John de 88
Longboys chace 148
Longespee, Stephen 21, 100
    William 100
Loring, Sir Nigel/Neil 8, 11, 146
Louth, William de 122
    William of, Bishop of Ely 21, 130
Louthe, Robert de 122
    Roger de 226
Loveceft, Richard de 144
Lucie, Sir Richard 82
Luxembourg, Lewis of see Ely, bishop of
Lytton, Robert 156, 158n
    Rowland (d. 1582) 156
    Rowland (d. 1674) 156
    Sir William (d. 1660) 156, 157
    William (d. 1517) 156
    William Robinson 159n

Man, Alice 176
Mandeville, de, family 130
Marche, John 150
Marescall, Roger 206
    Margaret, Countess of Norfolk 228

Margaret of Anjou, Queen 3, 65, 222
Margaret of France, Queen 62
Markyatestreet 94
Marshal, Earl 230
Marshal, Eleanor, Countess of Pembroke 228
    Gilbert, Earl of Pembroke 204
    William, Earl of Pembroke 10, 12, 228
    William, fifth Earl of Pembroke 21, 228
Marston 8
Mary, Princess/the Lady 124, 224 see also Tudor, Mary
Mary, Queen 58, 138, 163
Marzen, Frances 206
Mathams manor see Sawbridgeworth
Maune, Henry de 122
    Peter de 122
Mauny, Walter de 74
Maydencroft park see Ippollitts
Mead, Richard 96
Meesden 52, 134
Midday, Philip, parker at Standon 204
Middlesex 14
    Harefield 164
Mildmay, Thomas 194
    Walter 194
Mileson, Stephen 9
Milkley park see Standon
Milkley, Robert de 208
Minet, William 169
Moat 35–6, 48, 52, 54, 72, 80, 82, 86, 96, 131, 152, 176, 182, 184, 194, 196, 212, 218, 220, 226
Moels, John de 160
    John, Lord 160
    Nicholas de 160
    Roger de 160
Molis, Nicholas de 112
Monmouth, Earl of 182
Montagu, John, Earl of Northumberland and Marquess of 202
    John, third Earl of Salisbury 202
    Maud, Countess of Salisbury 202
    Thomas de, Earl of Salisbury 222
Moor Park, Rickmansworth 4, 182 see also Rickmansworth, The More
Morden, Robert, mapmaker 88
More, John, parker at Cheshunt 78, 81
Morley, Lord 21, 172, 220
    fifth Lord 218
    Lady Alice 220
    Robert, second Lord 218
    William, third Lord 170
Morrison family of Cassiobury 170
Morrison, Sir Charles 151
Mortimer, Edmund, Earl of March 206
    Philippa, Countess of March 206
    Roger 206
Mowbray, John, Duke of Norfolk 230
Much Hadham 6, 7, 11, 178–9, 206, 208 see also Hadham
    Moor Place 178
    old park 178–9, 179
    Old Park Farm 178
Munby, Lionel 4, 149, 151, 214

Munden Furnivall 221n *see also* Great Munden
Munden Magna *see* Great Munden
Mundens, the 56

National Archives, The 6, 94, 138, 162
National Nature Reserve 131
National Trust, The 162, 164
Nayll, William 65
Nevill, Alice 76
    Richard, Earl of Salisbury 76, 222
Neville
    earls of Warwick 94
    George, chancellor of England 180
    Richard de 194
Newenton, John de, parker at Berkhamsted 64
Newgate Street 30, 108, 112
Newport, Edward 98n
    Reginald de 112
    Robert 96
    William 96
Node, William, parker at Bedwell 90
Norbury, John 8, 11, 13, 80, 90, 160
Norden, John, mapmaker 4, 44, 48, 65–6, 68, 78, 82, 90, 94, 96,
    106, 108, 114, 118, 124, 138, 142, 151, 156, 164, 170, 174,
    182, 192, 194, 198, 202, 206, 210, 212, 214, 216, 224, 226
Norfolk 96, 212, 218
    Bradenham 212
    Castle Rising 80
    Hingham 98n
    Necton 94
    Wymondham Priory or Abbey 212
Norfolk, Thomas, Duke of 136
    earl of 36
Normandy, abbey of Saint–Evroul 222
Norris, Henry 136
North Mymms 221, 184
Northchurch 66, 162, 214, 216
Northumberland, Tynemouth 88
Nott, Roger 113
Nurse, Thomas 90
Nuthampstead 52
    Park Farm 52

Oak 32, 33–4, 112, 113, 116, 118, 120n, 124, 138, 151, 154, 164,
    166, 167, 168, 180, 204, 208, 228, 229–30 *see also* Trees
Oak bark 33, 167
    coppice 60, 204
    pales 28, 59, 64
    pollards 33, 60, 61, 104, 204, 222, 225, 229
    timber 28, 64, 154, 166
Offa, King 14, 17
Offley manor 31
Ogard, Alice 212
    Sir Andrew 11, 12, 13, 212, 214
    Henry 212
Oldhall, Sir William 14, 86, 136, 206
Oliver, John, mapmaker 80, 88, 108, 114, 118, 125, 139, 156, 170,
    182, 198, 201n, 206, 214, 226
Olyve, Walter, parker of Hatfield great park 112
Ordgar, William 114

Ordnance Survey 42
Ossevill or Osevill, Henry de 102, 218, 221n
Otes, William, parker at Little Hadham 168
Oxfordshire 9
Oxhey *see* Watford

Pace, James 126
    Reynold 126
Page, Sir Richard 94
Panetrye, John de la 114
Panfold, Richard 68
Pannage 3, 6, **31–2**, 232
    Benington 58
    Berkhamsted 24, 62, 65
    Cheshunt 78, 80, 81
    Essendon 90
    Great Munden 27, 102
    Great Offley 106
    Hatfield 112, 114
    Hertingfordbury 122, 124
    King's Langley 148, 151
    Knebworth 156
    Little Gaddesden (Ashridge) 162
    Little Hadham 166
    Rickmansworth 180
    Standon 204, 206
    Walkern 218
    Weston 228, 230
Parc, Richard ate 72
    Simon ate 44
Parco, Richard de 72
    Thomas de 72n
Paris, Matthew 114
Park Street 6, 192
Park, Adam atte 72n
    Cecil ate 52
    Richard atte 72n
    Richard de 72
    Rogus atte 72n
Parke, Johanes 72n
    John atte 44
    Roger 72n
    Symon 73n
Parker, Cecil le, of Barkway 52
    Elye/Elie (the), of King's Langley 148, 150
    Henry 96
    Henry le, Baldock 36–7
    Henry, Baron Morley 96, 99
    John le, of Gaddesden 37, 100
    John le, of Walkern 56, 218
    Ralph le, of Hatfield 112, 114
    Robert (le), bailiff at King's Langley 148
    Robert le, of Berkhamsted 22, 36, 62, 64
    Stephen le, of Ardeley 48
    Thomas le, of Knebworth 154
    Walter le, of Hatfield 112, 114
    Walter le, of Knebworth 154
    Sir William, Baron Morley & first Baron Mounteagle 96
    William le, of Eastwick 36–7, 86
    William le, of Hunsdon 136

William le, of Knebworth 154
William le, of Watford 36–7, 226
William le, parker at Standon 208
Parkesgate, Walter de, of Knebworth 30, 154
Parliament 4, 44, 80, 82, 88, 90, 139, 162, 204, 221, 224
Knight of the Shire 154, 158n
Member of (MP) 90, 94, 96, 118, 136, 160, 169, 172, 180, 198, 214
Parr, Lady Anne 103
Sir William 58
Pattmer, William 169
Pearce, Reverend Richard 95n
Peasants' Revolt 190
Pelham manor 225n
Pembroke, Countess of 12
Earl(s) of 11, 210
Joan, Countess of 3
Pembrugge, Richard de 50
Pendley see Aldbury and Tring
Perceval, John 156
Perers, Edmund de 154
Joan de 154
Richard de 154
Periers manor see Cheshunt
Periers, Richard de 12, 82
Philip, King 58, 138
Philippa, Queen 44
Phyppes, Henry 65
Pilkington, Sir John 65
Pirton 15
Pisho or Pishobury see Sawbridgeworth
Plumer, William 206
Podebat, Walter 64
Polyti, William 229
Pond 24, see also Fish and Fishponds
Benington 60
Berkhamsted 65
Bishop's Stortford 24, 68
Cheshunt 78
Great Munden 24, 102
Hatfield 116, 118
Hoddesdon 131
Hunsdon 138, 140n
Ippollitts 142, 144
King's Langley 24, 150
Knebworth 24, 154
Sawbridgeworth 194
Standon 207
Walkern 220, 221
Ware 225
Watford 180
Ponsbourne estate 108
Ponsbourne House 108
Pope, Sir Thomas 184
Potter, William 92
Pottere, John, of Essendon 112
Robert 112
Pride, William 176
Prince, Hugh 201n
Puckeridge 208

Punsho park see Albury
Putteridge 126

Rabbit **23**, 26, 159n, 214 see also Coney and Warren
Rabbit warren see Warren
Rabley Heath 157
Rackham, Oliver 4, 14, 30, 33, 34
Radwell 56
Railway Great Northern 116
London & North Western 216
Ramssey, John 169
Raven, Richard, parker at Berkhamsted 64
Raymond, John 210
Redbourn manor 118
Redvers, Baldwin de, Earl of Cornwall 194
Margaret de, Countess of Cornwall 194
Richard I 88
Richard II 64, 66, 80, 151
Richard III 136
Richard, first Earl of Cornwall, King of Germany 62
Richmond Park 164
Richmond, John, Duke of Brittany and Earl of 80, 82
Margaret, Countess of, 136, 222
Rickmansworth 8, 180–3
Moor House or Morehouse 182
park at The More **180–3**, *181*
Parson's Lodge or Astons Lodge 182, 183
The More 5, 8, 12, 13, 180, 182
Ridge 35, 184–7
Park Gate Corner 30, 186
Tyttenhanger fishpond 24
Tyttenhanger Heath 184
Tyttenhanger House 186
Tyttenhanger park 7, 8, 11, 13, 21, 30, 35, **184–7**, *185*, 187, 192
Rigby, Oliver 194
Rivers/valleys **20**
Ash 16, 18, 210
Beane 16, 18, 218
Colne 184, 186, 226
Dane End Tributary 172
Gade 100, 148, 151
Hiz 129
Lea 8, 16, 37, 80, 90, 122, 124, 131, 210, 212, 222
Mimram 16, 122, 124, 125, 126
Old Bourne 218
Quin 15, 18,
Rib 15, 16, 17, 18, 99, 172, 206, 222, 224
Stort 17, 18, 70, 194, 196, 200, 212
Ver 188, 190
Roche, Margaret 103
Rodes, John 210
Romayn, Robert 32
Rothais, wife of Richard de Tonbridge 10
Rowney Priory or Nunnery 102, 103, 104
prioress of 102
Rufus, William 144
Rushden 74, 102
Russell, Lord 151
Sir John 180
Rutland, Earl of 94

Rye, The *see* Stanstead Abbots 5, 13

Sacombe 56, 225n
Sacombe Green 103
Sadleir, Ralph 206
St Albans 7, 57, 148, 202
    abbey 17, 72, 88, 188, 192
    abbot(s) of 6, 8, 11, 13, 17, 21, 22, 24, 64, 72, 150, 151, 180,
        192
        Abbot Frederic 192
        Abbot John 72
        Abbot John de la Moot(e) 184, 188
        Abbot John of Wheathampstead 13, 184, 192
        Abbot Leofstan 14, 192
        Abbot Michael 184
        Abbot Paul de Caen 192
        Abbot Richard 184
        Abbot Richard de Wallingford 88
        Abbot Robert Catton 184
        Abbot Thomas de la Mare 4, 37, 192
        Abbot Thomas Ramryge 184
        Abbot William Heyworth 184
    Liberty 72
    Kingsbury manor 190
    monastery 88
    St Jermans or Germains 190
St Bartholomew *see* London
St Ledger, Geoffrey de 106
    John de 106
St Martin's-le-Grand *see* London
St Michael's, St Albans 188–91
    Batchworth manor 188
    Childwick Green 188
    Childwick manor 11, 188
    Childwick park 8, 11, **188–9**, *189*
    Childwickbury estate 188
    Derefold 7, 11, **190**, *191*
St Paul's, London
    canons of 11, 12, 24, 48
St Stephen's, St Albans 192–3
    Eywood park 11, **192–3**, *193*
    Sopwellbury 192
Salisbury Hall and Park *see* Shenley
Salisbury, Earl of 8, 14, 114, 169, 202
    Marquess of 116, 131, 169
    Robert Cecil, Earl of 112–13, 116 *see also* Cecil, Sir Robert
    Thomas, Earl of 13, 76
Salmon, Nathaniel 48, 69, 96
Sandes/Sondes, Thomas, parker at Cheshunt 78
Sandon, La More manor 102
Sawbridgeworth 8, 11, 20, 27, 29, 86, 138, 194–201
    Blunts Farm 200
    Lodge Farm 196
    mill 194
    Pisho or Pishobury manor 194, 200
    Pisho park 7, 17, 20, 29, 31, 35, 99, **194–6**, *195*, 198, 201
    Sayes or Sayesbury manor, 27, 196, 200
    Sayes park 7, 17, 22, 23, 27, 32, 35, **196–8**, *197*
    Sayes Park Farm 198
    Shingle Hall and Mathams, manor of 198, 200

Shingle Hall 5, 8, 13, 196
Shingle Hall park 99, **198–200**, *199*
Sweat Dews Farm 200
Yardley's Farm 200
Saxton, Christopher, mapmaker 4, 44, 48, 65, 68, 78, 82, 90, 94,
    96, 99, 106, 108, 114, 118, 124, 138, 139, 142, 151, 156, 164,
    170, 174, 182, 184, 192, 194, 196, 198, 202, 210, 212, 214,
    224, 226
Say, Elizabeth, Lady 80, 90
    Geoffrey de, second Lord 196
    Sir John 27, 90, 102
    Sir William (d. 1529) 22, 27, 30, 32, 35, 58, 60, 90, 92, 102,
        118, 172, 196, 201n
    William de (d. 1272) 11, 196
    William de (d. 1295) 196
    William de (d. 1375) 196
Sayes park *see* Sawbridgeworth
Scalers, Harduin de 72
Scales park *see* Barkway
Scales, de, family 52
Scales, Robert first Lord 52
Schyrlock, Richard 159n
Scot, Robert 230
Scrope, John, eighth Lord 194
    Richard, first Baron Scrope of Bolton 194
    Richard, third Baron Scrope of Bolton 194
Segrave, Sir Hugh 128
Seller, John, mapmaker 46, 80, 88, 90, 103, 106, 108, 114, 118,
    125, 139, 156, 164, 170, 182, 194, 198, 206, 214, 221, 226
Sexteyn, John, parker at Albury 44
Sexton, John 156
    Richard 156
Seymour, Jane, Queen 151, 206
Shenley 14, 202–3
    Holmes alias Cannons manor 202
    Salisbury Hall 14
    Salisbury Park 14, **202–3**, *203*
    Shenley Lodge 202, 203
Sheriff of:
    Cambridgeshire 13, 176
    Essex 13, 96, 118, 169, 176, 214
    Hertfordshire 13, 96, 118, 154, 158n, 169, 176, 198, 208, 214,
        224
    Leicestershire 222
    London 214
Shingle Hall *see* Sawbridgeworth
Shirley, Evelyn 4, 114
Site of Special Scientific Interest (SSSI) 131
Skot, John, parker at Walkern 218
Smith, John T. 46, 142
Somerset, Porlock 146
Somery, de, family 74
Sondes/Sandes, Thomas, parker at Cheshunt 78
Sopwellbury *see* St Stephen's
Southcote, Sir Edward 209n
Spramich, John 162
Staffordshire:
    Cannock Forest 152n
    Rugeley 21, 148
    Tixall 206

Stanborough 119
Standon 16, 204–9, 225n
    hospital 169, 208
    Latchford 204
    Lodge Farm 35, 207
    Lordship 99, 206, 207
    manor 10–11, 140n, 204, 206
    Milkley or Mentley manor 169, 208
    Milkley park 7, **208**, *207*
    park 4, 7, 19, 21, 22, 29, 30, 31, 32, 33, 35, 36, **204–8**, *205*
Stanley, Edward 100
    Rev. Francis 69
    Rev. William, precentor of St Paul's 69
    Sir William 136
Stanstead 136, 138, 225n
Stanstead Abbots 8, 210–13
    Easneye park 7, 19, **210–11**, *211*
    Easneye Wood 7
    Halving Farm 210
    Rye, The 5, 13, 212
    Rye manor 12, 212
    Rye park 18, 35, **212–13**, *213*
    Warren Farm 210
    Stanstead Bury estate 212, 99
    Great Farm of 210
Stanstead St Margarets 99
Stapleford 44, 98n
    Waterford Hall 44
Statute of Merton 21
Stevenage 34, 154, 157
Stigand, Archbishop 10
Stocking Pelham 8
Stokes, Edmund, parker at Cheshunt 80
Stortford 11, 20, 198, *see also* Bishop's Stortford
    castle 178
    manor 7, 69, 178
    park 17, 31, 36, **68–71**, *69*, 170n, 178
    Park Farm 69–70
    pond 24, 68
Stratford 37, 122
Strete, William, parker at King's Langley 151
Stretelee, Master John de 64
Suffolk 9, 57
    Clare 10, 204
    Hundon 209n
    Tendring Hall 136

Taillebois, Ralph 222
Talbot, Richard 122
Tany, de, family 86
    Laurence de 86
    Margaret de 86
    Richard de 86
Taylor, Pamela 178
Tewin parish 72
Theobalds estate 78, 112–13
Theobalds Park 82
Thorley 8, 99, 198, 200
Thornbury, Sir John 172
    Sir Philip 172

Thorpe, mapmaker 82
Thurkeld, John 68
Times, William Gorsuch 69
Tonbridge, Richard de 10
Tosny (later Tony), Lord 94
    Ralph de 94
Totteridge 8, 17
Trees 4, 6, 22, 24, **30–1**, 32, **33–4**, 36
    ash 33, 34, 58, 60, 124, 138, 151, 154, 163, 164, 168, 208, 229, 230
    beech 28, 31, 32, 33, 34, 44, 60, 64, 65, 66, 112, 116, 151, 154, 164, 180, 204, 210
    holly 60, 92, 94
    hornbeam *see* Hornbeam
    maple 92, 138, 151, 168, 180
    oak *see* Oak
Tregelles, J.A. 130
Tring 8, 12, 17, 214–7, *216*
    Pendley 5, 8, 12, 13
    Pendley House 214
    Pendley Manor 214–15, 217
    Pendley park **214–7**, *215*
Troghford, Thomas de, keeper of Berkhamsted park 64
Tudor, Mary 90 *see also* Mary, Princess
Turner, Richard 68
Tynemouth, Thomas, prior of 188
Tyttenhanger *see* Ridge

Valence/Valencia, Agnes de 122
    Aymer de, Earl of Pembroke 108, 122, 134
    Joan de, Countess of Pembroke 122
    Mary de, Countess of Pembroke 134
    William de, Earl of Pembroke 108, 114, 122
Valence, William, charcoal maker 33, 169
Vallans, William 225n
Valognes, Christina de 122
    Peter de 10, 56, 142
Vataile, John 44
Venison 3, 4, 6, 22, 27, 28, 64, 113, 192, 204, 206
Vere, John de 180
Verney, John (*fl.* 1472) 214
Verney, John (custodian of King's Langley park in 1534/5) 65, 151
Verulamium 190

Wainwright, Angus 162, 163, 164
Wake, Blanche 222
    Thomas, de Lydell 222
Walkern 56, 218–221
    Bridge Farm 221
    Bury 220
    Bury Farm 218
    Holmes Farm 221
    manor 7, 102, 172, 218, 220, 221
    parish 20, 56, 58, 60
    park 6, 7, 19, 21, 28, 31, 32, 35, 36, 59, 60, 154, 166, 168, 170n, 172, **218–221**, *219*
    Park Farm 220, 221
Wallington parish 74
Walsingham, Thomas 190
Waltham abbey and town 136

Waltham Cross 78
Waltham Holy Cross, abbey of 210
    abbot of 5, 7, 11, 80
Waltham park 90
Warburton, J., mapmaker 108, 125, 139, 206
Ware 7, 222–5, 225n
    Askell of 10, 222
    manor 10–11, 28, 222, 224
    park 3, 4, 6, 10, 18, 19, 28, 35, 99, **222–5**, *223*
    Westmill manor 224
Ware, Beatrice de 222
    Geoffrey de 28, 222
Ware, Robert, Cellarer of St Albans abbey 72
Warren **23**, 23n, 26
    Albury 44
    Ayot St Lawrence 50
    Barkway 52, 54
    Benington 58, 60
    Berkhamsted 23, 62, 64, 65, 67n
    Bishop's Stortford 70n
    Bushey 76
    Cheshunt 23, 80, 81, 83n
    Essendon 23, 90, 92, 93n
    Flamstead 23, 94
    Great Munden 102
    Hatfield 108, 113, 114
    Hertingfordbury 23, 122, 124, 126, 127
    Hormead 134
    Hunsdon 139
    Knebworth 23, 156, 157, 158n
    Little Munden 23, 27, 172, 175n
    Little Wymondley 23, 176
    Much Hadham 23, 178
    Rickmansworth 180
    Sawbridgeworth 23, 197
    St Stephens 192
    Standon 206
    Stanstead Abbots 210, 212
    Walkern 218, 220
    Ware 224, 225, 225n
    Watford 226
    Weston 228, 230
Warrener 94, 122, 124, 126, 157
Wars of the Roses 136, 180
Warwick, Guy de Beauchamp, Earl of 94
    Thomas, Earl of 94
Watford 8, 21, 36–7, 151, 180, 182, 226–7
    Cassiobury 151, 170, 221
    Oxhey 5, 8
    Oxhey Hall 226
    Oxhey Lodge 226
    Oxhey manor 226
    Oxhey park 21, **226–7**, *227*
    Oxhey Place 226
    Oxhey Warren 226
    St Cleeres/St Clowes 226
    Sandy Lodge 182, 183
    Sandy Lodge Farm 182
    Sandy Lodge Golf Course 182
Watford, Robert de 48

Welwyn Garden City 119
Wengham, John de, precentor of St Paul's 74
    Tomas de 74
West, John of Ayot St Lawrence 50
Westmill 134, 225n
Westminster 4, 204
Westminster abbey 14, 17, 170n
Weston 7, 10–11, 12, 228–31
    great park 7, 12, 32, 35, **228–30**, *229*
    Ipgrave park 7, 19, 29, 32, **228–31**, *231*
    Ipgrave Wood 31
    Lodge Farm 230
    park 21, 22, 30, 31, 33, 36, 102
    wood sales from the parks 24, 228, 229–30
Wheathampstead 14, 17
Whittingham/Whityngham, Agnes 214
    Sir Robert 12, 13, 212n, 214
Widford 8, 86
Wigginton 214
    Newground Farm 216
Wilkinson, Henry 210
William I, the Conqueror, Duke of Normandy 10, 56, 68, 80, 94, 192, 222
Williamson, Tom 11
Willoughby, William, later Lord 139
Wiltshire 108
Windsor Great Park 114
Wolsey, Cardinal Thomas 136, 180, 182
Woodland Trust, The 131–3
Worcester, bishop of 3, 64
    William of 212
Wormley 16, 80, 82
Wright, Richard 58
Wyatt's rebellion 163
Wylmyn, John 112
Wymondham Priory or Abbey 212
Wymondley Bury *see* Little Wymondley
Wynselowe, William 206
Wyte, John le 176

Yardley's Farm *see* Shingle Hall
York 3
York, Cicely, Duchess of 65, 151, 206
    Richard, Duke of 14, 136, 206
Yorkshire 5
    Bolton castle 194

Zenzano, Hannibal, farrier to Henry VIII 112
Zouche, William de la 94